Nancy W. Wilson

THE PRESCHOOL IN ACTION:
EXPLORING EARLY CHILDHOOD PROGRAMS

DR. RONALD K. PARKER
EDITOR

The Center for the Advanced Study of Education

Graduate Center
THE CITY UNIVERSITY OF NEW YORK

Sponsored by
The City University of New York

ALLYN AND BACON, INC.
BOSTON

©Copyright 1972 by
Allyn and Bacon, Inc.,
470 Atlantic Avenue, Boston.
All rights reserved. Printed in
the United States of America. No
part of the material protected by this
copyright notice may be reproduced or utilized
in any form or by any means, electronic
or mechanical, including photocopying,
recording, or by any informational
storage and retrieval system,
without written permission
from the
copyright owner.

Library of Congress
Catalog Card Number: 79-186843

Acknowledgments

The editor wishes to express his sincere gratitude to the many authors who contributed their time and effort to this volume. Difficult as it always is to respond to requests for presentation papers, it becomes doubly so when a certain format and length are specified. Special thanks are due to Benjamin Rosner, Dean of Teacher Education, The Center for the Advanced Study of Education, The City University of New York, for providing the financial support so essential to the success of the conference and the preparation of the final manuscript. Recognition must also be given to Mary Carol Day for her expert handling of the numerous details connected with the revision of the material as well as for her substantial contribution to the last chapter. Lastly, the invaluable assistance of Sueann Ambron, Gary Danielson and De Ansin Parker in organizing the conference and assuring that it ran smoothly is hereby gratefully acknowledged.

Contents

Foreword, *Benjamin Rosner*		ix
Introduction, *Ronald K. Parker*		1
1.	Poverty and Childhood, *Jerome S. Bruner*	7
2.	The Wrong Response: Is It to be Ignored, Prevented, or Treated? *Marion Blank*	36
3.	A Development Process Approach to Curriculum Design, *Shari Nedler*	59
4.	An Application of Piaget's Theory to the Conceptualization of a Preschool Curriculum, *Constance Kamii*	91
5.	An Evaluation of Logical Operations Instruction in the Preschool, *Frank H. Hooper*	134
6.	A Traditional Nursery Program Revisited, *David P. Weikart*	189
7.	Montessori: Myth or Reality? *Thomas J. Banta*	216
8.	A Model Program for Young Children that Responds to the Child, *Glen P. Nimnicht*	245
9.	A Comprehensive Approach to Early Education: The Discovery Program, *David C. Whitney, Ronald K. Parker*	270
10.	Rationale for the CHILD Curriculum, *Helen F. Robison*	301
11.	Extending Direct Instruction to Conceptual Skills, *Valerie Anderson, Carl Bereiter*	339
12.	An Ameliorative Approach in the Development of Curriculum, *Merle B. Karnes, R. Reid Zehrbach, James A. Teska*	353
13.	Toward Individual Competency — A Curriculum in the Child's Ecology, *James O. Miller, Janet C. Camp*	382

14. Infant Education Research Project: Implementation and Implications of a Home Tutoring Program, *Earl S. Schaefer, May Aaronson*   **410**
15. Minimal Intervention at Age Two and Three and Subsequent Intellective Changes, *Francis H. Palmer*   **437**
16. Comparisons of Preschool Curricula, *Ronald K. Parker, Mary C. Day*   **466**

Foreword

The faculties in Education of The City University of New York are much involved in the preparation of teachers for preschool children and the early childhood years, and have recognized a vacuum in the field regarding a systematic formulation of the theoretical foundation underlying preschool curricula.

We believe that preschool education is likely to become a major component of publicly supported education in the immediate future. Many curricula are being developed by public school personnel as well as by private enterprise, but these curricula and the instructional materials being generated frequently have little theoretical and research support. Accordingly, the general public may well be deluged by a multiplicity of programs and materials built upon little more than common sense or the author's particular beliefs.

Until now, the major contribution of psychology (and, more generally, of the social sciences) to education has been in the identification of individual differences among school age persons and adults. The psychology of individual differences and the instruments used to assess individual differences in cognition have had a greater impact on the operation of the schools than has any theoretical formulation in the field of learning or motivation. Recently, stimulated by the work of Piaget, educators and psychologists have begun to concern themselves with the processes of child growth and development, and it seems probable that the outcomes of this concern will have equally as great an impact on the organization of instructional programs and the design of curricula as the psychology of individual differences has had.

In order to provide at least a partial structure to the development of preschool curricula and to suggest some valid guidelines for the development of instructional materials, we believed it would be helpful to convene the proponents of the major theoretical systems underlying the cognitive, social, and emotional development of young children so that their viewpoints, the available research and needed research might be organized and made available to the professional education community as well as to the lay public.

The present volume evolves from papers presented at a conference on "Conceptualizations of Preschool Curricula" which was sponsored by The City University of New York. Its publication under the editorship of Dr. Ronald K. Parker, who was also coordinator of the conference, brings together in one place various educational and psychological theories around which preschool curricula are being developed today. We hope that in making these papers available to a wide audience we will have rendered a useful service to the community of early childhood educators.

Benjamin Rosner

Ronald K. Parker

Introduction

The editor invited a selected number of leaders in the field of early education to present papers representing their current thinking about curricula for young children. These individuals were selected on the basis of their pioneering ideas in early education or their major contribution in curriculum development.* The purpose of this conference was threefold: to provide each participant with the opportunity to describe his own curriculum conceptualization in the form of an original paper, to explore and examine together the various conceptualizations proposed, and finally, to reach wherever feasible a consensus on the need for clarifying, reorganizing, and updating some of the ideas and questions under discussion. These papers, taken together, form the body of this volume.

In the invitation to the conference each participant, apart from Bruner and Blank, was asked to include in his paper the following information: 1. A Theo-

---

* Since then, a recent survey (Parker and Ambron, 1972) conducted by the Office of Child Development has revealed that over 200 preschool curricula exist in various stages of development. Given this ever-increasing proliferation of materials, it has become close to impossible to separate out those curricula that represent promising approaches to early education. Furthermore, even where this can be done, it is very difficult on the whole to find concise statements elucidating their most salient features. Because this entire field is in a constant state of expansion and flux, the reader will appreciate the importance of selecting certain leaders to present clear conceptualizations of their curricula.

retical Orientation to Curriculum Development; 2. A Diagnosis of Need; 3. Curriculum Objectives; 4. A Selection of Content; 5. An Organization of Content; 6. A Selection of Learning Experiences; 7. The Role of Staff, and 8. A General Evaluation. Individual differences in style and approach often made it impossible for the participants to follow this outline exactly; however, in most cases, all of the major points were at least touched upon. For this reason, the reader would do well to keep in mind these eight breakdowns in studying each author's curriculum conceptualization.

Chapter 1 by Bruner and Chapter 2 by Blank provide broad guidelines and general information which have applicability to a wide variety of curricula — in particular, to those aimed at "disadvantaged" children. Bruner's chapter, entitled "Poverty and Childhood," offers a useful overview of three major topics directly involved with any conceptualization of preschool education for low-income children. After examining what is known today about the effects of poverty on child development in Western culture, he looks briefly at modern developmental theories from two vantage-points: whether they aid in the understanding of the general impact of culture as well as of the *particular* impact of poverty on a child's growth. This examination leads him to a discussion of the implication his findings have in terms of public policy and how early education ought to be conducted.

Blank presents 12 techniques that teachers can use when a child makes a wrong response, in addition to a discussion of the basic principles governing their use. Not only does this paper expand on her previous ideas concerning the use of programmed and didactic learning, but more importantly, it offers a systematic approach which she believes will facilitate the learning process and promote better teacher-child interchange.

Chapters 8, 10, 11, 12 and 13 represent both an updating and an extension of a number of curriculum conceptualizations that have previously appeared elsewhere. In Chapter 8, Nimnicht uses his work at the Far West Laboratory for Educational Research and Development to build on his earlier curriculum development project, The New Nursery School at Greeley, Colorado. However, the material reported here is much more extensive than any of Nimnicht's previous efforts, in that the long-range objective of his current program is to develop a responsive educational system that will be able to serve as a model for at least 90% of American children from the ages of three to nine.

The curricula of Robison (Chapter 10) and Karnes (Chapter 12) have been cursorily described in publications which report on empirical evaluations of their curriculum development. Nonetheless, their chapters represent original contribution since, for the first time, each of the programs receives an extensive conceptual treatment. Both Robison and Karnes are engaged in preparing new curricula for commercial publication, and the essence of their two papers is a general introduction to this "work in progress."

Anderson/Bereiter (Chapter 11) begin by clarifying some of the most common misunderstandings regarding the academic preschool and direct instructional model originally presented in *Teaching Disadvantaged Children in the Preschool* (Bereiter/Englemann, 1966). They then describe how the method of direct instruction can be extended to the teaching of conceptual skills, specifically those of communication and cognition.

In Chapter 13, Miller/Camp set forth a curriculum which, having grown out of one of the best-known preschool intervention programs (The Early Training Project of Gray/Klaus), focuses on the improvement of children's performance in preschool settings. The development of information-processing skills, positive motivation and attitudes conducive to maintaining and extending behavioral competencies are the main objectives of the Miller-Camp program.

Of the remaining chapters in this book, six of them (Nedler's, Kamii's Hooper's, Weikart's, Banta's and Whitney/Parker's) deal with curricula developed for preschool children between the ages of three and six. The other two, Chapter 14 (Schaefer/Aaronson) and Chapter 15 (Frank Palmer) discuss curricula which have been designed for children between 15 and 36 months old. As for Chapter 16 (Parker/Day), it is essentially a review of the preceding chapters and, as such, is best regarded as a summary statement.

Writing from the perspective of the Southwest Educational Development Laboratory, Nedler (Chapter 3) presents a method of curriculum design which she calls a "developmental process approach." The rationale for her paper is the fact that too few research workers have seen fit to describe in concrete terms the process by which a curriculum is developed. Nedler's model for curriculum development includes the following six design stages: 1. context analysis, 2. conceptual design, 3. prototype design, 4. pilot test, 5. field test, and 6. preparation for installing the curriculum in the preschool setting. It is Nedler's hope that this model will serve in the future development of other preschool programs, since it has applicability across most curricula.

The Piagetian theoretical orientation is represented in this book by two papers: one by Kamii (Chapter 4), the other by Hooper (Chapter 5). Kamii first identifies those concepts and hypotheses embedded in Piagetian theory having particular relevance to early education. The second task she sets herself is to develop a broad curriculum with cognitive and socio-emotional objectives that reflect the theoretical underpinnings of Piaget. As far as Hooper's approach to a cognitive curriculum is concerned, it has its theoretical roots in Piaget as well as in Werner, and focuses on such educational subcomponents as seriation, classification and memory discrimination.

Though Weikart (Chapter 6) is probably best known for his Cognitive Oriented Curriculum developed in the Yspilanti Public Schools, he was asked at the conference to discuss a less publicized facet of his research—the Unit Based Curriculum. This request was prompted by Weikart's report in 1969 that a "traditional" or unit-based curriculum was unusually successful in improving the performance of low-income and retarded children. In fact, based on measures such as the Stanford-Binet, Weikart was able to show that children in a unit-based curriculum did as well as those participating either in a cognitively-oriented curriculum or in the Language Training Curriculum developed by Bereiter and Englemann.

In Chapter 7, Banta traces the history of the Montessori movement prior to an analysis of the Montessori curriculum itself. His answer to the question of whether this curriculum is a myth or reality is an intriguing one and grows out of his Montessori Research Project conducted at the University of Cincinnati.

The Discovery Program by Whitney/Parker (Chapter 9) is a relatively new curriculum designed with the intention of involving parents in early education programs. This chapter represents the first complete statement of the Whitney/Parker approach to curriculum development, the scope of which has been extended since the conference to include the care and development of infants.

Because of the importance of early intervention during infancy, two papers were solicited by the editor which dealt with this subject. Schaefer/Aaronson (Chapter 14) were asked to contribute because an empirical evaluation of their Infant Education Research Project has shown it to be reasonably productive and to have a rather well-developed curriculum. In the case of Frank Palmer (Chapter 15), it was felt that his data describing the impact of "minimal intervention" (i.e., structured tutoring for 2 hours per week) on two and three-year-olds were very interesting. In fact, there is good reason to believe that his Concept Training Program may lend itself to one of the best longitudinal investigations of the impact of such intervention on very young children, since his plans call for following and assessing the progress of program participants over an eight-year period.

The purpose of Chapter 16, the last one in the book, is to provide a comparison between all of the preschool curricula presented by the conference participants. The main dimensions of this comparison are: 1. the foundations of the conceptualizations; 2. the goals and objectives of the curricula; 3. the methods for implementing the curricula, including instructional format, the role of the teacher, and parental participation; 4. the assumptions made concerning the motivation of children and the teacher's motivation and commitment to the program; and 5. the exportability of the curricula. For individuals with little background in the field, it is suggested that they might read Chapter 16 first as supplementary material to these brief introductory comments. On the other hand, the more experienced reader will no doubt find it more useful as a summary statement.

Bruner | *Introduction* | 1

Bruner examines the impact of social and cultural variables on the intellectual functioning of children from poverty backgrounds. The chapter provides a broad overview of the research literature on three topics. He first examines what is known about the effects of poverty on child development in western culture. Next, modern theories of development are presented as they aid in understanding the impact of culture on growth, generally, and the impact of poverty on growth, particularly. Lastly, Bruner highlights the implications of his analysis of poverty and developmental theory for public policy and for the conduct of early education programs.

Poverty has significant effects on children's problem-solving behavior, linguistic behavior, and what Bruner calls "patterns of social reciprocity." Each of these three areas are explored with extensive support from current empirical studies.

Theoretical formulations of development are assessed in terms of their strengths and weaknesses as they relate to early intervention programs. The "context-sensitive" theories may overemphasize environmental inputs while minimizing the universals of growth. "Context-free" theorists such as Piaget support an intrinsic anticulturalism while searching for universals.

Finally, reference is made to common features of successful intervention programs and illustrative principles for guidance in preschool curriculum development.

Jerome S. Bruner

Poverty and Childhood

1

I should like to consider what we know about the education of the very young, about what may be formative influences during infancy and early childhood upon later intellectual competence and how these influences may be more compassionately deployed. Our focus will be upon the manner in which social and cultural background affects upbringing and thereby affects intellectual functioning. And within that wide compass, we shall limit ourselves further by concentrating principally upon the impact of poverty and dispossession.

There is little enough systematic knowledge about what in fact happens to children during infancy and early childhood and even less on what its latter effects on competence may be. Indeed, in the current debates, it is a moot point as to what is properly meant by intellectual competence, whether or in what degree competence comprises soul, mind, heart, or the general community. Nor can the topic be limited to education. For the charge has been made by Royal Commissions and advisers to Presidents as well as by the anti-Establishment New Left that educational and socializing practice, before the school years as after, reflects and reinforces the inequities of a class system by limiting access to knowledge for the poor, while facilitating it for those better off. The charge is

---

Jerome S. Bruner is at Oxford University, Oxford, England. Portions of this paper were presented on the occasion of the Annual Citation Award of the Merrill-Palmer Institute, Detroit, Michigan, June 9, 1970. Printed by permission of the author.

even more serious: that our practice of education, both in and out of school, assures uneven distribution not only of knowledge but also of competence to profit from knowledge. It does so by limiting and starving the capabilities of the children of the poor by leading them into failure until finally they are convinced that it is not worth their while to think about school-like things. As Stodolsky and Lesser (1967) grimly put it, "When intelligence data and early achievement data are combined we have a predictor's paradise, but an abysmal prognosis for most children who enter the school system from disadvantaged backgrounds."

Why concentrate on the very young? The answer is, of course, in the form of a wager. For one thing, Bloom's (1964) careful and well-known work strongly suggests that a very major proportion of the variance in adult intellectual achievement, measured by a wide variety of procedures, is already accounted for by the time the child reaches the usual school-starting age of five. For another, there are enough studies to indicate, as we shall see, that certain possibly critical emotional, linguistic, and cognitive patterns associated with social background are already present by age three. But principally, I am moved to concentrate on the very young by my own research (for example, Bruner, 1969; Bruner, Lyons, and Kaye, 1971). The staggering rate at which the preschool child acquires skills, expectancies, and notions about the world and about people; the degree to which culturally specialized attitudes shape the care of children during these years — these are impressive matters that lend concreteness to the official manifestos about the early years.

Our first task is to examine what is known about the effects of poverty on child development in our contemporary Western culture — whether this knowledge comes from attempted intervention, from naturalistic studies, or from the laboratory. I do not wish to make a special issue of poverty, of whether or not it represents a self-sustaining culture, as Oscar Lewis (1966) urges; nor do I want to make the claim that poverty is in every culture the same. Yet there are common elements that are crucial wherever it is encountered and in whatever culture imbedded. We shall have more to say about these in context as we consider what it is that poverty and its attendant sense of powerlessness may do to the growing pattern of children.

Our second task is to look briefly at modern theories of development with a view to assessing whether they aid in the understanding of the impact of culture on growth, generally, and of the impact of poverty, particularly.

Finally, and again too briefly, we must examine what the implications of this exercise are for public policy and for the conduct of early education. As Robert Hess (1968) puts it, "The current growth of programs in early education and the large-scale involvement of the schools and federal government in them is not a transitory concern. It represents a fundamental shift in the relative roles and potential influence of the two major socializing institutions of the society — the family and the school."

Most of the work that compares children from different socio-economic backgrounds points to three interconnected influences associated with poverty. The first relates to the opportunity for, the encouragement of, and the management of goal seeking and of problem solving; it reflects differences in the degree to which one feels powerless or powerful, and in the realistic expectation of reward for effort. *What* the child strives for, *how* he goes about the task of means-end analysis, his expectations of success and failure, his approach to the *delay* of gratification, his *pacing* of goal setting — these are not only crucial, but they also affect how he uses language, deploys attention, processes information, and so on. The second influence is linguistic: by exposure to many situations and through the application of many demands, children come to *use* language in different ways, particularly as an instrument of thought, of social control and interaction, of planning, and so forth. The third influence comes from the pattern of reciprocity into which the child moves, whether middle-class or poor and dispossessed. What parents expect, what teachers demand, what peers anticipate — all of these operate to shape outlook and approach in the young. We must consider each of these in turn.

GOAL SEEKING AND PROBLEM SOLVING

A close reading of the evidence surely suggests that the major source of "cognitive" difference between poor and better off, between those who feel powerless and those who feel less so, lies in the different way goals are defined and how means to their attainment are fashioned and brought into play.

Begin with a general proposition: that one feels competent about oneself before feeling competent about others or about the world at large. Moffett (1968) observes how language complexity increases when the child writes or speaks about events in which *he* participated in a goal-seeking process. Consider these unlikely initial subordinate constructions from third-graders uttered in describing a task in which they have had a central, directive role:

> *If I place a flame over the candle, the candle goes out.*
> *When you throw alum on the candle, the flame turns blue.*

Or take two speech samples from lower-class black children, one describing a TV episode in "The Man From U.N.C.L.E.," the other a fight in which he, the speaker, was engaged.

> *This kid — Napoleon got shot*
> *And he had to go on a mission*
> *And so this kid, he went with Solo.*

> So they went.
> And this guy — they went through this window.
> And they caught him.
> And they beat up them other people.
> And they went
> and then he said that this
> old lady was his mother
> and then he — and at the end he say
> that he was the guy's friend.

And the fight:

> When I was in the fourth grade — no it was in the third grade —
> This boy he stole my glove.
> He took my glove and said that his father found it downtown on the ground.
> (And you fight him?)
> I told him that it was impossible for him to find downtown 'cause all those people was walking by and just his father was the only one that found it?
> So he got all (mad).
> So then I fought him.
> I knocked him all out in the street.
> So he say he give
> and I kept on hitting him.
> Then he started crying
> and ran home to his father
> And the father told him
> that he didn't find no glove.

As Labov (1969) remarks, the difference between the two is that the second has a consistent evaluative perspective or narrative line — from the speaker to the events that impinge upon him, and back to his reactions to these events.

A study by Strandberg and Griffith (1968) provides the third example. Four and five-year-olds were given Kodak Instamatic cameras and told to take any pictures that interested them. Their subsequent utterances about these pictures were compared with what they said of comparable pictures that they had photographed when told to do so in order to learn. In the first of the two excerpts, the child struggles — unsuccessfully — to find a context for an assigned picture. In the second, describing one he took on his own, it is built in. The speaker is a five-year-old.

> That's a horse. You can ride it. I don't know any more about it.
> It's brown, black, and red. I don't know my story about the horse.

*There's a picture of my tree that I climb in.
There's — there's where it grows at and there's where I climb up —
and sit up there — down there and that's where I look out at.
First I get on this one and then I get on that other one. And then I
put my foot under that big branch that are so strong. And then I
pull my face up and when I get a hold of a branch up at that place —
and then I look around.*

The bare, schoolish organization of the first seems so detached next to the intentional, active, egocentric perspective of the second.

Shift now, without benefit of transition, to much younger children — infants of four to six weeks, studied at the Center for Cognitive Studies. In this study, conducted by Kalnins (1970), infants control the focus of a lively motion picture by sucking at a preset rate on a special nipple. In one condition, sucking at or faster than the prescribed rate brings the moving picture into focus and keeps it there. In the other, sucking at this rate drives the picture out of focus and keeps it out. One group of infants starts with sucking for clarity and shifts to the suck-for-blur condition. The other begins with the suck-for-blur and shifts to the suck-for-clear condition — though the two conditions were never presented in the same session, or, indeed, on the same visit to the Center. Note two crucial points about performance. The first is that the infants respond immediately and appropriately to the consequences produced by their sucking — the pauses averaging about four seconds in suck-for-clear and about eight seconds in suck-for-blur. As soon as the consequences of sucking alters, the infant's response pattern shifts abruptly and appropriately. As a further feature of reacting to consequences in both conditions, the infant averts his gaze from the picture when it is out of focus — while sucking in the case of suck-for-blur, and while pausing in the other case.

For those not acquainted with the data on infant learning, these findings may seem a trifle bizarre though otherwise quite to be expected. They are, in fact, rather unexpected in the immediacy of the learning reported, particularly in the light of the painfully slow process of *classical* conditioning found in infants of comparable age by Papousek (1967), Lipsitt (1967) and others. Papousek's infants turned their head one way or another *in response* to an environmental event, as did the babies in the Brown University experiments. Kalnins' babies were learning to respond not to a stimulus, *but to a change produced by their own act*, and to store the information thus gained as an instrumental sequence involving their own action. Indeed, it may well be that a special type of recurring "critical period" is to be found in the few thousand milliseconds that follow upon a voluntarily initiated act. This is not the proper context in which to treat the matter in detail, yet it must be said emphatically that since the pioneer work of von Holst and Mittelstaedt (1950), the role of intention has become increasingly central in biology and psychology.

It was Held and Hein (1958) who first showed how crucial was the reafference output of "intentional" movement for adaptation learning. In their now famous experiment with yoked kittens adapting to prismatically induced angular displacement in the visual field, one kitten actively walked about an environment, the other was passively transported in a gondola through an identical path. The former adapted to the prisms, the latter did not. While we are still far from understanding the neural mechanisms of intentionality — variously called reafference, feed-forward, motor-to-sensory mechanism corollary discharge, or "Sollwert" — there are a sufficient number of leads to suggest that the pursuit will pay off.

In a word, probably the first type of acquired representation of the world the child achieves is in the form of an egocentrically oriented action scheme: a joint representation of action intended along with the consequences of that action — a matter to which Piaget (1954) has devoted some of his most exquisite descriptions.

But if one thinks of acquired egocentric orientation only as a phase out of which the child must grow enroute to becoming operational and decentered, then a crucial point may be overlooked. In Vygotsky's (1962) terms, the stream of action and the stream of language begin to converge in the process of interacting with the world in just such an egocentric orientation.

My colleague Dr. Greenfield (1969) notes, "Not only can people fail to realize goals, the environment can fail to provide a growth-promoting sequence for them. I should like to suggest that the goals set for the child by his caretakers and the relation of these to the child's available means is a critical factor in determining the rate and richness of cognitive growth in the early, formative years." She goes on to comment in this context, "If a mother believes her fate is controlled by external forces, that she does not control the means necessary to achieve her goals, what does this mean for her children?" The follow-up data from the Hess (1969) group's study of the relation between maternal variables and the development of intelligence (to which we shall turn shortly) shows that the more a mother feels externally controlled when her child is four years old, the more likely the child is to have a low IQ and a poor academic record at age six or seven.

Striking documentation of these points is beginning to be available at the intimate level of family interaction. One such study, now in progress, is Maxine Schoggen's (1969), an effort to elucidate differences in directed action that had been found in the children of the five-year study of Klaus and Gray (1968). She uses an "Environmental Force Unit" or EFU, which is defined as an act by any social agent in the child's environment directed toward getting the child to seek a goal. One crude finding already available — the data are only now in process of analysis — is that for lower-class families, some two-thirds of the children are below the total median rate for EFU's per minute, whereas only a quarter of the middle-income children are. This suggests how great a difference there may be in sheer emphasis upon goal directedness in the two groups.

One must note also that in the two major studies of how middle-class and poverty mothers instruct their children — Hess and Shipman (1965) and Bee, et al. (1969), a quite comparable trend emerged. They found, first, that middle-class mothers are more attentive to the continuous flow of goal-directed action. Secondly, they allow the child to set his own pace and make his own decisions more. Thirdly, they intrude less often and less directly in the process of problem solving itself. Fourthly, they structure the search task by questions that sharpen yet ease the search for means. Fifthly, they are more oriented toward the overall structure of the task than responsive to component acts in isolation. Sixthly, they react more to (or reinforce) the child's successful efforts than his errors (a practice far more likely to evoke further verbal interaction between tutor and child). These surely suggest some of the crucial differences that emerge in the goal-seeking patterns of economically advantaged and disadvantaged children.

To this evidence must now be added still another type of research finding, resulting from longer-term longitudinal studies tracing human growth from infancy through adolescence.

Kagan and Moss (1964) state in their well-known monograph, "It appears that the pattern most likely to lead to involvement in intellectual achievement in the boys is early maternal protection, followed by encouragement and acceleration of mastery behaviors." And then, "Following our best judgment in estimating the most desirable patterns to follow with young children, our educated guess remains that higher intelligence is fostered by warmth, support, and plentiful opportunity and reward for achievement and autonomy. Moreover, it is probably important to provide active, warm, achievement-oriented parental figures of both sexes after whom appropriate role patterns can be established" (p. 51). Add to this, finally, the conclusion reached by Robinson and Robinson (1968) in their review: "Children with a high degree of achievement motivation tend to become brighter as they grow older; those with a more passive outlook tend to fall behind their developmental potential (Bayley and Schaeffer, 1964; Sontag, Baker, and Nelson, 1958). The degree of achievement motivation is related to the sociocultural background of the child; middle-class children are more strongly motivated toward achievement than are lower-class children (Douvan, 1956; Lott and Lott, 1963; Mussen, Urbano and Bouterline-Young, 1961)."

There is a further multiplier factor in the effects we have been discussing: the impact of urbanization on the care of children. We have, until now, argued that poverty, by its production of a sense of powerlessness, alters goal striving and problem solving in those it affects, whether the powerlessness occurs in a depressed London working class borough, among Kurdistani immigrants to Israel, in a black ghetto, among uneducated and abandoned Greenland Eskimo mothers down-and-out in literate Copenhagen, or in the midst of Appalachia. The evidence points to a magnification of this effect when poverty moves to the city. Perhaps the most comprehensive study to date is by Graves (1969), who has compared rural and urban Spanish-Americans around Denver, as well as rural and urban Baganda around Kampala and Entebbe in Uganda. Interviews with mothers in her study show that urban mothers come to believe more than rural mothers that their preschool children cannot understand, cannot be taught ideas or skills, cannot be depended on. City mothers rated their children lower in potentialities for independence, for self-reliance, and for ability to help with the family. It is a cycle. When the poor mother moves to the city, she becomes trapped with her children — more irritable, more interested in keeping peace than in explaining and encouraging adventure. She often, then, produces the very behavior she rates down. At the same time the urban environment itself restricts outlets for the child, it also reduces the mother's confidence in her children's capacity for coping with those that are left.

Warren Haggstrom (1964), in a masterful review of the literature on the effects of poverty, comes to the conclusion that "the fact of being powerless, but with needs that must be met, leads the poor to be dependent on the organizations, persons, and institutions which can meet these needs. The situation of dependency and powerlessness, through internal personality characteristics as well as through social position, leads to apathy, hopelessness, conviction of the inability to act successfully, failure to develop skills, and so on" (p. 215).

Consider now some consequences of this pattern on the development of language usage in interactive speech, and likely as well in the internal use of speech in problem solving.

LANGUAGE AND POVERTY

It was perhaps the studies of Hess and Shipman (1965), inspired by Basil Bernstein (1961), that drew attention to *how* language was used in communicating with young children and what its significance was to the lower and the middle-class child. They asked mothers to instruct their own children to use an Etch-a-Sketch drawing pad, taking careful note of the mother's language and her mode of instruction. Their general conclusions have already been discussed. Looking in detail at linguistic considerations, we turn to a more recent study that used Hess and Shipman's system of classification with further elaboration. It documents the work carried out by Helen Bee and her colleagues (1969) at the University of Washington with four to five-year-olds. The Washington group also asked the mother to help her child accomplish a task (copying a house of blocks); in addition they observed mother-child interaction in the well-supplied waiting room and interviewed the mother afterwards about her ideas on looking after children. An excerpt from their paper can serve as summary.

> *The middle-class mother tended to allow her child to work at his own pace, offered many general structuring suggestions on how to search for the solution to a problem, and told the child what he was doing that was correct . . . The general structure offered by the mother may help the child acquire learning sets (strategies) which will generalize to future problem solving situations.*
>
> *In contrast, the lower-class mother did not behave in ways which would encourage the child to attend to the basic features of the problem. Her suggestions were highly specific, did not emphasize basic problem-solving strategies, and seldom required reply from the child. Indeed, she often deprived the child of the opportunity to solve the problem on his own by her non-verbal intrusions into the problem-solving activity.*

They comment on the fact that middle-class mothers ask so many more questions in an effort to help the child in his task, that their mode of operating linguistically could fairly be called "interrogative" in contrast to the more indicative and imperative modes of lower-class mothers.

Hess and Shipman (1965) had, of course, found quite comparable differences in mothers, though they distinguished three modes of communicating: cognitive-rational, imperative-normative, and personal-subjective. In the first the mother was task-oriented, informative, and analytic; in the second, she ordered and evaluated; and in the third, she pleaded for performance on grounds that it would please her. The highest concentration of the first mode was found among middle-class mothers.

Both studies point to early class differences in language use. One is the use of language to dissect a problem. In lower-class discourse, mothers more often order, or plead, or complain, than set up a problem or give feedback. Such usage possibly accounts for the "poor reinforcement value" of verbal reactions by the parents of less advantaged children (see, for example, Zigler, 1968): language is not usually used for signalling outcome or hailing good tries. What is most lacking in the less-advantaged mother's use of language is analysis-and-synthesis: the dissection of relevant features in a task and their appropriate recombinings in terms of connection, cause-and-effect, and so on.

The evidence surely leads one to the conclusion that there is more demand for as well as more use of analytic language among middle-class than among lower-class speakers. Turner and Pickvance (1970), for example, attempted to measure the difference by counting incidences of uncertainty in the verbal expressions of sixteen-year-olds from middle-class and poverty backgrounds who were making up stories or interpreting uncertain events. "Orientation toward the use of expressions of uncertainty is more strongly related to social class than to verbal ability . . . . In every case in which social class has been shown to be related to the use of expressions of uncertainty, it was the middle-class child who used more of them;" the middle-class child had more recourse to Wh-questions, to the use of "might be . . ." and "could be. . .," to *I think*, and to refusals to commit himself. As the authors say, "Bernstein's work suggests that the forms of socialisation typically employed in middle-class families are likely to give the children reared in these families greater scope for self-regulation, for operating within a wide range of alternatives. These socialisation procedures . . . are likely to give these children a greater awareness of uncertainty in certain areas of experience and are likely to encourage the children to be flexible in their thinking."

Other evidence also suggests a difference in analytic discrimination. Klaus and Gray (1968), among impoverished black children in Murfreesboro, Tennessee, and Robinson and Creed (1968), with slum children in London's Borough of Newham, agree in finding less fine discriminations made by lower-class than by middle-class children — at least in rather impersonal, school-like tasks. Marion Blank (1969) shows that tutoring children from poverty backgrounds to extract features from displays — distance, direction, form, for example — increases their measured intelligence (long a belief of Maria Montessori). Indeed, it is not surprising that Earl Shaefer's (1969) careful intervention study with one to three-year-old children in poverty families emphasizes such discriminative training, with good results in raising standard intelligence scores.

Another index of the analytic use of language is the accumulation of vocabulary. As Cazden (1970) puts it, "Consideration of vocabulary as an aspect of language cannot be separated from considerations of concepts as the whole of our personal knowledge. The content of our mental dictionary catalogs more than our knowledge of language; it catalogues our substantive knowledge of the world." Brown, Cazden, and Bellugi (1969) also point out that most instances of natural language instruction between parent and child relate to word meanings — true not only in their small Cambridge sample, but also for two lower-class black mothers in a Great Lakes city (Horner, 1968) and for mothers in Samoa (Slobin, 1968). It is of special interest then that Coleman (1966, pp. 292-295) noted that vocabulary subtests of an IQ test were more correlated with differences in quality of schools than were achievement tests in such more formal school subjects as arithmetic and reading. This suggests that the push to analysis, differentiation, synthesis, and so on, is accompanied by a push to achieve economy of means of representation in words. Again, the more active the intellectual push of the environment, the more the differentiation of concepts and of words, their markers. Hence the richer, better stocked vocabulary of the middle-class child.

Perhaps the most telling example of increased analytic-synthetic activity in speech *per se* comes from Joan Tough's (1970) study of two groups of three-year-olds, matched for IQ and about equal in verbal output, one of middle, the other of working-class background. Even at this age, middle-class children single many more qualitative features of the environment to talk about, and indeed, also talk much more of such relations between them as cause-and-effect. So there is good reason to believe that there is an early start to the differentiating process whereby children from one social class move toward a program of linguistic analysis-and-synthesis while the other move toward something else. Klaus and Gray (1968) remark of the "something else," "the children with whom we worked tended to have little categorizing ability except in affective terms; they were highly concrete and immediate in their approaches to objects and situations" (p. 16). Bernstein (1970) also comments on the fact that in carrying on a role-play type of conversation of the "he said/she said" variety, the child from the slum area is often richer and less hesitant in his speech, as if the more direct and concrete affective tone of human interaction were the preferred mode. Perhaps the "something else" is more thematic, personal, and concrete.

Let me then suggest a tentative conclusion from the first part of this much too condensed survey of class differences in language use. Bruner, Goodnow, and Austin (1956) drew a distinction between affective, functional, and formal categories. Affective categories involved the organization of events in terms of the immediate reactions they produced in the beholder, particular affect-laden reactions. Functional categories group objects and events in terms of fitness for the achievement of some particular goal or the carrying out of a particular task. Formal categories are those governed by a set of relatively universal criterial attributes in terms of which things can be placed without reference either to their use or to the "gut reaction" they produce.

It would seem to be the case, though I am aware of how very insufficient the data still are, that "middle-class upbringing" has the tendency to push the child toward a habitual use of formal categories and strategies appropriate to such categorizing — featural analysis of tasks, consideration of alternative possibilities, questioning and hypothesizing, and elaborating. It is a mode in which one uses language in a characteristic way: by constructing linguistically an analytic replica independent of the situation and its functional demands and manipulating the replica by the rules of language.

But note that it is *not* that children of different classes differ either in the *amount* of language that they "have," nor in the variant *rules* that govern their language. Cazden (in press) and Labov (1969) have compiled enough evidence from the extant literature to cast serious doubt on both the "less language" and the "different language" theories of class difference. The critical issue seems to be language *use* in a variety of *situations* and the manner in which home and subculture affects such usage. Or as Hymes (in press) puts it, children not only learn to form and interpret sentences but "Also acquire knowledge of a set of ways in which sentences are used." A striking experiment by Heider, Cazden, and Brown (1968), and an observation by Francis Palmer (1968), remind us again that the lower-class child, under appropriate conditions, *can* operate analytically quite well, though he might ordinarily or habitually not do so. Heider, et al. (1968) asked lower-class and middle-class ten-year-old boys to describe a picture of an animal in a fashion that would later permit distinguishing it from many other similar pictures. Some of the attributes they used in their descriptions were criterial in the sense of uniquely defining the target or reducing materially the range of possibilities; others were irrelevant for guiding one to the correct target. Both groups mentioned about the same total number of attributes, and moreover, both mentioned about the same number of criterial attributes, 18 out of a total of 67 for middle-class boys, 16 out of 69 for lower-class. Where they differed was in the number of adult prompts and requests that were necessary to get the attributes out of them: an average of 6.11 for the lower-class children, and only 3.56 for the middle-class. And by the same token, Palmer (1968) finds that if seven or eight hours of prior, rapport-establishing contact is assured before testing, most differences between lower-class and middle-class children become minimal. This point was also established by Labov (1968) when he concluded that Northern Negro English did not differ structurally or in underlying logic from Standard English.

What seems to be at issue again is the question of "personalness" and the egocentric axis. If the situation is personal, egocentrically organized, then the lower-class child can be just as complex as the middle-class one. But the lower-class child seems far less able to achieve "decentration," to analyze things in the world from a perspective other than his personal or local perspective. Perhaps this point will become more compelling when we examine a second feature of language that differentiates between social classes, to which we turn now.

This second feature involves communicating through language in a fashion independent of the situation. Grace de Laguna (1927, p. 107) says, "The evolution of language is characterized by a progressive freeing of speech from dependence on the perceived conditions under which it is uttered and heard, and from the behavior which accompanies it." She argues that the superior power of a written language inheres in this freedom from the contexts of action and perception, that all of its "semantic markers," to use a more familiar contemporary term (Katz and Fodor, 1964), are inherent in the utterance itself: they are "intrasemantic" rather than "extrasemantic."

Greenfield (1969) remarks on how the speech of technologically oriented societies (in contrast to preliterate, more traditionally oriented ones) becomes more like a written language in its increasing context-independence. The title of her paper, "On speaking a written language" is opposite not only, I think, to the trend in spoken language from a preliterate to a literate society, but also from working class to middle class society in Western culture. Basil Bernstein (1970) provides an interesting reason for the class difference. "We can see that the class system has affected the distribution of knowledge. Historically and now, only a tiny proportion of the population has been socialized into knowledge at the level of the metalanguages of control and innovation, whereas the mass of population has been socialized into knowledge at the level of context tied operations... This suggests that we might be able to distinguish between two orders of meaning. One we would call universalistic, the other particularistic. Universalistic meanings are those in which principles and operations are made linguistically explicit, whereas particularistic orders of meaning are meanings in which principles and operations are relatively linguistically implicit. If orders of meaning are universalistic, then the meanings are less tied to a given context. The metalanguage of public forms of thought as these apply to objects and persons realize meanings of a universalistic type. Where meanings have this characteristic, then individuals have access to the grounds of their experience and can change the grounds.... Where the meaning system is particularistic, much of the meaning is imbedded in the context of the social relationship. In this sense the meanings are tied to a context and may be restricted to those who share a similar contextual history. Where meanings are universalistic, they are in principle available to all, because the principles and operations have been made explicit and so public. I shall argue that forms of socialization orient the child toward speech codes which control access to relatively context-tied or relatively context-independent meanings." In short, it is the parochializing effect of a culture of poverty that keeps language tied to context, tied to common experience, restricted to the habitual ways of one's own group.

The comparative context dependence of the language of disadvantaged children shows up early. In Joan Tough's work (1970) on three to four-year-olds from middle and lower-class backgrounds in an English industrial city, the children were matched on Stanford-Binet scores and, roughly, on verbal output. "All of the children's 'items of representation'... were rated as to whether they required the presence of the concrete situation for effective communication. This concrete component constitutes 20.9 percent of the representation of the favoured children and 34.5 percent of the less favoured children. The most frequent form of the concrete component are pronouns whose only reference is to something pointed at in the environment. Such 'exophoric' reference is contrasted with 'anaphoric' reference, where pronouns refer to an antecedent previously supplied in words. The percentage of anaphoric references was 22.8 per cent for the favoured children and only 7.7 percent for the less favoured. This finding replicated Bernstein's research with children five to seven years old" (Hawkins, 1968). I do not know, save by everyday observation, whether the difference is greater still among adults, but my impression is that the difference in decontextualization is greater between an English barrister and a dock worker than it is between their children.

Two trends, then, seem to be operative in the *use* of language by middle-class children. One is the use of language as an instrument of analysis-and-synthesis in problem solving, wherein the analytic power of language aid, in abstraction or feature extraction, and the generative, transformational powers of language are used in reorganizing and synthesizing the features thus abstracted. The second trend is toward decontextualization, toward learning to use language without dependence upon shared percepts or actions, with sole reliance on the linguistic self-sufficiency of the message. Decontextualization permits information to be conceived as independent of the speaker's vantage point, it permits communications with those who do not share one's daily experience or actions, and in fact does, as Bernstein (1970) insists, allow one to transcend restrictions of locale and affiliation. Lower-class language, in contrast, is more affective and metaphoric than formal or analytic in its use, more given to narrative than to casual or generic form. It is more tied to place and affiliation, serving the interests of concrete familiarity rather than generality, more tied to finding than to seeking.

Both trends seem to reflect the kind of goal striving and problem solving characteristic of those who without protest have accepted occupancy of the bottom roles and statuses in the society that roughly constitute the position of poverty. It is not that the poor are "victims" of the system — they are, but so is everybody else in some way. It is rather that a set of values, a way of goal seeking, a way of dealing with means and ends becomes associated with poverty.

SOCIAL RECIPROCITY

Being socio-economically disadvantaged is no simple matter of deficit, of suffering a cultural avitaminosis that can be dosed by suitable inputs of compensation. It is a complex of circumstances at the center of which is usually a family whose wage-earner is without a job or where there is no male wage-earner. If there is a job, usually it is as demeaning in status as it is unremunerative. The setting is a neighborhood that has adapted itself often with much human bravura to "being at the bottom," with little by way of long range perspective or hope, often alienated by a sense of ethnic separation from the main culture.

This is not the place to examine the economic, social, and political means whereby some societies segregate social classes by restricting access to knowledge and eroding in childhood the skills needed to gain and use knowledge. Obviously, the techniques of segregation by class are not deliberately planned, and they often resist deliberate efforts of abolition. More to the point is to ask how the behavior patterns of the dispossessed are transmitted by the family to produce the forms of coping associated with poverty (or middle-class status).

We have already encountered a striking difference in the use of reward and punishment by the mother. One finding suggests that the transmission may be accomplished by so simple a factor as rewarding achievement in the middle-class while punishing or ridiculing failure among children of the poor (Bee, *et al.*, 1969).

Several studies point to a by-product in the form of a class difference in asking adults for help (for example, Kohlberg, 1968) or in showing doubt in their presence (e.g., Hawkins, 1968). The poor do much less of both.

Modelling of "class" patterns by adults — both in interaction with the child and in general — may be another source of family transmission. Hamburg (1968) draws some interesting inferences about such modelling from studies of higher primates. He writes, "The newer field studies suggest the adaptive significance of observational learning in a social context. Time and again, one observes the following sequence: 1. close observation of one animal by another; 2. imitation by the observing animal of the behavior of some observed animal; and 3. the later practice of the observed behavior, particularly in the play group of young animals." A like point is made for preliterate people, as in the close study of Talensee education and play by Fortes (1938) and the detailed observation of children's play among the Bushmen by Lorna Marshall (1963). They too point to the conclusion that observation and imitative incorporation in play is widespread and seemingly central.

Early language acquisition seems almost to be the type case of modelling. In a recent and detailed review of the language acquisition of the three children being studied at Harvard by Brown, Cazden, and Bellugi (1969), the importance of modelling is highlighted. But this work suggests that modelling is not a simple form of transmission.

The puzzling and challenging thing about learning language from a model is that the child is not so much copying specific language behavior from observation-and-imitation, but rather is developing general rules about how to behave from which various specific acts can be appropriately derived or interpreted. It is not at all clear how much we should attribute in early learning to the reinforcing effects of reward and/or punishment and how much to such rule learning acquired by observing or interacting with a model. Discussing the role of approval and disapproval as possible influences in the acquisition of grammar, Brown and his colleagues (1969) say, "In general, the parents fitted propositions to the child's utterances, however incomplete or distorted the utterances, and then approved or not according to the correspondence between proposition and reality. Thus *Her curl my hair* was approved because the mother was in fact curling Eve's hair. However, Sarah's grammatically impeccable, *There's the animal farmhouse* was disapproved because the building was a lighthouse... It seems then to be truth value rather than syntactic well formedness that chiefly governs explicit verbal reinforcement by parents — which renders mildly paradoxical the fact that the usual product of such a training schedule is an adult whose speech is highly grammatical but not notably truthful" (p. 70-71).

If it turns out to be the case that the young child is learning not only linguistic rules but also "rules about roles" and rules also about *ways* of thinking and *ways* of talking, then indoctrination in class patterns must be, in the linguists sense, generative and pervasive to a degree that is difficult to estimate. This would make even more meaningful the insistence of Smilansky (1968) that intervention programs emphasize *rationale* and *explanation* in order to reach the deep conceptual level where the class-pattern rules operate. In sum, both through compelling effects of approval and disapproval and by the modelling of "rule-bound" behavior, the family passes on class patterns of goal striving, problem solving, paying attention, and so forth.

Let me, in closing this section, make one thing clear. I am not arguing that middle-class culture is good for all or even good for the middle-class. Indeed, its denial of the problems of dispossession, poverty, and privilege make it contemptible in the eyes of even compassionate critics. Nor do I argue that the culture of the dispossessed is not rich and varied within its limits. (There are critics, like Baratz and Baratz (1970), who are too ready to cry "racist" to what they sense to be derogation of Black culture, or Yemeni culture, or Cockney culture.) But, in effect, insofar as a subculture represents a reaction to defeat and insofar as it is caught by a sense of powerlessness, it suppresses the potential of those who grow up under its sway by discouraging problem solving. The source of powerlessness that such a subculture generates, no matter how moving its byproducts, produces instability in the society and unfulfilled promise in human beings.

CULTURE AND THEORIES OF DEVELOPMENT

Thus far we have concentrated upon how a culture of poverty reflects itself in child rearing. But there is no reason to believe that the effects of such child rearing are either inevitable or irreversible — there are ways of altering the impact of middle-class pressures or of poverty. Better to appreciate this likelihood of change, we must look briefly at the nature of human development and at theories designed to explicate it.

There is a paradox in contemporary formulations. We have, on the one hand, rejected the idea of culture-free intelligence, and probably the Coleman Report (1966) put the finishing blow to the idea of school-free tests of intelligence. In this view, intelligence depends on the incorporation of culture. At the same time, there is a current vogue for theories of intellectual development promoting education strategies that presumably are unaffected (or virtually unaffected) by class difference, cultural background, and other conditions of the life of the child short, perhaps, of pathology. The only differences, according to such theories, are in time table, the steps being the same. It is a matter only of slower and faster, not of difference in kind. So on the one side we urge a context-sensitive view while on the other we propose that intelligence grows from the inside out with support from the environment being only in the form of aliments appropriate to the stage of development — a relatively context-free conception formulated most comprehensively by Piaget's Geneva school.

I suspect both kinds of theory are necessary — at least they have always existed. The strength of a context-free view is that it searches for universal structures of mind; its weakness is its intrinsic anti-culturalism. Aebli (1970) notes the Geneva dilemma: if the child only takes in what he is "ready to assimillate," why bother to teach before he is ready, and since he takes it in naturally once he *is* ready, why bother afterwards. The weakness of most context-sensitive views of development is that they give too much importance to individual and cultural differences and overlook the universals of growth. Their strength, of course, is in a sensitivity to the nature of the human plight and how this plight is fashioned by culture.

Two things, it seems to me, can keep us mindful of both universality and cultural diversity. The first is an appreciation of the universals of human culture, which revolve most often around reciprocal exchange through symbolic, affiliative, and economic systems. To alter man's participation in any of these systems of exchange is to force a change in how man carries out the enterprises of life. For what must be adjusted to is precisely these exchange systems — what we come to expect by way of respect, affiliation, and goods. Herein is where poverty is so crucial an issue — for poverty in economic life affects family structure, affects one's symbolic sense of worth, one's feeling of control. But beyond the universals of culture, there are universals in man's primate heritage. The primate series illustrates to an extraordinary degree the emergence of curiosity, play, planfulness, anticipation, and, ultimately, the human species characteristic ways of seeking, transforming, representing, and using information. Our review thus far has surely shown us how hope, confidence, and a sense of the future can affect the unfolding and nurturing of these capacities. If the conditions imposed by a culture can alter hopes and shrink confidence it can surely alter the use of these species–typical patterns of behavior. Theories of development are guides for understanding the perfectibility of man as well as his vulnerability. They define man's place in nature and signal opportunities for improving or changing his lot by aiding growth. A theory of development that specifies nothing about intervention is blind to culture. One that specifies only intervention is blind to man's biological inheritance.

ON INTERVENTION

With respect to virtually any criterion of equal opportunity and equal access to opportunity, the children of the poor, and particularly the urban poor, are plainly not getting as much schooling, or getting as much from their schooling as their middle-class age mates. By any conservative estimate of what happens before school, about a half million of the roughly four million children of each year of age in the United States are receiving sub-standard fare in day care, nursery school, kindergarten, guidance, whatnot. This is not intended as a psychological assessment but as a description of resources, of officially agreed-upon facilities (c.f. Sugarman, 1970). A few typical figures make the matter of facilities concrete. The kindergarten population in the United States in 1966 was 3,000,000 out of approximately 12,000,000 of the age group three through five. And the chances of a child in the lowest quarter of income being in kindergarten were immeasurably less than of a child in the top quarter. In 1967, there were 193,000 children in full-year Headstart, a definite improvement but a fraction of the estimated twenty-percent of the 8,000,000 three and four-year-olds who needed it, or 1,600,000. One should note that more than 80 percent of parents covered in the Westinghouse study (Cicirelli, 1969) said that their children improved as a result of Headstart, a fact to be reckoned with in the light of the Rosenthal effect (1968) and Graves' (1969) findings on the ebbing confidence of poor urban mothers in their children. Finally, in 1968 there were some 2.2 million working mothers in America with children three to five many of whom were the sole breadwinner in the family. In that same year, there were approximately 310,000 places for children in registered day care centers and in approved "private home" arrangement, one place per seven mothers. The present estimate, as of 1970, is that 9 percent of children two to five or 14 percent of children three to five with working mothers are catered for by day care.

I have been expressing the view that induction into this "culture of failure" begins early. In cities like New York, half the children born in poverty are illegitimate. Growing up in an urban ghetto, in the family structure often produced by such a setting, in the neighborhoods and schools that it spawns, surely diminishes the skills and confidence needed to use the benefits of modern industrial, democratic society on one's own behalf or on behalf of one's own group. Romanticism about poverty and its effects on growth is middle-class escapism.

Probably we cannot change this plight without changing the society that permitted such poverty to exist during a time of affluence. My first recommendation as a common-sense psychologist and as a concerned man is to transform radically the structure of our society. But that is not our topic. What can one do now, within the context of the changing society of today.

At a symposium of the "Education of the Infant and Young Child" at the American Association for the Advancement of Science late in 1969 (Denenberg, in press), I was asked to prepare a summary of reports on major programs of intervention. Several common themes running through the reports struck me.

The first was that there is an enormous influence exerted by the child's day-to-day caretaker, whatever the program. Programs had to consider the mother as a major factor. She had to be worked with, not compensated for.

Secondly, growth involves a small, step-wise acquisition of skill and competence on a day-to-day basis. Though theories of development emphasize principally the great leaps forward, it is in the management of day-to-day progress that discouragement or encouragement occur, where shaping has effect toward progress in one direction or another.

Thirdly, there is an enormous contribution to cognitive development from factors that, on the surface, are anything but traditionally cognitive. They are, instead, diffuse affective factors: confidence, the capacity to control one's environment, hope in the future, and the like. They too operate day-to-day, and they reflect the caretaker's mood.

Fourthly, it is now widely agreed that the idea of "enrichment" puts the child in the position of a passive consumer. One study after another showed that for a child to benefit he must be helped to be on his own, to operate eventually on his own activation. It is this activation that must be cultivated and supported.

Fifthly, and very practically, there seem to be a wide range of alternative ways to succeed in an intervention program — provided only they produce opportunities for mother and child to carry out activities that have some structure to them.

Beyond these specific conclusions, a general one stood out: the importance of initiative in the community as a means of activating parents and caretakers to do something for their children.

Haggstrom (1964) again makes telling points in discussing "the power of the poor." "In order to reduce poverty-related psychological and social problems in the United States, the major community will have to change its relationship to neighborhoods of poverty in such a fashion that families in the neighborhoods have a greater stake in the broader society and can more successfully participate in the decision making process. . . . The poor must as a group be helped to secure opportunities for themselves. Only then will motivation be released that is now locked in the silent and usually successful battle of the neighborhoods of poverty to maintain themselves in an alien social world. This motivation . . . will enable them to enter the majority society and make it as nurturant of them as it is at present of the more prosperous . . . One way in which the poor can remedy the psychological consequences of their powerlessness and of the image of the poor as worthless is for them to undertake social action that redefines them. . . . To be effective such social action should have the following characteristics:

1. The poor see themselves as the source of action.
2. The action affects in major ways the preconceptions, values, or interests of [those] defining the poor.

3. The action demands much in effort and skill. . .
4. The action ends in success; and
5. The successful self-originated important action [seen to increase the symbolic value of specific people who are poor]" (p. 7)

Haggstrom's list is admittedly ambitious. Even so, it falls short of dealing with some intractable correlates of poverty, as race in the case of the American Black, as nationality with the Italian Swiss, and so on. Yet it surely provides a sense of the role of community action in providing a background for countering the very problems of goal seeking, problem solving, and language usage we have been discussing.

Granted the importance of community action and revolutionary aspirations in the struggle against poverty's effects, one can still discuss psychological help for the child of poverty so that he may grow more effectively, not into a middle-class suburban child (who has problems of his own), but into one capable of helping himself and his own community more effectively. It is with some considerations along these lines that I should like to end this paper.

The expression, "no room at the bottom" means something. With an increase in technological complexity, capital-intensive rather than labor-intensive techniques come to prevail. Instead of *more* labor to run the economy, more intensively *skilled* labor is used. While school rejects can be absorbed in a society built on stoop-labor, they can no longer find a place in one where even the street sweeper gives way to well designed, motorized brushing machines. Since the first steps toward dropping out take place at home, the home is where the first remedies must be applied — only the first, for it avails little to give help in the nursery only to defeat the child later in school.

The objective of "curricula" for young children (as for older ones) is to produce the kind of generalist in skill, the "skill intensive" worker who is capable of acting as a controlling factor in the regulating, running, or curbing of a technology such as we are developing in the West, or one who is capable of understanding it well enough to serve, to criticize, to be controller rather than victim. I am assuming, to put it plainly, that man's cultural and biological evolution is toward general skill and intelligence and that the major difficulty we face is not in achieving such skill but in devising a society that can use it wisely. This means a society in which man feels at home and fulfilled enough to strive and to use his gifts. I am taking for granted that we do *not* want to curb idiosyncrasy, surprise, and the inevitable raucousness that goes with freedom.

My colleagues at the Center for Cognitive Studies, Drs. Greenfield and Tronick, have been devising a curriculum for a day care center at Bromley Heath in the Roxbury section of Boston. I have been enormously impressed with a set of implicit principles underlying their work (hopefully soon to be published) — principles that I have extracted from one of their memoranda, but with which they may not agree. Nonetheless, let me briefly run through them, not with a view toward comprehensiveness, but toward illustration. These will be many echoes from earlier parts of this paper.

1. **The active organism.** Human intelligence is active and seeking. It needs an environment to encourage such action.
2. **Effort after meaning.** The search for meaning and regularity begins at birth. There is a constant search for cues for significance that needs nurturing.
3. **Intentionality.** Action and the search for meaning are guided by intention, self-directed, and help can be provided to sustain such self-direction.
4. **Pace.** Each age and activity have a pace that requires respect and patience from those around the baby.
5. **Receptivity and state.** There is a state of alert awake receptivity when the child is hospitable to the environment. Use it for getting to the infant, rather than trying to break through unreceptive states.
6. **Cycles of competence.** Each newly emerging skill has a cycle of competence: initial crude effort, followed by consolidation and perfecting, followed by a period of variation. The phases require recognition to be helped to their completion.
7. **Prerequisites.** Skills require prior skills for mastery, as, for example, in the "fail-safe" method of sitting down from a standing position before risking walking. Opportunity to master prerequisites helps later skills.
8. **Appropriateness of play and objects.** Different activities have requirements that can be met by providing appropriate games, play, or objects. The child intent on exploring small irregularities with his fingers will work for hours on a board with irregular holes cut in it, each differently colored.
9. **Principles of the enterprise.** Activity, as the child grows older, is more temporally organized under the control of intention. It is dependent upon mobilizing means to achieve an objective. Provision of means and encouragement for such enterprises and protection from distraction is of utmost importance to growth.
10. **Principle of representation.** Useful memory depends upon finding effective ways of representing information — be it in customary action, in a well-liked game, in a vivid picture, or in words. Marking something for later use or recognition is an important aspect of growth.
11. **Analysis and synthesis.** Problem solving often consists of reducing a task or situation to its component parts and then reorganizing them. Taking apart and putting together games, objects, stories, problems is practice for such activity.
12. **Time perspective.** The future is constructed by each human being by coming to expect, by planning and achieving planned objectives, by

doing one thing so one may do the next, by learning how to hope and anticipate with realistic confidence. The process is long and begins early — probably with peek-a-boo.
13. **Principle of attachment.** Human young more than any other, perhaps, are dependent on a consistent caretaker who is there with warmth, certainty and effectiveness. It is in interaction with a caretaker that much of earliest learning occurs. A well-informed, decently satisfied, and hopeful caretaker is worth a pound of cure.

SUMMARY AND CONCLUSION

Persistent poverty over generations creates a culture of survival. Goals are short range, restricted. The outsider and the outside are suspect. One stays inside and gets what one can. Beating the system takes the place of using the system.

Such a culture of poverty gets to the young early — how they learn to set goals, mobilize means, delay or fail to delay gratification. Very early too they learn in-group talk and thinking and just as their language use reflects less long-range goal analysis, it also tends toward a parochialism that makes it increasingly difficult to move or work outside the poverty neighborhood and the group. Make no mistake about it: it is a rich culture, intensely personalized and full of immediate rather than remote concerns. The issue is certainly not cultural deprivation, to be handled, like avitaminosis with a massive dose of compensatory enrichment.

Rather the issue is to make it possible for the poor to gain a sense of their own power — through jobs, through community activation, through creating a sense of project in the future. Jobs, community action under community control, a decent revision of preschool and early school opportunities — all of these are crucial. But just as crucial is a sense of the change in the times — the insistence of the powerless that their plight is *not* a visitation of fate, but a remediable condition. If we cannot produce that kind of change, then our system that has worked fairly well (if exploitatively) since the industrial revolution will doubtless collapse, probably to be replaced by something premised far more on coercion for all rather than just for some. That is why the generation to be raised is so crucial a resource. It may be our last chance.

REFERENCES | 1

Aebli, H. Paper presented at the Center for Cognitive Studies, Harvard University, June 5, 1970.

Baratz, S. S. and Baratz, J. C. Early childhood intervention: The social science base of institutional racism. *Harvard Educational Review*, 1970, *40* (1), 29-50.

Bayley, N. and Schaeffer, S. Correlations of maternal and child behaviors with the development of mental abilities: Data from the Berkeley Growth Study. *Monographs of the Society for Research in Child Development*, 1964, *29* (6).

Bee, H. L., *et al.* Social class differences in maternal teaching strategies and speech patterns. *Developmental Psychology*, 1969, *1* (6), 726-734.

Bernstein, B. Social class and linguistic development: A theory of social learning. In A. H. Halsey, J. Floyd, and C. A. Anderson (Eds.), *Education, economy, and society*. Glencoe, Ill.: Free Press, 1961.

Bernstein, B. Social class, language, and socialization. Unpublished paper, 1970.

Blank, M. and Solomon, F. A tutorial language program to develop abstract thinking in socially disadvantaged preschool children. *Child Development*, 1968, *39*, 379-389.

Blank, M. and Solomon, F. How shall the disadvantaged child be taught? *Child Development*, 1969, *40* (1), 47-61.

Bloom, B. S. *Stability and change in human characteristics.* New York: John Wiley and Sons, 1964.

Brown, R., Cazden, C. B., and Bellugi, U. The child's grammar from I to III. In J. P. Hill (Ed.), *1967 Minnesota Symposium on Child Psychology, Minneapolis:* University of Minnesota Press, 1969.

Bruner, J. S., Goodnow, J. J., and Austin, G. A. *A study of thinking.* New York: John Wiley and Sons, 1956.

Bruner, J. S. Origins of problem solving strategies in skill acquisition. Presented at the XIX International Congress of Psychology, London, July 1969.

Bruner, J. S., Lyons, K., and Kaye, K. Studies in the growth of manual intelligence in infancy. *Monographs of the Society for Research in Child Development*, 1971.

Cazden, C. B. Language education: learning what, learning how, learning to. Presented at meeting of the Boston Colloquium for the Philosophy of Education, Boston University, April 13, 1970.

Cazden, C. B. The neglected situation: a source of social class differences in language use. *Journal of Social Issues*, 1970. In press.

Cicirelli, V. et al. *The Impact of Head Start; An evaluation of the effects of Head Start on children's cognitive and affective development.* Westinghouse Learning Corporation and Ohio University, April 1969.

Coleman, J. S., et al. *Equality of educational opportunity.* Washington, D. C.: U. S. Department of Health, Education, and Welfare, Office of Education, 1966.

Denenberg, V. H. (Ed.) *Proceedings of the American Association for the Advancement of Science Symposium on "Education of the Infant and Young Child"* (Boston, December 1969). London: Academic Press. In press.

Douvan, E. Social status and success striving. *Journal of Abnormal and Social Psychology*, 1956, *52*, 219-223.

Fortes, M. Social and psychological aspects of education in Taleland. Supplement to *Africa*, 1938, *2* (4).

Graves, N. B. City, country, and child rearing in three cultures. Institute of Behavioral Sciences, University of Colorado, 1969.

Greenfield, P. Oral or written language: the consequence for cognitive development in Africa and the United States. Presented at Symposium on Cross-Cultural Cognitive Studies, American Educational Research Association, Chicago, February 9, 1968.

Greenfield, P. M. Goal as environmental variable in the development of intelligence. Presented at Conference on Contributions to Intelligence, University of Illinois, Urbana, Illinois, November 15, 1969.

Haggstrom, W. The power of the poor. In F. Riessman, J. Cohen, and A. Pearl (Eds.), *Mental health of the poor.* New York: The Free Press, 1964.

Hamburg, D. Evolution of emotional responses: Evidence from recent research on nonhuman primates. *Science and Psychoanalysis*, 1968, *12*, 39-54.

Hawkins, P. R. Social class, the nominal group, and reference. Sociological Research Unit, University of London, Institute of Education, 1968.

Heider, E. R., Cazden, C. B., and Brown, R. Social class differences in the effectiveness and style of children's coding ability. *Project Literacy Reports*, No. 9. Ithaca, New York: Cornell University, 1968, pp. 1-10.

Held, R. and Hein, A. V. Adaptation of disarranged hand-eye coordination contingent upon re-afferent stimulation. *Perceptual and Motor Skills*, 1958, *8*, 87-90.

Hess, R. D. and Shipman, V. Early experience and socialization of cognitive modes in children. *Child Development*, 1965, *36*, 869-886.

Hess, R. D. and Shipman, V. C. Maternal influences upon early learning: the cognitive environments of urban pre-school children. In R. D. Hess and R. M. Bear (Eds.), *Early Education*. Chicago: Aldine, 1968.

Hess, R. D., *et al. The cognitive environments of urban preschool children.* The Graduate School of Education, The University of Chicago, 1969.

von Holst, E. and Mittelstaedt, H. Das reafferenzprinzip. *Naturwissenschaften*, 1950, *37*, 464-476.

Horner, V. M. The verbal world of the lower-class three-year-old: A pilot study in linguistic ecology. Unpublished doctoral dissertation, University of Rochester, 1968.

Hymes, D. On communication competence. In R. Huxley and E. Ingram (Eds.), *The mechanism of language development*. London: Ciba Foundation. In press.

Kagan, J. and Moss, H. A. *Birth to maturity: A study in psychological development*. New York: John Wiley and Sons, 1962.

Kalnins, Ilze. The use of sucking in instrumental learning. Presented as doctoral thesis at the University of Toronto, 1970.

Katz, J. J. and Fodor, I. A. The structure of a semantic theory. In I. A. Fodor and J. J. Katz (Eds.), *The structure of language: readings in the philosophy of language*. Englewood Cliffs, New Jersey: Prentice-Hall, 1964.

Klaus, R. and Gray, S. The early training project for disadvantaged children: a report after five years. *Monographs of the Society for Research in Child Development*, 1968, *33* (4).

Kohlberg, L. Early education: A cognitive-developmental view. *Child Development*, 1968, *39* (4), 1013-1062.

Labov, W. The logic of non-standard English. In James Alatis (Ed.), *Georgetown Monograph Series on Language and Linguistics*, no. 22, 1969.

de Laguna, G. A. *Speech: its function and development*. Bloomington, Indiana: Indiana University Press, 1927.

Lewis, O. The culture of poverty. *Scientific American*, 1966, *215* (4), 19-25.

Lewis, O. *The Children of Sanchez*. New York: Random House, 1961.

Lipsitt, L. P. Learning in the human infant. In H. W. Stevenson, E. H. Hess, and Harriet L. Rheingold (Eds.), *Early behavior: comparative and developmental approach*. New York: John Wiley and Sons, 1967.

Lott, A. J. and Lott, B. E. *Negro and white youth*. New York: Holt, Rhinehart, and Winston, 1963.

Marshall, L. and Marshall, L. The bushmen of Kalihari. *National Geographic*, 1963, *23* (6), 866-888.

Moffett, J. *Teaching the universe of discourse*. Boston: Houghton Mifflin, 1968.

Mussen, P. H., Urbano, P., and Bouterline-Young, H. Esplorazione dei motivi per mezzo di un reattivo: II. Classi sociali e motivazione fra adolescenti di origine italiana (Exploration of motives through a projective technique). *Arch. Psicol. Neurol. Psiciat.*, 1961, *22*, 681-690.

Palmer, F. Unpublished research reported at a colloquium at Harvard University, November, 1968. Cited in Kagan, J. S. Inadequate evidence and illogical conclusions. *Harvard Educational Review*, 1969, *39* (2), 274-277.

Papousek, H. Experimental studies of appetitional behavior in human newborns and infants. In H. W. Stevenson, E. H. Hess, and H. Rheingold (Eds.), *Early behavior: comparative and developmental approach*. New York: John Wiley and Sons, 1967.

Piaget, J. *The origins of intelligence in children*. New York: International Universities Press, Inc., 1952.

Piaget, J. *The construction of reality in the child*. New York: Basic Books, Inc., 1954.

Robinson, H. B. and Robinson, N. M. The problem of timing in preschool education. In R. D. Hess and R. M. Bear (Eds.), *Early Education*. Chicago: Aldine, 1968.

Robinson, W. P. and Creed, C. D. Perceptual and verbal discriminations of 'elaborated' and 'restricted' code users. *Language and Speech*, 1968, *2*, 182-193.

Rosenthal, R. and Jacobson, L. *Pygmalion in the classroom*. New York: Holt, Rinehart, and Winston, 1968.

Schaefer, E. S. Need for early and continuing education. In Victor H. Denenberg (Ed.), *Proceedings of the AAAS Symposium on "Education of the Infant and Young Child"* (Boston, December 1969). London: Academic Press. In press.

Schoggen, M. An ecological study of three-year-olds at home. George Peabody College for Teachers, November 7, 1969.

Shaw, J. W. and Schoggen, M. Children learning: Samples of everyday life of children at home. The Demonstration and Research Center for Early Education, George Peabody College for Teachers, 1969.

Slobin, D. I. Questions of language development in cross-cultural perspective. Presented at Symposium on "Language learning in cross-cultural perspective," Michigan State University, September 1968.

Smilansky, S. The effect of certain learning conditions on the progress of disadvantaged children of kindergarten age. *Journal of School Psychology*, 1968, *4* (3), 68-81.

Sontag, L. W., Baker, C. T., and Nelson, V. L. Mental growth and personality development: A longitudinal study. In *Monographs of the Society for Research in Child Development*, 1958, *23* (2).

Stodolsky, S. S. and Lesser, G. S. Learning patterns in the disadvantaged. *Harvard Educational Review*, 1967, *37* (4), 546-593.

Strandberg, T. E. and Griffith, J. A study of the effects of training in visual literacy on verbal language behavior. Eastern Illinois University, 1968.

Sugarman, J. M. The future of early childhood programs: An American perspective. Unpublished manuscript, 1970.

Tough, J. An interim report of a longitudinal study. Institute of Education, Language, and Environment, The University of Leeds, 1970.

Turner, G. J. and **Pickvance, R. E.** Social class differences in the expression of uncertainty in five-year-old children. Sociological Research Unit, University of London, Institute of Education, 1970.

Vygotsky, L. S. *Thought and language.* New York: MIT Press and John Wiley, 1962.

Zigler, E., and **Butterfield, E.** Motivational aspects of changes in IQ test performance of culturally deprived nursery school children. *Child Development*, 1968, *39* (1), 1-14.

Blank | *Introduction* | 2

In her previous and ongoing work with deprived children, Dr. Blank has focused on fostering the development of abstract thinking skills, and her main objectives have been the development of cognitively directed perception, the development of coding processes, and the development of the child's problem-solving strategies. Thus, Dr. Blank's emphasis is on process as opposed to content. Yet the manner in which the content is presented to the child and the corresponding task required of the child are vital — in terms of maintaining the child's motivation, providing him with problems which he can solve but which lead to a higher level of cognitive functioning, and providing him with models of problem-solving behaviors (models such as identifying relevant features of a situation, breaking down a task into smaller units, bringing known information to bear on an apparently novel situation, and experimenting to test assumptions).

In the following paper, Dr. Blank is concerned with the situation which arises when the child makes a "wrong" response. Explaining why ignoring and preventing the wrong response may allow the perpetuation of error patterns, she goes on to explain and demonstrate how a child's "wrong" responses may serve diagnostic purposes for the teacher and provide a valuable opportunity for the teacher and child to examine the "wrong" response. In examining the child's response and discovering with concrete objects or activities why it is inappropriate, the child is exposed to methods of evaluating thought which he may use at a later date.

Dr. Blank presents an impressive analysis of a variety of simplification techniques which may be used both to create a situation to which a child can successfully respond and to guide him toward completing the initially requested response (whether verbalization or motor activity). The techniques rely primarily on a "discovery" orientation which requires that the child be an active participant in the teacher-child dyad, although examples of occasions when didactic materials are considered appropriate are given. Mastery of the simplification techniques obviously poses a challenge to the teacher desirous of using them appropriately and immediately upon the occurrence of a wrong response. The challenge to using them in a small group situation as well as the one-to-one ratio described by Dr. Blank would be even greater. But much value may be gained from a large repertoire of teacher responses to "wrong" responses, and such a repertoire would enable "individualized" appropriate responses to each child. A major contribution of the paper is that it explicitly states techniques which teachers can use and describes the situations wherein their use is most advantageous. It is time "technology" came to the classroom, making the elusive "art" of good teaching more a possibility for all teachers.

Marion Blank

The Wrong Response: Is it to be Ignored, Prevented, or Treated?

2

The stimulus deprivation model has had an overriding influence in intervention programs for the preschool disadvantaged child. In this model, deficits in performance are the result of insufficient stimulation at critical periods in development and remediation rests on making such stimulation available. This assumption has led enrichment programs to focus on the part of the teaching-learning equation concerned with the imparting of information by the teacher. The other side of the equation – the child's incorporation of the material – is rarely mentioned. It is tacitly assumed that once the appropriate stimulation is offered, its effective incorporation is insured.

But what if this does not occur? What if the child ignores the information, misinterprets it, or is confused by it? Teachers have been sufficiently confronted by the wrong response (the refusal to respond, the irrelevant response, and the failure to respond[1]) to recognize that its occurrence is not unusual. A certain percentage of "wrong responses" are inevitable in learning and need be of little concern to the teacher. As indicated by their scholastic failure rate, however, errors in learning become a major factor in the performance of disadvantaged

Marion Blank is at the Albert Einstein College of Medicine, Bronx, N.Y. Printed by permission of the author.

children. It is easy to find scapegoats for this fact; depending upon one's bias, these scapegoats can be the child, the teacher, the "system," or the family. Unfortunately, the placing of blame does little to cope with a problem that must be overcome if the children are to maximize their functioning. The complexity of investigating the source of difficulty coupled with the rationale that children will and indeed should make mistakes has led us to ignore the fact that we have developed almost no systematic techniques for the management of "the wrong response."

At present, only two approaches even consider this problem — one is programmed learning and the second is didactic teaching. While both have important roles in the learning process, their handling of this problem is not sufficient for dealing with the difficulties of the disadvantaged child. First, let us briefly examine the usefulness of programmed learning. A basic principle of this approach is that the material be designed so that errors in performance be minimal (or nonexistent), since the aim is to build up positive learning while totally avoiding negative reinforcement. This goal is appropriate only if the wrong response represents chance behavior that can be bypassed with no ill effect. Wrong responses, however, often represent deeply ingrained error patterns or error sets (e.g., perseveration, rote imitation, attraction to salient perceptual characteristics, etc.) which must first be overcome if efficient learning is to take place. For example, if a child in a bright room were asked "What could we do to make this room darker?" he might well answer "Open the window" because his most common verbal and motor association to window is "open — close." It is certainly possible to avoid the occurrence of this error by building in the "correct" response through a carefully programmed sequence of learning. This approach relies on the hope that the wrong response will be extinguished through lack of reinforcement. Our experience suggests however, that the more likely result will be that the "correct" response will coexist with, but not displace or even dominate, the "incorrect" response. While this behavior may seem paradoxical, it is consistent with the well-established ability of children to interpret the same event both magically and with rational explanations.

The ineffectiveness of training children in the "right" response without eliminating the "wrong" response is evident in the tenuous grasp young children have of concepts such as "conservation" (Smedslund, 1964; Wohlwill and Lowe, 1962). These experiments might lead to the conclusion that training to overcome error sets is valueless unless the child has reached the "appropriate maturational stage." This assumes that all error sets are as resistant to modification as are those on the "conservation" task. Significant differences exist, however, between the type of error set represented by errors of "conservation" and the type of errors representing position set, rote association responses, perseveration, etc. In the latter instances, the child can be confronted with the clear, dramatic, and demonstrable inappropriateness of his response. For example, in the "window" illustration above, the child can be told "Okay, open it" and he can then be asked "Did that help to make the room darker?" This "confrontation with error" capitalizes on the preschool child's concreteness, for when faced with the perceptual verbal conflict, he is impressed by the inappropriateness of his verbalization. He is then quite amenable to seeking an alternative verbal explanation that is in accord with the perceptual reality. Even a superficial analysis indicates that the Piaget-type task is markedly different since no action or characteristic is available to reveal the inappropriateness of the child's initial response. Six beans spread out *look like* more than eight closely spaced beans and little can be done to show that this *verbalization* is an inaccurate representation of the visual impression. Thus, while all error sets cannot be overcome, it is possible to alter those error patterns where "proof" can be given to demonstrate the inadequacy of the child's response. This "proof" will, of course, vary with the developmental level of the child, e.g., while a young child is bound to concrete sensory-motor reality, the older child can deal with discrepancies on a purely verbal level.[2]

One further advantage obtains from actively dealing with error sets in contrast to methods which simply prevent them from occurring. The need to examine the "wrong" response not only solidifies the "right" response, but it also leads the child to internalize the "rules" used by the teacher to demonstrate the appropriate response. As a result, even when an adult is not present, the child has techniques by which to evaluate his thinking. These rules of course cannot be explicit in the preschool age child; rather, like language (Chomsky, 1957), they exist as an implicit framework for self-critical judgment.

Aside from programmed learning, the second major approach available for dealing with the "wrong response" is didactic teaching. As in the case of programmed instruction, this is a vital aspect of teaching for many types of children and many forms of information. For example, if a child holds up an object and asks the teacher its name, it would be foolish to apply discovery learning principles to the situation. Didactic teaching, however, is probably a poor method for most preschool age children since they are limited in their capacity to be the passive recipients of information. Didactic teaching is particularly inappropriate, though, for the disadvantaged preschool child. The wrong response or failure to respond in such children does not only indicate cognitive difficulties, but also reflects significant affective variables as well. Because of their learning difficulties these children experience anxiety in situations demanding intellectual skills. This leads them to say nothing that might condemn them (hence, the frequency of the "no response") or to say something — anything — that will remove the demands on them as quickly as possible (the "wrong" response). One might suppose that the removal of demands through didactic teaching would lead to learning for the possibility of failure is removed. Hence the child is free to devote his energy to the problem being discussed. In reality, however, the providing of information can often serve as a deterrent to learning. The child knows that once the demand is removed, the teacher will not "bother" him again and so he need not continue to attend (see Blank and Frank, in press). This result occurs regardless of whether the teacher herself or another child within the group supplies the information.

These difficulties make it essential to permit wrong responses to occur. At the same time, however, the teacher must be given techniques with which to cope when they do occur. The techniques outlined below represent an initial effort in this area. They were devised within the framework of a structured tutorial program for preschool children from disadvantaged backgrounds that is being developed by the present author (Blank and Solomon, 1968, 1969; Blank, in press). The basic premise underlying the techniques is that the problem confronting the child must be simplified, but not to the level where he is supplied with the answer. This is done to ensure the child's continued active participation in the problem solving situation. In almost all cases, the teacher was told that she should not be content with the child's having answered the simpler question. Instead, she should use these simpler questions to lead him back to the more difficult question which was posed initially. In addition, the teacher should not become dependent on any single technique in order both to prevent the child from becoming conditioned to only one kind of help and to give the teacher a wider repertoire to cope with the child's failure.

Perhaps even more important than the specification of the techniques themselves are the principles governing their use. Suggestions are therefore given as to when a particular technique is appropriate to the child and/or situation and when its use would be inappropriate. In general, the techniques proceed from those offering almost no degree of simplification to those in which the demands made upon the child are minimal. The following listing summarizes the techniques that are documented in this paper.

SIMPLIFICATION TECHNIQUES

1. Delay
2. Focus for attention
3. Repeats demand
4. Synonomous rephrasing
5. Partially completes task
   a. Verbal   b. Perceptual-motor
6. Focusing on relevant features
   a. Verbal   b. Perceptual-motor
      1. on relevant part
      2. action or function
      3. characteristic
7. Dissects task into smaller components
   a. Isolates individual components
   b. Introduces guide to emphasize unique characteristics of situations

8. Repeats demonstration for step by step clarification
9. Offers relevant comparisons
10. Relates unknown to the known
11. Directed action to recognize salient characteristics
12. Didactic
    a. Gives relevant facts or labels
    b. Gives known referent to mediate new concept
    c. Provides model

1. DELAY
This technique is specifically geared towards handling the impulsivity which exists in all young children and which dominates the behavior of some children. While delay alone is not sufficient, the need to delay at least affords the child the opportunity to interrupt his impulsive first response and rethink the problem confronting him. This technique should be used only when the teacher is almost certain that the child can perform the behavior demanded but has not done so because of his impulsivity.

WHEN THIS TECHNIQUE MIGHT BE APPLICABLE
1. When the child does not wait for full directions.
    Example — Teacher "Pick up the . . ." — child starts grabbing objects. Teacher "Wait a minute. Listen to what I want you to pick up."
2. When he quickly and automatically says "I don't know" to problems he has shown himself capable of mastering.
    Example — Teacher "What is the boy in the picture wearing?" Child "I don't know." Teacher "Hold it. Take a look and see if you can show me what I asked for."

WHEN THIS TECHNIQUE MIGHT *NOT* BE APPLICABLE
1. When the child has offered no response, particularly when he has been given a motor command.
    Example — Teacher "Lift up the big one over there." Child does nothing. Teacher "You have time. You don't have to rush. Just lift it when you want to."
2. Child has offered an incorrect response after obviously attempting to think through the solution.
    Example — Teacher "Look at these things (a strainer, a pot, a spoon). In which one could we heat the milk?" Child looks carefully at all and points to strainer. Teacher "No, take your time. Which one do you think we could use?" (Here the teacher's comment is merely a signal to child to change his response without indicating why his first answer is wrong.)
3. When child has offered an appropriate answer but not the one that the teacher "wanted."

Example — Child has spilled some milk. Teacher "What could we use to wipe it up?" Child "A paper napkin." Teacher "Yes, we could I guess. But think again, what else could we use?" (Here the teacher wants a different answer such as paper towel or mop, but she gives no reason, and there is no reason, why the child's first response is unacceptable.)

2. FOCUS FOR ATTENTION

Frequently a child makes an error on a task after having correctly initiated the action that was requested. This occurs most commonly in situations where the command is contrary to a usually performed rote sequence or where there are strong perceptual components which distract the child. In this case, the child can often be brought back to the original request by simply asking him to remember what was demanded of him.

WHEN APPLICABLE — The child has begun to execute an action correctly, but then fails to complete it accurately.
Example — Teacher "Go to the sink and get me the pot." Child goes to the sink and reaches for the first thing he sees which is a glass. Teacher "Do you remember what I asked you to bring?"

WHEN NOT APPLICABLE — When a child makes no move to carry out a command (either through fear and/or failure to comprehend), the request for expressive verbalization when he has not been able to fulfill the receptive language task serves to increase rather than decrease his difficulty.
Example — Teacher "Bring me the pencils on the desk." Child does nothing. Teacher "What did I just ask you to bring?"

3. REPEATS DEMAND

This technique is closely related to "Focus for Attention" and it often can be used in similar situations. The present technique, however, makes fewer demands since it eliminates the need for the child to verbalize the initial request. It is particularly useful if a child has failed to meet the demands of situations which are relatively simple for him. The demand (whether a question, command or statement) can either be repeated exactly or in a slightly altered form by changing the emphasis of the command.

WHEN APPLICABLE — When a child fails a problem because his attention was not fully directed to the task presented by the teacher.
Example — Teacher "Put your coat on the chair next to the table." — "No, not on the table; put it on *the chair* that's next to the table."

WHEN NOT APPLICABLE — The greatest danger with this technique is the possibility of the teacher persisting in endless repetition of the same unfulfilled demand. If after the first repetition the child still fails, an alternative technique must be tried even if the teacher is certain that the child can achieve the requested action.

>Example — Teacher "Taste the drink now. Is it sweet?" Child —. Teacher "Tell me how it tastes. Is it good and sweet?" Child —. Teacher "Did you taste it? Do you think it's sweet?"

4. SYNONYMOUS REPHRASING

A child often encounters difficulty with a task because he fails to understand the particular phrase or sentence used by the teacher. The adult may not appreciate the child's difficulty in this regard because of the strong temptation to think that the words we use with children "are so simple" that they must be understood. Nevertheless, many factors exist to interfere with the child's comprehension of simple words (e.g., lack of the particular information, dialect differences, focusing on a main word in a sentence and ignoring key terms such as adverbs, prepositions, etc.). These obstacles may be overcome if the teacher has a repertoire of *simple*, synonymous terms to offer the child.

>WHEN APPLICABLE — When the child appears to have attended to the verbalization but is having difficulty in proceeding with the task. Having reduced the task to the verbalization already available to the child, the teacher should then point out the equivalences between the two phrases.
>
>Example — Teacher "Lift the box off the floor." Child —. Teacher "I mean I want you to pick it up with your hands." Child does it. Teacher "See, you lifted it up."

>WHEN NOT APPLICABLE — When the child's failure is not caused by a lack of familiarity with the label *per se*, but rather by a failure to understand the concept represented by the label. This occurs particularly with relative concepts (like family relationships, size, etc.) where the concept cannot easily be defined in synonymous terms.
>
>Example — Teacher "Get me the tall doll." Child —. Teacher "The tall one is the one that's bigger than the others. No, not that one. I mean the one near the pillow." (In this case, the teacher's synonymous rephrasing has failed and her new phrasing is not an adequate representation of the initial concept she was trying to teach. In effect she has dropped the concept and substituted a known, different concept.)

5. PARTIALLY COMPLETES TASK

In certain complex situations, the teacher may begin to fulfill the demands she has placed upon the child and leave only a small part of the task unfinished for him to complete. This technique is particularly useful when the child's behavior indicates that he wishes to try to meet the demand but that he is almost totally immobilized in knowing how or where to begin.

WHEN APPLICABLE — This technique is most appropriate for relatively simple situations involving short, well-defined tasks which can be completed within one or two steps (e.g., sentence imitation, drawing of figures, counting, rote sequences (such as poems), etc.).

Example
A. Verbal — Teacher asks "What is a pail for?" Child says nothing. Teacher says "It can carry w_____."
B. Non-verbal — Teacher "Now you draw the triangle." Child does nothing. Teacher "I'll start. I'll make these two lines." She does so and says "Now you draw the rest."

WHEN NOT APPLICABLE
1. The greatest misuse of this technique is not its inappropriate use (i.e., using it in the wrong circumstances) but rather the tendency to disguise a didactic answer in a question form. As a result, it appears that the child has been left with a problem when in fact, the total answer has been supplied.

Example — Teacher asks "What do you call this?" Child —. Teacher Asks "Do you think it's a . . . ball?"

2. This technique should also not be used in cases where a relatively long, interrelated sequence is involved since a whole chain of answers (except for one item) must be supplied. As a result, one cannot be sure that the child had understood all the items and their interrelationships. This may lead the child to resort to random guessing when the teacher finally requests him to complete the task since he knows "something more is demanded" but he does not know what it is.

Example — Teacher "Now how did we build the chair yesterday?" Child —. Teacher "Well, we got nails, a hammer, we took the picture of the chair from the magazine and then we did what?" (In such a case, it would be preferable to break the task into individually manageable discrete components such as "What was the first thing we got?" and then "What did we do with it?", etc.)

6. FOCUS ON RELEVANT FEATURES

When confronted with complex questions, one of the great difficulties young children experience is a failure in knowing even how to begin to approach the problem. Frequently any progress on the problems requires the child to differentiate the relevant from the irrelevant features, and even prerequisite to this, to recognize that some features are relevant and others not. It is therefore extremely useful to the teacher to help the child focus on what is relevant in the situation —

The Wrong Response

this can vary in such a way that it might be either a part, action (function), or characteristic of the situation. (In a sense, all the simplification techniques help to focus the child on the required information. In this technique, however, the emphasis is on becoming cognizant of relevant properties associated with the phenomena under study.)

WHEN APPLICABLE

A) On verbal level

When teacher knows that the child possesses the necessary vocabulary (including comprehension of the referent) but he does not recognize that this concept is relevant in this situation.

> Example — Teacher "Why did you pull your hand away from the stove?" Child says nothing. Teacher "Well, how did the stove feel?" (Focus on relevant characteristic.) Teacher "Why did he think the little boy was sad?" Child —. Teacher "Well, what had he just seen the little boy doing?" (Focus on relevant action.)

B) On perceptual level

When child is non-verbal on an expressive level it is useful to reduce the task to receptive language so that he has only to act on the material.

> Example — Teacher points to a valise without a handle and says "Why couldn't we carry this valise?" (Silence) Teacher points to a valise with a handle. "Touch the part on this valise that lets us carry this valise." (Focus on relevant part.)

WHEN NOT APPLICABLE

A) On verbal level

1. When the child is very ill at ease with verbal material (especially in initial sessions).

> Example — Teacher "Now come on. I'm sure you know what's inside the box." Child —. Teacher "Look at the cover and tell me what you think is inside." Child —. Teacher "Well, if you don't want to tell me what's on the cover, tell me what you'd like to find inside. Just take a guess." (Here the teacher has abandoned the problem by not providing any framework to judge the appropriateness of the child's response.)

2. When attribute focused upon involves such a subtle characteristic that the child may fail to discern its relevance.

> Example — Teacher "Why do you think children wear sweaters?" Child —. Teacher "Well, how would you feel if you didn't have a sweater on?" (This is to be contrasted with clearly demonstrable function of clothing items such as shoes and winter coat.)

B) On perceptual level

When the perceptual field is extremely complex so that the child will not know where to direct his attention.

Example — Teacher "Well, what could we use if we wanted to make a house?" Child —. (Teacher points to a table covered with objects.) "Well, we'll need something hard — look over there and find something that is hard that we could use for building."

7. DISSECTS TASK INTO SMALLER COMPONENTS

The method of *focusing* outlined above was designed to enable the child to begin to analyze the relevant features of a complex situation. In some situations, however, all components of a task may be relevant and the child may be bewildered because of the number of units with which he must deal. In such a case, the teacher may dissect the task into its various components so that the child can complete the problem in partial steps. This goal can be accomplished in one of two ways; either the teacher can a) isolate individual components by sequentially focusing the child on the various subunits forming the totality or b) introduce some cue (perceptual or verbal) which restructures the situation so that its significant characteristics are emphasized. Both techniques share, in common, the fact that the teacher must decide which parts should be emphasized and the order in which the totality should be dissected. The second technique, however, requires greater ingenuity since the totality is not composed of clearly recognizable units. As a result, skill is required to discern how readily available, but not clearly related, background material can be brought in to dissect a seemingly indivisible situation.

A. Isolates individual components.

WHEN APPLICABLE — When the situation has clearly demonstrable components which will maintain some central aspect of their identity even if removed from the totality.

Example

1. Teacher gives a complex command such as "Fill the jar up to this line, stir the water with the spoon and then put the cap on the jar." Child —. Teacher "Okay, first fill the jar to this line. . . . Good. Now . . ., etc."

2. Teacher presents a group of blocks in a pattern and says "Now you make the same pattern over here with these blocks." Child —. Teacher "Show me the block at the bottom. Get one like it."

WHEN NOT APPLICABLE — When the teacher dissects the task into such simple components that some essential feature of the totality is now lost, with the likely result that the aspect causing the child the greatest difficulty was not coped with at all.

Example — Teacher "Draw this square." Child —. Teacher "Draw one line, now another line, etc." (In this case, the teacher has omitted directionality and has thereby omitted an essential component of configuration.)

B. Introduces guide to emphasize unique characteristics of situation.

WHEN APPLICABLE — When the child's behavior or thinking indicates that he has failed to perceive some essential element(s) of the situation confronting him.

Example

1. Teacher says "Now write the p and d". Child writes them both as p. Teacher "look at this." She points to the p and d and draws lines across them (p̶ d̶) as an initial guide to help the child recognize the importance of directionality in these letters. (It should be noted that the *introduction of these additional perceptual cues* serves to simplify a situation which is complex precisely because of its lack of distinctive features.)

2. Teacher "Why do you think we couldn't get this sponge into the (small) cup and we could fit the marble?" Child "Because it's a sponge." Teacher "Okay, *I'll cut this sponge into two.* Now it's still a sponge. Why does it go into the cup now?" (The teacher here has shown the child that "spongeness" is not the reason for the failure of the sponge to fit into the cup. In addition, she redirected the lesson onto size by manipulating and structuring the competing perceptual cues of the material in such a way that the relevant concept was emphasized.)

WHEN NOT APPLICABLE

1. The introduction of additional cues can often increase rather than decrease the complexity of a situation, particularly if the task demands a restructuring of a rote activity. While this use of the technique need not be avoided, the teacher should be aware of whether or not the restructuring is simplifying the task.

Example — Teacher has observed that the child easily executes the drawing of circles. She then puts a line through the circle O and says "Now just draw me the top part of the circle." (In this case, the child is being asked to change a well established motor sequence and thus this represents a major increase rather than a decrease in the cognitive demands.)

2. The restructuring can also be used in such a way that it serves the same role as a didactic answer. As a result, it does not simplify, but rather totally removes the demands.

Example — Teacher shows child a face and says "Show me the part of the face that we see with." Child —. Teacher takes a paper and covers all of the face save the eyes and then repeats her question. (In this case, the teacher has removed all need to think in terms of the function of the object and is now merely asking for a label of the exposed objects.)

The Preschool in Action

8. REPEATS DEMONSTRATION FOR CLARIFICATION

A child's behavior often indicates that he has failed to understand some central element in a phenomenon which has just been demonstrated. The repetition of the phenomenon may then be a useful technique to help the child absorb the information. This repetition is not simply a second exposure, but rather a demonstration in which the child's observation may be guided by the questions he failed after the first demonstration.

> WHEN APPLICABLE — When the focus of a particular idea has not been attained by the child either through a failure in attention or because he was dazzled by some more potent stimulus in the situation.
>
> Example — Teacher asks "Where did I put the key to get the door to open?" Child —. Teacher can say "Well, watch again. I'm going to do it over — and then you can show me."
>
> WHEN NOT APPLICABLE — When the child gives an ambiguous response which does not clearly indicate whether or not he has gained the information. Repetition of the demonstration should not be resorted to unless a more demanding level has first been applied to evaluate the extent of the child's information.
>
> Example — Teacher asks "Where did we just get the water for this plant?" Child points vaguely toward the sink. Teacher says "Wait. I'll get some more water for you and you can see where it came from." (In this case, it would have been preferable to say "Go over and show me the place it came from.")

9. OFFERS RELEVANT COMPARISONS

Of the range of possible simplification techniques, the one of offering relevant comparisons seems to straddle the line between didactic teaching (giving the correct information) and "discovery" learning (still requiring the child to determine the required information by himself). The teacher can begin to rely excessively on this method which only requires her to offer a series of contrasting responses, one of which is obviously correct (or obviously incorrect). Such excessive reliance not only restricts the teacher's repertoire, but more seriously, leads the child to know that if he waits the correct answer will be offered in the form of a fairly obvious choice. As a result, he will learn to abandon his problem solving efforts when difficulty occurs. Nevertheless, this technique is a useful one for the teacher to possess. In order to vary the teacher's repertoire with this technique, a number of different versions of the technique are illustrated.

> WHEN APPLICABLE — When the child has not been able to answer an open-ended situation or problem involving labels, facts, characteristics, or actions.
>
> A. Correct from Obviously Incorrect

Example — Teacher "What did we open when we came into the room?" Child —. Teacher "Well, did we open the door or the ceiling?"

B. Contrast Through Incorrect Alternatives

Example — Teacher "Where did the ball go?" (Ball is resting next to the door.) Child —. Teacher "Did it go under the table?"

(In this technique, it is important that the incorrect choice be selected from the same framework as the correct response. In this way, it can serve as a background which will bring the correct choice to the foreground. For example, if an object has dropped under the table, the mention of various locatives will help the child realize that "place" is the relevant dimension.)

C. Offers Correct for Comparison

Example — Teacher "Put these pieces together to form a face." Child manipulates pieces, does not complete puzzle correctly, but stops, saying he has finished the work. Teacher brings out identical model in completed form and says "Does yours look like this one?"

WHEN NOT APPLICABLE

a) Choices closely associated with the correct object (either in time or space) should not be offered since they are so closely linked in the child's mind that he may be unable to see them as distinct. As a result, they do not simplify the problem, but instead add to its complexity.

Example — Teacher "What can we write with?" Child —. Teacher "Can we write with a pen or a paper?" (Here the child might easily say "paper" because it is so closely associated with pen and the teacher would have difficulty in showing that paper was an inappropriate response.)

b) When the child readily spouts rote associations to particular categories, the use of this technique on a verbal level will further random guessing and thus reinforce his behavior in this regard.

Example — Teacher "Which block did I put in the box?" Child —. Teacher "Was it red?" (In this setting, the child may easily agree or begin to shout one color after another in the hope that by chance, he will hit on the correct one. It should be noted that when the child engages in this sort of activity, his behavior is barely influenced by his having seen the object; the same responses are likely if the teacher had shown no items and merely said "Say some colors." To prevent this, it is sometimes preferable for the teacher to reduce the task to a perceptual level by taking some differently colored bits of paper and saying "Find me a piece of paper that is the same color as the block you saw me put in the box." In such a case, if the child makes a wrong choice, it can easily be proven to him that his response was not correct since the color he selected can be compared directly with the block that had been hidden.)

10. RELATING UNKNOWN TO THE KNOWN

One of the best ways to help the child cope with difficulty is to have him realize that information already in his repertoire can be useful in handling new problems. This goal is perhaps most directly reflected in this simplification technique where the analogy between the known and the unknown is made explicit.

> WHEN APPLICABLE — When the child is confronted with a concept he already knows, at least in part, but he does not recognize its relevance in this situation.
>
> Example
>
> 1. Teacher "How do you think the boy felt when the teacher gave him an ice cream?" Child —. Teacher "Well, how might you feel if I gave you some ice cream now?" (This is to be distinguished from a simplification using "focusing" where the question might be "Well, look at his face. Does he seem happy or sad?")
>
> 2. Teacher "Now the spaghetti is hard. How do you think it will feel after it is cooked?" Child —. Teacher "Well, do you remember when we cooked the potatoes? How did they feel?" (Focus on relevant characteristic in analogous situation.)

> WHEN NOT APPLICABLE — When the child is confronted with a complex concept where any attempt to relate the as yet unknown concept to a "known concept" requires highly analogous reasoning which will only serve to confuse the child even further.
>
> Example — Teacher "See the red block measured this high on the ruler and the blue block this high. So what can we use the ruler for?" Child —. Teacher "Look at the scale. What is the same about the scale and the ruler?" (In this case, it would be preferable to contrive a situation where two objects of very similar height are separated so that the child cannot easily compare them on a simple visual basis. The teacher can then lead the child to use the rule to measure them and ask about the differences. "Where did the green block reach on the ruler and where did the purple block reach?" "Did they reach to the same place?" "Okay, what did the ruler show you about the two blocks?"

11. DIRECTED ACTION TO RECOGNIZE SALIENT CHARACTERISTICS

Nursery school educators have emphasized the need for the child to manipulate appropriate exemplars of concepts, before demanding their recognition on a verbal level. Although the teacher may accompany the child's actions with relevant verbalization, the situation rarely demands that the child attend to the verbal information so supplied. By contrast, the technique cited below structures the situation so that the child must incorporate the teacher's verbalization. The demands placed upon the child, however, are quite simple in order to reduce the anxiety generated by a concept which seems to be beyond him. This is achieved by a simple command which focuses the child on the central features of the concept (commands such as this should be differentiated from the many simple commands that occur in the course of a lesson such as "Get me the playdough now.").

> WHEN APPLICABLE — When a child is faced with a concept which he does not seem to understand, but which contains clearly demonstrable salient features.
>
>> Example — Teacher asks "How is the ice different from the water?" Child seems unable to predict and so the teacher can say "Turn over the cup of water and turn over the tray of ice." (This can be followed by such questions as "Which one spilled all over the floor?" "Why didn't the ice spill?", etc.)
>
> WHEN NOT APPLICABLE — When the action which the teacher demands will not reveal the properties which she is attempting to illuminate.
>
>> Example — A child does not understand mailing a letter (a concept that is unverifiable and from our viewpoint, unteachable). Teacher says "Here, put on the stamp because then we will be ready to mail it." (This in no way explains the action involved.)

12. DIDACTIC TEACHING

Didactic teaching was generally avoided in the tutorial program since it permits (but does not necessarily lead) a child to disengage himself from the learning situation. Nevertheless, there are certain forms of information which the child cannot possibly derive from the immediate situation (e.g., vocabulary, facts, etc.). In these cases it is appropriate and necessary that the information be given to him. *Once it is given, however, the child should be tested to see if the information has been incorporated correctly.*

A. Gives relevant facts to child

> WHEN APPLICABLE — If, in the context of an ongoing lesson, the teacher realizes that the child does not possess a particular label or fact relevant to the productive pursuit of the lesson.
>
>> Example — Teacher "Could you go over there and get me the strainer." Child goes to table and looks bewildered. Teacher "Do you know what a strainer is?" Child shakes head. Teacher "Look, this one is a strainer." (The incorporation of this information can then be tested by a demand such as the following. "First, before we use this strainer, go over to the cabinet and see if you can find another one like it.")
>
> WHEN NOT APPLICABLE — If the material being discussed is not a simple fact or label but rather represents some concept that can be derived by the

child (with suitable direction from the teacher) from the material already present.

> Example — Teacher "Look at these things, the wheel on the car, the doorknob and the dial on the radio. What's the same about all of them?" Child looks bewildered. Teacher "Well, they're all circles, aren't they?" In this case, the teacher might simplify by bringing in a contrast item such as a square, and saying "In what way are they different from this shape?"

B. Gives known referent to mediate new concept

Limited didactic teaching is also useful in teaching new concepts when the child has difficulty in abstracting their central features. He can select objects that are nearly identical to the initial example of the concept. For example, if you show the child the "corner" of a room and ask him to find another corner, he will readily make an appropriate choice. This only involves matching rather than selective judgment. If he is then asked to show the "corner" of the desk, however, confusion results since the perceptual differences outweigh any perceivable similarity. A common teaching procedure employed to overcome this difficulty is to provide the child with numerous and varied instances of the concept. This technique, though helpful, relies on the hope that the numerous examples will lead the child to independently abstract the essential similarity. Should this fail, the teacher must have additional means for facilitating the attainment of relatively abstract concepts. One such means is to didactically show the child how already attained concepts may serve to mediate the learning of the higher order concept.

> WHEN APPLICABLE — If a child is encountering difficulty with a concept, it is useful to show him how characteristics that he already understands can serve to identify exemplars of the new concept. It is most helpful if the characteristics shown to the child lend themselves to actions that he can easily perform, for, he then has a rule by which to test out new exemplars of the concept.

>> Example — Teacher "Now show me the top of the desk." Child —. Teacher "You know what top means? It means that you go up on something (takes finger and starts from bottom) until you can't go up any higher. See, now you can't go any more than this. This is the top of the desk. Okay, now show me the top of the coffee pot. Remember, you start all the way down and keep going up until you can't go any more. Good." (The movement can then be eliminated after one or two examples and the child should be asked simply "Now find me the top of the bookcase, the top of the waste paper basket, the top of your shoe," etc.)

> WHEN NOT APPLICABLE — When no clear perceptual correlate is available which the child could discern to help him mediate the concept.

Example — Teacher "You know why we have no more water when we left the pan on the radiator? Because the water dried up. It evaporated. Now think of something else that we can make dry up, make evaporate." (In this case, evaporate is perceptually equivalent to disappearing and as a result could have come about — in the child's mind — from pouring the water down the drain, someone drinking it, etc. The teacher has no means of demonstrating the *process* of evaporation by solely displaying the *end product* of the process with no intervening perceptual correlates.)

C. Provides model

WHEN APPLICABLE — In most instances, imitation should be avoided since it allows the child to complete a task by the simplest avenue possible instead of having to independently determine the appropriate course of action. Imitation can be useful, however, particularly in the early stages of teaching when the child has attempted to meet the demands imposed, but has not been able to do so. This form of didactic teaching is especially useful with insecure children who are fearful of making an error. The availability of an adult model provides the child with the necessary reassurance since it leaves no doubt as to the desired course of action.

Example — Teacher "Pour the water out of the glass." Child does nothing. Teacher "Watch, I'll do it first."

WHEN NOT APPLICABLE — Imitation should not be used if it so reduces the task that a number of intervening steps in the problem have been bypassed.

Example — Teacher "What could we use to clean these shoes?" Child —. Teacher "Watch, I'll clean this one and then you can do the other one." (Here it would be preferable if the teacher used a method which would tap some of the intervening steps between the initial request and the actual polishing, e.g., "Which could we use — the shoe polish or the pencil?")

This listing of techniques is by no means complete. Rather, it represents an attempt to define methods that will deal with "the wrong response" in such a way that the child does not abandon his efforts at problem solving. The techniques contain an implicit distinction between the diagnosis and treatment of error patterns. Diagnosis requires that errors be committed; once exposed, however, nothing is gained by having the child repeat the error. This merely reinforces the particular wrong response and fails to move the child beyond the error. Instead, the techniques of simplification should be so structured that the child is inevitably led to reach the "correct" answer. This often means that a single attempt at simplification is not sufficient since the task may have to be simplified by several steps.

The emphasis placed in this paper on the importance of identifying error sets reflects the assumption that such patterns of error vary considerably across individuals. Were this not the case — were error patterns uniform in all children — then there would be no need to reveal the errors since their existence could be assumed. It would then be sufficient to apply the same teaching material to all children since their manner of learning could be assumed to be identical. *The recognition of individual differences makes it vital to define the rules which govern the application of the simplification techniques relative to the type of child (his personality, strengths, and weaknessess), the task, and the cognitive process demanded.* For example, when there is a failure to respond, particularly that characterized by passive withdrawal, techniques which only reiterate the failed request (e.g., Repeats Demand, Focus for Attention, Repeats Demonstration) are unlikely to be useful. By contrast, techniques which reduce the demand by partially completing the task for the child (e.g., Dissects Task, Offers Comparisons, Provides Model) are much more likely to succeed. In the case of the hyperactive, overly impulsive child who tends to blurt out responses, it would be self-defeating to use techniques such as Offers Comparisons since it will reinforce his glib verbalization. Instead, it might be well to concentrate on techniques such as Delay (to control impulsivity) and Directed Action (to capitalize on his motor involvement, but in a controlled manner).

Even were these rules to be worked out, considerable problems remain with regard to the actual implementation of the techniques. It is relatively easy to conduct an arm chair analysis of how the techniques should be used since one can focus specifically on this problem. In an actual teaching session, however, the teacher is confronted with a host of variables — involving subtle attitudes, emotions, cognitive processes, and so on. When faced with a failed response she does not have the luxury of contemplating "Which simplification technique is now appropriate?" but instead she must readily and seemingly intuitively apply the correct technique.

It is easy to underestimate this difficulty since a common feeling exists to the effect that it is "so natural and easy" to speak to a young child. This impression, however, is dependent upon the almost unrecognized importance of active feedback role played by the well-functioning preschool child in most teaching situations. When the teacher asks a question, it is assumed that the child will answer and will even spontaneously elaborate on the material by offering questions, suggestions, criticisms, etc. The significance of the child's role becomes evident when he does not fulfill his expected feedback function. In such a case (e.g., being faced with a child who passively withdraws or conversely chatters on his own wavelength) the teacher is frequently left at a total loss as to how to cope (see Blank and Solomon, 1969). The absence of such response in any particular child does not interfere with group interaction since someone else in the group is bound to answer and salvage the feedback relationship. This fact, of course, does not help the child with cognitive difficulties since it merely permits him to retreat further and further into his ineffective patterns of response. These considerations in large measure determined the selection of a tutorial setting as a necessary component for effective teaching to take place.

Despite the difficulties in analysis and implementation, the simplification techniques have proven to be useful both clinically and for analysis of the teaching situation. For example, if almost every question posed to the child must be simplified by several steps, then it is clear that the level of questioning is well beyond the child's grasp. On the other hand, if no simplification techniques are required then the lesson is doing little to help the child grow beyond the level he was at before he entered the room. Similarly, the teacher's ability to handle children's difficulties can be evaluated by analyzing her behavior according to the categories specified. For example, even though the content of their simplifications may vary, certain teachers may consistently use only one or two techniques, with the result that they confine themselves to limited patterns and they initiate set expectancies in the child. This type of analysis may also reveal the appropriateness of the teacher's simplifications in particular situations or with particular types of children (e.g., regardless of her range, if most of her techniques do not yield success, they are by definition inappropriate to the child).

It is evident that considerable problems remain to be worked out regarding both the rules governing the techniques and methods for training teachers in their implementation. Nevertheless, it is hoped that these simplification techniques will be seen as a promising approach towards rectifying our previous neglect of the significance and treatment of "the wrong response."

FOOTNOTES | 2

[1] For brevity's sake, in the remainder of the paper, the term "the wrong response" will be used to represent all forms of error which children may display, including the fear or failure to respond.

[2] The correction of error sets need not be confined to material where "proof" can be given of the inappropriateness of the response. As will be indicated, it is also possible to overcome error sets which interfere with the learning of material involving defined rather than derived relationships, e.g., letter-sound associations, factual information, labeling, etc.

REFERENCES | 2

Blank, M. A methodology for fostering abstract thinking in deprived children. *Bulletin* of the Ontario Institute for Studies in Education. In press.

Blank, M. and Frank, S. M. Story recall in kindergarten children: Effect of method of presentation on psycholinguistic performance. *Child Development.* In press.

Blank, M. and Solomon, F. A tutorial language program to develop abstract thinking in socially disadvantaged preschool children. *Child Development,* 1968, *39*, 379-389.

Blank, M. and Solomon, F. How shall the disadvantaged child be taught? *Child Development,* 1969, *40*, 47-61.

Chomsky, N. *Syntactic structures.* The Hague: Mouton, 1957.

Smedslund, T. Concrete reasoning: A study of intellectual development. Monographs of the Society for Research in Child Development, 1964, *29*, 1-39 (Serial No. 93).

Wohlwill, J. F. and Lowe, R. C. An experimental analysis of the development of the conservation of number. *Child Development,* 1962, *33*, 153-167.

Nedler | *Introduction* | 3

The following paper presents a description of the *development process approach* to curriculum design, and, in addition, provides information concerning the specifics of a curriculum developed by the Southwest Educational Development Laboratory (SEDL) using the development process model. The development process model, in actuality, consists of a sequence of behavioral objectives for those involved in designing a preschool education program. The goal of SEDL from which the model evolved was "to produce and test replicable strategies designed to enable disadvantaged children from particular target populations to attain specific educational goals." The value of the model for others who are or will be involved in the development of a preschool program, or a program for any age level, resides in the fact that the six stages comprising the model and the criteria established for the successful completion of each stage may be used for the development of a program for any population and for any specific educational purpose. Following the model requires that the program developer 1. formulate a sufficient rationale for the program, 2. refer to appropriate theoretical models and relevant research for applicable information, 3. design a *replicable* prototype product – all objectives, materials, and teaching strategies are therefore written, and 4. test the prototype with various populations in various geographical areas, making appropriate revisions after each pilot test or field test. One of the valuable outcomes of following such a procedure is that the program may then be implemented by other individuals in other locations. The benefits derived from having sequentially stated criteria for program development are similar to those derived from having behavioral objectives for children's learning within the program.

Following the process development model, SEDL has developed a curriculum for three-to-six-year-old Mexican-American children who speak Spanish in their homes. The main thrust of the bilingual program centers on language development (both Spanish and English), but the language is closely bound to sensory-motor experiences and is considered to be a necessary prerequisite to reasoning and problem-solving activities.

Shari Nedler

A Development Process Approach to Curriculum Design

3

Even a most careful survey of the literature for guidelines to aid in the conceptualization of a curriculum for preschool children yields meager results. Although numerous institutions and research workers, during the past decade, have focused on the problem of designing and implementing compensatory programs for disadvantaged preschool children, the process of development has rarely been described. Piecemeal bits of information range from position papers specifying the program rationale to descriptions of the actual learning experience.

The process which I will describe in this paper has emerged from an intensive effort at the Southwest Educational Development Laboratory (SEDL) to produce and test replicable strategies designed to enable disadvantaged children from particular target populations to attain specific educational goals.

Educational development involves translating available relevant knowledge into a form that permits improved educational practice. The SEDL model for development includes six stages of a process for production and testing of a replicable strategy. These stages are context analysis, conceptual design, prototype design, pilot test, field test, and preparation for installation. This model has guided the conceptualization of the preschool curriculum and has enabled the

Shari Nedler is at the Southwest Educational Development Laboratory, Austin, Texas. Printed by permission of the author.

staff to revise and modify the instructional program systematically after each cycle in an effort to achieve prespecified outcomes successively.

An outline of the model follows.

"The process description related to a stage outlines each step within that stage. The criteria establish only broad guidelines that specific criteria for any given program would adhere to. The implication of development according to this model is that cycles will be made within each stage until criteria are satisfied. However, it is not essential that each stage be completed prior to beginning the next subsequent stage. In other words, the model is not entirely linear through each stage. Rather, in addition to cycling within each stage, cycles back to a prior stage may be necessary before satisfactory completion. Changes in an early stage usually would imply related changes in subsequent stages. The design of a prototype does not imply any given time period for training or instructions. In other words, a prototype might be a one-week training program for teachers, the first week of an inservice training program for teachers, or one year of curriculum for students. Within a given program a prototype would need to be defined in terms of its scope. The major characteristic of a prototype is that it is replicable. The flow chart (Figure 1) graphically portrays the cycling that might occur in proceeding through the development process." (Randall, 1970 a, pp. 3-5).

THE DEVELOPMENT PROCESS

DEVELOPMENT STAGES	PROCESS DESCRIPTION	CRITERIA	OUTCOMES
1. Context Analysis	a. Identification of social goal that is not being attained sufficiently well b. Identification of important barriers that prevent attainment of the goals c. Identification of barriers that will be attacked d. Identification of alternate strategies and selection of a strategy or general approach to overcome barriers	a. Relevance of social goal to problem focus of the Laboratory b. Empirical support that documents existence of barriers c. Justification that supports focusing on certain barriers d. Justification for strategy selection based on empirical data and relevance of solution strategy to important barrier	a. A document setting forth the rationale for selection of a solution strategy
2. Conceptual Design	a. Identification of theoretical framework b. Identification of components and elements in the model	a. Documentation from research and theoretical literature b. Consistency with rationale	a. A document that specifies the model with appropriate documentation

THE DEVELOPMENT PROCESS, (Continued)

DEVELOPMENT STAGES	PROCESS DESCRIPTION	CRITERIA	OUTCOMES
	c. Descriptions of the scope and sequence of each component	c. Adequacy of scope d. Relevance to culture and ethnicity of target population	
3. Prototype Design	a. Specification of objectives for each component and element	a. Clarity of objectives	a. A prototype product is ready for testing
	b. Specification of criterion measures for objectives	b. Consistency with model	
	c. Designation of activities to attain the objectives in writing	c. Replicability of prototype	
	d. Specification of materials equipment, and special arrangements required in activities	d. Unit-Cost ratio	
	e. Specification of costs		
	f. Integration of activities into a schedule that allows for sequential development		

4. Pilot Test*	a. Specification of procedures for each population included in test	a. Subject performance outcomes
	b. Designation of feedback evaluation system. A plan for use of feedback data and a revision system is specified with criteria to be applied	b. Side effects on subjects and users
	c. Implementation of a try out (time required, difficulty of use, etc.) for a cycle of time appropriate to the nature of the prototype	c. Costs to subjects and users (time, difficulty of use, money, extra personnel)
		a. Documents specify the application of criteria and results of the try-out
		b. Revisions are made prior to next cycle, if required
5. Field Test**	a. Specification and implementation of a plan for more widespread use and try-out of the revised prototype with provisions for comparison against alternate approaches	a. Extent performance requirements of prototype are met
		a. An evaluation report specifies the conditions, procedures and results of the validation effort

*Note: Each component may be cycled through a pilot test more than once, if necessary to meet criteria. A cycle may be designed to meet only part of the criteria.

**Note: Field Test may require several cycles (e.g., service testing, initial field test, extended field test). Criteria for each cycle must be specified.

THE DEVELOPMENT PROCESS, (Continued)

DEVELOPMENT STAGES	PROCESS DESCRIPTION	CRITERIA	OUTCOMES
		b. Extent strategy compares favorably with alternate in terms of effectiveness, side effects, and costs	b. Modifications, as required, are noted and made
6. Preparation for Installation	a. Identification and projection of benefits based on validation reports and existing cost benefit analyses. Benefits are related to cost	a. Relationship between costs and projected benefits	a. A document that describes the cost benefit rationale
	b. Development of means to disseminate widely	b. Flexibility of arrangement for dissemination	b. Capability for marketing and production (arrangement with publisher, etc.)
	c. Development of a manual of installation procedures and requirements	c. Adequacy of manuals	c. Manuals that facilitate marketing and installation
	d. Development of a technical manual	d. Usefulness of manuals	

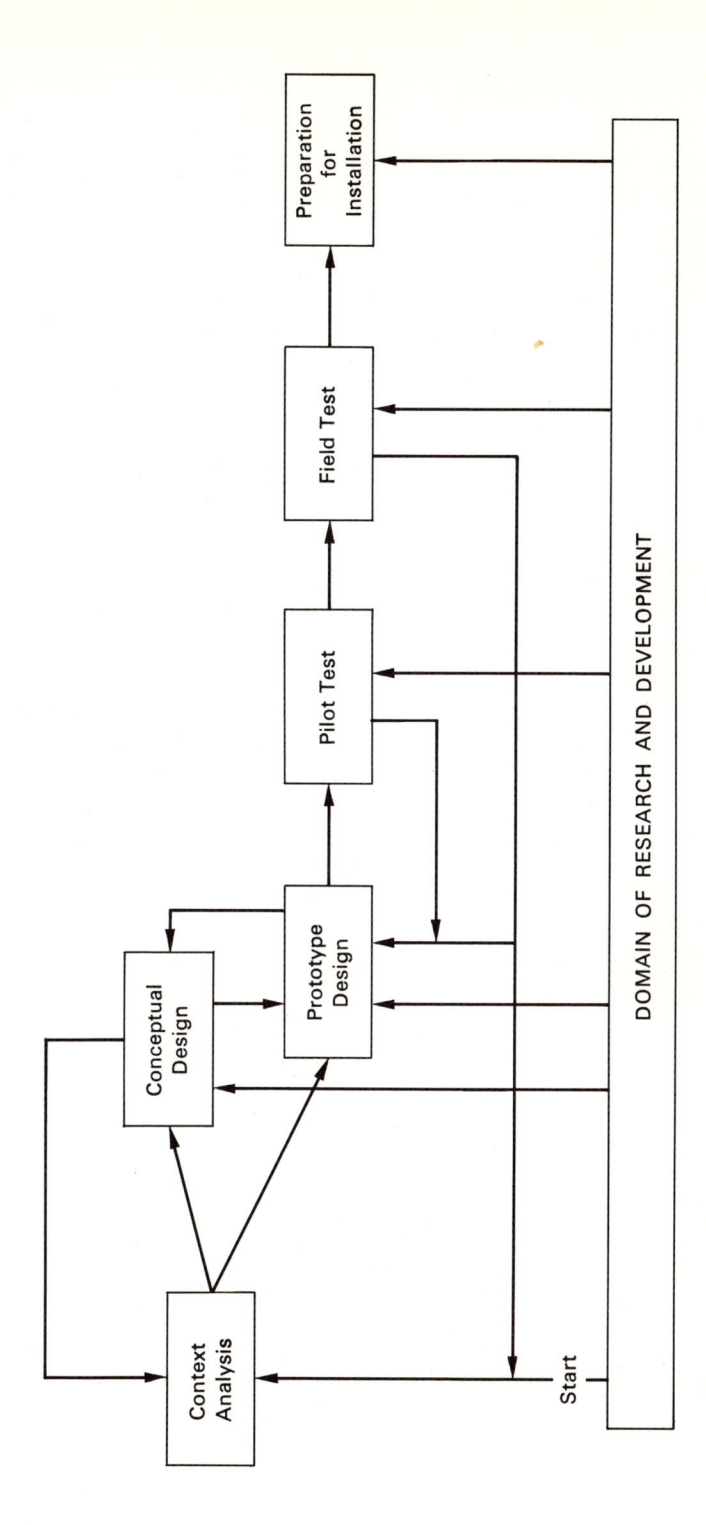

Figure 1. Flow Chart of Development Process

CONTEXT ANALYSIS

Although numerous early childhood projects have focused on the development of compensatory programs for the low income Black-American, relatively little attention has been given to those children in our society who enter school speaking a language different from that of the wider community. Approximately 40 percent of the more than 5,000,000 persons in the United States of Mexican origin or ancestry live in Texas. Most of these persons are native Spanish-speakers, living and working in an English-speaking society. The 1960 census in Texas reported that the median school years completed by the Anglo population over twenty-five years of age was 11.5 years, but only 6.1 years for the comparable Spanish surname population. Typically, the Mexican-American child — urban and migrant — with a home language of Spanish, reaches school age with little knowledge of English. His proficiency in Spanish likewise is often limited. One result of this language deficit is that a large percentage of Mexican-American children in Texas fail the first grade. (Some estimates are as high as 80 percent.) They fail becuase they are so involved in learning English they cannot master first grade content.

The problem of language differences affects learners in dramatically negative ways. Education becomes a frustrating experience, and school and failure become synonymous. The child becomes alienated both from the school itself and from other spheres of activity toward which his school experience leads. Under these conditions, the child may well be expected to move away from the legitimate opportunity structures of society to alternative opportunity structures, such as crime, rebellion, welfare, or other retreatist systems. When he matures and becomes a parent himself, he instills negative attitudes toward school in his own children.

Through context analysis, each of these problems is isolated and assessed. During the initial stage of context analysis two important questions are posed:

1. What components of the problem should be selected for attack? How should priorities be set?
2. What strategy (or strategies) should be selected to attack the given problem(s)?

Context analysis and evaluation involve the gathering of specific kinds of information. However, it would be impossible to attack all facets of the problem at once. A specific set of problems and problem components have to be identified in order to establish priorities and select a solution strategy.

We assume that intelligence is not fixed or determined at birth, and that much of development depends on the environment of the child, particularly the kind of intellectual stimulation he receives during his early years. Review of the literature suggests that appropriate stimulation and reinforcement are essential to the child's physical, emotional, and intellectual growth. Research indicates that early manipulation of stimulus and reinforcement can accelerate the development of intellectual and social competencies. A logical extension of these findings is to attempt to develop an intervention program for disadvantaged preschool Mexican-American children that will remediate and prevent cumulative deterioration of their social and intellectual performance.

To ascertain the needs of the disadvantaged Mexican-American preschool child, the Laboratory conducted research surveys in urban and rural neighborhoods with a high concentration of Mexican American residents. Relevant demographic data were compiled describing family structures, housing, income, language usage, child rearing practices, educational attainment, and levels of aspiration. The literature was reviewed, and ongoing experimental projects were studied. Critical problems were identified, including those related to:

Nutritional and medical needs
Language and intellectual competency
Parental attitudes and skills regarding the education of their children
Teacher preparation and teaching strategies
Economic needs

THE INTERVENTION STRATEGY

The project staff was best qualified to handle an educational attack, therefore, the development of language and intellectual competency was established. The major objective of the Early Childhood program was to develop new methods for the teaching of English as a second language to Spanish-speaking children between the ages of three and six. The preservation and reinforcement of the use of their native language was a corollary to the major objective. A feasible solution strategy had to be identified. Feasibility depends on the answers to many questions. Information related to each of the following variables was analyzed.

> 1. Cost-Benefit. What benefits will be likely to accrue as a result of applying the proposed solution? What will be the costs of various resources? Resources are always limited, whether expressed in terms of dollars, personnel, or time. Before a final decision was made, budget requirements, availability of qualified personnel, and a prediction of the time required for the strategy to have an initial effect had to be considered.

2. Testability. To what extent could the solution be tested? A proposed solution amenable to testing for potential effectiveness was preferred to one that was not.
3. Practicability. Could personnel be taught easily to apply the solution? Were necessary facilities available? Could *other* agencies be persuaded to invest money or resources in applying the solution?
4. Credibility. The solution had to be credible, both to the target audience and to the personnel who would implement it. Participants had to believe in the solution to make it work. Solutions that backfired could be worse than no solutions at all.
5. Exportability. Was the solution exportable? Solutions which were applicable in other places, by persons other than those who devised and engineered them, were more useful than those requiring continued sustenance.

Several strategies were considered. These included working directly with mothers in the home; developing a half-day instructional program; developing a day care program with an intensive instructional component; establishing neighborhood instructional centers staffed by para-professionals. Within the constraints of available resources, the approach that seemed most amenable to being tested, and most practical, credible, and exportable, was the development of a half-day instructional program. At that time our knowledge of how children learn, what they should learn, and the most effective way to teach them was extremely limited. Added to these basic teaching-learning uncertainties was the extra dimension of second language acquisition. The strategy of a half-day instructional program would permit systematic application of relevant research findings to various instructional strategies and would enable the staff to handle a reasonable schedule of daily classroom observation. Within the framework of limited knowledge, it appeared to be essential to involve the classroom teachers in the development process. The half-day teaching schedule, therefore, permitted the greatest degree of flexibility for achieving program goals.

Traditional preschool programs have focused primarily on the social and emotional development of the child. In traditional programs, children are provided with many opportunities to participate in play and manipulative activities, engage in creative art and music experiences, take field trips, listen to stories, and expand their experiential background. The teacher supervises and interacts with the class, but the children are free to engage in those activities which they find most appealing.

Specifically, emphasis is placed on:

Peer-group relationships — getting along together
Spontaneous sensory perceptual experiences

Language as a social rather than cognitive tool
Concern with immediate goals and present time orientation

Available research (Anderson, 1940; McCandless, 1967) indicated there is no significant difference in the academic achievement of these children whether they have preschool training or not, yet these children are typically the "achievers" in our educational system. Later studies indicate that many of the critical variables associated with academic competence can be found in the home, within the family structure and patterns of interaction. These critical variables include low adult-child ratio, the quality and quantity of language directed toward the child, and the high level of positive expectations for achievement reinforced by parental praise and encouragement. All of these factors appear to contribute to the child's achievement level.

A description of the environment of the disadvantaged Mexican-American child provides a dramatic contrast with that of the more advantaged child. His environment generally may be described as highly unstructured. These families usually are hard pressed to meet immediate needs and the present takes priority over the future. The language directed toward the child is used more for controlling behavior than for explaining, describing, or instructing. The child learns the values of cooperation and patience at an early age. He has to get along with his peers if he is to survive in the family system.

The disadvantaged Mexican-American child needs an educational program to complement his environment. We cannot assume that these children develop an organized fund of sensory and motor learnings which are basic to the development of language and conceptual skills. In many cases, the homes of these children fail to nourish their health, their emotional stability, or their intellect. Their behavior indicates they have not developed the skills essential for listening, focusing, and thinking through the answers to simple problems.

CONCEPTUAL DESIGN

The rationale for the program includes an analysis of the needs of the specific target population which supports the selection of a solution strategy. The next stage of the development process was the development of a conceptual design which specified the theoretical framework as well as the components and elements of the instructional model. This document provides a framework for major decisions related to the scope and sequence of the instructional program. As new research pertaining to developmental theory has appeared, and as data related to the instructional program has accumulated, the conceptual design has been revised.

Research on bilingualism indicates that whether or not bilingualism constitutes a handicap, as well as the extent of such a handicap, depends upon the way in which the two languages have been learned. Peal and Lambert (1962) reported that if the bilingualism was balanced, i.e., if there had been equal, normal literacy developed in the two languages, bilingual ten-year-olds in Montreal were markedly superior to monolinguals on verbal and non-verbal tests of intelligence. They appeared to have greater mental flexibility, a superiority in concept formation and a more diversified set of mental abilities.

Focusing specifically on the disadvantaged Mexican-American child, Manuel (1965) states that most Spanish-speaking children of the Southwest know neither English nor Spanish well. Generally speaking, their home language is a poor grade of Spanish. Even the fund of ideas which words express is limited. In their homes, they lack the opportunity and stimulus to develop the concepts which other children normally develop. In school, the growth of ability in their mother tongue is arrested by lack of instruction in the written forms of language, and the development of English is retarded by lack of sufficient contact with English.

Some of the specific problems related to second language learning, as described by Hakes (1965) include:

1. Sounds which do not appear in the person's native language. "In both speaking and hearing, the individual must learn to make additional discriminations in order to hear and produce sound differences which signal differences in meaning in the second language. In other words, sounds which are treated as the same in the native language may be treated as different in the second language, and having learned not to discriminate between them, the child must now learn to discriminate between them..."
2. Learning and selection of the appropriate response in the appropriate language; i.e., the child wishes to speak about a "dog." He has already learned the Spanish name for dog. He is now faced with the problem of learning the English name 'dog'.... In learning theory terms, the individual has acquired one response to the stimulus, dog. Attempting now to acquire a second response to the same stimulus provides what is referred to as a negative transfer situation. The previously learned response will interfere with learning the new response in the sense that *the new learning will be more difficult than if there had been no previous learning.*"
3. Interference at the grammatical level — Differences in word order must be learned; i.e., whether the adjective precedes or follows the verb, etc. Evidence indicates that interference and negative transfer are inevitable for the bilingual child to a far greater extent than for the monolingual. In addition, the bilingual has more to learn phonemically, semantically, and grammatically than the monolingual.

Whether the bilingualism of a child is to be an asset or a negative factor in his life appears to depend on the kind of education he receives in both languages. Research data indicate that the earlier a child begins a second language, the greater his facility in learning it.

Reviewing language development for the preschool child, Brophy and Stern (1961) state that recent theory and research stress the importance of language as the highest representational system. The most recent and perhaps most explicit statement concerning the relationship of language to intelligence and thinking is probably that of Bruner (1966). Bruner contends that language is the most sophisticated of the symbolic representational systems which form the highest stage of intellectual development. He indicates that the power of language as a representational system rests upon several of its properties — classification and hierarchical abstractness, ability to encode time and space, inclusion of function and causality. However, Bruner carefully indicates that the ability to speak and understand language *per se* does not automatically generate the highest forms of intellectual activity. In fact, *children must be induced to explore the logical implications of their language* before it becomes maximally useful for encoding experienced reality and for solving problems. Thus, Bruner suggests that most Western cultures force children to move to this highest level of language usage by giving them formal education ourside of the context of action... It appears likely that the systematic coordination of the child's emerging linguistic system with his earlier enactive and iconic experiential modes (Bruner, 1966) begins in the preschool period and is completed for many concepts in the middle-class child by the time he enters school. Thus, advantaged children enter the formal educational system with this process already begun, and school simply represents a continuation and reinforcement of familiar activity which builds upon an already solidly established base. It is likely that this does not occur in the case of many disadvantaged children.

Another conclusion suggested by recent research is that language is learned through the young child's interactions with adults who perform the functions of model, informer, and provider of feedback. This is suggested by the work of Brown and Bellugi (1964), Brown and Fraser (1964), and Cazden (1965), and is summarized in a lengthy review by Plumer (1968). It would appear that language learning requires a situation in which an adult carefully monitors what a child says and programs corrections according to the child's utterances. The simplified English which parents often use with children, and the precise, relevant feedback which they provide to the child (Brown and Bellugi, 1964) appear to be very good examples of providing the match as specified by Hunt (1961).

As yet, there is little direct evidence about how children learn to use language for problem solving and manipulating reality, but such learning must be closely related to what the child already knows experientially and must be carefully sequenced and programmed if it is to have maximum impact...

A Development Process Approach

Hunt (1961) suggests this when he describes the problem of the match. The "match" refers to an optimal relationship between the environment and the child's cognitive structures so that cognitive conflict is produced and cognitive development is stimulated. If the environment is too different or too similar to the child's level of development, there will be no match and further development will not take place. This same idea is also prominent in the work of Ausubel (1968) who suggests that the most important determinant of learning is what the learner already knows, and in the work of Gotkin (1968), whose programmed instruction approach provides teaching embedded in a curriculum game that systematically builds upon what the child knows and leads him toward what he doesn't know.

In addition to the need for matching instruction to what the child already knows, the other important condition for learning to use language as a problem posing and solving device is the availability of models who use language for these purposes. These models must support and reward such use by the child. That is, children must not only have certain structural skills involving language and concepts, but they must also use these skills in appropriate ways. The tendency to use the skills optimally can probably be learned only through imitation which is then successfully rewarded.

Marion Blank reports that in her studies with disadvantaged populations she did not find the perceptual deficits so frequently cited in the literature. When the learning tasks came to demand finer cognitive skills, however, the younger children and the disadvantaged children showed increasingly poor performance. She identifies the central deficit as being a deficiency in abstract thinking; i.e., in a set to use internal symbolic processes to organize and codify their world:

> *In the case of most children from middle-class surroundings, such opportunities are provided in the normally available environment, with the result that the immature thinking of the young child naturally matures with no apparent effort. In the case of the disadvantaged child, these opportunities are not available and the deficiencies in abstract thinking become entrenched with age.*
> *(Blank, 1967, p. 1)*

Disadvantaged children, according to Blank, do not lack perceptual experience or perceptual skills, but rather they lack the means for making these observations meaningful.

Hunt describes intelligence as a hierarchical organization of abilities acquired in the course of the young child's ongoing interaction with circumstances. He states that it should be possible to arrange institutional settings where children now culturally deprived by the accident of socio-economic class of their parents can be supplied with a set of encounters with circumstances which will provide an antidote for what they have missed. The trick, according to Hunt, is to capture each child's interest by making the circumstances which he encounters in the program relevant to the information already stored and to the skills already developed. The problem is to adapt the program to the child instead of waiting for the child to attain readiness for the program.

The Laboratory staff selected, as a strategy to achieve the goals described by Hunt, the design of a planned environment that would enable children to acquire those essential skills and concepts that underlie intelligent behavior.

The Leiter International Performance Scale was administered to all children enrolled in the program. Classroom observations and analyses of the data supported Marion Blank's contention that the majority of the children did not appear to have perceptual deficits. Eighty percent of the Leiter IQ scores fell within the average range of intelligence. In order to build on skills which the children had already developed, the conceptual model included sensory-motor skills as a major component. Appropriate learning experiences for each child were planned to include a variety of sensory-motor activities which are prerequisites to meaningful cognitive learning. Many of these activities — involving simple visual, auditory, and tactile perceptions — are ignored in the typical curriculum because they are thought to be skills which develop through normal maturational or casual experiences. The objective of this program component is to focus systematically on a sequential presentation of sensory-motor experiences to which language can be attached through various experiences.

The disadvantaged Mexican-American child suffers from language deficiencies in both Spanish and in English. Language skills in any language require that the child be competent in the areas of lexicology, phonology, and syntax. A language component, focusing on the development of linguistic competence in both Spanish and English, was designed to provide the basic conceptual knowledge necessary for abstract language functioning. Specific concepts were identified and introduced within the context of planned, relevant learning experience. Activities related to recognition, discrimination, and production of phonemes as well as the use and response to sentence patterns of increasing complexity were planned as part of the language component.

The systematic presentations of concepts, sensory-motor, and language activities were designed to support the development of thinking and reasoning skills. Generally, the disadvantaged child not only enters school inadequately prepared for the typical language tasks of the early grades but he also is severely handicapped in his capacity to use language as a tool in conceptualizing, reasoning, and problem solving.

Building on the development of cognitively directed perceptions, the skills needed for making observations meaningful in analyzing the surrounding "world" were programmed into lessons through carefully delineated questions related to activity-oriented learning experience. Expansion of this ability to handle the coding process, using language as the chief means for abstracting and internalizing an almost endless number of properties, formed the base for the development of abstract thinking skills. Within this framework of an integrated instructional program, the objective was to enable the child to generalize the prerequisite sensory-motor and language skills as they were acquired and apply them to problems requiring symbolic thinking.

THE THREE-YEAR INSTRUCTIONAL PROGRAM

A sequential three-year instructional program based on these major components has been designed for three, four, and five-year-old Mexican-American children. To date, five major training areas have been developed for the curriculum. These are visual, auditory, motor, English language, and reasoning and problem solving skills.

VISUAL SKILLS

The goal of the visual training program is to develop the child's total visual-motor functioning as it relates to the objectives for concept development. While there is little doubt that developmental maturation in visual-motor perception (and auditory-motor perception) is a prerequisite for success in the academic environment, there is no evidence that training should be limited to perceptual activity alone. The interaction of perceptual and conceptual activity was recognized by Hebb (1949), when he stated that perception involving variable stimulation would also involve conceptual activity.

The child progresses in a developmental manner from sensation through perception to conceptualization. On the level of sensation, input can occur without the child's attaching any meaning to the stimulus. On the perceptual level, details are perceived, discriminated, and integrated. As specific properties are gradually categorized and classified, a concept is formed. This concept is stored and can be retrieved when necessary. With this in mind, the objectives in the visual training program have been selected to aid the child not only in perceptual maturation, but also in concept formation.

The reciprocity of psycholinguistic functions makes it difficult to isolate various abilities either for purposes of evaluation or for training. However, some attempts must be made educationally. While Cruickshank (1957), Buktenica (1968), and others do not necessarily label these abilities identically, they discuss the same abilities generally. These abilities may be categorized as: perceiving position in space, eye-hand coordination, figure-ground perception, perceptual constancy, and analyzing spatial relationships. The objective of the visual training program is to develop the child's total visual-motor functioning, including visual-motor memory and sequence and the ability to accomplish visual closure.

AUDITORY SKILLS

The normal development of language comprehension depends upon the normal functioning of auditory processes for perceiving, remembering, and integrating sound experiences. The development of these auditory processes reportedly can be observed and traced in predictable steps.

According to Zigmond and Cicci (1968), it is only after listening skills have begun to develop and the child becomes aware of specialized sound and differences between sounds that language comprehension is seen. They further elaborate that as language skills develop, so do auditory, perceptual, and memory abilities. By three years of age, the child should have acquired the ability to comprehend language and should have developed skills in auditory localization, discrimination, perception of rhythm, sequencing, and memory.

An attempt has been made to include all areas of auditory development in the curriculum. These include auditory perceptual skills, localization of sound, foreground-background stabilization, discrimination skills, short-term memory span, long-term retention, closure, development of proper inflection and rhythm patterns, and production of sounds. Since educationally disadvantaged children have particular difficulty with auditory memory, emphasis has been placed on this area. Emphasis has also been placed on the discrimination of English speech sounds which give Mexican-Americans difficulty in speaking English.

Through the developmental sequencing of auditory skills, the teacher is able to identify any child having difficulty in this area. The auditory training program not only provides the necessary experiences for developing auditory skills, but also correlates these with related language concepts.

MOTOR SKILLS

Research clearly shows the relationship of adequate motor development and body image development to later academic achievement. The motor training program has been designed to detect possible motor deficiencies and to emphasize gross motor skills as they directly relate to developing body awareness, visual motor skills, and fine motor coordination basic to higher levels of functioning.

According to Schilder (1935), when the knowledge of our own body is faulty and incomplete, all actions for which this particular knowledge is

A Development Process Approach

necessary will be faulty. We need body awareness in order to start movements. Body awareness has been found, by many investigators, to be of crucial importance for the development of all psychological functions. Frostig and Horne (1964) have defined body awareness as being composed of three areas: body image, body concept, and body schema.

A child's body image is his subjective experience of his own body and his continuing impression of himself which is related to his emotional tone, interpersonal relationships, and culture. It is important, however, that the child's image of himself not remain on a receptive level. He should be able to express this self image through self evaluation, self expression, and self description.

A child's body concept is the intellectual knowledge that he has of his own body. This reportedly develops later than body image and is acquired by conscious learning. The child must first become aware of the existence of the parts and their names and then the precise location and function of the various parts.

Body schema reportedly is entirely unconscious and changes from moment to moment. The body schema regulates the position of the different muscles and parts of the body in relation to each other at any particular moment, and it varies according to the position of the body. Adequate body schema development involves the ability of the child to maintain equilibrium and make coordinated movements. Training activities have been developed in the areas of: gross motor patterns, laterality, midline and directionality movements.

Although the eyes and the visual system are said to be the master control system of the body, visual coordination is only one part of total body coordination. Many educators and clinicians have observed the need for motor training to be a total process, because there is very little one can do in motor performance that does not involve the eyes.

Getman and Kane (1964) state that the more the eyes are related to the motor activities in a training situation the better chance one has of developing the visual perception system and integrating vision with motor activities. The preschool years do not provide much more than the general and random patterning of eye movements that evolve from free play, personal interests, and the home life of the child. Since a much more specialized and directionally-oriented ocular control is necessary for reading and classroom activities, ocular control training has been incorporated into total body control activities.

Movement patterns begin in gross form, using extensive muscle systems, and through differentiation are refined so that they can be made with a less extensive muscle system. This is a learned process resulting from much experimentation on the part of the child. Although most disadvantaged children are fairly proficient in gross motor skills, many are not adequately prepared to handle the fine motor skills necessary for academic achievement. This is due in part to the child's environment and lack of opportunity to experiment with materials which help develop fine motor coordination. Appropriate training activities progress from manipulative experiences with concrete objects to chalkboard activities and finally to experiences with paper and pencil.

LANGUAGE SKILLS

"Man's use of the linguistic code in communicating involves two major processes: comprehension and expression of language. In comprehending the meaning of language, two aspects of linguistic utterances are involved; the lexicon, or the vocabulary used, and the structure, i.e., the syntax and morphology.... It is commonly held that understanding of a grammatical pattern antedates the oral expression of it.... and that passive control (comprehension) occurs before active control (production) of the same features." (Carrow, 1968, p. 101)

A vocabulary list of approximately 2,800 words has been compiled from previously published word lists. This core vocabulary represents those concepts which research indicates an average English speaking six-year-old will have in his receptive and expressive repertoire when he enters first grade. Basic concepts, as they have been identified through analysis of the word list, are emphasized in all sensory-motor activities. The teacher labels the objects and actions in Spanish and encourages the children to describe the activity. She often labels the objects for the children in English but she does not insist upon their production by the child.

The English language program begins during the fifteenth unit of the program for three-year-olds. Sustained and systematic instruction organized around specific linguistic content is presented daily. Terminal objectives specifying vocabulary, basic sentence patterns, and syntactic structures of increasing complexity have been developed and are integrated into the instructional program that covers a three-year time period.

The most efficient way to insure that a child learns the desired concepts is to plan and to sequence the lessons. Structured lessons provide a controlled and systematic approach to the acquisition of vocabulary and sentence structure for children learning English as a second language. These lessons provide the teacher with explicit instructions regarding the presentation of concepts. Specific tasks to be mastered by the child are clearly described. If the child does not respond or if he responds incorrectly, the teacher can provide immediate feedback by modeling the correct response.

REASONING AND PROBLEM SOLVING

To learn how to think and to solve problems is a prerequisite to competence and success in a scientific and complex society such as ours, where one must be able to cope with a vast body of knowledge. Robert Sears (1966) remarks that "such body of information requires *convergent* thinking for its mastery; there are right answers generally agreed upon. It is the duty of the school to develop this body of knowledge as a part of the repertory of each child. At the same time, however, the development of an understanding of the mechanisms by which science operates in both its pure and applied forms requires a type of thinking which can be described as *divergent* . . . demands novelty in the solution of its problems . . . each individual must become a master of divergent thinking . . . that is, problem solving."

It becomes obvious, upon reflection, that verbal processes enter into most, if not all, behaviors, above primitive level, directed toward "problem solving" or "solution-finding," divergent and convergent thinking. Until the child has some overt signs or a code for both concrete and abstract phenomena, his efforts toward retaining and communicating information result in a low level of competence in coping with his complex environment.

The Reasoning and Problem Solving component begins by training the child to understand and produce simple language forms in his native language and in English. As these skills develop, learning experiences are presented in which he must demonstrate the ability to describe objects, narrate events, generalize, explain and predict a variety of ideas related to these objects and events.

The content of these lessons has been very carefully selected to relate to both the child and to his environment. Using the content of the lessons as a tool, the child's competency to manipulate language in situations requiring various levels of cognitive skills should develop and emerge. Hopefully, each child will be able to use language to organize his thoughts, reflect upon situations, comprehend the meaning of events, and to choose among alternatives.

PROTOTYPE DESIGN

Skill outlines representing terminal objectives have been specified for each training area. The curriculum consists of sequenced series of lessons beginning with the lowest order of skill competencies and proceeding systematically to higher level tasks.

The techniques of behavior or component analysis (Gagné, 1962; Resnick, 1963) have been used to identify prerequisite skills and objectives. Resnick (1967, p. 7) states that "component analysis is a highly flexible technique in that it can be applied to any objective at any level of the curriculum. To begin the analysis, an objective at any "grade level" may be chosen; the analysis will always specify objectives that should come *earlier* in the curriculum. The initial objective itself may have been derived from an earlier analysis of a higher level objective. Similarly, any sub-objective identified in a given analysis may serve as the basis for a new analysis. The importance of the backward analytic procedure for an early learning curriculum is that it affords a method of identifying critical *early* behaviors—ones that may not have been identified before, or not identified as related to school performance. Purely logically, the process can be continued indefinitely. In practice, however, a component analysis not only provides ordered sets of skills for inclusion in the curriculum, it also specifies the skills a student needs to successfully enter the curriculum."

After ordered sets of objectives have been identified they are organized within the framework of a unit which determines specific conceptual content. A unit is composed of daily lessons in each of the five major training areas. The content of all activities, in most instances, is related to the unit topic so that the conceptual content can be explored through various senses. Subject matter relevant to the child's experience serves as the vehicle for carrying a process or developing a skill.

The dimensions by which objectives are selected for each unit include:

LEVELS OF OPERATIONS

The use of the term operations is modeled directly after Guilford. The categories include cognition, memory, convergent thinking, divergent thinking and evaluative thinking.

MODALITIES

Modalities are three different methods of presentation of information to be operated upon. That is, in setting the task for the child, the kind of information which is being dealt with may be in terms of visual sensations, auditory sensation, or in terms of his own action. Logically, these three methods of presentation could be used within each category of the five operations.

INFORMATION

The Information category represents a way of specifying the type of information required of the child performing a given task. The categories are different on the different levels of operations. For example, at the cognitive level, the information required may be discrimination: requiring the child to label two objects as same or different on some dimension. At the convergent level, predicting outcomes would involve forecasting what the outcome of a certain event will be given certain specifying conditions.

DIMENSIONS

The Dimensions category specifies particular dimensions on which informational discriminations can be made, such as color, size, volume, number, etc.

A Development Process Approach

REPRESENTATION

The Representation category refers to any dimension which might underly the abstractness or complexity of the presentation through any particular modality for any operational level. Thus, in specifying objectives at the cognitive level for the visual modality, objects, pictures, and figures should be considered. Specification of objectives for actions would include simple actions (clapping), meaningful actions (passing out papers), and product actions (drawing a circle).

LEVEL OF RESPONSES

The nature of the response demanded of the child must be considered in selecting objectives. For instance, the child might show a receptive mastery of the objective as indicated by his ability to locate or point to an appropriate picture. He might be required to supply a short answer to a question or graphically to illustrate a concept.

The lesson plan format includes a clearly stated behavioral objective, a description of the materials needed for presentation of the learning experience, and an outline of the teaching procedure designed to enable the child to achieve the specified objective. Media materials have been developed by specialists who have worked closely with the curriculum staff. Each teacher receives a packet which includes a thirty unit curriculum guide as well as pictures, transparencies, puzzles, audio tapes, and any manipulative materials for children that are needed for presentation of activities.

INTEGRATION OF ACTIVITIES

Skills that enable a child to learn from his environment and function well in the classroom are prerequisites to the higher order skills included in the curriculum. Resnick (1967) identifies these as orienting and attending skills. They include the ability to concentrate on a task and resist distractions, the ability to attend to appropriate details; to follow directions; to accept rewards which are delayed rather than immediate, and verbal rather than concrete. Acquisition of these kinds of skills leads to behavior which reflects persistence and an increased attention span.

The typical class consists of eighteen children, one teacher, and one assistant teacher. During the early weeks of the program attention is focused on establishing and maintaining a smoothly flowing routine that maximizes opportunities for the teachers to reinforce the desired behaviors related to orienting and attending. Materials for the classroom are carefully chosen by the teacher to relate to the unit and each child is encouraged to work independently. Through rotation, materials of increasing complexity are placed in the room to support the stimulation of independent problem solving abilities.

The language of instruction throughout the first fifteen units of the program is primarily Spanish. Concepts are initially presented in the child's native language and after mastery is demonstrated, the concepts are systematically introduced in English. Increased usage of English moves from approximately 20 percent the first year to 80 percent by the end of the third year. The teacher and assistant teacher working with small groups function as language models, monitoring what the child says and providing immediate feedback. Through careful programming of the environment the child hears natural speech in both languages at as many levels as possible, and he is encouraged to respond by using natural forms of language.

The daily schedule provides opportunities for both small group interaction and independent activity. The class is divided into three groups which cycle through alternating periods of direct instruction and self-selected activities. The instructional model for each child is outlined below (Figure 2). The teacher tests for attainment on each instructional activity. These teacher assessments are confirmed by diagnostic tests at the end of each unit.

PILOT TEST

Scriven (1967) describes formative evaluation as evaluation used to improve a curriculum during its development. It is evaluation which takes place at each stage of curriculum development and provides information which supports the changes to be made in the curriculum. A formative evaluation system which includes a plan for use of feedback data, and a revision system with criteria to be applied has been utilized at each stage of design and pilot testing of the early childhood curriculum.

Variables of concern vary somewhat with each stage of testing as follows:

1. *Design Testing* — Ethnicity of pupils and number of pupils. Since the concerns in several cycles of design testing are about appropriateness of format, materials, timing of the process and ease of usage, the effort is to get exposure of materials to a limited number of pupils within each ethnic group involved in the design testing. Mexican-Americans have been divided into two subgroups, migrant and stable populations.
2. *Initial Pilot Testing* — Initial pilot testing involves the first year-long testing of a curriculum and thus becomes the first attempt to replicate the designed curriculum at a given age level on a full year basis. The variables include ethnicity of pupils, number of classes and urban and rural subgroups for each, with a minimum of three classrooms for each analysis unit.
3. *Extended Pilot Testing* — Extended pilot testing is the second full year effort to replicate a design curriculum at one given age level for a full

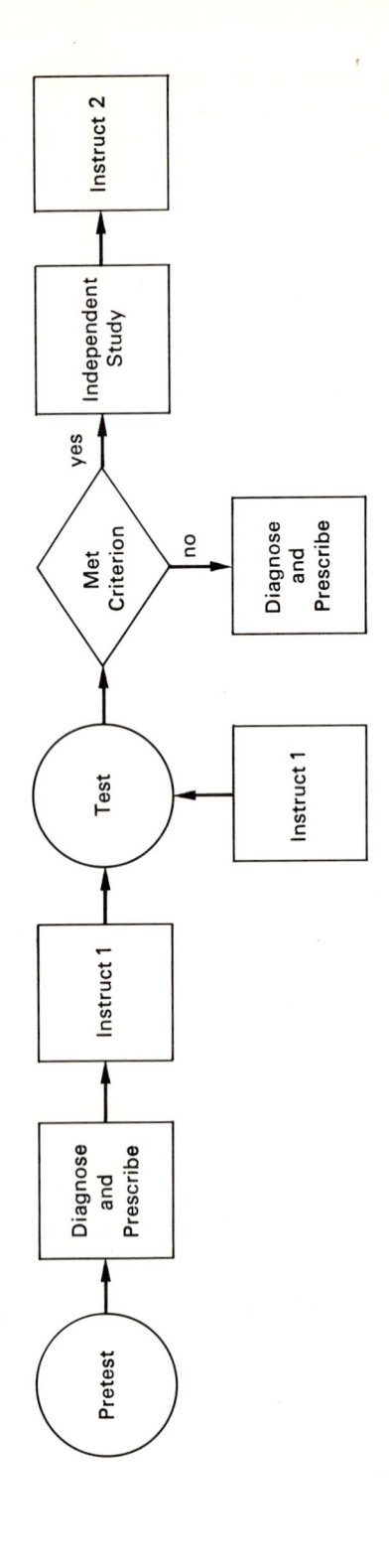

Figure 2. Pupil Instructional Model

year where hypotheses are tested related to revisions made as a result of initial pilot testing. Variables include all of those appropriate to initial pilot tests with the addition of length of day and ethnicity of teachers. The number of classes in each analysis unit increases to five.
4. *Initial Field Testing* — When the curriculum goes into initial field testing it has attained some demonstrated performance expectations and is ready for more widespread testing utilizing all of the variables involved in extended pilot testing with the addition of a geographic variable. At least three analysis units are required in each geographic area. An analysis unit is five classrooms with each ethnic pupil group, each different ethnicity of teacher, each length of day, in urban and rural settings.
5. *Extended Field Testing* — Extended field testing is necessary to test hypotheses related to changes or modifications made as a result of initial field testing with an expanded number of analysis units in each geographic area. The variables remain the same as those for initial field testing with an additional requirement of five analysis units for each geographic area.

Information is collected from three sources: Student achievements, teacher feedback, and observation.

1. Student achievement information — Four kinds of tests are administered.
   a. Pretest — This test covers important objectives from each unit for the year.
   b. Unit Test — These tests are developed for each unit and cover the major lesson objectives.
   c. Mastery Test — These tests cover ten units of material. One item is written for the most important objectives in each unit.
   d. Posttest — In order to develop an appropriate posttest, terminal objectives are identified for each training area. Ten items are written for each terminal objective.

In addition to the tests administered to each child, the teacher is asked, at the completion of each activity, to record responses of ten randomly selected children according to the criterion measure specified for each objective.

2. Teacher Feedback Information
   a. Structured teacher checklists are filled out at the completion of each activity by selected pilot test teachers.
   b. Oral conferences are held between the teachers and site coordinators. Coordinators use a questionnaire to guide the discussion.
3. Observation Information
   Structured and unstructured observations are recorded by the site coordinator or an observer trained to assess the effectiveness of the materials.

In Cycles I and II of design testing, criterion measures are stated for each objective within a program component. Validation of a sequence of activities involves having the teacher present the lessons to at least two small groups of children. The criterion of acceptable performance requires that eight out of ten children achieve the specified objective. The curriculum writers observe in the classroom and revisions are based on the teacher's suggestions at oral conferences, on the writer's observations of classroom operations, and on pupil performance achievement data. Structured forms are used in gathering this information.

When revisions are made, unit criterion tests are developed which are designed to measure mastery of unit objectives. The criterion of acceptable performance requires that 75 percent of the children master 75 percent of the items. Cycle III of design testing serves to trial test with another group of children the revisions made in Cycles I and II. Data from the classroom includes teacher checklists, oral conference questionnaires, daily pupil performance achievement measures, and unit criterion test results. After all of the data are analyzed, revisions are made and the materials are then introduced in Pilot Testing.

In initial Pilot Testing, materials are placed in classrooms outside the immediate area in which they were developed. They are tested for sequence, reinforcement, and applicability to specific target populations. Clinical information is obtained through teacher checklists, oral conferences using site coordinator questionnaires, and observations. Pupil performance data is obtained through mastery tests, unit criterion tests, and daily pupil performance achievement measures.

Three major criteria serve to determine the need for revision of materials for any specific ethnic group.

1. If 75 percent of the classrooms in each population had at least 75 percent of the pupils mastering 75 percent of the items, student performance on the unit criterion and post mastery test is considered adequate.
2. If 80 percent of the classrooms in each population group had at least 80 percent of the pupils mastering the terminal behavior as specified in the lesson objective, daily student performance is considered adequate.
3. If fewer than one-fourth of the teachers of a given population group report less than average pupil interest in response to any particular activity, it is considered that the criterion of student interest has been met.

If an activity meets these criteria, it is introduced, as is, into extended pilot testing. If any of the three criteria is not met, the activity is revised. To determine problems within the activity, all data pertaining to the lesson are analyzed.

Extended pilot test involves the introduction of materials into classrooms to test the effectiveness of revisions. In this phase of development, control groups are selected to measure the effectiveness of program materials against other early childhood programs and criteria. In general, the data collection instruments are the same with the addition of pre- and posttests designed to measure major terminal objectives.

When revisions are indicated, the general question that is asked is what needs to be modified? The program analyst examines all of the information available related to appropriateness of objectives, materials and presenter interaction.

Objectives may be too simple, too complex, or appropriate. The analyst examines the data in order to determine whether or not the objectives are appropriate. If the objectives were attained satisfactorily they are *not* too complex. They may be too simple (or okay). The test for simplicity is difficult, but the analyst can look at learner interest (attention to the learning task) and observer reports. It is difficult to maintain interest after objectives are attained in any learning session and observers can usually note that time was wasted. High performance of learners, low interest, and too much time reported by observers and teachers for the same learning session lead to questioning the objectives as being too simple for the time given for their mastery.

However, if objectives are not satisfactorily attained, the logical hypotheses are that: 1. objectives are too complex, 2. materials are inappropriate, and/or 3. presenter (teacher) interaction is inappropriate. Participant (learner) interest is again a good clue as are observer reports.

After evaluating the objectives the program analyst examines data to make decisions about the materials. Materials refer to any printed matter (teacher guides), pictures, or physical objects needed by the teacher or learners during a learning session. The materials can be judged as either appropriate or inappropriate. If materials enable the learners to attain the objectives to a satisfactory degree *and* maintain a reasonably high interest, then they can be judged appropriate, although, of course minor alterations might be of value. If objectives are *not* attained and interest is low, the likelihood is that materials are inappropriate. This can be confirmed by analyzing teacher comments about materials.

Presenter interaction may be inappropriate due to faulty management techniques (classroom management, organization, manipulation of materials, etc.), or motivation strategies. Faulty management techniques are usually related to a specific learning session, while motivation strategies are more general and related to most learning sessions.

In general, if learning performance is high, motivation processes are adequate. However, if performance is high, interest low, time is reported about right, the management techniques may be questioned. The reason is that something must account for the lack of interest. If materials are defective, either timing or performance would be off. If objectives are too simple, the time will likely be reported too lengthy. Hence, by elimination of other possibilities, faulty techniques seem the most likely cause.

In addition to the information that accrues to the curriculum design team, the evaluation system provides teachers with the diagnostic information that is needed for individualizing their assessment and teaching efforts. Each teacher assumes the responsibility for decisions regarding pacing and spacing of activities within the program. She is the final judge of how best to achieve the match between the child's cognitive structures and the experiences he will encounter in the learning environment. The objectives that have been specified represent minimal performance goals. It is hoped that every child enrolled in the program will achieve all of these objectives and that more challenging experiences will be provided for those children who are capable of moving beyond the program goals.

In conceptualizing the early childhood curriculum, cycles are made within each stage of the development process. Relevant information from the domain of research and development is constantly reviewed and significant findings are incorporated into the instructional model.

The outcome of context analysis was the development of a document which set forth the rationale for the selection of a solution strategy. The conceptual design stage focused on identification of the theoretical framework, the components and elements of the instructional model, as well as the scope and sequence of each component. Design of a replicable prototype product required specification of objectives, materials, criterion measures, and sequential activities. Revisions based on feedback data are being incorporated into the instructional program and will be tested with each target population selected for pilot test. In field tests, the program will be tested under a wider variety of conditions in different cultural and social environments, in different sized schools, in different sized communities, and with varying administrative organizations and varying population mixes.

Working within the framework of the development process, additional components of a comprehensive early childhood learning system are being designed. These include a staff development and a parent education program.

The challenge to those of us engaged in educational development is clear. Effective evaluation can accelerate the process of designing educational programs that respond to and meet the needs of disadvantaged children who have failed to benefit from traditionally based programs. We can no longer afford to explain away our failure to evaluate adequately by not having appropriate measurement techniques. If our programs are truly designed to serve children's needs, then we must accept the challenge by systematically evaluating each stage of our development efforts.

REFERENCES | 3

Anderson, L. D. A longitudinal study of the effects of nursery school training on successive intelligence test ratings. *National Society for the Study of Education 39th Yearbook*, 1940, Part I.

Ausubel, O. *Educational psychology: a cognitive view.* New York: Holt, Rinehart, and Winston, 1968.

Bereiter, C. and Englemann, S. *Teaching disadvantaged children in the preschool.* Englewood Cliffs, New Jersey: Prentice-Hall, 1966.

Bernstein, B. Language and social class. *British Journal of Sociology*, 1960, *11*, 271-276.

Blank, M. *A methodology for fostering abstract thinking in deprived children.* New York: Albert Einstein School of Medicine, 1967.

Blank, M. and Solomon, F. A tutorial program to develop abstract thinking in socially disadvantaged preschool children. *Child Development*, 1968, *39*, 379-391.

Blank, M. and Solomon, F. How shall the disadvantaged child be taught? *Child Development*, 1969, *40*, 47-63.

Bloom, B. S., Hastings, T., Madaus, G. *Formative and summative evaluation of student learning.* New York: McGraw-Hill. In press.

Bloom, B. S. *Stability and change in human characteristics.* New York: John Wiley and Sons, Inc., 1964.

Brophy, J. and Stern, H. *A project to develop a program to teach complex intellectual skills to preschool disadvantaged children in a tutoring situation, Project Proposal.* Washington, D. C.: U. S. Office of Education, Bureau of Research, 1961.

Brown, R. and Bellugi, U. Three processes in child's acquisition of syntax. *Harvard Educational Review*, 1964, *34*, 133-151.

Brown, R. and Frazer, C. The acquisition of syntax. *Monographs of the Society for Research in Child Development*, 1964, Serial No. 92, *29*, 43-78.

Bruner, J., Olver, R., and Greenfield, P. *Studies in cognitive growth.* New York: John Wiley and Sons, 1966.

Buktenica, N. A. *Visual learning dimensions in early learning series.* San Rafael, California: Dimensions Publishing Co., 1968.

Carrow, M. A. Sister The development of auditory comprehension of language in children. *Journal of Speech and Hearing Disorders*, 1968, *33*, 99-111.

Cazden, C. Environmental assistance to the child's acquisition of grammar. Unpublished doctoral dissertation, Harvard University, Cambridge, Massachusetts, 1965.

Cazden, C. Subcultural differences in child language: an interdisciplinary review. *Merrill-Palmer Quarterly*, 1966, *12*, 185-214.

Coleman, J. Rationale for the auditory training program, working paper. Austin: Southwest Educational Development Laboratory, 1969

Cruickshank, W. M., Bice, H. W., and Wallen, N. E. *Perception and cerebral palsy.* Syracuse: Syracuse University Press, 1957.

Frostig, M. and Horne, D. *The Frostig program for the development of visual perception.* Chicago: Follett Publishing Co., 1964.

Gagné, R. The acquisition of knowledge. *Psychological Review*, 1962, *69*, 355-365.

Getman, G. N. and Kane, E. R. *The physiology of readiness: an action program for the development of perception for children.* Minneapolis: P.A.F.F. Inc., 1947.

Gotkin, L. Programmed instruction as a strategy for developing curricula for disadvantaged children. *Monographs of the Society for Research in Child Development*, 1968, *33*, 1935.

Guilford, J. P. Intelligence 1965 model. *American Psychologist*, 1966, *21* No. 1.

Hakes, D. T. Psychological aspects of bilingualism. *The Modern Language Journal*, 1965, *XLIX*, 220-227.

Hebb, O. D. *The organization of behavior.* New York: John Wiley and Sons, Inc., 1949.

Hess, R. and Shipman, V. Early experience and socialization of cognitive modes in children. *Child Development*, 1965, *36*, No. 4.

Hunt, J. McV. The psychological basis for using preschool enrichment as an antidote for cultural deprivation. *Merrill-Palmer Quarterly,* 1964, *10*, 209-248.

Hunt, J. McV. *The challenge of incompetence and poverty.* Urbana, Illinois: University of Illinois Press, 1970.

Manuel, H. T. *Spanish speaking children of the southwest: their education and the public welfare.* Austin: University of Texas Press, 1965.

McCandless, B. *Children-behavior and development.* New York: Holt, Rinehart, and Winston, Inc., 1967.

Peal, E. and Lambert, W. E. The relation of bilingualism to intelligence. *Psychological Monographs: General and Applied,* 1962, *LXXVI*, No. 27, Whole No. 546, 1-23.

Penfield, W. and **Roberts, L.** *Speech and brain mechanism.* Princeton, New Jersey: Princeton University Press, 1959.

Plumer, D. Language problems of disadvantaged children: a review of the literature and some recommendations. *Monograph*, 1968, No. 6, Cambridge, Massachusetts: Harvard Research and Development Center of Educational Differences.

Randall, R. S. The development process, working paper. Austin, Texas: Southwest Educational Development Laboratory, 1970. (a)

Randall, R. S. Evaluation as an on-going experience and agent of change. working paper. Austin, Texas: Southwest Educational Development Laboratory, 1970. (b)

Randall, R. S. Knowledge about decision processes and information. A paper read at the American Educational Research Association Convention, Los Angeles, California, February 1969.

Resnick, L. B. Programmed instruction and the teaching of social studies skills. *Thirty-third Yearbook of the National Council for Social Studies*, 1963, *33*, 252-273.

Resnick, L. B. Design of an early learning curriculum, working paper 16. Pittsburgh: University of Pittsburgh Learning Research and Development Center, 1967, 7.

Schilder, P. *The image and appearance of the human body.* New York: International Universities Press, 1935.

Schulz, R. E. *The nature of educational development in education.* Athens, Georgia: University of Georgia, 1970.

Scriven, M. *The methodology of evaluation perspectives of curriculum evaluation: AERA monograph series on curriculum evaluation.* Chicago: Rand McNally and Company, 1967.

Sears, R. Introduction. J. Bruner (Ed.), *Learning about learning*, 1966, Washington, D. C.: Bureau of Research, Office of Education, U. S. Department of Health, Education, and Welfare.

Southwest educational development laboratory annual evaluation report 1968-1969, San Antonio urban education learning system. Austin: Southwest Educational Development Laboratory, 1969.

Southwest educational development laboratory; an overview of mechanism for planning, working paper. Austin, Texas: Southwest Educational Development Laboratory, 1969

Zigmond, N. K. and **Cicci, R.** *Auditory learning dimensions in early learning series.* San Rafael, California: Dimensions Publishing Company, 1968.

Kamii | *Introduction* | 4

The impact of Piaget's theory both on current research in developmental psychology and cognition and on the development of instructional programs for preschool and elementary school children has been tremendous. Although the actual relevance of Piaget's theory for the design of instructional programs and sequences has been much discussed (e.g., Sullivan, 1967), and Kamii states in her conclusion to the paper "What difference this theory can make to the education of disadvantaged children is a question that remains to be answered empirically," Kamii's program, based upon Piagetian theory, is a major step toward answering that question. In addition, as Frank Hooper pointed out during the conference, Kamii's program is providing a "considerable amount of normative data describing the cognitive functioning of the preoperational period (two to six years of age) child."

Kamii's efforts to adequately understand the implications of Piaget's theory and to accurately translate them into practice are obvious and thorough. In her paper, Kamii first explains concepts and hypotheses embedded in Piagetian theory which have relevance for education — specifically Piaget's definition and descriptions of intelligence, its course of development, and those particular actions (on the environment) and interactions (with peers) which are of major importance in its development. Given these concepts, Kamii posits as the main goal of her program developing the general framework of intelligence, intelligence being exemplified at its highest level by formal operations and socio-emotional maturity. Emphasis is placed on underlying processes rather than on external behavior. Thus, although objectives are divided into socio-emotional and cognitive, with subdivisions of each, there is no rigid series of behaviors to be learned. The child chooses from carefully selected materials those in which he is most interested, and the teacher functions to encourage his systematic exploration of his world and his curiosity by asking him questions and leading him to experiment.

Constance Kamii

An Application of Piaget's Theory to the Conceptualization of a Preschool Curriculum

4

As I go on with my sixth year of studying Piaget's theory, I keep finding in my own publications statements that reflect a misunderstanding of Piaget's theory. These errors can perhaps be viewed as evidence of how different Piaget's theory is from any other theory that is studied in American universities. The differences are too basic, too numerous, and too complex to discuss in an hour. Piaget's notions of "perception," "memory," "thinking," "intelligence," "learning," etc., are fundamentally different from the way in which we usually think about these terms. As I cannot possibly deal with any one of these topics today, I am forced to be selective and superficial in sketching the conceptualization of a preschool curriculum based on Piaget's theory. The conceptualization is by no

---

Constance Kamii is at the Ypsilanti, Michigan Public Schools. This program is part of the Ypsilanti Early Education Program, which is funded under Title III of the Elementary and Secondary Education Act of 1965 (No. 67-042490). The opinions expressed herein, however, do not reflect the position or policy of the funding agency, and no official endorsement by the Office of Education should be inferred. I am grateful to Robert Peper of the Ypsilanti Public Schools and Rheta De Vries of the University of Illinois at Chicago Circle for critically reading the manuscript and contributing many ideas, and to Hermina Sinclair of the University of Geneva, without whom the conceptualization presented in this paper would not have been possible. Printed by permission of the author.

means complete, as this paper reflects my views after less than three years of experimentation.

In order to give the rationale for the objectives of the preschool curriculum and the methods of teaching that will follow, I would like to highlight a few of the basic Piagetian notions concerning the nature of "intelligence," "knowledge," and "learning," and the relationship between cognition and affectivity. The theoretical underpinnings of the curriculum will be shown in a biological theory of intelligence that encompasses the intelligence of all the animals in the evolutionary scale at the lower end, and the intelligence of the human adolescent at the higher end of the continuum. We can better understand the nature of intelligence itself by taking a biological perspective, and we can conceptualize our short-term goals better once we have defined our long-term goals.

Piaget looked for laws of cognitive development in nature, rather than in the laboratory. His reason was that laboratories may provide "scientific" data, but they artificially limit what the organism is allowed to show to the experimenter. The laws of learning derived from the laboratory may, therefore, not be valid for education, and they may not even be valid for rats.

In *Biologie et connaissance* (1967), Piaget points out two methods which must not be used in studying behavior. They are:

1. Methods that project into less complex animals structures or phenomena that characterize more complex animals. For example, we may look at the bobbing head movements of a parrot and think that it is bowing to us, when in reality these movements are the stereotyped remnants of the parrot's desperate attempts to escape from its cage (Lorenz, 1952).
2. Methods that overlook the characteristics of more complex animals and reduce the analysis of their behavior to a level that is appropriate for less complex animals. An example is the approach to human intelligence in terms of what has been found with rats. In other words, human beings may learn certain things by association and reinforcement, but there may be much more to human learning than what can be found with animals.

Views of cognitive development may also be limited by our epistemological perspective. In psychology, we usually start studying cognition by looking at perception. In this approach, stimuli are thought to come through the senses and to be interpreted by the brain. Internal traces of perception are then assumed to remain in the organism in the form of images, and more "abstract" knowledge is believed to be constructed from perceptual knowledge according to principles of association and generalization. In this view, association and generalization are thought to be enhanced through language and various forms of reinforcement. I think education is generally limited by this perspective.

Piaget started his inquiry into the nature of knowledge not by looking at perception but by looking at all organisms, both extant and extinct. His starting point was the observation that all living organisms have the characteristic that they act and adapt to their environment. The very fact that an amoeba lives, or a crab or a lion or a human baby lives, indicates that it is acting and adapting to its environment. Otherwise, it would simply die.

Biological adaptation itself implies a degree of intelligence and knowledge. For example, fishes "know" enough not to jump out of water. Crabs run away from people. Some birds can travel to a specific place across a continent and return precisely to the original place the following year. Bees adapt not only to their physical environment but also to an elaborate social system. Babies know how to cry to announce their discomfort. Whether the mechanisms of adaptation are called "instinct," "reflex," or "intelligence," the fact remains that all living organisms have some kind of mechanisms that enable them to act in such a way that they adapt to their environment by meeting their biological needs. The basic biological needs of all animals are for nutrition, protection from physical harm, and reproduction. If adaptive mechanisms were not present, either the individual organism or the entire species would die off.

When Piaget talks about intelligence, he is talking about intelligence in this broad, biological sense. To be sure, some organisms are more complex and more intelligent than others. If there are genetic potentials, the organism develops far beyond mere biological survival. In the case of human beings, the baby's reflexes adapt to external objects and develop into the construction of the object, representation, reversibility of thought, and all the way up to formal operations. I think Piaget showed convincingly that there is a *complete continuity* between the newborn baby's reflexes and his later ability to think.

Before discussing this continuity in more detail, I would like to give a specific example. Let's take the example of the knowledge that Washington is the capital of the United States. If we tried to teach this knowledge to our preschool children, the most we would get would be rote recitation. The children would not even understand the statement because they do not have the general framework of knowledge into which they need to fit the statement in order to understand it. They need a framework of geography and political organization to understand this sentence. To have this framework, they have to have a general cognitive structure. Even the four-year-olds living in Washington would not understand that they live in Washington, or that they live in a city and a country *at the same time*. To them, "capital" may mean a person, or a building, or a fountain, or nothing at all. *Classification* is thus involved in understanding each of these words, as well as the relationship among the three main words. In addition, *space* has to be structured to understand the spatial relationship between Washington and the United States. If the child really understands this simple statement, we can conclude that he has a general cognitive structure that can coordinate all these abilities, and a lot more.

An Application of Piaget's Theory

A sixth grader can more or less understand that Washington is the capital of the United States. However, after six additional years of living, reading the newspaper, studying history and civics, and taking a senior trip to Washington, the same child in the twelfth grade will be able to derive much richer meanings from the same statement. If asked to free associate to the word "Washington," he might say, "Peace demonstrations, the White House. . ., Jefferson, Lincoln. . ., a square piece of land ten miles by ten miles, etc." If I asked you to free associate, you would probably put Jefferson and Lincoln at the end of the list and begin with things like "the Office of Child Development, OE, OEO. . ." Notice that, even in free association, few people would say, "The price of eggs in China. . ., Napoleon. . ., Charlie Brown. . ., and Marilyn Monroe!" These examples illustrate Piaget's view that since knowledge is organized in a coherent, whole structure, no concept can exist in isolation. Each concept is supported and colored by an entire network of other concepts.

The above example was given in order to lead up to the point Furth (1969) makes that, for Piaget, "knowledge" and "intelligence" in a broad sense are exactly the same thing. Furth says that to understand this statement, it is necessary to make the distinction between "knowledge" in a narrow sense and "knowledge" in a broad sense. Knowing that Washington is the capital of the United States is an example of knowledge in a narrow sense. The general framework that enables the child to understand the specific statement about Washington, on the other hand, is an example of knowledge in a broad sense. Knowledge in a broad sense is not a collection of specific facts but, rather, an organized structure that is qualitatively different. General knowledge is what makes it possible for the child to understand specific information. Piaget is not particularly interested in how the child acquires specific knowledge, but he is concerned with the development of the broad cognitive framework. This framework is what he calls "intelligence." The child understands and learns new things through this framework. "Knowledge" in a broad sense and "intelligence" are, therefore, exactly the same thing for Piaget.

"Learning," too, can be specific or general. The child can learn that something is called "a cup" or "the moon" or "a dinosaur," or that plants need water to grow. These are specific learnings. But the child can also learn to structure his space from his crib to his entire house, and then to the block he lives on, his city, his country, and all the way to outer space. He can also learn to structure his time from the present to infinity or to prehistoric times. He can learn to structure all the objects in the universe into hierarchical systems of classification. These are examples of learning in a broad sense. They comprise the basic elements of "knowledge," or "intelligence," in the broadest sense.

In formulating the objectives of a preschool curriculum, I think we need to put the accent on developing the general framework. But how to develop the framework is a question to which I have only partial answers. This is the question of our research. I am not even sure that a year of preschool makes any difference. There are empirical questions worth trying to answer. One thing I do know is that no amount of specific learning will result in greater general intelligence. Intelligence simply does not develop in an additive way. Another thing that I know is that schools generally function in ways that do not foster the development of intelligence.

The important question, now, is where this framework comes from and how it is built. According to Piaget, it is rooted in the baby's sensory-motor adaptive *actions* and is built as these actions are internally *coordinated.* Piaget saw cognitive structures in the baby's motor activities where others saw only preintellectual actions like motor coordination. One of his unique contributions is that he views intelligence as actions,[1] and sees a complete continuity between action and thought.

For the newborn baby, there are no objects. The reason for this phenomenon is that the baby has not differentiated himself from objects, and no discrete object can exist in the baby's mind until he has become able to impose a structure on the mass of incoming sensations. In *The Origins of Intelligence* (1952) and *The Construction of Reality in the Child* (1954), Piaget describes in great detail how the newborn baby's reflexes adapt to external objects and become sensory-motor schemes, or action patterns, through which the baby comes to recognize objects. He describes precisely how sensory-motor adaptive actions are repeated as long as the situation is similar, but are differentiated or combined in new ways if either the organism's needs or the external situation changes. The baby thus constructs objects and gradually comes to know each object by grasping it, putting it in his mouth, dropping it, picking it up, shaking it, transferring it from one hand to the other, etc.

If there were no action, therefore, there could be no object for the baby. If there were no object, time and space could not be structured, the notion of causality would never come into being, and there could certainly not be any representation, logic, physics, or history. In short, if there were no action, there would be no knowledge for the organism. There would be only sensations.

By acting on objects, babies gradually structure their space and time. Piaget gives the example of an experiment in which he placed an attractive toy on a pillow in such a way that the baby could reach the pillow but not the toy. (The toy was on the side of the pillow away from the baby.) Until a certain stage, it does not occur to the baby to pull the pillow to get the toy. However, once he has structured the spatial relationship between the two objects, the baby immediately pulls the pillow and never forgets this learning. This is an example of Piaget's theory that sensory-motor intelligence *is* coordinated actions.

Babies also find out about the physical nature of objects by acting on them. For example, by putting a cookie in the mouth and then a rattle and everything else in sight in the mouth, they find out that certain things can be eaten and others cannot. The foundation for classification, the notion of negation ("can*not* be eaten"), and the notions of size, shape, weight, and texture can all be seen in this familiar scene. If there were no action, therefore, there would be no physical knowledge.

Intentions come into being as the baby acts on objects. For example, he may fortuitously notice when he drops a rattle that it makes a noise. If he has reached a certain level of development, he will make use of this fortuitous discovery and repeat the same action intentionally to produce the same sound. Means-ends relationships, or problem solving, thus grow out of coordinated actions.

The action of walking greatly expands the baby's structuring of space and time. When he accidentally loses a ball by rolling it under a sofa, for example, the baby first looks for the ball where it disappeared. Later, however, under similar circumstances and even with a different sofa, he is likely to go around to the back of the sofa to look for the ball. This change demonstrates the baby's ability to structure space sufficiently to extend the movement of the ball into an area that he cannot see. There is a lot of elementary geometry and physics involved in these coordinated actions.

The baby who is just beginning to walk is likely to go down a step as if it were a flat surface. After one or two falls, however, he will anticipate the descent and adjust his actions accordingly. Anticipation is thus part of adaptation, and it is part of coordinated actions. Anticipation gives rise to new coordinations, and new coordinations in turn generate further anticipations. For example, the baby who has structured one step can go on to anticipate the structure of two steps. Before long, he will be able to anticipate running up and down the entire stairway. Eventually, he will become able to *think about* the stairway without actually engaging in the external action of running. In other words, knowledge is progressively created out of adaptive actions, and it has the function of facilitating the organism's greater adaptation to the environment.

I belabored the point that the child's cognitive framework is rooted in his adaptive actions, and that thinking *is* coordinated actions. This point was belabored because it has important implications for preschool education. If we believe that intelligence is rooted in the depth of biological adaptation, and if we believe that development is continuous and uninterrupted, and if we believe that intelligence is one coherent, integrated structure through which the child learns, then we will build a curriculum that *extends* these actions. If, on the other hand, we believe that intelligence develops through perception, association, and language, we are not likely to stress the coordination of actions.

In the remainder of this introductory section, I would like to discuss the relationship between the socio-emotional and cognitive aspects of human behavior from a phylogenetic perspective, and substantiate Piaget's assertion that, in reality, the two are inseparable. To do this, I would like to compare the various species first on the receptor side and then on the efferent side, and finally from the standpoint of social organizations.

Speaking of receptor organs, Piaget (1967) says that the degree of differentiation of receptor organs makes a difference in the organism's tendency to approach things that are desirable (food and sex) and avoid things that are undesirable (danger). He states that as long as the organism does not have differentiated sensory organs, external events are of concern to it only at the time of direct physical contact. Biological needs disappear as soon as they are satisfied, and reappear in periodic cycles.

On the other hand, when olfactory, visual, and auditory organs are differentiated, the organism's biological needs change because it becomes capable of sensing the presence of food, sex objects, and danger that are not in direct contact with it. More complex animals have organs with which to perceive food, for example, and they become capable of anxiety when there is no food in sight. In other words, the capacity for anxiety emerges as a result of the capacity to perceive things that are not in direct physical contact. A need to increase the probability of finding food thus emerges, and a new need for exploration is created. The ability to perceive distant enemies likewise generates anxiety and vigilance. Since more complex animals can perceive things with which they are not in direct physical contact, their cognitive milieu is larger. An animal's capacity for emotions thus goes hand in hand with its capacity for cognition.

According to Furth (1969)

> *Concerning the locus where modifiability occurs, Lorenz mentions a significant difference between the evolutionarily highest branches and lower ones. In lower animals it is predominantly on the receptor side that learning takes place. Animals learn to distinguish relevant cues, learn to aim better at objects which they approach, or acquire necessary information to complete an inbuilt behavior pattern.... However, freedom to acquire new motor patterns is characteristic of the highest mammals, as is witnessed by the development of that part of the brain which controls voluntary movements.*
>
> *The direction of this development seems of importance for a basic understanding of human intelligence. One notices that lower down on the scale of evolution animal behavior is rigidly fixed in its adaptation. Above this level there is increased modifiability in the form of greater responsiveness towards the environment on the receptor side, and finally there emerges the capacity to move freely and to act on and manipulate things of the environment. (p. 188)*

In other words, amoebas do not explore their environment, but dogs, rats, and human babies certainly do. Primates and humans have hands which immeasurably increase the organism's capacity to manipulate and explore objects.

The educational implication of the above passage is that from the standpoint of cognitive development, any training in perceptual discrimination is less likely to produce cognitive growth than developing the efferent side, i.e., "the capacity to move freely and to act on and manipulate things of the environment." The importance of developing children's curiosity and eagerness to explore and experiment becomes clear. The more curious the child is, the more he will explore, and the more knowledge he will gain. The more knowledge he has, the more advanced the nature of his curiosity will be, and the more systematic his exploration will be.

A corollary of the higher animal's capacity to act on its own initiative, rather than merely reacting to stimuli coming from the outside, is the capacity for play. Miller (1968, pp. 61-62) states:

> *No one, to my knowledge, has ever suggested that the single cell animals, the protozoa, play.... It is not until we get to the arthropods, jointed-limbed animals who have their skeleton on the outside of the body, that some observers have spoken of "play." (pp. 61-62)*

Play can be broadly defined as activities that the organism engages in for no reason except that the activity itself is pleasurable. In *Play, Dreams, and Imitation in Childhood*, Piaget (1962) classifies play into three types: practice games, symbolic games, and games with rules. All organs have a biological need to be used; otherwise they atrophy from disuse. Likewise, the capacity of higher animals to act on their own initiative has a biological need to be used. Play is, therefore, a characteristic of higher animals.

In other words, higher animals not only have the *capacity* to behave on their own initiative in a variety of ways, but also the *need* to actively use this capacity.

Piaget amply demonstrates in *Play, Dreams, and Imitation in Childhood* (1962), *The Origins of Intelligence* (1952), and *The Construction of Reality in the Child* (1954) that babies and children learn by playing. Play is one of the most powerful allies on the teacher's side. Unfortunately, we have not learned how to use play very well in our classrooms. This is the essence of what we are trying to do in our classrooms.

Adults, especially educators, have a tendency to classify human activities into "work" and "play," as if the two were mutually exclusive. We know that some play is hard work (e.g., skiing and playing the piano), and some work is fun (e.g., playing with ideas and hypotheses). The following matrix may clarify the relationship between work and play:

	Work Not enjoyed	Work Enjoyed
Play: Exploring, Making sense out of things, Games with rules, Symbolic games	?	X
Play: Practice games (repeating and exercising)	?	X

The ideal situation for learning falls in the cells marked "X." When education falls in the cells marked "?," as if learning were an unpleasant job the child has to be paid to perform, then it has to resort to motivational devices. There is something wrong somewhere when we have to use gimmicks to motivate preschool children to learn.

Another characteristic of more complex animals is that they create, and exist in, social systems. Amoebas do not have a social system, but more complex animals like ants, fishes, birds, bees, and humans do. The young of these species must adapt not only to their physical environment but also to their social environment. Social systems facilitate and regulate the species' biological needs for food, sex, and safety. Morality, values, attitudes, roles, interpersonal relationships, language, etc., are, therefore, an extension of our biological needs, and are part of our very nature. Even when he is alone, therefore, the child is, and always will be, a social being.

When Piaget discusses the importance of social collaboration in cognitive development, we can see that, in his thinking, he usually takes normal socio-emotional adaptation for granted. The desirability of teamwork among children is one of the few pedagogical principles he has explicitly stated (Piaget, 1969). He argues that by exchanging views and trying to resolve differences of opinions in social collaboration, children learn to coordinate different points of view. This coordination requires the child to get out of his egocentricity because his reality is not necessarily the same as other people's reality. The modifiability of human adaptation is thus enormous. We create a social system which in turn greatly modifies how we conceive of our environment.

By way of a summary, I would like to highlight the following conclusions from Piaget's biological theory of intelligence because of their relevance to preschool education:

1. Intelligence is rooted in the depth of biological adaptation, and there is a complete, unbroken continuity between the baby's reflexes and his higher mental processes.
2. Intelligence grows as an integrated whole structure, and not additively as a collection of skills. Neither perceptual skills nor specific information will result in developing the general framework that Piaget calls "intelligence." It is through this general framework that the child learns new things.
3. The child's socio-emotional life and cognitive life are inseparable.
4. Intelligence *is* coordinated actions, either externalized or internalized. Therefore, the way to develop intelligence is to extend the child's coordinated actions.
5. Higher animals have the following characteristics: (a) They have the capacity for voluntary actions and exploration, and use this capacity in the form of play. Human beings have both the capacity and the need to know and to make sense out of their environment. (b) They create social systems which regulate and modify their biological nature.

How to apply these principles to preschool education is a matter of opinion. I would like to present my May 1970 version below under the following headings: the formulation of objectives, teaching methods, and the evaluation of the curriculum.

I. THE FORMULATION OF OBJECTIVES

A. LONG-RANGE GOALS

The objectives of preschool education can best be conceptualized in light of long-range goals. I think one of the long-range goals of education should be formal operations and the socio-emotional maturity to use them in all kinds of situations outside the classroom.

The objectives of our preschool curriculum include physical knowledge, social knowledge, the structuring of space and time, classification, seriation, and number. By discussing the longitudinal outcome of these short-term objectives, I hope to show why we emphasize cognitive *processes* rather than external behavior. I hope to show that if we help the child to develop his cognitive processes, we may increase his chances of attaining formal operations. If, on the other hand, we teach the external behavior, or the final answer, we may end up decreasing his chances for later learning.

For example, seriation in preschool takes the form of arranging objects of graduated sizes (e.g., five dolls having heights of 6, 7, 8, 9, and 10 cm.). We are happy when children arrange the dolls in the right order, say, from the tallest to the shortest one. However, our real goal is not children's ability to arrange objects. In a sense, we don't even care whether or not they can arrange little dolls and sticks because, as adults, we never need to arrange dolls and sticks. Our real goal is to enable children to *generate the cognitive structure* of seriation when the necessity presents itself. After all, real problems in the world come with all kinds of ambiguities and shades of gray, and it is we who have to generate and impose the logical structure to even begin to isolate the relevant variables we want to think about. I would like to give two examples to illustrate what I mean, one in science and the other in history.

Inhelder and Piaget (1958, Ch. 3) describe an experiment dealing with the flexibility of metal rods. In this experiment, the child is given a number of metal rods, a number of dolls that can be screwed onto the end of the rod to make it bend when it is held horizontally, and the apparatus shown in Figure 1. The child is asked (a) to find out what kind of rods are flexible enough to bend and reach

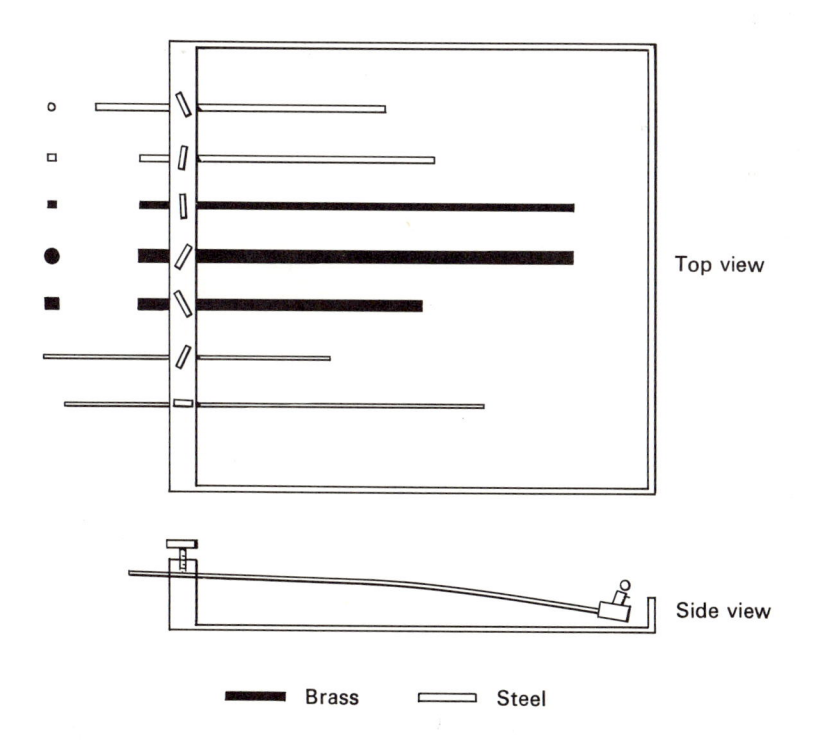

Figure 1. Apparatus Used by the Child to Test the Flexibility of the Rods.

the "water," and (b) to prove his conclusion. The rods vary along four dimensions: thickness (thin and thick rods); length (the child can adjust the length of the rod); cross-sectional shape (round and square rods); and material (brass and steel rods). The dolls are made of the same material but vary in size and, consequently, in weight (100, 200, and 300 grams). The child is encouraged to experiment freely with the objects to find out when the rod bends and when it does not. He is given help whenever he has any difficulty in manual dexterity.

The child in the period of concrete operations (from about seven to eleven years of age) can easily classify the rods by any of the attributes. However, in trying to figure out the factors that determine their flexibility, he is likely to put 100 grams on a long, thin, square, steel rod, and 200 grams on a long, thick, round brass rod. In other words, he holds only one or two factors (e.g., length) constant and varies all the other factors! The child who has reached formal operations, on the other hand, compares rods that are identical in every way except for one variable, such as length. Formal operations thus enable the child to incorporate into *one single system* all the variables that may be relevant, and to vary only one factor at a time. This systematic process of formulating and verifying hypotheses is a characteristic of hypothetico-deductive thinking.

The proof that the child considers to be necessary and conclusive also reveals whether or not he has attained formal operations. Below are examples of the ways in which a 9-year-old, an 11-year-old, and a 16-year-old responded to the request, "Could you show me that a thin one bends more than a thick one?"

A 9-year-old (in the period of concrete operations)
Places 200 grams each on a long thin rod, and a short thick rod. No amount of help enables him to see that his proof is not a proof.

An 11-year-old (not quite in the period of formal operations)
Places 100 grams on a round, steel, long, thick rod, and 200 grams on a rod identical with the first except for its thickness. The experimenter then says, "I would like you to show me only that the thin one bends more than the wide one. Is that way right?" The child replaces the 100-gram weight with a 200-gram weight.

A 16-year-old (in the period of formal operations)
Immediately picks up two rods that are identical except in thickness and gives the logical proof.

Classification and seriation schemes are generated in the above experiments. Without varying the lengths of the rods (i.e., establishing the serial correspondence between the length of the rod and the degree of bending), children cannot isolate the relevance of length. Without varying the thickness (establishing the correspondence between thickness and degree of bending), they cannot conclude that thickness indeed affects the flexibility of a rod.

In a study of formal operations in history, Hallam (1967) and Lovell (in press) gave to pupils of 11 to 16 years of age short passages to read on various historical topics such as the Norman Conquest and Queen Mary Tudor. After the children had read the passages and had any word explained that they did not understand, they were asked a number of questions. One of them related to the passage on Queen Mary Tudor was "Do you think it sensible to have conformity in religion in a country?" The children were allowed to re-read the passages as many times as they wanted to. In this research, Lovell and his collaborators found repeatedly that the pupils' answers could be classified as pre-operational, concrete operational, and formal operational, with many answers falling at intermediate points.

At the concrete-operational level, the children showed the following characteristics: ability to predict a result from the evidence, but inability to generate a hypothesis dealing with the possible; and ability to move from one point of view to another, but inability to coordinate the two or more points of view into a single system.

The formal operational adolescents, in contrast, were found to go beyond the given, to reason systematically by implication, and to attempt to relate a multiplicity of possible links and points of view. The following is an example given by an adolescent of 14 years and 8 months:

> *This is a very difficult question to answer because there are basically two ideas in the present day. On the one hand you have the idea that all should be subservient to the state and, on the other hand, you have the idea that choice is a good thing. There's a lot to be said for both sides. But religion, being essentially a private thing between man and God, should be divorced from politics whenever possible. However, where a situation arises where there are two conflicting religions or ideologies, I think that in such a case it is probably permissible to attempt to enforce a uniform front to hold together the country in time of stress. Two bitterly opposed religious parties is a thing that should be discouraged because neither thinks anything of the other and is prepared to go to any lengths because religious fanaticism, when entering into politics, is often a more evil thing and more dangerous than politics, although politics in its own way is often both.*

By using classification and seriation, the formal-operational scientist above constructed at least the following 32 combinations in trying to isolate the factors that are relevant to the flexibility of the rods:

$$2 \binom{\text{thick-}}{\text{thin}} \times 2 \binom{\text{long-}}{\text{short}} \times 2 \binom{\text{circle-}}{\text{square}} \times 2 \binom{\text{steel-}}{\text{brass}} \times 2 \binom{\text{bends-}}{\text{does not bend}} = 32$$

In reality, he was dealing with more than 32 combinations because each variable was not a dichotomy, but, rather, a continuum. The concrete-operational child can manage only two or three variables and mentally constructs matrices such as the following, which produces only four combinations:

	Bends	Does not bend
Long		
Short		

The formal-operational historian quoted above seems to have constructed the following six variables (there may be more, but six is all that I am able to isolate; maybe you can find more):

Religious freedom (vs. no religious freedom)
Political freedom (vs. no political freedom)
Physical danger (vs. safety)
The welfare of the individual (vs. the welfare of the group)
Fanaticism (vs. rationality)
What is permissible (vs. what is mandatory or forbidden)

The six variables yield at least $2^6 = 64$ combinations, assuming that each variable is dichotomous. In reality, there are more than 64 combinations because each variable is not a dichotomy, but, rather, a continuum.

I apologize for the detail I went into in the above discussion. The point I tried to make is that the long-term goals in classification and seriation are not to enable children to make little matrices and arrange little graduated sticks, but to use the *process* of classification and seriation to isolate relevant variables and to generate and test hypotheses in dealing with the real world.

B. SHORT-TERM OBJECTIVES

We have discussed the origins of intelligence on the one hand and some long-range goals of education on the other. The short-term goals of preschool education must be placed in this context to make sure that whatever children learn is firmly rooted in sensory-motor intelligence, and learned in such a way that the probability of future learning increases. Although the socio-emotional and cognitive objectives are discussed separately below, it must be remembered that, in reality, the two are inseparable.

1. SOCIO-EMOTIONAL OBJECTIVES

Our objectives are internal processes rather than external behavior. For example, one of our objectives is the development of curiosity. Whether curiosity manifests itself in constant experiments or endless questions, or both, is not of particular concern to us. We feel that each child has different ways of being curious, and the teacher's job is to encourage each child to be curious in ways that are comfortable for him. Some of the most important objectives are listed below.

   a. Intrinsic motivation to derive pleasure from using previously learned schemes.
      1. Children's busily doing things, many things, anything from rolling barrels to playing with a flashlight, with initiative, enthusiasm, and excitement.[3]
         Intelligence develops by being used. If children keep acting on things on their initiative, their intelligence is likely to develop by the very fact that it is being constantly used. As long as they have the initiative to keep doing *something*, each solution is likely to lead to a new challenge.
      2. Curiosity
         Curiosity is more focused than the above objective. Examples are
         a. Exploring things (e.g., magnifying glass, hair brush) to figure out how they are made and how they work.
         b. Experimenting with means-ends relationships with scales, balances, etc.
         c. Asking questions
      3. Confidence
         We want children to have the confidence that they *can* figure things out on their own (rather than depending on the teacher to provide the answer). Even when their answer is "wrong" from the standpoint of adult logic, we want children to speak their minds with confidence. Confidence seems to lead to the two objectives listed above.
      4. Creativity
         We want children not to come up with only one response, but to take pride in coming up with many different responses. Even with simple things like going down a slide, for example, we want chil-

dren to come up with many different ways of doing the same thing (e.g., coming down on the stomach, backward, with hands up, etc.).

I think the above objectives are likely to give more educational mileage than any of the specific cognitive objectives. If children are excited, curious, confident, and creative, they are bound to go on learning, particularly after they go home and after the preschool year.

  b. Controlling one's own behavior
    1. Ability to make decisions and plans, to carry them out, and to evaluate one's own activities
    2. Ability to respect rules and authority when necessary
  c. Relationship with peers
    1. Playing with other children
    2. Discussing things with other children
    3. Respecting the rights and feelings of other children
  d. Relationship with adults

2. COGNITIVE OBJECTIVES

Piaget delineated three areas of knowledge according to the different ways in which knowledge is structured. The three are physical knowledge, social knowledge, and logico-mathematical knowledge. Pens may be used to illustrate the differences among them.

Physical knowledge is structured from the feedback children receive from the objects when they do something to them. For example, by letting go of a pen, the child finds out that it does not break like a crayon when it hits the floor, and that it usually bounces once. If the child acts on the pen in a certain way, it reacts by making marks on paper, on skin, on cloth, and on walls.

Social knowledge comes not from feedback from objects, but from feedback from people. The fact that a pen makes a mark on the wall is physical knowledge, but the fact that Mommy gets angry when she sees the mark is social knowledge.

If I show you five pens, the fiveness is an example of logico-mathematical knowledge. If I show you five red pens and two blue pens, the fact that there are more pens than red pens is also an example of logico-mathematical knowledge. Each of these objectives, plus representation, will be discussed below in further detail.

a. PHYSICAL KNOWLEDGE

As stated before, physical knowledge concerns physical phenomena and the physical nature of objects. Time and space are also aspects of physical knowledge.

The child finds out about the physical nature of a pen, for example, by doing things to it, e.g., dropping it, trying to bend it, squeezing it, and trying to make marks with one end of the stick or the other. The object always reacts to the same action with regularity, and the child builds his physical knowledge by structuring the regularity of this feedback from the object.

The child can find out that while a pen does not bend, a metal rod does. In a similar way, he finds out that paper tears but cloth does not. He also finds out that fishes are happier in the water than out of it, and that no matter how hard he tries to make a block stay underwater by itself, it always comes back up with regularity.

There are three main objectives in teaching physical knowledge. One is enlarging the child's repertoire of actions he can apply to objects to explore their nature. The second is the process of experimentation when a problem is given. The third is the initiative to come up with a problem of one's own and to wonder about things.

For example, with a balance, the child first plays with the object and figures out how it works by thinking up different things to do to it. We might then put 8 washers on one side and 3 on the other, and ask the child to make the two sides balance. We are interested in the process of reasoning rather than the final answer. At the beginning of the year, some children put 2 on the side that is up, and then 2 on the other side that is already down! We want children to become able to reason more logically in an intuitive way, i.e., to better coordinate their actions.

After solving the problem that the teacher suggests, some children decide to play the same game with some other objects, e.g., marbles. This is an example of the initiative to come up with a problem of one's own. I think it is better that a child comes up with one question of his own than that he answers ten questions that he doesn't care anything about.

b. SOCIAL KNOWLEDGE

Social knowledge comes from people, e.g., the mother who gets angry at a mark on the wall. Other examples are:

> the names of all objects, both in spoken and written forms;
> the fact that neckties are for men, and not for women;
> the fact that dogs and plants can be brought into the house, but not worms and rabbits;
> the fact that we have to pay money to take home a bottle of pop;
> the fact that at certain times people insist that it's time to go to bed;
> the fact that firemen put out fires, maids clean rooms, and milkmen deliver milk; and
> the notions of religion, laws, and politics.

The ultimate source of this kind of "truth" is people, and the child can acquire social knowledge only from people.

Our objectives in social knowledge are usually not deliberately planned. Some content comes up incidentally (e.g., one child telling another child in sociodramatic play, "Daddies don't do that!"), and at other times children come up with questions (e.g., "What's this?" "A filing cabinet."). The reason for this unplanned approach will be given in the next section on teaching methods.

c. LOGICO-MATHEMATICAL KNOWLEDGE

Logico-mathematical knowledge includes three major categories: a. classification, b. seriation, and c. the construction of elementary number concepts. Logico-mathematical knowledge is the hardest to explain because people usually think that logic is socially derived. There is also a strong tendency to believe that logic is a matter of using language correctly.

Preoperational children think very differently from adults, and, particularly in the logico-mathematical realm, care must be taken to develop *their* cognitive processes according to the way *they* think. Since logico-mathematical knowledge is built from feedback from the cognitive structure that already exists, we will defeat our purposes in the long run if we push preoperational children into concrete operations. Therefore, our objectives remain well within the preoperational period.

1. CLASSIFICATION

According to Piaget's theory of classification, any criterion the child "invents" for grouping is correct, provided he uses it consistently. The objectives in teaching classification are the processes (not the final product) of a. inventing one's own criteria and using them consistently, b. shifting the criteria to group and regroup the objects in many different ways, and c. thinking independently rather than depending on others to judge the correctness of the conclusion.

Example of objects to be sorted
3 red pens
2 blue pens
2 red caps
8 blue caps (one is different from the other 7)
2 pencils (yellow)

With the objects listed above, for example, when asked to put together the things that are "the same in some way," the preoperational child may put a cap on each pen and pencil. We consider this response to be correct. Our objective in classification is not to have the child figure out how the teacher wants things grouped. We want him to come up with his own reason for grouping things and re-grouping them. A separate paper (Kamii and Peper, 1969) gives a fuller description of how Piaget's theory of classification differs from other theorists'.

After putting a cap on every pen and pencil, a high-level preoperational child may shift criteria and make the following four groupings:

> Grouping 1: 2 pencils and the 2 pens which have ink left in them, all the blue caps, all the red caps, and all the pens without any ink left inside. (Then, he removes the one blue cap that is different.)
>
> Grouping 2: all the pens, all the caps, and all the pencils.
>
> Grouping 3: all the pens (he puts caps on all the pens), and all the pencils.
>
> Grouping 4: all the blue things, all the red things, and all the yellow things.

If the long-range goal of classification were to group things by color, by shape, by size, or by genus, it would make sense to teach these classificatory schemes from the beginning. However, our long-range goal is formal operations. Therefore, the important thing for children to learn is the *process of generating and imposing a logical structure* onto all the ambiguities of the real world. Whether the logical structure he "invents" is based on color or shape is not the important thing.

2. SERIATION

Our goal in seriation is to have children become able to arrange series of graduated cups, dolls, blocks, etc., from the biggest to the smallest, or vice versa, by using the perceptual configuration (preoperational seriation). While this is our behavioral objective, in a sense we don't care whether or not children can arrange cups and dolls. It is more important to have the child seriously think about how to arrange the items than to have him mechanically apply a rule (e.g., "pick up the biggest one first, then the next biggest one, . . ."). The important thing is that the child become able to *generate the logical structure* when faced with real problems.

One day in water play, for example, a child was surprised to find out that a fairly heavy block floated. She got up to get a larger block, thinking that a larger one would sink. Upon finding out that the larger one also floated, she went to get another still larger one in an attempt to find one that would be heavy enough to sink in water. This spirit of generating a graduated order in a question raised by the child himself seems much more important than memorizing the generalization that wooden objects float regardless of size. In an intuitive way, this child learned that the phenomenon of sinking depends on something other than absolute weight and size.

3. CONSTRUCTION OF ELEMENTARY NUMBER CONCEPTS

Here, too, we would like the children to establish the numerical equivalence of two sets with about eight objects having a relationship of "provoked correspondence," and conserve the equivalence. However, the *behavior* of making one-to-one correspondence or giving conserving answers is not our objective. The structuring of the underlying *process* is our real objective. Since I wrote a separate paper on number (Kamii, 1969, in press) elaborating this statement, I will not say more about this area.

d. REPRESENTATION

Since Piaget's theory of the relationship among "thinking," "knowing," and "representation" is too unique and too complex to go into, I would simply like to refer you to Furth (1969, 1970). The only point I would like to make before delineating the curriculum objectives in representation is that it is *not* with pictures and words that children think. Therefore, the acquisition of knowledge is one thing, and the ability to represent this knowledge is quite another thing. Representation is taught in a Piagetian preschool in order to help the child to structure his knowledge and to communicate it to other people.

Piaget distinguishes three types of representation. They are (a) indices, (b) symbols, and (c) signs. They are elaborated below in outline form.

1. Indices
   a. Part of the object (e.g., part of a duck sticking out from behind a boat)
   b. Marks causally related to the object (e.g., footmarks in the sand)
2. Symbols
   a. Imitation (the use of the body to represent objects, e.g., walking like a duck)
   b. Make-believe (the use of objects to represent other objects, e.g., using a box to represent a duck)
   c. Onomatopoeia (e.g., uttering "Quack, quack!")
   d. Pictures and models (e.g., drawing a duck and making a duck with play dough)
3. Signs
   a. Words and other signs, e.g., algebraic signs

The index differs from symbols and signs in that it is part of the object that is being represented. Symbols and signs, in contrast, are differentiated from the objects. The difference between symbols and signs is that only the former bear a resemblance to the object represented. Signs do not resemble the real object at all.

Basic to Piaget's theory of representation is the notion that representation is an active process rather than a passive association. His biological theory states that the organism begins to represent objects as part of biological adaptation. As stated earlier, the child can walk down a stairway more easily, for example, when he can represent to himself the spatial structure on which he is walking. Later, he internalizes this action and becomes capable of evoking the object by only imagining the action. The result of this internalization is called the mental image, which has a visual, tactile, kinesthetic, and auditory reality for the child. The mental image is what makes it possible for the child to derive meaning from such external representations as pictures and words.

A Piagetian preschool, therefore, emphasizes the child's active construction of mental images (rather than the passive association of words and pictures with real objects). Socio-dramatic play and making symbols with play dough, blocks, paint, and pipe cleaners are examples of this active construction. If the process of creating symbols is strengthened, the resultant mental image is bound to be vivid, and the words the child uses are bound to have a solid sensory-motor foundation. Representation at the level of symbols (in the sense in which the term is used in the above outline) is an objective that we particularly stress, although language and the use of indices are also emphasized.

In concluding this section on objectives, I would like to stress that although Piaget divides knowledge into physical, social, and logico-mathematical knowledge for purposes of analysis, he believes that, in reality, the three are inseparable. Intelligence for Piaget is one coherent framework. Therefore, there cannot be any physical or social knowledge without a logico-mathematical structure.

II. TEACHING METHODS

By "teaching methods," I mean what the teacher does and uses to achieve the objectives of the instructional program. In this section, therefore, will be included the selection and organization of learning activities, and the selection and organization of the content. Since teaching methods differ according to our different notions of how the learner learns, I would like to discuss a few Piagetian principles of learning first in order to give the rationale for the principles of teaching that will be discussed later.

A. PIAGETIAN PRINCIPLES OF LEARNING

I will not deal today with the general relationship between "learning" and "development" that Piaget discussed in 1964 (Piaget, 1964). Instead, I would like to select three principles of learning that are particularly relevant to preschool education. The first one is that learning takes place from inside the organism by an active process of "construction," rather than by a passive process of "absorption."

The second principle is that if each cognitive structure is developmentally integrated with the previous structure, the developmental stages are longitudinally coherent, and the learning achieved in each stage is permanent. The third principle is that learning takes place within the general framework that Piaget calls "intelligence." Each of these principles is elaborated below.

1. LEARNING IS AN ACTIVE PROCESS
   OF "CONSTRUCTION" FROM INSIDE
   THE ORGANISM.

Fundamental to Piaget's theory is the notion that knowledge is not passively received from the environment but actively constructed by the organism. Piaget rejects the S→O→R model because it assumes that the organism perceives and receives the stimulus from the outside in a passive way. As Piaget puts it, there is nothing stimulating about the stimulus itself, and stimuli as such do not stimulate the organism. It is the organism that acts on the stimulus, and not the other way around. Piaget's view of the relationship between the stimulus and the organism is shown in the following diagram.

$$S \xleftarrow{} O$$
$$ \xdashrightarrow{} $$

Many examples can be cited from Piaget's writing to illustrate the above view of the stimulus. For example, the baby may be exposed to his bottle hundreds of times, but he does not *know* it well enough to recognize it until he has "constructed" the object in his mind. When the bottle is given to a hungry baby in such a way that only its bottom can be seen and the nipple is hidden, a six-month-old baby will not even recognize his own bottle. At about nine months of age, however, when he has "constructed" the object, he will immediately show recognition by grasping the bottle, turning it around, and starting to drink out of it. In other words, stimuli do not stimulate, and it is the organism that constructs even highly meaningful objects to which it has been exposed hundreds of times.

Let's take an example from a more advanced stage. Babies grasp and let go of the same object many times to study the regularity of the object's reaction. They then pick up and let go of other objects and find out whether or not they react in the same way. They also vary the position from which the object is dropped, and the trajectory by throwing things instead of just letting go of them. These endless, tireless activities can be interpreted as the baby's process of constructing an elementary notion of the force of gravity. It is thus not the object that stimulates the baby to react. It is the baby that acts on the stimuli that were around him all along. Objects which were not previously of interest can thus become interesting when the organism has developed enough ideas to perceive them differently.

2. LEARNING TAKES PLACE IN SUCH A WAY THAT THE DEVELOPMENTAL STAGES ARE LONGITUDINALLY COHERENT.

Piaget believes that no stage can be skipped if cognitive development is to have a solid foundation for future growth. This statement is obvious enough to any programmer. What is not obvious to adults is the fact that the cognitive structures of preoperational children are very different from those of adults, and that the sequence of development is not what adult logic leads us to expect.

Let's take the concept of weight as an example of the longitudinal evolution of stages. Between seven and eight years of age, most children believe that a clay ball and another identical clay ball flattened into a "pancake" do not have the same weight. Many of these children believe, however, that the clay ball and pancake have "the same amount" of clay. For these children, there is no *logical necessity* that "the same amount" necessarily implies "the same weight."

Six months to a year later, these children acquire the conservation of weight. In other words, the knowledge that did not lead them to the conservation of weight before (i.e., the knowledge that the two clay objects have "the same amount") now leads them to conclude that the two objects *must* weigh the same. Although these children now have the conservation of weight, their notion of weight is still not completely differentiated from their notion of volume. Faced with two balls of exactly the same dimensions, one made of clay and the other made of heavy steel, these children believe that the one made of steel will make the water come up higher than the one made of clay. The reason for this belief is that the heavier ball is believed to push the water more than the lighter ball, thereby making the water rise more. As long as weight and volume are thus not dissociated in the child's mind, the notion of specific gravity is impossible to construct. Specific gravity, after all, is the relationship between the weight of an object and its volume, each of which can vary independently.

At about eleven years of age, the child dissociates volume from weight, and he soon becomes able to construct the notion of specific gravity.

The evolution of the concept of weight is only one of the many examples that can be cited to show that later concepts develop out of earlier concepts, and that the child has to go through one stage after another of being "wrong" before he becomes able to think logically like adults. Piaget views children's "wrong" notions as intermediary stages that are necessary for the ultimate construction of adult concepts.

The child who cannot conserve weight may be "wrong" from the adult's point of view. However, there is a certain amount of intuitive correctness in the belief that the "pancake" weighs less "because it is flat." From the standpoint of the pressure one feels in holding a clay ball in the palm of one hand and a flattened clay ball in the other, the child is absolutely correct in thinking that if weight is distributed over a large surface, the pressure on each spot will be less than when it is applied only at one spot. In a sensory-motor way, ever since infancy the child understands weight in terms of the downward pressure he kinesthetically feels when he picks up an object. The seven-year-old's concept of weight may thus be "wrong," but pressure is a factor that is relevant to the concept of weight. Therefore, it has to be part of his construction of the concept of weight rather than being cued out if it is to develop eventually into the dissociation of weight and volume.

Each concept is thus rooted in the baby's sensory-motor intelligence and takes a long time to evolve into an adult form. Therefore, concepts can be taught neither in a month nor in a year or two. Any attempt to skip an intermediary stage or to cue out the "wrong" notions is likely to result in hindering later learning. When earlier concepts are shaky, they will not serve as the foundation that generates higher-order concepts. Therefore, rather than cuing out and suppressing "wrong" notions, the teacher must bring them out to the fore to be integrated with other notions.

When new concepts are integrated with previously acquired ones, the learning is solid and not likely to be forgotten. Each new stage then increases the probability that the next stage will be achieved.

3. LEARNING TAKES PLACE WITHIN
   THE GENERAL FRAMEWORK THAT
   PIAGET CALLS "INTELLIGENCE."

Let us go back to the example of the concept of weight to illustrate the theory that each concept is part of a general cognitive framework, and that each concept is related to all the other concepts that the child has constructed. I would like to discuss below the evolution of the concept of weight in the periods of sensory-motor intelligence, concrete operations, and formal operations.

In the infant's early sensory-motor intelligence, there is no differentiation between the self and the object, and the baby's concept of weight is limited to what he feels in his body. We can infer from his behavior that he can tell the difference between being held securely and being held uncomfortably. One of the accomplishments of the sensory-motor period is the differentiation between the self and the object. The concept of the weight of objects emerges as part of this development. The sensory-motor adjustments the baby makes between holding a heavy bottle and holding a light rattle illustrate both his notion of the objects' weight and the gradual differentiation between the self and the object.

Intelligence which has reached the stage of concrete operations (around seven or eight years of age) is characterized by reversibility of thought. By this time, the object has become clearly differentiated from the self, and it can exist in the child's mind regardless of whether or not it is in sight. In contrast to sensory-motor intelligence, which functions only as the organism acts directly on the object, concrete-operational intelligence involves *actions which are internalized*. Thought at this stage can take place without external actions and in two opposite directions at the same time, e.g., pouring and pouring back,[4] separating and reuniting subgroups,[5] pushing an object to the right and pushing it back to the left,[6] and viewing an object as being at the same time bigger than certain objects and smaller than certain other objects.[7]

The conservation of weight is part of the general framework of intelligence which has become able to function internally without external actions, and without being limited to actions going only in one direction. The child can now mentally transform the piece of clay back and forth into a ball and into a "pancake." Other concepts that are involved in the conservation-of-weight task are the physical knowledge about the nature of clay and how scales work. The concept of weight as being independent of the kinesthetic feeling of pressure, and the concepts of "same," "more," and "less" are also involved in the conservation-of-weight task. When we thus compare the seven-year-old's concept of weight with that of the infant, it becomes clear that each concept is part of a general cognitive framework which consists of a network of more concepts than we can imagine.

While concrete operations are operations on concrete objects (such as clay, water, and beads), formal operations are operations on operations (such as classification and seriation). When the child is about twelve years old, his cognitive framework becomes able to operate on operations. In the specific-gravity experiment, for example, the concrete-operational child's concept of weight is limited to absolute weight. As can be seen in the matrix below, concrete operations are inadequate to explain why things sink or float. Big things are usually heavy, and heavy things usually sink, but not always. Small things are usually light, but they don't always float. When a needle is found to sink (a small and light object) and a unit block is found to float (a big and heavy object), the child needs to operate on classes and series to generate the concept of specific gravity. This is precisely what the child cannot do at seven years of age because he is just becoming able to engage in operational classification and seriation.

I am not sure that I am being clear about the evolution of the concept of weight. All the details were given as an example to illustrate the point that each concept is made possible in the context of the general framework that Piaget calls "intelligence." Because concepts exist as part of this framework, every concept is related to every other concept in a network. The educational implication of this statement is that if we work through this framework, we are likely to maximize our educational mileage. If, on the other hand, we overlook this framework, we may well continue to make things hard and artificial both for children and for ourselves.

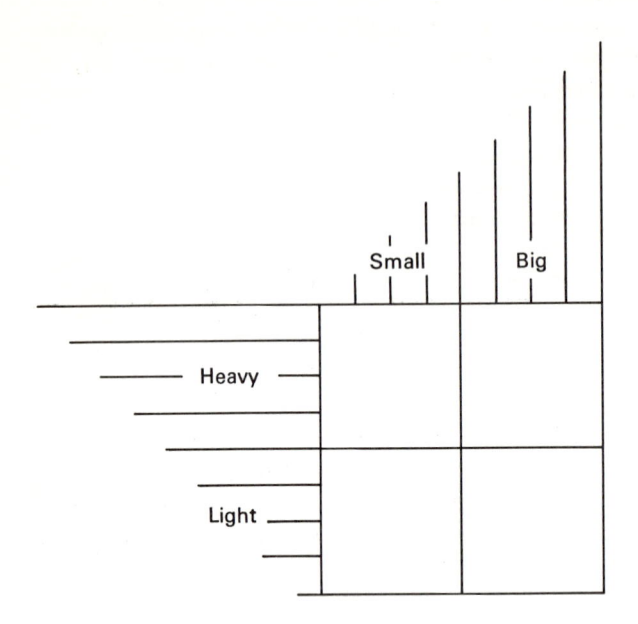

B. PIAGETIAN PRINCIPLES OF TEACHING

The question at hand now is how to achieve the objectives discussed at the beginning of this paper in ways that apply the above Piagetian principles of learning. The objectives of the preschool were said to be to maximize the child's chances of attaining the long-range goals of formal operations and adaptation to society by developing in the following areas:

1. Socio-emotional development
    a. Intrinsic motivation to derive pleasure from using previously learned schemes.
    b. Controlling one's own behavior
    c. Relationship with peers
    d. Relationship with adults

2. Cognitive development
   a. Physical knowledge
   b. Social knowledge
   c. Logico-mathematical knowledge
      1. Classification
      2. Seriation
      3. Construction of elementary number concepts
   d. Representation

The basic principles of learning were said to be

1. Learning is an active process of construction from inside the organism.
2. Learning takes place in a longitudinally coherent way.
3. Learning takes place within the general framework called "intelligence."

I would like to discuss now some principles of teaching under the following headings: (a) The role of the teacher in a Piagetian preschool, (b) the selection and organization of learning activities, and (c) the selection and organization of the content.

1. THE ROLE OF THE TEACHER IN A PIAGETIAN PRESCHOOL

According to Piaget, as it was stated above, there are three sources of knowledge — feedback from objects, feedback from people, and feedback from the cognitive structure that the child has already built. The role of the teacher in a Piagetian preschool, therefore, cannot be one of simply transmitting all types of knowledge to children. Her function is to help the child construct his own knowledge directly from feedback from objects and through his own reasoning with objects.

In physical knowledge, for example, if the child believes that a block will sink, she encourages him to prove the correctness of his statement. If he predicts that chocolate pudding will turn into chocolate, she says, "Let's leave it here until tomorrow and find out what happens." Most four-year-olds predict, before a marble is placed in one pan of a balance, that that side will go down, and that the other side will go up. When this prediction is given, the teacher does not say, "You are right," but, instead, says, "Let's find out." She lets the object give the feedback from the child's own action on objects. This is how she indirectly builds the child's initiative, curiosity, and confidence in his own ability to figure things out.

In the teaching of social knowledge, teaching in a Piagetian preschool is not different from traditional teaching, i.e., the teacher simply tells the answer and reinforces the correct responses.[8] Since social knowledge is man-made and can come only from feedback from people, the teacher feels quite free to tell the child, for example, that something is called a "pendulum" or a "tape recorder," that we have to pay pretend money to buy things from the play store, that clean-up time is not just for a few people but for everybody to clean up, and that we have different attitudes towards accidents and willful destruction. Social knowledge is the only area in the cognitive framework in which the teacher in a Piagetian preschool freely transmits ready-made knowledge. If the child believes that he can have two birthdays two days in a row, for example, she becomes the direct source of feedback.

The teacher's role in logico-mathematical knowledge is harder to explain because logico-mathematical knowledge is usually believed to be a kind of social knowledge. Classification, for instance, is often considered in terms of the "correct," or "more advanced," form of classification. An example of this point was given earlier in connection with the cognitive objectives of classification. In classification, the teacher should accept the child's way of thinking and proceed from there because, in the final analysis in classification, there is no "right" or "wrong" criterion for grouping things.

The role of the teacher in the logico-mathematical realm is thus not to reinforce the "correct" answer but to encourage the child's process of reasoning from his point of view. Young children have their own way of reasoning, and if we prematurely impose our ways, we only confuse them because they have no way of understanding why our classification is "better" than theirs. If we prematurely impose adult logic on young children, the lesson they will end up learning is that the correct answers always come from the teacher's head. Learning will then become a matter of guessing the desired response while scrutinizing the teacher's face for social approval.

The preceding statement is an example of the close relationship between cognitive development and socio-emotional development. If logico-mathematical processes are taught by social approval, we could end up making the child uncertain and lacking in confidence about his ability to figure things out. If the child feels that his own way of classifying things usually turns out to be considered wrong, he will end up having less and less confidence in his own resourcefulness, and more and more confidence in what is in the teacher's head.

I cannot overemphasize the importance of developing disadvantaged children's confidence in their own ability to figure things out. We find in our project that when children do not have this confidence, they will not experiment to find out the different effects of different actions. In fact, they will prefer to say, "I don't know" than to venture a response.

Chittenden (1969) emphasizes the difference between *in*struction and the child's *construction* of knowledge. We find in our project that when the teacher minimizes her *in*structional role and does whatever she can to facilitate the child's construction of knowledge through his own actions on objects, his initiative and curiosity increase. In fact, it seems to be in the nature of young children to have an insatiable amount of curiosity about everything. The Piagetian teacher's role, in summary, is not to transmit knowledge, but to enable the child to create his own knowledge.

2. THE SELECTION AND ORGANIZATION OF LEARNING ACTIVITIES

When I first came to the field of preschool education, I rejected the traditional nursery-school curriculum because its goals seemed too vague and sentimental. I found out, for example, that dramatic play was used for self-expression, for the development of children's imagination, for learning about the roles of fathers and mothers, and for a chance to feel like big people. I had no particular objection to these goals, but felt that for children in danger of failing in school later on, education had to do a lot more than what was good for middle-class nursery schools.

Later, I found in Piaget's theory many reasons why dramatic play, painting, block building, paper folding, Jell-O making, etc., were so relevant to education. The more I studied Piaget's theory, the more I came to respect the intuitive wisdom of the traditional nursery school. For example, Piaget (1962) showed that dramatic play provides an important entrance into the symbolic world. In other symbol-making activities like painting and making clay models, the child cannot directly externalize his mental image because he has to express it indirectly through paint and clay. In dramatic play, in contrast, he can externalize his mental image directly with his own body. If he wants to symbolize the idea of "father" in dramatic play, for example, he does not have to make the drawing or a clay model of a man. He can use his body directly to symbolize his ideas. Socio-dramatic play, therefore, provides the unique situation in which the child can be both the *symbol* and the *symbolizer* at the same time. (In other symbol-making activities, the child is a symbolizer, but not a symbol.)

Socio-dramatic play has the added advantage of movement, interaction, and continuity over time. The painting of a man cannot move and interact with other people, but the self as a symbol can. In socio-dramatic play, the child thus has a dynamic symbol rather than a static one. As the symbolizer, he has to maintain a coherent sequence of interactions over time, and also decenter from his own perspective to that of a father, brother, or policeman in order to interact with other children who are in complementary roles.

The significance of the above cognitive processes for the ability to read became clear. Reading in a mechanical sense cannot take the child very far because if the child's symbolic world is not a vivid, dynamic reality, the written and spoken word cannot have much meaning. Reading then becomes an empty, mechanical, meaningless chore. I think socio-dramatic play can help the child to make his symbolic world more real, more vivid, and more exact, but this hypothesis still remains to be tested empirically.

Since a complete Piagetian analysis of the traditional curriculum is beyond the scope of this paper, I would simply like to say that our general approach to preschool education is similar to the child-development philosophy. However, the way in which we use the traditional activities is different. In this section on how learning activities are selected, and the next section on how the content is selected, I hope to sketch a few examples of the way in which our curriculum differs from the traditional practices.

We have a daily schedule to give variety as well as to provide a framework for the children to enable them to anticipate the daily sequence of activities. This schedule includes individual activity time, group time, playground time, juice time, and bathroom time. Occasionally, there are field trips to the zoo, to the store to find out more precisely how to play "store," and to the neighborhood streets to collect leaves, sticks, and stones for use in physical knowledge, classification, seriation, and number.

The individual activity time is the longest and most important block of time. During this period, the children choose what they want to do from the range of possibilities that the teacher provides. The materials she selects to put in the classroom are, therefore, crucial. If she puts some paint and brushes, a number of blocks, house-keeping toys, puzzles, etc., in the classroom, there is a high probability that these things will be chosen by the children.

The teacher may make a pendulum, for example, by suspending a weight from the ceiling in hopes that the children will notice it and start playing with it. (By "playing," I mean the child's acting on the object to find out how it reacts.) After allowing a sufficient amount of time for the children to find out about the object, the teacher can introduce a game of knocking down a rubber doll which is standing on the floor. The rule of this game is to hold the weight at a particular spot and let go of it, rather than giving it a push. Either the teacher or the children can vary the position of the doll. The important thing in the selection of activities is that the teacher should have several possibilities in mind for the child's activity, but that the teacher should not force things in which the child is not intrinsically interested at a given moment.

There are times when children are not given a choice. For example, at playground time, everybody has to clean up and go outside. Most of the time, however, the children are told what the choices are, e.g., painting, socio-dramatic play, block building, table games, and playing with sand. We feel that it is desirable to let the child select his learning activity for several reasons. Among them are the following:

a. An activity that the child himself selects is likely to be at the right level of difficulty for him. Children seldom select things that are either too easy and boring, or too hard and meaningless.
b. Voluntary activities are those in which the child is maximally involved. Both the socio-emotional forces and the child's entire framework of intelligence are then likely to be active in the learning activity.
c. Asking children to make decisions is likely to enhance their initiative. We want children to take the initiative to learn both at school and after school hours, rather than waiting to be told what to do.
d. Children need to learn how to make decisions, rather than simply obeying orders all day. Selecting an activity and having to live with a decision for a brief period of time is in itself educational.

3. THE SELECTION AND ORGANIZATION OF THE CONTENT

The content can be conceptualized roughly in a matrix form, as shown in the following matrix. In the columns of this matrix are the various socio-emotional and cognitive objectives. In the rows are the objects we want children to know and use, e.g., the self, items of food, kitchen utensils, etc. The traditional nursery school has done well in finding out what objects appeal to young children; so we select mostly from these objects things that are likely to enhance certain cognitive processes.

At the beginning of the year, for example, we put in the classroom two sizes of many things, such as plates, pans, wooden and metal spoons, forks, rectangular and cylindrical blocks, paint brushes and containers, paper for painting, etc. We select these objects because we want children to become aware of size differences and classify things according to size as they play with the objects. At this point, classification and seriation are still undifferentiated, and we don't worry about number as such, yet. Making groups of things is an elementary activity in the construction of numbers, and this is all that we aim for at the beginning of the year.

Our philosophy in selecting and organizing the content is to (a) select the materials as suggested above to give a variety of appropriate choices to the child, (b) make a diagnostic evaluation of the child's level of functioning and train of thought once he has chosen an activity, and (c) follow up on his interests in the light of this diagnostic evaluation. In other words, the teacher constantly engages in diagnostic evaluation by keeping the theoretical framework in mind and locating the child's level of functioning in this framework. She has several possible objectives, both socio-emotional and cognitive, in mind for each child, but in her moment-to-moment interaction with the child, she picks up on his interests rather than imposing hers. She constantly works on the socio-emotional objectives as she works on the cognitive objectives.

Matrix I. The Content of a Piagetian Preschool Curriculum

	SOCIO-EMOTIONAL OBJECTIVES			COGNITIVE OBJECTIVES						
PROCESSES / MATERIALS	INTRINSIC MOTIVATION	CONTROLLING ONE'S OWN BEHAVIOR	RELATIONSHIP WITH PEERS	RELATIONSHIP WITH ADULTS	PHYSICAL KNOWLEDGE	SOCIAL KNOWLEDGE	CLASSIFICATION	SERIATION	NUMERICAL CONSTRUCTION	REPRESENTATION
The self										
Food										
Kitchen utensils										
Art materials										
Tools										
Animals										
Plants										
Rocks										
Colors										
etc.										

Note: Under "LOGICO-MATHEMATICAL KNOWLEDGE" are grouped CLASSIFICATION, SERIATION, and NUMERICAL CONSTRUCTION.

As stated above, the selection of objects to put in the classroom is crucial. The kind of objects and their variety and quantity are important considerations in determining what the children will select. Another consideration is the versatility of each object as can be seen in the following examples of how blocks might be used for the development of the child's physical, social, and logico-mathematical knowledge as well as representation:

    a. For representation
        If the child is building a gas station, the teacher can help him to

elaborate the streets around it or to introduce cars and customers to extend the play into a dynamic, symbolic experience.

b. For spatial reasoning

If the child does not seem to know what to do with the blocks, toy stove, sink, and dresser that he has collected, the teacher can arrange them into a room and ask him if he would like to make a room just like hers. If the child has a passion for trains, she would make a train station instead. (Spatial reasoning is similar to representation, but it involves making an exact copy or a precise modification of a spatial arrangement, rather than the externalization of a general idea.)

c. For pre-seriation

If the child is building a ramp, the teacher might make a bigger ramp and see how the idea strikes the child.

d. For physical knowledge

Blocks can be placed in a collection of objects for sinking-and-floating experiments.[9] Another game the teacher can introduce uses the sounds objects make when they are dropped on the floor. She can ask a group of children to close their eyes and to guess what she dropped on the floor. Blocks make sounds that are different from the sounds made by scissors, empty cans, and old magazines. The children can soon play this game without the teacher and add other actions on objects, such as hitting a block with a block, or a block with a pencil.

Piaget's theory makes it possible for the teacher to get a kind of X-ray picture into the child's cognitive processes. When the child does this in classification (Figure 2), the teacher knows that, with these objects, he is functioning not at quite the Stage-II level. Likewise, if in seriation a child arranges a group of cylinders of different heights by decreasing height, with one exception — the largest and second largest cylinders are switched around — the teacher knows that the child is clearly still in Stage I.

Figure 2. Classification of Beads: A Child Between Stages I and II.

An Application of Piaget's Theory

Our method of teaching applies Piaget's exploratory method of testing. If the child's answer is incorrect, the teacher asks another question to stimulate his thinking. For example, when a child is given a number of sticks arranged in a triangle on top of a rectangle, and copies the figure incorrectly by placing the triangle on the side of the rectangle, the teacher can ask whether or not the child could walk on his roof in the same way he could walk on the teacher's roof. (By the way, copying shapes with sticks is one of our reading-readiness activities.)

The specific items selected are of particular importance in the teaching of physical and social knowledge. If we want children to know how a swing works in the sense of physical and social knowledge, for example, it is imperative that there be a swing in the environment. For logico-mathematical knowledge, in contrast, the particular objects used do not matter as much. For example, numbers can be learned with dolls and hats just as well as with cups and saucers, as long as the two sets of objects involved have a qualitative one-to-one relationship that Piaget calls "provoked correspondence."[10] Classification, too, can be learned just as well with cars and blocks as with balls and toy shoes.

The approach advocated in this paper is not easy for the teacher to use in the classroom. It is much easier to take children through a pre-planned set of activities. However, if each child's knowledge is a construction from within, and if this construction is a continuous process of integrating the new with the old structure, and if no concept exists in isolation, learning cannot proceed in the same way and same sequence for all children. Therefore, the teacher must follow the learner's own way of learning and guide it, rather than imposing her sequence of objectives. Before concluding this section on teaching methods, I would like to make a few comments about the importance of children's expressing themselves. The importance of clear and open communication, as well as the importance of respecting other people's feelings and opinions, goes without saying. From the point of view of children's cognitive development, too, we must encourage children to say *exactly* what they mean rather than pressuring them into giving the "right" answer.

In the first place, unless children tell us how they think, we cannot get the diagnostic insights that are essential for diagnostic teaching. In the second place, I would like children to have confidence in their own processes of reasoning, rather than "learning" through social conformity. For example, in the situation shown below, if the child feels that 8 objects in the top row are "more" than 8 objects in the bottom row, I would like him to say so with confidence, rather than for him to be shaped into reciting the "right" answer. The space occupied, after all, is an important consideration in the construction of number

o   o   o   o   o   o   o   o

ooooooo

concepts, and any attempt to teach numbers must let the child himself work out the relationship between space and number through his own process of reasoning. If the process becomes well structured, the correct conclusion is bound to emerge. It is, therefore, on the underlying processes that we must work, not the answer or the surface behavior. There are two papers (Ezell, Hammerman, and Morse, 1969; Kamii, 1969, in press) which describe the method of work on the underlying processes for the construction of elementary number concepts.

There is another paper (Kamii and Derman, in press) giving the findings from an experiment which contributed to my belief that we must allow children to be honest with themselves. The six-year-old children who took part in this experiment were taught, among other things, to conserve weight and volume. They were found, for the most part, to give the correct answers, but usually in a sing-song fashion, as if they did not mean what they were saying. Their responses were not coming from the depth of their convictions. It occurred to me afterwards that teaching methods that attempt to involve the child's entire cognitive framework and to evoke enthusiasm must encourage him to say *exactly* what he means and *exactly* what he believes.

The teaching methods proposed on the basis of what I understand of Piaget's theory promise not to produce quick and spectacular results. However, changes that come from within an organism always come slowly. There is a phenomenon in embryology that Piaget points out: the fact that the more complex the organism's structure, the longer it takes the embryo to develop into a structured whole. There is no step that can be skipped in this process, and no way to force the rate of development. The only thing we can do to enhance biological development is to optimize the conditions under which the organism develops.

Disadvantaged children do not live under optimal conditions, neither in a physical-biological sense nor in a cognitive-biological sense. If I am wrong in the specifics of the curriculum conceptualized so far, I may still be right in saying that the best way to educate disadvantaged children should be sought in the laws of cognitive development *in nature*, and not in the laboratory.

In summary, the role of the teacher is neither to dictate "good" behavior nor to transmit ready-made predigested knowledge. Her role is to help the child to control his own behavior and to build his own knowledge through his own actions on objects, his own reasoning processes, and his own curiosity and excitement. To accomplish this task, the teacher selects a variety of objects to give a range of possibilities for the child to choose from. When the child has chosen his activity, the teacher diagnostically picks up on the child's interests by making suggestions and asking questions. Piaget's distinction among physical, social, and logico-mathematical knowledge and representation guides the teacher in deciding when to answer a question, when to let objects give the answer, and when to leave the question open. As stated earlier in this paper, the basic principle to keep in mind is that play is the most powerful ally on the teacher's side.

III. THE EVALUATION OF THE CURRICULUM

In a nutshell, I don't know how to evaluate this curriculum. It has taken almost four years to conceptualize the objectives presented above, and in some areas (i.e., physical knowledge and the structuring of time and space) the objectives and teaching activities are yet to be developed. While studying the theory, the children in the classroom, and education in general, I changed my mind many times about what the objectives of a Piagetian preschool should be. Since I am not sure about the objectives, I am even less sure about how to evaluate the curriculum.

I used to think that intelligence or achievement tests could be used to evaluate a preschool curriculum based on Piaget's theory. I later came to see, however, that it made no sense at all to use these tests. Some of the reasons for this statement can be found in Kohlberg (1968) and Kamii (in press).

By definition, a Piagetian approach can only be a long-term approach. However, long-term evaluation is not possible at this time because schools function in ways that are very anti-Piagetian. For example, we advocate children's voluntary activity and curiosity, but schools encourage passive receptivity. We believe in children's constant exchange of views, but schools prefer passivity. We think that the *process* of arriving at the answer is more important than the answer itself, but schools put the accent on specific facts and the "right" answer. In fact, we even believe in the importance of the child's going through many stages of being "wrong" before he becomes able to reason logically like an adult. We think that children learn to make decisions by making decisions, but schools emphasize obedience.

It may be worth sketching a few ideas about how the curriculum might be evaluated. I think the most important variables are the socio-emotional ones because if the children achieve our socio-emotional objectives, their chances for future learning are maximized. I think these data should be collected by observing the children in their real-life milieu, rather than in artificial test situations. The important thing in the evaluation of an educational program is not whether or not the child is able to do something under certain circumstances, but whether or not he actually uses his abilities from day to day under normal circumstances. Incidentally, I think it would be good to institute a system of exchanging evaluators among the various projects that are in existence. For the cognitive areas, the Piagetian tasks described in Kamii (in press) might be used, with the modifications that were found to be necessary after the chapter was written.

Before concluding this paper, I would like to make a few points about the use of psychometric tests, "accountability," and the long-range solution of social and educational problems. The scores obtained on psychometric tests like the Peabody Picture Vocabulary Test, the Stanford-Binet Intelligence Scale, and the Preschool Inventory may predict later achievement test scores, which indeed predict the pupil's survival in school. However, I would like to raise the question as to how much theoretical and practical validity these correlations have. They can perhaps be explained simply in terms of the peculiar way in which all psychometric tests are constructed and administered, and the way in which schools are run to teach specific facts and the "right" answer. Our perspective should be broader than payoff and "accountability."

I am well aware of the social crisis that we are facing today. Any quick method that can be found to increase the disadvantaged child's chances of getting through public schools is an enormous accomplishment. However, I am also of the opinion that any effort that perpetuates the present educational system will not result in the long-range solution of our social and educational problems. Atkin (1969) points out that the federal perspective of "accountability" is almost by definition a short-term perspective related to political payoff.[11] He argues convincingly that "to gear all of our new educational effort to attempt to solve deep (social) problems on a short-term basis may in the long run turn out to be a major misapplication of scarce resources." It is absurd to think that we can institute 500-750 hours of preschool education without changing the 10,000 hours of compulsory education that follow preschool and kindergarten.

The more I study Piaget's theory and the children in our project, the more I become convinced that Piaget's theory can make a contribution to education. However, the theory still needs to be digested, developed into a curriculum, implemented, and evaluated in longitudinal experiments. What difference this theory can make to the education of disadvantaged children is a question that remains to be answered empirically, not only to my satisfaction but also to the satisfaction of people like this audience and the teachers who actually teach the children from day to day. There is a long and thorny road ahead before this question can be answered.

FOOTNOTES | 4

[1] The significance of "actions" in this context is not the *external* behavior, but the *internal* processes that accompany the motoric actions. In early sensory-motor intelligence, the two are not differentiated. They become gradually differentiated, and the child becomes able to think about actions without actually engaging in them and to predict the results of his actions.

[2] The lobster, crayfish and other crustacea, and insects such as ants, bees, and wasps are the examples she gives.

[3] I would like to acknowledge the assistance of Eleanor Duckworth, of the University of Montreal, in conceptualizing this objective.

[4] Manifested in the conservation of liquid.

[5] Manifested in class inclusion.

[6] Manifested in mental images.

[7] Manifested in seriation.

[8] This statement refers to the teaching of social knowledge, which is not to be confused with socialization. Social knowledge refers to factual information, while socialization refers to the child's behavior and feelings. An example of social knowledge is the child's knowing that willful destruction of property causes people to become angry. Whether or not the child respects other people's feelings and belongings (in his behavior) is an example of socialization.

[9] In physical knowledge experiments, we do not ask children to *explain* any phenomena. We limit ourselves to having them *predict* the outcome of an action on objects, to *verify* the prediction, to *recall* what happened, and to *figure out means* of producing certain results.

[10] Four-year-olds who do not understand the terms "just as many" and "the same number" understand much more easily the idea of "*just* enough hats for everybody" when the two sets have a relationship of provoked correspondence. They understand from the nature of the objects that there can be only one hat that each doll can wear at a time, and only one cup that can go on each saucer.

[11] Atkin goes on to say, "The term 'political payoff' is not used in a pejorative sense. It is becoming a requirement, however, for a federal administration to show in a reasonably short period of time that large amounts of monies spent for social improvement result in significant changes. The short-term nature of the perspective brought to our tasks by federal officials represents one major issue that should be in the forefront of educational thinking as we examine new sources of funds from the federal government for novel programs." (Reprinted by permission of Kappa Delta Pi, Honor Society in Education.)

REFERENCES | 4

Atkin, J. M. On looking gift horses in the mouth: The Federal Government and the schools. *The Educational Forum*, 1969, *34*, 9-20.

Chittenden, E. A. What is learned and what is taught. *Young Children*, 1969, *25*, 12-19.

Duckworth, E. Piaget rediscovered. In R. E. Ripple and V. N. Rockcastle (Eds.), *Piaget rediscovered* (A report of the Conference on Cognitive Studies and Curriculum Development). Ithaca: Cornell University School of Education, 1964.

Duckworth, E. A child's eye view of knowing. In P. A. Olson (Ed.), *Reason and change in elementary education:* proceedings of the Second National Conference of the U. S. Office of Education Tri-University Project in Elementary Education, 1968.

Easley, J. A. Some pre-adolescent dynamic concepts of motion. A paper presented at the Conference on Spontaneous Learning, University of Illinois, March 1969.

Ezell, M., Hammerman, A., and Morse, S. Letter to the Editor. *Young Children*, 1969, *24*, 310-312.

Furth, H. G. *Piaget and knowledge*. Englewood Cliffs, New Jersey: Prentice-Hall, 1969.

Furth, H.G. *Piaget for teachers*. Englewood Cliffs, N. J.: Prentice-Hall, 1970.

Hallam, R. N. Logical thinking in history. *Educ. Rev.*, 1967, *19*, 183-202.

Inhelder, B. and Piaget, J. *The growth of logical thinking from childhood to adolescence*. N.Y.: Basic Books, 1958.

Inhelder, B. and Piaget, J. *The early growth of logic in the child*. N.Y.: Harper and Row, 1964.

Inhelder, B. and Sinclair, H. Learning cognitive structures. In P. Mussen, J. Langer, and M. Covington (Eds.), *Trends and issues in developmental psychology*, N. Y.: Holt, 1969.

Kamii, C. Preparing preschool children for the acquisition of elementary number concepts. In *Kindergarten curriculum – A forward look*. Proceedings of the

1968 New England Kindergarten Conference, Lesley College, Cambridge, Mass., 1969. In press.

Kamii, C. Piaget's theory and specific instruction: A response to Bereiter and Kohlberg. *Interchange: A Journal of Educational Studies,* 1970, *1.* In press.

Kamii, C. Evaluation of learning in preschool education: Socio-emotional, perceptual-motor, and cognitive development. In B. S. Bloom, J. T. Hastings, and G. Madaus (Eds.), *Handbook of formative and summative evaluation of student learning.* N. Y.: McGraw-Hill. In press.

Kamii, C. and Derman, L. The Engelmann approach to teaching logical thinking: Findings from the administration of some Piagetian tasks. To be published in the proceedings of the Conference on Ordinal Scales of Cognitive Development, Monterey, Calif., February, 1969. N. Y.: McGraw-Hill. In press.

Kamii, C. and Peper, R. A Piagetian method of evaluating preschool children's development in classification. Paper mimeographed at Ypsilanti (Michigan) Public Schools, July 1969.

Kamii, C. K. and Radin, N. L. A framework for a preschool curriculum based on Piaget's theory. In I. J. Athey and D. O. Rubadeau (Eds.), *Educational implications of Piaget's theory.* Waltham, Mass.: Ginn-Blaisdell, 1970.

Kohlberg, L. Early education: A cognitive-developmental view. *Child Development,* 1968, *39,* 1013-1062.

Lorenz, K. Z. *King Solomon's ring.* N. Y.: Crowell, 1952.

Lovell, K. Some problems associated with formal thought and its assessment. To be published in the proceedings of the Conference on Ordinal Scales of Cognitive Development, Monterey, Calif., February, 1969, N. Y.: McGraw-Hill. In press.

Miller, S. *The psychology of play.* Baltimore: Penguin, 1968.

Piaget, J. *The origins of intelligence in children.* N. Y.: International Universities Press, 1952.

Piaget, J. *The construction of reality in the child,* N. Y.: Basic Books, 1954.

Piaget, J. *Play, dreams and imitation in childhood.* N. Y.: Norton, 1962.

Piaget, J. *Psychology of intelligence.* Paterson, New Jersey: Littlefield, Adams, and Co., 1963.

Piaget, J. Development and learning. In R. E. Ripple and V. N. Rockcastle (Eds.), *Piaget rediscovered* (A report of the Conference on Cognitive Studies and Curriculum Development). Ithaca: Cornell University School of Education, 1964.

Piaget, J. *The child's conception of number.* N. Y.: Norton, 1965.

Piaget, J. *Biologie et connaissance.* Paris: Gallimard, 1967.

Piaget, J. *Psychologie et pédagogie.* Paris: Denoël, 1969.

Sinclair, H. and Kamii, C. Some implications of Piaget's theory for teaching young children. *School Review,* 1970, *78,* 169-183.

Sonquist, H., Kamii, C., and Derman, L. A Piaget-derived preschool curriculum. In I. J. Athey and D. O. Rubadeau (Eds.), *Educational implications of Piaget's theory.* Waltham, Mass.: Ginn-Blaisdell, 1970.

Hooper | Introduction | 5

The following paper by Dr. Hooper differs from other papers in this collection in that it describes a comparative assessment of the effectiveness of several short-term instructional sequences in improving performance on both criterion performance and transfer tasks. Specifically, the study is designed to investigate the "developmental interrelationships among classificatory, relationality, and conservation skills as mediated by Piagetian logical groupings."

In the initial sections of the paper, however, Dr. Hooper specifies the relevance of an organismic-developmental orientation for preschool curriculum design. His main points concern 1. the use of a developmental acquisition sequence for choosing program content and for determining the appropriate time for introduction of content, 2. the intrinsically motivating situation resulting from an optimal match between the task and the child's cognitive capacity, and 3. the importance of peer-group interaction in the child's cognitive development. Additionally, the utilization of Piagetian stage constructs offers a useful hierarchical developmental sequence and highlights the importance of transfer to other "stage-appropriate" behaviors.

A brief review of the variety of experimental studies which have attempted to induce or elicit Piagetian logical operations functioning precedes Hooper's description of his study. Unlike Kamii, Hooper stresses the importance of explicit feedback as to the accuracy of response, learning sets, and language in the development of logical operations functioning.

The study presented compares three instructional sequences – classification, seriation, and memory-discrimination – in terms of their effectiveness in increasing scores on criterion performance, near, and far transfer tasks. The middle-class children included in the study were 3 years 8 months and 4 years 7 months of (mean) age, and were taught in groups of four. Instructional sequences progressed from relatively simple to more difficult tasks. Explicit immediate feedback, children's correction and evaluation of each other, encouragement of peer-group interaction, and encouragement of explanations, descriptions, and general verbalization were features integral to all three training groups. The training sessions were carefully-planned and teacher-directed.

Studies similar in design to Hooper's are likely to provide specific information not available from more global preschool efforts. They enable careful examination of transfer of training and they provide the possibility for "disentangling the relative contributions of maturational limitations from experimental factors." Hooper's study indicates quite clearly the precise evaluations which may be made in assessing potential components of an overall preschool curriculum.

Frank H. Hooper

An Evaluation of Logical Operations Instruction in the Preschool

5

The developmental acquisitions which mark the general preschool period of two to five years of age are acknowledged to be of impressive magnitude and importance within the life-span of the human organism. The essentially nonverbal, sensory-motor oriented infant becomes an individual who has acquired the rudiments of sociopsychological functioning in his cultural milieu. Linguistic functioning shifts from the gesture-vocable level of the shared concrete context to the active production, manipulation, and comprehension of the language medium which approximates the mature adult model (Langer, 1969; Werner and Kaplan, 1963). Perhaps most importantly, this age interval is highlighted by the emergence of imitative schemas which are the genetic precursors of representational and operative thought of the concrete operational period. The focal questions remain; what is the potential role for the preschool setting as an active agent in the developmental change process, and what curriculum orientation offers the best opportunity for optimizing the positive cognitive and socio-emotional advances associated with the early childhood period?

Frank H. Hooper is at the University of Wisconsin. This article printed by permission of the author.

The status of experiential factors represented by preschool instruction as significant influences upon developmental processes is still an open issue. The recent evaluations of Head Start programs (Cicerelli *et al.*, 1969; Cicerelli, Evans and Schiller, 1970; Smith and Bissell, 1970) and the controversy over the relative contributions of genetic vs. experiential factors in cognitive acceleration (Albee *et al.*, 1969; Jensen, 1969$_A$, 1969$_B$; Vernon, 1970; and *Harvard Educational Review*, 1969, Nos. 2 and 3) attest to this. More specifically to present considerations, Elkind (1970) has evaluated the merits of the academically-centered preschool and stated that the economics, efficiency, and critical learning period aspects of preschool instruction are of questionable positive value insofar as the middle-class child is concerned. While the case of preschool enrichment for the disadvantaged child is not as clear-cut, Elkind concluded:

> *There is no preponderance of evidence that formal instruction is more efficient, more economical, more necessary or more cognitively stimulating than the traditional preschool program. Indeed, while there is room for improvement in the traditional preschool, it already embodies some of the most innovative educational practices extant today. It would, in fact, be foolish to pattern the vastly expanded preschool programs planned for the future upon an instructional format that is rapidly being given up at higher educational levels. Indeed, it is becoming more and more apparent that formal instructional programs are as inappropriate at the primary and secondary levels of education as they are at the preschool level. (Elkind, 1970, p. 139)*

Regardless of the general merits of preschool instruction, it is certainly true that a large number of programs have been proposed and demonstrated which differ markedly in orientation, content, instructional strategy, and demonstrated effectiveness (Hooper and Marshall, 1968; Parker *et al.*, 1970).

It is the contention of the present paper that the organismic-developmental viewpoint exemplified by the theoretical systems of Heinz Werner and Jean Piaget offer a fundamentally superior orientation to the design of an effective preschool curriculum. The relevance of Piaget's theory to educational application has been the theme of a number of contemporary writers, e.g., Aebli (1951), Athey and Rubadeau (1970), Beard (1969), Brearly and Hitchfield (1969), Bruner (1960), Furth (1970), Ginsberg and Opper (1969), Hooper (1968), Kamii and Radin (1967), Ripple and Rockcastle (1964), Sigel (1969), Sonquist and Kamii (1967), Stendler (1965), Wallace (1965). Kohlberg (1968) has contrasted the Piagetian orientation with other conceptions of developmental change as they relate to preschool enrichment. He views Piaget's constructive interactionism as intermediate between the conceptual polarities of maturational determinism and reinforcement contingency environmentalism. This "compromise" aspect of the organismic position emphasizes a clearly reciprocal relationship between the developmental status of the preschool child and the imposed curricula which constitute the event contingencies of the preschool setting. Assuming the validity of Piaget's system and associated developmental norms, there appear to be a substantial number of considerations concerning the developmental status, content-topic requirements, and instructional techniques which are germane to preschool education.

Initially, there is the general principle of utilizing a developmental acquisition sequence as a guide to *"what"* content or task situation represents the optimal curriculum subject focus and *"when"* this material may be most efficiently introduced (Hooper, 1968). This is particularly true of the organismic model of developmental change which explicitly recognizes the coequal status of environmental input and individual structural capacity as interacting to yield cognitive reorganization. This is the logical and systematic outcome of Piaget's assimilation-accommodation dyad, and underlies the fundamental dynamics of the equilibration model. Repeated encounters with the surrounding environment lead to structural changes in the organism, and presuppose a changing view of external reality relative to the individual's position in the ontogenetic sequence. Insofar as directed instruction is concerned, this orientation demands a very precise alignment between the cognitive capacity of the individual child and the task requirements imposed upon him.

The clear importance assigned to optimal structure-input alignment was initially elaborated by Hunt (1961) in his "match-mismatch" proposal. It specifies that the ideal learning condition involves just the right amount of discrepancy between the established cognitive schemas and the introduced problem setting. A careful match presents an intrinsically motivating task situation which neither bores nor overwhelms the child. It follows from this view that the final arbiter of curriculum design is the individual child's developmental status, not a demand or behavioral objective integral to a content or instructional domain.

The intrinsic motivational properties of an optimal cognitive structure-environmental input matching lead to a number of curriculum design implications. It is certainly similar in general orientation to the "self-discovery" learning position and, by implication, subject to common assets and shortcomings. The superiority of self-directed exploratory learning over direct instruction is agreed upon by traditional nursery proponents and the Genevan researchers, e.g., Elkind (1967), Kohlberg (1968), Piaget (1964). From this view, the child is the self-correcting monitor of his behavioral progress, and it is the child who determines what is relevant vis-à-vis his environmental surround. Thus, the ideal curriculum program is one which provides adequate stimulation of a sufficiently diverse and attractive nature, and which permits maximal individual exploration. The problems of cognitive overload or simple overstimulation is clearly not provided for, since any input beyond the immediate capacities of the individual child would be automatically screened and excluded. The issue of inappropriate or excessive stimulation in early infancy, especially that of an instrumentally noncontingent or random nature, has recently been discussed by Watson (1966, 1967, 1970). It is probably true that children of any age should be provided with explicit feedback concerning the effectiveness or degree of accuracy of their responses within any learning sequence.

Another aspect of the motivational dynamics of the organismic viewpoint involves the potential role of peer-group interactions as an effective route to qualitative cognitive change. The greater portion of the equilibration-induced cognitive reorganization that is fundamental to intellectual growth requires an active exchange of viewpoints, a sharing of personal perspectives, and a distinctive emphasis upon adult-child and peer-group interactions. As Flavell makes clear:

> *One of Piaget's firmest beliefs, repeated over and over in scores of publications . . . is that thought becomes aware of itself, able to justify itself, and in general able to adhere to logical-social norms of non-contradiction, coherence, etc., and that all these things and more can emerge only from repeated interpersonal interactions (and especially those involving arguments and disagreements) in which the child is actually forced again and again to take cognizance of the role of the other. It is social interaction which gives the ultimate* coup de grâce *to childish egocentrism. (Flavell, 1963, pp. 156-157)*

These considerations are certainly pertinent to the preschool age-range and offer an integrative theoretical basis for much of the social play generally encouraged and fostered in the nursery setting. Small group situations were the training formats selected for the instructional attempt reported later in this paper.

The timing and content considerations briefly outlined above follow from any consistent application of developmental theory and norms to an educational effort, but they become particularly explicit for a stage-dependent conception of human development. The utilization of a stage construct, as in Piaget's system, carries considerable theoretical and empirical relevance insofar as training and enrichment efforts are concerned. Stemming directly from the major criteria of stage specification for the Piagetians (Beilin, 1969_A; Inhelder, 1962) are two definite corollary conceptual features delineated by Wohlwill (1963) — the assumption of invariance and the prediction of correspondence or convergence in development for any and all behavioral patterns native to a particular stage or developmental period. This usage of the stage construct may be contrasted with the essentially nontheoretical descriptive or representational stage designations by such investigators as Bijou and Baer, the Kendlers, and Sheldon White, e.g., Reese and Overton (1970). In the first instance, the *hierarchical* nature of stage-sequential behaviors generates a series of developmental prerequisites and conceptually related subsequent behaviors of greater formal functional complexity. This implies an implicit curriculum sequence, for if initial assessment indicates the child to be operating at stage A, and stage C responses are desired, then stage B processes, strategies, and adaptations are the obvious instructional focus. There is a clearcut operational congruence here between the developmental stage proponents and the hierarchical learning models proposed by Gagné (1968) and experimentally demonstrated by Gelman (1969), Kingsley and Hall (1967), and Rothenberg and Orost (1969), among others.

In the second case, the within-stage correspondence postulate involves the *implicative* nature of stage-related behaviors which yield across-task generalization following enrichment experiences or training. In the present context, instructional experiences focused upon one behavioral domain should generalize or transfer to other classes of behavior which share the same theoretically based stage location. This is the essence of the distinction between specific task-transfer and nonspecific far transfer of the general learning-to-learn set variety, e.g., Brainerd and Allen (1970) and Goulet (1970). Not coincidentally, this is one of the primary experimental requirements of valid operational learning for the Genevan oriented researchers (Beilin, 1969a; Beilin, 1969b; Hooper, 1970; Inhelder and Sinclair-de-Zwart, 1969; and Laurendeau and Pinard, 1969), i.e., the induced acquisitions must transfer to logically related task situations. The current picture regarding this operational requirement is mixed, and whether a specific training study reveals near or far transfer to other response categories appears to be a joint function of the selected task situations, the developmental status or chronological age of the subjects, and the variety of training-enrichment procedures utilized.

To briefly recapitulate, the present acceptance of the organismic-developmental position makes certain demands upon any curriculum design endeavor. The focus upon the individual-environment interaction setting and the acknowledgement of the stage sequence postulate requires an accurate and specific pretraining assessment of the child to determine basal behavioral levels. This is an essential first step prior to actual implementation of the intervention strategies. Following this, and operating within the demonstrated normative developmental progression, a series of explicit operational objectives should be specified. These directly relevant behavioral objectives provide the "landmarks" of the teaching sequence and also constitute the most explicit test of the program's demonstrated effectiveness. In addition, the final arbiter of an individual child's program sequence and progress is the child himself. Thus, the child should be permitted to monitor and pace his own acquisition pattern throughout the curriculum program. This will generally require the provision of response feedback information concerning accuracy, appropriateness, etc., at each point in the curriculum hierarchy.

Hopefully the present contentions will become clear when applied to a specific behavioral domain. The general content area of the present study is the complex cognitive behaviors exemplified by the concrete operations period and its developmental prerequisites. Specifically, we are interested in the developmental interrelationships among classificatory, relationality, and conservation skills as they are mediated by the Piagetian logical *groupings*. As a preparatory step to the design of a possible preschool curriculum, it seemed appropriate to examine the short-term experimental attempts to induce or elicit Piagetian logical operations functioning in young children.

The experimental literature relating to the manipulatory induction of conservation acquisition has reached considerable proportions (Brainerd and Allen, 1970; Sigel and Hooper, 1968). An evaluation of these studies pertains directly to the crucial issue of maturationally based vs. experientially derived determinants of cognitive development. The training intervention paradigm, ideally as an integral component of a longitudinal assessment program, offers the most promising experimental opportunity to disentangle the relative contributions of maturational limitations or constraints from the role of experiential variables as factors in human cognitive growth. Unfortunately for present considerations, the evidence from the large number of Piagetian training attempts is certainly not conclusive. Interpretations range from a complete acceptance of the feasibility and practicality of conservation training (Brainerd and Allen, 1970; Goulet, 1970) to an elaborate denial of the cogency and validity of the demonstrated learning as evidence for qualitative cognitive change (Beilin, 1969_A, 1969_B; Inhelder and Sinclair-de-Zwart, 1969; Piaget, 1964; Wohlwill and Flavell, 1969). Beilin (1969_A) is particularly clear in assigning a subordinate role to experiential factors in the development of logical operations processes, preferring to emphasize the genetic pre-programming inherent in Piaget's theoretical system.

The final evaluation of the logical operations training, notwithstanding, it appears appropriate to examine the existing literature for guidelines to viable preschool curriculum design. Judging by the criteria for valid cognitive learning specified by Piaget (1964) — long term stability, increased operational and functional complexity, and demonstrated nonspecific transfer across conceptually related task settings — there are a number of studies which merit our attention.

Adequate feedback as to the correctness of response appears to be a critical determinant of learning a complex cognitive task. This was shown to be true of a quasi-conservation area concept task (Beilin, 1966) and represents an integral aspect of most successful conservation training strategies. This is certainly true of those studies which have employed a hierarchical learning-set orientation or task-analysis approach to concept acquisition. Kingsley and Hall (1967) applied Gagné's learning set analysis to instruction in length and weight conservation. Significant training effects were found for a group of five and six-year-old children, and the experimental groups also indicated improved ability on a transfer task of substance conservation. Rothenberg and Orost (1969) taught kindergarten children the probable steps necessary for number conservation. The effects of training were retained on a 3 month delayed posttest and conservation ability was found to generalize to a discontinuous quantity transfer task.

In a study which examined the role of numeration and comparison of discrete units of liquid quantity, Bearison (1969) found the training experiences facilitated conservation of continuous quantity and transferred to the conservation of area, mass, number and length. The experimental children (average age 5 years, 10 months) maintained their superiority over a 7 month interval and their conservation explanations were analogous to those elicited from a group of "natural" conservers. Gelman (1969) administered discrimination learning set training to a group of five-year-old children who were classified as nonconservers of length, number, mass, and liquid quantity. Posttests indicated near perfect specific (length and number) and approximately 60% nonspecific (mass and liquid quantity) transfer of training, and these results were stable over a 2-3 week period.

In addition to these positive findings concerning the role of learning sets, it is apparent that language processes are closely related to logical operations functioning. While the Genevan proponents (Beilin and Kagan, 1969; Furth, 1969; Inhelder and Sinclair-de-Zwart, 1969; Sinclair-de-Zwart, 1969) argue that operativity develops relatively independently of language acquisition and specific linguistic instruction, Bruner *et al.* (1966) stress the facilitatory aspects of language mechanisms in the general transition from perceptual-iconic to symbolic functioning. Gruen (1965) found a combination of verbal pretraining (relational terms) and cognitive conflict training to be effective in eliciting number conservation with some evidence of far transfer to length and substance conservation.

Beilin (1965) compared a number of conservation acceleration techniques and found verbal rule instruction to be significantly efficient for length and number conservation. Although the subjects (median age 5 years, 4 months) failed to show nonspecific transfer to a quasi-conservation area task, this task has been found to be of significantly greater difficulty than conventional area conservation (Beilin, 1964, 1966, 1969_B). While Beilin (1969_B) interprets these results as a case of algorithmic or "model" learning and questions the conceptual nature of such acquisitions, Smith (1968) found a significant improvement in weight conservation for both nonconservers and transitional subjects (first and second graders) using the verbal rule instruction approach.

Of greater relevancy to the present study are those enrichment-acceleration attempts which have a clear basis *within* Piagetian conceptions and theory. These include those investigations of the role of certain logical operations skills, i.e., reversibility, relationality, and classification, as they bear on conservation performance. Reversibility instruction significantly influenced number conservation (average age of children, 6 years, 11 months) in a study by Wallach and Sprott (1964) but the training failed to indicate clear-cut nonspecific transfer to a liquid quantity task (Wallach, Wall and Anderson, 1967). Sonstroem (in Bruner *et al.*, 1966) found a combination of reversibility and verbal labeling instruction to be an effective means of inducing conservation of continuous quantity (solids). Similar significant reversibility instruction effects were found for length conservation by Murray (1968). These results together with a review of additional positive attempts to train children on the concrete operations period tasks lead Brainerd and Allen (1970) to conclude that the inversion-negation form of operational reversibility is a critical condition for successful conservation induction.

The immediate antecedent research upon which the present study rests focused upon classification and relationality (seriation) abilities. Sigel, Roeper, and Hooper (1966) gave gifted preschool children (average Stanford-Binet I.Q. 143) structured small group experiences in multiple labeling of stimulus attributes, multiplicative classification and relationality, and a concluding session on reversibility aspects. Significant nonspecific transfer effects were found for substance and weight conservation. Sigel and Shantz in an unpublished study compared the performance of subjects given multiple labeling and classification instruction to that of a control group (average age 4 years, 10 months) on quantity, weight, and area conservation tasks. They also found significant gains on quantity and weight conservation.

In an extensive follow-up investigation, Shantz and Sigel (1967) evaluated the effects of multiple labeling-classification instruction experiences as compared to discrimination-memory training of equal duration. Thirty-six kindergarten subjects who passed a pretest of relational term comprehension (Griffiths, Shantz and Sigel, 1967) and failed all conservation tasks were randomly assigned to a training condition (there were four labeling-classification groups and two discrimination-memory groups with 6 children and a teacher in each group). Post-testing revealed very little difference between the two instructional conditions in the percentage of successful subjects for quantity, number and area conservation (a control condition was not included). Conservation ability did not relate to any of the logical operations tasks, with the exception of low order, significant relationships between reversibility and number conservation, and classification skills and area conservation.

There are a number of other studies which deal with the role of classification abilities as they relate to logical thought development. Notable among these are the research with lower-class Negro kindergarten children (Sigel and Olmsted, 1967, 1970, in press) and the work of Parker and his associates (Day, Danielson, and Parker, 1970; Parker and Ambron, 1970; Parker and Levine, 1970). Although Mermelstein and Meyer (1969) found a lack of significant training effects for a number of instructional techniques including Beilin's verbal rule instruction and Sigel's classification approach, the degree of relevance in the replication procedures used and the meaningfulness of their transfer task sequence is certainly open to question (Brainerd and Allen, 1970).

The present research assumes the basic validity and developmental salience of the Piagetian logical operations skills. From this viewpoint, classification and relationality conceptual abilities are of particular importance, e.g., their complimentary role in the growth of a mature number concept (Piaget, 1952). There are a number of similarities between the present training procedures and the preschool instructional program of Kamii and her associates of Ypsilanti, Michigan. Thus, both emphasize experiences with pre-classification grouping and preseriation ordering activities. In contrast to the Ypsilanti program designed explicitly for disadvantaged children, the present study included only middle-class children in a university laboratory nursery.

This study may be viewed as a replication and extension of the Shantz and Sigel (1967) research. In addition to the labeling-classification and discrimination-memory training sessions, we included a seriation instruction condition and appropriate comparison control groups. It should also be pointed out that the average age of the children in the Shantz and Sigel study was approximately 5 years, 6 months whereas the present subjects represent two younger age categories: 3 years, 8 months, and 4 years, 7 months.

The classification training sessions were based upon the labeling-classification training sessions from the training study by Shantz and Sigel (1967), the Ypsilanti Early Education Program presently in operation, and the training study by Sigel, Roeper, and Hooper (1966) for the acquisition of Piaget's conservation of quantity. The training sessions, while retaining the general orientation of Shantz and Sigel, were derived from the classification task acquisition sequence of Kofsky (1966). These tasks were found to be rank-ordered in terms of difficulty as follows: 1. consistent sorting, 2. resemblance sorting, 3. "some" and "all," 4. exhaustive sorting, 5. multiple class membership, and 6. the whole is the sum of its parts $(A + A')$. This sequence became the organizational focus of the classification training program. The training sessions followed this sequence to a certain level within each session and progressed in complexity to the twelfth session.

The type of materials used differed quantitatively and qualitatively as the sessions proceeded. There were more objects with fewer attributes in the beginning sessions. The later sessions utilized fewer objects with more attributes. Examples of training sessions are presented at the end of the paper.

The seriation training program also followed a developmental sequence. Children were given experiences in the following task settings: 1. comparisons between two sizes (absolute comparisons), 2. relative comparisons (unidimensional seriation), 3. serial correspondence, and 4. multiple seriation. The twelve training sessions were based on data from the Ypsilanti Early Education Program presently in operation and from the *Preschool Curriculum Development Project* by Hooper and Marshall, 1968.

Each material was approached first in its descending order whether its relation was height, width, or shades of color. Training the group of children to seriate in ascending order was contingent on the groups' mastery of the previous skill. Examples of several seriation training sessions are given at the end of the paper.

The memory-discrimination training program was adopted from Shantz and Sigel (1967) and follows from a theoretical analysis of the conventional conservation task format by Watson (1968). Watson's general operant discrimination analysis, stressing a non-mediational S-R orientation, conceives of the conservation task as consisting of three parts: (1) the initial static stimuli pair which establishes the state of quality, (2) the transformation of one stimulus, (3) the presentation of two perceptually different (but conceptually equal) static stimuli. Watson establishes the transformation interval or state as being the single most important element in the child's ability to conserve, i.e., it is the discriminative stimulus for correct conservation responses. This element is different from the static stimuli in that it is time-distributed, and it requires that the child not only discriminate the conservation transformation from a nonconservation transformation (such as adding something or taking something away), but he must also remember the transformation when phase three occurs. A similar view of the critical, essentially positive role for the transformational stimulus component is also presented by Beilin (1969_B).

Watson suggests that training the child to grasp the sequence of a series of changing events may induce conservation, e.g., training should emphasize the skills in attention, discrimination and memory for serial events, rather than emphasizing the logical operations postulated by Piaget. The primary aim of the present memory-discrimination instructional sessions is "to facilitate children's ability to remember a sequence of actions, to visually analyze pictures for details as well as memory for details, and to increase their ability to verbally express their ideas" (Shantz and Sigel, 1967, p. C-8). The first sessions emphasize memory for action sequences: initially, gross motor movements (hands on head, hands behind back, etc.); then copying complex block designs; and, finally, repeating verbal messages. The second group of sessions involve use of pictures, whose details must be remembered; the creation of pictures whose details must be remembered; the creation of picture stories from individual items; and the invention of story segments. The last sessions deal with story reading followed by recall by the children. Examples of several memory discrimination training sessions are also included at the end of the paper.

In addition to the content-specific features of each of the three instructional programs certain general considerations guided all the present curriculum endeavors. Explicit immediate feedback, in the form of the teachers' designations of "right" and "wrong" answers or action sequences, followed each child's responses. Later in the training sessions the children were encouraged to correct and evaluate each other's responses. Peer-group interactions were encouraged wherever possible. Explorations, descriptions, and general verbalization were stressed throughout the various instructional settings.

Each training format consisted of four age-matched children (two boys and two girls) meeting with an experienced preschool teacher in a small room separated from the general nursery area. Each session consisted of 20-30 minutes of organized activity, and there were 12 sessions over a three week period for each training condition. The various control group children had an equivalent amount of separate small group activity with a preschool teacher.

The general characteristics of the various experimental subsamples are presented in Table I. There were two age groups of 4 children each for each training and control condition.[2] Children matched for age were randomly assigned to conditions in each of the preschools involved. There were two pretest measures, the Peabody Picture Vocabulary Test and a test of relational terms comprehension (Griffiths, Shantz and Sigel, 1967), which were readministered following the training-enrichment interval.

The criterion dependent measures were administered in a posttest – only control group design (Campbell and Stanley, 1963). This design selection was predicated upon the relatively small number of available preschool subjects and the commonly recognized "self-instructional" influence of pretesting in the Piagetian training literature (Beilin and Franklin, 1962; Sigel, 1968; Smedslund, 1961). The various curriculum-specific measures which represent near transfer tasks for the respective instructional conditions were as follows:

A. Seriation task series:

1. *Absolute comparison* which involves the ability to identify large and small members of different pairs of objects (2 trials).
2. *Relative comparison* which involves the ability to identify the same object as now large, now small, depending upon the size of simultaneously present comparison figures (3 trials).
3. *Successive comparison* (unidimensional seriation) which involves the ability to apply relative comparisons in systematic fashion to each of a number of simultaneously presented objects (one composite trial with a possible score $0 - 7$).
4. *Additive seriation* which involves the addition of three blocks within an ordered series (adapted from Elkind, 1964, score $0 - 3$).
5. *Serial correspondence* between two ordered arrays (adapted from Coxford, 1964, score $0 - 3$).
6. *Multiple seriation* which involves a series of drawings varying in two dimensions. This task requires that the subject fill in one empty cell on a strip of four cells with a picture that included *both* values of two continuous dimensions from which the strip is constructed. For example, a series of leaves were presented with the top leaf being large and light green, and the following leaves decreasing in size and increasing in darkness ending in a small dark leaf. The subject selects a leaf from four choices: one leaf is a duplicate leaf adjacent to the empty cell in the

TABLE I
GENERAL CHARACTERISTICS OF THE SUBJECT SAMPLES*

	Age-Ranges (years & months)	Mean Ages (years & months)	Pretest PPVT Means	Pretest I.Q. S.D.	Posttest PPVT Means	Posttest I.Q. S.D.	Pretest Relational Terms Means	Pretest Relational Terms S.D.
Preschool – A								
Classification Training – I	4,3 – 4,8	4,4	108.80	8.58	112.00	9.35	7.75	1.64
Classification Training – II	3,4 – 4,1	3,8	106.30	7.29	118.25	6.06	5.25	2.59
Seriation Training – I	4,5 – 4,9	4,7	122.00	9.14	120.50	9.01	9.00	0.00
Seriation Training – II	3,4 – 4,2	3,8	105.00	17.71	114.70	11.78	6.25	1.79
Control Group – I	4,3 – 5,1	4,7	102.50	9.23	112.20	9.98	5.75	3.42
Control Group – II	3,0 – 4,1	3,7.5	102.80	6.61	107.30	10.94	2.75	3.70
Preschool – B								
Memory – Discrim. Training – I	4,7 – 4,11	4,8	113.30	5.31	109.00	3.00	9.00	0.00
Memory – Discrim. Training – II	3,8 – 4,3	4,0	114.80	14.94	112.50	28.19	9.00	0.00
Control Group	4,0 – 4,5	4,3	112.00	11.23	120.75	12.49	9.00	0.00

*N = 4 in all cases

strip, one is correct on both values, and two leaves have only one correct value (i.e., correct on size and incorrect on shade, or the reverse). The position of choices was randomized across strip choice sheets.

A total of four strips were constructed from the same combination of dimensions as the classification matrices (see Table II, below). The dimensions for the strips were continuous, however (such as shades of green) as compared to discontinuous in the classification matrices (color represented by green vs. yellow). The definitions of the continuous dimensions and values are presented below.

The four strips and choice sheets were presented by the administrator in a separate notebook one at a time in the following order: color-size (leaves) as the practice item, orientation-emptiness (bottles); number-color (tulips); and size-border (houses) (Shantz and Sigel, 1967, pp. 11-13). The score range on this task was 0 – 3.

B. Classification task series: (with the exception of task 7, all the classification tasks are taken from Kofsky's [1966] analysis of classification skills).

1. *Consistent sorting* (score range 0-1)
2. *Exhaustive sorting* (score range 0-1)
3. *Resemblance sorting* (score range 0-1)
4. *Class inclusion* ("some" and "all," score range 0-4)
5. *Multiple class membership* (score range 0-4)
6. *Class addition* (score range 0-4)
7. *Multiple classification* (score range 0-3) This task requires that the subject fill in one empty cell of a four cell matrix (i.e., a 2-X-2 matrix) with a picture that includes both subclass attributes relevant to the matrix. For example, in a color (green-yellow) and size (big-little) matrix, a large yellow clock, a small yellow clock, and a large green clock were presented in a matrix; the correct picture for completion would be a small green clock. Subject selected a clock from four choices: two clocks were duplicates of cells adjacent to the empty cell, one clock had irrelevant attributes, and one clock was correct. A total of four matrices were constructed from the following combinations of dimensions: color-size, orientation-emptiness, color-number, and border-size. The definitions of each dimension are presented below. The position of the correct choice was randomized across matrix sheets. The four matrices and choice sheets were presented by the administrator in a notebook one at a time in the following order: color-size matrix (clocks) served as a practice task to insure subject's understanding of the requirements of the task; orientation-emptiness (pitchers); number-color (apples) and size-border (trees). (Shantz and Sigel, 1967, pp. 11-13.)

Table II
DEFINITIONS OF DIMENSIONS ON
MULTIPLE CLASSIFICATION AND SERIATION TASKS*

Dimensions	Symbol	Classification	Seriation
Color	C	Yellow vs. green Red vs. green	Four values: Light green to dark green Light red to dark red
Size	S	Big vs. little	Four values: Big to little
Orientation	O	Up vs. tilted	Four values: 0° (up) 45° (upward tilt) 135° (downward tilt) 180° (upside down)
Number	N	2 vs. 3	1, 2, 3, 4
Border	B	Entirely bordered vs. no border	1/4 bordered 1/2 bordered 3/4 bordered totally bordered
Emptiness	E	Full vs. 1/4 full	Full 3/4 full 1/2 full 1/4 full

*From: Shantz and Sigel (1967, p. 13)

C. Memory-discrimination tasks: (These tasks were taken directly from the Illinois Test of Psycholinguistic Abilities, McCarthy and Kirk, 1963.)

1. *Visual-Motor Sequencing*
2. *Auditory-Vocal Sequencing*

In addition to the above measures each subject received three conventional conservation tests. These conservation tasks are considered nonspecific far transfer tasks in the present context.

D. Conservation task series:

1. *Conservation of continuous quantity* (3 trials with an empirical "check"). This task was adopted from Shantz and Sigel (1967). In this test, two clay balls are used, one representing the standard and the other one transformed into a cup, a pancake, and a hot-dog shape. To avoid creating an "equality" in front of the child, two new balls are used at the beginning of each trial. To pass the test, the child must be able to recognize equality in spite of the irrelevant transformation and present an adequate explanation. A final "check-trial" was made by subtracting a piece from one ball, thus presenting the child with an unequal transformation.
2. *Conservation of number* (5 trials). In this task we adopted the procedure of Rothenberg (1969) using a display board painted in two distinctive colors and a series of colored poker chips. The colored poker chips were lined up on their respective colors and referred to as a "yellow bunch" or "blue bunch" throughout the test, thus assuring similarity of language and questions throughout. After a warm-up item of equal subtraction from both rows, five trials of various transformations made on the experimenter's row were administered. The transformations used are: 1) lateral displacement, 2) collapsing of one row, 3) resubgrouping, 4) equal addition to both rows, and 5) unequal addition. The last (unequal addition) acts as a "check-trial" for number conservation by creating a deliberate inequality.
3. *Conservation of surface area* (3 trials with an empirical "check"). This task is drawn directly from Shantz and Sigel (1967) and is a format similar to the one used by Piaget, Inhelder and Szeminska (1960). Two green blotters serve as "fields of grass" and two plastic cows are placed, one in each field, to "eat the grass." Red Lego blocks, representing barns, are placed on the fields in three trials as follows: trial 1: three barns per field; trial 2: nine barns per field; and trial 3: six barns per field. On the standard field, the barns are lined up in a row along one side of the field. On the other field, a transformation is used in which the barns are scattered at random about the field. A check-trial is used, in which the standard field receives five barns and the transformation field receives only four, thus establishing an inequality.

Directing our attention initially to the curriculum-specific dependent measures, the results of the present study may be briefly summarized. Since analysis of the pretest Peabody Picture Vocabulary Test I. Q. means (Table I) indicated a significant difference between treatment groups (classification training, seriation training, and control groups) in Preschool-A (the older seriation training group was significantly superior), the following general comparisons included both analyses of variance and analyses of covariance with P.P.V.T. pretest I.Q. score as the covariate. Considering the classification task series, Table III presents the various individual subscores and the total scores for the respective subsamples. A 3 X 2 (treatment by age-level) factorial analysis of variance and a corresponding covariance analysis failed to indicate any significant main effects or interactions for the Preschool-A total classification scores. The anticipated post-training superiority of the groups which had classification instruction are notably absent, i.e., the total score combined age group means are 7.625, 8.750, and 9.625 for the classification, control, and seriation groups, respectively. In addition, inspection of the Table III subtask score patterns fails to reveal any marked differences among the experimental subsamples. A similar lack of significant differences was shown in an analysis of variance for the total classification scores in Preschool-B (memory-discrimination training and control groups).

In contrast, the seriation task series results presented in Table IV reveal clearcut distinctions for the Preschool-A children. The factorial analysis of variance utilizing the total seriation scores indicated a significant main effect for age-levels,[3] and treatment conditions,[4] and a significant age-level/treatment interaction.[5] In essential accord with these results, the factorial analysis of covariance indicated a significant treatments main effect,[6] and a significant age-level/treatment interaction.[7] Inspection of the total score means of the various groups (Table IV) show a uniform superiority for the seriation training conditions. With regard to the age-level/treatment interaction, individual comparisons indicated significant differences favoring the older seriation subjects,[8] and the older control subjects[9] over their younger counterparts, and a contrasting younger classification score superiority which fails to reach significance.[10] Thus, the total mean score comparisons for the seriation vs. the control groups indicate similar differences (12.50 vs. 7.00 and 19.71 vs. 12.0) for the two age-levels, whereas the superiority of the seriation training condition over the classification condition is notably greater at the older age-level (19.71 vs. 9.25) than at the younger age-level (12.50 vs. 11.75).

For the between-treatment comparisons, the younger classification and seriation instruction groups each differ significantly from the younger control group.[11] For the older age-level comparisons, while the classification and control groups do not differ significantly, the seriation group is significantly superior to the classification group[12] and to the control group.[13]

TABLE III
MEANS OF THE CLASSIFICATION TASK SERIES*

	Task 1 Means	Task 2 Means	Task 3 Means	Task 4 Means	Task 5 Means	Task 6 Means	Task 7 Means	Total Score Means
Preschool – A								
Classification Training – I	1.00	1.00	.75	2.50	1.75	.25	1.00	8.25
Classification Training – II	1.00	.50	.50	2.25	2.25	0.00	.50	7.00
Seriation Training – I	1.00	1.00	1.00	3.50	3.00	0.00	1.00	10.50
Seriation Training – II	1.00	.75	.75	2.75	2.50	.50	.50	8.75
Control Group – I	1.00	.75	.75	2.50	2.50	.25	1.50	9.25
Control Group – II	1.00	.75	1.00	2.25	2.00	.25	1.00	8.25
Preschool – B								
Memory – Discrim. Training – I	1.00	.75	1.00	2.25	1.75	0.00	.50	7.25
Memory – Discrim. Training – II	.75	.75	1.00	3.25	3.25	.50	.25	9.75
Control group	1.00	.50	1.00	2.75	2.75	0.00	1.00	9.00

*Task Designations:
1 = Consistent Sorting (Score range = 0-1)
2 = Exhaustive Sorting (Score range = 0-1)
3 = Resemblance Sorting (Score range = 0-1)
4 = Class Inclusion (Score range = 0-4)
5 = Multiple Class Membership (Score range = 0-4)
6 = Class Addition (Score range = 0-2)
7 = Multiple Classification (Score range = 0-3)

TABLE IV
MEANS OF THE SERIATION TASK SERIES*

	Task 1 Means	Task 2 Means	Task 3 Means	Task 4 Means	Task 5 Means	Task 6 Means	Total Score Means
Preschool – A							
Classification Training – I	2.00	.50	3.25	1.50	1.25	.75	9.25
Classification Training – II	2.00	.50	4.50	3.00	1.50	.25	11.75
Seriation Training – I	2.00	2.25	7.00	3.00	3.00	2.50	19.71
Seriation Training – II	1.75	.50	5.00	2.50	2.25	.25	12.50
Control Group – I	2.00	.25	4.25	2.75	2.00	.75	12.00
Control Group – II	2.00	1.00	2.25	.75	1.25	.25	7.00
Preschool – B							
Memory – Discrim. Training – I	2.00	0.00	4.00	1.50	1.00	.50	9.00
Memory – Discrim. Training – II	2.00	.50	4.50	2.25	1.75	.50	11.50
Control Group	2.00	.25	5.25	1.75	.25	.25	9.75

*Task Designations:
1 = Absolute comparison (Score range = 0-2)
2 = Relative comparison (Score range = 0-3)
3 = Successive comparison (Score range = 0-7)
4 = Additive seriation (Score range = 0-3)
5 = Serial correspondence (Score range = 0-3)
6 = Multiple Seriation (Score range = 0-3)

In addition to these seriation total score results, Table IV indicates notable superiority for both the seriation training groups on subtasks 3, successive comparisons, and 5, serial correspondence. The older seriation training group demonstrated distinctly higher scores on subtask 2, relative comparisons, and subtask 6, multiple seriation. These results, in conjunction with the seriation total score analyses, clearly substantiate the anticipated specific transfer effects of an instructional program designed to encompass the various fundamentals of seriation ability. The analysis of variance results for the total seriation scores for the Preschool-B children failed to reveal any significant differences among the experimental or control groups.

The Illinois Test of Psycholinguistic Abilities subtest score values, which are considered as specific transfer tasks for the memory-discrimination training groups, are presented in Table V. Considering the relevant instructional setting, Preschool-B, a cursory examination reveals very little difference in the subgroup means. This is confirmed in the analyses of variance results in which the visual-motor sequencing and the auditory-vocal sequencing tasks yielded treatment F values that were not significant.[14] There is no indication, therefore, of a training induced improvement for memory-discrimination instruction insofar as the present criterial tasks and age groups are concerned. A similar lack of treatment main effects or interactions was found in the factorial analyses of covariance for Preschool-A, although the main effect for age-levels was significant[15] for the

TABLE V
MEANS AND STANDARD DEVIATIONS OF
I.T.P.A. SUBTEST SCORES*

	Visual-Motor Sequencing Means S.D.	Auditory-Vocal Sequencing Means S.D.
Preschool – A		
Classification Training – I	13.00 2.55	16.75 1.64
Classification Training – II	9.75 4.92	7.00 5.00
Seriation Training – I	13.00 2.12	18.00 1.22
Seriation Training – II	9.50 .50	14.00 8.09
Control Group – I	11.75 1.92	17.25 .83
Control Group – II	12.00 7.62	18.25 5.02
Preschool – B		
Memory – Discrim. Training – I (N = 3)	11.67 2.85	18.33 3.32
Memory – Discrim. Training – II	11.00 .71	20.00 2.55
Control Group	10.75 2.68	21.00 3.67

*(N = 4, unless indicated)

Visual-Motor Sequencing subtest. These age-level differences for the classification and seriation group children are in the direction to be expected from the conventional test norms.

The results with regard to the planned nonspecific or far transfer tasks are distinctly nonambiguous. Three subjects of the overall sample of 36 from both preschool settings were classified as conservers, i.e., one child from the younger memory discrimination group and one child from the control group of Preschool-B passed the number conservation task, and one child from the younger classification condition passed the quantity conservation task. In addition, there was very little change in the P.P.V.T. I.Q. scores (Table I) from pretesting to posttesting following training for the various experimental conditions. The only significant improvement was shown by the younger classification training group.[16] The present intervention procedures thus had a very limited effect upon task situations designated as generalization or nonspecific transfer of training indices.

The implications of the present investigation considered as a single effort are rather straightforward. In contrast, the interpretation of these results in conjunction with previous related studies is much less clearcut. The classification and memory-discrimination instructional conditions did not produce the anticipated specific generalization on the respective criterial measures. Conversely, seriation training was notably effective in demonstrating distinctive specific transfer to tasks which were integral components of the particular curriculum design. Moreover, the seriation trained groups indicated a fairly uniform, although nonsignificant, score superiority on the classification task series and the I.T.P.A. auditory-vocal subtest as compared to their classification training counterparts.[17] Classification instruction also failed to indicate any influence on seriation or memory-discrimination measures. A similar lack of effect was shown by the memory-discrimination condition.

The differences between the older and younger classification trained subjects on the seriation measures (Table IV) merit some comment. Assuming the control condition subjects' score patterns as representative of normative age related changes, the lower seriation scores (subtasks 3, 4, and total score) shown by the older classification-trained children are surprising. In this regard, Shantz and Sigel (1967) found a drop in multiple seriation scores on posttesting for a group of children trained on multiple labeling-classification skills.

In comparison to the antecedent investigations, the most distinctive exception in the present results concerns the lack of nonspecific far transfer effects. Although the younger classification training group did show a significant P.P.V.T. I.Q. score increment following instruction, there was no consistent carryover from any of the instructional programs to conservation acquisition. This result, while certainly encompassed by the Genevan viewpoint regarding the role of training or instruction in conservation acquisition, fails to accord with the earlier

An Evaluation of Logical Operations Instruction

findings of Shantz and Sigel (1967) and Sigel, Roeper, and Hooper (1966). There are three related essential distinctions between the earlier research and the present case which may reconcile the contrary findings. First, the present classification instructional curriculum adapted the Sigel multiple labeling and classification program format but applied it to a new, developmentally based, sequence, i.e., the task difficulty series reported by Kofsky (1966). The degree to which this new application vitiates the replication aspects of the present study is unknown.

A second major distinction concerns the assessment design of the various investigations. The present comparisons are drawn from a "posttest only" design, while Sigel and Shantz (1967) and Sigel, Roeper and Hooper (1966) used the conventional pretest-posttest transfer of training design. Acknowledging the demonstrated influence of the testing situation itself on Piagetian concept performance, the Shantz and Sigel (1967) results may be biased to an unknown degree since a null control condition was not included in the experimental design. Additionally, although the Sigel, Roeper, and Hooper (1966) assessment design included control groups, the presence of pretest X instructional treatment interactions are present to an unknown degree.[18]

The final distinction centers upon the ages of the experimental subjects in the various logical operations training studies. The present children, especially those subjects in the younger training conditions, are clearly younger than their counterparts in the Shantz and Sigel (1967) study or in the great majority of the conservation training studies reported in the experimental literature (Brainerd and Allen, 1970). In the case of Sigel, Roeper, and Hooper (1966), while the chronological age-ranges approximate those reported here, the mental ages of their gifted children were probably in the 6-8 year range. The present seriation training results on the seriation task series and the marked absence of far transfer to the conservation tasks emphasize the critical role of age-related developmental status as a contributing factor in manipulatory studies of cognitive growth.

The major positive aspects of the present research stem directly from the results of the seriation instructional program. These results certainly indicate that an operational preschool curriculum is a feasible derivative of an empirically demonstrated developmental acquisition sequence. Recall that the observed developmental order of mastery provided the curriculum sequence or hierarchy, the content areas, and the specific dependent tasks through which the evaluative assessment was realized. While extrapolations to subject populations beyond the present middle-class children should be made cautiously, it is noteworthy that a group of five to six-year-old lower-class, disadvantaged children demonstrated adequate competence in unidimensional seriation and serial correspondence tasks similar to those employed in this study (Hooper, 1969). Thus, the implementation of a preschool curriculum which includes seriation-relationality concepts as an integral aspect may have quite general application relevance.

In conclusion, we should return to the fundamental contention of the organismic orientation as it applies to preschool curriculum design — the essential salience of the individual child's developmental status. As this study has amply shown, the developmental status of the curriculum target population will determine to a great extent the success or failure of an educational intervention effort. While this conclusion may appear "simple minded" to any competent nursery or preschool specialist, it runs counter to the traditional environmentalistic orientation which has characterized most learning theorists. The failure to induce nonspecific far transfer insofar as the operationally complex conservation tasks are concerned, essentially supports the recent statements of Beilin (1969_A), and Inhelder and Sinclair-de-Zwart (1969). It is clear that a major role should be assigned to the age-related maturational components in any attempt to modify the course of cognitive development or to mitigate the detrimental aspects of sociocultural impoverishment. In this respect the clear acknowledgment of individual factors, insofar as maturational and sequentially invarient developmental patterns are concerned, makes an organismic orientation the essential prerequisite for a viable preschool curriculum endeavor.

Examples of Multiple Classification, Seriation, and Memory-Discrimination Training Sessions[19]

MULTIPLE CLASSIFICATION TRAINING SESSIONS

Session I
Session II
Session VI
Session VII
Session XI
Session XII

SERIATION TRAINING SESSIONS

Session I
Session II
Session VI

Session VII
Session XI
Session XII

MEMORY-DISCRIMINATION TRAINING SESSIONS

Session I
Session II
Session VI
Session VII
Session XI
Session XII

MULTIPLE CLASSIFICATION TRAINING SESSIONS

SESSION I

MATERIALS: 4 small boxes; shells — 4 snails, 4 scallops, 4 conchs, 4 clams; round buttons — 4 red, 4 blue, 4 pink, 4 green.

A. 1. Introduce buttons.
Identify and discuss, use and shape.
2. Ask *S*s to identify the different colors by pointing to buttons.
3. Ask *S*s if some of the buttons look just the same or look alike.
4. Place 4 boxes on table. Have all *S*s put those buttons together in a box that are just the same, just alike, or put the buttons together that go together.
5. Empty boxes. Mix the buttons and have one *S* put the buttons together that go together. Ask *S*s if this is correct. Have a *S* make corrections if necessary.

B. 1. Introduce shells.
Identify — discuss where they are found, animals that used to live in them, etc. Name each type.
2. Ask *S*s if some look just alike, just the same.
3. Place 4 boxes on table. Have all *S*s put the shells in each box that are just the same, just alike, etc.

4. Empty boxes. Mix the shells. Ask a *S* to put the shells together that are just the same.
5. Remove boxes. Hold up a snail and a scallop. Ask *S*s how are they different? Probe and suggest ways after *S*s have exhausted possibilities.
6. Hold up a snail and a conch. Ask *S*s how they are the same or different. Probe and suggest if necessary.

C. 1. Place all shells and buttons on the table. Place two boxes on table.
2. Tell *S*s — "I have 2 boxes. I want to put all the things in these two boxes. I want one kind in this box and another kind in this box. How can we do this?" Probe, reward, until *S*s understand what their task is. Have *S*s place correct objects in each box.

SESSION II

MATERIALS: 4 boxes; 5 nuts, 5 bolts, 5 washers, 5 nails (each group identical in size, shape and color); 5 pecans, 5 peanuts, 5 walnuts, 5 almonds, 5 buckeyes.

A. 1. Introduce hardware.
   a. Identify — place one of each group in sight of *S*s; name each object; discuss their use.
   b. Multiple labeling for each object. Discuss with *S*s their shape, markings, by asking *S*s, "What can you tell me about this bolt?" Let children give spontaneous answers. Suggest others; probe, e.g., color, size, what is it made of? These objects do not lend themselves to lengthy labeling. Do not spend too much time at this point on labeling.
2. Place all hardware on table. Ask *S*s if some look just alike, or just the same. Have one *S* that answered question correctly show everyone two objects that are just the same.
3. Teacher sorts items together without the boxes, by shape, and places one wrong in front of *S*. Asks *S*s if she is right. Have a *S* correct mistake.
4. Have a *S* mix all the hardware together. Place 4 boxes on table and ask *S*s to put the ones together in a box that are just the same, just alike.

B. 1. Introduce nuts.
   a. Identify objects (one of each type), discuss what they are, where they are found, who eats them, where they grow.
   b. Multiple labeling — probe and suggest attributes for each nut. Do not labor over too many attributes for each nut.

2. Place all the nuts on the table. Ask Ss if some nuts look just the same or just alike. Have a S who answered correctly show the group two items that are just the same.
3. Place 4 boxes on the table. Ask one S to put the nuts in each box that are just the same. Ask another S if this is the right way.
4. Repeat previous procedure with another S.
5. Children make piles with mistakes for others to guess which are wrong.

SESSION III

MATERIALS: 4 blue combs (2 large, 2 small), 4 pink combs (2 large, 2 small); 4 blue toothbrushes (2 large, 2 small), 4 pink toothbrushes (2 large, 2 small).

A. 1. Introduce combs.
   a. Identify 1 large blue comb, discuss its use — present 1 large pink comb. "Are they the same?"
   b. Find similarities and differences. "How are they the same? How are they different?"
2. Present all the combs. Find similarities and differences. Have S pick up the comb he is discussing.
3. Place 4 boxes on the table. Have Ss place the combs in each box that are just the same. Ask for justification.
4. Have a S empty all boxes. Place 2 boxes on the table and ask Ss if there is another way we can fill just two boxes so that all the combs in one box will be the same, all the combs in another box will be just the same. Have Ss carry out this task. The teacher will make suggestions if necessary.
5. Have a S empty boxes and repeat previous procedure.
6. Ask Ss if all the large combs are blue. Are all the pink combs small?

B. 1. Introduce 1 large pink toothbrush.
   a. Identify, discuss reason for its use, when a person should use it.
   b. Present all toothbrushes. Find similarities and differences. Have S pick up the object he is discussing.
2. Place 4 boxes on the table. Have Ss place all the brushes that are just the same in each box. Ask for justification.
3. Have a S empty all boxes. Place 2 boxes on the table. Explain to Ss that you are going to put the brushes together that are the same in this box and those brushes that are the same in this box. Sort the objects on the basis of color and place one item incorrectly. Ask Ss if this is the right way. Why?

    4. Have *S* empty boxes and ask that *S* if he can think of another way we can put the objects so that they are just alike in this box and just alike in the other box. Why?
- C. Present all combs and all toothbrushes.
  1. Place 2 boxes on table. Ask *S*s for one dichotomy. Why?
  2. Pose question for second dichotomy — Why?
  3. Empty both boxes. Ask *S*s if everything blue on the table are combs? If all of the toothbrushes are pink? Why?

SESSION IV

MATERIALS: Complete set of shells, nuts, combs, hardware.

1. Present each set of objects, have *S*s label each set, explain function of each set.
2. Have a *S* mix all objects. Ask *S*s if they can put together the things that go together (without boxes).
3. Play a guessing game. The teacher is thinking of some things that are made of metal, that are found near water, that working men and daddies use, of something that helps you look nice, of something to eat, etc.
4. Pose question. "How are they all alike in one way?" e.g., (Hard, will not bend).
5. Place set of hardware, combs, and nuts in center of table. Ask one *S* if he can put the things together that go together. Ask *S*s if he is right. Repeat procedure until each *S* has a turn, but vary groups of objects used.

SESSION V

MATERIALS: Plastic car, metal car, metal dump truck, plastic fire truck.

- A. Introduce plastic car.
  Multiple labeling — "What can you tell me about this car?" Let children give spontaneous answers. Suggest others when they finish; or probe. For example, color, size, what is it made of, wheels, people ride in it, steering wheels, adult drives it, has seats, windows, etc.
- B. Introduce metal truck.
  1. Multiple labeling — probe and suggest.
  2. Find similarities and differences with the car. "Are they the same? How are they the same? How are they different?"
- C. Introduce metal car.
  1. Multiple labeling.

     2. Compare similarities and differences with truck.
- D. Introduce plastic fire engine.
    1. Multiple labeling.
    2. Similarities and differences.
- E. Are they all alike in some way? Is there a name for all of them?
- F. Teacher groups 2 objects that are alike in some obvious way and poses question — "Can you tell me one way these two are alike and not the others?" For example, color, substance, etc.
- G. Repeat with mail truck and fire engine.
- H. Repeat with plastic car and plastic fire engine.

SESSION VI

MATERIALS: Apple, banana, pear, orange, tangerine, lemon.

- A. Introduce orange.
    Multiple labeling — What can you tell me about this orange? What can you do with it? Probe and suggest. For example, color, shape, food, peel, eat it, sweet.
- B. Introduce banana.
    1. Multiple labeling
    2. Compare similarities and differences with orange.
- C. Introduce tangerine.
    1. Multiple labeling
    2. Compare similarities and differences with orange.
- D. Introduce lemon.
    1. Multiple labeling
    2. Compare similarities and differences with orange and tangerine.
- E. Introduce apple and pear.
    Compare similarities and differences.
- F. Compare similarities and differences with apple and banana.
- G. Pose question, "Is there something that you can call all of them?" Present idea of another food, cracker. "Would that be a fruit, too?" Why?
- H. Teacher groups lemon and banana together. "How are these two alike?" (Peel, color, etc.)
- I. Teacher groups apple and pear together. "How are these two alike?"
- J. Pose question — "Can you find me two that are alike in color and shape?"

SESSION VII

MATERIALS: Blue hat, brown leather glove, brown leather shoe, red rubber boot, red scarf, red shirt, blue tie.

A. Introduce all wearing things.
 1. Multiple labeling — "What can you call all of these things?" List attributes of each item, color, material, use, where do you wear it, does it keep you warm or dry?
 2. Compare similarities and differences with shoe and boot, tie and scarf.
B. Teacher suggests attributes of an object and each child has a turn in guessing which object it is.
C. Have each child choose two items that are alike and tell to group.
D. Teacher asks Ss if they can find two objects that are alike in two ways.
E. Play "teacher is wrong" game, name one item and list attributes with one wrong. Boot — is red, rubber, shiny, you can keep your foot dry, you wear it in the bathtub.
F. Have Ss name other items of clothing.
G. Class inclusion:
 1. Are there more red things or more clothes?
 2. Are there more things to wear around your neck or more clothing?

SESSION VIII

MATERIALS: Clothing from previous session; Fruit from previous session.

A. Present clothing.
B. Play "teacher is wrong" game (E of above). "The glove is brown, leather, soft, and you wear it on your head."
C. Class inclusion:
 Are there more things for your feet or more clothing?
 Are there more things to wear around your neck or more clothing?
D. Introduce fruit.
E. Teacher sorts items together using color as single attribute, places one wrong, asks Ss if she is right.
F. Have Ss take turns in finding a single attribute and sort correct items.
G. Guessing game — Tell Ss you are thinking of something red and plastic. Let them guess what it is. Have Ss find another red and plastic object. For example, something hard and shiny, something soft and red, etc.

An Evaluation of Logical Operations Instruction **161**

SESSION IX

MATERIALS: 1 Negro family of 4; 1 white family of 4; 1 Negro fireman, 1 white policeman.

A. Present 1 Negro father. Multiple labeling — probe and suggest attributes.
B. Present policeman.
   1. Multiple labeling — probe and suggest attributes.
   2. Find similarities and differences with Negro father.
C. Place all rubber people on the table. "Are they all the same in some way?" "Is there a name for all of them?"
D. Teacher groups the two boys together and poses question — "Can you tell me one way these are just the same?" How are they different?
E. Teacher groups 2 fathers together, and fireman and policeman together — poses standard question.
F. Ask one S to find 2 people that are alike in some way. "Now can you find me another one?"
G. Play "teacher is wrong" game. Group the children together, add policeman. Ask Ss if this is the right way. Let Ss correct grouping.
H. Ask one S to group all the people together that are alike. Let other Ss correct — have each S repeat procedure.
I. Class Inclusion:
   1. Are there more daddies or people?
   2. Are there more people or children?

SESSION X

MATERIALS: Family of 4; dishes (4 cups, plates, forks, spoons), toothbrushes (2 different sizes and colors); 2 boxes

A. Introduce family of four.
   Multiple labeling. "What can you tell me about this family?" There are 4 people, they eat, sleep, run, play, etc.
B. Introduce set of dishes — multiple labeling.
C. Present family and other mixed materials. Ask a S to put the things together that go together.
D. With a comb and a boy — pose question, "Can this comb and this boy belong together in some way?" Why?
E. Introduce a small blue toothbrush.
   1. Multiple labeling — probe and suggest.
   2. Present large pink toothbrush. Find similarities and **differences**.

F. Place all brushes on table and have a *S* put those brushes together that are just alike. Have *S*s check correctness of groupings.
G. Place two boxes on the table and have *S* find a way of putting the things together that go together another way.
H. With the same two boxes, ask a *S* to find another way of putting the brushes together.
I. Place a mother and large blue toothbrush in center of table. Ask *S*s if they belong together in some way.

SESSION XI

MATERIALS: Set of erasers; set of nuts; 12 inch × 12 inch cloth, set of keys.

A. Introduce erasers.
   Multiple labeling of entire set — "What are they? What color are they? What do we do with them? Where do they come from, etc."
B. Introduce set of keys.
   1. Multiple labeling
   2. Compare similarities and differences with two different objects.
C. Place all objects, mixed, in center of table. Play "teacher is wrong" game — tell *S*s that you are going to put the objects together that go together. Fail to place 3 items in correct groups. Let *S*s find mistakes and physically correct task.
H. Have a *S* mix both sets together. Have same *S* put the things together that go together.
I. Play a guessing game. Place 4 objects from keys group, 1 eraser in center of table. Tell *S*s to look very closely. Place cloth over objects and remove eraser. Remove cloth and have *S*s guess which one you have removed.
J. Repeat procedure 3 times — Each time with a different set with four of a kind, one different. Always remove the differing one. Let *S*s take turns in guessing. After the third time ask *S*s if they can tell which one you are going to remove before you take it away. Repeat procedure until they understand object of game or before novelty wears off.

SESSION XII

MATERIALS: Set of farm animals, set of dinosaurs, set of buttons, set of safety pins in 4 sizes.

A. Introduce dinosaurs.
   1. Multiple labeling

2. Compare similarities and differences.
B. Introduce Farm animals — ascertain similarities and differences; in item itself, function, the animal (such as what they eat).
C. Place farm animals and dinosaurs in group "What do we call all these things?"
   1. More animals than dinosaurs.
   2. More dinosaurs than animals (as in standard class inclusion question).
D. Introduce safety pins.
   1. Multiple labeling.
   2. Similarities and differences — largest and smallest.
E. Place buttons with pins — group according to similarities. Name for all these (fasteners) — functional similarity.
F. Sort all groups on table into two sets — animals and fastening things.

SERIATION TRAINING SESSIONS

MATERIALS FOR ALL SESSIONS:
1. 3 bowls, differing 2 inches in width.
2. 4 pitchers, differing 2 inches in height and width.
3. 10 green circles, differing 1/2 inch in diameter.
4. 10 cylinders, differing 1 inch in height.
5. 8 cylinders, differing 1/2 inch in diameter.
6. 6 nesting barrels, differing 1/2 inch in height and width.
7. 5 three inch squares, differing in shades of blue.
8. 2 sets of size graded objects, 5 squirrels, 5 trees, differing in width and 1 inch in length.
9. 10 green felt, Easter eggs differing 1/2 inch in length.
10. 2 sets of size graded objects, 5 sails, 5 boats, differing 1/2 inch in length.
11. 2 sets of size graded objects, 7 houses, 7 dogs, differing in width and 1/2 inch in length.
12. 5 hats, differing in shades of blue and 1/2 inch in length.
13. 10 tepees, differing 1 inch in height.
14. 10 paper glasses of milk, differing 1/2 inch in length.
15. 5 paper glasses of juice, differing in shades of red and 1/2 inch in length.
16. 7 felt-model children, differing 1/2 inch in length.
17. 7 baskets, differing 1/2 inch in width and height.

SESSION I

MATERIALS: 3 bowls; 4 pitchers.

1. Introduce 2 bowls of obvious size difference.

a. Comparison between two bowls. "Can you tell me which one is the biggest, smallest?"
   b. Introduce middle size bowl. Compare it to the smallest. "Is this bowl smaller or bigger than this one?"
   c. Compare middle bowl with largest bowl. "Is this bowl smaller or bigger than this one?"
   d. Ask one child — "Remember the story of Goldilocks and the three bears? These bowls look like they belong to Papa bear, Mama bear and Baby bear. Could you put them on the table for the three bears? First, the biggest for Papa bear, the next biggest for Mama bear and then the smallest one for Baby bear."
   e. Let each child have a turn. Repeat with each child — the biggest, the next biggest and the smallest one for Baby bear.
2. Introduce two pitchers of obvious size difference. "What are these?"
   a. Compare two pitchers. "Can you tell me which one is the biggest, smallest?"
   b. Introduce middle size pitchers. Compare with smallest, largest.
   c. Ask one child — "If you were a Mother and were putting these pitchers away on the shelf, show me how you would put the biggest, next biggest and smallest."
      For boy Ss — "If you were a man working in the service station, etc."
3. Introduce fourth size pitcher. "Look I have another pitcher, where shall we put this one on the shelf. Why?"
4. Teacher lines them up the wrong way and asks Ss if that is the right way. Let the Ss correct mistake. Repeat.
5. Have each child take a turn in seriating pitchers. Repeat biggest, the next biggest and the smallest one, if necessary.

SESSION II

MATERIALS: 4 circles, 5 cylinders (height); 4 cylinders (width).

1. Introduce three green circles — "What are these?"
   a. Ask a child to seriate — "Let's play these are balloons. One for Papa bear, one for Mama bear, one for Baby bear. Can you pretend you are giving one balloon to each bear? Give one to Papa bear first, etc." Repeat after child has completed task. "Yes, you gave one to Papa bear, etc."
   b. Introduce fourth circle — "Look here's another balloon. Is it the biggest one? Smallest? Where should we put this balloon? Perhaps this is Grandfather's balloon."
   c. Have two Ss seriate circles. The other Ss will check their work. Have other Ss complete task also.
2. Introduce four cylinders differing in width only. "What are these? How are they different?"

a. Can you find me the largest? Next largest? Next largest? Smallest?
   b. Divide the group. Ask one group to place cylinders from the largest to the smallest. Have second group decide if task is correct. Scramble objects, let second group place objects in correct order.
3. Introduce three cylinders differing in height only. "What are these? How are they different?"
   a. Ask one child to place them in the right order from largest to smallest. Ask group if it is correct.
   b. Introduce fourth cylinder. Ask Ss where this one belongs.
   c. Introduce fifth cylinder (next to largest). Teacher places this one incorrectly. Asks Ss if this is the right way. Why? Let Ss place cylinder in correct place.
   d. Ask one S to scramble cylinders and place them in the right order. Have each child take a turn.

SESSION III

MATERIALS: 5 shades of blue; 6 barrels; 7 cylinders (height).

1; Introduce three shades of blue. "What are these?"
   a. "Can you find me the darkest? Next darkest? Lightest?"
   b. Divide group. Ask one group to place them in order from darkest to lightest. Have other group check. Scramble them. Ask other group to repeat task.
   c. "Here is another shade of blue. Where do you think it belongs? Why?"
   d. "There is one more shade of blue. Where shall we place this one? Why?"
   e. Scramble objects. Have each child seriate shades of blue, calling on other Ss to correct if necessary.
2. Introduce barrels. "What are these? You have used these before."
   a. Have a S show how we have used these before.
   b. Remove from nesting position. "There is another way we can use these." Place the first, third, and fifth barrel in order.
   c. "Can you find me the largest barrel? Next largest? Smallest?"
   d. Present the remaining two barrels. "Where do you think we should put the barrels so they will be in just the right place?"
   e. Have a S mix the objects. Have each S seriate barrels, always having other Ss correct if necessary.
3. Present 5 cylinders — Have a S seriate.
   a. Present sixth cylinder — "Where shall we place this one?"
   b. Scramble — Have 2 S's seriate.

c. Present 7th cylinder. Repeat b.
   d. Scramble — Let each S have a turn ordering objects.

SESSION IV

MATERIALS: All previous materials.

1. Introduce bowls with reference to Papa bear, etc.
    a. Let S be teacher. Encourage S to ask for largest, next largest, smallest. Have S ask a child how can we place these bowls in order. Let S check.
2. Present four pitchers.
    a. Teacher places pitchers in wrong order. Asks Ss if this is the right way. Why? Have Ss place them in correct order.
3. Present circles (7).
    a. Have S place in correct order. Ask Ss if correct.
    b. Present fifth circle (fourth in series). Ask Ss where can we place this one? Why?
4. Present five shades of blue. Have S place in order. Ask Ss if he is correct.
5. Present 8 cylinders differing in height.
    a. Have S place them in order.
    b. Present fifth (second in series). Ask Ss where this one should go. Why?
6. Present 6 cylinders differing in width.
    a. Have S place in order.
    b. Present fifth cylinder, the largest, ask Ss where this one belongs. Why?

SESSION V

MATERIALS: 8 cylinders; 5 squirrels; 5 trees; 5 circles.

1. Introduce 4 cylinders. "How are these different?"
    a. Divide group. Ask one group to place cylinders from the largest to the smallest. Have second group decide if task is correct. Scramble objects, let second group place objects in correct order.
    b. Introduce remaining 3 objects. "Where shall we place these, so they will be in just the right order. Each one has a very special place."
    c. Have a S scramble objects and seriate all cylinders. Have other Ss help if necessary.
    d. Play catch the teacher in a mistake. Teacher seriates objects, places one incorrectly. Have a S correct. Repeat with 2 items in incorrect order.

2. Introduce a squirrel and corresponding tree.
   a. Identify and discuss; squirrels have their homes in trees, what do squirrels eat, where do they find nuts? etc.
   b. "But we have 5 squirrels and 5 trees. We will have to find each squirrel his very own tree." Place the trees in the center of the table alone. Divide group. Ask one group to place them in order from the largest to the smallest. Have other group correct.
   c. Place squirrels in center of table. Have second group place squirrels in order.
   d. Ask *S*s, "Can you think of a way to find each squirrel his very own tree?" Probe and suggest if necessary.
   e. Scramble objects. Ask *S*s if they can find a way to place each squirrel in his very own tree. Show them if necessary by asking them to put first the trees together, then which is the largest tree, etc. Repeat with squirrels.
   f. If this task is difficult, scramble objects and repeat.
3. Introduce 5 balloons.
   a. Suggest the squirrels will now have a birthday party and these circles are their balloons.
   b. Repeat procedure used with squirrels and trees.

SESSION VI

MATERIALS: 10 Easter eggs; 5 sails; 5 boats; 9 green cylinders; 5 squirrels.

1. Introduce 5 Easter eggs. "How are they different?" "What could we pretend these are?" Discuss color, shape, etc.
   a. Ask one *S* to place them in order from largest to smallest. Ask group if it is correct.
   b. **Present a sixth egg.** Ask *S*s where this one belongs.
   c. **Present seventh egg.** Teacher places this one incorrectly. Asks *S* if this is **the right way**? Why? Let *S*s place in correct order.
   d. Ask one *S* to **scramble objects** and place them in the right order. Have each child take a turn.
2. Introduce a sail and a boat. "What is this? Where do we find boats? Have you ever been in a boat? etc."
   a. We have 5 sails and 5 boats. Each boat has its own sail. Can you think of a way we can find the right sail for each boat? Refer to how every squirrel found his tree. Repeat sequence as with squirrels and trees.
   b. Repeat procedure for each *S* to have a turn.
3. Introduce green cylinders.

168   *The Preschool in Action*

a. "Let's make a stairway for our squirrels to climb." Let each *S* have a turn. Let *S*s playfully have their squirrel climb the stair.
   b. Present 6th cylinder, 7th cylinder. Have a *S* place in order.
   c. Present 8th cylinder, 9th cylinder. Repeat b.
   d. Scramble. Let each *S* seriate.

SESSION VII

MATERIALS: 4 pitchers, 8 green circles; 5 squirrels, 5 trees, 8 cylinders differing in width.

1. Introduce 4 pitchers.
   a. Can you find me the largest? Next largest? Next largest? Smallest? As *S*s pick up each pitcher, teacher places them in correct order.
   b. Scramble objects. Teacher lines up objects incorrectly and asks *S*s if that is the right way. Let *S*s correct mistake. Repeat.
   c. Place 3 pitchers in random order. Have one *S* seriate. Present fourth pitcher and have the *S* insert correctly. Repeat for *S*s that need this foundation.
2. Introduce 5 circles, "Here are these balloons again. Now there are more." Have *S*s count.
   a. Can you find me the largest? Smallest?
   b. Ask a *S* to place them in correct order. "There is going to be a birthday party and we want the balloons to be in just the right places."
   c. "We are having two more children come to our party. Where shall we put these balloons so they will be in just the right place?"
   d. Scramble. Refer to balloons floating all around. Now they have landed on the table and we must put them in just the right places again.
3. Introduce 5 squirrels and 5 trees in random order.
   a. Make up a story about the squirrels out finding nuts for their supper. They want to find their very own tree again. Ask a *S* if he can find the squirrels their homes. If no response, repeat previous sequence of placing them in order. If group responds readily, repeat procedure, giving each child a turn.
4. Introduce 5 cylinders.
   a. Do you remember these? How are they different?
   b. Which one is the largest? Which one is the next largest? etc. Teacher places them in order as *S*s pick up correct one.
   c. Scramble. Have each *S* seriate.

SESSION VIII

MATERIALS: 7 houses, 7 dogs, 10 Easter eggs, 6 barrels.

1. Introduce 4 houses in random order. Discuss features.
   a. Ask a *S* to find the largest house, smallest house; ask a *S* to finish building this street of houses, so that each one is in just the right place.
   b. Present another house. Have a *S* find where this house belongs.
   c. Present another house. Repeat b.
   d. Repeat c.
   e. Scramble houses. Divide group. Have one group seriate items. Repeat with second group.
2. Introduce 7 dogs. Explain to *S*s that in each house lives a dog. These dogs have all been out to play and now they must find their very own home. Ask *S*s if they know of a way to find each dog a house.
   a. If no response, repeat sequence as with squirrels and trees. Otherwise, have *S*s working together to find correct order.
   b. "Now the dogs want to run out to play again." Separate dogs from houses. Ask a *S* to find correct order again, continuing with story.
3. Introduce 5 eggs.
   a. Have *S*s place in order. Scramble — rearrange, providing *S*s with playful discussion about the eggs.
   b. Present remaining 5 eggs, one at a time, having a *S* take turns placing in order.
   c. Play teacher makes a mistake, giving each *S* a turn in finding the mistake.
   d. Take 5 smallest eggs and suggest that each dog has his very own egg.
   e. If *S*s are receptive, place 2 more eggs and dogs for them to work with.
4. Present 4 barrels as cans of dog food.
   a. Have a *S* arrange in order. Stress largest, next largest, etc.
   b. Present 2 more barrels. Have a *S* seriate.
   c. Present 6 dogs. Have each *S* find a can of dog food for each dog.

SESSION IX

MATERIALS: 10 Easter eggs, 5 squirrels, 10 tepees, 10 glasses of milk and 5 blue hats.

1. Introduce 7 easter eggs. Discuss color. "How are they different?"
   a. Teacher lines them up the wrong way and asks *S*s if that is the right way. Let *S*s correct mistake.

b. Repeat procedure. Ask one *S* if the order is correct. Have that *S* correct seriation.
   c. Present another egg. Explain to *S*s that this one has a very special place and ask one *S* if he can put this in just the right place.
   d. Repeat procedure with ninth egg, tenth egg.
2. Present 5 eggs, 5 squirrels.
   a. "These little squirrels each has his very own Easter egg. See if you can find each squirrel his egg."
   b. Scramble, let each *S* have a turn.
3. Introduce 7 glasses of milk in random order. Tell *S*s that a little boy is going to have a birthday party and they should put all the glasses of milk on the table, but they look messy that way. "Is there a way we could put them in order so they will look better?" If no response suggest they find the largest glass, the next largest, etc.
   a. Have a child scramble the glasses. Let that *S* play teacher and show others how to place the glasses so each glass has a special place.
   b. Present eighth glass. Tell *S*s that another child has come to the party and ask *S*s where we should place his glass.
   c. Present ninth glass. "Here comes another child to the party. Where must we place his glass?"
   d. Present tenth glass. "This child is really late. There may not be any birthday cake left for him. Where shall we place his glass of milk?"
4. Introduce 10 tepees. What are these? Discuss. Tell a brief story about Indians and tepees.
   a. Have *S*s arrange in order.
   b. Suggest that they might find the right order by beginning with the smallest. Try to have each *S* verbalize his actions, e.g., the fact that now he is finding the smallest object from the remaining group of unordered objects.
5. Introduce 3 blue hats. "How are these different?"
   a. "Can you find me the darkest, the next darkest, the lightest?"
   b. Repeat with size difference.
   c. "Here are two more hats" Have a *S* place in order.
   d. Scramble and have *S*s arrange. Have each *S* take a turn.

SESSION X

MATERIALS: 6 barrels; 5 paper glasses of juice; 7 houses; 7 dogs, and 10 green cylinders.

1. Introduce 6 barrels. Discuss what they are and ask *S*s, "What can we do with these?"

a. Have a *S* operate nesting task. Have others correct.
b. Pose question — "What else can we do with these barrels?" Have another *S* place barrels in order.
c. After task is completed, ask a *S* to point to the largest one, another *S* point to the smallest one. Verbally reinforce — "Yes, this is the largest," etc.

2. Introduce 5 glasses of juice in random order. "What kind of juice could be in these glasses?"
   a. Comment on juice time at school. Suggest to *S*s that they should be placed just right on the table, for each glass has its very own place. Have a subject complete task.
   b. Play teacher makes a mistake game — place them in a disorderly arrangement. Ask a *S* if this is the right way. Why? Have that *S* arrange them in order.
   c. Repeat procedure until each *S* has a turn.

3. Introduce 7 houses and 7 dogs. Explain that these little dogs are lost. Each dog has his very own house.
   a. Ask a *S* if he knows a way to help the dogs find his very own home. If no response, repeat sequential steps for the *S*s to see how the dogs find their homes.
   b. After dogs are in their homes, tell *S*s that now the dogs would like to go out to play. Have a *S* help them find their homes again.
   c. Repeat sequence with different stories until each *S* has a turn.

4. Introduce 10 cylinders.
   a. "Remember how we made a stairway for our animals to climb?" Have *S*s take turns performing the task. If possible have them verbalize the operation they use, beginning with the smallest or largest.
   b. Have *S*s cover their eyes. Remove a cylinder. Let each *S* have a turn in replacing a cylinder into the stairway.

SESSION XI

MATERIALS: 10 green circles; 5 squirrels, 5 trees, 10 tepees, 7 felt-model children.

1. Introduce 7 children. "Now we can really have a birthday party, we have some children. How are they different?"
   a. Present 7 balloons. Have *S*s take turns finding a balloon for each child.
2. Present 10 circles as balloons. Have *S*s pretend they are balls. Ask each *S* to place these balls on the shelf in a store. Help *S*s verbalize their actions, choosing largest or smallest to begin task.

3. Introduce 5 children, 5 squirrels. "Now each child can have his very own pet."
   a. Let each *S* have a turn finding each child his very own pet.
   b. Place 5 trees on table. Have pets run back to their very own home in a tree. Have *S*s perform this task.
4. Introduce 10 tepees. "Do you remember who lives in these?" Discuss. Have each *S* place in order. Help *S* verbalize this action.

SESSION XII

MATERIALS: 7 baskets, 10 Easter eggs; 5 glasses of juice; 5 boats; 5 children; 10 cylinders (height).

1. Introduce 7 baskets. Discuss. How are they different?
   a. "Can you find me the largest, smallest?"
   b. Have each *S* place in order. Help *S*s to verbalize their actions.
2. Present 7 eggs. Discuss.
   a. Ask *S*s to find just the right egg for each basket. Scramble, rearrange.
   b. Remove baskets, add 3 more eggs. Have *S*s place these eggs in order.
   c. Have *S*s cover eyes. Let each *S* have a turn in placing an egg back into the arrangement, that the teacher has removed.
3. Introduce glasses of juice. "How are these different?"
   a. "Can you find me the darkest and the largest? The lightest and the smallest?"
   b. Have each *S* place objects in order.
4. Introduce 5 boats, 5 children. "Our children haven't taken a boat ride yet." Provide a brief story for interest.
   a. Have each *S* find each child his very own boat.
5. Introduce 10 cylinders.
   a. "Let's make a stairway for our children to climb." Let each *S* have a turn.

MEMORY-DISCRIMINATION TRAINING SESSIONS

SESSION I: *Motor imitation ("Copy cat game"):*

FORMAT: The children sit in a circle with the *E*. *E* presents a series of gross movements; *S*s must reproduce movements in correct sequence.

1. Copy cat game using one arm.
   a. Single arm movements.
      1. Flex elbow; touch shoulder; arm up.
      2. Tap head, circle arm out front; touch nose; drop arm to side.
      3. Ask children to make up a series for others to copy.
2. Double arm movements in copy cat game.
   a. Both arms extended to sides; clap hands; swing arms by side.
   b. Rotary arm movements at sides; touch shoulders; arms over head; drop arms by side.
   c. Ask one *S* to make up double arm series for others to copy.
3. Trunk movements in copy cat game.
   a. Hands on hips; bend at waist to left; jump.
   b. Turn around; bend forward at waist; stand; cover mouth with two hands.
   c. Ask children to make up a series for others to copy.
4. Statue game: *E* does series of movements and says stop; *E* holds position and *S*s try to reproduce series.

SESSION II   Block games:

FORMAT: Children sit with *E* at a table.

E makes a design using the blocks and *S*s copy the end-product of the design.

E makes a design and *S*s copy sequence of design building as well as the end-product.

1. Simple design, flat on surface.
   a. *E* makes design.
   b. Each *S* copies design only.
2. Simple design and movements
   a. *E* makes design in this sequence.
   b. Directions: "Watch *how* I build this; watch which block comes first, then second, then third and the last one." (Destroy model.)
3. Complex design.
   a. *E* makes:
   b. Each *S* copies design only.
4. Complex design and movements.
   a. *E* makes design in number sequence.

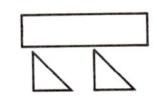

b. *E* destroys model.

c. *S*s build model as a group.

5. Continue as time permits.

SESSION III   Commands ("Message Game"):

FORMAT: Subjects sit in circle with *E*.

Repeat a few sequences of the "copy cat game" asking the children to make up sequences of movements.

E gives series of verbal commands; one *S* tries to reproduce sequence; other *S*s check his accuracy.

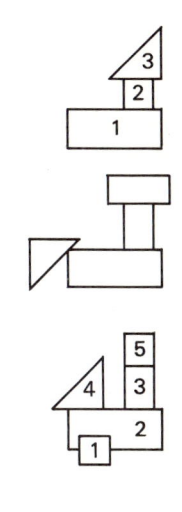

1. *E* does two things; *S*s tell what *E* did verbally.
2. Two commands (no demonstration — just tell).
   a. Blink your eyes, tap your toes.
   b. Run to the corner, then clap your hands.
   c. Choose one *S* to give two commands — either to other *S*, or whole group.
3. Three commands.
   a. First go to the door, hop once, then open the door.
   b. Put this block in that corner; turn around in the corner, and come back to me.
4. Four commands.
   a. Put this penny on the table; bark like a dog; touch the scales (or run around the circle); and sit at the table.
   b. Pick up the pencil; go touch the doorknob; give me the pencil; and tell us your name.
5. Have each *S* think up a series of two commands, or three if they can; have them whisper it to *E* first to check whether feasible.

SESSION IV: Review:

REPEAT a series of block sequence trials, having the children copy them.

SESSION V: *Visual memory and analysis*

FORMAT: Present picture; *S*s label items in it; hide picture; *S*s recall items.

1. Family scene picture.
   a. Have *S*s label as many items in picture as they can; suggest ones they miss.
   b. Hide picture: "Now, this is the game... how many things can you remember in that picture? Tell me everything you remember."
   c. Return picture and check accuracy; point out omissions.
   d. Hide picture; have *S*s tell a story about the picture.
2. Magazine sheets of scenes and items.
   a. Label each item; on some talk about them.
   b. Hide sheet.
   c. *S*s recall items.
   d. Check accuracy; omissions noted.
3. Magazine sheets of scenes and items.
   a. Show sheet for several minutes: NO labeling or talking.
   b. Hide sheet.
   c. *S*s recall items; check accuracy.

SESSION VI: *Review and verbal memory game:*

1. *Repeat* picture items from memory without previous labeling.
2. Verbal memory game: Say out loud several items and have *S*s remember them in sequence.
   a. mud-pencil-orange juice-car.
   b. moon-birthday-blackboard-snow.

SESSION VII: *Picture arrangement ("Make a picture story"):*

FORMAT: Children sit at a table with the *E*.
Present pictures one at a time in jumbled order for *S*s to talk about; lay all on the table mixed up; have *S*s put pictures in sequence to make a story; have other *S*s check it.

1. Block building story — four parts — boy on slide.
2. Colored picture stories — four parts — fire engine sequence.
3. Colored picture stories — four parts — milk story sequence.

SESSION VIII: *Review:*

FORMAT: Subjects sit at the table with *E*.

Repeat: picture sequence arrangements.
1. Hospital sequence — colored picture stories — four parts.
2. Mail sequence — colored picture stories — four parts.
3. Supermarket sequence — colored picture stories — four parts.

SESSION IX: *Story reading and questions:*

REPEAT: Pictures from memory — large colored animal pictures — no talking is permitted until pictures are hidden.
Read story: *Brown Bear, What Do You See?*
Check on memory for details — get spontaneous recall; then elicit other details.

SESSION X: *Story Reading Review:*

FORMAT: Children seated in circle while *E* reads story. Get spontaneous recall; then elicit other details by asking about events or objects in the story. If interest and time permit, allow *S*s to recreate parts of the story from memory.

SESSION XI: *Review:*

FORMAT: Subjects sit in a circle with *E*

Repeat stories from memory for details:
1. *Brown Bear, What Do You See?*
2. *The Very Little Boy.*
3. *Madeline.*

Repeat: Sequence picture, to see they remember the correct order.

1. Fire Engine Sequence.
2. Hospital Sequence.

SESSION XII:

FORMAT: Children sit in circle with *E*, who uses a number of items from previous sessions to help to consolidate skills:

1. Copy Cat Game.
    a. Arm movements: hands on knees; arms out straight and wiggle fingers; cross arms at waist.
    b. Trunk movements: turn around; touch one elbow; cover eyes; sit down.
2. Message game.
    a. 3 commands: go to door; sit on that chair; and bring me the pen.
    b. 4 commands: put this pen on that chair; say, "the pen is on the chair"; bring the pen to me; go to the door.
3. Visual memory.
    a. Use picture sheets for *S*s to look at without labeling; hide picture; have *S*s recall as many items as possible.
    b. Have children make up stories about pictures.
4. Show and Tell using children's own clothing and items they have brought with them.

FOOTNOTES | 5

[1] The preschool research project reported here is the result of a cooperative effort by Mrs. Wanda Franz, Research Assistant, the Division of Family Resources, West Virginia University, Mrs. Carolyn Kincaid, Director of the West Virginia University Laboratory Nursery, and the present author. We acknowledge the assistance and cooperation of Mrs. Lee McIntyre, Director of the ABC Village Day Care Center of Morgantown, West Virginia, and Diane Papalia, Mrs. Sherrie Wyant, and Joseph Fitzgerald of West Virginia University. Acknowledgment is also extended to Dr. Carolyn Shantz of the Merrill-Palmer Institute, Detroit, Michigan and Dr. Constance Kamii, Curriculum Director of the Ypsilanti, Michigan Early Education Program for the extensive use of curriculum outlines and programs.

[2] An unfortunate loss of subjects in the Preschool-B setting prior to posttesting required the combining of the control children into a single group of intermediate age range characteristics, i.e., see Table I. There was very little difference among the group performances, except for control group-II, on the relational terms pretest which has 3 subparts, each with a score range of 0-3, Griffiths, Shantz, and Sigel (1967).

[3] $F = 5.72$, df = 1/18, $p < .05$.

[4] $F = 9.27$, df = 2/18, $p < .01$.

[5] $F = 4.72$, df = 2/18, $p < .05$.

[6] $F = 6.71$, df = 2/17, $p < .05$.

[7] $F = 4.63$, df = 2/17, $p < .05$.

[8] $F = 12.01$, df = 1/17, $p < .01$.

[9] $F = 5.71$, df = 1/17, $p < .05$.

[10] $F = 1.43$, df = 1/17, $p < .25$.

[11] F values of 4.45 and 6.91, df = 1/17, $p < .05$, respectively.

[12] $F = 25.18$, df = 1/17, $p < .01$.

[13] $F = 13.719$, df = 1/17, $p < .01$.

[14] F values of .5522 and .0749, df = 2/8, respectively.

[15] $F = 4.688$, $df = 1/17$, $p < .05$.

[16] $t = 2.53$, $df = 6$, $p < .025$.

[17] It should be recognized that the present experimental effects are potentially confounded by teacher differences, i.e., one instructor worked with the classification and memory-discrimination groups, one instructor worked with the seriation instructional groups, while a third teacher conducted all of the control group experiences. However, the author has no information which indicates differential teacher effectiveness and this was substantiated by periodic interviews during the instructional period and observation of television tape recordings of the training conditions.

[18] Until adequate psychometric data concerning the reliability and validity of Piagetian tasks in general, and the present criterial measures in particular, are available, the possible confounding effects of repeated task administrations in developmental training research shall inevitably be present (Baltes, 1968; Wohlwill, 1970). A small additional matched control group (N=3) which received both pretests and posttests on the present task arrays showed one subject (age – 4 years, 8 months) who conserved number on pretesting but failed the task on posttesting. The only experimentally adequate design for research of the present type would appear to be the relatively demanding Solomon Four Group Design, Case 5, in Campbell and Stanley (1963).

[19] Copies of the entire multiple classification, seriation, and memory-discrimination training programs are available upon request from Dr. Frank Hooper, Associate Professor of Child Development, College of Agricultural and Life Sciences, School of Family Resources and Consumer Sciences, University of Wisconsin, Madison, Wisconsin, 53706.

REFERENCES | 5

Aebli, H. *Didactique psychologique: Application à la didactique de la psychologie de Jean Piaget.* Neuchâtel: Delachaux et Niestlé, 1951.

Albee, G. W., *et al.,* Statement by the society for the psychological study of social issues on current I.Q. controversy: heredity versus environment. *American Psychologist,* 1969, *24,* (11), 1039-1040.

Athey, I. J. and Rubadeau, D. O., (Eds.), *Educational implications of Piaget's theory: a book of readings.* Waltham, Mass.: Blaisdell, 1970.

Baltes, P. B. Longitudinal and cross-sectional sequences in the study of age and generational effects. *Human Development,* 1968, *11,* 145-171.

Beard, R. M. *An outline of Piaget's developmental psychology for students and teachers.* New York: Basic Books, 1969.

Bearison, D. J. Role of measurement operations in the acquisition of conservation. *Developmental Psychology,* 1969, *1* (6), 653-660.

Beilin, H. Perceptual-cognitive conflict in the development of an invariant area concept. *Journal of Experimental Child Psychology,* 1964, *1,* 208-226.

Beilin, H. Learning and operational convergence in logical thought development. *Journal of Experimental Child Psychology,* 1965, *2,* 317-339.

Beilin, H. Feedback and infralogical strategies in invariant area conceptualization. *Journal of Experimental Child Psychology,* 1966, *3* (3), 267-278.

Beilin, H. Developmental stages and developmental processes. Paper presented at the Invitational Conference on Ordinal Scales of Cognitive Development. Monterey, California: California Test Bureau, 1969a.

Beilin, H. Stimulus and cognitive transformation in conservation. In Elkind, D. and Flavell, J. H. (Eds.), *Studies in cognitive development: essays in honor of Jean Piaget.* New York: Oxford University Press, 1969b.

Beilin, H. and Franklin, I. C. Logical operations in area and length measurement: age and training effects. *Child Development,* 1962, *33,* 607-618.

Beilin, H. and Kagan, J. Pluralization rules and the conceptualization of number. *Developmental Psychology,* 1969, *1,* 697-706.

Brainerd, C. J. and Allen, T. W. Experimental inductions of the conservation of "First-Order" quantitative invariants. *Psychological Bulletin.* In press.

Brearly, M. and Hitchfield, E. *A guide to reading Piaget.* New York: Schocken Books, 1969.

Bruner, J.S., et al., *Studies in cognitive growth.* New York: Wiley, 1966.

Bruner, J. S. *The process of education.* Cambridge, Massachusetts: Harvard University Press, 1960.

Campbell, D. T. and Stanley, J. C. Experimental and quasi-experimental designs for research. In *Handbook of research on teaching.* Chicago: Rand McNally, 1963.

Cicirelli, V. G., et al. *The impact of Head Start: An evaluation of the effects of Head Start on children's cognitive and affective development.* The report of a study undertaken by Westinghouse Learning Corporation and Ohio University under contract B89-4536 dated June 20, 1968 with the Office of Economic Opportunity (Washington, D.C.: Office of Economic Opportunity, June 12, 1969).

Cicirelli, V. G., Evans, J. W., and Schiller, J. S. The impact of Head Start: A reply to the report analysis. *Harvard Educational Review*, 1970, *40* (1), 105-129.

Coxford, A. F. The effects of instruction on stage placement in Piaget's seriation experiments. *The Arithmetic Teacher*, 1964, *1*, 4-9.

Day, M. C., Danielson, G. I., and Parker, R. K. The learning and transfer of double classification skills from perceptual to functional and abstract attributes. Harlem Research Center, 144 West 125th Street, The City University of New York, 1971.

Elkind, D. Discrimination, seriation, and numeration of size and dimensional differences in young children: Piaget Replication Study VI. *Journal of Genetic Psychology*, 1964, *104*, 275-296.

Elkind, D. Piaget and Montessori. *Harvard Educational Review*, 1967, *37* (4), 535-545.

Elkind, D. The Case for the academic preschool: fact or fiction? *Young Children*, 1970, *25* (3), 132-141.

Flavell, J. H. *The developmental psychology of Jean Piaget.* Princeton, N.J.: Van Nostrand, 1963.

Flavell, J. H. and Wohlwill, J. F. Formal and functional aspects of cognitive development. In Elkind, D. and Flavell, J. H. (Eds.), *Studies in cognitive development: essays in honor of Jean Piaget.* New York: Oxford University Press, 1969.

Furth, H. G. *Piaget and knowledge: theoretical foundations.* Englewood Cliffs, N.J.: Prentice-Hall, 1969.

Furth, H.G. *Piaget for teachers.* Englewood Cliffs, N.J.: Prentice-Hall, 1970.

Gagné, R. M. Contributions of learning to human development. *Psychological Review*, 1968, *75*, 177-191.

Gelman, R. Conservation Acquisition: A problem of learning to attend to relevant attributes. *Journal of Experimental Child Psychology,* 1969, 7, 167-187.

Ginsburg, H. and Opper, S. *Piaget's theory of intellectual development: an introduction.* Englewood Cliffs, N.J.: Prentice-Hall, 1969.

Goulet, L. R. Training, transfer and the development of complex behavior. *Human Development,* 1970 (in press).

Griffiths, J. A., Shantz, C. U., and Sigel, I. E. A methodological problem in conservation studies: the use of relational terms. *Child Development* 1967, 38, 841-848.

Gruen, G. Experiences affecting the development of number conservation in children. *Child Development,* 1965, 36 (4), 963-979.

Hooper, F. H. Piagetian research and education. In Sigel, I. E. and Hooper, F. H. (Eds.), *Logical thinking in children: research based on Piaget's theory.* New York: Holt, Rinehart and Winston, 1968, (pp. 423-434).

Hooper, F. H. The Appalachian child's intellectual capabilities — deprivation or diversity? *The Journal of Negro Education Yearbook,* 1969, 38, (3), 224-235.

Hooper, F. H. Review of: Beard, R. M., *An outline of Piaget's developmental psychology for students and teachers.,* and Brearly, M., and Hitchfield, E., *A guide to reading Piaget., Harvard Educational Review,* 1970, 40, (1), 146-153.

Hooper, F. H. and Marshall, W. H. *The initial phase of a preschool curriculum development project.* Final Report, United States Department of Health, Education, and Welfare, Office of Education Contract No. O.E.C. 3-7-062902-3070.

Hunt, J. Mc V. *Intelligence and experience.* New York: The Ronald Press, 1961.

Inhelder, B. Some aspects of Piaget's genetic approach to cognition. In Kessen, W. and Kuhlman, C. (Eds.), *Thought in the young child. Monographs of the Society for Research in Child Development,* 1962, 27, 19-34.

Inhelder, B. and Sinclair-de-Zwart, H. Learning cognitive structures. In Mussen, P. H., Langer, J. and Covington, M. (Eds.), *Trends and issues in developmental psychology.* New York: Holt, Rinehart and Winston, 1969.

Jensen, A. R. How much can we boost I. Q. and scholastic achievement? *Harvard Educational Review,* 1969a, 39, 1-123.

Jensen, A. R. Criticism or propaganda? *American Psychologist,* 1969b, 24, (11), 1040-1041.

Kamii, C. and Radin, N. A framework for a preschool curriculum based on Piaget's theory. In I. J. Athey and D. O. Rubadeau (Eds.), *Educational implications of Piaget's theory: A Book of Readings.* Waltham, Mass.: Blaisdell, 1970.

Kingsley, R. C. and Hall, V. C. Training conservation through the use of learning sets. *Child Development,* 1967, 38 (4), 1111-1126.

Kofsky, E. A scalogram study of classificatory development. *Child Development,* 1966, *37,* (1), 191-204.

Kohlberg, L. Early education: A cognitive-developmental view. *Child Development,* 1968, *39,* 1013-1062.

Langer, J. *Theories of development.* New York: Holt, Rinehart and Winston, 1969.

Mermelstein, E. and Meyer, E. Conservation training techniques and their effects on different populations. *Child Development,* 1969, *40,* 471-490.

McCarthy, J. J. and Kirk, S. A. The construction, standardization and statistical characteristics of the Illinois Test of Psycholinguistic Abilities. Champaign-Urbana, 1963.

Murray, F. Cognitive conflict and reversibility training in the acquisition of length conservation. *Journal of Educational Psychology,* 1968, *59,* 82-87.

Parker, R. K. and Ambron, S. A comparison of the matrix and overlapping rings in teaching multiple classification to young children. Research Proposal, Center for Advanced Study in Education, City University of New York, 1970.

Parker, R. K., Ambron, S., Danielson, G. I., Halbrook, M. C., and Levine, J. A. Overview of cognitive and language programs for 3, 4, and 5-year-old children. Center for Advanced Study in Education, The City University of New York, 1970.

Parker, R. K. and Levine, J. A. Instruction in representation and its effect upon classification skills. Research Proposal, Center for Advanced Study in Education, City University, New York, 1970.

Piaget, J. *The child's conception of number.* London: Routledge, 1952.

Piaget, J. Development and learning. In Ripple, R. E., and Rockcastle, V. N., (Eds.), *Piaget rediscovered.* Ithaca, New York: Cornell University, 1964.

Piaget, J., Inhelder, B., and Szeminska, A. *The child's conception of geometry.* New York: Basic Books, 1960.

Pinard, A. and Laurendeau, M. "Stage" in Piaget's cognitive-developmental theory: exegesis of a concept. In Elkind, D. and Flavell, J. H. (Eds.), *Studies in cognitive development: essays in honor of Jean Piaget.* New York: Oxford University Press, 1969.

Reese, H. W. and Overton, W. F. Models of development and theories of development. In Goulet, L. R., and Baltes, P. B. (Eds.), *Life-span developmental psychology: research and theory.* New York: Academic Press, 1970.

Ripple, R. F. and Rockcastle, V. N., (Eds.), *Piaget rediscovered.* Ithaca, N.Y.: Cornell University, 1964.

Rothenberg, B. Conservation of number among four and five-year-old children: some methodological considerations. *Child Development,* 1964, *40,* (2), 383-406.

Rothenberg, B. and Orost, J. H. The training of conservation of number in young children. *Child Development,* 1969, *40,* (3), 707-726.

Shantz, C. U. and Sigel, I. E. *Logical operations and concepts of conservation in children: A training study*, 1967, Final Report: Project No. 6-8463, U. S. Department of Health, Education and Welfare.

Sigel, I. E. "Reflections." In Sigel, I. E., and Hooper, F. H. (Eds.), *Logical thinking in children: research based on Piaget's theory*. New York: Holt, Rinehart and Winston, 1968 (Chapter 7, pp. 504-524).

Sigel, I. E. The Piagetian system and the world of education. In Elkind, D., and Flavell, J. H. (Eds.), *Studies in cognitive development: essays in honor of Jean Piaget*. New York: Oxford University Press, 1969.

Sigel, I. E. and Hooper, F. H. *Logical thinking in children: research based on Piaget's theory:* New York: Holt, Rinehart and Winston, 1968.

Sigel, I. E. and Olmsted, P. P. Modification of cognitive skills among lower-class Black children: A Follow-Up Longitudinal Study. In Helmuth, J. (Ed.), *The disadvantaged child*. Bruner and Mazel. In press.

Sigel, I. E. and Olmsted, P. P. Modification of classificatory competence and level of representation among lower-class Negro kindergarten children. In: Passow, H. A. (Ed.), *Reaching the Disadvantaged Learner*. New York: Columbia University Teachers College Press, 1970.

Sigel, I. E. and Olmsted, P. P. Styles of categorization among lower-class kindergarten children. Paper presented at the American Educational Research Association Annual Meeting, New York City, 1967.

Sigel, I. E., Roeper, A., and Hooper, F. H. A training procedure for acquisition of Piaget's conservation of quantity: a pilot study and its replication. *British Journal of Educational Psychology*, 1966, *36*, 301-311.

Sigel, I. E. and Shantz, C. U. A study of classification training in conservation acquisition. Cited in Shantz, C. U., and Sigel, I. E. *Logical operations and concepts of conservation in children: a training study*, 1967. Final Report: Project No. 6-8463, U. S. Department of Health, Education, and Welfare.

Sinclair-de-Zwart, H. Developmental psycholinguistics. In Elkind, D., and Flavell, J. H. (Eds.), *Studies of cognitive development: essays in honor of Jean Piaget*. New York: Oxford University Press, 1969.

Smedslund, J. The acquisition of conservation of substance and weight in children: II external reinforcement of conservation of weight and of the operations of addition and subtraction. *Scandanavian Journal of Psychology, 2,* 71-84.

Smith, I. D. The effects of training procedures upon the acquisition of conservation of weight. *Child Development,* 1968, *39* (2), 515-526.

Smith, M. S. and Bissell, J. S. Report analysis: the impact of Head Start. *Harvard Education Review,* 1970, *40*, (1), 51-104.

Sonquist, H. and Kamii, C. Applying some Piagetian concepts in the classroom for the disadvantaged. *Young Children,* 1967, *22*, 231-245.

Stendler, C. B. Aspects of Piaget's theory that have implications for teacher education. *Journal of Teacher Education,* 1965, *16*, 329-335.

Vernon, P. E. "Genes, 'g,' and Jensen." Review of *Environment, heredity and intelligence* by A. R. Jensen. *Contemporary Psychology,* 1970, *15* (3), 161-163.

Wallace, J. G. *Concept growth and the education of the child.* The Mere, Upton Park, Slough Bucks: National Foundation for Educational Research in England and Wales, 1965.

Wallach, L. and Sprott, R. L. Inducing number conservation in children. *Child Development,* 1964, *35*, 1057-1071.

Wallach, L., Wall, J., and Anderson, L. Number conservation: The roles of reversibility, addition-subtraction, and misleading perceptual cues. *Child Development,* 1967, *38*, 425-442.

Watson, J. S. The development and generalization of "contingency awareness" in early infancy: some hypotheses. *Merrill-Palmer Quarterly of Behavior and Development,* 1966, *12* (2), 123-135.

Watson, J. S. Memory and "contingency analysis" in infant learning. *Merrill-Palmer Quarterly of Behavior and Development,* 1967, *13*, 55-76.

Watson, J. S. Conservation: an S-R analysis. In Sigel, I. E., and Hooper, F. H., (Eds.), *Logical thinking in children: research based on Piaget's theory.* New York: Holt, Rinehart and Winston, 1968, (pp. 447-460).

Watson, J. S. Cognitive-perceptual development in infancy: setting for the seventies. Paper Presented at the Merrill-Palmer Conference on Research and Teaching of Infant Development Meetings, Detroit, Michigan, February 1970.

Werner, H. and Kaplan, E. *Symbol formation.* New York: John Wiley, 1963.

Wohlwill, J. F. Piaget's system as a source of empirical research. *The Merrill-Palmer Quarterly,* 1963, *4*, 253-262.

Wohlwill, J. F. Methodology and research strategy in the study of developmental change. In Goulet, L. R., and Baltes, P. B. (Eds.), *Life-span developmental psychology: research and theory.* New York: Academic Press, 1970.

Weikart | *Introduction* | 6

The focus is shifted from the curriculum to the operational model of the preschool program in the following paper. This shift of emphasis was precipitated by the results of a comparison of the effectiveness of three programs by the Ypsilanti Preschool Curriculum Demonstration Project. The comparison indicated that the children involved in three programs, having quite different curricula, all improved in performance on test scores, with no significant differences found between groups. "The basic conclusion is that the operational conditions of an experimental project are far more potent in influencing the outcome than the particular curriculum employed." The operational model includes, 1. the curriculum content, 2. the manner in which the program is implemented, and 3. the staff model that supports its operation.

The unit based program described in Weikart's paper is a child-centered program focusing primarily on the social and emotional well-being of the child. The main objectives of the program are attitudinal and motivational in nature, with the exception of one — the formation of complete sentences. However, the unit-based program has a cognitive component; indeed, the first period of the child's day was both teacher-directed and focused on "cognitive" content. Teachers followed no specified curriculum, but rather were free to plan each day on the basis of their own experience, intuition, and judgement, while considering the needs of each individual child.

The emphasis on careful planning and evaluation for each child (required within the operational model) is somewhat at variance with the typical description of a traditional child-centered preschool, and greatly increases the similarity in implementation between the unit-based and more structured programs (structured in terms of teacher curriculum and methodology guides). Additionally, home visits were made, *two* teachers were responsible for each classroom, and a supervisor asked teachers questions "to establish clarity" and "to provide discipline so that the focus of the curriculum would remain constant."

In sum, it seems that Dr. Weikart's unit-based curriculum was different in several respects (involving curriculum and implementation) from the traditional nursery school, although similar to the traditional nursery school in the freedom allowed teachers in choice of content and overall teaching method. The unit-based curriculum was similar to structured programs in the planning and evaluation required for adequate individual instruction of each child. Thus, different curricula (although all had "cognitive" or "academic" components) and similar procedures of implementation (planning, evaluation, individual instruction) fostered comparable changes. Whether the success of the unit-based curriculum was due primarily to its excellent teachers, or whether any teacher functioning under the same requirements could effect comparable changes is a question deserving of immediate research.

David P. Weikart

A Traditional Nursery Program Revisited

6

INTRODUCTION

Against the current background of urgent social clamor and uncertainty, the limited success of compensatory education for disadvantaged children is being recognized by both professionals and parents, and the results are disquieting. Professionals are openly pessimistic and are often ready to reduce support for programs and limit their own involvement. Parents of disadvantaged children are increasingly aggressive in their demands for action. They are determined that someone assume the blame for the years of waste of human potential while ivory tower theorists wrestled with minutiae and the educational "establishment" promoted its own interests. The worst is yet to come, as the limitations of current compensatory education programs become more widely known by the public.

Professional educators and psychologists are expressing in public observations and conclusions limited to private conversations several years ago. As Jencks pointed out in the New York Times Magazine (1968), "Unfortunately, none of these (compensatory or remedial) programs has proved consistently

David P. Weikart is at the High-Scope Educational Research Foundation, Ypsilanti, Michigan. Printed by permission of the author.

successful over any significant period." This indictment has been verified by a group of researchers from the American Research Institute who reviewed compensatory programs covering preschool through 12th grade for the period 1963 to 1968; Hawkridge, Chalupsky, and Roberts (1968) found only 21 compensatory education programs which met a criterion of improved intellectual or academic functioning in a total sample of over 1000 such projects nominated for the study from throughout the country.

Parents of all minority groups are becoming increasingly outspoken in their criticism of the schools. At a recent meeting of the advisory committee for a Follow Through program in Harlem, a parent asked when the experimental project was going to teach her kindergarten youngster his ABC's. Strongly supported by the other parents with vigorous head nodding and such comments as "You tell it" and "That's right," the mother proceeded to denounce the school in which her children had failed to learn and to place the blame on the teachers, the curriculum, and the administration. This parent had no concern for the theoretical basis of curriculum development; she wanted education for her child *now*. She was especially bitter about the implication, common in professional circles, that children fail because their parents fail as parents. Such parents seem to be convinced that placing the blame for learning failure squarely on the shoulders of the school system will miraculously produce a reformed institution providing adequate education which is both relevant to and respectful of their children.

The concept of compensatory education for disadvantaged children evolved in the late fifties as a result of the emerging desire that social and educational equality, as well as political equality, be considered legitimate goals for a democratic society. It was nourished by the resurgence of the environment-oriented interaction theory of intelligence, in which compensatory education was seen as an answer to the achievement problems facing large numbers of youth from low socio-economic backgrounds. Pump in enough money, lower the teacher-pupil ratio, introduce new teaching techniques and new materials, be more responsive to the individual's needs for self-worth, and any child can be successful in an educational system which offers the technology and skills required for entry into the successful working and middle-class groups.

But today, at the start of the seventies, assessments of the situation are uniformly pessimistic. A recent review of compensatory education results by Roger Freeman (1970), while overwhelmingly discouraging in its entirety, was most biting in its conclusion: "It is too much to hope that the latter-day alchemists in our public schools will see the futility of their quest in less time than it took their spiritual ancestors to accept the fact of life that gold can be found only where nature placed it."

Preschool education for disadvantaged children has not escaped the increasing cloud of doubt that surrounds compensatory education efforts. The very small number of demonstrably successful projects has dampened the early enthusiasm generated by the "potential of preschool" and does little to counter Freeman's conclusions. Indeed, after the publication of the critical Westinghouse Report (Cicirelli, 1969), Head Start sustained its first major budget reduction after five years of expansion.

The response to the problem of slight long-term gain by preschool participants has created two sets of explanations and some action. Fowler (1966), among others, pointed out that the decline in the years after the initial Head Start experience is the result of inadequate curricula. Instructional programs must be greatly improved to attain the desired goals. On the other hand, Campbell and Frey (1970) have pointed out that the fade-out of effects can be explained in terms of learning theory. What has been learned is gradually forgotten. The action that has been generated has taken the form of curriculum improvement efforts both within and outside of Head Start.

Parker *et al.* (1970) have summarized many of the more promising efforts. Head Start has begun a systematic program of planned variations, attempting to look at eight preschool methods devised by eight National Follow Through sponsors in a series of specially selected preschool centers across the country. Preschool curriculum development projects are being funded to explore a wide range of programming ideas.

In this paper, the assumption is made that curriculum efforts are going to be limited in their success unless other factors, especially those relating to the operational model of the program, are given primary consideration. The basis for this contention is the outstanding success that a traditionally operated preschool has had when operated in the same style as experimental curriculum development projects (Weikart, 1969).

The next section will present a discussion of the place of curriculum; it will be followed by a look at a successful teacher-derived traditional nursery school program.

PLACE OF CURRICULUM

Until recently, the main goal in preschool education research was to develop *the* curriculum for optimally influencing the general development of the child. The basic reason for the failure of compensatory preschool education was assumed to be the inadequacy of treatment methods. In general, the major differences among the various curricula offered for use in preschools have been in the focus and amount of structure and in how this structure is thought to affect the general development of the child.

The major viewpoint in the early education field is that of the traditional nursery school educators. This position is best characterized as child-centered and permissive. The teacher provides the curriculum structure and bases it upon her intuitive grasp of the child's stage of development. The best examples of this method are found in the classes of master teachers, but what a master teacher does to achieve her results is a matter of personal expression.

Another point of view is held primarily by researchers new to the early education field. This position is best characterized as oriented toward structured programming, and it is usually based on a specific educational theory. A theoretical position might be derived from Piaget or Guilford, for example, and the primary goals would be cognitive and language development. The typical structured program is a carefully sequenced presentation of teacher-planned activities. While some structured programs may utilize traditional nursery school materials and activities, others turn directly to the task of teaching reading, writing, and arithmetic without even a nod toward traditional nursery school format. The structure may be derived from the curriculum materials themselves as well as from teacher commitment to a specific set of educational methods. In a structured program, the teacher is generally expected to understand how the activities will be used to achieve predetermined goals, and her teaching methods may range from the more traditional social controls to the newer behavior modification technology.

Since 1962, there have been a number of structured preschool education programs in operation (Klaus and Gray, 1968; Karnes, *et al.,* 1969; Weikart, 1967, 1968). These projects have submitted to different child development theories and have been organized around diverse teaching strategies. The central theme of each, however, has been the imposition upon participating children of carefully designed sequences of activities. While these projects have not been uniformly successful, the data have been encouraging in terms of both the immediate measurable impact on general functional ability and the long-term gains in areas such as academic and social performance. Several of these projects were accepted as successful by the Hawkridge *et al.* (1968) study. While there is little theoretical agreement among these researchers as to what constitutes a good nursery school program, they do agree that systematic teaching is essential.

The Ypsilanti Preschool Curriculum Demonstration Project was established in the fall of 1967 to determine which of two well-developed structured programs was most effective in meeting the needs of disadvantaged and functionally retarded children. The programs selected were the Cognitively Oriented curriculum and a language training curriculum. The *Cognitively Oriented Curriculum* had been developed over the previous five years by the Ypsilanti Perry Preschool Project (Weikart, 1968, 1970). This curriculum is a carefully structured program specifically designed for disadvantaged children who are functionally retarded. It is based on methods of "verbal bombardment" or verbal description of our own design, on principles of socio-dramatic play as defined by Sarah Smilansky (1968), and on child development principles derived from Piaget's theory. The

Language Training Curriculum was developed by Bereiter and Engelmann (1966) at the University of Illinois. This is a task-oriented program employing many techniques from foreign language training; it includes the direct teaching of language, arithmetic and reading. In order to complete the spectrum, a third program was established that would represent the traditional, or child-centered, approach to education. This program is called the *Unit-based Curriculum*, and it emphasizes the social-emotional goals and teaching methods of the traditional nursery school.

Much to our surprise, each of the three programs did unusually well on all criteria (Weikart, 1969). The findings indicated no differences among the three curricula on almost all of the many measures employed in program assessment: i.e., several intelligence tests (Stanford-Binet IQ gains by three-year-olds of 27.5, 28.0, and 30.2 points, for example, in the first year), classroom observations, observations in free play settings, ratings of children by teachers and independent examiners, and evaluations by outside critics. These data have now been replicated with essentially the same findings at the end of the second year. The basic conclusion is that the operational conditions of an experimental project are far more potent in influencing the outcome than the particular curriculum employed.

Until this study, it was our viewpoint that the traditional nursery education approach was ineffective in assisting disadvantaged children. The data supporting this position seem overwhelming (Weikart, 1967; Gray, 1969). However, with the evaluation of this study indicating the same excellent results with all three curricula, a serious look at the traditional method, at least as expressed in this project, is called for. After a brief review of the traditional nursery education position, we will discuss the actual program operated in this research project under the *Unit-based Curriculum*. The writings of the teachers who have been implementing the *Unit-based Curriculum* will be employed to illustrate the program.

TRADITIONAL NURSERY ORIENTATION

One of the most thorough summaries and reviews of the general position of traditional nursery schools is presented by Sears and Dowley (1963). This summary and several others, such as that by Swift (1964), are the last to appear before the current group of compensatory projects.

Sears and Dowley (1963) summarize the traditional methods as "watching and waiting for the child's needs to emerge and (to) determine the timing of different activities...." The specific aims of the traditional nursery program are (p. 822):

1. Meeting organic needs and establishing routine habits: Eating, elimination, sleeping, washing, dressing, undressing.

2. Learning motor skills and confidences: Climbing, running, jumping, balancing; learning to use the body effectively.
3. Developing manipulatory skills: Using scissors, crayons, paste, paints, clay, dough, etc.; building with blocks, working with puzzles, beads, tying, buttoning.
4. Learning control and restraint: Listening to stories, sitting still, reacting to music, etc.
5. Developing appropriate behavior: Independence-dependence in adult-child relations; coping with fear, angry feelings, guilt; developing happy qualities, fun, humor, healthy optimism.
6. Psychosexual development: Identification, sex role learning, formation of conscience.
7. Language development.
8. Intellectual development: Cognitive learning, concept formation, self-understanding and self-esteem, creativity, academic subject matter.

Presenting the curriculum focus in this way, however, fails to emphasize the constant goal in the traditional nursery school approach of influencing the general emotional well-being of the child. "One aim of preschool education ... is the achievement by the child of some emotional independence of adults, without undue side effects such as anxiety or insecurity" (p. 823). Or again, "Warmth and nurturance, given by adults to young children, clearly affect performances by children on concept formation...." (p. 828)

The sequence of the eight objectives above is not an accident. It represents, in rapidly decreasing importance, the concerns and interests of the traditional program. Indeed, Sears and Dowley recognize this when they comment, "It is curious that in the stated aims and purposes of the nursery school, intellectual development of the child has been very little considered. The review of objectives cited in the literature hardly refers to these cognitive aspects of a child's development." The kinds of concern and focus that *are* given attention in the traditional nursery schools are somewhat quaint, from our vantage point of 1970. For example, in a burst of social reform, Katherine Reed (1960) states, "Naps or rest periods are individual rather than group affairs and can usually be managed better at home than at school." (p. 25) Or again, in discussing child management, she states, "A set schedule for going to the toilet has the disadvantage of not meeting individual needs, or not meeting changing needs of the same individual." (p. 137) Then Sears and Dowley (1963) comment that in the postwar years of the 50's, "parents formed groups to share common concerns and problems in the education of their young children, under the guidance of professional educators," a situation that would be little tolerated by the vocal parent groups of today.

On the whole, however, the key outcome of the traditional nursery school curriculum approach is that it permits the teacher to deal independently and intuitively with the educational program for the children enrolled in her class. She does not follow a specified curriculum based on a specific cognitive theory or language theory. She does respond to the "needs" of the children as seen from the vantage point of general knowledge of child development and personal wisdom and experience.

THE UNIT-BASED CURRICULUM

This section was selected from a paper prepared by Mrs. Mary Lou Malte and Mrs. Mary Martin, creators of this *Unit-based Curriculum*, for presentation in workshops in Seattle, Washington; Ypsilanti, Michigan; and London, England, during May and June, 1970.

INTRODUCTION

The unit-based program is basically child-centered, having evolved from the traditional nursery program; the social and emotional development of each child are uppermost in our planning. The youngsters in our program are not of the typical preschool variety. Our children tend to be lacking in self-concept, self-esteem, and self-control; they require discipline, consistent handling, and structure. We find that a great deal of teacher-pupil interaction is necessary in working with disadvantaged children. We can take cues from the children, but we often have to be the instigators of new ideas, especially in role playing situations.

We feel that it is essential to have a well-planned day and to have the room prepared for the children before they arrive. Activities planned for the day generally are tied into the unit theme to make them more significant. There are many activities planned to interest all the children in a variety of ways. Since the children are free to make individual choices, they maintain a high degree of interest in the activities they choose. Once rules and routines are established, however, we are consistent about enforcing them. We ask the children to keep large blocks and mobile equipment in specific areas and not to bring them across designated lines. They are also reminded that they must share and take turns with the equipment. At the beginning of the year, we find it necessary to reduce the amount of material available so that the children are less distracted by outside stimuli. The class is then slowly introduced to new materials.

Since the children will be going into a large group situation in the school years ahead, we provide an opportunity for group experiences at the beginning of each day (Circle Time). This is the most highly structured period of the day. The children are required to remain in their chairs for the entire 1/2-hour period. During this time, we introduce unit-related materials, read stories, present music and rhythm experiences, work with puppets, and emphasize counting, colors, shapes, facial features, body parts, and other such "cognitive" goals. There are times when a child is not able to contain himself during our Circle Time activities. When this happens, we may remove him from the circle and give him the opportunity to find a quiet activity. This will keep him involved, and he will not disturb or distract other children.

There is a great deal of flexibility in our program, and a great deal of attention is given to each child. We can extend and develop a child's knowledge about a subject, depending on his particular needs or interest at the time. There is also flexibility concerning the planning for the day. When we feel the children are restless or not interested or not comprehending, we can quickly make a substitute plan. A well-planned program is essential, but there is also room for intuitive decisions by the teacher. We can and do change course in midstream. The specific plans are formulated on a day-to-day basis, since the plans for one day depend on the successes and failures of the day before. Just as important as the planning is the evaluation immediately following each day. During the evaluation, each child is discussed and his individual needs are identified.

Responses are not demanded in this program, but there is much verbal interaction. At the beginning of the year, we must initiate any and all conversation. As the children begin to talk on their own initiative, we reinforce them. Eventually there is a great deal of lively and spontaneous conversation, not only between teacher and child but also among children. These interchange situations are ideal for this type of program since it is basically one in which the teachers take the cues from the children. Obviously the teacher can tune in to the child's needs more easily if the child feels free to express them.

OBJECTIVES

The purpose of the *Unit-based Program* is to supply preschoolers with the necessary educational and social skills to adapt readily to a kindergarten curriculum. We look for the following characteristics in the child's development:

1. Sustained attention
2. Ability to stick to a task for increasingly long periods
3. Positive interaction with peers and teachers
4. Ability to use sentences in conversation

5. Positive attitude toward school
6. Impulse control
7. Good manners
8. Sense of well-being
9. Feelings of accomplishment

DAILY SCHEDULE

8:45 a.m. Arrival
9:00 a.m. Circle Time and Music Time
9:45 a.m. Discovery Time (free play) and Cleanup
10:30 a.m. Juice Time (story or directed activity and juice)
10:45 a.m. Outdoor Time
11:00 a.m. Dismissal

ACTIVITY AREAS

Housekeeping Area (dolls, kitchen utensils, dressup clothes)
Large Motor Area
Quiet Table (small blocks, books, tinkertoys, matching games, etc.)
Art Area

We found that it was practically impossible to take program cues from the children at the beginning of the year. The children showed very little interest in using the building blocks, paste, crayons, scissors, doll houses, etc. It was necessary to show them ways to use the many available materials. We divided the children into small groups before Juice Time in order to show them how to play with the variety of materials. We also found that the room was too stimulating with all the materials in full view, so we removed a majority of the toys and tools; we reintroduced them slowly.

The transition periods during the day were very difficult for the children. It was hard for them to move from one activity to another once a game or task had caught their attention, so we changed our routine and schedule by combining Music Time and Circle Time. We also added a story or a directed activity to Juice Time. These changes eliminated the difficulty of moving bodily from one activity area to another. The juice period was left to the end of the day, with outdoor play following.

SAMPLE WEEK LESSONS

September 30-October 3
(first week of school)

Goals

1. Learning names
2. Learning symbols
3. Learning routine for day
4. Learning body parts
5. Learning to listen to stories
6. Establishing limits
7. Acquainting children with school environment

Games for First Week

1. Roll Ball (Call Ball)
2. Jack Be Nimble
3. Do What I Do

Stories for First Week – Flannel Board

1. From *Our Kindergarten Book*, "The Three Bears," set to music
2. "The Three Bears"
3. "Three Billy Goats Gruff"
4. "The Three Little Pigs"

Songs for First Week

1. "Open, Shut Them"
2. "Where is _____?"
3. "Let Everyone Clap Hands"
4. "Hey, Everybody Touch Your Head"
5. "Happy Birthday"

GOALS

1. LEARNING NAMES

The first day of school is usually a frightening experience for the majority of our three-year-olds; therefore we felt it necessary to make the children feel at home by acquainting them with one another as soon as possible. The children quickly gain a great deal of security by having others identify them by name. During the week, we take every opportunity possible to emphasize the use of names. As the children get off the bus, one of us calls them by name. As the children enter the room, one of us is always present to welcome them with a friendly smile. Later, during Circle Time, and again during Juice Time, the children are introduced individually. During the day we use the children's names frequently. We also introduce the children to one another during free time and give them opportunities to play with one another in groups.

At the beginning of the week, a couple of children did not recognize their names when they were called, but by the end of the week they did. One of us would make a game of this activity by covering her mouth as she quietly called the child's name. The children have to listen very intently. "Where is _____?" and "Jack Be Nimble" and "Call Ball" are excellent games and songs for learning names. The children are delighted to hear their own names being called. They also enjoy looking for the child whose name is called in the song "Where is _____?" In the game "Call Ball," a child catches the ball and then names another child in the group to be the receiver. When the children are on the school bus going home, the aide has an excellent opportunity to talk about whose house is next, again emphasizing the use of names.

2. LEARNING SYMBOLS

Each child is assigned a "symbol" on the first day of school. The symbol might be an airplane, a dog, a circle, etc. cut from construction paper. This symbol is put on the child's chair, on his cubby, and on anything else in the classroom that he should be able to identify as his. Each symbol is distinct and simple enough for quick identification. The children learn to identify their symbols quite readily and adapt quickly to the idea of having symbols for the purposes of identification.

The symbols give the children a sense of security and belonging and make routine functions such as hanging up coats and finding a chair go very fast and smoothly. They are small and easy to handle, and the children are usually able to tell what a symbol depicts even the first time they see it, so that the teachers can soon begin asking, "Whose picture is the dog?"

The symbols are also used in transition times, when the children move from area to area. Two or three symbols are held up, and as a child recognizes his, he goes with the teacher to the art table, housekeeping area, etc.

3. LEARNING THE DAILY ROUTINE

The day is divided into five segments: Circle and Music Time, Discovery Time (free time) and Cleanup, Story Time or Directed Activity, Juice Time, and Outdoor Time. On the first day of school, the children are introduced to the routine for the day while they are on the bus. They are told to go into the school room, hang up their wraps, use the bathroom facilities, and find their chairs for Circle Time. With the four-year-olds as leaders, the younger children soon learn to follow this procedure.

The children are asked to remain seated during Circle Time. During the first week, only one child seemed unable to cope with this part of the routine, but he was able to go to the quiet area to look at books. Later he wanted to rejoin the group, and he has been able to stay seated during Circle Time ever since. Circle Time is the most structured part of the day. This is the time when we work on the themes and concepts which make up the "intellectual" component of the curriculum, such as learning body parts and categories (foods, furniture, etc.) and identifying shapes.

After Circle Time, the children are asked which area they would like to go to for Discovery Time. Each one is asked individually; then he is told to pick up his chair and take it to the table or area he has chosen. The children usually follow their plans though they are not forced to. During Discovery Time, the children may choose among many activities; they return the toys and games to the shelves when they are finished using them.

A signal is given on the piano to indicate Cleanup Time. The children have to be encouraged to return everything to specific places in the room. In each area, pictures and examples of objects from that area are attached to flannel boards, helping to make this task easier for the children. A paper hat is sometimes given to the best helper.

After Cleanup, the children are told that we will have juice as soon as everyone is sitting quietly at his table. Books are put out on the tables to give the children a quiet period in which to get settled. Sometimes we read a story. At other times a directed activity such as coloring, pasting, or matching is planned for this period.

During Juice Time, the children take turns passing napkins, cups and cookies. Each child pours his own juice. The children are asked to throw away their cups and napkins when finished and return to their seats. Then they go to the bathroom, put on their wraps, and sit in their cubbies waiting to go out to the playground.

4. LEARNING BODY PARTS

The identification of body parts is such a vital concept that we did no more than introduce it during the first week of school. We introduced many of the names of body parts by talking about them, pointing to them and emphasizing them through various songs and games. The first day we talked about our hands and fingers. We teachers wiggled our fingers and asked the children to imitate us. The response was not too good the first day because the children, especially the three-year-olds, were somewhat frightened since the whole situation was so new to them. The "Open, Shut Them" song was picked up by the children fairly quickly. The words are very simple, and their fingers add the action to the song.

Facial features were also discussed. From a practical point of view, it was necessary for the children to become aware of the relative position of eyes, nose and mouth in preparation for making pumpkins and masks for Halloween. When we began talking about facial features, most children were able to point to their eyes, nose, mouth and ears. The body parts were then emphasized in songs and in the "Do What I Do" game. The response from the children was good; next we started to talk about the relative positions of these features.

5. LEARNING TO LISTEN TO STORIES

Learning to listen is a crucial initial step in the reading readiness program in our curriculum. For the children to have an interest in words, stories, sequence, and imagination, they must first develop the ability to listen. We knew from past experience that the children would not be able to remain attentive very long. We also knew that the first step for developing attention span was through the use of flannel board stories. The children are usually fascinated by the introduction of the bright, colorful figures as the teacher relates the story. The teacher can help to dramatize the story through the tone and tempo of her speech; she can modulate her voice and use gestures for characterization. She can also ask "What's going to happen next?", "What does she have in her hand?", "Who is knocking at the door?"

6. ESTABLISHING LIMITS

The children are quite free during their day at school, but there are several limits within which they function. First is the daily routine. We begin each morning with our Circle Time music. The chairs are placed in the circle before the children arrive; when they come, they are expected to remove their coats and sit in their chairs for the duration of the activities presented during this period. Responses are encouraged, but not required. The only alternative to Circle Time activities is to look at books in the quiet area. This choice is offered to the child only when he feels he cannot contain himself and remain in the circle.

After Circle Time is over, each child is expected to take his own chair and place it at the table in the play area he has chosen to go to for Discovery Time. The children were confused about this initially, and one of us had to send the children over to the tables individually while the other showed them where to put their chairs. By the end of the first week, the children had caught on to this routine, but they continue to need encouragement.

The specification of play areas is an important aspect of Discovery Time. The large motor area has a visible boundary — a red line made from Mystik tape — that is vital to our classroom structure. The first day we talked about how this line was the furthest limit for large trucks and large blocks. The main reason for this limit is that these very large playthings must be contained in one area to prevent them from getting underfoot and disrupting the play in other areas. Also, being together in a bounded area seems to encourage interaction between the children. The children do not fully grasp the idea behind the boundary line yet, so this has to be reinforced through a variety of techniques. Often when a truck strays over the line, one of us "drives" it back and points out the line to the child. When a child is building close to the line, we suggest that he build farther back so he does not go over the line. So far, by using this line, we have avoided many problems that arise from having large equipment all over the room. This was about the extent of setting limits for the first week. Other problems, such as fighting, will come up, but the children are still so new and shy that it will take some time for these things to develop.

Some limits are set for outdoor play. These are strictly enforced because they are safety precautions; they include playing on the grass rather than on the driveway, allowing only one child on the slide at a time, and keeping sand in the areas designated for sand.

7. ACQUAINTING CHILDREN WITH THE SCHOOL ENVIRONMENT

To familiarize the children with toys and games in the room, we introduced a few toys during Circle Time. We showed the children how to use them and how to return them to their proper places on the shelves. We pointed out the various areas as we took a trip around the room. The children were then asked which area they would like to go to for free play time.

For the first week of school, we did not put out very many toys because we thought it best to eliminate as many distractions as possible. We spent a great deal of time showing the children how to paste, color, etc., because these children generally do not have materials for these activities in their homes.

SAMPLE UNITS

1. FALL UNIT

For the duration of a unit, we try to key in as much as possible to the central theme through stories, art activities, songs, pictures, etc. Using Fall as the theme of the first unit seemed natural since the Fall season makes children more aware of their environment — one of our goals running through the entire year.

The first day we talked about leaves — how they change and fall to the ground and what colors they turn: red, yellow, brown, orange — using pictures of trees and flannel board pictures of leaves. The children listened, but their responses were few; they couldn't identify colors by name but were able to match them. During the course of the week, we offered numerous activities relating particularly to leaves, such as coloring ditto sheet pictures of leaves.

The weather was very pleasant all week, and we were able to implement our new unit with a couple of field trips. Short ones are good at this time; we build up to longer ones later in the year.

2. HALLOWEEN UNIT

We decided to introduce the unit on Halloween because we wanted to be sure the children had an opportunity to see the pumpkins growing in the fields. We planned a trip to the pumpkin patch for Friday, devoting time during the early part of the week to discussions about Halloween and pumpkins. The children were given many opportunities to see pictures of pumpkins, use flannel pumpkin cutouts, color pumpkins, compare pumpkins with other fruits and vegetables, color and paste facial features on Jack-O-Lanterns, etc. We talked about the color of pumpkins and found other things in the room that were the same color. We also discussed the weights of pumpkins (little ones are light and easy to pick up; big ones are heavy and difficult to pick up). On the way to the pumpkin patch, we discussed what we would see when we arrived — pumpkins growing on vines. The children helped pick out five pumpkins, and back in the classroom we discussed how we could make Jack-O-Lanterns out of them: "What can we do to the pumpkins to make them Jack-O-Lanterns?" "Put candles in them!" "How can we get inside the pumpkin to put the candle in it?" "Cut it."

3. APPLE UNIT

Most of the activities in the classroom revolved around the identification and characteristics of apples. The children saw and touched real apples growing on trees at the apple orchard and saw, touched, cut, peeled, cooked, and ate them at school. They also played with artificial apples and had fun identifying apples during games. A favorite game was "What's Missing?", using apples and pumpkins hidden under a hat and asking the children to tell which one was hidden.

The children made apple sauce in class, and on subsequent days were encouraged to pretend that they were fixing it in the housekeeping area. In the large block area, some of the children used apples in their trucks and transported them to market. Many children made apples out of clay, play dough, art foam, etc. They also pasted apples on trees, used flannel board cutouts of trees and apples, and matched apple shapes to outlines of apples.

A Traditional Nursery Program Revisited 203

4. THANKSGIVING

We began the Thanksgiving unit by showing pictures of turkeys and discussing the various attributes of said winged creature: it is a bird; it has feathers, a head, eyes, feet, beak, and toes. After this, the children were able to pick out the turkey picture among several pictures of different birds.

Since we felt that the historical background of Thanksgiving would have little meaning for children, we more or less neglected it. Instead, we concentrated on tangibles like food and art activities like hand turkeys: spread out your fingers, trace your hand, make your thumb the head and fingers the feathers, just add feet and imagination and presto! A ready-made bird! We colored turkeys, talking about the colors in a real turkey. Another opportunity for discussing colors arose when we pasted real feathers of green, rust, gold, and orange on a pre-cut construction paper turkey. The children also painted paper plates brown, stapled on head and feet, and pasted on real feathers. Spatter-screen paintings of turkeys were also made. "Gobble, Gobble Turkey" was the only turkey song we sang. We felt that if we sang only one song, the frequent repetition of the words would result in greater participation.

5. FOODS

For our unit on foods we followed a few simple recipes. We had the children help make Jello, pudding, marshmallow sandwiches, and Rice Krispie squares. The children saw the Jello and the pudding harden (we used ice cubes to speed the process). They also enjoyed using a knife to spread the marshmallow fluff (which was very sticky) on graham crackers. We melted miniature marshmallows to help make the Rice Krispies stick together for Rice Krispie squares. What the children helped make during Discovery Time was consumed by one and all during Juice Time.

We also played food games to reinforce food identification. We played relay games — pass the banana to the person behind you; walkie-talkie; go to the store, pick up one apple, and bring it to me — and guessing games — what foods did teacher put under the towel and which one did she take away? The children also used foods in the store and housekeeping areas. Food puzzles, coloring sheets, and magazine pictures were available for tracing, coloring, cutting, and pasting. We used a number of Peabody and magazine pictures of foods during Circle Time. The children were enthusiastic about identifying foods they knew.

To combine our unit on foods with listening activities, we read a story about the supermarket; this started a discussion about various items that might be purchased at the supermarket.

SAMPLE SUMMARY OF MONTH

In the past month we have noticed substantial gains in many areas. The children have grown emotionally; the initial crying, hitting, random actions, and frustrations are no longer visible. Some children still need help with impulse control, but there has been improvement. For example, John, an extremely hyperactive and impulsive child, has managed to settle down during Circle Time and remain in his seat for the entire period. He is also able to wait for his turn during Juice Time and does not eat before others have been served. He knows now that we all eat together after everyone has been served, and after we have sung "Open, Shut Them."

The routine for the day has been well established, and the children need very few reminders about what happens next. As they enter the room, they find their cubbies, hang up their coats, use the bathroom, find chairs for Circle Time and sit down. This period usually lasts twenty to thirty minutes (including the music), during which the children are attentive but not as responsive as we eventually expect them to be. They imitate our actions in songs and stories, but they don't talk about what they're doing. They know "Open, Shut Them" the best, but Willie, Brian, Sharon, and Jackie still don't say the words. It is difficult for them to remember a series of words, and we are still working with the phrase, "Not by the hair of my chinny, chin-chin" from the "Three Little Pigs."

The children's attention span has increased; they are listening to stories with fewer props. Each child knows his own symbol as well as the symbols of his classmates. Most of them call their classmates by name, although the three-year-olds find this a little more difficult, of course.

During Discovery Time the children are definitely getting more involved with each other. Willie, a four-year-old, has been virtually nonverbal and has had extreme difficulty getting involved with the other children. However, during the past week he has been quite actively playing with Eddie. He and Eddie like to take turns pushing each other on the large truck.

Michael and David are the construction workers in the large block area. They involve many other children in their projects and use a great deal of imagination in building their structures — castles, motorcycles, cars, trucks, swimming pools, garages, and apartments. Their structures often reflect school activities. For example, if we have been reading "Three Billy Goats Gruff" or "Three Little Pigs" during Circle Time, they build a bridge for the billy goats and houses for the three pigs. There is a great deal of sharing, taking turns, helping each other, and talking to one another during these projects.

We also have some busy homemakers. Usually Sharon, Anna, Janice, Andrea, and Angela can be found in the housekeeping corner. Lisa likes this area, too, but she doesn't always interact with others. Anna is the leader and always attempts to interest others in her particular make-believe situation.

A Traditional Nursery Program Revisited

The children usually like to do an art project each day, but it is still very difficult for the three-year-olds to cut and paste. They know how to use paste, but they have a hard time pasting, cutting out and matching the cutout to a similar outline. It is necessary to turn the shape over to paste it, and this is hard for them to remember.

There are other areas in which the children are progressing. In addition to simple table manners like "Please" and "Thank you," they are used to taking turns passing cups, napkins, and cookies. They are also able to pour their own juice. A few were hesitant and shaky at first, but they gained confidence as time went on, because when they spilled juice in their attempts to pour, no big fuss was made, and they were encouraged to try again.

Cleanup seems to be going very well. Several children are the leaders in this area, but just about every child puts at least one thing away. Jackie and John still seem to want to continue playing, but verbal encouragement to help clean up seems to be working to some extent.

DISCUSSION

It is difficult to read these excerpts from the teachers' reports without noting the strong intuitive and practical base from which they have built their program. They have not reported any influence by outside theorists, such as Piaget or Bruner, or attributed any of their thinking to traditional nursery school curriculum advocates, such as Macmillian or Froebel from the early years, or Reed or Sears from more recent years. They talk instead of their general assumptions about children, the kinds of demands they feel they should make based on their experience with disadvantaged children, and the values of specific program activities and operations derived from their personal teaching experiences. Let's turn briefly to each of these areas.

ASSUMPTIONS ABOUT CHILDREN

When the children are specifically mentioned, it is most often in terms of emotional security needs. "The response was not too good the first day because the children were somewhat frightened." Or, "Children gain security by having others identify them by name." And again, "Symbols give the children a sense of security and belonging." In addition to being concerned about the emotional well-being of the children, the teachers do a number of things because they feel the children respond well to them. For example, they help children attend either by reducing the amount of material available to control outside stimuli or by increasing stimuli, "Children are fascinated by introduction of bright, colorful figures." The teachers also attribute to children certain characteristics that they value; for example, "Since children are free to make individual choices, they maintain a high degree of interest in the activities they choose." On the whole, the teachers feel very comfortable enacting program decisions based on a set of working assumptions about the children they teach.

DEMANDS ON CHILDREN

The teachers give considerable attention to individual children and describe their program as flexible and intuitive. However, this does not mean that they do not make extensive demands upon the children. The program has many of the characteristics of the "manners-and-morals" teaching of the traditional nursery program. The children are reminded that they must share and take turns with available equipment; they must stay seated during Circle Time; they must carry out the routine of picking up their own chairs and taking them to the tables or area they have chosen to work in; they must wait until all have been served before they eat their cookies or drink their juice; and they must sit in their individual cubbies while waiting to go out to the playground. Further emphasis is given to using manners and responding properly. The teachers often use some overt rewards such as the "paper hat ... sometimes given to the best helper," but generally it is the social approval of attention or the spoken word that the teachers employ as reinforcement for the child.

In general, then, while the atmosphere is openly permissive, the teachers do expect considerable compliance from the children in areas of routine, behavior control, and general manners.

ASSUMPTIONS ABOUT
OPERATION AND PROGRAM

Traditional nursery school teachers draw heavily upon personal beliefs about program and operations to guide their curriculum and teaching decisions. The unit-based teachers say, "We find that a great deal of teacher-pupil interaction is necessary in working with disadvantaged children." In carrying out this view they state, "We often have to be the instigators of new ideas." In handling planning and evaluation, the teachers "feel it is essential to have a well-planned day and to have the room prepared for the children before they arrive ... but there also has to be room for intuitive decisions by the teacher." They also feel that it is essential to have a clear focus on the individual child. "[We have] a great deal of flexibility in our program, a great deal of individual attention," and "Just as important as the planning is the evaluation ... [during which] each child is discussed and his individual needs identified."

Program activities in the traditional nursery curriculum are derived from the expressed interests of the children. These teachers followed that practice in part but also included a number of ideas of their own, drawn from intuitive assumptions about child development and learning or direct needs of the program. For example, they comment that learning body parts is a vital concept from the practical point of view: learning facial features is crucial to making pumpkins and masks for Halloween. This represents a definite shift into the intuitive area. The teachers know that the children will be going into a standard kindergarten program with large group instruction. Therefore, they provide opportunity for group experience within the nursery school. They select the program units on a very intuitive basis. "Using Fall as the first unit seemed natural since the Fall season makes the children more aware of their environment." Halloween became a unit "because we wanted children to see pumpkins growing in the field." When presenting a unit on Thanksgiving, the teachers decided that the historical background would have little meaning, so ". . . we concentrated on tangibles like food and art activities." Practical needs even influenced decisions about songs. "We felt that if we sang only one song, the frequent repetition of the words would result in greater participation." For the unit-based teachers, then, program decisions regarding actual curriculum plans were made on a practical intuitive basis rather than on a theoretical basis, making the particular curriculum a direct expression of their own views of preschool education.

Primarily, it is apparent that on the surface level the teachers did little ". . . watching and waiting for the child's needs to emerge and [to] determine the timing of different activities. . . ." On a deeper level, however, they did exactly that. After trying the usual techniques, the teachers found that the children could not respond. They then immediately made adjustments for the youngsters. They set many limits in order to avoid random play and impulsive and aggressive behavior: they consistently enforced rules and routine; they encouraged a great deal of teacher-pupil interaction; they instigated new ideas, especially in the area of dramatic play; they reduced the amount of material available so the children would be less distracted by outside stimuli; and they provided quiet alternative activities for youngsters who could not join the group activities. The children were allowed a great deal of flexibility, and much attention was given to each child. The teachers drew from their practical classroom experiences rather than from theoretical issues for the basis for critical program decisions. They also considered the child's general emotional state. The emphasis throughout the planning and evaluation was on the projected and actual impact of the daily activities on the individual child.

Perhaps the most important thing that can be said about this particular expression of the traditional nursery school program approach to teaching disadvantaged children is that it works unusually well in terms of measured intellectual and academic gains; it is one of the few examples of the traditional approach that does. This issue will be discussed next.

Unfortunately the focus of recent preschool research has been on the search for *the* curriculum to employ with disadvantaged children. The traditionally oriented curriculum presented in this paper was originally established as a "straw man" in the Ypsilanti Preschool Curriculum Demonstration Project, a study of the relative efficacy of several curriculum styles. When it was discovered that the measured results of the three curricula were essentially the same, considerable re-thinking was necessary.

This particular traditionally oriented *Unit-based Curriculum* was successful because it was required to function in the same setting with the same operational procedures and staff model goals as the experimental structured preschools with proven success records. Some of these issues have been discussed elsewhere (Weikart, 1969). Success in this program, then, seems to stem primarily from (1) the particular situation within which the program was operated, (2) the curriculum content included, (3) the manner in which the program was operated, and (4) the staff model that supported its operation.

1. THE SITUATION

The program was operated as part of the most recent of a sequence of preschool research projects. Over two thousand people visited the project, attending for periods ranging from one day to two weeks. The project was adequately funded with sufficient materials, space, and supplies. The entire eight-hour work day of the teachers was focused on the children; they taught for two and a half hours in the morning, made one and a half hour home visits in the afternoon, and spent the remaining time in program preparation. Visits by outsiders have enormous impact upon staff because it creates a need for constant attention to details as well as duty. The staff must be prepared at all times and must learn to be open-minded about their work. They must learn to be tough-minded and to accept criticism in the interest of research and exploration. If the teachers permit themselves to be deeply affected by the often thoughtless and insensitive comments of visitors, the project could not function. Having adequate funds for materials and supplies and a work load that "tells you" the administration feels that what you do with children is important gives teachers support in the areas in which they need it the most. But a demanding situation alone is not enough to produce the outstanding results these traditionally oriented teachers obtained. There have been many preschool research projects with visitors, adequate funding, etc. that have produced minimal or insignificant measured gains in children.

2. THE CURRICULUM

While the curriculum was traditionally oriented in its focus, the unit-based teachers did not hesitate to join the increasing number of traditionally oriented nursery schools which include extensive direct teaching of cognitive and language activities. For example, they taught coloring, pasting, and paper cutting, they read stories, worked with puppets, taught colors and shapes, and provided ample opportunity for free play with a doll corner, blocks, trucks, etc. Yet they also included an extensive language input component especially when the children did *not* respond. They taught body concepts, established temporal sequences, presented materials at various levels of representation, dealt with spatial relations, impulse control, classification, etc. Although the teachers did not use cognitive terminology in their discussion, the examples of activities illustrate the teaching of cognitive concepts. Thus, while the curriculum was traditional, it did include an extensive cognitive training component in a generally systematic way. The inclusion of some cognitive and language training appears to be a critical addition to successful preschool programs. However, it may not be for the training it provides the child but rather for the discipline it demands of the teacher.

3. THE OPERATION

The actual operation of the program included some fortuitous features that were the outcome of five years of preschool operational experience with disadvantaged children in the Ypsilanti Perry Preschool Project. Perhaps the most important of these procedures was a home teaching component. Each family (mother and child) received a 90-minute home teaching visit by the preschool teacher every two weeks. The goal of this visit was not so much to teach the mother how to teach her child but rather to help her become familiar with the educational process and to indicate how she may support that process in her youngster whenever possible.

A second factor in the preschool operation was the mixture of three and four-year-olds in the same classroom. The "cross-age" relationship with the resulting child-child interaction is a critical variable and one that the staff feels influenced the results of the program.

Most important, however, it was the intense focus on planning and evaluation that the teachers discuss in the excerpts. Lessons were planned for each week and each day of the week. Individual children were discussed and specific procedures evolved to assist them in taking the next step in the program. The individual child was the direct concern of the teachers, and aspects of program operation, such as the home visits, made that concern a reality. In concert with the planning was the evaluation that the planning process entailed. The evaluation procedures helped to create a focus for further planning.

4. STAFF MODEL

The staff model employed by the project determined its success. In this project, the classroom was established as a team-teaching setting without a head teacher.

This meant that the solutions developed for problems encountered by each of the two teachers could be utilized to improve the program. The common interest of the two staff members in creating an effective model program and in "fending off the world" at times also led to intense curriculum focus. Another essential part of the staff model was a supervisor who could deal directly with the teachers. The role of the supervisor was not to instruct the teachers in their tasks but to ask questions to establish clarity, to provide discipline so that the focus of the curriculum would remain constant, and to insure that problems inherent in program operation were not ignored and the opportunity for development they presented missed.

There are many components to a staff model, and it is difficult to identify the key one that will enable a curriculum to work. However, if one additional one had to be selected, it would be the need for a deep personal commitment of teachers to their program and children. It is this force that permits all else to occur and that enables them to teach and act like master teachers. . . . and obtain the same results that master teachers have historically produced.

CONCLUSIONS

From the initial assumption of the need for a specific, theoretically sound curriculum for successful preschool education, we have moved to a new view. The general search for the single technique or theory that would permit effective preschool experiences for disadvantaged children with specific activities, language training, equipment, and experiences is felt to be fruitless. The effort must go toward a much more complex and unexplored goal: How do we draw groups of adults and children together so that each can provide the situation with his unique contribution in terms of quality teaching and effective learning?

These two traditionally oriented unit-based teachers devised a program based on their own educational backgrounds and their perception of the children. What is to be emulated is not the curriculum they devised, but their efforts to create it, not the solutions they found for their problems, but their process of resolving those problems. If these teachers have demonstrated anything, it is that quality preschool education is available for those who need it if they are taught by people who can create the necessary environment. Our task is to provide teachers and children with the opportunity for success.

REFERENCES | 6

Bereiter, C. and Engelmann, S. *Teaching disadvantaged children in preschool.* Englewood Cliffs, N.J.: Prentice-Hall, 1966.

Campbell, D. and Frey, P. The implications of learning theory for the fade-out gains from compensatory education. In Hellmuth, J. (Ed.), *Disadvantaged child, Vol. 3, Compensatory education: A national debate.* New York: Bruner-Mazel, 1970.

Cicirelli, V., *et al.* The impact of Head Start; An evaluation of the effects of Head Start on children's cognitive and affective development. Westinghouse Learning Corporation and Ohio University, April 1969.

Fowler, W. Longitudinal study of early stimulation in the emergence of cognitive processes. Paper prepared for Social Science Research Council Conference on Preschool Education. University of Chicago, 1966.

Freeman, R. The alchemists in our public schools. In Hellmuth, J. (Ed.), *Disadvantaged child, Vol. 3, Compensatory education: A national debate.* New York: Bruner-Mazel, 1970.

Gray, S. Selected longitudinal studies of compensatory education – a look from the inside. Paper prepared for the annual meeting of the American Psychological Association, 1969.

Jencks, C. An alternative to endless school crisis – private schools for black children. *The New York Times Magazine,* November 3, 1968.

Karnes, M. B., Teska, J. A., and Hodgins, A. S. A longitudinal study of disadvantaged children who participated in three different preschool programs. Paper presented at the annual meeting of the American Educational Research Association, Los Angeles, California, 1969.

Klaus, R. and Gray, S. W. The early training project for disadvantaged children: A report after five years. *Monographs of the Society for Research in Child Development,* No. 120, 1968. Also see: Gray, S. W., and Klaus, R. The early training project: A seventh year report. Nashville: John F. Kennedy Center for Research on Education and Human Development, George Peabody College, 1969.

Hawkridge, D., Chalupsky, A., and Roberts, A. *A study of selected exemplary programs for the education of disadvantaged children.* Palo Alto: American Institutes for Research in the Behavioral Sciences, 1968.

Parker, R., Ambron, S., Danielson, G., Halbrook, M., and Levine, J. *Overview of cognitive and language programs for 3, 4, and 5-year-old children.* Center for Advanced Study in Education, City University of New York, 1970.

Reed, K. H. *The nursery school: a human relationships laboratory* (3rd Ed.). Philadelphia: Saunders, 1960. (1st Ed., 1950).

Sears, P. S. and Dowley, E. M. Research on teaching in the nursery school. In N. L. Gage (Ed.), *Handbook of research on teaching.* Chicago: Rand McNally, 1963.

Swift, J. Effects of early group experiences: The nursery school and day nursery. In Hoffman, M., and Hoffman, L., *Review of child development research.* New York: Russell Sage Foundation, 1964.

Weikart, D. Preliminary results from a longitudinal study of disadvantaged preschool children. Paper presented at the convention of the Council for Exceptional Children, St. Louis, Missouri, 1967.

Weikart, D. P. (Ed.), *Preschool intervention: Preliminary report of the Perry Preschool Project.* Ann Arbor, Michigan: Campus Publishers, 1967.

Weikart, D. A comparative study of three preschool curricula. A paper presented at the biennial meeting of the Society for Research in Child Development, Santa Monica, California, March 1969.

Weikart, D. and Lambie, D. Z. Preschool intervention through a home teaching program. In J. Hellmuth (Ed.), *The disadvantaged child, Vol. 2.* Special Child Publications, Inc., Seattle 1968.

Weikart, D., Deloria, D., Lawser, S., Weigerink, R. *Longitudinal results of the Ypsilanti Perry Preschool Project.* Washington, D.C.: U.S. Department of Health, Education, and Welfare, Office of Education, Bureau of Research, 1970.

Weikart, D., Rogers, L., Adcock, C., and McClelland, D. *The cognitively oriented curriculum: A framework for preschool teachers.* Washington, D.C.: National Association for the Education of Young Children, 1970.

Banta | *Introduction* | 7

A brief history of the American Montessori Society (AMS), a description of the theoretical base and educational philosophy underlying the operation of Montessori preschools, and a review of relevant research are presented in the following paper. In the introductory portion of the paper, Dr. Banta describes the formation and growth of the AMS amidst ever-increasing social interest, the problems arising as a result of social pressure for rapid growth, and the attempts to maintain "quality control" while expanding in numbers and geographic locations. As a program based upon a definite educational philosophy and having carefully specified materials and techniques, the AMS has already been faced with the problems and extensive responsibilities which may well be confronting directors of other preschool programs in the near future.

Particularly, Dr. Banta stresses the critical role of the teacher in implementing the program and the difficulties inherent in training teachers to "direct," in a consistent and uniform manner, a preschool program which may or may not be consistent with their own teaching styles and attitudes. Thus the *written* philosophy of a preschool program constitutes the "myth," the variety of implementations of the myth constitutes reality, and the goal is congruence between myth and reality.

The American Montessori Society is based upon the developmental theory, educational philosophy, and instructional materials formulated and developed by Maria Montessori. The main goal of the AMS preschool is to provide the setting and materials through which the child, intrinsically motivated, may himself develop his intellectual, physical, and psychological abilities.

The key Montessori concept is the planned environment, and all materials are carefully designed to hold the child's interest and to teach. Each piece of material is part of a graded series, and each has built-in error control, i.e., the material itself indicates that an error has been made so that the child may correct himself through experimentation. The Montessori environment is usually divided into the three categories of motor education, sensory education, and language and mathematics education.

The Montessori teacher's role is to facilitate learning, to facilitate the development of concentration. The teacher carefully demonstrates the appropriate use of materials and then allows the child to use them on his own while she maintains a classroom atmosphere which is orderly and conducive to concentration and while she observes the child. The child is free to work with materials of his own choice (and therefore at his own cognitive level), and to proceed at his own pace. Overall, the Montessori preschool is designed to provide the child with "freedom within limits."

Thomas J. Banta

Montessori: Myth or Reality?

7

THE AMERICAN MONTESSORI SOCIETY

Mr. Gilbert E. Donahue, the American Montessori Society's sociologist and historian, has pointed out that "...when you touch the preschool child within the American family, you are touching a vital nerve in the body politic within our society and are exposing deep-rooted values, hopes, as well as anxieties" (Donahue, 1966, p. 3). This analysis reflected the ambivalence of American Montessorians when the word "Montessori," several years ago, was written on education pages of almost every newspaper in the country. The Montessori materials made good visual presentation, and the philosophy of freedom within structure made good copy. Usually the journalists' claim was that your child could be taught to read by the age of three. The historical setting was a fertile one for news of this educational reform.

The Montessori method, as described in the mass media, suggested to many persons that here was an answer to the anxieties raised by Russia's Sputnik. In 1960, Nancy McCormick Rambusch started the first Montessori training course in the U.S. While this program undoubtedly began with dreams of future success, little did the original supporters know (how could they know precisely?) that they were about to be overwhelmed by passionate curiosity and endless inquiries by

Thomas J. Banta is at the University of Cincinnati. Printed by permission of the author.

educators, both public and private, both professional and amateur. As Donahue (1966) indicated:

> ... *when the time for an idea has arrived, it frequently transcends and makes feeble the efforts of its originators to control it. In the social unrest and popular concern with education during this period, the agitation started by Mrs. Rambusch evoked a response which soon overwhelmed the limited resources available to her for any orderly and systematic development of the movement. Unless it has been experienced, the social pressures of a popular response, such as those which confronted Mrs. Rambusch, are simply unbelievable (p. 3).*

The American Montessori Society was born out of this overwhelming interest. "Organized in 1960 with the support of the Trustees of Whitby School who were also its initial Board, the American Montessori Society was originally the name given to the promotional and 'extension' activities of Mrs. Rambusch as she encouraged the development of a community of Montessori associations and schools in this country" (Donahue, 1966).

The development of Montessori schools continues. Eleven years ago there was one Montessori school in the U.S.; today there are 762 operating, of which 172 are affiliated with AMS. "Affiliated" means that there is at least one American Montessori Society (AMS) certified teacher on the school's staff, and that the school complies with standards established for affiliation. The maintenance of these standards is accomplished through the AMS's Visitation Program. The Visitation Team is described (American Montessori Society, 1970) as providing "... effective counseling, suggestions for curriculum enrichment, guidance, exchange of information and innovative data. Visitation is mandatory during the first two years of affiliation, at the school's expense" (p. 2). Thus, the 11,732 children who are today being educated in AMS-affiliated schools have the benefit of some degree of quality control from this centralized operation. After the first two years, the visitations are arranged at least once every three years.

The three main functions of the AMS are 1. information and promotion of the basic Montessori philosophy, 2. teacher training and certification, and 3. the maintenance of quality controls. Each of these functions is much more complex than this simple summary appears, and there are other subsidiary functions as well. The "basic Montessori philosophy" is continuously undergoing change, either in the form of different interpreters or in the form of modifications of the original conceptions in the light of psychological and child development research.

"Teacher training" varies from location to location, and "quality controls" are difficult to maintain on the basis of a few hours' visitation. Thus, there is a fairly uniform Montessori philosophy and less uniform practice. The same is true of all educational systems. There is the uniform and continuous myth, which guides the non-uniform and discrete fact of everyday life in the classroom.

There are virtues, it should be noted, in such non-uniformity. The importance of individual differences in teaching style are not inhibited, nor is innovation stifled by rigid interpretation of what Dr. Montessori wrote in the early part of this century. The AMS is aware of this problem, and it is worth noting that they have achieved a "negative identity" with their European counterpart, the Association Montessori Internationale (AMI) (headed by Montessori's son Mario Montessori) which the American group regards as much more rigid and primarily dedicated to the charismatic attraction and perpetuation of Maria Montessori, the mythic character.

The AMS is a complex organization reacting to and adapting to complex inputs. It is currently searching for its "positive identity," its major points of emphasis, and the directions of its most productive growth. Its leadership has not always been united as to what constitutes these emphases. For example, AMS has always been in the curious position of necessary caution about more publicity and more interest in the movement, "creating demands which it could not fulfill with proper quality in a responsible, professional manner" (Donahue, personal communication). As Donahue (1966) indicated, "For AMS a substantial increase in the demands for its services might worsen its financial health . . . if you are operating at a deficit, increasing your operations will only increase your deficits and intensify the strain on already overloaded personnel" (p. 8). At the same time, refusal to expand could lead to loss of support and in effect would be a failure to fulfill the objectives of the organization.

There is now greater pressure in the area of teacher training. Current AMS President, T. E. Calleton, (1970) points out that ". . . those parents, boards, and schools who were satisfied with any teacher a few years ago are now demanding a better product from the teacher training course" (p. 1). In the past three years Master's Degree programs have been established in the Schools of Education at Xavier University in Cincinnati, and at Oklahoma University in Norman, Oklahoma. Five other training programs exist in: Chicago (2); Drayton Plains, Michigan; Los Angeles; and Belmont, California. There were 160 new teachers last year; this year there will be 120, and there are currently over 100 teacher vacancies listed. One recommendation to committees setting up Montessori schools is that they sponsor a teacher's training with the understanding that the teacher return to the school upon receiving certification.

The key problem today for AMS is the maintenance of quality training for teachers. The teacher is in the critical position in the interface between the method and the child. All other AMS functions, from an education perspective and from the child's perspective, are subordinate to teacher quality.

However high the priority on teacher quality, the organization in fact must attend to other business as well. Aside from internal issues arising from administration of the society, fee structures and the like, Donahue (1966) again has done a thorough job of emphasizing the main programs which need development or maintenance by AMS. The following 12 areas were cited: 1. developing and distributing information to its members, to the educational and scientific communities, and to the general public on various aspects of Montessori activities; 2. collecting and evaluating current research; 3. cooperating at national and local levels with other organizations to further the well-being of American children; 4. establishment of additional Montessori schools; 5. maintaining standards on Montessori schools; 6. establishing training programs and standards; 7. teacher certification and awards; 8. fostering in-service and continuing education programs; 9. provision of teacher placement services and benefit plans; 10. supervision of preparation, manufacture, and distribution of materials and equipment; 11. development of research facilities and programs; and 12. representing the Montessori movement in legislative and other public policy situations.

This is an extensive, complex, and demanding program. The AMS may or may not be able to carry out all such plans. With a large budget and greater centralization of organization, it might be done efficiently. But as Donahue shows, historically, "The AMS . . . has never been a centralized 'corporate-type' organization with branches in various parts of the country, but has evolved as a federation of semi-autonomous affiliates" (p. 10). The AMS is several things: it is a voluntary association incorporated under the laws of Connecticut; it is an "amateur" society of parents and other laymen "who share a concern that their own children and others in our society obtain a better education than has been available through other alternatives"; and it is potentially a professional society for teachers, staff members of the AMS, researchers, and salaried administrators. No organization can be all things to all people. While AMS had tried to do this in the past, it is currently at the stage where it must consolidate its energies and programs.

PARENTHESIS ON WHAT IS, WHAT IS THOUGHT TO BE, AND WHAT CAN BE

Is the Montessori Method a myth or reality? Is there sufficient uniformity so that in reality there is a method? "With myth, everything becomes possible," says one anthropologist (Levi-Strauss, 1967, p. 204). Thus as we read through the many volumes of Montessori's lectures and essays, and as these writings become interpreted variously by professionals and laymen, by the AMS, by Americans for Americans, we become aware that our knowledge of *any* educational method is mythic in character. The day-to-day behavior of teachers and children can only partly be characterized by abstract verbal descriptions.

In a one-page summary of the Montessori Method, distributed by the AMS, certain key ideas appear, by which they wish Montessori to be mythically known. Virtually all Montessorians are quick to agree that in practice these ideals are implemented in different ways by different teachers for different populations of children. Still there is the fundamental belief in a fundamental core of "Method," of basic strategies for structuring the interaction between the child, his environment, and the "teacher." For example, these fragments are frequently repeated among Montessorians:

> ...freedom – a freedom to be – achieved through order and self-discipline...mastery of himself and his environment..."prepared environment"...develop at his own speed, according to his own capacities...noncompetitive atmosphere..."Never let a child risk failure, until he has a responsible chance of success," said Dr. Montessori...years between three and six...acquisition of good manners and habits, to take his place in his culture...teaching materials are designed to make conscious his understanding and to signal appropriate responses...self-motivation...teacher prepares the environment..."inner discipline"...concentration, stick-to-itiveness, and thoroughness...programmed learning and non-teacher....

These ideals, of course, have been incorporated in other types of programs, yet this makes them no less central to the Montessori orientation. The quality-conscious Montessorian, however, in my experience has insisted that not all classrooms show these features at their best. Some of the same themes are apparent in another brochure put out by the AMS Public Relations Committee. The brochure begins with the question about Montessori Education, "What is it?" Here is their answer:

> *This system of education is both a philosophy of child growth and a rationale for guiding such growth. It is based on the child's developmental needs for freedom within limits, and a carefully prepared environment which guarantees exposure to materials and experiences through which to develop intelligence as well as physical and psychological abilities. It is designed to take full advantage of the self-motivation and unique ability of young children to develop their own capabilities. The child needs adults to expose him to the possibilities of his life but the child himself must direct his response to those possibilities.*

Key premises of Montessori education are:

1. Children are to be respected as being different from adults, and as individuals who differ from each other.

2. The child possesses unusual sensitivity and mental powers for absorbing and learning from his environment that are unlike those of the adult both in quality and capacity.
3. The most important years of growth are the first six years of life when unconscious learning is gradually brought to the conscious level.
4. The child has a deep love and need for purposeful work. He works, however, not as an adult for profit and completion of a job, but for the sake of the activity itself. It is this activity which accomplishes for him his most important goal: the development of himself — his mental, physical, and psychological powers. (American Montessori Society)

It is well agreed within the Montessori movement that these are fundamental ideals to be pursued in early education. Not too much emphasis on curriculum and content, but more emphasis on style and approach toward purposeful, self-chosen work. Thus, such brief description for the general public constitutes a mythic ideal, which is something to aim at; it does not describe the gun which does the shooting. Detailed descriptions become the next step. In another brochure, "Developing a Local Montessori Organization and School," two books are highly recommended: *The Montessori Method* by Montessori and *Learning How to Learn* by Nancy McCormick Rambusch. It is further suggested that "It is helpful to visit an established Montessori school."

Thus, one is guided from the general to the specific, and as one so moves, it becomes increasingly clear that the myth must be looked to for uniformity. Practice makes, not perfect myth, but imperfect myth. From the one-page statement, to the two-book description, to the many-faceted observations of an actual school, variety is inherent in Montessori practice. The teacher as observer, as preparer of the environment, and as participant in the AMS "federation of autonomous local units" is free to interpret and put into practice a *personal* version of the mythic "Montessori." The standard materials are there, true; but the teacher is watching the child, not the material, and it is that human interaction that becomes significant. No one expects a one or two-year training program to *transform* the person to a standard form or function.

My own conviction is that the electronic medium will be the appropriate message for sharing in the Montessori myth. Videotape can help capture the expert teaching episodes. Glen Nimnicht is already doing this with his New Nursery School format. There are master teachers of the Montessori persuasion. A high priority item is the capturing of this talent on electronic tape for visual and auditory retrieval, so that the coming teachers may more effectively capture the method and practice, and so that we non-Montessorians may better be able to sit in judgment. What follows is my best effort to capture the Montessori Method in linear, verbal form. I have omitted much of the charismatic, spiritual-religious quality of the original writing. One of my graduate students thanked me for that; her own experience of reading Montessori was so obscured by the objectional mystical qualities that the scientific-clinical virtues were all but lost. The material below is a presentation of Montessori Method as it can be and as it might be.

Certainly one of the outstanding features of the Montessori Method, and the one which impresses most persons who view a classroom for the first time, is the array of attractive materials. The first impression is that a lot of money has been spent on well-made toys, but further observation shows that they are in fact carefully designed teaching materials, each with a specific purpose. Each piece of material in the graded series was originally carefully developed through observation of retarded children's reactions. Each piece had to fit the child's hand properly; each item was attractively colored; a set of items was designed to emphasize *one* dimension to be learned and did not present a distracting or confusing array of stimuli, especially in the elementary materials. In short, the material had to *hold the child's interest,* and it had to *teach.*

How do materials teach? The major concept Montessori used was that of *error control* built into the materials. That is, each piece of equipment was built so that when an error is made, the material itself reveals the error and provides a way for the child himself to correct it through experimentation.

The knobbed cylinders provide a good example of error control. The material consists of ten small cylinders all of the same height, but with a diameter decreasing from thick to thin. The exercise consists of removing all the cylinders, mixing them up, and replacing each in its proper place. The child first makes a few trials. Many errors are made; the child attempts to place a large cylinder in a small hole, then he places it in a larger hole. Trying and testing each one, he typically finds that almost all the cylinders have been replaced, but there are one or two that do not fit. Thus it is evident from the material itself that more work needs to be done. Some cylinders have too much room, and this is discovered by the child. The assumption is that the child need not be told, need not be interrupted, in order for him to succeed at a task that interests him.

Once the cylinders have been replaced properly, many children will continue the exercise, repeating it many times. For example, in *Dr. Montessori's Own Handbook* (Montessori, 1965), she says, "Little children from three to three-and-a-half-years-old have repeated the exercise up to *forty* times without losing their interest in it." Not everyone immediately sees the value of such repetition. In one copy of the book I examined, an unsympathetic reader added a comment in the margin: "So what?" This indignant annotation reveals a common misunderstanding about the mental life of the child, and modern psychology is just rediscovering what Montessori became convinced of early in this century — intellectual development comes through sensory development and it is this expression of triumph which is shown in repetition of an activity. For the child of mental age three, self-initiated repetition is an important avenue to impressing

The Preschool in Action

simple concepts upon his mind. At this stage of development, repetition is an expression of interest, and Montessori, first and foremost, knew the value of interest in effective educational procedures.

It is always fascinating to note how interested children are in watching the slow, deliberate, knowing illustration of the teacher. If this were a meaningless exercise in compulsive routine, the child would be the first to let you know it. The proof is in the observation of many children who attend carefully to such instructions and intensively use what they have learned in completing the exercise. It was part of Montessori's genius that she emphasized detail and saw its importance *in light of the child's behavior.* Above all, she was an excellent observer and would never have retained a purposeless aspect of a lesson if children did not respond to it with interest. That is a good perspective for all teachers—the burden of correct teaching is not on the child, but on the teacher and the discovery of good methods.

Another detail should be noted. The shape of the solid wood in which the cylinders are inserted has been cut to a shape convenient for a small hand to grasp and hold easily. Thus, from the very start of the exercise, which involves the child's removing the material from its place on a shelf, the child finds that this is an activity which fits him. The act of bringing his own material to his table or rug is not confounded by awkward movements or outsized material. The entire process is guaranteed to enhance the arousal of the child's interest and intelligence.

Before we leave this example, it is worth noting some further details about the design of this particular exercise. For example, the knobs on top of each cylinder are not just convenient handles, but are designed to help the child develop fine motor coordination — in this case, finger-thumb opposition, similar to that involved in grasping a pencil. Thus, the teacher, when demonstrating this material, carefully shows the child how to pick up each piece by hand with two fingers and a thumb, rather than in the fist, as some children are at first inclined to do. Each step — grasping the knob, slowly lifting the cylinder, placing it *quietly* on the table, etc. — is given detailed attention by the teacher.

Each and every piece of Montessori equipment was designed to serve the child's natural tendency to work and learn. It is worth examining the range of material available. The Montessori environment is usually divided into three categories: 1. motor education; 2. sensory education; and 3. language and mathematics. The most relevant material for the trainable retardate is the motor and sensory equipment.

Motor or muscular education has reference to the organization and control of the spontaneous movements of the child (which some persons unfortunately have viewed as "never keeping still," "always getting into something," or "unruliness" and "naughtiness"). Montessori sought to outline exercises which organize and coordinate such movement so they will be useful. She saw the relevance of the following procedures for effective development:

Movements of everyday life (walking, rising, sitting, handling objects).
Care of the person.
Management of the household.
Gardening.
Manual work.
Gymnastics.
Rhythmic movements.

Dressing and undressing is seen as the first step in the care of the person. Several frames for teaching lacing, buttoning, buckling, and snapping are used. This exercise, with its own built-in error control, is taken seriously as a precursor to effective intellectual development. Without such motor coordination and impulse control, future development of higher mental processes is not effective. The child is shown, by the teacher, slowly and deliberately, how the material must be brought together so that the edges line up from top to bottom; then the teacher shows, step by step, the separate aspects of completing each buckle, button, or other fastener.

Similarly, pouring, polishing, and shoe polishing are practiced, as well as other relevant household management activities, such as table setting, washing, sweeping, and mopping. There is not space here to describe in detail each of these procedures but it is important to note that these are real, not "play" activities. The table is set because the children are going to eat or have a snack. Mopping is done when something is spilled. Real glass is used rather than plastic since glass when dropped provides its own error control through breakage. But small glasses are used, mops are scaled down to the child's size, and the bucket is suitable for the child to carry. As Nancy Rambusch (1970) has pointed out, "Montessori did not arbitrarily divide work from play. She liked the word 'work' better than the word 'play'" (p. 6). The key idea here is that work and play need not be separate and alienated one from the other.

Singing and rhythmic exercises are likewise used to develop motor coordination and a sense of order and organization. Each exercise is a meaningful activity; it is done with a sense of purpose, interest, and enjoyment, never as a routine or ritual. *Completion* of work is kept in view. When Montessori first taught retarded children, she put everything away herself when the child finished but noted that the children wanted to get up and follow her to the shelves. Montessori capitalized on this curiosity and interest and showed each child how to walk slowly and carefully, carrying each item securely in two hands. Children readily adopted this practice, and on any Montessori classroom day, one can see children taking great pains to replace their material exactly where it belongs. There is evidently a sense in which competence, however simple it may appear to the adult, is a valuable part of the child's world. There is a manifest sense of pride and satisfaction when the child shows a good finish to his work.

Sensory education and language education are developed through the graded didactic materials. The child may show little interest in these materials at first, in which case the directress follows the lead of the child and allows him to work with the practical life and other motor education materials. Until he shows a readiness to work in a sustained purposeful way when introduced periodically to the didactic materials, no special emphasis is placed on them. However, when the child shows interest, the teacher nurtures this with individual instruction or includes him in a small group lesson.

There is a wide variety of didactic materials designed to improve perception of touch, hearing, and vision. Other materials emphasize concepts of volume, length, weight, etc. Following is a list of the best-known materials. For more detail, see *The Montessori Method* (1964), *Dr. Montessori's Own Handbook* (1965a), and *The Montessori Elementary Material* (1917).

Knobbed cylinders: a. varying in diameter only, b. varying in height only, and c. varying in both diameter and height.

Three sets of solids, in graduated sizes, including: a. the *Pink Tower,* consisting of ten wooden cubes diminishing from ten centimeters to one centimeter; b. the *Broad Stair,* ten wooden prisms painted brown, each twenty centimeters in length, and like the Pink Tower, the square sides diminish from ten to one centimeter; and c. the *Long Stair,* ten rods, four centimeters square, and marked off alternately in red and blue, varying length from ten centimeters to one meter.

> Various geometric solids — prism, pyramid, sphere, cylinder, cone, etc.
> Rectangular tablets with rough and smooth surfaces.
> Small wooden tablets of different weights.
> Colored tablets of varying shades.
> A chest of drawers containing plane insets.
> A series of cards with outlines corresponding to the geometric shapes of the plane insets.
> A series of cylindrical, closed boxes, identical in shape but matched in pairs for sound when shaken.
> A series of paired musical bells.

All these materials serve to acquaint the child with basic discriminations learned through systematic sensorial inputs. The geometric solids, for example, are looked at, handled, named, and compared. Exercises are performed, when the child is ready, with blindfold: touching, identifying, and naming.

It should be noted that materials are interrelated. When the Pink Tower is mastered, the Broad Stair is introduced; still, ordering in terms of volume is the key concept being learned. Similarly, the Long Stair involves only variations in length, based on the already familiar unit of ten centimeters, touched and handled while working with the Pink Tower and Broad Stair.

Montessori: Myth or Reality?

In all sensorial material, one principle or organization of the lessons is very important. Montessori found that the best order of procedure in every sensory training method was to proceed as follows:

1. recognition of *identities* (the pairing of similar objects or the insertion of solid forms into places which fit them);
2. recognition of *contrasts* (the presentation of the extremes of a series of objects); and lastly,
3. discrimination between objects very *similar* to one another.

All this provides the basis for moving on to discrimination and judgment involved in the language and mathematics materials. These materials include sandpaper letters, to be traced with a finger to familiarize the child with the sensory aspects of letter shapes; colored cardboard alphabets for spelling; sandpaper and cardboard materials for sensory aspects of numerals' shapes; boxes of sticks for counting; and beads and cubes for counting from one (a one-centimeter bead) to one thousand (a 10 x 10 x 10-centimeter cube of beads).

Proper use of the materials takes many hours of observation and practice. But there is no reason why good teachers cannot adapt the parts of the method that appeal to them in their work with the child. Ideally, one should see these materials and methods in practice.

It is now necessary to turn to other characteristics of the method and to review some of the research findings which throw some light on the validity of the method.

ANALYSIS OF THE METHOD

Essentially, there are three main areas which provide a basis for analyzing Montessori Methods: 1. her developmental theory; 2. her educational program and didactic materials; and 3. her views on the role of the teacher and the teacher-child relationship. All three areas are currently points of controversy between Montessorians and "non-Montessorians." "Non-Montessorians" is in quotes because until recently, the best alternative label for nursery school practice has been "traditional," the most non-specific and unhelpful designation. But now we have other systems (Bereiter, O. K. Moore, Nimnicht, or the behavior modifiers) competing for our attention. Some educators have suggested that Montessori ideas have taken hold in part because they are *named*. It has not been very distinguishing or prestigeful to be called a traditionalist or a non-Montessorian.

It is very encouraging to see that Nimnicht, for example, references some degree of debt to the ideas of Montessori in the development of his New Nursery

School curriculum. In some respects, Nimnicht's work is more in the spirit of Montessori's experimental ideas than some of the work of the Montessori adherents themselves, who are simply bent on mechanical application of her didactic materials and deification of the dottoressa. I cannot believe, however, that Montessori herself was rigid, mechanical, or ritualistic. She was too much a scientist, too sensitive an observer for that.

> At the Bicêtre, where I spent some time, I saw that it was the didactic apparatus of Seguin far more than his method which was being used.... The teaching there was purely mechanical; each teacher following the rules according to the letter.
> *(The Montessori Method, p. 36)*

DEVELOPMENTAL THEORY

Put simply, Montessori had great faith in the positive growth tendencies of the child, normal and retarded alike. In *The Montessori Method* (Montessori, 1964), she says, "To stimulate life — leaving it then free to develop, to unfold — herein lies the first task of the educator." She postulated four normal growth periods. The first is from birth to six, and this is made up of two sub-phases, birth to three and three to six. In the first sub-phase, the child's mind is not subject to direct approach or influence. Certainly she would now change that position in the light of recent experimental findings. The second sub-phase consists of the same mental type (mainly learning from sensory-motor contact with the environment), but with the possibility of direct adult influence resulting in profound changes in personality. Between three and six, nursery school age, she states that the mind begins to control the child and in this period, the child needs help in acquiring self-directed concentration and abilities.

Montessori emphasizes that even under six, a child's real interest is to be always at work. Rambusch (1970) points out "Montessori knew that young children learned through movement, and that at no time in the growth and development of a young child ought an adult inhibit movement arbitrarily except for very real and serious reasons" (p. 3). This is similar to Piaget's recent admonition, "you cannot teach concepts verbally; you must use a method founded on activity" (Hall, 1970, p. 30).

Montessori's developmental theory and educational procedures apply to the "retarded" just as they apply to "normal" children. The retarded child is simply a human being who comes to be interested in materials that are lower in the graded scale of sophistication, a person who takes longer to move from one level of difficulty to another, and one who may need closer attention from the directress or her assistant. But in no case is the ideal of a child concentrating on self-chosen projects sacrificed. The teacher's job is that of preparing the environment so that the child can prepare himself for life. "Retarded" and "normal" are, in a sense then, inappropriate labels. All are members of the same species; all exist on the same continuum; the differences are a matter of degree.

Montessori's view of retardation is an essentially optimistic one. Although trained in medicine, she was reluctant to conceptualize retardation in terms of disease or other relatively permanent status. She said, "I felt that mental deficiency presented chiefly a pedagogical, rather than mainly a medical, problem." How closely this resembles "modern" psychological thought!

> *If you watch a child of three, you will see that he is always playing with something. This means that he is working out, and making conscious, something that his unconscious mind has earlier absorbed.... The hands are the instrument of man's intelligence.*
> (The Absorbent Mind, p. 26)

The next period, from six to twelve, brings the flowering of conscience and socialization. Once the concentration and self-direction comes, a child becomes joyful, careful, and conserving of things; responsible toward and loving of his fellows. This is a period of growth unaccompanied by other change; it is a period of calm, health, and assured stability.

The third period, from twelve to eighteen, Montessori says "is a period of so much change as to remind one of the first." The final period of full maturity is not marked by further physical changes, and Montessori has little to say about the role of later socio-cultural effects on adult education.

It is part of Montessori's genius that she was able to profit from what others have seen as "just obvious." She noted that educational theorists have been slow to see that if at six a child can go to school, understand directions, find his way around, etc., he surely had already learned a great deal and undergone considerable cognitive development. Her aim then was to capitalize particularly on this sub-phase of the first period where adult influence can be felt and during which much useful learning occurs.

> *Development is a series of re-births.*
> *(The Absorbent Mind, p. 17)*

One should note that the Montessori developmental periods not only coincide with the official educational designations but also generally agree with the developmental periods of Piaget: Sensory-motor, Pre-operational, Concretely Operational, and Formally Operational. Similarly, she views these periods, not simply as sequential events, but as manifestly different psychological types, different ways of viewing the world. To understand the child at each age, it is necessary to communicate with him in appropriate mental terms. Thus, when the child repeats and repeats an activity, one does not criticize him for his repetitiveness. The teacher understands that between three and six, washing a mirror over and over, for example, is a form of important learning, there being so many learnings about smooth, flat surfaces, reflecting surfaces, angles of incidence, rectangular forms, edges, right angles, etc., that are most profitably acquired through repetition of sensory-motor activities.

EDUCATIONAL PROGRAM AND DIDACTIC MATERIALS

The "planned environment" is a key Montessori idea. The classroom in every detail is designed exclusively for the child. The weight and size of furniture, the height of wash stands and shelves, reflect consideration for the appropriate environmental scale suitable for the three and four-year-old child. Ideally, the program permits freedom of movement, requires orderliness, and prevents improper uses of materials. "Improper use" does not mean restrictiveness or discouragement of creative variations. The didactic materials were carefully designed to provide important basic learning for the child, and random, disruptive, or destructive uses are looked upon as improper. Thus, careful demonstrations of key qualities of each set of materials are typically provided, either individually or in a group, before the material is made available for free use in the classroom.

The relevance of the care with which Montessori describes her lesson technique is shown clearly when we summarize the six steps of initiating a new learning with didactic material. Exceptionally good detail is given in *The Discovery of the Child* (Montessori, 1948), the chapter titled, "The Technique of the Lessons." *Isolating the object* is first: "the child's attention must be isolated from everything but the object of the lesson. She will therefore take care to clear a table of everything else and place on it only the material she wishes to present" (p. 169). Next is *working exactly:* this consists of showing the child how to use the material properly, and typically, she "performs the exercise herself once or twice, removing, for example, the cylinders from the solid insets, then mixing them up, and putting them back in position by a process of trial and error." Then she emphasizes *rousing the attention:* whenever a teacher offers an object to a child, she should not do so coldly but rather display a lively interest in what she is doing and attract the attention of the child to it. *Preventing errors in using the material* is divided into two parts: errors controlled by the material itself, which will be corrected by further development of the child, and errors "due to a kind of ill will, to negligence on the part of the teacher. When material is used wrongly so as to create confusion, or for needs that it cannot satisfy, it is .... not really used at all.... It cannot be said that one learns by making mistakes of this type. The longer one persists in such an error, the farther removed he is from the possibility of learning." Then, *respect for useful activity* covers the child's tendency to repeat successful learnings: "the teacher will permit him to continue to repeat the same exercise or make his own experiments as often as he wants without interrupting him in his efforts, either to correct slight errors or to stop his work through fear of his becoming tired." Finally, *a good finish:* "when a child has spontaneously given up an exercise . . . .the teacher, if need be, can, and indeed must, intervene so that the child puts the material back in place and everything is left in perfect order."

Since one goal of the Montessori curriculum is to communicate specific ideas to the child, the teacher's intervention sometimes is useful to diagnose the degree of learning that has been accomplished. The famous three-staged lesson, originally used by Seguin, has been found useful not only for "defective" children but for normal children as well. The First Stage consists of associating sense perceptions with names. The teacher says of one surface, "It is smooth"; of another, "It is rough." Both object and name should come to the child's understanding at the same time. In the Second Stage, the teacher checks to see if her lesson has had good effect. Several moments later, the teacher asks the child "Which one is *smooth?*"; "Which one is *rough?*" The child indicates his answer by pointing, and the teacher persists in asking the child many times. If the child does not attend well or is otherwise distracted, the lesson is terminated. In no case does the teacher insist upon the exercise. Learning is the child's choice, and when he makes a mistake, it indicates his lack of readiness at that time, not his inability or inferiority. Montessori points out that for the teacher to say "No, you are mistaken," would make more of an impression on the child than the learning of the names. The Third Stage checks on the child's ability to generate the object name himself. "What is this?" If the child is ready, "he will reply with the proper word: 'It is *smooth.*' 'It is *rough.*' " If the child does not pronounce clearly, the teacher makes note of it and follows up with corrective exercises in pronunciation at a later time.

The above examples provide some idea of the degree of attention to the small matters of education that make a difference. All these teaching procedures are supported by well-designed didactic materials which are part of the total educational program. For Montessori, these materials are not just toys, but "learning preparations" to facilitate the child's innate interest in the world when something interesting is provided.

> *The first essential for the child's development is concentration. It lays the whole basis for his character and social behavior. He must find out how to concentrate, and for this he needs things to concentrate on.*
>
> *(The Absorbent Mind, p. 221)*

To summarize, the program involves three areas of effort that are more or less in sequence:

1. Exercises of practical life: polishing, pouring, buttoning.
2. Sensory discriminations: texture, weight, shape, temperature, rhythm, tones, odors, tastes.
3. Conversion of manual dexterity into writing, visual and auditory into reading, and all of this into physical and mathematical concepts.

There are two important aspects of each of the pieces of equipment; each piece is part of a *graded series,* and each piece is designed to provide feedback to the child when errors are made *(error control).* The graded series provides a wide array of difficulty. This facilitates the child's choosing at his own level of cognitive development, so that he can proceed to the more difficult task when he is ready, or stay with simpler materials. Error control built into the material itself permits the child to function autonomously, without unnecessary dependence on the adult.

One is tempted to conjecture that the prepared environment is a good reality-contact "teaching machine." Montessori pointed out that "it is not simply the object used for the training of the senses and developing habits but the whole environment that is designed to make it easy to correct mistakes.... Bright colors and shining surfaces reveal stains. The light furniture, when it is tipped over or noisily dragged over the floor, tells of movements which are still clumsy and imperfect. The whole environment thus becomes a kind of instructor or sentinel always on the alert" (Montessori, 1948).

Thus the *materials* and the *prepared environment,* built to provide error control; along with a *teacher,* demonstrating appropriate use; and a *child,* interested in the world around him, combine to make the effective learning setting. In addition, there is intentionally only one set of materials for the entire classroom. This sets up a condition of necessary cooperation as a means to fair access to these attractive materials. Social skills, combined with individual effort, are part of the prepared environment's intended effect.

> *I was often asked, "But how do you make these tinies behave so well? How do you teach them discipline?" It was not I. It was the environment we had prepared so carefully and the freedom they found in it.*
> *(The Absorbent Mind, p. 223)*

THE TEACHER AND TEACHER-CHILD RELATIONSHIPS

What then is the role of the teacher in the carefully prepared environment? Certainly her attitude is one of humility. The word "teacher," in fact, may carry too much of a connotation from conventional education, centering too much on the accomplishments of the adult, rather than the accomplishments of the child.

The translation from the Italian of Montessori's word is "directress," although this itself is not quite accurate. One of the very fine Montessori teachers here in Cincinnati who studied with Montessori, Hilda Rothschild, suggested that her teaching is *indirect*. Perhaps, "indirectress" is the accurate designation for the Montessori teacher. In any event, her function is that of facilitating learning, not one of pushing, forcing, or insisting.

The teacher may interact freely with new young children to make them comfortable and to allow them time to learn their way around and familiarize themselves with other children and the new equipment. The teacher ultimately wants to withdraw into a position of being indirective — her job is not to talk but to arrange for the child's emergent motivation to work with the materials and model the older or more advanced children's behavior. The teacher's mastery of presentation of materials permits her to study the child's behavior and thought patterns intensively. Thus the teacher's role as observer is enhanced, making for an additional gain from using the standard equipment. Rather than mechanizing the teacher-child relationship, the Montessori materials humanize the relationship.

The child is not rewarded, graded, corrected, scolded, nor congratulated when working. He is simply shown. The teacher may divert a child who would otherwise create a disturbance to others. She may prevent destructive actions, but she will not punish nor scold a child. Montessori's chapter "Discipline" in *The Montessori Method* (Montessori, 1964) is a favorite of many teachers, and in it she cautions that the will of the child should be encouraged, not destroyed by punishment.

"So what must she look out for?" Montessori asks, and her answer is clear: "That one child or another will begin to concentrate" (Montessori, 1949, p. 277). First, the new children will be restless, and to the uninitiated this will seem so predominant and so salient that one might wonder if the classroom will ever come to anything at all. But in this first stage such behaviors are to be expected and at this time the teacher's attention should not be focused on the children but on the appearance of the room, the materials, and herself. Her job in this stage, like all stages of the Montessorian education, is to be a good *observer*.

> One who follows my method teaches little, observes a great deal, but rather directs the psychic activities of the children and their physiological development. This is why I have changed her name from teacher to that of "directress."
>
> *(Discovery of the Child, p. 179)*

The teacher's observations center on signs of the child's interest in work. But the approach is indirect and the teacher must use her personality and skills in clever ways. Montessori pointed out that "Every action of the teacher's can become a call and an invitation to the children" (Montessori, 1948, p. 279). Thus a lively teacher, interested in those things which attract children, from a walk in a garden to polishing a brass jug, is the beginning of development of interest on the part of the child.

For the child who persistently annoys other children, Montessori recommends a simple tactic. Interrupt him. When the child is involved in work, never interrupt him, but here the procedure is just the opposite; break the flow of his disturbing activity. "'How are you, Johnny? Come with me, I have something for you to do.' Probably, he won't want to be shown, and the teacher will say, 'All right, it doesn't matter. Let's go into the garden,' and either she will go with him or send her assistant."

The first indication of interest in something by the children is to be carefully noted by the directress. Usually this interest is first shown in the exercise of practical life; Montessori was convinced through experience that starting with the sensorial materials or the more advanced cultural materials is useless and sometimes harmful. She emphasizes that after the child's entrance into the classroom, this first step is fragile and delicate, and that any interruptions may set the child back severely. This is a time when many teachers go wrong. In their enthusiasm for this first important step, the teacher may say "good" or "fine" and this distracts from the child's own self-directed interest to the point that the task may be abandoned for weeks thereafter.

> ... *as soon as concentration has begun, act as if the child does not exist.*
>
> *(The Absorbent Mind, p. 281)*

The directress must be free of preconceived ideas about the level at which the child is functioning. To this end, the teacher's main job is facilitating the development of concentration and this is in part a social problem. The child absorbed in his work must not be disturbed by his companions, and one of the most important duties of the directress is to maintain order. A well-run Montessori classroom is a peaceful place. Only in this setting it is argued, can the child perform optimally. A child who disturbs others, or a classroom that is confused and disorderly, is never to be considered the fault of "bad children" but of bad teaching. The Montessori teacher is responsible for the environment. It is she who prepared it, and the ineffective classroom is her responsibility and must be reviewed and evaluated in that light.

> *Coins usually have two faces, one being more beautiful, finely chiselled, bearing a head or allegorical figure, while the other is less ornate, with nothing but a number or some writing. The plain side can be compared to freedom, and the finely chiselled side to discipline. This is so true that when her class becomes undisciplined, the teacher sees in the disorder merely an indication of some error she has made; she seeks this out and corrects it.*
>
> *(The Absorbent Mind, p. 287)*

RESEARCH

Early Montessori education was not followed up in any systematic way. Only recently have research funds and research interest increased to the point of subsidizing adequately designed studies. At this point, there have been a number of observational studies scattered around the country, but for the most part, they have not been carefully designed with sufficient care to consider them as more than expressions of opinion. Typically, these studies have not been related to any theory, nor have they provided adquate controls or relevant comparison groups.

An excellent exploratory study was reported by Dreyer and Rigler (1967) at the Eastern Psychological Association. They found plausible results from a comparison of traditional Montessori classroom effects with a "Cooperative nursery school ... representative of the large proportion of modern progressive nursery schools with its opportunities for 'unstructured' play." Montessori children in the testing situation were "highly task oriented," while the nursery school children viewed it as "an opportunity to be involved socially with the examiner." Consistent with this observation, Montessori children tended to describe objects in terms of physical characteristics (square, made of wood, green) rather then the *function* served by the object (to play with); spent less time in solving a hidden figures test (but did just as well); and on the Picture Completion Test showed some creativity, but significantly less than the nursery school children. Thus, they were more object-oriented, more efficient, and less creative. It is tempting to "run away" with these data that confirm the stereotype, but it is necessary to withhold judgment since this study applies to one Montessori teacher only and as will be documented later, great differences abound between Montessori teachers. A lot depends on the teacher, Montessori or otherwise.

A second study was conducted in Chicago under the direction of Kohlberg (Hess and Baer, 1968). This study too, involved just one Montessori classroom during a summer Head Start program, compared with two other curricula, one "run by an elementary school teacher stressing readiness for public school," while the other "was run by a teacher who had previously worked in, and believed in, a permissive child-development oriented pre-school" (Hess and Baer, 1968, p. 105). The permissive classroom showed a significant *decrease* of five I.Q. points on the Stanford-Binet, while the other two classes increased, but only two or three points. The permissive classroom significantly increased in distractibility, while the other classes showed a slight decrease. There was a high correlation between I.Q. drop and distractibility (.63). The greater the distractibility, the more the I.Q. decrease.

Kohlberg then went on to study a year-long Montessori program with ten ADC Negro children who showed a 17 point I.Q. increase between October and

January, with middle-class children in the same classroom showing a mean increase of ten I.Q. points. The I.Q. increase correlated highly with ratings of attention (the opposite of the distractibility measure) increase (.65).

In summary, Kohlberg's results showed significant improvement in attention and in conventional cognitive functioning (I.Q.) in this classroom. In addition, he found that these two variables were highly related to one another.

The Montessori Research Project at the University of Cincinnati was initiated in 1965 (see progress reports, 1965 to 1968). The Project was oriented toward understanding the development of autonomy in young children and to what extent early education has an effect. "Autonomy" was defined as *self-regulating behaviors that facilitate effective problem solving*. An important feature of this approach involves the idea of looking at the various strengths of the child, rather than placing emphasis on a single indicator like I.Q. (see Banta, in press, 1969b).

We have operated on the faith that no one number, like I.Q., can represent the many complex effects early education can bring about. For this reason, we set about to design tests that made good theoretical sense for evaluating early education. A child's strengths may show up in many ways, if only we have the wisdom to look for them in various areas of behavior and thought processes. The name of our tests is The Cincinnati Autonomy Test Battery (CATB) (Banta, 1970). The CATB, in its present form, provides test scores on fourteen variables. The variables were selected so as to reveal a wide variety of behavior tendencies on the part of three to six-year-old children. The tests do not favor Montessori methods and do not contain any materials which resemble those of Montessori. The following brief definitions give an idea of the ranges of behaviors assessed which are relevant to autonomous functioning:

Curiosity: Tendency to explore, manipulate, investigate, and discover in relation to novel stimuli.

Innovative Behavior: Tendency to generate alternative solutions to problems.

Impulse Control: Tendency to restrain motor activity when the task demands it.

Reflectivity: Tendency to wait before making a response that requires analytic thinking, when the task demands it.

Incidental Learning: Tendency to acquire information not referred to in the instructional stimuli.

Intentional Learning: Tendency to acquire information specified in the instructional stimuli.

Persistence: Attention to a problem with solution-oriented behavior where the goal is specified.

Resistance to Distraction: Persistence, with distracting stimuli present.

Field Independence: Tendency to separate an item from the field or context of which it is a part.
Task Competence: Ratings of tendency to deal effectively with problems of many kinds.
Social Competence: Ratings of ability to work comfortably with adults.
Kindergarten Prognosis: Ratings of ability to do well in conventional kindergarten.
Curiosity Verbalization: Tendency to engage in fantasy, expressed while exploring a novel subject.

Detailed descriptions of the tests and testing procedures are provided in my chapter, "Tests for the Evaluation of Early Childhood Education: The Cincinnati Autonomy Test Battery (CATB)," in a book titled *Cognitive Studies* (Hellmuth, 1970).

A brief summary of findings is presented from our first two-year study based upon Cincinnati Montessori classrooms, which we have studied closely. Of the three classrooms, one was highly structured, one was less structured, and the third was very permissive. This serves to indicate the wide range of personal choice involved in the teacher's management of a Montessori classroom.

When you open the door of a highly structured classroom, you do not hear much noise; children are seated quietly working with didactic materials; group activities are limited; children are organized and controlled sometimes by obvious instructions ("Now go over and get something to work with."), and sometimes by subtle directions (a look of disapproval when materials are used improperly). When you walk into a highly permissive classroom, you hear many sounds; children singing or furniture being moved about to construct forts or houses; some children are working by themselves while others are organizing a march or a family; the teacher may be holding a child or leading songs; the teacher is more of a participant than a detached observer; there is much more body contact between teacher and child. The highly structured classroom is task oriented while the highly permissive classroom is fantasy oriented and free-play oriented.

Both kinds of classroom occur within Montessori philosophy and Montessori training because the teacher brings to the teaching situation a whole life history of relationships with children. It would be strange psychology indeed if one were to expect that a few months or years of training would modify basic patterns of structure or permissiveness on the part of the teacher. The teacher's personality has a direct bearing on what will happen (or what can't happen) in the classroom.

Two classrooms we compared showed that the actual amount of time children used the didactic materials varied tremendously from class to class, even though all classes were run by Montessori-certified teachers. Based on 42 hours of observation, we found that the highly structured classroom ranged from 10 percent to 21 percent didactic activity in any one day, while the relatively unstructured classroom ranged from only one-half of 1 percent to 7 percent didactic activity. More detail of this study is reported in the paper, "Is There Really a Montessori Method?" (Banta, 1969).

The CATB was administered to the lower-class Negro children in each of these two classrooms and to a relatively high-tuition school for white middle and upper-class children. In addition, some comparisons are based on control groups of lower-class Negro children who did not attend preschool classes. Here are four provisional generalizations about types of classrooms and their different effects on disadvantaged children.

1. *Innovative behavior is lacking among the lower-class children; it can be modified through prekindergarten experience, but the upper-class children have a considerable head start.* In a test which involves a game of "getting the dog to get to his bone" via varying routes, 23 percent of lower-class children found *no* new or novel routes for the dog to get to his bone. *All* upper-class children found at least one novel route and their scores were dramatically higher. Lower-class children tended to confine their behavior to imitations of the demonstration provided by the tester, as though this is the only "safe" way to go. Lower-class Montessori classrooms showed improvement over matched non-prekindergarten children, but it appears that the highly permissive classroom had the greatest affect.

2. *Field Independence (or analytic thinking) can be trained in structured prekindergarten classrooms, but again, the upper-class child had the advantage.* We test field independence by asking the child to find a picture of an ice cream cone embedded in other, more complex, figures. This is somewhat like the games in a typical Sunday newspaper comic section where the reader is asked to look at the picture of a tree and to find as many outlines of faces as he can in the drawing. Again, it turned out the Montessori classrooms differed, and here the differences were even more dramatic. This time, however, the greatest improvement was found in the highly structured classroom. Almost no gains were found in the social, expressive, emotion-oriented classroom at the end of the first year. These results go contrary to some theories of the development of analytic thinking which suggest that such patterns are laid down very early in the child's life and are relatively non-modifiable. The finding holds out considerable hope for training productive thought processes among the disadvantaged. It appears that structured, controlled classrooms do this best.

3. *Learning processes are greatly improved through kindergarten experience, and under certain conditions, lower-class children do slightly better than upper-class children.* We have developed a test for two kinds of learning. One kind of learning reflects ability to master a task set by an adult for the child; this is called *intentional* learning. Another kind of learning reflects the ability of the child to learn things *other than* those which the child is told to learn; this is called

incidental learning, the learning of aspects of the problems incidental to the main task. In incidental learning, lower-class children do at least as well as upper-class children and the prekindergarten children do slightly better. In *intentional* learning, the prekindergarten children, whether lower or upper-class, did much better than children who did not go to school. There appeared to be no important differences between upper and lower-class children after prekindergarten on this intentional learning task. Whatever the component parts of this complex kind of learning, the prekindergarten experiences greatly improved the lower-class child, regardless of whether they were highly structured or highly permissive Montessori classrooms.

4. *Highly structured classrooms reduce curiosity motivation and exploratory behavior.* We studied curiosity and exploratory behavior with what we call the "curiosity box." The curiosity box is a wooden box with many gadgets, switches, holes, handles, springs, and shiny attractive materials attached to it. The child can look in the box, can stick his hand inside the box to explore it tactually, and can open up one end of the box which is closed with a latch. The curiosity box is placed in front of each child and the tester says, "Here is something for you to play with." Nothing more is indicated. Most children begin to explore the box, gradually becoming more and more interested in what it has in store for them. Upper-class children generally did more exploring, more talking while exploring, and tended to move around more. Lower-class children, by contrast, talked less, explored less, and appeared disinterested.

There were dramatic differences, however, as a result of different kinds of prekindergarten experiences. By far the highest scores obtained by lower-class Negro children were found in the permissive classroom (average score, 21). *The lowest exploratory behavior score of any prekindergarten classroom we have studied came from the highly structured Montessori children,* and these were middle to upper-class white children from relatively advantaged homes (average scores, 8 and 3). The less structured classroom showed curiosity and exploratory behavior between that of the other more extreme groups (average score, 15).

In summary, we have found that classrooms function on an either-or basis: either analytic thinking or curiosity and innovative behaviors are improved. But at present, we cannot have everything. All classrooms do appear to improve conventional learning processes. It is our hope that we can eventually develop procedures that will produce not only improved conventional learning processes, but produce improvement in analytic thinking *along with* maintenance of curiosity motivation, exploratory behavior, and innovative behavior. At the present time, it appears that teaching practices do not improve *all* factors in autonomous problem solving within one classroom. Educational innovations are sorely needed which optimize autonomous functioning in all areas.

Another line of evidence comes from a study we have been conducting on the effects of continuing Montessori education into the primary grades. One group of children had the benefit of Montessori preschool experience and were then enrolled in a non-graded Montessori experimental classroom in the public school. It appears that this is a very beneficial arrangement. When compared with three other groups of children in the same school (matched on age and sex and from the same socio-economic background), the Montessori class obtained the highest average scores on nine of the ten tests administered. The results, however, should not be taken to unequivocally support the Montessori method. One of the comparison groups came in a very close second and obtained highest scores on one. This comparison group was also a non-graded primary class which had had the benefit of preschool experience, but had at no time been exposed to Montessori methods.

The general configuration of the results went like this: Montessori continuity from preschool to primary grades did best, but *non*-Montessori continuity from preschool to primary grades did very nearly as well; a group of children who received *no* preschool exposure and who then went on to a *graded* primary class did poorest; finally, another group, *with* preschool experience but *graded* primary exposure showed results intermediate between the top two non-graded classes and the lowest group that did not have preschool.

In summary, non-graded primary combined with preschool experience showed the best overall results; subtracting either preschool or non-graded practices reduced the progress of the children.

Before summarizing the specific changes which occurred, it is important to clarify the meaning of the above results. When one observes and analyzes the educational experiences of the Montessori and the non-Montessori non-graded primary classes, one is impressed with the commonalities more than the differences. I think that if Maria Montessori were to visit the very skillful work of the so-called "non-Montessori" non-graded class, she would endorse its freedom for the children (moving about, working alone), its planned environment (innovative methods with tape recorder, live rabbit, etc.), its non-punitive character (an "incorrect" answer deserves help, not anger; original answers are reinforced, but other answers are pursued); and its emphasis on concentration (the children can sustain activity without supervision for relatively long periods of time). This class is more teacher oriented than Montessori might perhaps approve of, since there are frequently group lessons and little equipment that emphasizes individual effort. Thus, there is no reason to believe that many aspects of Montessori thinking cannot be incorporated into the teacher's personal style, in a useful and effective way. One might say that the teacher manifests his particular genius through selective reading and use of Montessori ideas and methods which are varied and rich indeed.

The Montessori continuity group had, since preschool, exposure to a relatively indirect teaching method combined with materials that were well suited to individual work. Whatever slight edge the group had in our study might be tentatively attributed to this feature.

The specific results were as important as the overall outcome. The significant advantages of the non-graded primary groups showed up not only in terms of innovative behavior, but even more strongly in what we call conventional intelligence measures; the ability to repeat sentences accurately after hearing them read just one time; or the ability to match objects which are conventionally thought to "go together," like a gun and a holster, or a bottle with a baby. This was important in terms of the children's ability to *shift* from conventionally intelligent functioning to innovative functioning. Such shifting ability gives the child flexibility in his attack upon problems; he can draw on traditional, culturally sanctioned answers or he can move out with novel solutions when the task demands it. This is a key idea in the theory of autonomous functioning (Banta, 1968; Hartmann, 1939, 1947).

REFERENCES | 7

American Montessori Society. General Information. Distributed by the American Montessori Society, 175 Fifth Avenue, New York, New York, 10010, April 1970, mimeograph.

American Montessori Society. Montessori Education: Questions and Answers. Distributed by the American Montessori Society, 175 Fifth Avenue, New York, New York, 10010.

American Montessori Society. The Montessori Method. Distributed by the American Montessori Society, 175 Fifth Avenue, New York, New York, 10010. mimeograph.

Banta, T. J. "The Montessori research project: Project reports." Mimeographed, 1965 to 1968.

Banta, T. J. "Is there really a Montessori method?" American Montessori Society Bulletin, 1969. In press.

Banta, T. J. "Tests for the evaluation of early childhood education: the Cincinnati autonomy test battery (CATB)." In J. Hellmuth (Ed.), *Cognitive Studies, Vol. I.* New York: Bruner/Mazel, 1970.

Calleton, T. J. Highlights of the AMS Board Meeting, Cincinnati, February 21-23, 1970. Distributed by the American Montessori Society, 175 Fifth Avenue, New York, New York, 10010. mimeograph.

Donahue, G. E. The American Montessori Society, Inc. Distributed by the American Montessori Society, 175 Fifth Avenue, New York, New York, 10010. Reprinted from *Constructive triangle*, May 1966.

Dreyer, A. and Rigler, D. Personal communication and dittoed paper presented at the 1967 Eastern Psychological Association.

Hall, E. A conversation with Jean Piaget and Barbel Inhelder. *Psychology Today*, May 1970, 25-32.

Hartman, H. Ego psychology and the problem of adaptation. New York: International Universities Press, 1958. (Originally published in German in 1939.)

Hartman, H. "On rational and irrational action." In *Psychoanalysis and the Social Sciences, 1.* New York: International Universities Press, 1947.

Hess, R. and Baer, R. *Early education.* Chicago: Aldine Press, 1968.

Kilpatrick, W. H. The Montessori system examined. Boston: Houghton Mifflin, 1914.

Levi-Strauss, C. *Structural anthropology.* New York: Anchor Books, 1967.

Montessori, M. *The Montessori method.* New York: Shocken, 1964. (Originally published in English – New York: F. A. Stokes, 1912.)

Montessori, M. *Dr. Montessori's own handbook.* New York: Shocken, 1965a. (Originally published in English – New York: F. A. Stokes, 1914.)

Montessori, M. *Spontaneous activity in education.* New York: Shocken, 1965b. (Originally published in English – New York: F. A. Stokes, 1917.)

Montessori, M. *The Montessori elementary material.* New York: F. A. Stokes, 1917.

Montessori, M. *The discovery of the child.* Madras, India: Theosophical Publishing House, 1948.

Montessori, M. *The absorbent mind.* Madras, India: Theosophical Publishing House, 1949.

Rambusch, N. M. The modern Montessori approach. Reprinted in *The American Montessori Society Bulletin,* 1970, *8,* whole issue.

Nimnicht | *Introduction* | 8

Believing that schools have been designed to meet the needs of only a certain type of child and that this restricted design is responsible for the unnecessary failure of many children, Nimnicht, at the Far West Laboratory for Educational Research and Development, is in the process of developing and implementing a rather extensive educational system which responds to the child, rather than requiring the child to respond to it. The resulting program is similar to the Montessori program in the freedom allowed the individual child (in selection and pacing of his own activities) and in the emphasis placed upon autotelic (self-rewarding) activities.

The two main objectives of this responsive learning environment are to help the child develop a positive self-image with regard to learning and to develop his intellectual ability. The emphasis is placed on learning how to learn (process) instead of specific content. However, the content (i.e., materials) is chosen with specific objectives in mind. Parents play an important role in determining the content objectives of the program. Parents also are involved extensively in a Parent/Child Toy Library, which is designed to enable parents to help their own child toward achievement of the two main objectives.

The long-range goal of the Far West Laboratory is more extensive than that of most programs described in this book, in that it "is to develop a model responsive educational system that will serve at least 90% of the children from age three to at least age nine." To accomplish this goal, five system components are being developed, four of which could be used separately as well as together, thus providing a flexibility sufficient to meet the lesser or greater needs of particular communities.

With an extensive (in terms of age range and separate programs) educational system, Nimnicht is facing the teacher training problems which many "preschool curricula" will be facing in the future or are facing now, as Banta pointed out in the preceding paper. Nimnicht's strategy may be instructive for others who are in search of or presently developing a viable model for teacher training. Two strong points of Nimnicht's method are that the training procedures do not require all of the Laboratory staff's time and yet they are sufficient to maintain a high level of performance in a manner considered characteristic of the curriculum.

Glen P. Nimnicht

A Model Program for Young Children that Responds to the Child

8

THE PROBLEM

The public schools are failing to educate large numbers of students. A large percentage of these students come from one or more of the following groups:

1. CHILDREN FROM
   IMPOVERISHED HOMES

A large number of children from impoverished homes are coming to school at age three, four, or five with skills and abilities that are vital and useful in the life situation in which they are growing and learning, but these skills and abilities are not congruent with the kind of skills and concepts that are currently valued by the school and used to measure the intellectual ability or the achievement of these

---

Glen P. Nimnicht is at the Far West Laboratory for Educational Research and Development. This paper is a modified statement of the Basic Program Plans for the Program, Education Beginning at Age Three, Far West Laboratory for Educational Research and Development, Berkeley, California, 1970. Printed by permission of the author.

children. The result is that the actual achievement of these children is underestimated and the school continues to fail to recognize that what the child knows and can do is more important to the child than what the schools value. Of course, every child will need the intellectual skills the school values, but these are in addition to those that he currently has and that are essential for daily existence. The schools must learn to respond to his needs.

2. CULTURALLY AND ETHNICALLY DIFFERENT CHILDREN

These children may or may not come from impoverished homes. To be culturally or ethnically different, however, increases the chances of being impoverished because of prejudice and repression by the dominant white society. To be culturally different also increases the chances of failure in school, not because the child is handicapped in some way but because the school does not respond to the cultural differences.

3. CHILDREN WITH SPECIFIC LEARNING DISABILITIES

There is a wide range of opinion in medical groups on the existence or nonexistence of specific learning disabilities and/or their causes. But we, as educators, know that a sizable percentage (10% or more) of children have the ability to learn according to I.Q. tests and other cognitive measures, but are failing in school because of specific problems with reading, writing, and sometimes mathematics — at least as they are now taught. These disabilities are usually complicated by other psychological problems related to school and learning.

4. OTHERS

In addition to these groups, there are many other individuals the schools are failing: 1. many highly intelligent and creative students think that classroom activities are boring and that the school is a jail; 2. students whose values do not correspond to those of the teachers also have difficulty in school.

The basic problem is that the schools are designed to serve students who are quiet and submissive and who hold the same values as the teachers. Either they are white, middle-class children or they aspire to emulate white, middle-class adults. The schools respond to these children and nurture their development. This is evident in both procedures and content.

The procedures are built around the concept that all children at a given age are ready to learn the same thing (with some consideration given to inherited ability) and are motivated by the same factors. That is, such children will avoid failure, low marks, or retention in grade, and will work for success, high marks, and praise from the teacher. Following this concept, most instruction takes place in front of groups of twenty-five or more students. The content is designed to be generally interesting to the average student and the major motivating force is threat of failure or promise of success.

Head Start and Follow Through programs represent an effort to recognize that children from impoverished homes need help if they are to respond to this system or that the system needs to be changed. But few examples exist of schools' making any concessions to children who are culturally different or who have different life styles. Some programs exist which recognize that, since English is a second language for Spanish-speaking children, it should be taught from that point of view. Yet only a few experimental programs are concerned with developing bilingualism and fewer still have any content that is relevant to the child's background. One of the causes of the problem is that neither the parents of those children nor the children themselves have had an effective voice in shaping their education.

The failure of the schools to educate these students is reflected in our society by the following:

1. The low-achievement (as defined by the school) and the high dropout rate of children who are from impoverished homes and children from racial or ethnic minority groups.
2. The obvious disenchantment shown by large numbers of high school and college students.
3. The negative attitudes of minority-group leaders toward the school system.

Presently, the Education Beginning at Age Three program's major focus is on children from impoverished homes and culturally and ethnically different children. The Laboratory is focusing on these children because: a. their needs are the greatest, b. they include the largest numbers whom the current educational system is failing, and c. improving the educational opportunities for these children has been given a high national priority.

The Laboratory's second priority focus will be on children with specific learning disabilities and other children the schools are currently failing, but this has not been considered in the detailed program planning that follows.

However, although the program is specifically aimed at the groups mentioned, it is not thought of as a special program suitable only for select or special children. Success with these groups of children will offer a workable alternative to the current approach to education for all children.

THE MAJOR OBJECTIVES
OF THE PROGRAM

The long-range objective of the program is to develop a model responsive educational system that will serve at least 90% of the children from age three to at least age nine. The major objectives of the system will be to help children develop a positive self-image as it relates to learning in the school and the home, and to develop their intellectual ability.

A child has a positive self-image in relationship to learning and school, if:

1. He likes himself and his people.
2. He believes that what he thinks, says, and does makes a difference.
3. He believes that he can be successful in school.
4. He believes that he can solve a variety of problems.
5. He has a realistic estimate of his own abilities and limitations.
6. He expresses feelings of pleasure and enjoyment.

If a child has a positive self-image in relationship to learning and school, he will behave in the following ways. When compared with other children from a similar background, he will:

1. Attend school more frequently.
2. Be tardy less frequently.
3. Say more positive things about the school, the teachers, and the things he is learning.
4. Make better estimates of his ability (that is, he will not greatly over-estimate or under-estimate his ability to perform a given task).
5. Make more positive statements about himself and his racial, cultural, or ethnic group.
6. Be more willing to take reasonable risks of failure when confronted with a problem he can probably solve.
7. Express more confidence in his answers to a question or solutions to a problem.
8. Express feelings or opinions more frequently, with fewer non-committal responses, fewer stereotypes, and a greater variety of responses to such questions as, "How do you feel about _____?" or "What do you think about _____?"
9. Respond when given a problem to solve or a task to perform that is within his capability.
10. Have an immediate response when asked, "What are you looking forward to today?" or "What have you done today that you enjoyed?"
11. Express himself more freely in his writing, painting, or picture-drawing.

A nine or ten-year-old child is developing his intellectual ability if he can solve a variety of problems. These problems can be roughly classified as non-interactional, interactional, and affective. A non-interactional or one-person problem involves an individual manipulating his physical environment but not being manipulated by it in the same way. The results of a physical problem are highly predictable. Solving puzzles is a good example of a non-interactional problem. In fact, intelligence tests are primarily a test of an individual's ability to solve puzzles. The present school curriculum deals mainly with this kind of problem-solving.

An interactional problem involves two or more people (or machines) and requires a person to think, "If I do this, what is he likely to do?" The individual is being manipulated at the same time he is manipulating. Games like bridge, poker, and chess are good examples; so is hide-and-seek. Interactional problems are not so predictable as non-interactional problems.

It is possible to think about these two kinds of problems without any emotional overtones but emotion is usually involved. When the emotional aspects of the problem become the dominant consideration, the problem becomes affective. And, of course, the more affective it becomes, the more difficult it is to cope with. An educational system must help children learn to cope with all three kinds of problems; for, in many instances, the learner cannot solve non-interactional or interactional problems until he has solved some affective problems. To solve these problems, a child must develop:

1. His senses and perceptions because the senses are the sources of data for the thought processes.
2. His language ability because language is a tool of the thought process.
3. His concept formation ability because he needs to be able to deal with abstractions and to classify information.

Therefore, the child will:

1. Have achievement scores on tests of school-related skills at least six months higher than would be predicted from the present programs.
2. Have better achievement of solutions to non-interactional, interactional, and affective problems than will comparable children who have not been involved in the program.

In order to accomplish these objectives, the model system will have the following characteristics:

1. The procedures are based upon the following heuristic principles:
    A. The learning environment satisfies the following conditions:

a. It permits the learner to explore freely.
   b. It informs the learner immediately about the consequences of his actions.
   c. It is self-pacing, with events occurring at a rate determined by the learner.
   d. It permits the learner to make full use of his capacity for discovering relations of various kinds.
   e. Its structure is such that the learner is likely to make a series of interconnected discoveries about the physical, cultural, or social world.
 B. The activities within the environment are autotelic; that is, the activities are self-rewarding and do not depend upon rewards or punishments that are unrelated to the activity. Stating that learning activities should be self-rewarding does not imply that a child never receives praise. However, the essential satisfaction should come from the activity and not from something alien to the experience itself. This means that the program must be individualized to provide many ways for children to learn a specific skill.

 The learning environment is not completely free, of course, because someone must choose what to put into, or leave out of, the classroom. The teacher plans this environment in terms of the objectives she would like to accomplish. A responsive classroom includes individual, small-group, and large-group activities. The child, however, is free to explore the available choices. Within broad limits, he can spend as much time on any activity as he likes, and no one will ask him to stop one activity to begin another.

 A responsive classroom is arranged so that the child is likely to make discoveries about his physical and social world because a child better remembers what he discovers for himself, and he can only learn to solve problems when the learning environment encourages problem-solving.

 Obviously, then, the responsive model emphasizes learning how to learn rather than learning specific content.

2. The system includes the participation of parents and their involvement in the decision-making process. The system must not only be responsive to children by the procedures that are followed but respond to them in terms of the content. Since children from age three to nine are not sophisticated enough to choose what skills or concepts they need to learn, someone must make those choices for them; thus the teacher is making choices when she chooses what to place in, or exclude from, the classroom. The best individuals, however, to make these judgments are informed parents, so they need to participate to become informed about the program and its contents and then to be involved in the decision-making process.

It seems safe to assume that unless an individual is opposed to the whole concept of education, he would agree that the major objective is to help individuals learn to solve a variety of problems; but the way this goal is approached and the content of the educational program are open to a variety of choices.

The educational program would obviously deal with skills and concepts such as color, shape, size, and counting that have no cultural basis; but an obvious choice for the parents is the extent to which culturally relevant material is included in the curriculum.

Another example of the kinds of decisions parents should be making is the approach to language development. Should English be taught as the primary language or as a second language or should the school offer a bilingual program?

3. The system will be composed of a variety of alternatives that can be combined to form the total system. For any educational system to have much chance of being implemented in a variety of communities with different kinds of administrative arrangements, it will have to be flexible. It should be designed so that any combination of the following components can be incorporated into it:
   a. Head Start programs that are sponsored by the school district or other agencies.
   b. Day-care programs of all sorts including public, private, and business-supported day-care centers.
   c. Parent/Child Toy Library programs which provide an alternative to having all three and four-year-old children in classrooms every day — by enabling the parents to help the child learn specific skills and by providing an educational toy library for their use. (This component will be described in greater detail later in this paper.)
   d. Public school systems, of course, would be the essential element for the program from kindergarten through the third grade but the system would also be open to private schools serving children of the same age.
4. The system will be economically feasible. Economic feasibility means that the system would be comparable to other model programs that are being developed but probably more expensive than most existing programs. When comparisons are made, however, of the cost related to the achievement, the system should be more efficient than the ones it replaces. Furthermore, some of the additional expense will have other social values, such as employment of impoverished parents as teaching assistants in the classrooms.

SELECTION OF THE APPROACH

The selection of this model educational system for development was based upon three basic considerations:

1. The model appears to correct some of the obvious defects in the present system by responding to the learner instead of asking the learner to respond to the system. The responsive model program:
   1.1 Assumes that all children are not ready to learn the same thing at the same time.
   1.2 Assumes that all children are not motivated by being rewarded with good grades or being punished with poor grades.
   1.3 Recognizes differences in the cultural, ethnic, and racial backgrounds of children and responds to those differences.
   1.4 Recognizes the need to involve parents in the decision-making process.
   1.5 Uses procedures that are based upon sound psychological principles.
2. One component of the system — a model Head Start program — had been developed and tested prior to the Laboratory's selection of this approach and the initial evaluation indicated that the desired educational outcomes could be achieved.
3. By cooperating with other model testers and designers in the Head Start and Follow Through programs, the Laboratory has access to information on a variety of other approaches that will enable the Laboratory to compare results and modify the Laboratory's system accordingly.

THE COMPONENTS OF THE SYSTEM

In order to accomplish the major objectives of developing a responsive educational program for children from age three to at least age nine, the development of five components has been undertaken. They are:
   A. A model Head Start program for three and four-year-old children.
   B. A model Follow Through program for children from five to nine.
   C. A Parent/Child Toy Library program for parents of children from three to nine.
   D. A model Day Care program for children from three to nine.
   E. The System Development component.

The strategy the Laboratory has followed has been to introduce one component at a time and develop each one on a fairly independent basis so that each component, with the exception of Component E, can stand alone or become a part of the total system. This means that each of the first four components have a set of objectives that are independent of the total system but must be accomplished if the majority of objectives of developing the system are accomplished.

The following chart shows how the components have been or will be phased into the program. Components A, B, C, D have three primary objectives:

CHART 1. STRATEGY TO ACCOMPLISH OUTCOMES

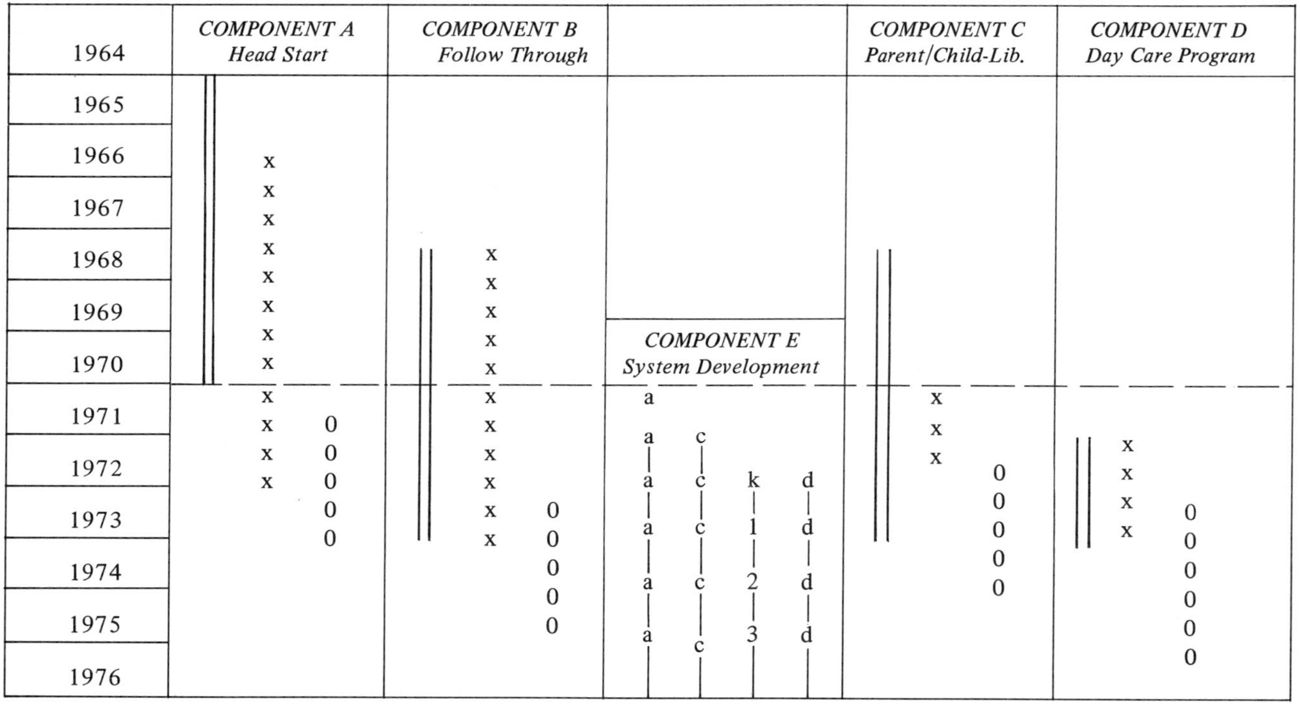

	COMPONENT A Head Start	COMPONENT B Follow Through	COMPONENT E System Development	COMPONENT C Parent/Child-Lib.	COMPONENT D Day Care Program
1964	━━━━━━				
1965	x				
1966	x				
1967	x				
1968	x	x ━━━━━			
1969	x	x			
1970	x	x			
1971	x	x	a		
1972	x o	x	a — c	x ━━━━━	
1973	x o	x	a — c — k — d	x	x ━━━━━
1974	x o	x o	a — c — 1 — d	x	x
1975	x o	x o	a — c — 2 — d	o	x o
1976	o	o	a — c — 3 — d	o	x o
				o	o

━━━━━━ Develop program for children
xxxxxxxxx Develop training for teachers and assistants
000000000 Implementation
Letters in Component E refer to other components

a – Component A
c – Component C
d – Component D

K – Kindergarten
1 – First Grade
2 – Second Grade
3 – Third Grade

253

1. To develop a model program for children (or parents in Component C).
2. To develop a model inservice training program for teachers.
3. To establish and test the model program in a variety of situations.

The fifth component, E, has one major objective; i.e., to combine the first four components into a system of education.

The logic for organizing the program into these particular components is based upon political rather than educational reasons. Currently the components are consistent with the way existing systems are organized and the way people think about them. Educational programs for three and four-year-old children, such as Head Start, are administered as special programs whether they are a part of the public schools or not. Kindergarten through the third grade is a part of the elementary school. The Parent/Child program can stand alone for parents of three and four-year-old children or be a part of a Head Start program. It will become apparent under the discussion of the fourth component, Day Care, that the educational program will be the same as the Head Start program but at the present time most people make a distinction between the two programs. Day Care usually starts with younger children and may extend to older children by providing after-school services and care. If each of these four components is to stand alone or fit into a system, it is important to recognize these distinctions even though they are not logical distinctions from an educational point of view.

Component A, Head Start for three and four-year-old children, was initiated in 1966 when the Laboratory, in cooperation with the New Nursery School in Greeley, Colorado, started to develop and test a training program for Head Start teachers and assistant teachers to enable them to carry out the responsive Head Start program for children that had been developed at the New Nursery School. Since then, the Laboratory has also been expanding and revising the model program for Head Start children. The development of the training procedures for teachers is currently in the performance testing stage; that is, the procedures have successfully completed a preliminary test and must go through an operational test before being released for general use. Since it will probably be necessary to recycle the testing and conduct a second performance test, the objectives of this component will not be accomplished until August, 1972. But the current training procedures are adequately developed to initiate Component E by starting to install the system beginning with Head Start classrooms in two (Fresno and San Francisco) and possibly three (Flint, Michigan) communities.

Component B, Follow Through for children in kindergarten through the third grade, was initiated in June, 1968. The development of the model program for the children and the inservice training program for the teachers and assistants are being developed and tested simultaneously. During the 1968-69 school year, the development started with kindergarten. This year (1969-70) the development was started in the first grade, and one grade level will be added each year.

The training program for kindergarten teachers was recycled through a second preliminary test this year, but based upon the experience the staff is gaining, it may be possible to omit the performance test for the teachers in the third grade. If this is possible, the objectives in this component could be achieved by 1974. But the development and testing at the kindergarten level will have reached the point that these procedures can be phased into Component E in September, 1971.

Component C, is the Parent/Child Toy Library for parents of three and four-year-old children. Since this component has the same general objectives as the other components but its focus is on working with parents rather than directly with children, the specific objectives need to be stated. They are:

1. Helping their child develop a positive self-image.
2. Aiding the child's intellectual development, using toys and games that are designed to teach children specific skills, concepts, or problem-solving abilities.
3. Aiding the child's intellectual abilities by improving the interaction between parents and children in aspects of cognitive development.
4. Participating in the decision-making process that affects the education of their children.

This component was initiated in January, 1969. It has been through a preliminary test and the performance test will be completed by June, 1970. After a series of operational tests during the 1970-71 school year it should be ready for release for general use beginning in June, 1971. But by January, 1971, this component can be phased into the system testing.

Component D, the Day Care program for children from three to nine, has not been initiated. According to current plans, we will start in September, 1970, to develop a model center in cooperation with the Berkeley Public Schools. Since the primary effort will be simply to modify the procedure and products developed in Components A and C so that they can be applied in a different kind of administrative arrangement, the objectives of creating a demonstration center for public-support day care centers should be accomplished by June, 1972.

Another objective of this component will be to create a model of a business-supported day care program. This should serve two purposes: 1. provide the input to encourage business or industry to join in the model system that the Laboratory plans to test; and 2. provide business and industry in general with a model. The approach will be to use the Laboratory itself as a model in this instance by creating a day care center for the children of the Laboratory's own staff. The financial arrangements would range from free day care services for some female employees to a sliding fee basis for other staff members. This goal might be accomplished by the Laboratory alone or by cooperation with some local industrial firm. The plans are to initiate this part of the component in January, 1971, with a viable model ready for demonstration by June, 1972.

Component E, Systems Development, will be initiated in September, 1970, by starting the training of Head Start teachers and assistants. The Parent/Child program can be phased in starting in January, 1971, and the first phase of Follow Through (kindergarten) could start in September, 1971. Under the best of circumstances the earlier date for the achievement of the objectives of this component, which is the major program objective, would be August, 1975, but the probability that such a system can be successfully developed and tested before 1977 is not very high.

MAJOR TASKS TO BE PERFORMED

In order to develop such a system, the Laboratory will have to undertake five major tasks which apply to all of the components.

THE FIRST MAJOR TASK

The first major task is to develop material and processes to enable the program to function in the classroom. For example, a variety of educational toys and games are essential to provide a wide range of learning activities. Programmed material and simple machines are necessary to provide a broad source of activities that give the child immediate feedback. The Laboratory does not, however, intend to create an entirely new curriculum or set of instructional materials. The strategy is to evaluate existing materials and modify or supplement them only when necessary.

In addition to developing material and processes to use in the classroom, we must develop learning units for teachers and their assistants to enable the teachers to use the materials and processes we are developing.

THE SECOND MAJOR TASK

The second major task is to integrate the learning units that have been developed for the teachers and assistants into a cohesive training program. The teachers will receive the initial training they need. We will also provide continuous training to maintain a high level of performance for the teachers who have been trained and provide training for new teachers entering the system. This goal must be accomplished without the continuous involvement of the Laboratory's staff in the training program.

The strategy the Laboratory is testing is to select individuals from a local community who can become trainers of teachers. We call these individuals Program Advisors (P.A.'s); the P.A. receives training from the Laboratory's staff and in turn trains ten teachers and ten assistant teachers.

The initial training for the teachers, conducted in their own classrooms, should last for two years to insure that at least 80% of the teachers reach a high level of performance. After the initial two years, the P.A.'s can maintain the program through continuous inservice training with 20 teachers and 20 assistants cycling the training on a yearly basis. The Laboratory will provide twelve weeks of training for the P.A.'s during the first two years and, after that time, the Laboratory will continue to supply new training units and developments for the classroom. But except for a week-long seminar at the beginning of each year, the P.A.'s would be responsible for the training of the teachers.

THE THIRD MAJOR TASK

The third major task is to develop an effective program to enable parents to participate in the education of their children and to involve parents in the decision-making process.

The strategy the Laboratory is following is to develop a course for parents built around the notion of showing parents how to use toys and games to help children learn some specific skill or concept. In the process, the parents learn some basic principles about child growth and development as well as ideas to help children develop a healthy self-concept. The parents also learn how to be more effective in influencing the education of their children. Examples include ways of appealing a decision of a teacher or principal or ways of making a recommendation that is likely to be accepted.

The second strategy is to form parent advisory groups to the Laboratory and in the communities.

THE FOURTH MAJOR TASK

The fourth major task is to install, maintain, and institutionalize the components of the system and finally the system itself into existing institutions.

The strategy the Laboratory will follow is to install the component by surveying the existing institution, select points of intervention, and monitor the progress and intervene in the system when necessary. Then the Laboratory will help maintain the program by acting as a catalyst — disseminating information about the program, encouraging spreading of the program, building support among stakeholders in the parent system, and encouraging the necessary changes in the parent system to accommodate the new program as an integrated part of the system.

THE FIFTH MAJOR TASK

The fifth major task is to conduct a continuous evaluation of the system and all of its sub-parts — from determining whether a toy or game is sufficiently interesting and effective to evaluating the total effect of the program on the behavior of children who have been involved.

The following illustrates how the five major tasks apply to all of the components in the program. Except for the second major task, developing and testing the training system, four senior staff members are each responsible for one of the major tasks in all components of the program and they supervise the activities of the other staff members assigned to that task within the component. This assignment of staff according to task across components provides a way for the activities or products developed in one component to be utilized in others. Each component is administered by a coordinator who is responsible for the coordination of the tasks within that component and for the development and testing of the inservice system for teachers and assistants (the second major task).

THE TRAINING PROCEDURES

Currently the program has three components — a model Head Start Program for three and four-year-old children, a Follow Through program for children aged five to nine and a Parent/Child-Toy Library program for parents of children from three to nine. The first two components not only include developing a model program for children but also developing a training process and materials to help teachers and their assistants carry out such a program.

The training program has been organized around the use of a Program Advisor. The Program Advisor is a local person who works with teachers and assistants in ten classrooms to develop a quality program in the local community with limited support from the Laboratory.

The Laboratory trains the Program Advisor and provides training materials for teachers and assistants. Initially, the Laboratory also provides some on-site training for teachers.

At the present time, we believe that two years of intensive training is required to obtain a high level of performance in 75% or more of the classrooms.

After two years, continuous inservice training will be provided to maintain the program and train new teachers.

The first year's training program has been organized into:

1. A series of four seminars (one two-week and three one-week sessions) plus on-site training for Program Advisors. The seminars will be held at the Laboratory or some central location. The on-site training for Program Advisors will involve someone from the Laboratory observing teachers working with parents or school administrators and critiquing videotapes of classroom activities.
2. A four-day workshop for teachers prior to the opening of school.
3. Three twelve-week training cycles to cover the first year of training. Each cycle consists of eight units of training and provides for four weeks of time for the Program Advisors and each teacher and assistant to decide what needs to be reviewed from the previous eight weeks or what particular problems to focus on, or what activities to undertake that will expand or broaden the training. This also provides time for the teachers to meet with the psychologist, parent coordinator, social worker and nurse to discuss these services and their relationship to classroom activities and parent participation.

The inservice training is organized to relate a weekly workshop for teachers and assistants to activities in the classroom. The sequence may be altered according to the Program Advisor's and Teacher's judgment of what the priorities should be, but the principles that are involved are important. They are:

1. Discuss, illustrate and/or demonstrate the understandings and skills that are involved.
2. Practice the skills or behavior in the classroom.
3. Discuss the results and then, perhaps, practice the same skills or behavior again or move on to the next unit. (Note that the twelve-week cycle does not have to be eight weeks of training units followed by four weeks of review. The review can come any time that the Program Advisor and teachers desire.)
4. Do not try to learn or practice too many different things at one time.
5. Evaluate the results and go back and practice those skills that still need improvement.

The outline in Table I covers the four-day workshop for teachers and the first four training units in the first 12-week training cycle. The third workshop for teachers and the fourth classroom unit will illustrate the typical content of a training unit. The unit contains a suggested focus, color, as an objective for the week, i.e., determining the number of colors each child can recognize and name and help the children who cannot recognize and name colors to do so.

TABLE I

Outline of The Four-Day Workshop Before School Opens
And The First Four Training Units

FOUR DAY WORKSHOP AND TEACHER ACTIVITIES BEFORE SCHOOL BEGINS

Four Day Workshop Prior to School
Overview of the Program
Classroom Organization
Classroom Control
Observations of Children's Behavior
Planning
Adult Relationships
Evaluation
Parent Participation

Before School Begins
Home Visitations
Organization of Room Materials
Plans for the First Week

**WEEKLY WORKSHOPS AND CLASSROOM ACTIVITIES
FOR TEACHERS AND ASSISTANTS**

First
Classroom Unit

1. Help Children Adjust to School
    Provide name tags
    Provide individual space with full name and photo
    Practice calling each child by name
2. Establish Rules and Routines For Children
3. Observe Class Behavior
    What they do and do not do
4. Establish Adult Relationship
    Working as a team

(Check when Covered)

_____1. Discuss Children's Adjustment To School
_____2. Discuss and Evaluate Rules and Routines
_____3. Discuss Teachers Observations Of The Class
_____4. Discuss Adult Relationships
_____5. Demonstrate One Of The Activities For Children
    Songs using children's names
_____6. Discuss Specific Language For Teachers
    To Practice
    Use verbs to describe action

First
Workshop
For Teachers

TABLE I. (Continued)

WEEKLY WORKSHOPS AND CLASSROOM ACTIVITIES
FOR TEACHERS AND ASSISTANTS

Second
Classroom Unit

1. Continue To Help Children Adjust To School
2. Post Rules And Routines For Easy Reference
3. Continue Observations Of The Class
4. Teachers Allow For Planning And Evaluation Time Together
5. Practice Using Action Words (verbs) To Describe Children's Play
6. Use Songs With Children's Names

____ 1. Discuss Observations Of The Class
____ 2. Discuss Songs Using Children's Names
____ 3. Discuss Use Of Specific Language To Describe Children's Actions (verbs)
____ 4. Discuss Planning
   Available materials in activity areas for free exploration
____ 5. Discuss Use Of Classroom Control Technique Anticipating Problems
__X__ 6. Discuss Responsive Environment Test (R.E.T.)

Second
Workshop
For Teachers

Third
Classroom Unit

1. Continue To Observe The Class
2. Continue To Use Songs With Children's Names
3. Continue To Use Verbs To Describe Action — Indoors And Outdoors
4. Organize Materials To Be Available To Children
   Change during the day according to children's interests and needs
5. Practice The Classroom Control Technique — Anticipating Problems
6. Complete Child Data Sheets For Testing

A Model Program for Young Children

TABLE I. (Continued)

**WEEKLY WORKSHOPS AND CLASSROOM ACTIVITIES
FOR TEACHERS AND ASSISTANTS**

_____ 1. Discuss Planning For The Week
    A Focus – Color
    Free Exploration with color during
    spontaneous play
      Concept Area
      Art Activities
      Manipulative Toys, e.g.,
      Cuisenaire rods
      Needed materials to make color lotto game
_____ 2. Continue To Discuss Classroom Control Technique
    Of Anticipating Problems
      Teachers consistency of rules/limits
_____ 3. Responsive Test (R.T.)
_____ 4. Observations Of The Class

Third Workshop For Teachers

Fourth Classroom Unit

1. Provide Experiences For Free Exploration
    With Color
2. Practice Anticipating Problems
3. Begin Testing With R.E.T.
    A few children a day
4. Continue Using Songs With Children's Names
5. Continue Describing Children's Action
    Indoors and Outdoors
6. Continue To Observe The Class

_____ 1. Continue To Focus On Color
    Add another color – free exploration, e.g.,
    Easel paints, water trays or play dough
    Make color lotto game
    Discuss color lotto #1
_____ 2. Discuss Developing The Concept Of Size During
    Spontaneous Play – Demonstrate with Unit Blocks
    Longest and Shortest
_____ 3. Discuss Classroom Control Technique
    Making Positive Statements – Positive Redirection
__X__ 4. Review Testing
    Understanding Of the procedures
_____ 5. Discuss Use Of Volunteers In the Room

Fourth Workshop For Teachers

The idea is not to concentrate on one objective to the exclusion of everything else, but to focus the teacher's attention on one or two objectives so she and her assistant can train themselves to see the possibilities that exist in the room to help the child to achieve the objectives. The training units suggest that the teacher first study each area of the room and determine how it might be used to accomplish the objective. The second step is to choose several learning episodes that will help accomplish the objective. A learning episode is a brief statement that states the objective, and describes the procedures to use with a game or toy to accomplish that objective. In this instance, the learning episodes are designed around a color lotto game that the teacher can make. The episode either accompanies the training unit or is contained in the *New Nursery School* pamphlet (Nimnicht, McAfee, and Meier, 1969).

The training unit recommends that the teachers and assistants practice on language behavior or classroom control techniques. In this instance, it is anticipating problems. The teacher anticipates problems when she does such things as:

1. Offers a game or toy to a child who is restless or moving aimlessly through the room.
2. Sees possible conflict between two children and suggests that one of them play elsewhere or helps them share.
3. Moves closer to the place where a conflict may arise.

The training unit provides for the demonstration of some learning episodes. In this instance, because it is at the beginning of the year, the learning episodes are the Responsive Test.

The training units provide form for the teachers and assistants to use in observing individual children in the classroom. The teachers are asked to conduct one five-minute observation of a different child each day.

THE PARENT/CHILD COMPONENT

The way the principles of a Responsive Program are carried out in the classrooms has been described above. The Parent/Child-Toy Library component applies those same principles to the situation where the parents are helping their own children. The program was designed to aid the parents in:

1. Helping their child develop a positive self-image.
2. Aiding the child's intellectual development, using toys and games that are designed to teach children specific skills, concepts or problem solving abilities.

3. Aiding the child's intellectual abilities by improving the interaction between parents and children in aspects of cognitive development.
4. Participating in the decision-making process that affects the education of their children.

The basic approach is to offer parents an opportunity to meet once a week for ten weeks. At these meetings, the parents are told about some general ideas in child development. They see toys or games used to teach skills and concepts and practice using the games. They are asked to practice some skill that would help their child with language ability as well as improve interaction between the parents and the child. After the ten-week course, the parents have access to a toy library where they can check out educational toys, games or other materials as long as they like. Each two-hour session includes:

1. An informal fifteen-minute period for unstructured conversation on such topics as selection of children's books and local concerns.
2. A fifteen to thirty-minute slide or film presentation on some aspect of child development followed by discussion.
3. An explanation of one technique to help the child develop his language to promote a better interaction between the parent and the child, or to help the child develop a better self-image.
4. Evaluation of the toy the parents had taken home the previous week.
5. A demonstration and role-playing with new games followed by a discussion of the instructions and purposes.
6. A topical discussion on school or community concerns of the parents; for example, how to make recommendations to the school or how to appeal a decision of the school.

The instructions that accompany the toy are called learning episodes, and there are several learning episodes for each toy or game. Each learning episode states the purpose of the game and gives simple instructions for playing. The general instructions are always the same:

1. The parent is to play by our rules unless the child changes the rules, then the parents should play by the child's rules.
2. If the parent asks the child to play and the child does not want to play, the parent cannot ask again that day. But if the child asks later during the day, the parent can play with him.
3. The child can stop playing anytime he likes and should not be asked why. The parent then puts the game away.

These general rules are to prevent the parents from unintentionally pressuring a child to do something he is not able to do and to help maintain a healthier interaction between the parent and the child when they are playing the game.

The Parent/Child-Toy Library program was designed to serve parents who are above the income level qualifying their children for Head Start but who cannot afford a private nursery school. The program can also become a part of Head Start or day care programs as a means of encouraging parents to participate in and to understand the purpose of such programs.

The support system for helping to establish and maintain the Parent/Child-Toy Library program will include:

1. A two-week course for the teacher-librarians that is conducted by the Laboratory's staff.
2. A detailed manual for the teacher-librarian outlining the course and instructions for establishing and maintaining the Library.
3. A set of toys, games and other materials with learning episodes.
4. A cross reference filing system to aid the librarian in recommending games and toys.
5. A set of strip films and audio tapes to demonstrate the use of the toys so that the parents can see the way the toy is used before checking it out of the Library.

To reduce the amount of training required for the teacher-librarian, the plans are to eventually film the part of the ten sessions that include the overview of some aspect of child development, the explanation of one technique to help the child develop his language, the demonstration of how to use the games or toys; and develop training films for the teacher librarians.

EVALUATION

The final evaluation of the program will be based upon how well it meets the objectives stated earlier. In the meantime, the various components of the program are being systematically evaluated. The Laboratory uses a systematic development process with four major steps:

1. Selection of approach and designing prototype.
2. Preliminary testing with a limited sample.
3. Performance testing with a larger sample but under careful supervision of the Laboratory.
4. Operational testing under normal field conditions with limited involvement of the Laboratory.

At any point, the process can be recycled if the desired results are not obtained.

The development and testing of the model program for children and the training program for teachers and assistants are parallel developments. The first concern in evaluating the program is to determine how effective the training program is in producing the desired changes in teacher behavior. The primary techniques that are being used are periodic classroom observations by trained observers and audio and video recordings of classroom behavior of teachers.

After the teacher's performance is satisfactory, the second concern is to determine the effects upon the children. Does the changed teacher behavior significantly affect the growth of children toward the objectives of the program?

We have collected baseline data for evaluation of the children by using standardized tests of intelligence and achievement, but we do not consider these tests as adequate measures of the program; so we are developing a responsive achievement test to assess the children's achievement in intellectual development. The emphasis will obviously be on a child's problem-solving ability. We are currently devising situational tests and observational techniques to assess a nine- or ten-year-old child's behavior on the indicators of healthy self-concept stated earlier as objectives of the program.

In the meantime, we are relying upon observations to make some estimate of a child's self-concept at earlier ages.

The Laboratory does not anticipate having a final evaluation of the first phase of the total program for at least four or five years, but in the developmental process there are enough check points to ensure against a complete failure. One thing seems to be certain, if the program does not meet our expectations, the alternatives are to revise the program until it does or replace it with a better model — we cannot return to current practices.

REFERENCES | 8

Gowan and Demos. "Definitions, statistics, identification," *The Disadvantaged and Potential Dropout,* 1966, 105-106.

Labov, W. and Cohen, P. Systematic relations of standard rules in grammar of Negro speakers. *Project Literacy* No. 7, 1967.

Labov, W. The logic of nonstandard dialect. In J. Alatis (Ed.), *School of Languages and Linguistics Monograph Series,* No. 22. Georgetown University, 1969, 1-43.

Leary, M. E. "Children who are tested in alien language: mentally retarded?," *The New Republic,* May 30, 1970.

Nisbet, J. "Family environment and intelligence," Halsey, Flood, Anderson, (Eds.), *Education, Economy, and Society,* Free Press of Glencoe, Inc., New York, 1963, pp. 273-287.

Stewart, W. "Continuity and change in American Negro dialects," *The Florida FL Reporter,* Spring, 1968.

U.S. *Congressional Record,* November 3, 1969, Vol. 115, No. 179.

White, B. L. Pre-School Project: "An overview of the project," symposium presented at Society for Research in Child Development, Santa Monica, California, March 26-29, 1969.

Whitney, Parker | *Introduction* | 9

An analogy is appropriate when describing the central feature of The Discovery Program. It may be viewed as a comprehensive system composed of interacting components which must function smoothly together so that the total system can operate successfully. These components are described as either people (the parents, children and staff), places (the educational environment) or programs (the various facets of the child development program). Like Miller and Camp, Parker and Whitney are concerned with the total ecology in which the child is functioning and how the various parts of the ecological system fit together in a state of balance. The curriculum is seen as only one part of the comprehensive system.

Additional salient features of this program include: 1. its parent involvement program; 2. its behavioral orientation; 3. its program development; 4. its monitoring and feedback system; and 5. its accountability.

The parent involvement program combines visits to the centers for the child and parent plus an elaborate take-home educational program. For the child, the center visits guarantee that the child's skills are appropriately diagnosed in order to prescribe an appropriate match between the child's development and the educational program. For the parent, the center visits provide appropriate role models and staff consultation to aid the parent in understanding the program and her child's development. The take-home program insures that the parent will reinforce and extend the educational program providing a continuous planned educational experience for the child.

An important feature of the program is its behavioral orientation. A unified taxonomy has been developed of the program's objectives which encompass over

1,800 behavioral objectives classified into 43 areas. This feature is admirable at a time when many developing programs are incapable of stating more than general program goals.

The Discovery Program is developed to include multimedia educational materials especially developed to facilitate the attainment of the program's objectives, an educational environment designed around the program's objectives and a complete teacher training program.

The monitoring and feedback system provides for accurate monitoring of the program in practice by feedback from the staff, parents, and child. Flaws in the learning materials are quickly detected since approximately 1,500 children use the materials. This responsive system therefore enables program revisions to be made quickly and efficiently.

Lastly, the Discovery Program is theoretically accountable to the consumers since the developers have so clearly specified their objectives. Since the public schools have historically been unaccountable to anyone, it is refreshing to see preschool program developers suggest that they should be held accountable for their program's impact.

David C. Whitney
Ronald K. Parker

A Comprehensive Approach to Early Education: The Discovery Program

9

The Discovery Program is a comprehensive educational system designed to enhance the learning of preschool children through involvement of both the children and their parents. In the eight months from October 1969 to May 1970 the Discovery Program has successfully involved more than 1,500 preschool children and their families in nine Discovery Centers operated by Universal Education Corporation (UEC) in five northeastern states: New York, New Jersey, Pennsylvania, Connecticut and Massachusetts. These children range in age from two to six years with the median age 3.7 years. Most of the children are from middle-income families who pay tuition for the program. Approximately 1,000 low income children will receive the Discovery Program in day care centers in Pennsylvania during 1971.

In recent years much emphasis has been placed on innovative approaches to curricula for early education, but with little discussion of the total context in which the curricula exist. Viewed from a broad perspective, a curriculum represents the core of a complex set of interacting components that must function

David C. Whitney is at the Universal Education Corporation, Educational Systems Division, New York, N. Y. Ronald K. Parker is at the Graduate Center of the City University of New York. Printed by permission of the authors.

together smoothly for the curriculum to have its maximum impact on a child. The curriculum may be thought of as only one component of a comprehensive program, the component that determines *what* the learner should learn, while the other components create an environment that makes it possible for the learning to occur.

The purpose of this discussion is to describe the Discovery Program from the perspective of a comprehensive early education program. In doing so the discussion will include four overviews: 1. conceptualization of the curriculum; 2. interacting components; 3. operation of the entire program; and 4. research.

THE CONCEPTUALIZATION OF THE DISCOVERY PROGRAM CURRICULUM

The importance of early education is now widely accepted. A body of research findings exists that details the potential for learning in the preschool years. Among those who have provided theoretical structure and observational evidence concerning the potential for early learning are Jean Piaget, Marie Montessori, Jerome Bruner, J. McVicker Hunt, Benjamin Bloom, Urie Bronfenbrenner, Martin Deutsch, Robert Glaser, Ira Gordon and Myrtle McGraw. The last five of this group serve as consultants in the development of the Discovery Program.

It is also widely accepted that many, if not most, children fail to realize their potential during the preschool years. In terms of intelligence, Benjamin Bloom (1964) has reported that the greatest development takes place between birth and the age of eight. Many research studies with low income children have demonstrated that intelligence as measured by standard I.Q. tests can be enhanced by the application of early education in the preschool years.

Nevertheless, relatively few children are enrolled in prekindergarten educational programs. Statistics compiled by the U.S. Office of Education show that only 6.9 percent of the children in the three to five age group are enrolled in prekindergarten early education.

To help meet this problem, the Discovery Program was conceptualized on the following hypotheses: 1. that, quantitatively, the bulk of learning for preschool children has always taken place and is likely to continue to take place in the home environment rather than in structured institutional environments; 2. that, qualitatively, most learning among preschool children has been of a haphazard, or unplanned nature, largely dependent on the quality of the home environment; and 3. that, if dramatic changes are to be brought about in both the quantity and quality of preschool learning, the focus of the early education program must be on the family, rather than merely on the child. In other words, the educational program must work cooperatively with the parents, as well as with the child, if it is to be effective.

One important consequence of these hypotheses is that the curriculum and the interacting components must be described in terms that have positive connotations and are understandable to parents who play an important role in implementing the curriculum. The label "Discovery Program" was selected because it has a positive connotation among the lay public and because it describes one effective method by which young children acquire new information.

Historically, discovery-learning was contrasted with reception-learning, the main difference between the two approaches being whether the principal content of what is to be learned is discovered by the learner himself or is presented to him. To quote Ausubel (1968), "in reception-learning, this content is presented to the learner in the form of a substantive or non-problem-setting proposition that he need only understand and remember. In discovery-learning, on the other hand, he must discover this content himself by generating propositions that represent either solutions to the problems that are set or successive steps in their solution."

From a professional standpoint, we are aware of both the positive and negative connotations of the term "Discovery." Ausubel's (1968, pp. 467-504) brilliant discussion of discovery-learning noting the lack of solid empirical support for this approach for school age children, leaves little doubt in our minds that discovery-learning per se does not have the widespread applicability that some of its early advocates supposed (Hendrix, 1961). It does seem, however, that what has been called "*guided* discovery-learning" has important implications for preschool curricula. Structured discovery methods that lead the learner to a desired generalization through the use of carefully organized materials and experiences have some demonstrated empirical validity (Beberman, 1958; Gagné and Brown, 1961).

Regarding the question of a "match" between the method of instruction and subject population, it may be that guided discovery-learning is even more appropriate for the preschool age than for older children. Although the empirical evidence on this point is limited, many important figures in developmental psychology have discussed the rapid developmental changes during the first seven years of life and the special needs of the preoperational child for concrete experience. Piagetian and Montessori enthusiasts have focused on the use of learning materials and experiences during the preschool years with heavy reliance on sensorimotor manipulation and exploration of materials. Even critics of the discovery techniques, such as Ausubel (1968), find reason for using this approach at the younger years on the grounds that "the acquisition and transfer of intuitive insights may possibly facilitate the later acquisition of abstract understanding" (p. 482). Lastly, the use of guided discovery methods is useful only for certain pedagogical purposes and in certain educational circumstances.

It is evident that the young human being must receive considerable instruction but also that he should be eternally vigilant in making additional observations. His life is a complicated blending of in-

struction and discovery. Many facts will be handed to him outright: At the same time, during every day of his life, he will be engaged, almost unknowingly, in inductive reasoning, the process of bringing together a number of experiences and extracting from them some common factor. The issue becomes, then, not instruction versus discovery, since both are essential, but a consideration of the relative importance to be accorded each in the educational process (Stanley, 1949, p. 457).

In addition to the application of discovery-learning principles in some parts of the Discovery Program, there are many other salient features of this curriculum conceptualization that will be discussed under the following headings: 1. behavioral orientation and objectives; 2. learning and development; 3. instruction and development; 4. motivation and development; 5. continuous education; 6. continual evaluation of skill and concept acquisition; 7. cognitive development program; 8. language development program; 9. affective support program; 10. motivational program; 11. socialization and social development program; 12. physical development program; and 13. accountability.

BEHAVIORAL ORIENTATION AND OBJECTIVES

The field of early education is filled with dedicated individuals who want to help children by focusing on the whole child without ever clearly identifying their specific educational objectives, specifying the program to attain those objectives, or determining whether the objectives have been attained. It is easy to fault the thousands of applied preschool programs that not only have failed to identify their educational objectives but also have never even considered what their specific objectives are or should be. The distressing fact in the 1970's is that so many of the "research" preschool programs have not identified their specific educational objectives or made explicit their educational programs. A recent overview (Parker, Ambron, Danielson, Halbrook, and Levine, 1970) of the literature surveying the preschool programs for three, four, and five-year-old children concluded "... that most programs do not have an operational statement of their curriculum. Literally hundreds of programs were reviewed for this paper that did not have any written curriculum" (p. 120). Without a written curriculum one would hardly expect to find behavioral objectives in these programs. Perhaps Bereiter and Englemann's (1966) most important contribution to early education was a clear specification of their behavioral objectives even though the publicity surrounding their program has centered more on their method of adult-child interaction.

The Discovery Program has, therefore, carefully defined its behavioral objectives in order to avoid some of the ambiguities that characterize most preschool programs.

Three somewhat incompatible criteria guided the selection of the behavioral objectives: 1. the objectives should present a comprehensive view of child development; 2. the list of objectives should be manageable; and 3. each objective should be easily understood by learning staff members and parents. The criterion of comprehensiveness has been met by insuring that behavioral objectives were selected across all areas of child behavior, including cognitive, linguistic, affective, motivational, social, and physical development.

The current list includes more than 1,800 key behavioral objectives representing the combined efforts of our staff and consultants to enumerate those key skills and concepts that lead a child to future success in school and in life. We recognize that the list is not, and very likely never will be, totally comprehensive — because if it were it could become unwieldy and unmanageable. It will, however, probably be expanded as we continue our finegrained analysis of child development.

After the behavioral objectives were identified, they were classified into thematic skill areas and then organized into a comprehensive taxonomy of behavioral objectives for early education. The term "skill area" in this context may be defined as a cluster of behavioral objectives that have been grouped together for thematic and conceptual clarity. Obviously, some of these skill area groupings are more arbitrary than others. The 43 skill areas in the Discovery Program are presented below.

LIFETIME SKILL AREAS
A. Creativity
B. Reasoning
C. Perception
D. Work and Study Skills
E. Understanding the World
F. Communication
G. Self-Confidence
H. Initiative

BASIC LEARNING SKILL AREAS
1. Observing
2. Listening
3. Expanding Vocabulary
4. Improving Memory
5. Recognizing Characteristics
6. Classifying
7. Solving Problems
8. Predicting and Testing
9. Touching
10. Understanding Shapes
11. Knowing Color
12. Speaking
13. Following Directions
14. Counting
15. Understanding Numbers
16. Telling Time
17. Measuring
18. Sticking to a Task
19. Understanding Rules
20. Tasting and Smelling
21. Finger Dexterity
22. Drawing and Design
23. Making and Building
24. Using Tools
25. Knowing the Alphabet
26. Relations with Others
27. Self-Care and Safety
28. Understanding "What?"
29. Understanding "Where?"
30. Understanding "When?"
31. Understanding "Why?"
32. Understanding "How?"
33. Understanding "Who?"
34. Making Sounds and Music
35. Physical Coordination

Recognizing the need for a unified taxonomy of behavioral objectives that does not present a fragmented picture of a child, we have attempted to integrate the skill areas with one another by coding them in such a way that a specific behavioral objective may be included in more than one skill area and be internally cross-referenced. For example, in the skill area 1.00 OBSERVING, the sub-skill "1.01 Understands the words *same* and *different*," also carries the cross-reference "equals 5.03." Within the skill area 5.00 RECOGNIZING CHARACTERISTICS, the sub-skill "5.03 Understands *same* and *different*" carries the cross-reference "equals 1.01."

To establish the interrelationships among behavioral objectives across skill areas is an extremely difficult task. The most inviting error is to begin thinking as a faculty psychologist and divide the child into self-contained parts. While such an approach might simplify the task of developing a comprehensive taxonomy of preschool behavioral objectives, it would violate the integrity of the organism and lead to an over-simplified conceptualization of the program. For example, even the binary division of a child's behavior into "mental" and "motor" skills on the Bayley Scales (1969) possesses many dangers because any sample of behavior does not clearly fall into only one of these categories. With full awareness, therefore, of the inherent risks in specifying distinct skill areas, we have continued to work out the complex relationships across skill areas in the belief that the logical and conceptual clarity gained from this approach is worth the risks. Lastly, we feel that we are only beginning the task of a sophisticated taxonomy of behavioral objectives for preschool children. As Bloom, Krathwol and others have discovered, to develop a taxonomy of behavioral objectives is a time-consuming, expensive, and difficult task.

LEARNING AND DEVELOPMENT

Several key assumptions about learning and development guide the Discovery Program: 1. normative developmental data provide important leads for preschool educational programming; 2. principles of learning, such as transfer of learning and overlearning, must be embedded in the educational programming; and 3. heterogeneous grouping of children according to age enhances the opportunities for individualized learning experiences.

In attempting to plan a comprehensive early education program which covers the various facets of child development we have examined the developmental literature for educational programming leads. In examining normative developmental data for preschool educational programming, a central assumption is present: to a large degree development proceeds in an orderly manner across time but specific experiences may modify the rate or pattern of development. In areas such as physical development, the general pattern of development is very similar across American children with the rate of development varying somewhat depending on experience (McGraw, 1966). In other areas of development such as mastery of standard English (not language) the pattern and rate of mastery varies tremendously depending on experience. As an operating principle, therefore, the developmental data were used as general guides to suggest behavioral objectives and to provide leads indicating the degree of variability within an area assuming that the larger the variability, the more likely experience interacting with genetics would modify the pattern and rate of development. Unfortunately, most developmental data is either too general or too incomplete to be of maximum benefit. For example, in spite of the rather large volume of data on the various Piagetian "stages" of development, these data are not very valuable for educational programming because the data cover several years of development with only a few observations such as the differences between the pre-operational and operational child. Our needs are for a very specific behavioral analysis of developmental data in small time steps. In other cases such as social development, our program is organized around a crude data base. Finally, after behavioral objectives have been organized developmentally, the main requirement is to determine the proper "match" between the child's developmental level and the developmental hierarchy of objectives.

Noticeably absent from the field of early education are programs which explicitly capitalize on the contributions from the psychology of learning literature. The Discovery Program is guided by the application of the following principles of learning: 1. task analysis; 2. successive approximation; 3. learning sets; 4. overlearning; 5. transfer; 6. generalization; and 7. reinforcement.

The children, ranging in age from two to six, are grouped heterogeneously during a Discovery Session because 1. it is a natural method of grouping paralleling the family structure, 2. older children serve as excellent models for younger children (White, 1961) and 3. older children reinforce their own learning while teaching younger children, thus learning important social skills that cannot be taught in any other way (Woolman, 1968).

From observing an older child a younger child may acquire motivation to learn, learn strategies and methods of seeking and receiving help, and learn something about a particular skill.

INSTRUCTION AND DEVELOPMENT

Several explicit theoretical assumptions about instructional materials and experiences guide the Discovery Program: 1. concrete sensory experience is important for maximum development; 2. multimedia materials are important in promoting maximum learning; 3. educational diagnosis is important in providing the "match" between a child's developmental level and planned learning experiences; and 4. differentiated staffing provides the best use of staff resources.

Following the insights of Piaget and Montessori, the educational environment is planned to promote concrete, multisensory experiences; however, an equal emphasis is placed on extending this concrete experience to a more abstract level by verbal exchange with the staff. While it is very important for preschool children to manipulate materials per se, this should not be the terminal objective in using a material.

Not only are multimedia materials (video tapes, audiotapes, etc.) used in the Center, but they are a part of a program in which the child goes from one media to another in an integrated plan. For example, following a film on the concept of tall and short, the child is immediately able to play with materials designed to consolidate and extend the film material. Programs like Sesame Street have fortunately begun to include manipulable materials to reinforce the audiovisual presentation.

Simply stated, educational diagnosis is important in order to know where a child is in a developmental skill area before proceeding to a more advanced level. The behavioral observations taken by the learning staff during planned activities and during free time enable the staff to be of maximum benefit in facilitating the child's development. Without the diagnosis, one cannot attain the proper match between a child's level and the needed "next step" of instruction. After the educational diagnosis is obtained, the staff is trained to use the planned activities or self-selected activities to capitalize on the knowledge of a child's level of development.

Lastly, the differentiated staffing pattern of the Centers reflects a discovery philosophy and a conscious attempt to incorporate these theoretical assumptions about instruction. (This will be discussed later.)

MOTIVATION AND DEVELOPMENT

The challenge in planning a well-designed educational program and environment is to capitalize on a child's general motivation in order to attain certain important behavioral objectives without interfering with his curiosity and exploration. The Discovery Program has employed five techniques successfully: 1. allow the child time to self-select his own activities after each planned activity; 2. plan the total environment so carefully that no matter what materials he self-selects they can be used to achieve specific behavioral objectives; 3. allow children of different ages to work together; 4. provide planned learning experiences with high interest value designed to stimulate a child to work with the materials to achieve specific behavioral objectives; and 5. apply contingent social reinforcement to shape and strengthen particular behaviors. During a two-hour Discovery Session, five planned activities are alternated with Discovery Time in which a child is free to self-select any play materials in the Center. The learning staff initiates the planned activities but they do not direct them. For example, when it is "TV time" a staff member makes this announcement and begins watching TV (i.e., initiates the activity), other children join in the TV viewing (social facilitation); however, a child is free to participate or to not participate in the activity. Likewise, when the TV time is over and the relevant learning materials are present, a child may or may not involve himself in activities related to the TV time. The staff members do not insist (i.e., direct) that the child behave in one particular manner. In general, this relaxed structure of learning experiences coupled with contingent social reinforcement when a child is participating in activities has been successful in providing a balance between total free play or self-selection at the one extreme and over-control from a teacher at the other. This balance leads to high motivation and active participation by the children.

CONTINUOUS EDUCATION

The limited contact time between any child and the typical preschool program makes it imperative that the child's parents be involved in his early education and development. Additionally, as early education programs begin earlier and earlier, it is advisable to work with the parent during the first two years of life. Gordon (1968), Levenstein (1969), Weikart (1969), and Nimnicht (1970) are among those who have included parent education and/or home visitation in early education programs.

    This program was designed around parental involvement in order to involve the major figures in the child's life more deeply in his development and to provide the child with a continuous educational experience that extends beyond the visits to the Discovery Center. While the parent involvement aspects will be discussed more thoroughly later, it provides Take-Home Materials that include: 1. weekly materials answering questions about various facets of child development; 2. suggested daily activities at home appropriate to a child's development; 3. specific learning materials, such as worksheets and educational toys; 4. parent instructions for use of the materials with the child at a range of ability levels; and 5. a parent observation form to summarize and report strengths or weaknesses of the Take-Home Materials and the week's activities.

CONTINUAL EVALUATION OF
SKILL AND CONCEPT ACQUISITION

On a regular basis the learning staff observes and evaluates the child's skill acquisition. A complete record of all observations and learning activities is kept for each child to assure proper planning and appropriate continuity of experiences for the child. The staff obtains needed detail by talking with the child and by watching him at play. One of the prime ingredients in staff development is the training of staff members to observe and listen to the child in order to guide him to activities that will help him build his abilities from his existing level of skills and concepts. It should be emphasized that children are not "tested" in the Discovery Program; they are evaluated. This is an important distinction, because typical testing programs lead to an evaluation of the child relative to the child's own prior ability level. Testing also introduces elements of stress and anxiety, detracting from play and learning.

COGNITIVE DEVELOPMENT PROGRAM

The Discovery development programs (cognitive, language, affective, motivational, social, and physical) are interlaced to represent as closely as possible the interactions that occur in real-life situations. These programs move away from standard classroom educational techniques in which one area of the curriculum is assigned to a specific period within the schedule and another curriculum area to another period. Although for clarity several programs are discussed as separate entities, they are in fact integrated throughout a Discovery Session.

Within the cognitive development program, challenges for the individual child are based on his current knowledge and state of development. Solving problems, classifying, understanding numbers, predicting and testing, and knowing the alphabet are illustrative of some of the basic skill areas involved. For each of the sub-skills within the basic skill areas, specific learning experiences have been designated to contribute to the development of the skill or concept. As an illustration, the following learning activity is designed to develop skills in the areas of observing and recognizing characteristics. This activity is aimed specifically at developing the concept of "same and different." The activity is initiated by the viewing of a videotape created for this purpose and titled "Same and Different." It runs for three minutes, involves two puppets, and focuses on distinguishing objects that are identical and those that are not. Following the viewing, the staff invites the children to play the game just as "Pip and Squeak," the TV puppets, did, and with the same materials — unit blocks. As the games are played, each child is given an opportunity to demonstrate or learn the use of the words "like," "not like," "alike," "not alike," "same," and "different." Similar activities are used to develop and reinforce other concepts with each child.

LANGUAGE DEVELOPMENT PROGRAM

Skill in communication is basic to reasoning and to social development. A child learns to communicate by listening, observing, and then by responding through the use of speech. Systematic building of larger listening and speaking vocabularies makes it easier for children to communicate. Later, reading and writing develop as the basic skills of communication that largely determine the child's understanding of the world. The key to successful communication, however, is not only the addition of words to a child's vocabulary and the addition of patterns of speech, but also the development of his confidence in his own ability to make himself understood by others. Within the Discovery Program, the children's use of speech is enhanced as they learn to tell stories, to take part in group discussions, and to play communications games. Great emphasis is placed on stimulating conversation among children and between children and adults by the use of audio-visual films and tapes and by carefully selected learning materials whose manipulation naturally elicits conversation.

AFFECTIVE SUPPORT PROGRAM

This program concentrates on the emotional adjustment of children, assisting the dependent child, the aggressive child, and others to overcome problems that might otherwise impede their success. Of great importance to this aspect of the program is the continual training and monitoring of the staff to encourage them to maintain a warm, sympathetic, and enjoyable relationship with each child. Through imitation learning these adult-child relationships help promote social skills, behaviors, and motives that are essential for maximum personal growth and development. Activities within the program help children learn to identify different emotions and to role-play social skills and behaviors.

MOTIVATIONAL PROGRAM

This program assists children in attaining control over their environment in such areas as self-confidence, creativity, initiative, work and study skills, sticking to a task, responsibility, and self-control. By giving children an opportunity to master new skills and concepts at their own pace, without pressure or failure, the Discovery Program helps them build self-confidence and establish an image of themselves as successful human beings. As a child learns new ways to put thoughts, information, and skills together, he finds joy and excitement in his new ability to express ideas that are his alone. In this program a child has the opportunity to use his imagination in playing, in pretending, in thinking, in acting, in drawing, and in building. The development of imagination in a child encourages the blossoming of his creativity. Initiative is developed as each child is given great latitude to experiment — to initiate action on his own — and to be rewarded with praise for his positive accomplishments. The children are encouraged to develop good work and study skills and to stick to a task as they are motivated with activities and materials that appeal to their individual interests. They then develop habits of patience and concentration that enable them to persevere with other tasks that are sometimes less rewarding or are somewhat frustrating.

SOCIALIZATION AND SOCIAL DEVELOPMENT PROGRAM

This program permeates all aspects of the Discovery Program system by providing continual opportunities for the child to acquire skills in working cooperatively with others and to learn techniques for non-destructive resolution of personal and interpersonal problems. A staff thoroughly trained to understand positive approaches to the child's rule-testing and rule-breaking is crucial in helping the child develop patterns of responsible behavior. The learning staff is trained to recognize the child's attempts to solve personal and interpersonal problems and to deal with them in an understanding and positive manner through the use of contingent reinforcement to enable the child to develop positive self-concepts. In the group activities in each Discovery Session a child has many opportunities to work cooperatively with adults and other children to achieve mutually rewarding goals.

PHYSICAL DEVELOPMENT PROGRAM

To a child, agility and physical development are often goals in and of themselves. A child is proud of his physical accomplishments, and they in turn contribute to his good health. By playing simple, active games, the children develop eye-hand coordination, muscle tone, and a sense of confidence in their physical abilities. The physical activities are carefully integrated into the total program, cutting across the cognitive, social, and language programs to reinforce past and current achievements.

ACCOUNTABILITY

Because the Discovery Program is designed around behavioral objectives, the system can be held accountable as to whether or not the children attain the established objectives. A parent can readily understand the step-by-step approach to learning within each skill area because the objectives are clearly stated in lay terminology. Thus, the parent can readily determine whether the immediate objectives are being met. Because parents are free to withdraw their children from the Discovery Program at any time, the system must be constantly accountable to the parents in terms of the results with the individual child. We feel that, because it is so easy for a parent to withdraw from the program, we have been exceedingly fortunate in achieving an average weekly retention rate of more than 96 percent of the parents and children remaining in the program — this despite the many withdrawals caused by families moving to other communities among a highly mobile population.

THE INTERACTING COMPONENTS
OF THE DISCOVERY PROGRAM

The design of the Discovery Program includes consideration of its component structure, requirements and design of facilities, programs and services, staff requirements, staff development, and fiscal planning. In addition, the interaction and relationships among the people, places, and programs have been taken into account in the planning. These include: *People* — the parents, the child, the staff, the administration, and the community; *Places* — physical facilities and locations for Discovery Centers, homes, schools, and other community institutions; *Programs* — cognitive growth, language development, socialization and social development, values and motivations, emotional adjustment, physical development, and special services to meet individual, family and community needs.

THE INTERACTING HUMAN COMPONENTS

PARENTS

In the Discovery Program's conceptualization of its curriculum, the parents play the key role in facilitating the child's development. The program, first, focuses on parent education in the broad area of child development, and, second, supplies the parent with the necessary materials and toys to provide a continuing educational experience in terms of helping the child attain specific behavioral objectives. This orientation is dictated not only by common sense, but through recognition that high quality and economical early education programs can be successfully delivered only with parent involvement.

To help motivate the parents' involvement, interactions were designed with all the other subsystems. For example, consider the parents' interactions with the learning staff. During a Discovery Session, a member of the staff discusses with the parents the activities being conducted in the Center that day and indicates why they are important. While a Discovery Session is in progress, the parents watch the child interact with the staff either directly or over closed-circuit TV; this provides two benefits to the program — 1. the learning staff members constantly perform at their best because they are under close scrutiny from the parents, and 2. the learning staff members serve as role models for the parents on how to interact with the child. At the end of a Discovery Session a member of the staff demonstrates the Take-Home Materials to the parents and answers questions the parents may have. In addition, members of the staff have conferences with parents to report on individual achievements of the child and to suggest individualized approaches to meet the needs of the child.

THE CHILD

As mentioned earlier, the children in the Discovery Program range in age from 2 to 6 with a median age of 3.7. The interactions of the child with the other subsystems have been designed to motivate the child to succeed. For example, both staff and parents are encouraged to reinforce the child's positive accomplishments and to refrain from criticizing his failures. The planned activities at the Discovery Center and the suggested activities to be accomplished at home are designed to be fun and entertaining, with their educational objectives being attained incidentally, so far as the child is concerned.

The planned activities *must* be entertaining and motivating, because the child has the prerogative to join or reject each activity. Alternating with the planned group activities, the child has the repeated opportunity in "Discovery Time" to select materials and activities that appeal to his individual interests. The child participates in the planned activities as part of a learning group of no more than twelve children. Two staff members are assigned to each learning group in an adult-child ratio of 1:6, thus insuring that there is ample opportunity for individualized interaction with each child.

LEARNING STAFF

The learning staff of each Discovery Center is composed of a Learning Director, Learning Advisors, and Learning Aides. The term "teacher" is consciously avoided in the belief that the conventional connotation of the word "teacher" is antithetical to the learning environment of the Discovery Program. To many persons, the term "teacher" connotes an authority who stands before a group of children, lecturing and giving lessons. The Discovery Program learning staff avoids direct teaching in the conventional sense of "you do this because I tell you to do it." Instead, the learning staff organizes the environment and presents interesting activities that stimulate a child to use materials and concepts. The staff members diagnose a child's strengths and weaknesses, guiding him to discover relationships and concepts through careful verbal probes and demonstrations designed to help him acquire specified behavioral objectives. The qualifications and job descriptions of the members of the learning staff are in brief: 1. *Learning Director:* A teacher with five years of experience and a degree in early education. Her specific responsibilities include: a. staff supervision and training; b. Discovery Program administration; and c. relations with parents. 2. *Learning Advisor:* A teacher with two or three years experience and a degree in early education. The primary responsibility of a Learning Advisor is to interact with the children to assist them in the learning process. Specific responsibilities include: a. conduct of the Discovery Program sessions; b. guiding children to meet individual learning needs; c. insuring accuracy of child records; and d. relations with parents. 3. *Learning Aide:* A man or woman, usually a college graduate, who is specially trained in observing and working with children using Discovery Program techniques and procedures. He or she is responsible for recording observations as to each child's achievements and assists the Learning Advisor in implementing a Discovery Session with a particular learning group of children.

EDUCATIONAL CONSULTANTS

Each Discovery Center is assigned a Ph.D. educational-school psychologist who functions 1. as a consultant to the parents, 2. as a consultant to the center staff, and 3. as an arm of the research program. Routine consultation is provided free to the parents in the form of brief individual conferences and regular group conferences.

To have easy access to a professional doctoral level psychologist is an attractive feature of the program for many parents. The Center staff relies heavily on the psychologist's professional expertise in working with children, in implementing certain aspects of the program, and in crisis consultation. The psychologist's role as a part of the research staff centers around developing and administering instruments to measure the impact of the program on the children and comparing results of the Discovery Program with those of more traditional approaches to early education.

PERSONNEL DEVELOPMENT

Probably the most critical aspect of implementing any preschool program is a good training program for the staff. Weikart (1969) has suggested that staff training and other noncurriculum concerns may have more to do with the success or failure of a program than its curriculum content. The learning staff members are trained through a four-step procedure: 1. thorough familiarization with the Learning Staff Handbook; 2. assignment to a fully operating Discovery Center for pre-service training; 3. placement in a continuing training program using videotape training materials; and 4. field monitoring by staff development personnel using the Learning Staff Inventory. To be candid, designing and implementing this personnel development program has been extremely difficult because of the time and talent required to produce and organize the written materials, video tapes, and other educational materials and equipment used in the program. After eight months of operation, the staff development program is undergoing continued revisions so that paraprofessionals or multipurpose workers can be trained as Learning Staff members in Discovery Centers.

RESEARCH STAFF

The research staff is comprised of a director of research (Ph.D. developmental psychologist), four Ph.D. psychologists, an M. S. statistician, and several consultants. The most positive aspect of research in this setting is that the staff does not have to deal with many of the usual problems (such as permission to use subjects and problems of scheduling) found when conducting research in school systems as an "outsider."

CENTER ADMINISTRATIVE STAFF

A Center Director manages each Center. He or she has had several years of experience in educational administration. The Center Director is responsible for fiscal management of the Center, demonstrating the Discovery Program to prospective enrollees, scheduling new learning groups, and in general operating the Discovery Center. He is assisted by a Registrar who enrolls new children into the program and is responsible for the flow of recorded information between the Center and UEC headquarters.

UEC OPERATIONS STAFF

A national operations staff administers the operation of the Centers, providing logistical support with materials, and monitoring the operation of each Center.

UEC EDUCATIONAL SYSTEMS DIVISION STAFF

A highly-trained staff develops, produces, evaluates, and acquires materials and equipment for the Discovery Program. All instructional materials used within the program are developed and produced by this staff. On the other hand, most of the learning materials, such as educational toys, have been acquired from other producers after these materials have been evaluated and tested with children. This division administers the staff development program for the learning staffs of the Centers. In addition the division produces many of the audio-visual materials used in the Discovery Program, including TV-tapes, slide/sound shows, film strips, and audio-tapes.

THE INTERACTING MATERIALS AND EQUIPMENT COMPONENTS

Many of the interactions within the Discovery Program system are stimulated by the manipulation of materials and equipment. Special attention is given to determine the best use of each of these components to insure that it fulfills its purpose. Of course, all of the ideas, procedures, assumptions, and programs discussed in the section of the conceptualization of the curriculum may be considered important components, but their interactions with the comprehensive program as a whole already have been detailed and will not be repeated here. Otherwise, the three major types of materials and equipment include: 1. instructional materials; 2. learning equipment and materials, including books, educational toys and equipment used directly in learning processes; and 3. the physical environment of the Discovery Center.

INSTRUCTIONAL MATERIALS

The instructional materials comprising more than 2,300 pages, all of the printed handbooks, notebooks, and booklets that contain the specific instructional information about the Discovery Program.

THE LEARNING STAFF HANDBOOK

The learning staff handbook includes all of the policies and procedures needed to understand and implement the Discovery Program. Its fifteen chapters serve as the basic handbook for the learning staff, and include: 1. the basic principles of the Discovery Program; 2. the detailed responsibilities of each member of the learning staff; 3. the uses of the various handbooks, booklets, notebooks, and report forms of the program; and 4. suggestions concerning the best methods of interacting with children and parents.

THE CHILD DEVELOPMENT CHART

The Child Development Chart contains the taxonomy of over 1,800 behavioral objectives classified into skill areas and coded numerically across each skill area. Earlier we discussed the criteria for selection of these objectives and the organization of the objectives into a taxonomy. Appendix A illustrates a sample of the Child Development Chart.

THE LEARNING MATERIALS HANDBOOK

The Learning Materials Handbook includes: 1. a picture of each learning material used in the Discovery Center; 2. a brief discussion of the way to use the material; and 3. a list of behavioral objectives that may be addressed using this particular material. This handbook is used extensively by the learning staff 1. to help them understand the flexible uses of the learning materials; and 2. to relate each material to the total objectives of the Discovery Program.

THE LEARNING GROUP NOTEBOOK

Separate 16 to 32 page Learning Group Notebooks (40 of which have been completed thus far) serve as guides for the learning staff in conducting specific sessions. Each notebook is a guide for the learning staff in conducting a specific Discovery Session. Each includes: 1. a table of contents; 2. answers to queries from the staff about policy and procedures; 3. an outline of the planned activities, locations, and materials for the entire session; 4. separate pages of step-by-step instructions for conducting each of the planned activities; 5. a set of behavioral objectives for each planned activity with space for the Learning Aide to record observations of each child's achievements; and 6. a Session Research Form to be filled out by the Learning Advisor and sent to UEC headquarters at the conclusion of the session. Use of these notebooks insures a measure of uniform quality control in the presentation of each session at all preschool sites.

THE PARENT SUGGESTION NOTEBOOK

A separate 24 to 36 page Parent Suggestion Notebook also is prepared and printed for each of the numbered sessions of the Discovery Program. In the first eight months of operation of the Discovery Program, forty of these notebooks have been developed. Each notebook is a guide to parents and is given to a parent to take home at the end of a session. Each notebook contains: 1. a description of each of the planned activities presented in the session and an explanation of its importance in terms of its behavioral objectives; 2. answers to questions about child development that have been asked by the parents; 3. a list of suggested Home Discovery Activities that may be used with the child during the forthcoming week; 4. a weekly planning calendar on which the parent may schedule various suggested activities with the child throughout the week; 5. instructions for the use of workbook material which has been given to the child to reinforce skills or concepts presented during the Discovery Session; 6. step-by-step instructions for activities to be conducted with the child at a range of ability levels from early to middle to advanced, utilizing the educational materials or toys that have been given to the child at the end of the session; and 7. a Parent Observation Form for the parent to fill out and return to the Discovery Center, reporting on the week's activities at home.

PARENT REPORT LETTERS

Parent Report Letters are sent each month to parents with children enrolled in the Discovery Program. These letters detail each of the behavioral objectives achieved by the child during the month and provide suggestions as to ways the parent can help reinforce these skills and concepts. To handle the large volume of letters, computerized information retrieval system was designed. Separate paragraphs were written for each of the behavioral objectives in the Child Development Chart, and these paragraphs have been stored in the computer. A letter is compiled by the computer when a child's account number and code numbers of the behavioral objectives the child has attained are given to the computer. The computer also stores the data on each individual child for use in research evaluation.

RETAIL MATERIAL BOOKLETS

Retail Material Booklets have been prepared for each of the educational toys and games that are available for purchase by the parents at the Discovery Center. Each booklet contains a picture of the material, a description, and a series of early, middle, and advanced level activities to engage the child in achieving various behavioral objectives. The content of these booklets is similar to that of the Parent Suggestion Notebooks and encourages parent-child interaction with the learning materials.

LEARNING EQUIPMENT AND MATERIALS

Most learning activities center around 600 different learning materials that have been evaluated and tested for use in the program. Each item of educational material has been selected for effective interaction with a young child, and much care was taken in choosing the objects and equipment. The furniture and room arrangement are designed to promote learning by taking into consideration the children's needs and the requirements of different activities. Each toy, book, slide projector, microscope, television set, concept builder, set of creative materials, is carefully evaluated both for its role in learning and for its quality.

The following are examples of educational materials and equipment that have been developed and are used in the Discovery Centers:

1. A multimedia system which is housed in a single compact unit. A set of controls permits a given medium as well as combinations of media to be selected. For example, presentations have been prepared which interweave audio tapes, motion picture films, and slides. The devices in the unit include a cassette audio player, a single concept 8mm movie projector, a 35mm slide projector, a projection microscope, and a 35mm strip film projector.
2. A Portable TV Studio on Wheels, complete with its own TV camera, TV Tape recorder, and viewing screen that can be used by the children themselves in producing cooperative TV shows. It is also used in presenting single-concept educational TV tapes for planned activities and in recording group activities for teacher training and parent instructions. The use of this TV equipment with instant playback is particularly effective in enabling children and staff members to see themselves on TV as others see them.
3. A "Chatterbox" device that enables children to freely select printed cards showing letters, words, and numbers which the machine reads aloud to them, allowing a child who cannot read to obtain information that he wants from print. Use of this device encourages reading readiness, reading, and understanding of number concepts.

4. A learning device that enables a child to press buttons to respond to programmed slide/sound materials in learning the alphabet, beginning reading, beginning spelling, and beginning arithmetic. Use of this device helps a child to learn at his own pace with minimal intervention by staff.
5. A closed-circuit TV system designed to provide the parents and Center Director with unlimited opportunities to make unobtrusive observations of the staff and children during a session. Various components are located in three places in the center. The director's office houses a video-tape recorder, a desk top TV monitor, and switching controls. In the learning area of the center a small TV camera and microphone are mounted on the wall. A TV monitor on a swivel base is located in the parent's waiting area. In actual practice, the present system does not provide a complete visual image of the activities throughout the center. The addition of additional cameras with zoom lens and additional microphones would solve the problem, but the cost has been prohibitive.
6. A computer terminal is hooked up to a computer on a time-sharing arrangement. The uses of this equipment range from simple letter matching and identification to reading and math programs.
7. Educational TV tapes designed around the program's objectives that use puppets to introduce new concepts and processes in a dramatic manner to stimulate and motivate young children.
8. Slide/sound programs that assist children in understanding concepts of the world around them, such as the microscopic world that can be seen through magnifying glasses.
9. Audio tapes for synchronization with color motion pictures geared to the understanding of preschool children.
10. A collection of books by outstanding authors and artists, including many Newberry and Caldecott award-winning titles, that have been selected for their relevance to the Discovery Program as well as for their ability to interest preschool children.
11. A cassette tape recorder is used during conversation time to record and play back cassette tapes. A multiple earphone strip permits as many as eight pairs of earphones to be plugged in at one time to allow several children to listen privately to an audio tape cassette.
12. A portable phonograph and record library are used frequently by the children during Discovery time.

The Take-Home Materials in the Discovery Program are given to the child at the end of each Discovery session to take home and keep. Each of these materials is accompanied by Suggestions to Parents and a Parent Observation Form to be used in reporting back to the Center on the child's use of the material. The crux of the Discovery Program is the parent-child use of the Take-Home Materials.

A few Learning Materials have been manufactured in limited numbers as research prototypes for the Discovery Program. These materials were developed for special needs in the program that could not be met by commercially available materials. Because these materials are for use only in the Discovery Centers, the learning staff reports regularly on the usage of these materials, on the interest of children in them, on their value in developing skills and concepts, and on their durability.

PHYSICAL ENVIRONMENT OF THE DISCOVERY CENTER

The Discovery Center environment was carefully planned to implement the educational philosophy and behavioral objectives of the Discovery Program. Each Center is colorfully decorated and is comfortably furnished and air-conditioned to provide year-around temperature control.

Many pieces of equipment were specially designed and manufactured to fit the needs of the preschool environment. Large plastic Learning Circles were constructed, enabling small children to sit around a low table in group activities. The Learning Circles are mounted on casters to provide greater flexibility in the use of space. Low portable partitions enable the learning staffs to subdivide the space of the learning area in order to provide closure for separate learning groups. Colorful Learning Corners provide low desk space for one child and shelf space for learning materials. Because these Learning Corners are portable, children can arrange them for a variety of play activities. The lowest shelves of A-frame storage units along the walls of the learning area are used as work surfaces by young children.

Some Discovery Centers were carpeted and some were tiled in an effort to learn which type of floor covering was most useful. It has been decided in future Centers to carpet most of the learning area, but to tile an area reserved for art activities.

Because the Discovery Centers vary in size and arrangement of space, no two Centers can have their materials organized in exactly the same way. Therefore, each Learning Director finds unique ways of making the best arrangement of materials for a particular Center so that they are accessible and inviting to the children.

The learning materials are grouped in 16 activity centers of related materials, including a reading corner, a listening post, a science laboratory, a number corner, a store, an office, and a music center.

OPERATION OF THE ENTIRE DISCOVERY PROGRAM

To help provide an understanding of the Discovery Program as a whole, this section will discuss 1. what happens during a typical Discovery Session, 2. the modification of the program through feedback information, and 3. the variables that either facilitate or impede the program's operation.

A TYPICAL DISCOVERY SESSION

Whether a child has or has not been to a Discovery Center before, he requires some time to become adjusted to the new environment. The children of a learning group are not immediately plunged into a guided activity, because during their period of adjustment to the Discovery Center environment they are unlikely to be able to function at their best.

The Learning Advisor guides the children to one of the Learning Circles. She sits down and invites them to sit with her. Both the Learning Advisor and Learning Aide introduce themselves and encourage the children to tell their names. They ask a few questions about pets or brothers and sisters. But they do *not* force any child to talk who does not wish to, either by direct questions or by innuendo.

The staff may divert the attention of the children from themselves by showing them a tape recorder. They record some conversation, play it back, and encourage the children to use the tape recorder themselves to record each other's voices. If the children are very young, the use of the tape recorder may frighten them. If it seems to, the staff does not use it.

During the conversation period the Learning Aide records observations about each of the children — especially in the Basic Skill Areas: 3. EXPANDING VOCABULARY, 12. SPEAKING, and 26. RELATIONS WITH OTHERS.

If the children of the group have never before attended a Discovery Session, the staff members take them on a tour of the various Activity Centers, such as the Reading Corner, the Workshop, the Village, and so on. If one or more of the children spontaneously pick up and begin to use materials or equipment at one of the Activity Centers, the staff does NOT try to force them to continue the tour.

The object of the tour is not the tour itself but to make the children feel at home in the Discovery Center. If a child stops and begins using a Learning Material, it means that he is feeling comfortable about being there and does not really need to go any farther with the tour.

Before reaching the end of the tour all of the children in the group may have dropped off one-by-one at various Activity Centers. They find out about the other Activity Centers on a later visit to the Discovery Center.

About half of the time during a session is devoted to Discovery Time, or free play, between each of the planned activities. Each child is free to choose materials or activities that suit his needs. If the Learning Advisor is not familiar with the particular material that a child chooses to use, reference to the *Learning Materials Handbook* will suggest various uses for the material to which the child may be assisted.

The Learning Aide refers to the *Learning Materials Handbook* to determine what observations of concepts and skills may be made as to the child's use of the materials. These observations may be entered directly into the Child Records or may be entered on black Observation forms for transfer later to the Child Records.

The planned Learning Activities called for by the Session Schedule are spaced out during the session, allowing for Discovery Time after each Learning Activity. The Learning Advisor carries out the instructions on the Learning Activity forms, giving individual assistance to those children who need it. The Learning Aide observes the children, recording the prescribed observations on the Observation form for that activity.

About fifteen minutes before the session is over the staff gathers the children together for the final planned Learning Activity, which always is a demonstration of that session's Take-Home Material. While the Learning Aide demonstrates activities suitable to the skill levels of the children, the Learning Advisor talks with the parents about the use of the Take-Home Materials at home during the forthcoming week.

At the conclusion of the session, the children are guided to the reception area by the Learning Aide, where they meet their parents.

The staff makes sure each child has his Take-Home Material and that each parent has a Parent Suggestion Notebook with appropriate activities checked for the individual abilities of each child.

In conversing with the parents, the staff always makes *positive observations* about skills or concepts that the child has demonstrated during the session.

As soon as the children have been returned to their parents, the Learning Advisor and the Learning Aide spend whatever time is needed to transfer observations from the Observation forms to the Child Records and to discuss the observations made on the various children. They also fill out the Session Report form to provide evaluative data on the results of the session.

MODIFICATION OF THE PROGRAM THROUGH FEEDBACK INFORMATION

To insure continual improvement of the Discovery Program based on its usage by staff, parents, and children, several feedback loops were built into the program: 1. weekly reports by the Learning Director of each Discovery Center containing statistical data on child attendance as well as specific parent and staff comments about the successes and failures of specific activities, materials, and equipment; 2. daily session reports filled out by a Learning Advisor each time a session is conducted, so that data is accumulated as to the success of each activity in each session in terms of length of time an activity held the interest of the children involved, and learning staff suggestions for the improvement of the activities in the specific session; 3. child profile forms sent into UEC Headquarters once each month on each individual child, enumerating the skills and skill levels accomplished each month by each child; and 4. weekly reports by each parent detailing the accomplishments of the child in using Take-Home Learning Materials and the parent's suggestions for improvements in the activities and the materials.

In the eight months since the Discovery Program was initiated, more than 150,000 items of information have been recorded and analyzed from these feedback loops. Information derived from this feedback system enabled the Educational Systems Division staff to produce, print, and distribute the first revision of the program in March 1970, only six months after the first version of the program had begun to be used.

As quickly as feedback indicates a weakness in the program, appropriate modifications are made in the session activity materials, the take-home materials, or in the total curriculum. The instructional information accompanying a session, such as the Learning Group Notebook, may be modified and distributed to the Centers in as little time as two weeks, while a change in a video-tape or a Learning Material may take as long as four or five months. Parenthetically, the parents generally have been very happy with the Take-Home Materials, and our least-liked Take-Home Material is rated as useful by over 50% of the parents. As a rule, we consider replacing a material if over 20% of the parents indicate that it is not useful.

In sum, the operating system provides a large data base that makes rapid and precise modifications of any facet of the curriculum possible and feasible.

VARIABLES THAT FACILITATE THE PROGRAM'S OPERATION

A program may be said to be operating smoothly when all of the components are *in balance.* The key to a balanced operating program is *to provide* 1. *a mechanism for decision-making and* 2. *the support components to implement the decisions.* When the Discovery Program operates smoothly, it does so because techniques of sound management have been used to remove the usual ambiguities in operating an early education program. An organized personnel development program insures a well-trained staff while the various handbooks and notebooks allow proper implementation of the program. This concern with organization and efficient management does not, however, remove the staff's flexibility and creativity but it serves to channel the expression of these behaviors as they interact with the children and parents.

VARIABLES THAT IMPEDE THE PROGRAM'S OPERATION

The Discovery Program's total system fails to operate smoothly 1. when the mechanism for decision-making is in error; 2. when the support elements fail to implement the decisions; or 3. when certain human biases cannot be overcome.

In any new program, rules for operation are established and they later must be modified in the light of experience. One erroneous decision made early in the operation of the Discovery Program was to schedule overlapping sessions, in which new sessions began every 30 minutes with different groups of children. While the decision seemed sound in theory, in practice chaos resulted as each new group entered the Center and disrupted the activities of other groups; the practice was discontinued shortly thereafter.

A clear example of a program in a state of imbalance is provided when the support elements fail to implement the decisions. During the first few months of a new Center's operation, one of the most difficult problems is to provide the necessary session material on schedule. It is a tribute to the ingenuity of many a Learning Director that the staffs of various Centers were able to improvise session materials when the warehouse failed to provide needed session materials.

Probably the variable that most frequently impedes the operation of the Discovery Program is human bias. The parents and staff share certain common biases yet each group has a few unique group biases that sometimes throws the system into a state of imbalance.

Five troublesome biases, or beliefs, are frequently exhibited by the parents and staff. *First*, the belief that "education" should take place in an institutional setting rather than in the home. Because many public schools have actively discouraged involvement of parents in their children's education at home, it is easy to understand why both teachers and parents unconsciously resist this aspect of the Discovery Program. Additionally, some parents indicate that, although they believe that parent involvement is important, they feel that to become involved would require them to rearrange their lives to provide more time to fulfill this responsibility. *Second*, the parents and staff are sometimes upset because they feel too little *direct* teaching takes place in a Discovery Session and that too little emphasis is placed on recitation of facts. *Third*, there is a strong bias by parents and staff against heterogeneous grouping of children by age. We have been unable to convince some parents and staff members of the benefits of heterogeneous grouping by age, even though research data gathered in the project indicates that age differences among three to five-year-olds are of little value as predictors of a child's skills or grasp of concepts. *Fourth*, the parents and the staff have a difficult time breaking with a traditional school set in which a Learning Staff member is seen as a "teacher" and the Take-Home Materials are seen as "homework," thus negating basic tenets of the Discovery Program. The *fifth* common bias shared by the parents and staff concerns the view of a business corporation involved in education. The profit motive is suspect and the Discovery Program is viewed with some doubts because it was developed by a business corporation. This reservation is understandable because historically, curriculum development has been a preserve of the educational establishment, with business corporations relegated to the role of producing textbooks or other materials used to implement curricula. Parenthetically, it should be noted that almost all of the nursery schools in America are operated privately on a for-profit basis.

Three biases are relatively unique to the parents. *First*, many parents do not realize how important the early years are for learning and development. Consequently, it is difficult to convince some parents that there is any need to enroll their three-year-old in *any* preschool program. Government statistics show that only a small minority of American children are enrolled in preschool educational programs. We believe that the majority of children do not attend nursery school or other preschools mainly because their parents are not convinced of the potential benefits of preschool. *Second*, many parents do not recognize that learning is a continuous process in or out of a formal setting and that they, as parents, play the key role in promoting and facilitating preschool learning. Consequently, these parents find it difficult to believe that a program that only requires their child to be present in an institutional setting for one or two sessions each week can have a significant effect on the child's future. Originally, a parent was offered only one two-hour session per week, but more flexible schedules have been developed for those parents who feel strongly that their child should attend sessions in the Center more than once a week. *Third*, many parents, and some staff members, perceive specific educational toys as being more appropriate to one age level than another regardless of the potential uses of these toys for multiple activities at various levels of difficulty. For example, a Take-Home Toy such as the Giant Snap-Lock Beads has been dismissed with such comments as, "He had that when he was a baby," or, "She is too old for those" — even though the Parent Suggestions call for use of the beads in relatively sophisticated sequencing problems that older children enjoy.

The biases that are unique to the Learning Staff can be classified into entry biases and later biases. Two major entry biases of the Learning Staff often impeded the smooth functioning of the Discovery Program. Most of the members of the original Learning Staffs were drawn from the ranks of early educators and they possessed a strong bias against a behavioral approach to preschool education. This behavioral approach was often completely misunderstood and after working within the Discovery Program for some time, most of these staff members have come to recognize that the behavioral approach is very responsive to the needs and interests of the children, as well as providing the Learning Staff with specific means of guiding learning. A second entry bias of many members of the original staff, as with many traditional early educators, was a belief in what has been called the "sunshine theory of learning" — a view of the teacher as the source of light for growth and development and of the child as a recipient of the radiance emanating from the teacher. The Discovery Program calls for a reversal of this bias, with the child becoming the focus of learning, and the staff member adjusting to meet the needs of the child.

Two later staff biases emerged after the Discovery Program had operated for some time. The first was a bias that developed against the recording of data necessary for feedback on evaluation and improvement of the program. The data gathering became regarded as an imposition on the staff and was not seen as an integral part of the program's operation. The forms were subsequently modified to make the data recording and reporting easier and the staffs were briefed on the critical need for this feedback for the program to stay in balance. However, these changes revealed a second later staff bias — a bias against changes in the report forms or other changes in the program. In other words, within six months the program had become "established" and the staff had become loath to change patterns of behavior that they had come to accept as routine.

RESEARCH PROGRAM

The research program focuses on activities designed 1. to improve and evaluate the Discovery Program and 2. to contribute valuable developmental data to benefit all researchers in early education. Each of these activities will be briefly described in its present stage.

DATA STORAGE

Behavioral observations are stored on computer tape to be used in reporting to the parents on a child's performance and to be analyzed to improve the program.

LEARNING STAFF SELECTION

After review of their academic credentials, members of the learning staff are selected on their performance on a behavioral test of 17 dimensions while engaging a child in learning activity, and while monitored by two observers. Staff are scored according to how closely their behavior approximates the ideal learning staff member. While this procedure has face validity, it remains to be seen whether it has accurate predictive validity.

SESSION OBSERVATIONS

Earlier the Session Report Form was discussed by outlining the behavioral observations taken at each session. This information is used immediately in prescribing some of the learning experiences for the children.

WEEKLY OBSERVATIONS

A small study is currently underway which was designed 1. to isolate exactly what a child learns from one week's use of a particular Take-Home Material and

2. to discover the relationship between the amount of time the parent and child use the material and the amount of learning.

MEASURING THE IMPACT OF THE PROGRAM

For the past several months, we have been gathering data to measure the impact of the Discovery Program on children, using three dependent measures administered at various times across twelve months. This between-group design varies treatment (Discovery, nursery school, and no preschool) and age (three, three-and-one-half, and four-years-of-age). The Discovery Evaluation Instrument, a test designed to measure the session and Take-Home objectives, is administered every five weeks; the Curiosity Test, from Banta's Cincinnati Autonomy Test Battery (1970), is administered at three-month intervals; and the Binet is administered as a pretest, after six months, and as a posttest.

PARENT'S OBSERVATIONS

The Parent Observation Form provides space for the parents to report their perceptions of the children's learning. One of our major research interests is to determine how accurately parents observe their children's behavior.

The Discovery research program hopes to add to the developmental literature important longitudinal data as we track Discovery children across time. A scarcity of clean developmental data exists across all preschool behavioral areas. Possibly our standard recording system can be used to gather systematic descriptive developmental data on large numbers of children.

Finally, if parents are accurate observers of their children's behavior, we hope to enlist a large cadre of parents to make specific observations that will complement and extend our Center observations.

REFERENCES | 9

Ausubel, D. P. *Educational psychology: A cognitive view.* New York: Holt, Rinehart and Winston, Inc., 1968.
Bayley, N. Bayley scales of mental development. Psychology Corporation, 1969.
Banta, T. J. Tests for the evaluation of early childhood education: The Cincinnati autonomy test battery (CATB). In J. Hellmuth (Ed.), Cognitive Studies, Volume *I*. New York: Bruner/Mazel, 1970.
Bloom, B. S. *Stability and change in human characteristics.* New York: John Wiley and Sons, 1964.
Beberman, M. *An emerging program of secondary school mathematics.* Cambridge, Massachusetts: Harvard University Press, 1958.
Bereiter, C. and Englemann, S. E. *Teaching disadvantaged children.* Englewood Cliffs, New Jersey: Prentice-Hall, 1966.
Gagné, R. M. and Brown, L. T. Some factors in the programming of conceptual material. *Journal of Experimental Psychology,* 1961, *62,* 313-321.
Gordon, I. J. *Reaching the child through parent education.* Institute for Development of Human Resources, College of Education, University of Florida, 1968.
Hendrix, G. Learning by discovery. *Mathematics Teacher,* 1961, *54,* 290-299.
Levenstein, P. *Cognitive growth in preschoolers through verbal interaction with mothers.* Mimeograph (n. d.), 1969.
McGraw, M. *Neuromuscular Maturation of the Human Infant.* Reprinted, Hafner Publishing Co., 1966.
Nimnicht, G. *Toy lending library.* Far West Regional Educational Laboratory, 1970.
Parker, R. K., Ambron, S., Danielson, G. I., Halbrook, M. C., and Levine, J. A. *Overview of cognitive and language programs for three, four, and five-year-old children.* The City University of New York, 1970.
Stanley, J. C. The role of instruction, discovery, and revision in early learning. *Elementary School Journal,* 1949, *49,* 455-458.
Weikart, D. P. *Comparative study of three preschool curricula.* Paper presented at the biennial meeting of the Society for Research in Child Development, 1969.
White, M. A. and Harris, M. W. *The school psychologist.* New York: Harper and Brothers, 1961.
Woolman, M. *Take-off: A micro-social learning environment system for improving school readiness (a progressive choice system).* Vineland Public School District and the New Jersey Education Program for Seasonal and Migrant Families, June 1968.

Robison | *Introduction* | 10

The CHILD Curriculum, developed and described by Dr. Robison, is comprehensive in its base in the empirical literature and theory, in the content areas included in the curriculum, and in the instructional strategies employed. The main goal of the CHILD Curriculum is "maximum cognitive functioning in school," and special emphasis is placed upon language and cognition. Language goals of the program include encouraging developmental progress toward mature speech in the native dialect while teaching standard English as a second dialect to inner-city children. Cognitive goals include encouraging playfulness with a variety of self-selected objects to stimulate learning of all types, stimulating verbalizations, providing success experiences in cognitive tasks, and providing practice with varied content of school learning.

Drawing from the theories of J. Piaget and O. K. Moore, Robison emphasizes the importance of play, games, and active experiences in learning. However, given that all goals cannot be achieved through play, direct instruction in tutorial situations is used for finding each child's level of competence and thereby structuring appropriate teaching episodes. The child's autonomy, as exemplified in his choice of activities, is respected wherever and whenever possible. Thus the instructional techniques used in the CHILD Curriculum range from spontaneous, unstructured play to direct tutorial instruction.

Eight content areas comprise the curriculum: cognitive skills, music, language, mathematics, science, sociology, geography, and economics. The "cognitive skills" area focuses on "conceptual needs basic to all content areas." Each content area includes a summary, a list of behavioral objectives, and "structure models" — detailed suggestions for tutorial teaching keyed to the child's responses and designed to provide both success and challenge.

The teacher's central position in planning each day's work is stressed, but at the same time detailed teacher guides are available to provide direction. The CHILD Curriculum has been used by many regularly appointed public school teachers and has pointed to the main problems which may arise when and if individual pacing on the basis of diagnostic tests becomes a widely adopted instructional technique within the present structure of school systems. The teachers of the CHILD Curriculum taught two classes of children daily, and within this context the time-consuming nature of individual diagnosis and prescription became a problem. Either a low pupil-teacher ratio or, as Robison suggested, a new specialist (Teacher Diagnostician) in individual planning is necessary if teaching is to take into account the present abilities, interests and learning rate of each child.

Helen F. Robison

Rationale for the Child Curriculum

10

Neuropsychology may soon furnish the physical and scientific basis for learning theory which will eventually replace supposition with knowledge. In a recent article on the functional organization of the brain, Luria (1970, p. 66)[1] concluded that such complex human functions as speech and writing are not localized in specific centers of the brain but are self-regulating systems, each managed by a complex apparatus which coordinates various brain structures. Based on research on specific behavioral disorders involving brain lesions, Luria (1970, p. 78)[2] hypothesizes that "training or habituation changes the organization of the brain's activity, so that the brain comes to perform accustomed tasks without recourse to the process of analysis. It is challenging to push this metaphor to explain the differences in observed and tested behavior of young children, contrasting those from middle and low SES backgrounds, in terms of degrees of automatic self-regulating functioning.

In the early 60's, many studies of young children's behavior in economically depressed areas pinpointed the same prime areas of educational need, that is, perceptual-cognitive, language, experience, conceptual and self-concepts (Deutsch, 1965; Dreger and Miller, 1960; Strodtbeck, 1964).[3] Retarded or poor speech development and lack of "experience" were frequently cited as the two most important points of impact for early schooling. Inferior perceptual functioning for low SES children was inferred from scores on tests for auditory discrimination.

Helen F. Robison is at the Bernard M. Baruch College of The City University of New York. Printed by permission of the author.

Medical data which became available through Project Head Start, while generally partial and incomplete, indicated possible higher than average rates of emotional disturbance, and untreated congenital and physical ailments for this population (Stine, 1969).[4] For the most part, however, despite higher rates of prematurity, congenital defects and untreated ailments, the vast majority of children in this population must be viewed as lacking physical or perceptual impairment and capable of normal sensory-motor functioning. Yet on the Wepman Auditory Discrimination Test, these children scored low. Apparent symptoms of deficits among these children were numerous.

Lower than average IQ scores were among the most visible symptoms of economic disadvantage. In fact, it became routine for researchers to find confirmation for their assumption of disadvantage in a sample group, if IQ scores averaged about one standard devation below the mean, or around 85. Bloom's (1964)[5] study of longitudinal changes in IQ scores served to create a mantle of respectability for the previously discredited notion that IQ scores may change with changes in environmental factors.

Almy (1966)[6] found that, on Piagetian-type tasks of conservation, young children in a low SES group were moving at a slower pace of cognitive development than their age-mates from middle-class homes. While Piaget's theory of cognitive development requires a constant series of adaptive interactions between the child and the environment, with a limiting maturational factor, Piaget has not studied the nature of different environmental inputs or their differentiated impacts on cognitive growth. His conception (Inhelder and Piaget, 1964)[7] of intelligence as a resultant of the transactions between the child and his environment, and of the cumulative nature of intellectual growth, suggests several points at which the environment may exert resistance to growth. Hunt (1964)[8] emphasized the necessity to find the match between the child's achieved intellectual functioning and the school's efforts to stimulate further development.

Kohlberg's studies of Montessori education for low SES children, and his analysis of Piagetian theory, led him to conclude that this theory is compatible with a variety of preschool programs, insofar as they define cognitive goals developmentally and "center on relatively active and self-selective forms of cognitive stimulation of the child (Kohlberg, 1968).[9] However, Kohlberg concluded that little could be expected of any preschool programs in the way of significant change in cognitive functioning, because of the difficulty of equating any school experience with the massive daily living experiences available to the middle-class child in his environment. A logical conclusion from Kohlberg's pessimism about the low potency of part-time schooling might be an implication from Bettelheim's study of the schooling of young children in the Israeli Kibbutz. Bettelheim (1969) found that twenty-four-hour care of young children, away from home, can generate the required potency to accelerate cognitive functioning. This is one of many points where value questions intrude.

There are cures which may be worse than the disease. One such cure might be separation of the young child from his family, in order to give him the constant, massive experiential base which is alleged to be missing in his home environment. The American urban ghetto is so different from the Israeli Kibbutz that what works in Israel cannot be assumed to work in Harlem. Nor is there any basis for assuming either that poor families wish to part from their children or that good can come of such separation.

The most hopeful avenue for beneficial change in school functioning of children of the poor would appear to be increased motivation through economic improvement for the family. Better housing, jobs, and hope for equality in living and earning would surely contribute more to alleviation of the problem than any other form of intervention. In the interim, however, while poverty and problems of schooling prevail in the nation's inner cities, the challenge continues to improve the school's contribution to the education of the children of the poor.

DIFFERENCES BASED ON SOCIAL CLASS

Most middle-class children, by age four, have almost mastered a form of English which is close enough to the standard dialect, so that they do not have to master a new dialect or a new language when they enter school. Many slum children, however, either speak English as a second language or they speak an English dialect, with structures and phonemic patterns sufficiently different from the standard dialect to cause interference with the acquisition of the standard English dialect required of practically all American reading programs. It would be infinitely less stressful for the children if their earliest schooling featured their native speech, whether this is Spanish-Puerto Rican or Mississippi-black dialect. Since, for a variety of reasons, this is not always possible, the young ghetto child faces the formidable problem of learning a new dialect or language, at the same time that he is expected to learn a whole new communication system based on symbols and the new rules and unfamiliar content of the school culture. By this time, the middle-class child is already oriented to the new communication system based on symbols, and he has already been socialized to a system within the family which is not too different from the one which operates at school.

It happens that language learning is not a particularly difficult achievement for young children. In fact, they are better at it than anyone else. It seems paradoxical that the young child, with his great linguistic plasticity at the preschool level, should find it difficult to learn the standard English dialect. This is sufficiently unlikely that it must be that the problem resides in the school rather than in the child. It seems likely that the school is dealing with the wrong problem, to the child's detriment. A realistic assessment of the young inner-city child as

Rationale for the Child Curriculum

linguistically different, but not necessarily inferior, suggests goals and procedures for school language development which are different from those often selected.

Slow cognitive development, as indicated by standard IQ scores or by school achievement tests, has been attributed to a complex of factors. The recent Jensen (1969)[10] articles and counter-arguments have resulted in fresh evaluations of data, most of which is not new. Contrary to Jensen's assertion that compensatory education has apparently failed, most personnel involved in compensatory education efforts would surely agree that the money, efforts, and mechanisms so far directed at this target are miniscule and woefully inadequate to the task.

Since environmental inadequacy of huge proportions seemed implicit in the slower intellectual development of young children in the slums, it became fashionable to point to their lack of experience, especially with such symbols of the cultural mainstream as the museum, zoo, art gallery, and other places of cultural interest. The relationship of cognitive growth to visits to places of cultural interest is obscure. While young ghetto children live rather segregated lives in the inner city, television — a penetrating window on the cultural mainstream — is almost universally available. In addition, slum children are less protected from the seamier side of life than middle-class children, and their experiences tend to be not too few, but perhaps too many, too unselected, and too emotionally abrasive. Here again, there is experiential difference, with some important differences related to the frequency, quality, and content of adult-child relationships.

Sylvia Ashton-Warner's (1963)[11] development of an "organic" method of teaching reading to disadvantaged young Maori children, using words of high affect selected by the child, suggests the irrelevance of many types of trips and visits to the acquisition of specific reading skills. This is not to negate the relationship of specific experience to understanding content and vocabulary, however, which is another matter.

On the whole, there seems no barrier to learning to read which stems from any child's ordinary life experiences. Children everywhere, with a few dramatic exceptions, experience life in families with the usual gamut of human relationships involved in satisfying basic needs, even on welfare checks, or on pitifully inadequate wages. Life may be difficult, often unpleasant and changeable, but the ghetto child can not be said to lack "experience."

Perceptual deficiency, especially in auditory discrimination, is suggested by lower scores on the Wepman Auditory Discrimination Test. But Baratz (1969)[12] found that non-standard dialect speakers have better auditory discrimination for their own dialect than for standard English, while white speakers of standard English have better auditory discrimination for their own dialect, than for non-standard dialects.

Rigrodsky and Morrison, speech specialists who tested prekindergarten children in classes using the CHILD Curriculum during the 1967-68 school year in New York City, indicated that auditory discrimination scores might reflect the bias of standardized tests in favor of the standard English dialect, in addition to the difficulty evidenced by these children with the concept of "same-different" when applied to speech sounds (Robison, 1968).[13] When these researchers (Rigrodsky and Morrison, 1969)[14] subsequently tested an auditory discrimination program based upon auditory feedback and phonemic distinction theory with this population, training centered on recognition of sound differences produced by another speaker. A specially constructed test was administered, requiring differentiation of word pairs as "same" or "different." Included in this test were ten word pairs which are not differentiated in the black dialect and ten pairs which are. An instructive finding was that, while 17 of the 102 four and five-year-olds in the training group could not be trained to take the pretest, all 102 were able to take the posttest. However, in a control group, 13 of 83 children could not be trained to take the pretest, and 7 of the 83 were also unable to take the posttest.

The Rigrodsky-Morrison evaluation and speech training studies with children in the CHILD Curriculum population suggest the possibility of raising scores on sound and word discrimination tests through training. While the transfer value of such training to reading competence has not yet been demonstrated and requires further study, it seems likely that specific training in sound and word discrimination may sufficiently facilitate acquisition of reading skills by black dialect speakers to justify the time and teaching commitment required.

Poor self-concepts are often cited as one of the many deficits of the slum child which act to retard learning. Yet the relationship of low self-valuing to learning in school has yet to be delineated reliably. A recent doctoral study (Samuels, 1969)[15] found middle-class five-year-olds tended to have higher self-concepts than low SES children, although there were no significant differences in either class based on race. In a study of the effectiveness of selected preschool programs in New York State, Di Lorenzo (1969)[16] reported that disadvantaged prekindergarten children had lower self-concepts than their more advantaged controls, and that black disadvantaged young children had lower self-concepts than white children who were disadvantaged. Since none of the programs reported by Di Lorenzo appeared to have any effect on the children's self-concepts, this variable may be the resultant of a mixture of school-out-of-school factors which resists manipulation. However, another study of older children found that "disadvantaged children do not necessarily suffer from lower self-esteem and a lower sense of personal worth (Soares and Soares, 1969).[17] Self-concept data are difficult to secure in reliable form from young children, and it may be that adequate instruments have not yet been devised. Difficulties in measurement or in effecting change, however, are not sufficient grounds for discarding the commonsense view that teacher reflections to children of valuing and of succes expectations may be prime ingredients of effective strategies for young children.

IMPLICATIONS OF OBSERVED DIFFERENCES

Value questions challenge the educator at every decision point in curriculum design. Whether to change the child or the school is a basic value question. But even when the decision is to change the school, difficult as this is, in the short run there remain the usual questions of "to what purpose?" and "what knowledge is of the most worth?" These value questions received answers based on researcher bias and empirical testing in the form of operationally defined goals of a new curriculum design, which is described below. A more empirical question is related to the reality of social class differences and their implications for schooling.

LANGUAGE DIFFERENCES

The nonverbal stereotype of the young child in the inner city is a myth which is readily dispelled by his teacher. Some children are initially shy in school and many come with the admonition to "be good and keep quiet"; thus, the early weeks of school are often relatively silent as children gauge their new experiences and learn expected behaviors. Thereafter, where teachers permit and stimulate conversation, these children are talkative. In Central Harlem and the South Bronx in New York City, however, black children speak in an English dialect with patterns equally distinct but different from the standard English dialect. Project CHILD researchers reported that they had to visit a classroom for several weeks before they could "hear" or understand what the children were saying. Early in the school year, it was difficult to decode the children's tape recorded speech sufficiently to make typescripts. It was not clear whether the children's phonemic pronunciation shifted slightly toward the standard dialect, by virtue of hearing school models from teachers, or whether researchers gradually learned to decode the different pronunciations of familiar words and the unfamiliar syntactic forms they heard from the children. Probably, both tendencies operated, to improve the ability of the observers to record and transcribe the children's speech.

Sample typescripts were examined early in the study for identification of non-standard and standard speech. During the first year of the study (in 1966), comparisons were made between tape-recorded language samples taken early and late in the school year (Robison and Wann, 1967).[18] Seven relatively homogeneous (i.e., black and low SES) prekindergarten classes were involved in the comparisons. It was concluded that:

1. There was notable decline of infantile speech such as substitution of "w" for "r" sounds, which could be expected from maturation and development through speech usage.

2. The children's fluency and ease of verbal communication improved.
3. Monosyllabic responses, brief phrases and gestural responses tended to be replaced by a surprisingly high proportion of complete, if simple, sentences without phrases or clauses.
4. Articulation seemed to improve. There was a noticeable decline in slack lip position, mumbling, uneven flow of words, word "tangles," and baby talk.
5. The children generally had a considerable fund of school-acquired information available for spontaneous verbalization.
6. There was a notable vocabulary increase. Names and descriptive words were greatly multiplied or more readily elicited and used.
7. Verb omission was surprisingly uncommon on end-of-year samples.
8. Most children moved back and forth from non-standard to standard language patterns, using many typical non-standard forms as well as many standard forms.

Linguists point out that the observer exaggerates the extent of non-standard forms used by dialect speakers, since the novelty of these aspects of dialect speech tends to obscure the other important aspect of non-standard dialect, which is that it shares a large proportion of the features of the standard dialect. If the school decision is to teach non-standard dialect speakers the standard dialect, the nature of the problem needs more precise definition than it usually receives.

With young children of four or five years of age, decisions about language teaching can benefit from study of the research on early language development. So far, this research is rich in mapping the course of spontaneous language development, but yields are still slight regarding effective teaching of language to young children. Cazden (1969)[19] suggests that children may need specific types of help, such as grasp of word meanings or such general cognitive strategies as focusing attention in school or on tests. As Cazden and other linguistic researchers are pointing out, the commonsense view that children learn language by imitation is true only in a general way. The evidence suggests, rather, that the young child is born with a rule-making capacity in learning language spontaneously, that he is "wired in" for language learning (Bellugi and Brown, 1964; Lenneberg, 1966).[20] In this view, the child must hear a great deal of language in order to form hypotheses about grammatical structures, and then test these out in use, with feedback from adults used to monitor and change generalizations about syntax and pronunciation. This, of course, refers to learning one's native language.

That early language learning is not primarily or entirely imitative is attested to by the fact that young children make utterances they could not have heard before, in forms adults do not use. Language development seems very different from other forms of early cognitive learning, not only in its apparent rule-making process, but also in its early maturity, with many four and-five-year-olds producing speech almost as mature and perfect as adults.

Rationale for the Child Curriculum

Second dialect learning is in many respects easier and in some respects more difficult than first dialect learning. Learning the standard English dialect does not require non-standard dialect speakers to learn everything new. Dialects, however, tend to interfere with each other because they are so alike, yet different. Labov (1969a, 1969b)[21] has pinpointed a selected list of "interferences" to be considered before making school decisions on second dialect learning. Labov suggests concentrating on ten major grammatical forms which, he says, seem to present the most difficulty in the acquisition of the standard dialect. He includes such grammatical features as negative concord, the regular past tense form (ed), and yes-no questions with main verbs.

Observations and studies of the speech of these young black children in New York City emphasized vocabulary needs. Rothenberg (1969)[22] noted, in a recent study of number conservation among four and five-year-olds, that lower SES children seemed to have a "less than complete" understanding of such key words as "same" or "more," and therefore, that low SES children are more often wrongly assessed as "non-conservers" than high SES children because of key vocabulary problems. Project CHILD testers reported early in the study that children tended to score low on the various tests used because they evidenced lack of comprehension of such essential words as "same-different," "more-less," and many terms of number, time, and spatial relationships.

The decision that teachers could value the children's natural speech without destroying or suppressing it, while teaching standard English as a second dialect, was based on assessment of current realities. Standard English is the language of literature and of school learning. Parents in the ghetto are eager to equip their children for success in today's world where education is highly prized in all vocational channels which afford upward mobility. Many classes include non-English speaking or bi-lingual children. The great diversity of native languages among inner-city children in the complex metropolis that is New York City, added to the high turnover of children in schools, makes impracticable alternatives based on maintaining the child's native speech in the early grades of school without adding standard English.

In practice, teachers are ambivalent about valuing the child's native speech while teaching a second dialect with the unmatched prestige of standard English. They find it very difficult to refrain from "correcting" a child's faultless utterance in a non-standard dialect, such as, "I ain't got no cookie." This is, however, chiefly a matter of teacher training and study of linguistic research.

Two further types of language experiences were identified as needs for this population. The first need was practice in decoding and encoding verbalization related to cognitive tasks. The confusion these children evidenced in test situations and in typical cognitive tasks seemed to reflect lack of experience in this kind of behavior. The rapid progress most children made in learning these cognitive uses of language confirmed the utility of selected forms of structured teaching for this purpose. For example, in patterning tasks the "structure models," or suggested teaching sequences, specify that after a pattern of objects has been copied with objects, teachers encourage children to touch objects and to label them as follows: "The first one in my row is"; "the next one in my row is"; "the last one in my row is." This sequence furnishes the opportunity for the child to verbalize his actions after the fact, while habituating a left-right direction of "reading" and establishing in context the meaning of the word "row." It soon appeared that this encoding practice also facilitated the child's ability to decode further task instruction.

A final need, which seems well documented and which is reflected in children's school behavior, is repeated exposure to and practice with various symbolic forms of information — especially, but not only, letters and numerals (Robison and Mukerji, 1966).[23] Abundance of books and reading for pleasure seem to be encountered infrequently in low SES homes. Therefore, the school curriculum seemed to require incorporation of, exposure to, and practice with various symbolic forms of information, including books and such representational forms as photographs and pictures, as well as graphs, tallies, charts, letters, and numeral symbols. Sigel's and Olmsted's (1968) study suggested that classification of pictures by young black children from low SES homes was poorer than classification of pictures by middle-class children.

To summarize, the language development goals were as follows:

1. Acceptance and valuing of the young child's spontaneous speech, without constraint or correction, while encouraging developmental progress toward mature speech in the native dialect.
2. Teaching standard English as a second dialect, to develop receptive and productive efficiency through games, active experiences, and tutorial teaching.
    a. Saturating the classroom with taped and live models of standard English dialect.
    b. Developing dialectal flexibility in children's linguistic behavior.
3. Practice in language uses for cognitive tasks on a systematic, planned basis, using game-like strategies.
4. Planned forms of vocabulary expansion, through action, experiences, games, and play.
5. Planned practice with various symbolic forms of information, including books, letters, numerals and pictures.

COGNITIVE DIFFERENCES

The observed inferiority in cognitive functioning of young black children of low SES may be more apparent than real. The language dimension of almost all cognitive tasks may account for a high proportion of the problem. Nevertheless, the Hess-Shipman (1968)[24] studies highlight differences in mother-child interactions on cognitive tasks which seem to add further difficulties for the low SES child. They found that the "cognitive environment of the culturally disadvantaged child is one in which behavior is controlled by imperatives rather than by attention to the individual characteristics of a specific situation."

If mother-child studies of young black slum children are valid, there seems to be a need to create discontinuity or cognitive dissonance for such children, with problems to solve or tasks to complete which require task definition and attention to task characteristics. A corollary requirement would include work with parents to bring about more unity in school-home behavioral expectations.

It seemed possible that young ghetto children might have available more complex cognitive functioning than was being elicited at home. To elicit and foster the child's highest level of achieved cognitive functioning, and to reinforce its routine occurrence under good practice conditions, would in itself be a worthy goal of a preschool curriculum. But Vygotsky (1962)[25] pointed out that good teaching is more than this — it marches ahead of current achievement and seeks to cause the child's cognition to stretch in the direction of complexity. Cognitive stimulation could emanate from teachers and peers at school with the possibility of accelerating sluggish rates of development.

Piaget's (1964)[26] interactional view of the development of intelligence includes social interactions and active manipulation of things as important sources of cognitive growth, in addition to maturation and day-to-day living experiences. While Piaget's feature of self-equilibration coordinates actions tending toward assimilation and those tending toward accommodation within the child, the school, which has no access to this internal process, may be able to structure the environment to accentuate desired inputs in order to power this process indirectly.

It seems possible to raise the power of school inputs to a strong charge which vastly increases the sources of both accommodation and assimilation for the child. Environmental structuring, which is open to teacher manipulation, includes the teacher's choices of equipment and materials for children's use, structuring of tasks, and teaching children constructive forms of cognitive behavior through adult behavior models and through direct teaching, with appropriate reinforcement strategies.

With problem-solving and task mastery as important cognitive goals, capable of creating dissonance or conflict with prior learned behavior and therefore likely to have effect on cognitive development, the problem of methodology became central. O. K. Moore (Moore, 1965; Moore and Anderson, 1968)[27] suggests that children "play their way to social competence," learning through what he calls folk models, which consist of such forms as puzzles, games of chance, games of strategy, and the normative qualities of aesthetic experience. Playful school experiences are common, of course, to most early childhood programs. But there was no evidence that children's spontaneous play in school situations would, by itself, close the cognitive gap between the slum child and his middle-class peers. Designing environmental inputs to magnify the chances that children would use them fruitfully for cognitive growth was the major challenge in this project. Bloom's model (1968)[28] of "learning for mastery," suggesting pacing and differentiated instruction appropriate to the needs of each student, is a clear statement of the decision to base the CHILD curriculum on an individual tutorial basis, wherever possible.

To summarize the cognitive goals of the program, they were:

1. One-to-one relationships with teachers in playful, game-like experiences, to challenge the child to active physical manipulation, attentiveness, task mastery and problem solving.
2. Self-selected playfulness with a varied assortment of objects, to stimulate forms of sensory discrimination learning, skill practice, social interaction, and learning rules of games.
3. Teacher intervention in play to stimulate verbalization of skills of ordering, classification, and other forms of relationships.
4. Structured, individual game-like teaching sequences, featuring problems which challenge sensory evidence.
5. Exposure to and skill practice with varied content of school learning, including reading, mathematics, science, selected social sciences and the arts — content unlikely to be encountered by young ghetto children outside the school.
6. Success experiences in cognitive tasks.
7. Reinforcement of learning, primarily through social approval techniques.
8. Extinction of undesirable behavior, primarily through environmental restructuring, non-reinforcement and tutorial teaching.

In addition to the language and cognitive goals of the curriculum design, several other criteria guided the testing and fashioning of the new curriculum. One was the requirement of child autonomy, or respect for the child's choice of involvement or participation in any activity where choices could be offered. Despite the abundant literature about the authoritarian nature of relationships within families in the slums, this value had so high a priority in the research design that the only question considered was how to bring it about. The importance of play in the child's total development was another featured value, not only for its expected contribution to the child's social and cognitive growth, but also for its role in satisfying the young child's need for spontaneous behavior and for such psychological needs as fantasy and discharge of tension. A final value, in art activities, was viewed as an important expressive and constructive need, to enhance personal meaningfulness of the child's school experience and to introduce him to satisfying forms of aesthetic experience. In other words, an intellectually stimulating program was regarded as a complex mix of activities, drawn from many and varied sources, in order to offer the child a culturally rich matrix in which to experience growth-inducing content.

RATIONALE FOR A CURRICULUM DESIGN

The goals which have been listed above do not lead ineluctably to one curriculum design. There must be countless models which could follow from the selected goals. There are, in fact, numerous decision points in the construction of this design which will benefit from research, now in process in other projects or in need of initiation. The intent was to construct one viable model which would be mapped clearly enough for replication and testing that empirical data could accrue and that problems and additional needs could be identified. It was not intended that the end product would be a final teacher-proof package, incapable of variation and change.

The CHILD Program is an example of a type of curriculum which has been very scarce in early childhood education, in its specificity and breadth, written form, and detailed delineation of content areas for teaching young children. The rationalization rests on value decisions and extensive empirical tryouts with many different teachers in classrooms for young children in inner-city schools in New York City. Accepting a Piagetian view of children's natural development and Moore's notions of how children play their way to learning their own culture, the rationale accords with the Hess-Shipman views of the need for young ghetto children to experience more cognitively-stimulating adult guidance than is usual in their own families.

The rationale for the CHILD Curriculum assumes that most young children of the poor are deficient neither in sensory functioning nor in cognitive potential, although their behavior may frequently belie this assumption, primarily because of experiential differences. A value decision contributes the goal of maximum cognitive functioning at school with the responsibility resting on the school to bring this into effect. Stress on teaching cognitive behavior at school does not imply over-valuing this type of functioning, but rather features special program emphasis required to balance de-emphasis or differences in models and forms of adult guidance at home.

In order to elicit and foster the young child's highest attained level of language and cognition, as a basis for stimulating more advanced functioning, it seemed necessary to strive at the same time for both spontaneity and challenge. Children who experience much constraint tend to suppress their natural exuberance and playfulness. On the other hand, play activities may tend to exaggerate sensory-motor forms of behavior with children whose experiences tend to be physical and motoric. The motivation, intensity of involvement, long attention span, and the intrinsic nature of the reward in play activities presented the most attractive and efficient possibilities for young children's learning. But spontaneous play precluded learning of new behaviors, content, and skills. This problem was resolved by featuring play wherever possible as a parallel to tightly structured, specifically planned forms of teaching. Thus, the continuum of play activities ranged from the most spontaneous, unsupervised types of play to the most highly structured forms of teacher-supervised games or direct teaching.

A packaged curriculum was developed in written form, in order to blueprint for teachers examples of precision teaching designed to help children move toward specified behavioral goals. The specific models were needed to help teachers grasp methodology and content which was different from their usual programs. Earlier models of a more general, flexible nature, were discarded because teachers tended to assimilate them to their ongoing programs, assuming no need to change. The unaccustomed precision of the "structure models" precluded ready assimilation and, instead, required various forms of teacher restructuring of the schedule, use of materials, content and methodology. In one class after another, as soon as a teacher began to implement the program in earnest, she conveyed her progress by communicating distress about classroom management procedures and a desire for assistance in instituting the substantial changes required.

Behavioral goals were used to guide program design because 1. they encouraged greater specificity of design features, 2. they required demonstrable relationships between goals, procedures and outcomes, and 3. they also served as criteria for performance and diagnostic testing. With the selection of playfulness with objects, people, and ideas as the embodiment of intellectual stimulation for young children, the program design sought to activate or to energize children to pursue activity and to practice behaviors which impel them into cognitive processes which tend to add to their perspectives of the world. "Playfulness" has been defined by Moore, Dewey, Huizinga, and many others, not only as representing unique involvement and interest, but also as an enduring value which gradually takes on such adult characteristics as the joy of knowledge for its own sake, open-mindedness, creativity, scientific experimentalism, flexibility in thinking, and the ability to reorder or transform abstract conceptions (Dewey, 1933; Huizinga, 1955; Moore, 1965).[29]

Since the target population evidenced a wide range of ability, interest, and skills, the curriculum seemed to require open-endedness at the entrance as well as the exit. Assuming therefore neither a floor nor a ceiling to the probable range of progress over a two-year period for children aged four and five, the project staff undertook to collaborate first with scholars in delineating content goals and then with teachers in testing out a preselected body of content, methodologies, and procedures.

The content selection stemmed from consultations with scholars in various disciplines, although in all cases the early childhood specialist staff made final decisions on the specific behavioral goals to be pursued, based on possibilities for generating teaching and learning activities appropriate to the target population. While the curriculum design was written primarily in separate content areas, such as mathematics and language, an overarching area designated as "basic cognitive skills" abstracted and integrated the major types of cognitive behavior which recurred in specific structure models, clothed in the varieties of content selected. Basic cognitive skills referred to such key forms of cognitive behavior as patterning, comparison, contrast, and classification.

The curriculum design required the identification of multiple and complex goals. Curriculum writing called for considerable ingenuity to combine several behavioral goals in the same activity for maximum efficiency. It was found that children could continue to benefit from the curriculum design over a two-year period — through their year in prekindergarten followed by the kindergarten year. There were no "standards" for children's achievement other than specified forms of diagnostic testing to suggest pacing, and reminders to teachers of the possibility that some children could usually be identified who were capable of moving to more complex tasks in various areas.

Tutorial teaching, or direct teaching in a one-to-one relationship, was selected as a natural format for teachers to find each child's level of competence and to structure a teaching episode to accord with the individual child's pace, skill and style of learning. However, suggestions for tutorial teaching were specified in detail to provide teachers with models carefully designed to give the child success experiences and new challenges keyed to his responses. Since these structure models were tested by many teachers, with many different children, teacher and researcher feedback contributed to constant revision and further testing, over a period of about three years. Teacher ingenuity added to project staff's knowledgeability, helped to produce a written curriculum which was selective, detailed, and sequenced in many cases, and which could be accepted as "teachable" by other teachers.

The rationale for the curriculum design, as it has finally emerged, may be summarized as follows:

1. Play-centered activities, playfulness and independence in learning constitute the most efficient forms and the highest values in young children's school learning.
2. Since the current state of the teaching arts precludes achievement of all goals through play, wherever possible activities feature play, but it is necessary to parallel play with direct teaching in tutorial instruction, planned experiences, and games.

3. To keep motivation high and to support the child's autonomy and control over specified areas of his experience, the child's right of choice of activity from itemized options is respected.
4. Play, games, real-life experiences, and tutorial teaching are the major avenues to eliciting the highest achieved levels of the child's cognitive functioning and of stimulating more complex cognitive behavior.
5. Teacher success in stimulating children's cognitive progress tends to cause positive change in teacher expectations, attitudes, and aspirations for the children. Teacher willingness to change pace, to continue tutorial teaching with slow-paced children, and to offer more complex challenges as children evidence progress all contribute to the creation of an intellectually stimulating classroom climate for learning.
6. A written packaged curriculum design, with precision of statement in goals, procedures, use of materials and collection of feedback, makes it possible for the teacher to undertake unaccustomed roles and strategies with unfamiliar content successfully with training.
7. The richness of content derives from the authentic material contributed by scholars in selected disciplines, analyzed and synthesized by early childhood specialists, and finally tested by various teachers in classroom settings for teachability and appropriateness.
8. Children increase their attention-span in task-oriented school activities and they learn new behaviors in structuring knowledge through direct teaching in tutorial instruction and through teacher modelling in one-to-one relationships. Children's learnings contribute to their independence in purposeful activities, social interactions and play.
9. Children's spontaneous language is accepted, elicited and supported, so that verbalization in school grows in fluency, complexity and level of mastery.
10. Second-dialect learning is programmed through games, playful activities and specified experiences. Dialectal flexibility is the goal, with increasing differentiation of school-appropriate and home-appropriate dialects.
11. Cognitive uses of language are practiced in games, tutorial teaching and specifically developed practice play, such as work with puppets.
12. Diagnostic testing samples children's progress and offers teachers the feedback required for pacing and selection of individual learning tasks.

DESIGN OF THE CURRICULUM

The final version of the CHILD Curriculum, pending revision through future field testing, consists of 8 content areas: cognitive skills, music, language, mathematics, science, sociology, geography, and economics. Each area includes a summary and list of selected behavioral goals, followed by a series of structure models or detailed structures for teaching for specified goals. Art and esthetic experiences are not listed in a separate heading but are detailed in several content areas, in addition to further specification in the teacher manual.

WHY CONTENT AREAS

Division into content areas, in an early childhood curriculum, appears to require explanation. On the debit side are the strong feelings of many persons, especially in developmental psychology, that content is irrelevant to young children's learning and that time wasted on content selection could be better spent by teachers on monitoring children's learning or studying children's behavior. Another disadvantage is the admitted lack of preparation of early childhood teachers in math, science, social sciences, or even in reading instruction, since such teachers have traditionally been "child-centered," not "subject-centered." Another argument against subject-matter division of content is that it may be too "academic" and formal for young children, whose education is best fostered in informal, "cognitive-developmental" programs.

There are, however, some powerful advantages to the content-centered program. Articulation with later elementary school learning is an obvious but minor asset, since there are great needs for change in primary and elementary education content and learning procedures. More important advantages are:

a. Rich program resources resulting from detailed scrutiny of subject-matter content.
b. Exciting program possibilities developing from cross-disciplinary collaboration involving early childhood specialists with subject-matter specialists.
c. Intellectual challenge to early childhood teachers to learn new content in order to teach it.
d. Teacher need to monitor children's learning very closely, because of the specific behavioral goals and the need to structure plans for the child's continuous learning.
e. Dissonance of teachers' perceptions of program with their prior understandings of teacher roles, strategies and appropriate children's activities, with less likelihood of assuming, "We're already doing that" — an assimilative response which often stifles new ideas at the classroom door.
f. Possibilities for sending signals for curriculum change into the primary grades, to articulate with the new early childhood prekindergarten and kindergarten curriculum.
g. Ease of maintenance of "cognitive-developmental" program features, including children's spontaneity, autonomy in choices of activity, in-

formality, individual child-centeredness and program adaptation to each child's needs, pace and interest.
- h. Possibilities for clearer focus and specific purpose for recording children's behavior and testing for selected learning needs-procedures which give teachers more information and more specific types of information than they had before about the behavior of each child.
- i. Ease of sharing defined and specified teaching roles with Aides, other paraprofessionals, parents and volunteers in order to multiply children's opportunities to practice skills and learning tasks in one-to-one relationships with adults.

Of course, some of the above-listed benefits would attach to any program which is specific, written, and capable of being tested through observation or test of children's mastery. The point is that content selection has to be accomplished in some fashion and a disciplines-based design has as much, or more, logic than other types. One further argument for subject-matter content is the possibility of attracting to early childhood education some teachers who find too little intellectual challenge in the "nursery-school" type of program but who like young children and would like to become their teachers. There surely is room to meet the demanding needs in the education of young children of the poor for varieties of teachers, and especially for those who can supplement kindly, maternal personalities with intellectually challenging interests.

SELECTED CONTENT AREAS

It was not possible to select content from subject-matter programs devised by other researchers because there was very little available for children under six. What was available was usually out of harmony with the values or preferred methodology of the CHILD Program.

Of the eight content areas, the one designated "cognitive skills" is an overarching area of conceptual needs basic to all content areas, featuring comparison, contrast, patterning, and simple classification. Some of the competencies stressed in cognitive skill tasks include several forms of "same-different" relationships, matching objects one-to-one, perceiving, copying, extending and creating various types of simple patterns and "reading them off," (i.e., verbalizing the pattern type and differentiating pattern types). These competencies receive further practice in the math area, in the language of simple sets, and in classification activities in the science area. An important strategy children learn in the cognitive skill area, applicable to all other areas, is the need for and some procedures in self-checking.

Teachers found the cognitive skills area especially useful in training children to play tutorial games, to experience success in cognitive tasks, and to learn some simple cognitive uses of language, along with vocabulary and communication skills. Children enjoyed mastery in these early tutorial games and once they had been learned, children were often observed initiating these tasks, teaching each other, or simply using the materials playfully, alone or with a friend. Playful use, in the sense of variation, extension or application, was regarded as evidence of internalization of learning and conceptual mastery.

Tests for conceptual mastery, featuring playfulness, were attempted but not completed because of limitations of time and personnel. However, teachers often reported instances of such behavior. After learning some of the patterning tasks, some children spontaneously patterned with paints at the easel, with sets of manipulative materials, with felt letters on the flannel board, with letter stamps, or at the typewriter.

Some teachers, while enthusiastic about the patterning games, found it difficult to conceptualize the purposes well enough to explain it to Aides or parents. It was suggested that patterning is a way of structuring knowledge and much of school learning can be regarded as patterning activities. Learning to read can be viewed as perceiving the patterns we call words, both as a whole and as a series of units called letters, which comprise the whole. Patterning words involves directionality (from left to right, in English), specific order (letters cannot appear in random order but only in a specified order), and finiteness (the word has a beginning and an ending letter, as well as a space separating one word from another, so that it is possible to know whether a word appears once, twice or any other number of times).

As teachers began to view patterning as a prototype of many forms of learning, they invested great creativity in planning transfer tasks, especially in devising the countless craft projects which seem so appealing to parents, supervisors and visitors. Project staff sought to minimize or eliminate craft projects, as time-consuming and less productive forms of classroom activities. Finding teachers firmly wedded to these craft projects, the CHILD staff tried to make a virtue of them by re-admitting them to the curriculum, but only for purposeful learnings which could be specified and related to any other behavioral goals. Some teachers misinterpreted this to mean that art activities could only be programmed for specific purposes, but the Teachers Guide is clear that art activities are available practically all the time, and that these are distinguishable from craft projects in that the former are exploratory, expressive kinds of activities which permit children to work independently and spontaneously with art media, with very little adult guidance or constraint.

Mastery of the simpler patterning tasks is a prerequisite to initial tasks on sets in mathematics, as well as for name replication and beginning reading in language. Classification tasks are coordinated with similar tasks in science and in sociology, where many of the craft projects are concentrated in connection with celebration of national holidays.

MUSIC

The usual goals of spontaneous enjoyment in movement and song are built into a series of fun tasks in music, involving differentiation of tone, pitch, rhythm, accent, melody, mood, dynamics, and timbre. For example, children learn to delineate the steady beat vs. the melodic pattern of a simple song by clapping, jumping, or through other actions.

In one kindergarten class, the teacher used the terms "steady beat" and "melodic pattern" in context, while demonstrating and leading a class practice session. She asked the children to clap the steady beat of "Mary Had A Little Lamb," a song which the children chose. Praising this very skillful performance, the teacher asked the group to change the task — to clap the melodic pattern. She did not define her terms, she said afterwards, because the children had already learned the meanings. The next step was to divide the class into two groups, one to clap the steady beat, the other to clap the melodic pattern. The two groups clapped at the same time with some initial success. As the clapping patterns melted into an indistinguishable one, the teacher called for two children to demonstrate clapping the two rhythms at the same time. The first pair of children were very competent, the second pair were not, but the third and fourth showed great skill in maintaining the two patterns simultaneously. This scene was typical of many others recorded by observers.

Unlike the tutorial games which usually feature a teacher and one child, in music the tasks are either small-group or total group-oriented, because of the pervasive quality of music and its attraction for children's participation. Music skills featured in practice games and esthetic experiences include singing, movement, rhythm, playing rhythm instruments, and discrimination of musical sounds.

Some musical activities are relatively unstructured, although purposeful and planned, and include spontaneous movement, singing, and exploring a rhythm instrument. Other musical activities are tightly-structured tasks, similar to the mathematics or cognitive skill tasks, especially in differentiation of pitch, tone or timbre. Music is also used for tension release or to set or change a classroom mood, as from noisy to quiet. In addition, there is a direct transfer from the practice in rhythmical chants to some of the language games used to practice standard forms of syntax.

LANGUAGE

Language goals run the gamut from spontaneous speech production to beginning reading. Children who make rapid progress in reading and who need tasks beyond the beginning reading stage are expected to be encouraged to continue their interest in reading and their skill development within the school's reading program, with the advice of the school's reading specialist or early childhood supervisor.

The series of goals in language are as follows: spontaneous speech production, listening, vocabulary development, creative dramatization, name and word recognition, replication and writing, syntax, phonics and beginning reading. Primer typewriters are used in the kindergarten, but not in the prekindergarten where few children have the small muscle coordination required. The program makes no other distinction between four and five-year-olds, on the assumption that each child has a unique pace of learning and brings different interests, skills and prior experiences. One of the most advanced readers the program produced happened to be a four-year-old in a prekindergarten class, but this was a chance occurrence.

Work with letters of the alphabet and with standard English syntax is introduced early. It may be instructive to describe the development of fruitful syntactic skill practice as an example of the process of curriculum development represented in the CHILD Curriculum.

When Labov suggested the use of his list of selected standard English grammatical forms for skill practice, it seemed obvious that very little practice would occur unless it took a form that was attractive to teachers and children. Puppet play seemed a promising activity, so various puppet dialogues were written, to elicit desired responses from children. Teachers were not enthusiastic about these suggested dialogues, and they simply ignored them. Finally, one prekindergarten teacher agreed to try out a dialogue and to bring it to life with her class of four-year-olds. Her session was tape recorded and transcribed, and typescripts were shared with other teachers who then found it possible to try some of their own variations of the dialogue. Staff study of the typescripts revealed some very effective dialogue possibilities and, as these were shared with more teachers, improved prototypes were written which offered more dependable and lively forms of puppet play to help children produce selected forms of standard syntax.

Alphabet letter learning, on an individual tutorial basis with respect for children's choices of involvement, turned out to be one of the most important elements of the program for securing parental interest and cooperation. Many inner-city parents have such great anxiety about children's learning to read and their experience has so often been disappointing, that no curriculum seems to receive much parental or community support unless it visibly features reading skills. Since so many middle-class families now insist on teaching their young children to read at home, it is realistic for low-income parents to regard early reading experiences as a requirement of good schooling.

It is interesting to note that letter name knowledge seems to show a consistent relationship with reading competence. Among other studies, Dykstra (1970, p. 7) recently reported: "It is clear that children who can identify the letters of the alphabet prior to the beginning of reading instruction stand a good chance of learning how to read effectively regardless of whether they are enrolled in conventional basal, code-emphasis, i.t.a., or language experience programs." Even if letter name knowledge is not the basic characteristic which distinguishes potentially good from potentially poor readers, at the very least parents and teachers applaud letter name knowledge and, if this predisposes a child to expect success and to enjoy being successful, such motivational force seems well worth the effort.

Replication of names on name cards with felt letters, magnetic or sandpaper letters, and letter stamps, or, for five-year-olds, on the typewriter, was a high interest activity which practically every child sooner or later proudly mastered. Using color Polaroid photographs of children with name cards guaranteed interest and helped children to find their name cards independently and learn their names well, for identification, replication, writing, or typing.

From names, letter and word learning followed children's interests and classroom activities. Each teacher used the structure models in constructing little duplicated booklets based on common class experiences, such as cooking pancakes or taking a trip to the zoo. Some children copied these stories on the typewriter. When children took these little booklets home and "read" the books, parental approval of the child, the activity itself, and the program was expected to feed the child's motivation to "read" more books.

As children demanded to hear more stories, teachers tape-recorded many of their trade book stories and arranged a combination box with head sets and books in a listening center, so that children could follow the story by looking at the pictures as they turned the pages appropriately. Some children also dictated stories to the tape recorder and recorded them at the typewriter with the teacher's help.

The reading program introduced decoding procedures in an adaptation of the Merill Linguistic Readers. All instruction in decoding was individual and tutorial, but teachers were urged to permit other children to watch while awaiting their turns at the typewriter. The watchers often seemed to learn as much as the child being instructed, but avoiding group teaching insured that the teacher would in each case ascertain from the child his level of interest, skill, and understanding.

It was noted how high interest in typing and decoding was among boys, who loved to manipulate anything mechanical. Since children were not discouraged from waiting their turns, there was often a group of boys clustered around the typewriter, helping the learner who was typing while learning what he was typing.

Phonics practice was introduced primarily through objects and homework assignments. In keeping with the linguistic approach, sound-symbol relationships were featured only for invariant consonant sounds, omitting such variable ones as "C" and "K" and blends. Some teachers sent home notes requesting contributions of simple objects for the "M" box, such as a mitten whose mate was lost. Shoe or hosiery boxes, or transparent plastic boxes were used to house such object collections and were clearly marked with the consonant symbol, in both upper and lower-case.

MATHEMATICS

The Nuffield material in mathematics (Nuffield Mathematics Project, n. d.)[30] was one of many sources from which the math program developed. Several math consultants suggested various lists of learning goals and, over a period of several years, with teacher and project staff feedback, a list of behavioral goals emerged which appeared to be realistic and fruitful. Project staff found agreement with Lovell (1968),[31] in that "the concepts do not develop in an 'all or none' fashion," but rather tend to become stable over time with practice. Videotape recording was an important vehicle of study and analysis of suggested structure models or teaching sequences. Some videotapes were replayed many times before revising structure models.

Teacher language and the order and clarity of the tutorial sequences were successively revised until they became not only "teachable" but also "learnable." Teachers had great difficulty with the math area, initially, because of the precision required with unfamiliar terms in a subject area in which most teachers were uncertain, untrained, and fearful. None of the teachers who participated in the CHILD Curriculum field tryouts had training in the language and concepts of the "new" math, and they balked at learning such formidable terms as sets, equivalence, cardinal sequence, arbitrary linear measurement, ordinal sequence, and conservation.

Despite the teachers' candid reluctance to learn the "new" math in order to teach it, by virtue of workshops, demonstrations, and videotape study most of the teachers became comfortable with their newly acquired math language. This area, however, presented more difficulty to teachers than any other part of the program. The need to retrain teachers as conceptions of content areas change, will soon become a constant, and this problem will surely have to be solved for teachers at all grade levels in need of periodic re-education. Some combination of in-school supervision and training with college courses or workshops would appear to be a continuing necessity.

In the math area, symbol learning was structured to cover not only numerals but also tallies, arbitrary symbols, math symbols such as "+ " or "-" and simple graphing to represent some aspect of reality. While symbols were not used in the initial sequences, and no structure models were written which were not based on manipulation of objects which a child could check visually or tactually, symbols were introduced along with notions of "more," "less," "add," and "zero" in order to associate the symbol with the concept and the word.

Teachers learned a great deal about children's unique cognitive development in pace and level, as they tested for conservation of number and discovered how readily the child could be confounded by his senses. Teachers also learned while watching videotape replays how many visual, gestural and verbal cues they tended to give children in teaching. As a result, teachers realized that cues could be helpful in initial learning stages but that rigorous testing to find children's conceptual mastery required the removal of such cues. Differentiating teaching from testing became clearer to teachers, both as to purposes and techniques.

SCIENCE

The Karplus SCIS program (Karplus and Thier, 1967)[32] was the original model of science goals and activities. Since the CHILD population was younger than the one for which SCIS was designed, basic goals were restricted to identifying properties of objects, classifying objects on observed properties or on results of simple interaction experiments, and predicting and checking results of simple interaction.

The science program was fashioned to provide children with frequent opportunities to make observations about objects and to manipulate objects in ways that reveal information about their properties, as well as to use appropriate descriptive and naming vocabulary. For example, attempting to roll a ball and a box is an active experience which offers the child much physical and visible information about the properties of these objects. Informal, playful manipulation of objects is expected to provide children with the sensory-motor and verbal base which is required for simple sorting and classification skills.

Teachers are urged not to "tell" children anything they can have the pleasure of finding out for themselves. A problem-solving attitude by the teacher usually sparks delighted self-propelled activity by children.

Many craft projects are included in the science area in addition to water play, woodworking, cooking, art, and music explorations. In effect, the science area integrates activities from several other areas, assuring multiple-purpose learning activities. To transform a cooking activity into a science experience, for example, teachers are asked to start with duplicate trays, and to foster comparison of the two sets of objects before and after the transformation by cooking of one set. Tasting and eating constitute one important source of information about the properties of objects and, fortunately, young children are usually eager to participate in such scientific explorations.

SOCIOLOGY

Aspects of sociology featured in this program are self-knowing and self-valuing, and group and community membership. Self-knowing brings into clear focus a child's unique attributes, such as his appearance, name, voice and activity products. Self-valuing as a competent task-oriented worker flows, hopefully, from pride in known achievements and products, reflected by teachers and parents.

Membership, or a sense of belonging to one's family, one's classroom and to the larger community is pursued through holiday celebrations, production of craft products related to holidays, and familiarity with features of one's own neighborhood. Flag-making for Lincoln's birthday — requiring patterning of red and white stripes — produces a product which the child associates with the idea of "holiday" which usually means that the school is closed to celebrate something. Focus is on the product, on the child's sense of pride of accomplishment, and on his anticipation of parental praise of his work.

Art and woodworking activities are also featured here, since both contribute products which are exploratory and expressive in nature and which further the goals of self-knowing and self-valuing. Sociology tasks are arranged chiefly to dovetail with activities in other content areas and with holidays as they occur.

GEOGRAPHY

Basic goals in geography are orienting oneself in space, distinguishing details and features of the local neighborhood (related to sociology), representing these features with objects, and developing a sense of directionality.

Walks in the school building, around the school block, and to various places nearby (e.g., a grocery store, pet shop or firehouse) are followed by representing physical space with physical objects in the classroom. While block play is a valued form of regular classroom play, block play becomes more structured in attempts to recreate known aspects of physical space with blocks and other objects. Photographs are used to help children remember some features of physical space they are trying to represent. Photographs of the children, taken at the zoo, on the street on which the school stands, or elsewhere are studied by the block builders, to help them decide what aspects of space they wish to represent with blocks.

Games are used to practice orientation in space with appropriate verbalization (such as an obstacle game) and other games are geared to left-right orientation. For example, combining directionality with a musical action game, children make simple colored construction-paper bracelets which they wear only on the right wrist, to help distinguish left from right for "Looby-Loo," "Hokey-Pokey," or other action song-games which specify such actions as "Put your right hand in."

ECONOMICS

Economics goals relate to buying and selling, store play, and classification of food packages (related to cognitive skills, in putting like things together, and to classification in the science program).

Children role-play buying and selling, and as they learn from common experiences in making real store purchases, they make finer differentiations of roles and activities in the dramatic play in the store area. Use of toy money is related to math concepts. Children read and write numerals as they fix prices of foods. Classifying foods is introduced after sorting experiences in cognitive skills and science.

Language is also fostered in store play as children first read pictures and symbols, then gradually food labels, differentiating cartons, cans and packages.

The economics content area offers children an interesting and familiar source of information for playful practice of skills in math, science and language. In addition, it fosters abundant dramatic play which tends to be imaginative as well as imitative, where every child can find a part to play and use his own store of information about food buying, money, and family eating habits.

USE OF THE CURRICULUM

The CHILD Program received a series of field tryouts in New York City public schools, all of which were designated "special service." This term implies that the school population includes a high proportion of "disadvantaged" children, that the school is eligible for Title I funds, and that school achievement scores are on the low side. From 1966 through 1969 the number of teachers with whom the CHILD Project staff worked varied from 4 to 17 in any one year. During the 1968-69 academic year, kindergarten and prekindergarten classes were included in the field tryout, although only prekindergarten classes were involved before that.

The teachers involved in the CHILD field tryouts were all regularly appointed public school teachers, most of whom had been teaching the same grade level in the same school previously. The CHILD Project staff had no authority to hire teachers or to determine which teachers would be involved with the project. Project staff planning for retraining these teachers prior to the opening of the school year was circumvented each year by disputes, resulting in strikes between the Teachers' Union and the New York City Board of Education. Since retraining plans could not be used, inservice training procedures were developed. These procedures offered Project staff frequent opportunities to make classroom observations, to work as members of the teaching staff in demonstrating new methodology or content, and to hold regular weekly meetings with the teachers for further training and for evaluation of the Program.

Originally, weekly lesson plans, which resembled Chinese menus, were written sampling each content area weekly with as many children as possible. Teachers were asked to move to the next behavioral goal in each area for those children who demonstrated mastery of the preceding goal. While supervisors approved of these weekly lesson plans, most teachers did not.

Teachers expressed a sense of pressure to keep up with the proposed schedule, even though there was no requirement about which, if any, children were to be introduced to new learning tasks each week. As a result of sampling teachers' reactions systematically through open-ended tape-recorded individual interviews, open-ended questions, and the use of a semantic differential attitude questionnaire, it was concluded that teacher acceptance of the program required elimination of weekly plans prepared for them. For example, of 16 teachers responding to the semantic differential during the 1968-69 academic year, highest mean scores were found for such terms as "coordinated," "organized," "relevant," "child-centered," "interesting," "inner city," "successful," and "restricted" (Rusalem, 1970).[33]

More than half of the teachers responded with positive views about the new curriculum on an incomplete sentences blank: that it is a worthwhile instructional tool, its organization is good to excellent, it provides more structure and purpose than usual programs, it is relevant and worthwhile, and the curriculum guides are helpful and explicit. Negative responses related primarily to modifying or adding to the content, as indicated above, and the management problems of individual and small group instruction.

Rusalem (1970)[34], summarizing the extreme mean scores on the incomplete sentences blank, suggested that the 16 teachers who responded to the questionnaire during the 1968-69 school year had these attitudes about the CHILD Curriculum:

1. Although the Curriculum is imperfect, it is a new and promising tool worth using again.
2. It is well organized and coordinated.
3. It is relevant for our times in urban areas.
4. It promotes growth in both teachers and children.
5. It focuses upon the interests and needs of children.

However, detailed planning is obviously necessary to move through a packaged curriculum, no matter how much leeway a teacher has as to pacing and adaptation of program suggestions to individual children and to her own interests. Even if teachers were willing to be guided by suggestions for pacing, it would still be necessary to make decisions, daily and weekly, as to what these suggestions would mean in practice. Since in the CHILD Curriculum tasks are voluntary, and each child has some options to choose from, better planning would seem to flow from detailed analysis of each day's work and each child's progress than from general pacing suggestions.

Teacher planning in detail has other important advantages. A teacher is more likely to invest her creative energy in making a success of a project in which she has made active choices. Each choice she makes is a personal commitment which presents a possibility for revision, for personalization in some features, or for redesign. Also, each choice the teacher makes gives her reaffirmation of her own autonomy. From the excellent perspective of hindsight, teacher insistence on control of their own planning and decision-making can only be regarded as positive and constructive. Teacher autonomy has the same value as child autonomy, and teacher models are required for children's social learning. However, teacher autonomy does not automatically foster child autonomy.

The chief drawback to the elimination of the suggested weekly lesson plans was the tendency, observed in most of the teachers who participated in the field tryouts of the curriculum, to pace children too slowly. However, it was recognized that these teachers were working their way through a new curriculum for the first time and that pacing was less a matter of following children's readiness to move on than of the rate at which the teacher felt ready to proceed. This observation was reinforced during the 1969-70 year when a group of teachers were working with the CHILD Curriculum for the second year. With just one year's experience, teachers demonstrated far more ease and expertise in planning. They introduced many structure models earlier in the year to more children, at a more rapid pace generally, and even used the same activities to combine multiple learnings, so that more progress was made in more areas during the same time periods.

The problem of pacing individual children is also a factor of teacher load. When teachers have two classes of young children daily, each for a half-session, even with an Aide the teacher load is too heavy to leave time or energy to analyze records of task mastery or diagnostic tests in order to plan for optimum pacing of each child. This suggests the need for freeing teachers for work on records and plan-making, either by increased staffing of professionals or paraprofessionals or both, or by restructuring the children's or teachers' schedules. Perhaps a new specialist is needed on early childhood staffs, a Teacher-diagnostician, who would have specialized training and responsibilities in working with groups of teachers and paraprofessionals to help them plan for individual children, using good records and regular analysis of the records.

In the CHILD Curriculum, it was decided to replace the weekly lesson plans with detailed teacher guides, in order to offer teachers as many suggestions as possible, but at the same time to stress the teacher's central position in decision-making and planning. The teacher guides, sampling the experiences of many different teachers, makes available to each teacher a far larger repertoire than she might be able to devise by herself.

TESTS AND DIAGNOSIS OF LEARNING

Another original feature of the program, to which some teachers responded negatively, was the requirement of brief diagnostic weekly tests. A series of such tests was constructed by project staff to help the teacher collect systematic feedback on children's progress toward selected behavioral goals, such as color differentiation, alphabet letter name learning, simple classification and various simple types of math tasks. Here again, the teachers sometimes felt too pressured.

Although some teachers were indicating their negative feelings about these diagnostic tests, they were also reporting frequent surprises about children's performance on these tests. Project staff concluded that a large part of teachers' negativism about these tests stemmed from their discomfort on learning that tasks which they had worked carefully to structure, and which they assumed most or all children had mastered, were in fact not yet fully mastered by some or all of the children. This is not to negate the time pressures teachers found uncomfortable. Nevertheless, it seemed possible that teachers may have been more inclined to welcome the testing procedures and the results had these been seen as more ego-gratifying, in confirming rather than contradicting expectations. This suggests specific needs in teacher training, or re-training, to help develop attitudes about diagnosis and instructional planning for young children which would be more realistic about the slow course of conceptual growth and objective and data-oriented.

All teachers who worked with the CHILD Curriculum came to accept the need to record some measure of children's performance on structured tasks, even though this is time-consuming. Hence, it was decided to eliminate the requirement for weekly diagnostic testing in favor of a test battery which teachers could use for their own purposes. The test battery, which samples the content and skills in the CHILD Curriculum, may be used for pre- and posttesting, for frequent testing of specific children or specific skills, or in other ways. Recording suggestions are made to teachers to offer procedures for those teachers who need assistance in this respect. While many teachers demonstrated considerable capability and inventiveness in devising their own procedures, some teachers were grateful for any assistance provided. Therefore, a set of recording forms is made available, with a simple coding system, to record a child's progress.

However, negative teacher reactions to data-gathering requirements through diagnostic tests appear to be a further reflection of lack of time, and energy, and expertise. It seems essential to help teachers find time for diagnostic testing, in order to give far more attention to individual children's learning, to plan more specifically for each child's progress, and to conceive of teaching as data-based, child-based, and plan-based.

WORK WITH PARENTS

Throughout the life of the project, efforts were made to reach parents in various peripheral ways, none of which were successful. Parents were sought and welcomed as volunteers in the classroom, project staff agreed to address many meetings for parents on the subject of the CHILD Curriculum, and suggestions were made for parental reinforcement of children's learnings at home. It was felt that few parents were effectively reached, either by project staff or by the extensive efforts made by school personnel, in terms of home reinforcement of the school's educational program.

In the 1968-69 academic year, when the school opening was delayed almost to Thanksgiving Day by a teacher strike in New York City, it was decided to develop a small pilot parent program in one school to back up the CHILD Project. One staff member was assigned to the parent project and, despite the brief experience of a five-month study, the parent program yielded some interesting insights about future structure and development of such experiences (Robison, in press).[35]

Without going into detail about the parent project at this point, it can be said that parents appear to be more eager for and capable of home reinforcement of children's school learning than is usually assumed. Where the school is attempting to provide massive opportunities for children's practice in new content or skills, failure to work with parents effectively is an invitation to failure.

RESULTS OF CHILD CURRICULUM

With teacher turnover, school changes in programs, continual modification of the CHILD Program, and other uncontrolled variables, it was difficult to gauge the effect of the CHILD Curriculum on children's academic progress. In several instances, it happened that children who experienced the CHILD Program in the prekindergarten were assigned to some other "follow-through" program for the kindergarten and first grade, rendering any longitudinal assessment impossible. Assessment difficulties also stemmed from the "outsider" position of the project staff, which made it impossible to achieve any desired level of congruence with the written program.

During the 1967-68 year when four prekindergarten teachers were working with an earlier version of CHILD, comparisons were made with prekindergarten children in a nearby school, those children who appeared to be of a comparable population. It was not anticipated that, shortly after pretesting, the comparison group would be assigned to a new program, with increased staffing and strong emphasis on reading and math concepts. Based on PPVT scores, the two groups evidenced remarkably similar progress, in both cases gaining about a fifteen-point increase to posttest means of 86 (Robison, 1968).[36] It was impossible to follow these groups for the reasons listed above.

In the following academic year (1968-69), which included the long teacher strike, project plans for teacher training and for control group selection were disrupted. When a comparison group was finally made available, it was found after pretesting was well advanced, that this group had a white minority of about 30 percent, rendering it quite different from the population in which the CHILD Program was in use. A new test was devised, called the "Child Behavior Test," which was comprised of the items related to the behavioral goals of the new program and which seemed to tap some of the cognitive and behavioral variables featured. In view of the population differences, it is interesting to note that no significant differences were found between the groups on an analysis of co-variance, either on the new CBT or the PPVT series. The children using the CHILD Program appeared to have some advantage on the subtest of the CBT on patterning-classification. However, a significant difference in scores (at the 5 percent level) in favor of the children in the CHILD Program was found on the Metropolitan Readiness Test administered in the first grade in the fall of 1969, in 3 schools in which some kindergarten classes had participated in the experimental program. Mean scores were 55.1 for those children who had experienced the CHILD Curriculum in the kindergarten and 49.1 for those who had not, with standard deviations of 10 for both groups. Since in these schools, kindergarten classes may be regarded as randomly constituted, although teacher self-selection introduces bias in the teacher variable, these results suggest that continued use of the CHILD Program is warranted for further data collection.

The CHILD Curriculum now seems ready for testing in a research design capable of yielding more definitive information about its effects on children's academic progress. One vital ingredient of such a design must be a measure of the extent to which teacher behavior samples indicate that the curriculum is actually experienced by children. Better tests are needed, however, than those which have been available to determine the contributions of an early childhood program to such desirable, but elusive, values as playfulness with ideas, self-valuing, autonomy, independence in learning, and dialectal flexibility.

FOOTNOTES | 10

[1] A. R. Luria, "The functional organization of the brain," *Scientific American*, Vol. 222, March 1970, p. 66.

[2] *Ibid*, p. 78.

[3] Martin Deutsch, "The role of social class in language development and cognition," *American Journal of Orthopsychiatry*, Vol. XXXV, January 1965, pp. 78-88; Ralph Mason Dreger and Kent S. Miller, "Comparative psychological studies of negroes and whites in the United States," *Psychological Bulletin*, Vol. 57, Sept. 1960, pp. 361-402; and Fred L. Strodtbeck, "The hidden curriculum of the middle class home," in C. W. Hunnecutt (Ed.), *Urban education and cultural deprivation*, Syracuse, N.Y., Syracuse University Press, 1964.

[4] Oscar C. Stine, "Selected neurologic and behavioral findings of children entering an early school admissions project from culturally deprived neighborhoods," *Journal of School Health*, Vol. XXXIX, No. 7, Sept. 1969, p. 476.

[5] Benjamin S. Bloom, *Stability and change in human characteristics*, N. Y., Wiley, 1964.

[6] Millie Almy, *Young children's thinking*, New York City, Teachers College Press, 1966, p. 84.

[7] Barbel Inhelder and Jean Piaget, *Early growth of logic in the child*, New York, Harper and Row, 1964.

[8] H. L. Hunt, "The psychological basis for using pre-school enrichment as an antidote for cultural deprivation," *Merrill-Palmer Quarterly*, Vol. 10, July 1964, pp. 209-248.

[9] Lawrence Kohlberg, "Early education: A cognitive-developmental view," *Child Development*, Vol. 39, No. 4, Dec. 1968, pp. 1013-1062.

[10] Arthur R. Jensen, "How much can we boost IQ and scholastic achievement?", *Harvard Educational Review*, Vol. 39, No. 1, Winter 1969, pp. 1-123.

[11] Sylvia Ashton-Warner, *Teacher*, New York, Simon and Schuster, 1963.

[12] Joan Baratz, "A bi-dialectal task for determining language proficiency in economically disadvantaged negro children," *Child Development,* Vol. 40, No. 3, Sept. 1969, pp. 889-901.

[13] Helen F. Robison, "Data analysis, 1967-68," Teachers College, Columbia University, mimeograph, pp. 47-48.

[14] Seymour Rigrodsky and Eleanor B. Morrison "Report of auditory discrimination program conducted in the prekindergarten and kindergarten classes at P. S. 140, 1968-69," Teachers College, Columbia University, October, 1969.

[15] Louis T. DiLorenzo, *Prekindergarten programs for educationally disadvantaged children,* Final Report, Project No. 3040, Contract No. OE-6-10-040, The University of the State of New York, The State Education Department, Office of Research and Evaluation, 1969.

[16] Shirley Samuels, "Investigation into self concepts in early childhood of kindergarten children from middle and lower-class homes," unpublished doctoral study, New York, Teachers College, Columbia University, 1969.

[17] Anthony T. Soares and Louise M. Soares, "Self-perceptions of culturally disadvantaged children," *American Educational Research Journal,* Vol. 6, No. 1, Jan. 1969, pp. 31-45, p. 43.

[18] Helen F. Robison and Kenneth D. Wann, "Status report: study of intellectual stimulation of disadvantaged pre-kindergarten children, sponsored by Center For Urban Education," Teachers College, Columbia University, July 7, 1967.

[19] Courteney B. Cazden, "Studies of early language acquisition," *Childhood Education,* December 1969, pp. 127-131.

[20] Eric B. Lenneberg (Ed.), *New directions in the study of language,* Boston, MIT Press, 1966, and Ursula Bellugi and Roger Brown (Eds.), *The Acquisition of language,* Monographs of the Society for Research in Child Development, Serial No. 92, Vol. 29, No. 1, Lafayette, Indiana, 1964.

[21] William Labov, "The logic of non-standard English," Georgetown Monograph Series on Language and Linguistics, Monograph No. 22, 1969, and "Some suggestions for ordering the problems of non-standard English used by prekindergarten negro children," November 1969, dittoed.

[22] Barbara B. Rothenberg, "Conservation of number among four and five-year-old children: some methodological considerations," *Child Development,* June 1969, Vol. 40, No. 2.

[23] Helen F. Robison and Rose Mukerji, "Concept and language development in a kindergarten of disadvantaged children," Monograph, Cooperative Research Project, S-320, U.S. Office of Education, 1966.

[24] Robert D. Hess and Virginia C. Shipman, "Maternal influences upon early learning," in Robert D. Hess and Roberta Meyer Bear, *Early Education,* Chicago, Aldine Publishing Co., 1968.

[25] Lev Semovich Vygotsky, *Thought and language,* Edited and translated by Eugenia Hanfmann and Gertrude Vakar, Boston, The MIT Press, Massachusetts Institute of Technology, 1962.

[26] Inhelder and Piaget, *Op. Cit.*

[27] O. K. Moore, "The responsive environments project and the deaf", *American Annals of the Deaf,* November 1965, Vol. 110, No. 5, pp. 604-614, and Omar Khayyam Moore and Alan Ross Anderson, "The Responsive environments project," in Robert D. Hess and Roberta Meyer Bear (Eds.), *Early education,* Chicago, Aldine Publishing Co., 1968.

[28] Benjamin S. Bloom, "Learning for mastery," *Evaluation Comment,* CSEIP, Vol. 1, No. 2, May 1968, Los Angeles.

[29] John Dewey, *How we think* (2nd Ed.), Boston, D. C. Heath and Co., 1933; O. K. Moore, "The responsive environments project and the deaf," *American Annals of the deaf,* Vol. 110, No. 5, Nov. 1965, pp. 604-614, and Johan Huizinga, *Homo ludens,* Boston, The Beacon Press, 1955.

[30] *Nuffield mathematics project,* published for the Nuffield Foundation by W. and R. Chambers and John Murray, New York, John Wiley and Sons, n.d.

[31] K. Lovell, *The growth of basic mathematical and scientific concepts in children,* London, University of London Press, Ltd., 1968.

[32] Robert Karplus and Herbert D. Their, *A new look at elementary school science,* Chicago, Rand McNally, 1967.

[33] Herbert Rusalem, "Independent evaluation of project CHILD Curriculum," Teachers College, Columbia University, March 25, 1970.

[34] *Ibid.,* pp. 12-13.

[35] Helen F. Robison, Monograph-Final Report on CHILD Project, in press.

[36] Helen F. Robison, "Data analysis, 1967-68," Teachers College, Columbia University, mimeograph, p. 20.

REFERENCES | 10

Almy, M. *Young children's thinking.* New York, Teachers College Press, 1966.

Ashton-Warner, S. *Teacher.* New York: Simon and Schuster, 1963.

Baratz, J. "A bi-dialectal task for determining language proficiency in economically disadvantaged negro children" *Child Development,* Vol. *40,* No. 3, September, 1969, pp. 889-901.

Bellugi, U. and Brown, R. (Eds.) *The acquisition of language.* Monographs of the society for research in child development. Serial No. 92, Vol. *29,* No. 1.

Bettelheim, B. *Children of the dream.* New York: MacMillan Co., 1969.

Bloom, B. S. "Learning for mastery" *Evaluation Comment.* CSE 1P, Los Angeles, Vol. *1,* No. 2, May, 1968.

Bloom, B. S. *Stability and change in human characteristics.* New York: Wiley, 1964.

Cazden, C. B. "Studies of early language acquisition" *Childhood Education.* December 1969, pp. 127-131.

Deutsch, M. "The role of social class in language development and cognition," *American Journal of Orthopsychiatry.* Vol. *XXXV,* January, 1965, pp. 78-88.

Dewey, J. *How we think.* 2nd Edition. Boston: D. C. Heath and Co., 1933.

DiLorenzo, L. T. *Prekindergarten programs for educationally disadvantaged children.* Final Report, Project No. 3040, Contract No. OE-6-10-040. The University of the State of New York, The State Education Department, Office of Research and Evaluation, 1969.

Dreger, R. M. and Miller, K. S. "Comparative psychological studies of negroes and whites in the United States," *Psychological Bulletin.* Vol. *57,* Sept. 1960, pp. 361-402.

Dykstra, R. "Relationships between readiness characteristics and primary grade reading achievement in four types of reading programs." Paper read at AERA Conference, Minneapolis, Feb. 1970.

Hess, R. D. and Shipman, V. C. "Maternal influences upon early learning." In Hess, R. D. and Bear, R. M. *Early Education.* Chicago, Aldine Publishing Co., 1968.

Huizinga, J. *Homo ludens.* Boston: The Beacon Press, 1955.

Hunt, H. L. "The psychological bases for using pre-school enrichment as an antidote for cultural deprivation," *Merrill-Palmer Quarterly.* Vol. *10,* July 1964, pp. 209-248.

Inhelder, B. and Piaget, J. *Early growth of logic in the child.* New York: Harper and Row, 1964.

Jensen, A. R. "How much can we boost I.Q. and scholastic achievement?" *Harvard Educational Review.* Vol. *39,* No. 1, Winter 1969, pp. 1-123.

Karplus, R. and Thier, H. D. *A new look at elementary school science.* Chicago, Rand McNally, 1967.

Kohlberg, L. "Early education: a cognitive-developmental view." *Child Development.* Vol. *39,* No. 4, Dec. 1968, pp. 1013-1062.

Labov, W. "Some suggestions for ordering the problems of non-standard English by prekindergarten negro children." New York: Columbia University, dittoed, Nov. 1969(a).

Labov, W. "The logic of non-standard english." Georgetown Monograph Series on Language and Linguistics. Monograph No. 22, 1969(b).

Lenneberg, E. B. (Ed.) *New directions in the study of language.* Boston: MIT Press, 1966.

Lovell, K. *The growth of basic mathematical and scientific concepts in children.* London: University of London Press, Ltd., 1968.

Luria, A. R. "The functional organization of the brain." *Scientific American.* Vol. *22,* March 1970, p. 66.

Moore, O. K. "The responsive environments project and the deaf." *American annals of the Deaf.* November 1965, Vol. *110,* No. 5, pp. 604-614.

Moore, O. K. and Anderson, A. R. "The responsive environments project." In Hess, R. D. and Bear, R. Meyer (Eds.), *Early Education.* Chicago: Aldine Publishing Co., 1968.

Nuffield *Mathematics project.* Published for the Nuffield Foundation by W. and R. Chambers and J. Murray. New York: John Wiley, n.d.

Piaget, J. *Play, dreams and imitation in childhood.* New York: W. W. Norton Co., 1962.

Rigrodsky, S. and Morrison, E. B. "Report of auditory discrimination program conducted in the prekindergarten and kindergarten classes at P. S. 140, 1968-69." New York: Teachers College, Columbia University, Oct. 1969, typescript.

Robison, H. F. and Mukerji, R. "Concept and language development in a kindergarten of disadvantaged children." Monograph, Cooperative Research Project S-320. U.S. Office of Education, 1966.

Robison, H. F. "Data analysis, 1967-68." New York: Teachers College, Columbia University, mimeo, November 1968.

Robison, H. F. and Wann, K. D. "Status report: study of intellectual stimulation of disadvantaged pre-kindergarten children, sponsored by Center for Urban

Education." New York: Teachers College, Columbia University, July 7, 1967.

Rothenberg, B. B. "Conservation of number among four and five-year-old children: some methodological considerations." *Child Development.* June 1969, Vol. *40,* No. 2.

Rusalem, H. "Independent evaluation of project CHILD Curriculum." New York: Teachers College, Columbia University, March 25, 1970. Typescript.

Samuels, S. "Investigation into self-concepts in early childhood of kindergarten children from middle and lower-class homes." Unpublished doctoral study. New York: Teachers College, Columbia University, 1969.

Sigel, I. E. and **Olmstead, P.** "Modification of classificatory competence and level of representation among lower-class negro kindergarten children." Detroit, Michigan: The Merrill-Palmer Institute, 1968.

Soares, A. T. and **Soares, L. M.** "Self-perceptions of culturally disadvantaged children." *American Educational Research Journal,* Vol. *6,* No. 1, Jan. 1969, pp. 31-45.

Stine, O. C., *et al.* "Selected neurologic and behavioral findings of children entering an early school admissions project from culturally deprived neighborhoods." *Journal of School Health.* Vol. *XXXIX,* No. 7, Sept. 1969, pp. 470-477.

Strodtbeck, F. L. "The hidden curriculum of the middle class home," in Hunnecutt, C. W. (Ed.), *Urban Education and Cultural Deprivation.* Syracuse, New York: Syracuse University Press, 1964.

Vygotsky, L. S. *Thought and language.* Edited and translated by E. Hanfmann and G. Vakar. Boston: The MIT Press. Massachusetts Institute of Technology, 1962.

Anderson, Bereiter | *Introduction* | 11

The conceptualization of an academically-oriented preschool for disadvantaged children was presented in *Teaching Disadvantaged Children in the Preschool* by Carl Bereiter and Siegfried Englemann. The curriculum described in the book focused on three areas (language, arithmetic, and reading), and the teaching method used was that of direct verbal instruction. In the following paper Dr. Valerie Anderson and Dr. Carl Bereiter describe an extension of the method of direct instruction to teaching conceptual skills, specifically communication and thinking skills.

However, in the initial portion of the paper the authors focus on clarifying some of the most frequent misunderstandings of the academic preschool and the direct instructional model. They present rationales for the preschool's academic curriculum and for the choice of a preschool as the most appropriate place to begin instructional change. For some, the negative connotations that direct instruction carries, and especially when used in conjunction with preschool education, may be vitiated by a description of direct instruction which includes responsiveness to the child, fun, and success.

The extension of the direct instructional model to conceptual skills was made in response to the needs of a particular population, just as was the original focus on pre-academic skills. Many middle class children learn at home those skills taught in the academic preschool, so the curriculum was expanded to include areas of greater difficulty and broad transfer value — communication and thinking skills. The skills included in the communications area are defined by the action which the child makes in the communication process, and thus there are clearly defined behavioral objectives. In addition, the picture of the child as a passive recipient of information fades, for the child is following instructions, giving instructions, and asking questions — all of which require active participation. The thinking skills component requires practice on different types of thinking problems, progressing from simple problems to more and more complex ones. Several sub-skills are included in this component, and analytical processes as well as productive thinking are included. This extension is most valuable in demonstrating that direction (specification and programming of skills, primarily teacher directed), as well as being used didactically, may also be used in ways which require the child's overtly active participation.

Valerie Anderson
Carl Bereiter

Extending Direct Instruction to Conceptual Skills

11

The academic preschool, as defined in *Teaching Disadvantaged Children in the Preschool*, was a response to a definite need in education. The advent of Head Start and other special programs represented a demonstration that a particular group of students were in educational difficulty. Disadvantaged young people did not do well in school and the hopes were high that if they could begin their education early enough, they might not have that difficulty. Certainly the emphasis was not on changing the society and schools to fit the disadvantaged, but on changing the disadvantaged to fit the society and schools.

The beginning efforts to do so varied slightly from program to program, but by and large they were modelled after a traditional preschool model. The prevailing feeling, in spite of the general acknowledgment that disadvantaged youngsters were somehow "different," was that the same preschool that met the needs of the "whole" middle-class child would also appeal to and make "whole" the lower-class child, plus adequately prepare him to cope with middle-class or advantaged schools, teachers, and curricula in the same way that advantaged children were able to cope with them. At that time, few educators saw a necessity to change the schools or the preschools for these children. *Teaching*

Valerie Anderson and Carl Bereiter are at the Ontario Institute for Studies in Education. Printed by permission of the authors.

Disadvantaged Children in the Preschool was written in response to a need that required more than the increase of existing preschools to facilitate more children or an extension of existing preschools to include the disadvantaged; it was written in response to a need for instructional change.

The choice of the preschool as an appropriate place to initiate change amounted to more than a belief in the need for early education or accelerated learning. The first consideration in that choice was that the preschool was a place where change might be the *easiest* to initiate in that it had fewer educational commitments, fewer concrete goals, fewer ties to the educational establishment, and fewer years of existence. In short, it did not appear to have the middle-class "hang-ups" that the later school years so blatantly imposed upon the lower-class student. Had the elementary or even the secondary schools allowed for the same sort of speculation, the effort and the book would have been different. Beyond ease of change, the preschool certainly offered another advantage: children who, by virtue of their age, were particularly teachable, unfrustrated by the inability to meet adult demands, untainted by the arbitrary nature of the school system, and who, while they may or may not have been taught, were certainly willing to learn. The preschool also seemed like the most likely area to find cooperation from many in an honest effort to help children. And, if changes seemed impossible within the schools themselves, then early education was the *only* place to prepare children for what they had in store.

The choice of an academic preschool over any other type was made partly because of what was in store for the children. Disadvantaged children typically have the most difficulty with the skills that schools require of them in the early grades. If deficits begin then, they seem to be carried throughout the school years. The question of whether or not the schools do an adequate job of teaching those skills is overshadowed by the fact that many children do learn them. The disadvantaged, more often, do not. Language, reading, and arithmetic skills were chosen as those most likely to build a foundation for the skills that might be further developed both in and out of school. Other activities were less direct in nature but were geared to reinforce the academic aspects of the curriculum.

The age of the children in the academic preschools ranged from late three to early six. This seemed to be the best time to initiate a program which could utilize language as a vehicle for instruction. The way of teaching was direct. This seemed the most obvious way to teach anything once decisions were made about what would be taught.

Before discussing how direct instruction was extended and applied to conceptual skills, or how that extention might be conceptualized into preschool curricula, it seems (unfortunately) necessary to discuss what actually was included within the direct instructional model, simply because it has been rather grossly misunderstood by a number of educators. Preschool education has, in the last eight years, changed a great deal, in order to offer many program alternatives to young children. It has become more considerate of the various needs of children, more willing to set specific goals, and more willing to accept various means of attaining more global goals. The recognition of this has produced a certain amount of complacency regarding the acceptability of direct instruction in school circles, but this complacency gets rocked from time to time by some vague acknowledgement, such as, "Oh yes... Isn't that the program where they yell at the kids all the time?" There seems to remain a substantial difference between how we see ourselves and how others see us (primarily those who have not seen us). Because this discrepancy has been so obvious, it is important to restate the facts, since they provide a better basis for further program development than the surmises.

The field of early education is beginning to move away from a strong tie to platitudes and glorifications of childhood. The disadvantaged child's plight is not a glorious one, nor is the plight of thousands of children who perform poorly in school in spite of advantaged environments. *Teaching Disadvantaged Children in the Preschool* avoided platitudes in an effort to provide solutions. Little was said about the beauty of childhood, the promise of a glorious future, or the personal fulfillment of the individual. The book tried to be as specific as possible about what to teach and how to teach it. This alone caused a great deal of controversy in that it was felt that a program that was so specific about the teaching of skills could not possibly have considered the emotional aspects of the child. On the contrary, we cared about the children and we considered their emotional future as carefully as we considered their academic future. Concern for the child's emotional stability was the justification for such careful programming of skills — to make learning a less frustrating experience. In fact, it was considered so carefully that it went without saying: no one in his right mind would overlook the child's emotional stability. And since the sentimentality already entrenched in the field of early education seemed to negate consideration of the more practical issues of teaching disadvantaged children, we felt that practical issues should take precedence. Resulting assumptions have created descriptions of the method ranging from mildly punitive to monstrous, but all equally unfounded.

Just for the record, the most odious should be denied. The following teaching "uglies" have been carefully avoided and are certainly *NOT* to be considered as a part of direct instructions: beating, physically punishing, deriding, frustrating, browbeating, brainwashing, or badgering children; locking children in closets or refusing to feed them; shouting at children in anger; pushing children beyond their capabilities; deliberately discouraging or undermining creativity, free expression, and peer interaction; conditioning children into behaving like robots, encouraging rote learning or attempting to impose middle-class values. There are undoubtedly other accusations that do not come immediately to mind; but these are enough. All of these "uglies" are things that direct instruction should, as we conceive it, do away with. Any one of these could be accompanied by further explanation as to why or how it was avoided through direct instruction, but within the scope of this paper, it seems enough to state that all of these bad practices *have been avoided* because they are detrimental to the emotional state of the child.

Discussions of punishment in the book cover some three of its three hundred pages of instructional techniques and procedures which, when implemented, do away with virtually any need for punishment. Those three pages, for many, have sadly evolved to a statement of program philosophy. The following principles have actually prevailed and may clarify the manner in which discipline problems were handled. If nothing were said at all, it might be assumed that discipline problems have never been encountered or that there is no way of dealing with them. There certainly are ways of dealing with them and to say we have encountered no discipline problems would not be completely honest, even though it's almost completely true.

1. Punishment is a *last resort* for those very few children whose behavior is dangerous to themselves or others in that the effects of the behavior promise to be more detrimental than the effects of its immediate extinguishment.
2. Positive means of changing behavior work better than negative means. The rewards a teacher receives for barking at or punishing children may be more immediate than those she receives for positively reinforcing nondestructive behavior — but her reward is far less lasting.
3. Changing behavior should be a highly individualized form of teaching.
4. There is no need for punishment if the teacher regards all behavior as something to be taught, informs the children of her wishes honestly and consistently, and rewards children for their cooperation. Unfortunately, this combination is rarely seen, but where it occurs both teacher and children are happy.
5. Being dishonest with children is perhaps the most punishing thing a teacher can do regardless of how pleasantly she goes about it. If a child's behavior is dangerous to himself or others, he should know it clearly and dramatically. If it were an easy thing to learn, he would know it already.

Critics have also regarded direct instruction as an educational regression, a step backward from the more enlightened forms of modern unrestricted education, a return to "hickory stick" techniques. Certainly these old techniques were direct, but they lacked three major characteristics of modern direct instruction. These are responsiveness to the child, fun, and success. While direct instruction proposes a number of specific things to be taught, the child's interests and abilities determine just what and how much will be taught at any time. Second, direct instruction is designed to be fun. No value is assigned to hard work for its own sake. Finally, direct instruction is programmed so that the child experiences continual success, whereas in the old schools it was accepted as inevitable that many children would experience failure most of the time. A close look at even the more enlightened forms of modern unrestricted education seldom reveals a satisfactory combination of these three characteristics. It is felt that such a combination is important enough to overrule considerations of content in any curriculum.

The academic preschool was designed for a particular group of children. Since its inception, however, the methods have been used and extended to many kinds of children, both more and less able. Since direct instruction requires verbal communication for its effects, the most specific requirement for its adoption has been the readiness of the children to verbalize. For this reason, the experience of the program has continued to be with children within the age range of three to six, and it is to that age range that this paper is addressed.

The needs of disadvantaged children differ from those of other children; the priorities are different. In designing a preschool curriculum that can apply to all children, regardless of socio-economic status, the academic preschool can only provide a base upon which to begin. Direct instruction, however, can go beyond that base. Many of the skills taught in the academic preschool have been acquired or nearly acquired by more advantaged children. Thus the curriculum has been expanded so that the needs of these other children might also be met.

In expanding the curriculum, some areas were first identified that are not learned by enough students to be claimed as accomplished goals in education, areas in which even advantaged children have difficulty. A broad range of these could be identified: social skills, physical coordination, mechanical ability, artistic ability, communication skills, mathematical problem solving, creative writing, and thinking. While direct instruction could be applied to all of these areas, so far, the effort has been concentrated on communication and thinking skills.

We have not begun with a theory of thinking. Rather, the approach has been first to design a number of thinking tasks that seem reasonably teachable to young children and then to try them out. Wherever the children have had difficulty, lower level tasks have been designed that eliminate the difficulties and allow the children to learn the skills. Although we cannot define thinking, one negative statement can be made about it; if you can describe the behavior that you're teaching, then you're not teaching thinking. Thinking is a kind of residual. If the behavior to be taught can be described accurately, then, at best, some kind of mechanical process will be taught. For example, to teach long division, the behavior that the child is to execute can be described in quite explicit detail. It therefore lends itself nicely to teaching. The great advances that have been made in teaching have been made whenever people have taken some kind of performance that previously had not been described very well behaviorally, and have done so — and then it became teachable. In other words, when a person can be shown how to do something, thinking is not required in order to do it. It is a rote action. Advances in teaching children to read have come about largely by *finding ways* of showing them how to do it. Previously, they first memorized words, and as they went ahead and rattled off those words, sooner or later they might learn how to read new words. But with some attention to the engineering of the task, they can be shown how to figure out what a word is — and then, when they have been taught how to read, reading no longer requires the kind of thinking that it formerly did. The kinds of things loosely referred to as thinking are solving problems, reasoning, drawing deductive and inductive inferences, and creativity, in the sense of generating new ideas. In all of these it may be possible to define the performance that is expected of the child — what he is expected to accomplish — but one can't provide a definition as to how to accomplish it. This leaves the behavioral engineer at somewhat of a loss for tools. His most powerful tool, which is that of describing explicitly the behavior he wants, and then setting up some way to achieve the goal, proceeding from where the child begins by reinforcing steps in the right direction, is lost because he doesn't know what the behavior is that he is trying to reinforce.

There are two ways to methodically try to teach thinking without knowing what the behavior is that you want. Both are inadequate, but they are probably the only ways. One of these is to forget about thinking altogether and simply try to teach the children other things which may enhance the quality of their interaction with the environment in such a way that they'll learn everything better — and then hope that thinking will be included among the things that they learn better. For instance, one may teach them how to ask more questions, more different kinds of questions, and how to use questions for more varied purposes. This in itself is not teaching thinking, but it is not unreasonable to suppose that if a child is able to ask more and better questions that it will lead eventually to his having more experiences that will enhance learning and thinking. That is one way of doing it and our current work is pursuing several tactics along those lines. We have developed a communications skills program that's concerned with three aspects of language use:

Instruction-following. This doesn't have much to do with thinking at all. It is just a practical thing for children to know in school — how to follow different kinds of instructions of increasing complexity. A number of simple descriptive concepts are isolated and taught within this area for those children who have not learned them.

Instruction-giving. This seems to have more relevance to thinking. A typical instruction-giving task is one where the children are given a diagram of some kind and they instruct the teacher in how to reproduce it; that is, they tell her verbally what to do step by step so that she can reproduce their picture. The children are able to work their way up to becoming quite proficient in giving rather complex instructions. For example, the picture may have a triangle in the upper left-hand corner and a circle at the bottom and a line connecting them and, in the middle of the line, a square with a horizontal line sticking out on the left and right side of it. The children include all of those details so that the teacher can adequately follow their directions and reproduce their picture. This communication skill seems as if it might be helpful to children in learning to think in that it gives them greater proficiency and confidence in specifying exactly what they would like someone else to do instead of expressing a very general wish or simply letting someone know that they're uneasy about something. It helps them to be very specific about what they want.

The third communication skill is *question asking*, where again we strive to help children learn to be very specific about getting the information that they need and want.

The premise that we're operating on, in advocating this kind of instruction, is drawn from Piaget, who used to talk a lot about how important social interaction was for learning to think. For the child to acquire points of view other than his own (which Piaget saw as the basis for decentered thinking), Piaget held that it took "friction" of one mind with another. More broadly, Piaget sees intellectual development as occurring through an experimental process as the child acts on the environment, something happens and, as a result, the child's cognitive structure changes. The application of this idea is obvious for fiddling around with blocks, but in the social environment, how does a child experiment? One way is by telling people to do something and seeing what happens as a result of the instructions; another is by asking questions. These are analogous to physical manipulation, so that by developing these skills we are trying to teach children to be better experimenters with the social environment. The premise is that if children are able to do more things in the social environment, act on people in more precise and various ways, they will surely learn more as a result of it. Thus, we draw from Piaget a theoretical justification for a very direct and non-Piagetian sort of teaching.

The skills — instruction following, instruction giving, and question asking— are designated in terms of the action taken by the child in the communication process. A set of objectives of this kind is well defined behaviorally. There are, of course, problems of sampling and taking account of chance success, but objective evaluation is clearly possible. Communication objectives of this kind can cover all that people have previously been striving for in the way of language goals, without involving dubious inferences about language competence and without forcing children into predetermined linguistic forms. They specify what the child should be able to accomplish through language rather than specifying the linguistic features themselves and in this way they have a good deal more potential relevance to major educational goals. One of the advantages of substituting communication goals for language goals is that we are less tempted to suppose that in teaching children the grammar of a language that we are teaching them logic or a thinking system.

The other way of trying to accomplish the teaching of thinking is through simply isolating more and different kinds of thinking problems — more kinds of thinking performance — and operating on them separately. This amounts to the most primitive kind of teaching there is, straight practice — when in doubt about how to teach something, just give people practice. This is probably the only way that anybody tries to teach thinking. The more glamorous thinking programs are, upon closer examination, simply fancy types of practice. No one is ever shown how to think; one is only given practice in thinking. That is where we are: all we know how to do is give practice. It can be fun-practice. It can be exciting practice. But in the end it is just practice. First, we give children practice on easy things and then we work our way up to hard things. Somehow or other we hope the children stay with us and can go from easy to difficult. We don't know how they get there. We just observe that they do.

How can this crude procedure be improved upon? One way is to give practice on more kinds of thinking sub-skills. The following point out some of these that we have been working on. They are not listed in any particular order, but they give a sense of the kinds of things that are viewed as lower-level kinds of performance.

RELEVANCE

Relevance is very important to thinking. You have to know whether or not a statement is relevant to an issue to think rationally about it. While a general understanding of relevance is difficult even for adults, we've tried to strip it down to the simplest kind of relevance task for children in which the child asks the teacher a question. When the teacher answers, the child must decide whether or not she answered the question. Not whether the answer was right or wrong, but whether it was answered at all. This proves to be a very difficult thing, not only for five-year-olds but for second-graders — even fairly bright second-graders — to handle. Since we don't know how to teach anybody how to decide whether something is relevant or not, the only thing to do is try to get down to an easy form of the problem that the children can already do, and then work our way up by degrees. One way to do it is to give glaringly irrelevant answers. If the children ask, "What's your name?", you say something like, "Today is Tuesday," so that there is no resemblance between the question and the answer; then ask, "Did I answer your question?" so that they can say, "No." Another way is to separate out the sources of difficulty. Some children feel any answer is relevant simply because it is directed toward them. This can be cleared up by having two or three children ask different questions, answering only one of them and asking the children to identify whose question was answered and whose was not answered. Where children have real problems on the relevance task is in confusing rightness and wrongness with answers and non-answers to questions. If they ask you, "What month is this?" in May, and you say, "September," they know it's not September and they often maintain that you have not answered their question. They're just not willing to admit that you have answered their question because your answer was wrong, and they do not consider wrong answers to be relevant to a question. The difficulty can be avoided by always giving them true statements, which simplifies the task initially. We start out with answers that are radically irrelevant but always true statements, so that they can't quarrel with the truth of it. Now they only have to judge whether or not the question has been answered. This gets the task down to a five-year-old's level, and then it's a simple matter of working up, giving answers that are less and less obviously irrelevant until the children are fairly finely tuned-in on whether their question has been precisely answered.

Another way we protect children from confusing correctness and relevance and still cover the relevance of incorrect answers is to have them ask questions *about* some object that is held behind a book. Once they ask about the thing, e.g., "What color is it?", they are told, "It's orange. Did I answer your question?" They don't know whether they've been answered rightly or wrongly because they don't know what the thing is, but they *can* decide whether the question was answered. After their judgment is acknowledged, they are shown that the object is white and told, "Yes, I answered your question . . . Did I answer your question? (Yes) . . . Did I answer it right? (No)" and so on.

After the children have reached the point of judging an answer to their question, they can be introduced to the more potentially confusing business of the *truth or falseness* of statements about objects. Simple true and false statements can be related to relevance but require special attention. Truth and falseness deal with a relationship between a statement and an actual object or situation. Determining whether a statement is true or untrue of an object requires both observing an object *and* judging a statement about it. Children have considerable difficulty in forming statements that express such judgments, particularly when negatives are involved. For example, when shown a pencil and asked to judge the statement, "This is not a pencil," as true or not true, they often say that the statement is true; further, when the pencil is offered with the statement, "This is not an elephant," the children will insist that the statement is not true. The children's effort is basically a descriptive one (e.g., "Yes, it is a pencil" or "No, it is not an elephant") which evades taking the additional reasoning step required to judge the statement (e.g., Yes, it is a pencil; therefore the statement — It is not a pencil — is not true. No, it is not an elephant; therefore the statement — This is not an elephant is true). Another sort of problem arises when the children are asked to produce statements that are *not* true about an object. With a pencil, for example, they often offer true statements such as "It's not an apple" or "It's not a dog," thus regarding any negative statement as an untrue statement. While the task is quite difficult, it is simplified by introducing the statements through puppets or pictures of well-known characters (e.g., a clown, a parrot, etc.) in order to strongly emphasize the presence of both the object *and* a spoken action upon the object. Children also have difficulty in using *only* available evidence to make and judge statements. For example, they may confirm untrue statements such as "That pencil belongs to a little girl" even though there is no evidence or proof simply because it is likely. Likewise, they may reject unlikely but true statements such as "This pencil does not have an eraser," maintaining that the eraser has been removed. This, like other aspects of the task, can be mastered by the children — by presenting a series of questions that systematically reveal the processing steps required — often more ably than their teachers who show considerable confusion in judging the children's responses. It might be asked to what end these things are taught. Simply because both our experience and the task have revealed that children have some interesting and rather persistent problems in dealing with common negative and positive true and false statements.

The areas of relevance, truth, and falseness are stressed here because they nicely illustrate the strategy of starting out with some kind of behavior that looks important, but that's beyond the typical five-year-old, and trying to find some way to get that same performance simplified to where the child is actually able to do it at age five, by working the way up through grades of difficulty. The same strategy applies to many other areas: for example, *detecting incongruities* — such things as missing parts, wrong parts, things that are the wrong size and so on. The kinds of incongruities children are asked to detect can get endlessly subtle. But on the other hand, they can begin at a point where the incongruity is so obvious that any five-year-old or the four-year-old can spot it immediately. When shown a chicken with a square egg rural children will spot it, but city children just see a chicken with a block beside her and recognize no incongruity at all. But show them a picture of a man with windows where his eyes should be and they get it right away and, furthermore, can tell you what's wrong with him. From easy examples, the children again work up through other levels of difficulty. Although children notice more or less subtle incongruities, their observations may amount to little more than noticing similarities and differences (e.g., a car with square or no wheels is different from other cars which have round wheels), thus reducing a potentially valuable skill to a simple matching process. Incongruity tasks can involve more and more complex presentations in which a set of pictures and questions are used to lead the children to detect, explain, correct, adapt, or justify incongruities or to judge their possible consequences.

DEFINING SOLUTION SETS

Defining solution sets is another area of thinking. One task presents the children with a problem that can have many solutions. For instance, there are all kinds of things that could be used to hold down pieces of paper, but instead of just learning to name all of them the children learn how to discover the common attribute or attributes that they have: they all have to be heavy; further, they should all be dry rather than wet things that are heavy.

DEFINITIONS

Definitions is another area. Generating definitions can require a lot of trial and error processing. To some children, it is easier just to memorize definitions as they hear them and avoid the bother. One way of simplifying definition skills is to illustrate the processing problems in a clear but entertaining way. The children are told a short story about a fictitious person whose inadequate definitions get inadequate results. For example, he wants a pillow, so he asks for something soft and white and then gets a marshmallow. These stories are simple enough for even very young children to learn from and they provide a starting point from which to build tasks that enable children to get involved in forming as well as judging definitions and predicting the outcome of an inadequate definition. A group of six-year-olds, who mastered these abilities very quickly, illustrate the kind of involvement we're talking about. They had agreed that they wanted a dog but that they would ask for one without saying the word "dog." After one attempt with "Can I have an animal that's around the house that hates cats?" a second child said, "You might get a mouse," to which the first child quickly countered, "All right then, I'll ask for a grown-up puppy."

In setting up these objectives for the preschool in the areas of communications and thinking, we have limited ourselves to short-term goals; that is, goals that can be achieved in the time available. Short-range goals provide a teacher with a number of instances of what can be done; long-range goals, on the other hand, tell the teacher only what ideals she should aspire to. And the danger of shooting for those long range *objectives* at the expense of those that are more possible is that nothing at all may be accomplished.

It may well be asked how one can ever hope to decide upon short-range goals without first having decided upon the long-range goals which they are to serve. To this question, which is one of the most nagging ones in educational practice, John Dewey has provided the most reasonable answer in his concept of education as growth. Dewey has claimed that short-range educational achievements are valuable insofar as they increase the future options available to the learner. Dewey rejected the whole question of ultimate values and asserted that educational goals should grow out of potentialities discovered in the present situation.

Following Dewey, we tend to reject all such long-range value statements as that — children should develop into creative, expressive individuals, revolutionaries, responsible citizens, competent scholars and the like, simply on the grounds that these goals, if seriously pursued, would lead to limitations on individual freedom and to the forcing of children into some predetermined mold. If it is argued that short-range goals inevitably reflect one's biases with respect to long-range values and purposes, we should reply that this is a potential source of corruption that should be watched for and guarded against to the best of our abilities. Corruptive biases should be identified and pointed out and goals should be altered so as to remove as much as possible the influence of such biases. This is the proper application of intelligence and reflective thinking to the determination of goals.

Karnes, Zehrbach, Teska | *Introduction* | 12

The Ameliorative Curriculum described by Merle Karnes was developed for the education of three, four, and five-year-old disadvantaged children. Its primary goal is "to prepare the young disadvantaged child for effective participation in a standard school program." The program developers considered the primary task in developing an effective preschool program to be the formulation of principles for making decisions pertinent to all aspects of the program. Thus, the principles and theories used may be applied to any group of children in any setting to develop a preschool program which is matched to the particular needs of the children, family, and staff. Karnes, Zehrbach, and Teska point out that the Ameliorative Curriculum is only one of the many curricula which could be developed from the same principle.

Within their main goal of preparing children for success in school, the authors have identified eight sub-goals which include many components of the child's development (cognition, language, motivation, information-processing, social and emotional, self-concept, motor skill) and parental and staff involvement. Although the content was carefully selected for its relevance to early elementary school requirements, top priority was assigned to process. The three main content areas are mathematics, language, and science-social studies. Process theoretical models served as guidelines for developing the curriculum and for establishing behavioral objectives and guiding teacher behavior on a day-to-day basis. The psycholinguistic model as exemplified in the ITPA was used to guide language instruction, and Guilford's Structure of the Intellect model provided guidelines for instruction in intellectual function (i.e., cognition, memory, convergent and divergent production, and evaluation.)

Behavioristic principles were also incorporated, with such principles including behavioral objectives, criterion performance tasks, hierarchical sequencing of materials and learning experiences, and positive reinforcement. A highly structured game format was the teaching strategy used in small groups of one teacher to five children. Much emphasis was placed on providing instruction appropriate for the individual child, and initial diagnostic tests, criterion tasks, and diagnostic observations were employed to develop the most effective curriculum.

The comprehensiveness of the Ameliorative Curriculum, and the values derived from its firm base in the research literature and its use of theory for guiding teacher behavior and curriculum development are most apparent in the following paper.

Merle B. Karnes
R. Reid Zehrbach
James A. Teska

An Ameliorative Approach in the Development of Curriculum

12

I. INTRODUCTION

A series of preschool studies conducted over the past five years at the University of Illinois has produced an Ameliorative Curriculum for the education of young disadvantaged children. "Ameliorative" is defined here as an approach which "improves or makes better." Implicit is the assumption that the environment of disadvantaged children is inappropriate for developing the skills, knowledge, and attitudes requisite for success in schools with middle-class orientation. Further, it is assumed that appropriate experiences provided disadvantaged children at an early age in a preschool setting can contribute to their optimal development. The effects, then, of cultural deprivation are reversible if intervention is introduced at ages 3, 4, and 5. This approach views the child positively and may be considered enhancing as well as preventive. The causes for potential school difficulty are seen to reside in the discrepancy between the experiences provided in the disadvantaged child's environment and those needed to ensure success in the middle-

Merle B. Karnes is Professor, R. Reid Zehrbach, Associate Professor, and James A. Teska, Assistant Professor, in the Department of Special Education, Institute for Research on Exceptional Children, University of Illinois, Urbana-Champaign campus. Printed by permission of the authors.

class school rather than to exist as a deficiency within the child. From such a point of view, one can appropriately regard the child as having a positive potential for growth which has been denied by inappropriate experiences. The Ameliorative Curriculum, then, was a special curriculum designed to meet the unique needs of children whose development had been impeded by environment.

The generating ideas behind this curriculum differ quite clearly from those embodied in a remedial approach which focuses on incapacitating deficiencies and which relies on highly specialized techniques of instruction. Children who need remedial instruction have experienced a preponderance of failures, they have learned poor habits and are ineffective learners. Their problems are more complex than those of children who merely lack the training needed to be successful in school, and the specificity of intervention is more difficult to determine.

Prior to discussing the conceptualization of the Ameliorative Curriculum, it will be helpful to summarize the program briefly. The Ameliorative Program was developed with black and white 3, 4, and 5-year-old disadvantaged children in a central Illinois community of 100,000. A class consisted of fifteen children of one age level. Each class was divided into three subgroups on the basis of Binet IQ, with one teacher for each subgroup, a teacher-pupil ratio of 1 to 5. Groupings were flexible, however, so that children who needed extra supervision or instruction could be more evenly distributed or children who did not perform according to test indications might be more appropriately placed. The daily schedule centered around three 20-minute structured learning periods: math concepts, language, and science-social studies. A large room where the fifteen children could gather for group activities was available; however, most of the instruction took place in relatively small cubicles off the main room. Each cubicle contained materials appropriate to one of the three content areas, and each teacher moved from one cubicle to another with her group of five children.

Each group remained with the same teacher for the three structured periods, for juice, and for field trips. The low teaching ratio allowed for differentiation of instruction to provide a high success ratio for each child. Immediate correction of incorrect responses (often through repetition of model sentences or duplicate layouts of small, manipulative materials) and reinforcement of appropriate responses (usually through praise) assured the children of their competencies in handling curricular requirements and enhanced their intrinsic motivation to learn. Frequent review extended content previously presented and provided opportunities to use further the vocabulary and sentence structures which had been taught.

Children formed their own peer groupings during the music period and during a brief period of directed play which stressed visual-motor activities such as puzzles, blocks, clay, and pounding sets. No use was made of outdoor play equipment or traditional preschool toys such as dolls, toy appliances, cars, or trucks. Concepts taught during the structured periods were reinforced during directed play and especially during the music period. For example, when body parts were introduced in science or counting in math, these concepts were stressed in songs and in rhythmic activities during music.

The general goals of the social studies and science curriculum were to teach useful vocabulary, to develop skills of classification, and to provide simple experiences in developing sensory discriminations and in observing natural phenomena. The curriculum began with a unit on body awareness and self-concept developed through the use of body exercises, songs, precut unassembled figures, and body outlines of the children. A unit on family members and immediate home environment followed, using integrated pictures, rubber play people, and family puppets; clothing cut from catalogs and sorted according to body parts, family member, or season; furniture items cut from catalogs and sorted according to type or appropriate room; go-together pictures such as a hand and a mitten, a chair and a table. A kitchen science unit, through the demonstration of simple scientific principles, provided opportunities for careful observation and verbalization of what had been seen, heard, tasted, or touched. Additional units in this curriculum were germination of seeds and plant growth, farm and wild animals, fruits, vegetables, community buildings and workers, vehicles, weather, seasons, and time sense.

Objectives of the math curriculum involved the development of basic number concepts, appropriate manipulative skills, and a useful vocabulary. The general areas included the identification of five geometric shapes, one-to-one matching and its relationship to copying patterns, matching quantity, and establishing sets and verifying their equivalency; dimensional terms and seriation; counting as a functional concept; the introduction of numerals as visual symbols; and beginning addition and subtraction with manipulative objects such as popsicle sticks, bottle caps, and peg boards.

Multiple copies of inexpensive books were the most important instructional material in the language curriculum. As the teacher read, each child held his own copy of the book. He learned to hold the book right-side-up, to turn the pages singly and in sequence, to associate the pictures with the story being read, to develop left-to-right progression, and to associate the printed symbol with meaning. In addition, the small group storytime provided opportunities for reinforcing and elaborating upon vocabulary previously taught, for short- and long-term memory acitvities, for sequencing events to show cause and effect and time relationships, and for making inferences and divergent responses. Finally, as the story was read, the child heard acceptable syntactical models and the familiar constructs of the language. He absorbed the rhythms and stresses of standard, informal English. This curriculum also included activities which developed visual-motor coordination and which emphasized the rather fine visual and auditory discriminations requisite for reading readiness.

Language development received major emphasis throughout the day, especially during the three structured periods. Verbalizations in conjunction with the manipulation of concrete materials were considered to be the most effective means of establishing new language responses. The game format (card packs, lotto games, models and miniatures, sorting, matching, and classifying games) created situations where verbal responses could be made repeatedly in a productive, meaningful context without resorting to rote repetition; often the child could visually and motorically assess the correctness of his thinking before he made an appropriate verbalization. If the child was unable to make a verbal response, the teacher supplied as appropriate model; when he began to initiate such responses, the teacher had the opportunity to correct, modify, and expand his verbalizations. Teachers initially accommodated their teaching strategy to the performance of the children on a battery of tests. Instructional models derived from the Illinois Test of Psycholinguistic Abilities and the Guilford Structure of the Intellect were used to plan instructional strategies.

The primary task in developing a viable and effective preschool program was considered to be the formulation of principles for making decisions rather than the production of static curricular materials. The curriculum developed at the University of Illinois, however, represents only one specific application of these principles. Another research staff working with different children and teachers in another area of the country and within the framework of public schools, for example, would develop a somewhat different curricular product. Two such curricula, however, having evolved from the same principles, would theoretically be equally effective. The effectiveness of the Ameliorative Curriculum is supported in both short- and long-term research findings.

The overriding goal of the Ameliorative Curriculum is to prepare the young disadvantaged child for effective participation in a standard school program. The goal of preparing children for a "standard school program" does not imply satisfaction with schools as they are. Nothing could be further from the truth. Schools can and must change. Change, however, is more likely to occur if the *input* to the schools becomes substantially different; that is, if children come to school with good processing abilities, a strong content base, and positive attitudes. The schools can then employ more flexible formats and innovative curricula. In devising the Ameliorative Curriculum, the local elementary school program was analyzed to determine content, processes, and attitudes essential for successful participation in that program. Such preliminary action obviously resulted in the development of a preschool program which met local needs but which represents only one application of general principles.

II. CHARACTERISTICS OF THE DISADVANTAGED CHILD

Although the needs of specific disadvantaged children may differ as sharply as the needs of children within the general population, curriculum development requires an attitude of generalization as well as the tactics of individualization. The necessity for such a synthesis emerges from the specifics of a case study which, although unique, nevertheless echo the problems of many disadvantaged children.

> *Jane, a four-year-old Caucasian child, was the next to the youngest in a family of eight children living in an integrated housing project. Her father, whose formal education ceased after four years of elementary school, had been intermittently employed as a laborer on a construction crew. He deserted the family when she was 12 months of age. Her mother withdrew from school at the age of 16 to marry. At that time she had repeated three grades and was in the sixth grade. After her husband's departure, she relied on Aid to Dependent Children for an income.*
>
> *The mother appeared to be overwhelmed by her responsibilities and experienced periods of depression during which she showed little interest in her children. On occasion she frequented local taverns, leaving the oldest child, a ten-year-old, in charge of the other children. Jane, as was true of all the children, had few toys with which to play. No printed material was in the home, and the environment provided little in the way of intellectual stimulation. The school-age children had histories of school failure and poor attendance.*
>
> *At the age of 15 months, Jane had been a subject in a research project. Records indicate that her IQ fell well within the average range of the Cattel Infant Scale. At age 4, however, a follow-up assessment of her intellectual abilities (Stanford-Binet Individual Intelligence Scale, Form L-M) indicated that she was functioning in the borderline mentally retarded range. She was below the norm, which extends downward to 2½ years, on three subtests (Verbal Expression, Grammatic Closure, and Auditory Association) of the Illinois Test of Psycholinguistic Abilities. On the other subtests she scored from 8 to 12 months below her chronological age.*
>
> *During a testing session Jane was unable to label common objects in her environment (chair, bed, tree) and did not respond to simple directions ("Go to the door and open it."). She was unable to repeat a four-word sentence correctly. She was reluctant to try new tasks and prone to give up easily. Her attention span was markedly retarded for her chronological age. One may anticipate that Jane's future intellectual behavior will approximate her mother's unless effective intervention occurs.*

Many of the characteristics found in Jane can be observed in large numbers of disadvantaged children. Although disadvantaged children come from all nationalities and all races, from rural as well as urban communities, and pose a variety of problems, similarities do exist. Young disadvantaged children differ markedly from their middle-class peers in language development (McCarthy, 1930; Cazden, 1966). Their communication skills are frequently limited to gestures and single words or, at best, phrases. They have not mastered the language structure characteristic of the predominant culture (Fries, 1952; Templin, 1957; Bernstein, 1960). Not only have these children failed to acquire expressive skills, but their listening or receptive skills are underdeveloped also (Deutsch, 1963). They learn to tune out many of the auditory stimuli in their environment, and in the classroom this may include the teacher (Deutsch, 1964). Much of what is said in the school setting is not understood by disadvantaged children because they are unfamiliar with the middle-class mode of expression (Fusco, 1964). Conceptually they lag behind because their environment has not been conducive to developing skills of inquiry, of labeling, classifying, and generalizing, of perceiving cause and effect relationships, and of solving simple problems of divergent and productive thinking. Disadvantaged children often fail to profit from what they see and hear becuase they have not acquired refined skills of information processing.

Disadvantaged children come to first grade poorly prepared to cope with the expectations dictated by middle-class culture and soon feel inadequate. In addition to inadequate language and cognitive development, they often have not acquired the social skills necessary to good school adjustment. A succession of failures reinforces a poor self-image and leads to further alienation. Their environment has not taught them how to learn or rewarded them for learning, and thus, they respond poorly to the challenge of learning. The educational problems of the disadvantaged child are cumulative (Deutsch and Brown, 1964). Generally, public schools do not develop the cognitive skills of these children, fostering instead their feelings of inadequacy and frustration.

III. GOALS AND OBJECTIVES

As stated previously, the overriding goal of the Ameliorative Curriculum is to prepare the young disadvantaged child for effective participation in a standard school program. To reach this goal, the following subgoals were established:

1. *To enhance cognitive development with particular prominence given to the development of language.* A preschool curriculum that helps the disadvantaged child develop his optimum potential must stimulate intellectual development. Jackson (1958) suggests that intervention between the ages of 9 months and 5 years is critical. Due attention must be given to what Hunt (1964) calls the "proper match"; that is, learning activities must be congruent with the child's present cognitive development while, at the same time, providing for further cog-

nitive development. Since disadvantaged children are deficient in language development as judged by the criteria of middle-class culture, a curriculum which prepares these children for effective school participation must provide for the development of communication skills and language processes which are the correlates of academic success.

2. *To develop motivation conducive to learning.* Optimal achievement requires a high level of motivation. To become motivated, the child must experience success. Further, he must be able to validate the appropriateness of his responses and, therefore, requires immediate feedback specific to his behavioral or linguistic response to ensure his own recognition of his success. Initially, a child may strive for extrinsic rewards such as verbal praise; but, as Hunt (1964) points out, when the child finds the act of learning rewarding, his motivation has become intrinsic. Since young children have not yet internalized this need to achieve, their learning is usually stimulated by the inherent interest-arousing qualities of the situation. Motivation is also contingent upon the quality of the teacher-child interaction. A teacher, for example, who rewards positive rather than negative behavior obviously facilitates the development of the motivation to learn.

3. *To acquire effective information-processing skills.* Disadvantaged children require specific training in the basic operations of information processing if they are to cope successfully with school tasks.

4. *To develop a positive self-concept.* Providing the child with experiences where success is possible and where immediate feedback informs him of the appropriateness of his response helps build an adequate concept of self. The acquisition of skills and knowledge requisite for academic achievement enables him to cope with school expectations and further enhances his self concept. He learns he is a competent learner.

5. *To enhance social and emotional development.* White (1959) holds that competence plays a major stabilizing role in the development of personality; as the child makes progress in cognitive areas, his affective behavior is also positively influenced. This point of view challenges the validity of the argument that a cognitively oriented curricula for the disadvantaged has ill effects on personality development. As Caldwell (1968) points out, socio-emotional progress and cognitive development on the whole are positively rather than negatively correlated.

6. *To promote motor skill development.* Precise and effective control of bodily movements encourages the child's realistic perception of the world about him and of himself as a successful individual. Disadvantaged children must, therefore, be provided the opportunity to maintain and enhance development in this area.

7. *To assure parental participation.* Parents are teachers of their children whether or not professional educators want to accept that fact. Parents can become better teachers of their young children (Karnes, 1969) when professional personnel help them to acquire the necessary competencies. The child-rearing

environment of the disadvantaged (Pavenstedt, 1965) is determined largely by impulse. The planning of activities of benefit to both parent and child is lacking but may be promoted in conjunction with the educational program offered the child.

8. *To enhance staff competencies.* To ensure the success of a program, there must be a dynamic, professional growth program. An important aspect of such a program should be its sincere emphasis on the positive growth and development of both children and teachers.

IV. PROCESS AND CONTENT GUIDELINES

Historically, curricular goals and objectives have been determined by the judgments and values held by scholars, administrators, and teachers. Typically, goals were stated in broad general terms such as to develop independent thinkers, to transmit the cultural heritage, to develop salable skills. Recently, studies have revealed the existence and importance of content and process domains.

In the development of a curriculum, a series of decisions must be made regarding the selection of content and process. Content materials to be taught must be selected. The processes to be used by the child must be determined. Content and process are independent concepts, but classroom implementation requires their integration. The critical decision requires consideration of the amount of time and energy to be spent in selecting and teaching content as opposed to the emphasis to be placed on the selection and utilization by the child of processes. *Process refers to the ability to obtain, organize, manipulate, synthesize, integrate, and communicate information.* Programs that focus on process are concerned about the way in which children think, evaluate, and seek out new information. A preschool based on the "discovery" method provides an example of a process-oriented school. Emphasis is placed on the processes involved in observing, relating, hypothesizing, and manipulating. Particular content areas are of relatively limited importance. The strength of such an approach is that it prepares the child for the continuing acquisition of knowledge. Its weaknesses appear to be its slow development of a body of information and its frequent failure to include bodies of information that may be crucial to the later development of knowledge and process.

Content, on the other hand, is defined as facts, information, and concepts. Concern here is for what a child learns rather than how he learns it or what he does with what he learns. Classroom activities which require strict attention to specific words and concepts, to the reinforcement of these concepts, and to the day-to-day sequencing of these concepts are content-oriented. The goal is to teach the information needed to function adequately in standard classrooms. In such a preschool program, the minimal content necessary for effective learning in later school has been identified and sequenced for presentation to the child. Such an approach establishes a finite body of material to be taught but may fail to provide the child with the opportunity to relate what he has learned to other tasks and areas. Further, since our society is changing at a rapid rate, considerable effort is required to ensure that the content is always relevant.

The process-content controversy merits particular consideration in curriculum development for disadvantaged children who typically lack certain types of concepts, particularly in the language areas, but also have difficulty in processing information in a school setting. These children need to acquire additional processes for organizing and internalizing their experiences as well as the content typically held by middle-class children.

The characteristics of the pupils that a classroom teacher is working with help determine the position that she must take on the process-content continuum. If the children being served have the broad informational background typical of middle-class school oriented children, then the teacher will be able to move more toward the process end of the continuum without encountering lacks in the content area.

The Ameliorative Curriculum assigned top priority to process; however, since process can be developed through a variety of content and since disadvantaged children lack certain types of content, process was to be developed using that content which most effectively bridged the gap between the disadvantaged culture and the school culture.

In addition to the definition of the content and process areas, studies of language development, thought processes, and learning have led to the development of a variety of theoretical models. Theoretical models were selected to serve as guidelines for developing the curriculum and guiding teacher-behavior in the Ameliorative Program. Process models were selected on the basis that the behavior described in the model might be amenable to change through an appropriate educational program.

THE PSYCHOLINGUISTIC MODEL

Since inadequate language development represents one of the greatest problem areas for the disadvantaged child, it seemed obvious that the curriculum include a strong language component. Psycholinguistic theory as exemplified in the clinical model of the Illinois Test of Psycholinguistic Abilities appeared to afford a practical and yet theoretically powerful approach. Figure 1 provides a graphic portrayal of the three-dimensional ITPA model (Kirk, McCarthy, and Kirk, 1968).

This language model was derived from Osgood's theoretical model (1957) by Kirk and McCarthy in 1961, and was modified by Kirk, McCarthy, and Kirk in 1968. Briefly, psycholinguistic abilities are analyzed along three dimensions:

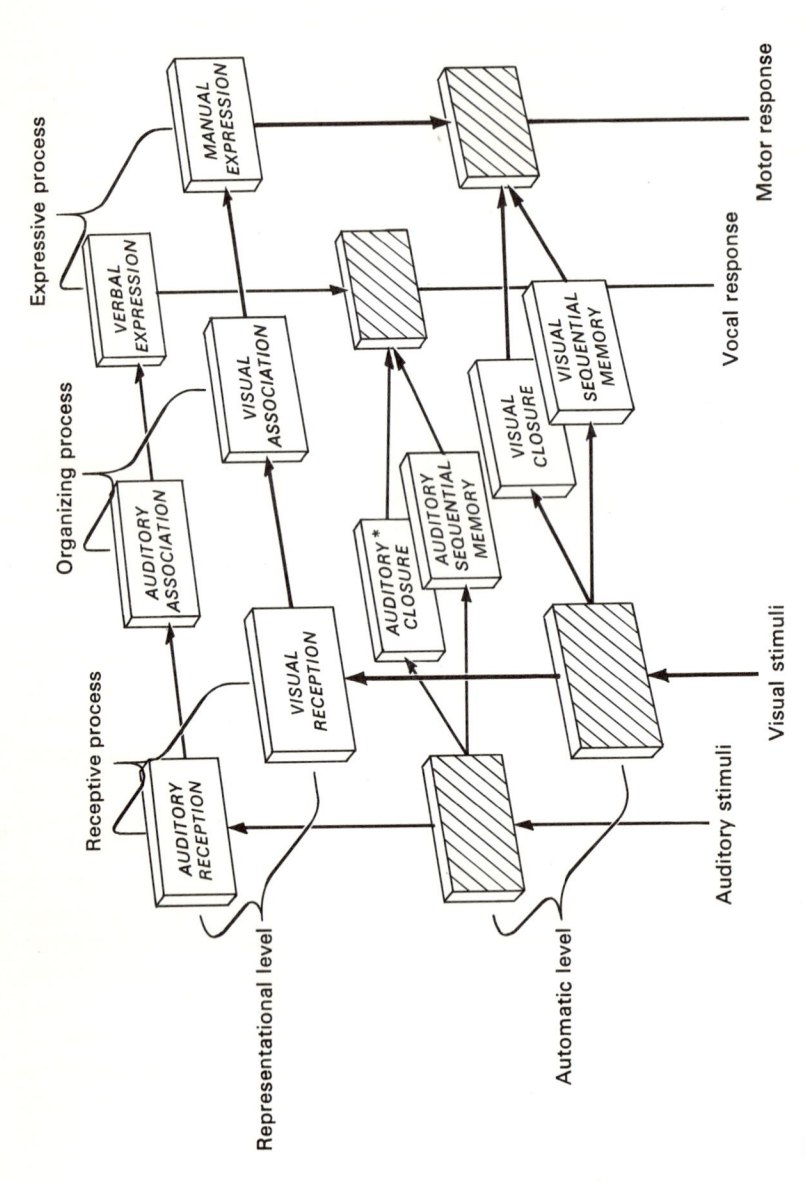

Figure 1. Three-Dimensional Model of the ITPA

* Auditory Closure, Grammatic Closure, and Sound Blending Subtests

* Model reprinted by permission of University Press, University of Illinois at Urbana-Champaign.

levels of organization, psycholinguistic processes, and channels of communication. The levels of organization refer to the degree of complexity required of the symbols used in the mediating process. In the model there are two degrees of complexity — the representational and the automatic. At the representational level, the mediating process is complex with symbols carrying considerable meaning. At the automatic level the individual functions in a highly organized but somewhat involuntary manner. Psycholinguistic processes are divided into receptive, organizing, and expressive areas. The channels of communication describe the sensory-motor path by which linguistic symbols are received and produced. Avenues of reception chiefly involve visual and auditory channels while motor and vocal channels are the major avenues of response.

One of the advantages of this model is that the test derived from it can be used diagnostically to ascertain the assets and weaknesses of individual children of commonalities in a small group of children. Further, each subtest in the ITPA is deemed highly relevant to the development of language and reading skills. Another strength of the psycholinguistic model lies in the structure that it provides professional teachers and paraprofessional personnel. When the model has been mastered, it provides a convenient connection between diagnosis and the development and implementation of an educational program. During the evaluation process, a psychologist, teacher, or trained observer can use the model to observe and evaluate the strengths and weaknesses of each child. These data can be gathered through the formal administration of the ITPA by a psychologist or through less formal observational procedures used by the teacher. Once the initial information has been obtained, decisions and planning relative to curricular offerings are made for each child to ensure that he is provided with the appropriate experiences to correct his weaknesses and to enhance his strengths in the various language facets included in the model.

The model was implemented both during the overall planning phase and in day-to-day classroom activities. The psycholinguistic model guided the development of the overall curriculum; yet, it was sensitive enough to direct day-to-day teacher planning. Using a model to guide instruction provided teachers with a basic structure which ensured certain learnings and yet allowed latitude for creative teaching. Teachers were better able to plot the direction of daily instructional periods as well as to reinforce fortuitous learnings that occur in the classroom.

The evaluation of classroom activities must occur at two levels—the overall or general level and the individual level. Teachers used this model to ascertain whether or not they spent appropriate amounts of time and energy in each of the areas covered by the model. Further, the model guided teachers in the development of criterion tasks that assessed the behavioral objectives appropriate to instructional goals on a day-to-day and week-to-week basis.

The use of an asset and deficit model required teachers to adopt one of several theoretical points of view: efforts may be focused on eliminating deficits by direct attack; deficits may be ignored and strengths may be utilized; a third approach, and the one adopted in the Ameliorative Curriculum, used strengths to alleviate weaknesses. The utility of the model in this respect can be appreciated when one notes (Karnes, 1969, p. 75) that certain types of disadvantaged children are deficient in Vocal Encoding (Verbal Expression), Auditory-Vocal Automatic (Grammatic Closure), and Auditory-Vocal Association (Auditory Association). These children demonstrated relative strengths in Auditory-Vocal Sequencing (Auditory Sequential Memory), Visual-Motor Associations (Visual Association), and Visual Decoding (Visual Reception). The teacher may, for example, develop a task whereby strengths in Visual Reception and Visual Association are used to improve functioning in an area of deficit, Verbal Expression.

STRUCTURE OF THE INTELLECT MODEL

Disadvantaged children have been shown to be deficient in reasoning and problem solving as measured by standard intelligence tests such as the Stanford-Binet. An analysis of the intellectual functioning tapped by the Binet and the ITPA reveals that the types of intellectual functioning assessed by the Binet are similar to only a few of the ITPA subtests. Total dependence on the ITPA model, then, is ruled out since it does not provide teachers with an adequate guide for the development of intellectual functioning. A more comprehensive model, the Guilford Structure of the Intellect (Guilford, 1967), was chosen to provide teachers with guidelines for curriculum development.

The Guilford Structure of the Intellect is organized along three dimensions: content, operation, and product. The content dimension contains four subcategories—semantic, symbolic, figural, and behavioral. The first three focus the teacher's attention on such important qualities of stimuli as the semantic content of the situation or task, the meanings attached to a symbol, or the need for a child to be aware of figures. Continued awareness of these dimensions and their utilization in developing the Ameliorative Curriculum helped to ensure that the teacher provided the child with a broad range of appropriate experiences. She was helped to guard against the development of a "set" to teach only one type of content.

The behavioral content dimension of the Guilford model has not been as highly developed as the other three and, consequently, was of less assistance to the teacher. Nevertheless, knowledge of this dimension provided the teacher with an organizational structure for viewing information about human interaction.

The operation dimension is divided into five parts—cognition, memory, convergent production, divergent production, and evaluation. Most traditional instructional programs place great stress on memory, cognition, and convergent production. Group intelligence and achievement tests also stress these operations. To develop effective problem-solvers among individuals who must enter an alien culture, such as the disadvantaged, requires emphasis on all types of intellectual operations. Precisely because the young disadvantaged child lacks experiences that provide him with flexibility of thinking and the ability to evaluate situations, preschool teachers must emphasize divergent productive and evaluative thinking. This position is supported by evidence (Torrance, 1960; Karnes, Zehrbach, Studley, and Wright, 1965) which suggests that there is as high a correlation between divergent productive thinking scores and achievement as there is between intelligence scores and achievement.

The third dimension of the Guilford structure has to do with products which are subdivided into units, classes, relations, systems, transformations, and implications. Analysis of this dimension suggested to teachers ways in which various concepts can be manipulated, such as organizing them into classes, placing them within a systematic structure, relating them to other products, transforming them into different perspectives, or discerning implications given certain premises.

In the Ameliorative Program, the structure of the intellect model complements the ITPA model. It provides an extension and expansion of the structure of the intellectual processing domain without confusing discrepancies between models.

PRINCIPLES OF CONTENT SELECTION

Research reveals that culturally disadvantaged children have marked gaps in their backgrounds of knowledge and information as well as deficiencies in processing information which limit their participation in standard school activities. Since the major goal of the Ameliorative Program is to equip the child to function effectively in subsequent school experiences, the first step in the selection of content was to determine the information base required of children in the early elementary years. In the initial selection of content for the Ameliorative Curriculum, data were obtained from the following sources: 1. A review of the literature regarding grade placement of content in mathematics, science, social studies, and language. 2. An inspection of courses of study and curriculum guides. 3. An examination of instructional materials such as basal readers and social studies, science, and mathematics books designed for young children and commonly used in the schools.

Obviously more content was available than could possibly be taught during the preschool years, and it was, therefore, necessary to select that content which seemed most relevant. In making this selection the following principles served as guides:

1. *Frequency of occurrence of content in sources examined.* For example, the frequency with which farm animals were found in basal readers, social studies books, storybooks, songs, and educational games for young children indicated that this content area should be included in the curriculum.

2. *Information that can be organized to form a logical category.* An example of content that fits together logically is information concerning foods—their color, taste, method of production, or preparation.

3. *Information that organizes into a logical sequence.* In mathematics, for example, it seemed efficient to introduce certain concepts such as one-to-one matching before teaching the concept of numbers or the recognition of numerals.

4. *Information that encourages generalization and transfer.* Since acquiring processing skills is viewed as highly important and is developed by the child as he ascertains relationships within and between areas, content areas must be broad. For example, the selection of a content area such as foods permits the child to learn relationships within an area such as vegetables, fruits, meats. Further, he can transfer concepts such as yellow vegetables to the area of physical health.

5. *Feasibility of providing concrete experiences.* One of the community helpers included was the fireman. Providing direct experience with this individual at the fire station enhanced the children's understanding of his role.

6. *Relevancy to the immediate community.* The Ameliorative Curriculum was developed in the Midwest. Changes in season are readily observable and provide logical content. If this program were initiated in California, less emphasis would be given to seasons, and content involving ocean life might well be an alternative.

7. *Interest and background of teachers.* The Ameliorative Program, in addition to providing for individual differences among children, also provided for individual differences among *teachers*. Since the method of content selection resulted in more facts and concepts than could be used in the classroom and since the enthusiasm of the children is greatly influenced by the interest of the teacher, teachers were permitted to select content they felt most competent to present.

8. *Staff knowledge of the child's strengths and weaknesses in content areas.* Staffings were held for each child prior to his entrance into the Ameliorative Program. At this time the psychologist, social worker, teacher, and other staff members shared data. Specific content weaknesses and strengths were noted in these discussions and were used to develop guidelines for the selection of the facts and concepts to be taught to that child. In addition, throughout the year the teacher determined individual deficiencies in information and concepts.

V. OTHER GUIDING PRINCIPLES

The models and guidelines discussed in the preceding section provided teachers with procedures for organizing instruction. Research and experience produced other guiding principles that were gradually incorporated into the present Ameliorative Program.

BEHAVIORAL OBJECTIVES AND CRITERION TASKS

Mager (1962, 1968) has provided educators with a thought-provoking presentation of the need for writing educational objectives in behavioral terms. The original impetus for his work seems to have derived from the need to encourage teachers to establish their objectives in terms that could be submitted to evaluation as an integral part of the instructional process. In addition to meeting this goal, his efforts have proved useful to researchers and administrators as they attempt to determine the effectiveness of current programs and the definition, development, and assessment of new programs. It was, thus, decided to adopt this approach in the Ameliorative Program.

Criterion tasks team well with behavioral objectives in developing new programs and ensuring the continued success of mature programs. Specifically, once a behavioral objective was defined, a criterion task was established which permitted the teacher to observe each child in a structured setting and to formulate an objective evaluation of his behavior. Children who succeeded on the task were then scheduled for the next phase of the program while children who did not attain the specified competency were recycled for additional instruction. Further, the teacher was immediately aware of the success of her instruction when large numbers of children achieved criterion or of the failure of her instruction when large numbers of children failed to meet criterion. Teachers also developed greater insight into the needs of children through this attentiveness to specific behaviors.

ORDERING OF LEARNING EXPERIENCES

The sequencing of instruction has been of concern to educators for many years. Some authors, such as Bruner (1961), have suggested that sequencing is of limited importance because many concepts can be taught prior to the age that had been thought possible, if the learning experience is appropriately structured. Although this may frequently be the case, once the learning experience has been specified, there seems to be a lower limit at which a child can be taught. In addition, it seems appropriate to present ideas to children in a hierarchical order so they can use previous knowledge to learn new knowledge. Furthermore, when children with limited backgrounds are taught ideas that are unique to them, a hierarchical approach provides the teacher with needed structure. In social studies, for example, instruction in the Ameliorative Curriculum began with the child as an individual and moved outward to the family, neighborhood, and larger community.

POSITIVE REINFORCEMENT

Some controversy has existed in the literature regarding the efficacy of positive as opposed to negative reinforcement. Although the controversy is yet to be resolved, it is not unreasonable to speculate that disadvantaged children might learn well under negative reinforcing conditions to which they have become attuned in their daily lives. On the other hand, to continue such procedures in school may merely reinforce a learning style which tends to result in passive or active resistance or minimally conforming behavior. Positive reinforcement coupled with explicit remarks delimiting the reasons for praise was chosen, since it was felt that such an approach would eventually help the child to internalize the ability and the need to work for positive reinforcement. Mitzel's article (1970) is the latest in a series of studies and theories which suggests that learning may be best accomplished by positive reinforcements that meet the needs of the learner. Thus, praise from an adult, the child's own recognition of his completion of a concrete object (such as a picture), winning in a competitive setting, or work for symbols (such as tokens that can be later exchanged for a selected reward) may have differential effects on learning. Preschool programs should provide for the use of various types of positive reinforcement to ensure the best possible learning and to help children learn how to work toward different types of rewards.

LOW TEACHER-PUPIL RATIO

Explicit positive reinforcement obviously required a low teacher-pupil ratio. Additional support for the low teacher-pupil ratio lay in the fact that disadvantaged children have a deficit in language, particularly oral language, and require a high level of verbal interaction with the teacher. The planning and implementation of individualized instruction required a commitment of time that can only be achieved with a low teacher-pupil ratio. Individual programming required that the teacher have a thorough knowledge of each child.

CAREFULLY STRUCTURED PROCEDURES

Children who have not been sensitized to stimuli that are considered important by the classroom teacher must be provided with an environment where what is to be learned differs significantly from the irrelevant. In other words, the figure-ground contrast for learning activities should be high.

Precise planning of daily learning experiences defined another aspect of structure in the Ameliorative Program. Daily learning experiences were carefully planned to cover those aspects of process, content, and attitude that had been selected for consideration at a particular time. Large-group, small-group, and individual activities were planned to meet the needs of each child. The structure provided by this approach increased the effectiveness of the teacher by reducing the number of decisions she made during the actual learning period. The teacher knew what she was going to do and how she was going to do it; thus, she was free to focus on the unfolding behavior of the child in the learning situation and to provide an optimum learning experience.

Another aspect of structure derived from the belief that learning occurs best when the child develops a basic framework to which additional concepts can be attached in a meaningful manner. Carefully presented ideas that are continually related to prior learnings to develop a conceptual structure seemed to be an efficient method of teaching young disadvantaged children. Again, programmatic benefits may have accrued as much from helping the teacher organize and plan her work as they did from providing the children with a conceptual framework.

BELIEF IN THE INDIVIDUAL WORTH OF EACH CHILD

Research indicates that the disadvantaged child typically develops feelings of inadequacy and limited personal worth (Ausubel and Ausubel, 1963). Teachers, from their own feelings of insecurity or from their need to succeed, frequently view disadvantaged children as unworthy and of limited potential. To prevent the development of a negative self-concept in the children, it was deemed important to develop a program that fostered feelings of personal worth. In the Ameliorative Program the child had a high degree of success in activities that he felt were meaningful; his success was reinforced by the teacher to enhance his positive self-image. Recognition and appropriate labeling of feelings and the development of ways to safely express these feelings also facilitated emotional growth.

TEACHER ENHANCEMENT PROGRAM

Educators have long recognized the need for the continued professional growth of teachers. Inservice training programs too frequently are held at the end of the day when teachers are tired and frustrated; program content often consists of announcements and routine administrative detail. The Ameliorative Program, in contrast, adopted the position that an intensive, dynamic participatory program designed to enhance teacher competencies and emotional well-being was critical to the success of this curriculum. Positive attributes of this teacher enhancement program included the daily planning of activities. After teachers had implemented these plans to the best of their abilities, a debriefing session was held during which successes were recounted, objectives restructured, and new plans evolved. Such a learning-centered approach encouraged the externalization of concerns, fostered open discussions, and encouraged positive outcomes. The debriefing sessions also served to relieve built-up frustrations, to provide for the recognition of success, and to foster positive attitudes of teachers.

Since the educational objectives were developed so that each child could be successful, teachers also felt that their teaching was successful. Frequent opportunities for teachers to discuss their problems with ancillary personnel—psychologists, social workers—were felt to be important. Ancillary personnel were encouraged to help the teachers focus on their successes as well as their deficiencies. The basic goal was to plan positively.

VERBALIZATION CONCURRENT WITH MULTI-SENSORY PRESENTATION

Learning occurs best when experiences provide for multi-sensory stimulation. Activities requiring concurrent visual, auditory, and motoric behavior facilitate effective learning. Thus, the game format which lends itself to this concept was adopted as a basic procedure.

REPETITION IN A MEANINGFUL CONTEXT

To ensure permanency of learning, repetition is necessary. Repetition in a meaningful context was also facilitated through the use of the game format.

PROGRESSION FROM CONCRETE TO ABSTRACT

The initiation of conceptual learning should proceed from the concrete to the abstract. Since young disadvantaged children have a restricted experiential background, their learning must start with specific, concrete referents in their environment. Development of a realistic perception of these concrete referents is basic to the development of more abstract concepts. Games developed to implement the curricula were constructed to start with concrete, multi-sensory experiences before progressing to more abstract games.

PARENTAL INVOLVEMENT

Research has revealed that middle-class parents provide their children with a hidden curriculum (Strodtbeck, 1965). On the other hand, lower-class parents have typically been excluded from participating in school-related activities because of lack of knowledge or lack of acceptance by public school personnel. Recent research by Karnes (1969) revealed that lower-class parents can be taught procedures that will be reflected in the accelerated intellectual and academic growth of their children.

Active parent involvement in the Ameliorative Program was adopted as a guideline because it gained support for the program within the community and because parents could learn to extend and reinforce the knowledge gained by the children in the school. Family involvement included having parents work with their young children in the home setting, teaching in the classroom setting, helping other parents acquire improved teaching competencies, and training older siblings to teach younger children.

VI. ORGANIZATION OF PROCESS AND CONTENT

These is no best way to organize content and process. For example, it has already been mentioned that many concepts can be taught sooner than was previously thought possible if the learning experience is structured appropriately. On the other hand, there must be some organization of content and processes if children are to engage in activities consistent with their "range of challenge." Some of the criteria that were used to organize content and process are briefly presented below.

Assistance for organizing processes was derived from the psycholinguistic and intellectual structure models. Attention to the relationships of the processes within and between the models indicated ways of organizing and sequencing processes. For example, when the decision was made that the processes of Auditory Reception, Auditory Association, and Verbal Expression were to be strengthened, it was obvious that the Auditory Reception process must be improved first so that new competency in this area would assist in developing

Auditory Association. The development of both of these processing skills preceded Verbal Expression.

Content was organized around a framework which incorporated the content to be learned initially and which would facilitate the integration of subsequent learnings. The additional requirement was imposed that the content be that which disadvantaged children will need for entrance into the first grade and which they will not learn at home. For example, in mathematics, the concept of one-to-one relationships is an important central concept not likely to be learned at home.

At the heart of any attempt to organize curriculum should be an emphasis on individual differences. The content and processes of the curriculum were organized so that each child met the behavioral objectives set for him; different objectives were provided for different children. A child was placed in a learning setting only when an appropriate behavioral objective had been established for him.

Content can be viewed within an organized hierarchy; "orange," for example, can be viewed as a sensation, as a member of the class of colors, as a member of the class of fruits, as a member of the class of nutritional necessities, as a complex mixture of acids, bases, and vitamins. When the child begins to learn, he will function at the lowest level of his hierarchy, but as he develops, he must remain flexible enough to reorganize and integrate his thinking from level to level within the hierarchy. Content in the Ameliorative Curriculum was organized to facilitate the development and integration of similar hierarchies.

Since these preschool disadvantaged children had so much to learn and so little time, the content they were taught was selected to have as general an application as possible. Content was considered to be applicable at home and at school, to reading as well as mathematics and other school subjects, to group as well as to individual work.

VII. SELECTION AND ORGANIZATION OF LEARNING EXPERIENCES

"Learning experience" in this paper is defined as the process that a child undergoes when confronted with a teaching-learning situation. The importance of the term "process" cannot be underestimated in this definition because learning occurs only when the child undergoes some change in behavior. The efficacy of the learning situation is evaluated by determining the degree to which the child's behavior meets or exceeds the criterion established for that situation.

The selection of learning experiences for the Ameliorative Program required the evaluation of the complex interactions between the needs of the individual child, the presentation of content and processes identified by the previously described guidelines, the capabilities of the teacher, the availability of instructional materials, the interpersonal relationships within the classroom, and the physical characteristics of the classroom. Since the needs of children and the guidelines for content and process have been discussed previously, they will not be reiterated except to point out that they are extremely important areas to consider in the selection of an appropriate learning experience.

For too long, the literature has viewed teachers as being all things to all people. Administrators of programs for the disadvantaged quickly learned that many teachers cannot be effective teachers of the disadvantaged. In the Ameliorative Program, teachers were selected on the basis of their ability to relate to disadvantaged children, and their interest in implementing this highly structured program.

Teachers frequently lack enough materials to establish the kind of learning experiences they would like to provide or find that the materials they have are inappropriate. If the teachers have the time, energy, and creative ability, experience indicates that they can make or adapt free or inexpensive materials to suit their educational objectives. The use of models and highly specific objectives frequently stimulates teachers to develop materials. One reason why the Ameliorative Program seems so adaptable is that the emphasis on process permitted the use of a greater variety of content and a more flexible and creative use of the materials that were available. For example, a set of pictures were used to teach specific vocabulary, to develop visual reception, and to stimulate storytelling designed to increase verbal expression and divergent productive thinking.

Experience with preschool children suggests that physical setting plays an important part in structuring or modifying behavior. For example, disadvantaged children who live in crowded apartments often seem to feel more comfortable in a small room or in an enclosed corner of a large room than in the center of a large room. Aggressive behavior, on the other hand, seems amplified by propinquity. Dark, dingy rooms seem to subdue behavior and curiosity while light rooms promote activity. Rooms with too many bright colors and a high level of visual and/or auditory stimulation may disrupt learning. Awareness of these factors helped teachers of the Ameliorative Program to construct the type of situation most conducive to learning. Thus, classrooms were cheerful, uncluttered, and provided space for small-group instruction in small rooms and large-group activity in a more spacious room.

Educational activities were organized into three types of settings—large group, small group, and individual. Within each of these settings a highly structured game format was adopted as the teaching strategy. The game format was adopted because it provided 1. a positive approach to learning, 2. an opportunity for the teacher to establish a high degree of structure, 3. for flexible programming of process, content, and attitudinal variables, 4. for hierarchical ordering of concepts, 5. for utilizing paraprofessional and parental assistance, 6. for immediate feedback for parent and teachers, 7. for high motivation, 8. for repetition which was not mere rote, 9. opportunities to enhance self-image, and 10. opportunities for individualized instruction in a small-group setting.

Although considerable information is available about the needs of disadvantaged children in general, this information does not tell us what a specific group of children or a child within the group is like. Each class must be studied carefully to determine its needs and the needs of individuals within the class. Of course, special attention must be given to areas where research has indicated the likelihood of weaknesses or deficits. Initially, assistance was obtained from psychologists, experienced teachers, social workers, and others who could offer relevant information. Psychologists, for example, administered the Illinois Test of Psycholinguistic Abilities and the Stanford-Binet Individual Intelligence Scale or made structured observations of individual children or of the class. Similarly, an experienced teacher, a speech therapist, or a social worker viewed a child or the class from a particular point of view and provided the teacher with pertinent information. When the needs of the class or of an individual child were identified, the teacher specified objectives, selected strategies, and developed activities to meet these objectives.

After the initial diagnosis had been made and a prescription translated into practice through the formulation of objectives and the development of suitable strategies and learning experiences, the teacher began to conduct diagnostic observations and to evolve appropriate curricula. Reference to the structure of instructional models provided guidelines for ongoing diagnoses. One example of how this process was implemented is found in the following illustration wherein teachers used the ITPA model to formulate behavioral characteristics of children with deficiencies in the various areas assessed by the ITPA.

Auditory Reception (ability to understand what is heard).
Inability to follow oral directions appropriate to his age group.
Frequent asking of "What?" or "Huh?"
Relatively expressionless face during story-time or when teacher is reading to class.
Distortion of words.
Confusion when spoken to.

Visual Reception (ability to understand or interpret what is seen).
Difficulty with simple sorting exercises (sorting nails from pins, butterfly seals from flower seals).
Holds book upside down or looks at other pictured material from a wrong direction.
Difficulty in identifying familiar objects presented in pictures.
Inability to identify his own belongings (coat, sweater, art work).

Auditory Association (manipulation or transfer of ideas received through the auditory channel).

Difficulty understanding similarities or differences between concepts presented verbally.

Difficulty in generalizing from information well known to him.

Confusion and inability to respond to questions of a "what if" or "why" nature.

Few spontaneous statements such as "That's the same as _____."

Poor answers to questions requiring more than strict recall.

Lack of awareness of interrelationships and similarities and differences appropriate for his age level.

Difficulty with classification and connecting ideas which go together.

Vocal Encoding (generation and vocal expression of ideas).

Relies on gestures for much of his communication.

Never volunteers any information (personal, anecdotal, as well as recitative).

Difficulty expressing himself verbally even though he has the information or understanding.

The incorporation of behavioral objectives and criterion tasks into the curricular structure provided the teacher with a built-in strategy for conducting continuous diagnosis. The teacher was able to observe each child functioning in a structured setting daily. The development of skills, knowledge, and attitudes were observed, deficits were noted, and strengths were reinforced. Failure to reach criterion by a child or a group of children was apparent, and procedures were instigated to promote growth in the deficit area. When criterion was reached, the teacher expanded the child's knowledge at that level or promoted an advanced level along the same dimension. This procedure applied to areas of deficit as well as to areas of strength.

VIII. EVALUATION

Evaluation must be conducted with regard to specific criteria. Further, evaluation requires attention to long-range criteria, termed goals, and short-range criteria, termed objectives. The evaluation of long-term goals usually requires data that answer two types of questions. First, the evaluator (teacher, administrator, researcher) needs to know to what extent the children in the program reached the goals set for them. Second, the evaluator needs to know how well the children in the program did when compared with similar children on traditionally accepted measures, such as achievement, language, or intelligence tests.

Long-term studies (Karnes, 1969) using standardized tests have revealed that children in the Ameliorative Program attained significantly better achievement test scores than did children in three other types of programs—Traditional, Community Integrated, and Montessori—and attained similar scores to those in the Bereiter-Engelmann program. Since the goals of the program were to raise the children's level of functioning so they could be effective in a standard school program, the long-range program goal is considered to have been met. Although these disadvantaged children as a group are achieving as well as or better than the average middle-class child, improvements within the program might produce even higher gains.

Continued application of the criterion task approach to the evaluation of a program can be used to clarify the answer to three types of questions: 1. What is being learned? (This is a cow.) 2. What is the relationship between what is being learned and that which is to be learned? (This is a cow. A cow gives milk.) 3. How does the learner compare, on referent tasks or tests, to similar children? Of the three questions, the last has received greatest attention in schools, i.e., compared to children of the same chronological age, how many children are at, above, or below the 50 percentile? For preschool programs, the relevancy of the comparison depends on the extent to which the child is approaching the age where he will be grouped with children who come from backgrounds that have prepared them for effective school learning. From this point of view, advantaged children and disadvantaged children are perceived as starting from widely separated points and only tend to reach an appropriate commonality when they enter first grade. The results of standardized tests, then, become most meaningful as the child is entering school or after he has attended school for a year. Of greater importance are the first and second questions where the concern is for what the child is learning and how it relates to the next step in his instructional program.

Since the goals of the Ameliorative Program focus on process, content, and personal growth, evaluation was conducted in each of these areas. Criterion tasks relative to content were comparatively easy to construct and readily implemented by the classroom teacher. Process and personal growth, however, are slow to develop and difficult to assess. Measures of rate of change such as is provided by the daily recording of the number of times a given behavior occurs were useful in detecting changes in rate that might not have been observed with a less-precise approach.

By setting goals, establishing daily objectives, and keeping careful records one is able to gather information that will support the development of new knowledge of how children learn and develop. Since the classroom teacher is collecting the information, she will be the first, not the last, to benefit from the new knowledge. The teacher's use of objective goals and criterion tasks enabled her to make controlled observations of children's learning. Only through controlled observation can the teacher gain the high quality of information needed for the rapid productive improvement of teaching.

IX. CONSIDERATION FOR THE FUTURE

Since the Ameliorative Curriculum is an evolving one, developers are constantly engaged in modification and innovation. Current interests are outlined below.

GAGNÉ MODEL

When behavioral objectives and criterion tasks have been identified, the teacher is in a position to become concerned about the conditions under which learning occurs. Gagné (1967) conducted a careful analysis of conditions of learning and described eight types in detail. Although the inexperienced teacher may not be ready to implement all of these ideas, a review of Gagné's writings proves helpful to many. In the future, efforts will be made to help teachers in the Ameliorative Program learn how to utilize this information. For example, the concepts of stimulus-response learning, "chaining," verbal association, multiple discrimination, and concept learning may well add to the knowledge base of the teacher.

TEACHER-PUPIL INTERACTION

Teacher-pupil interaction has recently risen to the forefront as an area of concern because it focuses on the effect the teacher has on the child and on the effect the child has on the teacher. Since the teacher is involved in the setting, it is hard for her to take an objective point of view. Use of objectives and criterion tasks plus other aides such as video tapes, audio tapes, trained observers, or fellow team teachers can help gather the data needed to analyze the setting. Evaluation, then, should be based on the rationale and value system of the classroom.

PARENTAL INVOLVEMENT

Evaluation of parental involvement can utilize much of the rationale, principles, and techniques considered in teacher-pupil interaction with these differences: 1. Greater concern must be expressed for the personal worth of the parents. 2. Greater opportunities must be provided for parents to make choices regarding goals they want to work toward and how they want to include themselves. 3. Greater care must be used in applying procedures that might be viewed as entering the privacy of the individual.

REFERENCES | 12

Ausubel, D. P. and Ausubel, P. Ego development among segregated negro children. In A. H. Passow (Ed.), *Education in depressed areas.* New York: Teachers College Press, Columbia University, 1963.

Bernstein, B. Language and social class. *British J. Sociology*, 1960, *XI*, 271-276.

Bruner, J. S. *The process of education.* Cambridge: Harvard University Press, 1961.

Cazden, C. B. Subcultural differences in child language: An interdisciplinary review. *Merrill-Palmer Quarterly*, 1966, *12*, 185-214.

Caldwell, B. M. What is the optimal learning environment for the young child? In S. Chess, M. D., and A. Thomas, M. D. (Eds.), *Annual progress in child psychiatry and child development.* New York: Brunner/Magel, 1968, pp. 149-165.

Deutsch, C. P. Auditory discrimination and learning social factors. *Merrill-Palmer Quarterly*, 1964, *10*, 277-296.

Deutsch, M. The disadvantaged child and the learning process. In A. H. Passow (Ed.), *Education in depressed areas.* New York: Teachers College Press, Columbia University, 1963, pp. 163-179.

Deutsch, M. and Brown, B. Social influences in negro-white intelligence differences. *J. Social Issues*, 1964, *20*, 24-36.

Fries, C. C. *The structure of english.* New York: Harcourt Brace, 1952.

Fusco, G. C. Preparing the city child for his school. *School Life*, 1964, *46*, 5-8.

Gagné, R. M. *The conditions of learning.* New York: Holt, Rinehart and Winston, Inc., 1967.

Guilford, J. P. *The nature of human intelligence.* New York: McGraw-Hill, 1967.

Hunt, J. McV. The psychological basis for using preschool enrichment as an antidote for cultural deprivation. *Merrill-Palmer Quarterly*, 1964, *10*, 209-248.

Jackson, E. G. The impact of environment on racial achievement. *J. Human Relations*, 1958, *6*, 47-63.

Karnes, M. B., Zehrbach, R. R., Studley, Wm. M., and Wright, W. R. *Culturally disadvantaged children of high potential: Intellectual functioning and edu-*

cational implications. Champaign, Ill.: Champaign Community Unit 4 Schools, Sept. 1965.

Karnes, M. B. *Research and development program on preschool disadvantaged children.* Vol. *I.* Urbana, Ill.: Institute for Research on Exceptional Children, May 1969.

Kirk, S. A. and McCarthy, J. J. *Illinois Test of Psycholinguistic Abilities, Examiner's Manual.* Urbana, Ill.: University of Illinois Press, 1961.

Kirk, S. A., McCarthy, J. J. and Kirk, W. D. *Illinois Test of Psycholinguistic Abilities, Examiner's Manual* (Rev. Ed.). Urbana, Ill.: University of Illinois Press, 1968.

Mager, R. F. *Preparing instructional objectives.* Palo Alto, Calif.: Ferrin, 1962.

Mager, R. F. *Developing attitude toward learning.* Palo Alto, Calif.: Ferrin, 1968.

McCarthy, D. *Language development of the preschool child.* Minneapolis: University of Minnesota Press, 1930.

Mitzel, H. E. The impending instruction revolution. *Phi Delta Kappa*, April 1970, *LI*, (8) 434-436.

Osgood, C. E. Motivational dynamics of language behavior. In *Nebraska Symposium on Motivation.* Lincoln: University of Nebraska Press, 1957.

Pavenstedt, E. A comparison of the child-rearing environment of upper-lower and very low-lower class families. *American J. Orthopsychiatry,* 1965, *35,* 89-98

Strodtbeck, F. F. The hidden curricula in the middle-class home. In J. D. Krumbaltz (Ed.), *Learning and the educational process.* Chicago: Rand McNally, 1965, pp. 91-112.

Taba, Hilda. *Curriculum development: Theory and practice.* New York: Harcourt, Brace, and World, Inc., 1962.

Templin, M. C. *Certain language skills in children: Their development and interrelationships.* Minneapolis: University of Minnesota Press, 1957.

Torrance, E. P. *Educational achievement of the highly intelligent and highly creative: Eight partial replications of the Getzels-Jackson study.* (Research Memoranda BER 60-18). Minneapolis: Bureau of Educational Research, University of Minnesota, 1960.

Watson, G. *What psychology can we trust?* New York: Teachers College Press, 1961.

White, R. W. Motivation reconsidered: The concept of competence. *Psychological Review,* 1959, *66,* 297-333.

Miller, Camp | *Introduction* | 13

James Miller and Janet Camp present a conceptualization of a preschool curriculum which is focused on the development of the child's competence, his ability to effectively cope with his world. Man's ability to predict and thereby control his environment is viewed as the essence of competence, and prediction requires an ability to impose a structure upon the environment and to effectively process the information provided by the environment. Thus, the development of information processing skills and the development of motivations and attitudes conducive to maintaining and furthering the development of these skills are the main objectives of the program. Content is viewed as "a vehicle for the development of skills," and thus is secondary to process in importance, i.e., to conceptual skills.

    Miller and Camp's ecological, or interactional, approach emphasizes the importance of the objective (material) and instrumental (human) environments in fostering or inhibiting the child's attainment of effective information processing skills. The total intervention study, therefore, included curricula for the members of the "child's learning ecology," in addition to the child. The research literature provided information concerning the variables important to developing the child's competence, and these variables — cognitive, motivational, personal style, and nutritional — were considered in designing the curricula for the disadvantaged children. An information-processing model provided the overall structure for the curriculum, and those processes important in a child's interaction with his environment were categorized into sensory skills (receiving and decoding skills), abstracting and mediating skills (organization of input), and response skills (expression of the prior two processes verbally and motorically). The conceptual dimensions used by the major sense modalities offered further guidelines for instructional emphasis. Content was organized into units to encourage meaningful learning.

Developmental sequencing, careful introduction and ordering of new material, and steps of just manageable difficulty are considered extremely important, and a teacher-child ratio of one-to-five enables individual and specific reinforcement of desired behaviors. Evaluation is considered integral to the instructional program. The program is teacher directed, although the child himself is very active. Task analysis was used to specify behavioral objectives within each of the categories.

James O. Miller
Janet C. Camp

Toward Individual Competency — A Curriculum in the Child's Ecology

13

INTRODUCTION

In this paper we will describe the rationale and skill development portion of a curriculum for three to five-year-old children which is a part of a second major longitudinal intervention program carried out at Peabody College (Miller, 1970). The specific research project with which this curriculum was associated grew logically out of an earlier study, *The Early Training Project* (Gray, Klaus, Miller, and Forrester, 1966; Klaus and Gray, 1968), and represents the continuing developmental nature of the intervention studies in which we have been engaged. It underscores the concept of an open-ended curriculum which is never developed, but is in a continuing process of development. While the total intervention study engaged members of the family beside the target child (three to five years of age), including curricula for the various members of the child's learning ecology, we will limit this presentation to a discussion of the program for the target child.

James O. Miller is at Emory University, Atlanta, Georgia. Janet C. Camp is at George Peabody College, Nashville, Tennessee. Printed by permission of the authors.

RATIONALE

In our work with disadvantaged children and their families, we have taken the stand that environmental inadequacy is the primary factor leading to progressive intellectual retardation and the inability to cope effectively in an increasingly complex society. The cycle of defeat and failure is self perpetuating, creating an ever more apparent gap between those caught in its grip and those reaping the benefits of an affluent society. The choice point for intervention in the cycle has been during early childhood, around three years of age.

In designing an intervention strategy based on the assumption of environmental inadequacy, two major dimensions of the environment have received attention. The first two of these dimensions we shall call the *objective environment,* or the world of things which the child manipulates. The objective environment provides stimulus input which must be processed, contributing materially to intellectual and motivational development. The objective environment provides feedback to the child as to the relevance of his attending and exploratory behavior, which in turn affects his ability to efficiently process information and utilize it effectively. It provides reinforcement for his manipulative behaviors, and this helps to develop a concept of personal control over his world and himself.

The second dimension, perhaps the more important, is the *instrumental environment* or the world of people. The instrumental environment consists of those significant others who mediate between the child and the objective environment by imposing temporal and spatial order upon it. The effective instrumental agent interacts with the child, continuously providing behavior models and arranging appropriate reinforcement contingencies which encourage and sustain continued development and motivation. These considerations mediate for an active, or participating, involvement with a child rather than a passive, or observing, detachment if positive change is to occur.

The child, then, is seen as a part of an ecological system whose elements are in continuous interaction. This interchange can be stimulating and supportive, providing the conditions for continued growth and development of competency or, if either of these major environmental dimensions are inadequate, the interaction will inhibit, restrict or pervert development. Only by attending to all the essential elements of the system can we expect positive development to occur and be sustained.

During the child's early formative years, the instrumental environment is primarily the family and, more specifically, the effective instrumental agent is the mother. Our intervention strategy has been directed at the mother as well as the child while self-consciously recognizing that our intrusion adds another factor in the basic ecological system.

A prime source for identifying the variables associated with the development of competency has been the research literature. Particularly, the body of comparative literature which has lent support to the hypothesis of environmental inadequacy has given direction to the development of the instructional programs for both the mother and the child. For purposes of organization, these variables have been divided into four major classes: 1. *cognitive variables,* those skills and abilities which are necessary to function at a level of abstraction required to be competent in a highly technical society, including such abilities as language and conceptual and perceptual skills; 2. *motivational variables,* sustaining states which support continued skill development and maintenance and orient the individual toward a high level of task performance, including such things as need achievement, delay of gratification, and interest in cognitively stimulating tasks; 3. *personal style variables,* those variables which define approach behaviors in problem-solving situations such as self-concept, success-failure orientation, impulsivity-reflectivity, and time orientation; 4. *physical variables,* such variables as nutritional conditions, large and small-muscle coordination, and other physiological factors which are necessary to sustain continued performance output.

An exhaustive survey of the literature will not be presented on these four functional categories related to competence, but some representative research findings will be presented as the cornerstone for the development of intervention strategies with both the children and their mothers in our second major project.

COGNITIVE VARIABLES

Lesser, Fifer, and Clark (1965) studied differential and mental abilities, including verbal ability, reasoning, number facility, and space conceptualization, as they relate to social class and ethnic group membership. A large group of first grade children was divided into middle and lower-class socio-economic groups according to their ethnic background: Chinese, Jewish, negro, or Puerto Rican. Social class placement was associated with significant differences in ability patterns. Ethnic group differences were related to both absolute level of each mental ability and the patterns among these abilities. Interestingly, social class and ethnicity interacted to affect absolute ability *levels,* but not to affect ability *patterns.* Since the pattern of performance within ethnic subgroups was similar across social class levels, it appeared that a selective perceptual and learning set was exerted upon the membership. Ethnic groups also apparently place differential importance upon skills, depending upon the child's sex. The findings of these investigators suggest that ethnic group membership, the child's sex and patterns as well as level of performance must be taken into consideration when planning intervention programs.

When compared with middle-class subjects, disadvantaged children have been shown to be deficient in many aspects of language ability, both qualitatively and quantitatively (Siller, 1957; Bernstein, 1961-1962; Deutsch, 1965; Jensen,

1963; Irwin, 1948a, 1948b). Lower-class children spend less time in interaction with adults (Keller, 1963); and when in communication with adults, their verbalizations are significantly shorter (C. Deutsch, 1964). Hess and Shipman (1965) believed the paucity and impoverishment in the mother-child communication system is the heart of the lack of language development among the disadvantaged. Their assessment of mother teaching styles and information processing strategies clearly indicated that the verbal output and the level of conceptualization, as well as the quality and focus of the mother-child interaction, are significantly poorer among lower-class subjects. On tasks which require precision and abstract language and conceptualization, Deutsch (1965) found that middle-class children were superior. Their superiority increased from the first to the fifth grades, leaving them to conclude that early intervention is necessary to offset the accumulative deficit these data reveal.

Recognition vocabulary, vocabulary of use, length of remark, and complexity of sentence forms are all significantly below norms for disadvantaged children (Jones, 1966). These findings are consistent with those of Bernstein (1965), who interpreted his findings as indicative of differential encoding processes between classes. It is his observation that lower-classes use a restricted language pattern which functionally retains group integrity and status. Group solidarity is maintained through such a restricted encoding pattern by excluding non-group members from sharing in the in-group communication. It restricts the ability of the lower-class person to communicate effectively with those outside the group. On the other hand, the middle-class develops elaborated codes which are capable of transmitting information at high-levels of intensity and meaning within a variety of social contexts.

Such elaborated codes require a high level of abstract usage. The ability to label and classify, use hierarchical categorization, and discriminate relevant stimulus cues and dimensions is related to effective informational processing and is substandard among the disadvantaged (Ryckman, 1966; Spain, 1962; Clark and Richards, 1966; Jensen, 1966). Ryckman (1966) concludes from his factor analytic study of cognitive abilities, "Since general language ability is the major differentiating characteristic between class groups and is a central element for information processing, it appears highly essential to give language training a central place in the (intervention) program framework."

MOTIVATIONAL VARIABLES

This category consists of those learned attitudes which maintain the task orientation of the individual and retain task relevant involvement necessary for achievement. They seem to be highly related to reinforcement contingencies and types of rewards available in the environment. Disadvantaged children prefer concrete rewards over more abstract reinforcement in learning tasks (Terrel, Durkin, and Wiesley, 1959), while advantaged children perform at a higher level and prefer abstract reinforcements (Zigler and de Labry, 1962). Disadvantaged children prefer immediate reinforcement over delayed reinforcement even when greater rewards would be obtained under the delay condition. The ability to delay gratification is related to socio-economic status, higher intellectual functioning, and such family variables as father presence or absence and conditions of family disorganization (Mischel and Metzner, 1962; Mischel, 1961; Kahl, 1965; Maitland, 1966; Steen, 1966). Strauss (1962) has documented the relationship of deferred gratification and need achievement to social class.

The affluent society has been characterized as an achievement-oriented society. It is not surprising to find that members of the affluent mainstream would evidence a high degree of achievement motivation. McClelland and his associates (1955) have provided much of the stimulation for study of n achievement. Of particular interest is the relationship of n achievement to family variables. Rosen and d'Andrade (1959) demonstrated that parents of high n achievement boys were more competitive, took more pleasure in problem-solving experiments, and were more involved with their children than parents of low n achievement boys. Fathers of high n achievement boys stressed independence and tended to let their sons develop self-reliance by giving hints to the solution of problems, rather than doing the problems for them. This is an interesting contrast to the mother teaching styles of Hess and Shipman's (1965) lower class subjects. Just as Hess and Shipman found greater language facility with their middle-class subjects, who presumably show greater n achievement, so Buehr (1965) found that high n achievement boys manifest less dialect in their speech under achievement oriented situations.

PERSONAL STYLE VARIABLES

It is much more difficult to draw a direct line between this group of variables and adequate achievement. Gordon and Wilkerson (1966) suggest that such a variable as self-concept may not be an important dimension of the problem since either positive *or* negative self-regard may be related to high achievement. With that word of caution in mind, we can say that disadvantaged children do evidence significantly lower self-esteem than more advantaged children (Long and Henderson, 1967; Coleman, 1966; Keller, 1963). These feelings of inadequacy seem to be related to failure experiences in the school environment. The concept of personal control implies a feeling of responsibility for that which happens to one and is related to social class (Battle and Rotter, 1963). Disadvantaged boys lack persistence in a school-related task and evidence a lower sense of control over the environment than more advantaged children. Poor achievers among the disadvantaged groups give higher evaluative ratings for school subjects in which they are achieving poorly than do better achievers (Greenberg et al., 1965). These findings seem to be consistent with a greater discrepancy between actual performance and level of aspiration found among the disadvantaged (Hieronymus, 1951; Keller, 1963).

Academic achievement is related to a personal style dimension which Kagan has labeled "impulsivity-reflectivity." The more reflective response tendency is related to higher reading achievement, social class, and intellectual ability (Kagan, 1965; Miller and Mumbaure, 1967).

Disadvantaged children are more present-oriented than future-oriented (Le Shan, 1952). In a study of the relationship of home environmental variables to high and low potential success in school among Mexican-American children, Henderson (1966) found that the low potential families were more concerned with meeting daily needs than providing experiences that will have a future educational payoff.

M. Schoggen (1967) of our laboratory, in her ecological studies of disadvantaged homes, reports that disorganization can be characterized in terms of lack of temporal and spatial organization. The most disorganized homes do not even have a regular mealtime. Regular mealtime represents the most basic time ordering event by which one can begin to develop time concepts and a future orientation.

PHYSICAL VARIABLES

A basic need for productive achievement is a reasonable state of physical health. However, among the disadvantaged, the wherewithal to provide adequate medical care is unavailable. The proportion of the population suffering from chronic ill health because of the lack of medical care rises sharply as income decreases. The incidence of chronic health problems is almost four times as great among disadvantaged families (income under $2,000) when compared with more advantaged families ($7,000 annual income and up) (MacDonald, 1966).

Nutritional deficiencies are probably the greatest single deterrent to adequate physical health. Inadequate and substandard diets, particularly when sustained by the pregnant mother, are the cause of a higher rate of infant mortality, prematurity, and birth defects among the disadvantaged than any other single cause. Liebow (1967) points out that pregnant disadvantaged women often eat as many as four boxes of Argo laundry starch a day.

SOCIALIZATION FOR COMPETENCY –
THE CHILDREN'S PROGRAM

The ecological observations which Maxine Schoggen of our laboratory has been conducting in the homes of disadvantaged families confirm our assumptions concerning the inadequacy of the role the mother takes as an instrumental agent in the child's ecological system. Perhaps the observation of greatest impact has been the relative lack of structure or organization evident. Few attempts have been observed to impose order upon the physical and temporal environment of the kind with which we are all familiar. Certainly this is not confined to the homes of lower socio-economic groups, but it is an observation that is relatively general among them. It may well be a crucial defining variable in the operational definition of disadvantage.

Following George Kelly's (1955) thesis that man is basically a scientist and predictor, we would suggest that structure, order, indeed redundancy, are necessary to developing predictive accuracy. When he can predict events, he can choose appropriate behavioral alternatives to cope with the events, thus exercising a minimal control over them. As predicting skills increase both in accuracy and over greater intervals of time, he is able to exercise even greater control, increasing his opportunity for innovative and creative solutions to the problem which confront him. This is the essence of competency.

Evidence from a variety of sources in the psychological literature suggests that man strives to impose order and structure upon the environmental chaos in which he finds himself. More importantly, there is evidence to suggest that organizing and structuring skills are learned. As the child learns to impose order and structure upon his environment, he is able to process information much more economically and efficiently. Efficient informational processing is essential to predicting environmental events. We have assumed that this learning takes place relatively early and is particularly susceptible to retarded development given an inadequate instrumental agent.

Using an informational processing model, the skill development program was carefully constructed to consider all of the conceptual dimensions used by the major sense modalities in the ordering process. For instance, color, shape, size, volume, time, numerical, positional, and whole-part-whole relationships representing relatively invariate conceptual areas were task analyzed according to the molar sensory processes needed to assimilate information. In this fashion the decoding skills for each of the major sense modalities were specified. Skill development objectives were organized in three categories of processing skills — sensory skills, abstracting and mediating skills, and response skills. Each of these three skill groups were subdivided into skill areas which through continuous refinement have been translated into sequences of specific behavioral expectations. Once these specifications were made, the abstracting skills necessary for appropriate responses could be generated. On an *a priori* basis, the developmental sequence of matching (simple discrimination), recognition (appropriate response to a verbal label or command), identification (appropriate response to introduction of the stimulus), to response of choice (appropriate initiatory activity), became an instructional strategy. Evidence subsequently collected empirically demonstrated such ordering to be correct (Gilmer, 1969).

This elaborate and detailed work, when accomplished, provided a sequential road map around which appropriate activities could be designed to develop the complex of skills we feel are necessary for the child to be competent and able to cope effectively with later school activities.

Careful introduction and ordering of new material and steps of just manageable difficulty helped in moving motivations from an extrinsic to an intrinsic locus. Such a strategy also insured success, which helped to develop task orientation in school-related activities. Since the curriculum was directed toward the development of skill and placing order upon one's environment, content — as such — took a secondary role. The basic conceptual skills were assumed to be relatively invariant while content changes over time. Much more important than changing content is the ability to recognize a set of three or five, to understand the positional concepts before, behind or through, and to discriminate rough from smooth or hot from cold. Content then became a vehicle for the development of skills. A unit approach was adopted which moved from the child himself through the family, school, local community, to urban and farm life. The unit emphasis was upon social studies, language, and science. Thus, within the context of ever broadening content areas, the skill development program increased in scope and the child developed ever more finely tuned capabilities.

Equally important to the development of coping skills was the development of attitudes necessary for sustaining developed skills and continuing the developmental momentum. Positive attitudes relating to school type activities, ability to delay reward, persistence, achievement motivation, and so forth, were a few of the major sustaining attitudes which were systematically programmed into the curriculum. By carefully sequencing activities and tasks to develop these motivations, the child gained greater control over himself and his environment.

Central to the aptitude and attitude development was the careful programming of reinforcement schedules to move the child from a concrete and extrinsic reward system to an abstract and intrinsic one. Careful contingency management was critical to the child's progress and his rapid development in the program.

SKILL DEVELOPMENT PROGRAM

A road map has been provided (Table I, at the end of the chapter) of the breakdown of the skills into the three major areas and sub-areas previously mentioned.

SENSORY SKILLS

The first division of skills, Sensory Skills, can be labeled "Input" skills. These are the processes which must operate in order to receive and decode environmental stimuli through the senses. The skill development program was carefully constructed to consider all of the conceptual dimensions used by the major sense modalities — visual, auditory, tactile-kinesthetic, taste-olfactory — in the ordering process. Such conceptual areas as color, shape, size, volume, time, texture, temperature are a few of the relatively invariant dimensions for the organization of environmental stimuli. These areas were then task-analyzed according to the sensory processes needed to assimilate information.

The most basic sensory process is what we call the *Orienting or Attentional Skill*. This is a basic learning skill whereby a child learns to focus attention on the relevant stimuli in his environment. For example, in dealing with the visual modality, our concern is that the child develops an awareness of color, size, shape, position, number, etc., as consistent conceptual dimensions by which he can order the visual stimuli he receives. In the initial stages of the classroom program, we attempt to develop the Orienting Skill by carefully controlling stimuli in order to make salient those which are relevant.

A second sensory process is the *Discriminatory Skill* — the ability to perceive likenesses and differences among stimuli received by the four sensory modalities. A more complex process is involved with a third sensory process, the *Relational Skill,* where a child must deal with interrelated stimuli which occur simultaneously. An example of this skill in the visual modality is the child's ability to work a puzzle by perceiving the relationships among the parts and constructing the whole. The fourth sensory process is the *Sequential Skill,* by which the child learns to perceive a repeating pattern of stimuli which occur in a certain spatial or temporal order.

The development of each one of these four sensory skills, for each of the sensory modalities, is programmed over time through a carefully developed sequence of behavioral expectations which require increasingly finer and more precise discrimination, with stimuli which become more complex and abstract. For example, the Discriminatory Skill in the visual modality begins at a gross level with the perception of likenesses and differences of whole concrete objects (as with two cups and a spoon) and then moves to discriminations among similar objects on the basis of likeness and difference in parts, color, size, shape, number, or position. As this skill is gradually refined, the child is able to discriminate fine differences among small, detailed, abstract configurations and symbols such as designs, words, numerals, and letters.

ABSTRACTING AND MEDIATING SKILLS

The second division of information processing skills, Abstracting and Mediating Skills, is concerned with what could be termed "Organization" processes. This area includes skills which are critical in the assimilation of stimuli into a logical and orderly cognitive framework to facilitate retrieval of information and to foster transfer of learning. We have designated these skill areas as Conceptual, Association, Classification, Sequencing, and Critical Thinking.

The development of Conceptual Skills and Association Skills occurs concurrently. Initial emphasis in the program is on developing awareness of the stimuli in the child's immediate environment through the child's observation and manipulation of concrete objects. Through frequent encounters with and exploration of objects, the child develops concepts of identity. As the child observes and manipulates the objects, the teacher, and later the child, labels the nominal and functional attributes which correspond to each object. The child learns, through association, to relate a label with each identity concept. Pictures of objects are introduced to encourage the child to relate the object with its representation and to associate the same nominal and functional labels with the representation as with the object itself.

As Sensory Skills develop, attention is focused on additional, more formal attributes of objects. When the child is able to attend to relevant stimuli in his environment and has developed the ability to discriminate among stimuli perceived through the four sensory modalities, basic ordering concepts begin to develop based on the invariant conceptual dimensions used in the sensory ordering process. The Basic Ordering Concepts include such concepts as color, shape, size, number, position, volume, texture, weight, temperature, motion, taste, time, age, affect. As with nominal and functional concepts, the teacher labels each basic concept as it is perceived by the child. When the child can both recognize and identify a concept, every opportunity is taken to set the stage so that it is necessary for the child to use the label.

As the program progresses, the child's environment is expanded. New and different objects, concepts, and experiences continue to be presented to the child. Through association processes, the child develops meaningful relationships between objects, concepts, and events which are spatially, temporally, or functionally related. He learns to associate labels with every object, attribute, representation, and symbol he encounters.

We work on the assumption that the more sophisticated Classification Skills develop through the process of association. During planned activities, the child is directed to associate or group certain objects or concepts which all share a particular characteristic to form a class of objects or concepts defined by the common characteristic. The child sorts objects first on the basis of attributes (nominal, function, or basic ordering concepts such as color) and later on

Toward Individual Competency

the basis of subordinate and superordinate relationships. The child learns to classify deductively by sorting objects with a common characteristic into their appropriate categories which are identified by the teacher. He then learns to classify inductively, by abstracting a shared characteristic of given objects or concepts and formulating the class defined by the common characteristic. Activities are sequenced to increase the amount of conceptual differentiation demanded of the child and to move the child from the classification of objects or concepts using concrete or representational materials to the classification of objects or concepts using verbal labels only.

Sequencing skills are the tools used by the child to arrange concepts and experiences in a logical spatial or temporal order. These are the mediating skills utilized by the child in ordering motor and verbal responses when dramatizing the action patterns of stories or events; when executing a series of verbal directions; when verbalizing the serial order of numbers, days of the week, seasons of the year; and when verbalizing the sequence of episodes of familiar stories and events or activities which the child has experienced. Eventually the child utilizes this skill at a very abstract and complex level as he learns to develop his own stories exhibiting a sequence of events in a logical order. In activities of this type, the child is also using many complex Critical Thinking processes which are emphasized in the program when working with stories and problem situations. These are the very complex and abstract skills of drawing relationships, making inferences, analyzing problems, synthesizing ideas, hypothesizing, evaluating, drawing analogies, and analyzing absurdities. With the Abstracting and Mediating Skills, as with Sensory Skills, the curriculum is organized to develop increasingly more sophisticated schemata for organizing information to encourage the continuous segmentation and differentiation of the child's cognitive field.

RESPONSE SKILLS

The third division of information processing skills, Response Skills, can be called "Output" skills. These are the processes required to express, through both motor and verbal responses, the resultant product of the decoding and organizational processes. The curriculum for this process area is designed to develop the verbal and small motor coordination skills essential for self-expression and the effective communication of thought processes.

The objectives in the subdivision of Verbal Response Skills are concerned with both quantity and quality of verbalization. The learning milieu of the classroom is organized to stimulate individual expression. Each child spends approximately two-thirds of his time in a small group situation with four other children and a teacher. Individual expression is reinforced with specific verbal praise, with physical gestures of approval, and sometimes, with a concrete reward. Many activities are planned and many instructional devices are utilized to augment the quantity of verbalization. Conversation of child with teacher and child with child is encouraged, particularly in small groups during the snack and lunch periods.

Quality in verbalization is developed through the use of very carefully developed reinforcement schedules to realize continuous improvements in articulation and in sentence structure. The child is reinforced for closer and closer approximations of complete sentence structure in encoding declarative (affirmative and negative) and interrogative statements. Lessons are planned whereby the child can develop the ability to use present, past, and future tense forms in actual situations. Certain sentence patterns are reinforced because they demonstrate evidence of complex thinking operations: negative statements used in classification activities to indicate objects or concepts which do not belong to a designated class; comparative statements used to describe the relationship between two objects exhibiting comparative forms of polar concepts of size, texture, weight, etc.; "if-then" statements used to state deductions when certain qualifying conditions are given; statements with "or" used to imply choice. Succinctness of expression is developed by encouraging the child to reduce redundancy in consecutive sentences through consolidation of adjectives, verbs, and nouns using the coordinating conjunction "and."

Use of "standard" grammatical forms and sentence patterns (a reflection of environment and thought process) is secondary in importance to the ability to use many variant forms employed in both the child's environment and a school-type situation. Since verbal expression is a primary method of communication as well as a tool and indicator of cognitive functioning, it is felt that the child should be able to comprehend and use alternative grammatical and structural forms. Without this versatility, comprehension handicaps and communication impediments might well develop with individuals from differing environments in later school-learning situations.

The objectives for the Motor Response Skills are concerned primarily with the development of eye-hand coordination since these particular children tend to be extremely well coordinated in tasks involving gross motor skills. Again, as with Sensory Skills, classroom activities are sequenced throughout the program to refine coordination from the relatively gross control required in manipulating objects, modeling with clay, painting on large surfaces, drawing, stringing beads, and cutting to the fine control required in tracing, following dots, coloring in small areas, and printing.

CONTENT

As previously stated, the focus of the curriculum is not on the learning of specific information but is on the development of skills needed to process information more effectively. The basic conceptual skills are assumed to be relatively invariant while content changes over time. Content plays the role of the vehicle for the development of skills. Although the content is subsidiary in importance to skill development, it must be carefully selected and organized to ensure maximal opportunities for the development of the information processing skills.

A unit approach for ordering content was adopted on the assumption that learning experiences organized around a central theme would encourage more meaningful learning for the child. In addition, this organizational plan would aid the teacher in presenting the learning situations in an order of increasing complexity and abstraction, following the sequencing directions for skill development. In the implementation of the unit approach, both the activities within a unit and the units themselves are sequenced to augment the continuing growth of more abstract and complex skills. Units chosen for the initial stages of the classroom program are those which provide opportunities for the development of Sensory Skills and basic ordering concepts in very concrete situations. Subsequent units utilize these basic learning skills and concepts to build more complex concepts and to develop skills in organizing and expressing experiences.

Table II (at the end of the chapter), an excerpt from a forthcoming curriculum publication, illustrates the articulation of the skill development program with the instructional activities which are organized around a unit theme. This particular unit is one developed on plants. Basic activities are augmented by extension activity. Evaluation is an integral part of the instructional program. Conscientious attention to the skills to be developed provide direction for the development of instructional content.

By using an interrelated unit approach, each successive unit utilizes concepts and skills in each of the preceding units and develops then to a higher level of sophistication. For example, the first unit used is about the child himself. The content is exciting to the child and obviously offers the most concrete and real situations for learning. The concepts and skills developed here are transferred to, and repeatedly utilized in, a sequence of units on family and home, neighborhood, and city. With this interrelated unit approach, skills in experiencing, in organizing experiences, and in expressing experiences become increasingly more refined and complex. The child is steadily carried from proximal to distal situations in space orientation, encouraging him to move from reliance on perceptual media into the use of conceptual and language media for learning.

Similarly a sequence of units on animals moves the child from the concrete, proximal environment to the abstract, distal environment beginning with pets, followed by farm animals, small woods animals, and sometimes large wild animals. This series of units provides maximum opportunities for developing Association and Classification Skills using both basic concepts and more complex concepts as the building blocks for hierarchical class formation. A series of units on the four seasons provides opportunities to develop Sensory Skills and concepts basic to seasonal change and to review and expand them over a period of one full year. This series is particularly effective in developing Association Skills and in encouraging the drawing of relationships between seasons as their sequential order is recognized.

Although the units which have been implemented appear very similar to those of most preschools, our curriculum approach is far different. The content itself is not the primary focus; the main thrust is on the aptitude development. The DARCEE instructional program, therefore, makes a pronounced departure from the traditional nursery school program. It is a structured program in which every moment has a designed instructional purpose in terms of an established objective.

Our goal has been to develop a curriculum based on substantive research and theory with clearly defined goals and objectives. In this way we believe we are able to delineate the step-by-step procedures for obtaining our objectives which can be communicated easily for application in other contexts and with other populations.

TABLE I

I. SENSORY SKILLS

Orienting and Attentional Skills

Visual
Auditory
Tactile-Kinesthetic
Taste-Olfactory

Discriminatory Skills

Visual
Auditory
Tactile-Kinesthetic
Taste-Olfactory

Relational Skills

Visual
Auditory

Sequential Skills

Visual
Auditory

II. ABSTRACTING AND MEDIATING SKILLS

Conceptual Skills

1. Identify Concepts
   nominal and functional

TABLE I (Continued)

II. ABSTRACTING AND MEDIATING SKILLS (Continued)

   2. Basic Ordering Concepts

color	pitch		taste
shape	length	auditory	flavors and odors
size	volume		time
number	texture		age
position	weight		affect
volume	temperature		
	motion		
	speed		

Association Skills
1. Object with object, attribute, representation, symbol
2. Attribute with attribute, representation, symbol
3. Representation with representation, symbol
4. Symbol with symbol

Classification Skills
1. Deductive, by attribute and hierarchy
2. Inductive, by attribute and hierarchy

Sequencing Skills
1. Motor — executing a sequence of action, directions, events
2. Verbal — verbalizing a sequence of concepts, events

Critical Thinking Skills
1. Drawing relationships
2. Making inferences
3. Making predictions
4. Analyzing problem-situations
5. Synthesizing ideas
6. Hypothesizing
7. Evaluating
8. Drawing analogies
9. Analyzing absurdities

III. RESPONSE SKILLS

Verbal Response Skills
1. Fluency
2. Articulation
3. Syntax

TABLE I (Continued)

III. RESPONSE SKILLS (Continued)
- a. Single-word level — identification of objects, actions, sounds, concepts
- b. Phrase level
- c. Complete sentence level
  simple declaratives
  interrogatives
  negatives
  "and" statements
  "or" statements
  "if-then" statements
  "I don't know" statements
  complex sentence — adverbial clauses

Motor Response Skills

1. Small-Motor coordination (eye-hand coordination) in:

pasting	cutting
modeling	lacing and weaving
painting	tracing
coloring	solving mazes
stringing	following dots
drawing	printing

2. Orientation
   left-to-right progression
   top-to-bottom progression
   front-to-back progression

TABLE II

UNIT UNDERSTANDING: A. All trees, bushes, flowers, vegetables, grasses, vines, mosses, and ferns are plants.

BASIC SKILLS TO BE DEVELOPED	INSTRUCTIONAL ACTIVITIES

SENSORY SKILLS
Visual Skills
  Focuses attention on mural
  Isolates each plant type in mural
  Discriminates differences in colors and sizes among the plants
Auditory Skills
  Listens to questions
  Listens to labels for plants, color, size, and position concepts
ABSTRACTING SKILLS
Conceptual Skills
  Knows types of plants — tree, bush, vine, flower, grass
  Recognizes color concept — green
  Recognizes size concepts — tall, short; tallest, shortest; fat, thin; fattest, thinnest
  Recognizes position concepts —
    above, below
    top, bottom
    at the side
    beside
    between
    in the corner
Classification Skills
  Comprehends the class of plants
RESPONSE SKILLS
Verbal Skills
  Labels types of plants
  Identifies concepts of color, size, and position
	1. *Basic Activity*
	Make a colorful mural picturing various kinds of plants and place it in a prominent space on the classroom wall. Show a variety of plants such as a tree, a shrub, flowers, grass, and a vine which are found in your area. Be sure to use some of the colors with which the children are already familiar and to show all the parts of a plant including the roots below the ground.
	
	This mural may be used to introduce plants. Question the children to see if they can identify any of the plants. Be careful to label each one which the children cannot identify. Discuss each plant at length, asking the children to identify the various colors. Emphasize the fact that most plants have some parts which are green. Compare the sizes of the plants such as tallest, shortest, thickest, thinnest. Talk about the positions of the plants and their parts using such labels as above, below, top, bottom, at the side, beside, between, in the corner.
	
	Evaluation
	Assess carefully which children can and cannot do the following:
	  1. label the types of plants
	  2. identify the color, size, and position concepts illustrated by the plants.

TABLE II (Continued)

BASIC SKILLS TO BE DEVELOPED	INSTRUCTIONAL ACTIVITIES

SENSORY SKILLS
Visual Skills
    Focuses attention on pictures
    Isolates plant within picture
    Discriminates likeness and differences among plants in pictures and plants in the mural
ABSTRACTING SKILLS
Conceptual Skills
    Recognizes number sets
Association Skills
    Relates a picture of a plant with the representation of that plant in the mural
RESPONSE SKILLS
Verbal Skills
    Counts plants in the mural
    Identifies number sets
SENSORY SKILLS
Visual Skills
    Focuses attention on plants during the walk
    Focuses attention on objects and drawings after the walk
    Distinguishes parts of plants from other objects seen on the walk
    Discriminates among types of plants seen
Auditory Skills
    Listens to discussion on walk and after walk
    Listens to labels for types of plants and plant parts
	Use the mural during the unit to develop the concepts which the children cannot label or identify.
	
	Extension Activity
	
	Collect a number of study prints or magazine pictures which look as much like the plants in the mural as possible. Show each picture to the group and ask one of the children to match it to one of the plants on the mural. Possibly the child will be able to label the plant by type.
	
	The mural should be used throughout the unit to further develop the basic concepts of color, size, position, number and visual likeness and difference skills. It should also be used as a visual aid to illustrate the other understandings in the unit.
	
	2. *Basic Activity*
	
	Take the children on an observation walk or "plant hunt." It would be a good idea to look over the area beforehand in order to find the best places to observe plants. The area around the classroom may be sufficient, but a nearby park or farm might offer a wider variety of plants.
	
	Before beginning the walk, explain to the children that they are going on a trip to look for plants. Give each a small bag in which to put the things he finds from plants such as seeds, flowers, leaves, twigs,

TABLE II (Continued)

BASIC SKILLS TO BE DEVELOPED	INSTRUCTIONAL ACTIVITIES

Tactile-Kinesthetic Skills
    Discriminates likenesses and differences in textures of plant parts which are touched
 	
ABSTRACTING SKILLS
Conceptual Skills
    Knows types of plants — tree, bush, vine, flower, grass
    Knows parts of plants — flower, twig, seed, leaf, etc.
    Recognizes color concepts
    Recognizes size concepts
    Recognizes texture concepts
Association Skills
    Relates a plant part with the plant from which it comes
    Relates drawings of plants with real plants seen on the trip
Classification Skills
    Comprehends the class of plants
 	
RESPONSE SKILLS
Verbal Skills
    Labels types of plants and parts of plants
    Identifies concepts of color, size, and texture
    Identifies the source of plant parts collected
 	
SENSORY SKILLS
Visual Skills
    Focuses attention on objects collected on walk
	or nuts. During the walk, point out specific examples of various plants. Hopefully, you will find some plants similar to those on the mural or to the pictures they have seen. Note the colors of the plants, the various sizes, and textures of the parts. Encourage the children to identify the types of plants and their characteristics (tree, bush, vine, flower, grass) and collect leaves, etc.
	
	Assessment Activity
	
	After the walk discuss the things they collected. Take each object and ask the children where it came from. When the child answers, draw a simple picture of the plant on a chalkboard or large sheet of paper asking, "Did it look like this"? Purposely draw some that are the wrong kind of plant or draw objects which are not plants such as a car, or piece of clothing.
	
	Extension Activity
	
	The objects which are collected on "plant walks" or the plants which the children may bring from home may be kept on a

TABLE II (Continued)

BASIC SKILLS TO BE DEVELOPED	INSTRUCTIONAL ACTIVITIES
Distinguishes very small parts of each object	special table, the "Science Table," to be viewed often during the unit. A magnifying glass could be left on the table for closer observations.

SENSORY SKILLS
Visual Skills
  Focuses attention on pictures and teacher as she models actions
  Isolates the objects in the pictures
  Scans the pictures from left to right
Auditory Skills
  Listens to words of action verse
  Distinguishes the voice intonation used with each line
ABSTRACTING SKILLS
Conceptual Skills
  Knows tree, bush, building, crack, ball, pancake, giant, mouse
  Recognizes size and shape concepts — tall, short; wide, narrow; round, flat; big, tiny
  Understands the order of objects mentioned in the action verse
  Understands the sequence of actions
Association Skills
  Relates each picture with the correct label in the action verse
	3. *Basic Activity*
	Teach the children a fun action verse called "Tall as a Tree." To aid in developing the concepts included and the sequence of the verses, collect pictures of a tree, bush, building, crack, ball, pancake, giant, and mouse. Before introducing the action game, discuss the pictures with the children, labeling and describing them together. With each object, emphasize and dramatize the descriptive word which will be used in the verse: tall (tree), short (bush), wide (building), narrow (crack), round (ball), flat (pancake), big (giant), tiny (mouse). Place the pictures in front of the children, arranging them from left to right in the order the objects are mentioned in the action verse. Model the entire action verse for the children, saying the words and demonstrating the motions. Use a loud voice tone for lines that include tall, wide, big. Use a softer voice tone on the remaining lines. Then ask the children to recite the words with you as you point to each picture. When the children seem quite familiar with the words, add the motions for each verse and play the entire action game together.

TABLE II (Continued)

BASIC SKILLS TO BE DEVELOPED	INSTRUCTIONAL ACTIVITIES
Relates each line of the verse with the appropriate action **RESPONSE SKILLS** *Verbal Skills* Labels objects in the pictures Describes objects in the pictures Recites the verse clearly and accurately Uses loud and soft voice intonations appropriately *Motor Skills* Reproduces the actions appropriate for each line	*Evaluation* Note carefully which children can and cannot do the following: 1. Label and describe the pictures 2. Recite the verse accurately and clearly 3. Reproduce the correct action for each line
ABSTRACTING SKILLS *Conceptual Skills* Recognizes size and shape concepts *Classification Skills* Comprehends classes of tall objects, short objects; round objects, flat objects; big objects, tiny objects **RESPONSE SKILLS** *Verbal Skills* Identifies objects which belong to a defined class	*Extension Activity* In order to assess whether the children understand the size and shape concepts involved, ask them to name other objects which are tall as a tree, short as a bush, wide..., narrow..., round..., flat..., big..., and tiny..., "Tall as a Tree" is useful not only for the development of size concepts but is also a good stretching exercise. The children will probably enjoy playing it often.
SENSORY SKILLS *Visual Skills* Focuses attention on objects and pictures Isolates plant pictures in the magazines	4. *Basic Activity* Classify objects which are plants and objects which are *not* plants. Begin the activity by showing the children several real objects such as: plants — flowers, grass, small

402   *The Preschool in Action*

TABLE II (Continued)

BASIC SKILLS TO BE DEVELOPED	INSTRUCTIONAL ACTIVITIES

Auditory Skills
 	
    Listens to discussion of each object and picture
 	
ABSTRACTING SKILLS
 	
Conceptual Skills
 	
    Knows the objects
    Recognizes the objects which are plants
 	
Classification Skills
 	
    Comprehends the class of plants
 	
RESPONSE SKILLS
 	
Verbal Skills
 	
    Labels the objects and pictures of objects
    Identifies the objects which are plants
    Identifies the objects which are *not* plants
    Uses negative statements
 	
Motor Skills
 	
    Manipulates scissors to cut around pictures
    Manipulates paste and paper
	branch; non-plants — cup, article of clothing, rock. When selecting items for the non-plant category, include objects with which the children will be familiar, such as objects discussed in the previous unit. Do not include foods or objects made of wood since these objects come *from* plants and may confuse the children.
	
	Hold up each object and ask the children to tell whether it is a plant or not. If no, what is it? Encourage the children to speak in complete sentences and use the word "not": "It is *not* a plant. It is a cup." After the children have successfully classified the concrete objects, repeat the same procedure using study prints or pictures from magazines. Again be careful when selecting the pictures.
	
	Assessment Activity
	
	Give the children old household magazines to find and cut pictures of the various types of plants. Have the children paste them on a piece of construction paper as they identify the types of plants.

REFERENCES | 13

Battle, E. S. and Rotter, J. B. Children's feelings of personal control as related to social class and ethnic group. *Journal of Personality,* 1963, *31,* 482-490.

Bernstein, B. Social class and linguistic development: A theory of social learning. In A. H. Halsey, J. Floud, and C. A. Anderson (Eds.), *Education, economy, and society.* New York: Free Press of Glencoe, 1961, pp. 288-314.

Bernstein, B. Linguistic codes, hesitation phenomena and intelligence. *Language and Speech,* 1962, *5* (1), 31-46.

Bernstein, B. A socio-linguistic approach to social learning. In J. Gould (Ed.), *Penguin survey of the social sciences.* Baltimore: Penguin Books, 1965, pp. 144-168.

Buehr, R. F. Need achievement and dialect in lower-class adolescent negroes. *Proceedings of the 73rd Annual Convention of the American Psychological Association,* 1965, 313-314.

Clark, A. D. and Richards, C. J. Auditory discrimination among economically disadvantaged and nondisadvantaged preschool children. *Exceptional Children,* 1966, *33* (4), 259-262.

Coleman, J. S. Equality of educational opportunity. Washington, D. C.: U. S. Government Printing Office, 1966. Office of Education 38001.

Deutsch, C. P. Auditory discrimination and learning: Social factors. *Merrill-Palmer Quarterly,* 1964, *10* (3), 277-296.

Deutsch, M. The role of social class in language development and cognition. *American Journal of Orthopsychiatry,* 1965, *35,* 78-88.

Gilmer, B. R. Intra-family diffusion of selected cognitive skills as a function of educational stimulation. *DARCEE Papers and Reports,* 1969, *3,* No. 1 (Peabody College).

Gordon, E. W. and Wilkerson, D. A. *Compensatory education for the disadvantaged: Programs and practices – preschool through college.* New York: College Entrance Examination Board, 1966.

Gray, S. W., Klaus, R. A., Miller, J. O., and Forrester, B. J. *Before first grade: The early training project for culturally disadvantaged children.* New York: Teachers College Press, 1966.

Greenberg, J. W., Gerver, J. M., Chall, J., and Davidson, H. H. Attitudes of children from a deprived environment toward achievement concepts. *Journal of Educational Research,* 1965, *58* (2), 57.

Henderson, R. W. *Environmental stimulation and intellectual development of Mexican-American children:* An exploratory study. (Doctoral dissertation, University of Arizona) Ann Arbor, Mich.: University Microfilms, 1966. No. 66-15, 258.

Hess, R. D. and Shipman, V. C. Early experience and the socialization of cognitive modes in children. *Child Development,* 1965, *36* (4), 869-886.

Hieronymus, A. N. Study of social class motivation: Relationships between anxiety for education and certain socio-economic and intellectual variables. *Journal of Educational Psychology,* 1951, *42,* 193-205.

Irwin, O. C. Infant speech: The effect of family occupational status and of age on sound frequency. *Journal of Speech and Hearing Disorders,* 1948, *13,* 320-323. (a)

Irwin, O. C. Infant speech: The effect of family occupational status and of age on use of sound types. *Journal of Speech and Hearing Disorders,* 1948, *13,* 224-226. (b)

Jensen, A. R. Learning in the preschool years. *Journal of Nursery Education,* 1963, *18* (2), 133-138. (b)

Jensen, A. R. Social class and perceptual learning. *Mental Hygiene,* 1966, *50* (2), 226-239.

Jones, K. L. *The language development of Headstart children.* (Doctoral dissertation, University of Arkansas) Ann Arbor, Mich.: University Microfilms, 1966, No. 66-11, 609.

Kagan, J. Reflection-impulsivity and reading ability in primary grade children. *Child Development,* 1965, *36* (3), 609-628.

Kahl, J. A. Some measurements of achievement orientation. *American Journal of Sociology,* 1965, *70* (6), 669-681.

Keller, S. The social world of the urban slum child: Some early findings. *American Journal of Orthopsychiatry,* 1963, *33* (5), 823-831.

Kelley, G. A. *The psychology of personal constructs.* New York: W. W. Norton and Co., Vol. *I,* 1955.

Klaus, R. A. and Gray, S. W. The early training project for disadvantaged children: a report after five years. *Monographs of the Society for Research in Child Development,* 1968, No. 120.

LeShan, L. L. Time orientation and social class. *Journal of Abnormal and Social Psychology,* 1952, *47,* 589-592.

Lesser, G. S., Fifer, G., and Clark, D. H. Mental abilities of children from different social-class and cultural groups. *Monographs of the Society for Research in Child Development,* 1965, *30* (4), Serial No. 102.

Liebow, E. *Tally's corner: A study of negro streetcorner men.* Boston: Little, Brown, 1967.

Long, B. H., and Henderson, E. H. Social schemata of school beginners: Some demographic correlates. *Proceedings of the 75th Annual Convention of the American Psychological Association*, 1967, *2*, 329-330.

Maitland, S. C. *The perspective, frustration-failure and delay of gratification in middle-class and lower-class children from organized and disorganized families.* (Doctoral dissertation, University of Minnesota) Ann Arbor, Mich.: University Microfilms, 1966. No. 67-866.

McClelland, D. C. *Studies in motivation.* New York: Appleton, 1955.

Miller, J. O. Disadvantaged families: Despair to hope. Invited address, Division I, American Psychological Association, Washington, D. C., September, 1969. In *Psychology and the Problems of Society.* Washington, D. C.: APA, 1970.

Miller, J. O. Cultural deprivation and its modification: Effects of intervention. In H. C. Haywood (Ed.), *Proceedings of Conference on Social-Cultural Aspects of Mental Retardation.* Nashville, Tennessee: George Peabody College for Teachers, June 1968.

Miller, J. O. and Mumbauer, C. Intellectual functioning, learning performance and cognitive style in advantaged and disadvantaged preschool children. Unpublished manuscript. George Peabody College for Teachers, 1967.

Mischel, W. Preference for delayed reinforcement and social responsibility. *Journal of Abnormal and Social Psychology,* 1961, *62*, 1-7.

Mischel, W. and Metzner, R. Preference for delayed reward as a function of age, intelligence, and length of delay interval. *Journal of Abnormal and Social Psychology,* 1962, *64*, 425-431.

Rosen, B. D. and D'Andrade, R. The psycho-social origins of achievement motivation. *Sociometry,* 1959, *22*, 185-218.

Ryckman, D. B. *Psychological processes of disadvantaged children.* (Doctoral dissertation, University of Illinois) Ann Arbor, Mich.: University Microfilms, 1966. No. 66-12, 417.

Schoggen, M. Research, change, and social responsibility: Studies of imprint of the low-income home on young children. In *Research, change, and social responsibility: An illustrative model from early education. DARCEE Papers and Reports,* 1967, *2* (3).

Siller, J. Socio-economic status and conceptual thinking. *Journal of Abnormal and Social Psychology,* 1957, *55*, 365-371.

Spain, C. J. Definition of familiar nouns by culturally deprived and non-deprived children of varying ages. Unpublished doctoral dissertation, George Peabody College for Teachers, 1962.

Steen, M. T. *The effects of immediate and delayed reinforcement on the achievement behavior of Mexican-American children of low socio-economic status.* (Doctoral dissertation, Stanford University) Ann Arbor, Mich.: University Microfilms, 1966. No. 66-8594.

Strauss, M. A. Deferred gratification, social class, and the achievement syndrome. *American Sociological Review,* 1962, *27* (3), 326-335.

Terrel, G., Jr., Durkin, K., and Wiesley, M. Social class and the nature of the incentive in discrimination learning. *Journal of Abnormal and Social Psychology,* 1959, *59,* 270-272.

Zigler, E. and deLabry, J. Concept-switching in middle-class, lower-class, and retarded children. *Journal of Abnormal and Social Psychology,* 1962, *65,* 267-273.

Schaefer, Aaronson | *Introduction* | 14

The Infant Education Research Project is a one-to-one tutoring program which is unique in that it is the only program described in this book which takes place in the child's home. Although this location has its disadvantages, it eliminates the problems associated with taking a young child from his familiar home setting and increases the possibility of involving mother and siblings in the teaching process. The children, who are tutored for one hour a day, five days a week, enter the program at 15 months of age and continue to 36 months of age. Whereas the long-range goal of the project was to increase the academic achievement of the participating children, the more immediate objective was to increase intellectual ability, with special emphasis placed upon the development of language skills. A positive relationship with both the child and the family was considered to be extremely important to achieving these goals.

No set curriculum was implemented, and the tutors developed curricula, following general guidelines, which responded to the needs and interests of each individual child. Providing varied and increasingly complex experiences and age-appropriate language stimulation were major goals of the tutors. Because the tutors played such an active role in developing the program and because their relationship with the child and his family was so important, the maintenance of dedication and enthusiasm was critical. And the techniques which maintained those critical characteristics may have relevance not only for tutors in special programs, but also for teachers in other educational settings and for mothers, as Schaefer and Aaronson point out near the end of the paper.

The investigators also emphasize other implications of the home tutoring program which may be important to consider in the development of future educational programs. They stress that education should begin early (even earlier than

15 months) and should continue in order to be effective in increasing intellectual functioning. Furthermore, given the major importance of the family (and especially the mother) in affecting the cognitive and language growth of the child, educational programs should be extended to include the entire family and more emphasis should be placed on the child's education in the home. To accomplish training in child care and education and those things necessary to maintaining enthusiasm (e.g., meetings with others for advice or simply sharing experiences), new but inexpensive toys occasionally should be available to parents. Perhaps of most far reaching importance is the statement that "educational planning should recognize that each person is both a teacher and a student throughout the life span." Education focused on developing teaching skills would have the double function of preparing individuals for aiding the development of others and of reinforcing and clarifying the knowledge of the individual who assumes the teacher's role.

Earl S. Schaefer
May Aaronson

Infant Education Research Project: Implementation and Implications of a Home Tutoring Program

14

The Infant Education Research Project was designed to facilitate the intellectual development of disadvantaged children through a program of home tutoring during the second and third years of life. The initial motivation for the development of the project was provided by research data that showed that most social groups reach a stable IQ level during the preschool years. A reported negative correlation of mean IQ with age for a sample of minority group elementary school children was interpreted as produced by the sampling method which resulted in unrepresentative samples in the upper and lower age ranges (Kennedy, Van de Riet, and White, 1963). The critique concluded that "a low mean IQ developed during the preschool years and remained stable during the elementary school years" and suggested "a need for research on factors related to intellectual development in the preschool years and for preschool programs designed to raise the level of intellectual functioning of culturally deprived children" (Schaefer, 1965).

Earl S. Schaefer is at the University of North Carolina, Chapel Hill, N. C. May Aaronson is at the Center for Studies of Child and Family Mental Health, National Institute of Mental Health. Printed by permission of the authors.

410

A review of research on early intellectual development suggested that differences between social groups in intellectual functioning emerge during the second and third years of life. Mean IQ's by fathers' occupations, reported by Terman and Merrill (1937) showed that differences between occupational groups for children between two years and five and one half years of age were comparable to those for later ages. Bayley (1965) reported no significant differences between groups in comparison of scores for ages one through fifteen months by sex, birth order, race, parental education, or geographic residence. Francis-Williams and Yule (1967) have confirmed these findings for an English sample. Hindley (1965) also found little difference between socio-economic groups for English children at eighteen months of age, but substantial differences by three years of age. Van Alstyne (1929) also reported substantial correlations of socio-economic indicators with Kuhlman-Binet scores and vocabulary scores at three years of age.

These replicated findings of essentially no difference between social groups in mental test scores at fifteen to eighteen months but substantial differences at three years suggested that mental-test scores may be measuring different functions at different ages. Bayley's (1949) intercorrelations of mental test scores from repeated tests between birth and eighteen years have been factor-analyzed by Hofstaetter (1954) and reanalyzed by Cronbach (1967). Both analysts agree that the intercorrelations show that the tests are measuring different functions at different ages. Cronbach (1967) convincingly argues that the analysis cannot reveal distinct qualitative stages of mental development, but he suggests that "Many sorts of developmental research provide a basis for arguing that the available tests tap different processes at different ages, and for arguing that mental development goes through qualitative stages." Different correlations with socio-economic status variables at different ages provide some evidence that the tests are measuring different functions at different ages.

Unpublished findings of substantial intercorrelations of mental and motor tests during the first year of life, but insignificant correlations as the child approaches two years of age, also suggest that different functions are being measured at those ages. Since neither the early mental nor the early motor tests have significant correlations with later mental tests, the importance of early sensory-motor development for subsequent intellectual functioning or achievement is questionable. These data suggested that other variables should be stressed to achieve a long-term goal of higher intellectual functioning. The analysis also suggests that the importance of early sensory and motor development for later intellectual development must be proven rather than assumed, for existing longitudinal data would not support that view.

The findings of very low correlations between early mental-test scores and later mental-test scores would not support an assumption that accelerating an early stage of development would accelerate or increase level of functioning at a subsequent uncorrelated stage of development. The need for additional longitudinal research on the interrelationships of differences in cognitive functioning at different ages and the need for study of both long-term and short-term effects of early intellectual stimulation is suggested by these analyses of mental-test data.

Evidence that early mental and motor skills do not predict later development, and that differences between social groups emerge during the second and third years of life, influenced the major focus of the Infant Education Research Project. Examination of infant mental tests showed an increasing emphasis upon language-development items during the second year of life that parallels the child's rapid increase in the use of language. Van Alstyne (1929) had reported very high correlations between Kuhlmann-Binet scores and scores on her vocabulary test at age three. Miner (1957) reviewed the literature on the intercorrelations of vocabulary scores and Wechsler-Bellevue and Stanford-Binet scores and found that typically the correlations are above .80. Miner also found that vocabulary correlates as highly with these two major mental tests as they correlate with one another. Bradway (1945) analyzed Stanford-Binet items from tests given during preschool years into verbal, non-verbal, and memory components and reported that verbal scores had higher correlations with later intelligence than did the non-verbal scores. Bayley (1966) isolated several factors from mental-test items administered between two and six years of age and found that a factor of verbal knowledge yields the highest predictions of later intelligence. The research that provides evidence that verbal scores are better predictors of future intelligence, that vocabulary is highly correlated with mental test scores and with occupational and academic achievement, and that differences among socio-economic groups in intellectual functioning emerge during the second and third years of life — the period of early verbal development — dictated both the focus upon language development and the choice of fifteen months as the age at which tutoring was begun.

The hypothesis that providing additional intellectual stimulation could produce higher levels of intellectual functioning in lower-socio-economic-status Negro infants was derived from both correlational studies and intervention studies on early intellectual development. Van Alstyne (1929) had found sizable correlations between parent practices such as reading to the child, and the child's vocabulary even after partialling out the effects of the mother's intelligence. Milner (1951) reported that low scorers on readiness tests less frequently shared mealtime conversations with their parents, experienced less affection from their parents, had fewer books and were read to less often, and had received more direct physical punishment. Bayley and Schaefer (1964) found that maternal behavior ratings during the first three years of life of Equalitarianism and Positive Evaluation of the Child were positively correlated; and Irritability, Punitiveness, Perceives the Child as a Burden, and Ignoring were negatively correlated with intelligence-test scores of sons during the school years. Hurley (1965, 1967) has also reported that measures of parental acceptance versus rejection are correlated with intelligence-test scores of children.

Socio-economic status variables tend to be correlated with parental care of children as well as with intelligence test scores of children (Bayley and Schaefer, 1960). Moore's (1968) finding, that parental variables correlate with intellectual development of the child even after partialling out socio-economic status, suggests that socio-economic status gains much of its predictive power as an index of environment rather than as an index of genetic influences. Research that has demonstrated changes in intellectual functioning following changes in environmental influences would support this interpretation.

Skeels and Harms (1943) and Skodak (1939) found that children in adoptive homes acquire far higher intelligence than their mentally retarded or lower-socio-economic-status natural parents. Skeels and Dye (1939) found that children transferred from an orphanage nursery with little stimulation to the care of older girls in an institution for the mentally retarded showed large gains in IQ, while a contrast group showed losses in IQ in the orphanage. Dawe's (1942) program of verbal stimulation for orphanage children produced marked gains in intelligence, and Kirk (1958) reported significant gains for children enrolled in a special training program for children committed to an institution, while control children showed decreases in mental-test scores. Irwin's (1960) finding that reading stories to children between 13 and 30 months old produced significant increases in language usage also demonstrated that experience can influence language development. Hunt's (1961) book *Intelligence and Experience* and Fowler's (1962) review of *Cognitive Development During Infancy* provided further support for the hypothesis that changes in intellectual stimulation could produce changes in IQ in lower SES Negro infants.

FORMULATION OF OBJECTIVES

The review of correlates of early intellectual development and of intervention research designed to improve intelligence-test scores contributed greatly to determining the objectives of the project. Although the ultimate objective of the project was to increase academic achievement, increasing level of intellectual functioning, particularly in the area of language skills, was the major immediate objective, and criterion of success, of the project. Formulation of subordinate objectives was influenced by the longitudinal data from the Berkeley Growth Study on maternal behavior, child behavior, child intelligence-test scores, and their intercorrelations from infancy through adolescence (Schaefer and Bayley, 1963; Bayley and Schaefer, 1964). Major findings of that research included evidence that maternal loving acceptance had significant positive correlations while maternal hostile rejection had negative correlations with task-oriented behaviors as well as intelligence-test scores, particularly for males. Task-oriented behaviors that were included in that study included consistent cooperation, attentiveness to instructions, low distractibility, persistent effort, interest, and systematic methods of task-performance. These findings of the relationship between maternal care and task-oriented behavior suggested an objective of developing cooperation interests, attentiveness, and persistence in completion of tasks. The relationships that were found among task-oriented behaviors, intelligence, the child's positive relationships, and the quality of maternal care influenced the plans for infant intellectual stimulation.

Review of research on intellectual development suggested that the major components of an infant-education project should be: 1. development of a positive relationship with the child, and in a home-tutoring project, with his family; 2. providing the child with varied and increasingly complex experience; 3. providing the child with age-appropriate language stimulation. This conceptualization of an intellectual stimulation program did not suggest a specific, limited curriculum but rather the need for a broad range of methods for promoting development. Therefore, the program of home tutoring was designed to provide the types of experience and verbal interaction that typically occur in a highly motivated, middle-class family.

PROJECT DESIGN

An experimental group of 31 negro male infants and a control group of 33 negro male infants were selected from door-to-door surveys of two lower-socio-economic neighborhoods in Washington, D. C. Although experimental and control cases were chosen from different neighborhoods, children from the two neighborhoods have comparable readiness scores at school entrance. Only families that had agreed to participate in either the experimental or control group were included. Families that did not meet two of the three criteria — family income under $5000, mother's education under 12 years, and mother's occupation, if any, either unskilled or semiskilled — were excluded as were homes judged to be too crowded or unsuitable for home tutoring. Comparisons between the groups revealed only small differences, many of which favored the control group, on family variables that might be expected to influence the child's intellectual development.

Tutors visited the home of each experimental infant for an hour a day, five days a week, beginning when the infant reached 15 months of age and continuing through 36 months. Participation of the mother and of other family members in the education of the infant was encouraged but not required.

Intelligence tests were administered at a center, by experienced psychologists, to both experimental and control infants at 14, 21, 27, and 36 months, and ratings were made of test behavior. From their observations of the experimental group during tutoring sessions, tutors provided data on the home environments and experiences of the infants, on maternal behavior, and on the social and emotional behavior and language development of the infants. Reliability of these data could be determined from the independent reports of the two tutors who visited an infant on alternate weeks. Daily visits to the home over an extended period yielded more valid data on the home environments of the experimental infants than are usually obtained in behavioral research.

Recognition of the tutor-child relationship as the most important part of the program led to an emphasis on staff selection, training, supervision, and support in the development of the project. The curriculum was to be developed during the course of the project from methods and materials evaluated by the tutors. Because of the initiative and innovativeness required from the tutoring staff, the training, supervision, and group support of the tutors was designed to develop and maintain enthusiasm, morale, and an optimal performance level.

SELECTION OF TUTORS

Tutors were selected from among college graduates because of the high level of functioning required for participation in curriculum development and collection of scientific data. Applicants were judged for pertinent training and experience on the basis of written applications and interviews. Brief essays on structured topics, incorporated as part of the written applications, helped the staff to explore motivations for affiliation with the project and attitudes toward disciplining and interrelating with young children. Personal interviews helped to provide information on warmth of personality, sense of dedication, and personal familiarity with ghetto conditions, as well as on previous training and experience with young children. The tutors selected came from diverse backgrounds. The educational supervisor, or head tutor, was a speech therapist. Others had backgrounds in psychiatric nursing, psycholinguistics, child development, and as teachers in nursery school, Head Start programs, Montessori preschool, and elementary school. Dancing, music, special education, psychology, and sociology degrees were represented. All had previous inner-city involvement and experience with young children.

TRAINING OF TUTORS

Training proceeded simultaneously with recruitment of the sample. Even though, of necessity, recruitment was the first task assigned to the tutors, it in fact proved to be a valuable training device. Their efforts, which took them from door-to-door in both the experimental and control neighborhoods, and required them to complete interview schedules on over two hundred families, caused them to learn first-hand of the effects of poverty and over-crowded living conditions, and to become acquainted with a variety of children and parents in their home environments.

The training program alternated group sessions and workshops with field observations and actual practice with babies. Outside reading was encouraged, and a small library was established of pertinent books, pamphlets, and journal articles covering a broad range of relevant subjects from Montessori and Russian Day Care of Infants to The National Safety Council's Safety Guidelines for Babysitters. Films were shown on early child care. *Palmour Street*, depicting the daily life of a Negro family in a small Southern town, described both negative and positive influences that parents can have on the mental and emotional development of their children. *Abby's First Two Years* demonstrated the physical and behavioral changes of infancy and childhood in reverse sequence from two years down to two months.

Throughout the initial training period, and as part of on-going training after the tutoring was under way, various specialists spoke to the tutors on subjects related to child development. Particularly effective were those who related first-hand accounts on "how-to-do-it." Among these was a mother who had published a book on the education of her physically and neurologically handicapped infant son. Another demonstrated language-development techniques which had proved successful in the education of her two adopted children. One of the tutors, a former Montessori teacher, gave a series of talks on preparation of the learning environment and Montessori-oriented language instruction. Her talks stimulated interest in the written works of Maria Montessori, of which *The Absorbent Mind* (1963 translation) was most read and discussed. Stoner's (1914) most detailed "how-to-do-it" book, describing her precocious daughter's early education, stirred lively discussions of methodology and principles of education. Pertinent scientific journal articles were read and discussed. Representative was Dawe's (1942) report of a successful orphanage intervention program with a curriculum based on training the children in the comprehension of words and concepts, looking at and discussing pictures, listening to poems and stories, and going on short trips and excursions.

The tutors made observations of fifteen-month infants in a variety of settings including orphanages, a welfare department's institution for homeless and neglected children, and middle-class homes. Middle-class mothers contributed lists of toys, activities, games, music, books, pictures, descriptions of trips and room decorations used in the education of their young children.

Each tutor conducted practice sessions at the Center with non-sample infants, observed and evaluated in turn by the others. This was followed by a two week pilot trial of all procedures developed for intervention, reporting, and data collection, each tutor visiting the home of a non-sample baby every day in the prescribed manner. The tutors reported that this last exercise gave them the assurance they needed to undertake the intervention.

STAFF RELATIONSHIPS

The unique nature of the collaboration with the tutors, participation of the entire staff in planning and trouble shooting, and morale-building elements embedded in the network of interrelationships, all contributed immeasurably toward sustaining a high level of enthusiasm and dedication among the personnel. Most of the tutoring took place in environmentally difficult situations in which the tutors were not always able to remain aloof from the stresses and traumatic events that invaded the lives of the families. Overcrowding, compounded when school-age children were home for holidays and the summer months, sometimes raised almost insurmountable obstacles to the child-centered approach of the program. The tutors were continuously being faced with problems which required group support and deliberation and, at times, staff intervention. The remarkable ability of the racially integrated staff, consisting of the principal investigator, project director, project supervisor, educational supervisor, nine tutors and a secretary to function as a coordinated unit to promote their common goals, was one of the project's greatest assets.

The project supervisor was responsible for general management at the project, as the principal investigator and project director were not housed at the project. He was to a great extent also responsible for the general atmosphere under which the others worked. He was a soft-spoken, albeit authoritative person, who expended much effort at making the rather dreary and dilapidated project quarters cheerful and homelike. The walls were filled with pictures of project children, curriculum and holiday materials, and teaching suggestions. He treated the tutors with respect and consideration, and was resourceful in finding ways to assist them. The families cooperated when he made suggestions; and it was he who could get a mother to clean up a special area for the tutoring, or convince her not to withdraw her child from the project. When a tutor felt the need of protection or the support of an authority figure, he could be depended upon to respond effectively and diplomatically.

The educational supervisor, a contemporary of the tutors, played the role of collaborator rather than superior, actually participating by tutoring a subject herself. Their meetings were conducted on the order of workshops at which the tutors had fullest participation, exchanging ideas, making suggestions, assisting one another, freely sharing both successes and failures. She presided over brief daily staff meetings with the tutors at which curriculum and data-collection information were exchanged and problems aired. Once a week the agenda was broadened to include an invited specialist, or discussions of educational techniques and learning theory; and these meetings were attended by the entire staff. She conducted special case conferences focusing on the environmental conditions and educational progress of a single subject from time to time, which were attended by the two concerned tutors and the supervisory staff. With time thus allotted for the special consideration of the progress and development of a particular subject, solutions to difficult tutoring problems frequently evolved.

The principal investigator and the project director developed personal relationships with the tutors, made themselves accessible, elicited suggestions, listened. The fact that they regularly attended weekly staff meetings and case conferences, participated in curriculum workshops, and aided in the deliberation of family problems, served to communicate to the tutors the scientific importance of the intervention. But most important of all, the tutors were highly motivated, dedicated people with a personal interest in the well-being of the children and of their families.

HOME TUTORING RELATIONSHIPS

The process of attempting to establish a good relationship between the designated tutors and the members of the family in each home was the first order of business and proved to be a task about which few generalizations can be made. In some instances the mothers were sincerely interested in the education of their children; they cooperated to the best of their abilities and participated in the tutoring sessions whenever they could. At the other end of the continuum were mothers who showed so little response that one must conclude that they participated in the experiment only because they were paid for the tutoring sessions. In between there were mothers who showed varying degrees of interest and who at times cooperated more with one tutor than another. There were some lonely mothers who so welcomed the tutors' visits that they tended to monopolize the tutoring time with their conversation. In these instances the tutor would play the role of sympathetic listener and at the same time attempt to direct the mother toward active involvement in the tutoring. Whether the mothers would be able to tolerate the invasion of privacy and restriction of movement occasioned by receiving a visiting tutor into the home day after day was an initial concern but caused no great problems.

According to data that was collected, those mothers who failed to become positively involved in the tutoring usually were either hostilely involved with, or tended to ignore their children, and the tutoring did not fare well for both reasons. One such mother is described by the tutors at a case conference.

> Mrs. T regards the children as a burden and seems quite insensitive to their emotional needs. B apparently bears the brunt of her frustrations and, as a result, is showing signs of becoming disturbed. Frequently, the tutors have been unable to get into the apartment at the time for the session or have found the children alone. The mother will often become entangled in the explanations she gives and contradict

herself, making it obvious that she is not being honest. On Monday, the tutor learned that W had swallowed lighter fluid and had been taken to the hospital. On Tuesday, the tutor worked with W, but Mrs. T was very short-tempered, shouting threats at the children throughout the session.

Many of the subjects were found to be passive and inactive, engaging in repetitious unimaginative play with one toy or object over long periods of time. When the tutoring was initiated, the tutors entered their new environments as quietly and unobtrusively as possible, considering their mere presence almost a sufficient source of stimulation. Few toys were brought along — perhaps a ball, some keys, or inexpensive objects in the tutor's pocketbook. Food tins, graduated in size, collected by the mother, were covered with brightly colored paper by tutor and mother, together, and used by the subject as a nesting or towering toy.

Traumatic events which affected the family, such as evictions, fires, disturbances in family relationships, and shifts in caretakers, usually disturbed the child, rendering the tutoring less effective or interrupting it entirely.

Staff meetings and case conferences helped to solve or at least to modify a variety of problems in the area of tutoring relationships. To illustrate, when it was noted that a particularly unmotivated and uncooperative subject liked cars, the tutors were able to achieve a breakthrough by following the staff's suggestion to conduct future tutoring sessions in a car. In another instance, a tense, withdrawn, and uncommunicative child was assigned to only one tutor, who was instructed to take him along on her rounds to the homes of her other subjects once a week with a stop for lunch or ice cream at a restaurant. Increased affect and language resulted from the more intensive relationship that she was able to establish. A third child, restrained in his crib most of the day, would run about aimlessly when released for tutoring, resisting all attempts to gain his cooperation and focused attention. When the tutors became discouraged at their inability to effect progress, it was recommended that the project supervisor replace the tutors temporarily. The restraints that a kindly authoritative male was able to impose proved effective, and the tutors were able at a later date to resume the tutoring with better results. Another type of problem developed when the Welfare Department prepared to take custody of the children of a family being evicted from their quarters, thus threatening the project with the loss of a subject. The staff provided temporary housing for the children and successfully assisted the mother in obtaining new quarters.

DEVELOPMENT OF LANGUAGE SKILLS

As stated earlier, increasing the level of intellectual functioning of the subjects, particularly in the area of language skills, was the major immediate objective and criterion of success of the project. This was to be accomplished through the provision of varied and increasingly complex types of experience and verbal interaction utilizing a broad range of methods, materials, and activities for promoting development, rather than a specific limited curriculum. Thus, while a brief overview of the programming, techniques, experiences, and materials which were used will be presented here, there is no intention to represent that these are the only specific plans and stimulus materials that could have been used. Rather, the orientation of the tutors was that whatever they did use would be exploited to the fullest for its stimulus value in teaching basic vocabulary, receptive and expressive language, and concept formation.

Even though the tutors were encouraged to vary their methods to meet the needs of the individual subjects, curriculum guidelines developed by the staff, the many interactions and discussions among the tutors, and other mechanisms to be described tended to bring about certain uniformities in the tutoring program. All tutors were instructed to reinforce positive personality characteristics that should help the child succeed in school (*e.g.,* cooperativeness, friendliness, attentiveness, concentration, perseverance, curiosity, resourcefulness, and goal-directed behavior). The child was to be encouraged to develop feelings of competence and of human worth and to assert himself in a positive way. Toys, materials, and experiences were to be used to broaden the subject's comprehension and meaningful use of language. Time was to be spent, preferably at the beginning of the tutoring session, in varied activities with books. The particular selection of books, toys, and ideas that were provided tended to somewhat shape and direct the tutor's efforts. Methods discussed at meetings spread from tutor to tutor, thus developing shared interests and activities. Their very collaboration in pairs for the tutoring of a single child superimposed a common order on their planning. The fact that they for the most part collaborated with a different partner for each child tutored, effected a further spread of the same ideas.

Written materials were developed as guidelines, and also to stimulate the tutor's production of like materials. The educational supervisor developed a detailed list of activities with suggested language to accompany each activity. The list included gross motor, fine motor, and sensory behavior, activities of daily living, and cultural activities. Examples are, "climbing in and out of boxes" accompanied by, "Get up. Get down. You're in the box. Get in. Get out," and "presence and absence of sound," accompanied by, "I hear it. All gone. It's quiet. Shhh. Turn it off. Turn it on." She also developed a rather comprehensive list of specific toys, materials, and learning situations, listing graduated levels of difficulty, *e.g.,* "Puzzles. 1. Can take pieces out of board, 2. Attempts to put pieces in wrong position, 3. Succeeds in putting one piece in successfully, 4. Can put all pieces in correctly." Twenty-four such gradations are listed under "Books."

As the tutoring progressed, curriculum items were developed, incorporating language and concept formation skills designed to accelerate the pace of the tutoring and provide more action-oriented development of speech. Processes by which simple materials could be easily and quickly transformed into useful toys and articles were described, as were numerous methods for sorting and classifying, differentiating, and discriminating materials. To illustrate, a dozen uses were proposed for jingle bells, using big ones, little ones, colored ones, gold and silver ones, and including sorting, counting, making ornaments and rhythm instruments, playing games, and singing. The tutors caught the spirit of writing the items and began generating many more which they used with the subjects.

The following descriptions of tutoring techniques and materials, summarized from tutors' reports, represent only a sample of the total array. Listed under subheadings of Labelling, Books, Experiences, Jigsaw Puzzles, Games, Music and Rhythm, and Toys, the selection of topics and subdivisions is arbitrary; they are not arranged in chronological sequence; however they were all used toward a common goal, the development of language skills.

LABELLING

Teaching the child to be aware of and to learn the names of objects in his environment played an important part at the beginning of the program. "Oh, Oh! There's a mirror. Let's look at Johnny in the mirror. He has two eyes, two ears, a nose and a mouth," the tutor would say while pointing to the head parts. "Show me your nose and your eyes," she would continue, helping him with his response when necessary. A valuable game that most subjects enjoyed was, "Let's look out the window and see what we can see." After the child would mention what he could see, the tutor would point out additional things, such as animals, people, vehicles, stores, houses, flowers, birds, trees, or what people were doing. At times she might call his attention to unusual occurrences, such as wind and rain storms, snow falling, fire trucks, or an ambulance. A less direct method of labelling might take place as part of an activity. "Look what I have – a red rubber ball. Let's sit, spread our legs apart, and roll it. Here it comes. Oh, it rolled under the chair. Can you get it?"

The project children reacted to labelling in different ways. Some took great pride in naming things for parents, relatives, friends, and the tutors. Others played the role of the tutor and asked, "What's that?" indiscriminately pointing to both familiar and unfamiliar objects. No matter which way they reacted, they were learning that things have names, and what they didn't know they could ask about.

BOOKS

The project made a systematic effort to acquaint the children with both picture books and the printed words. Tutors were expected to allot some time to books every day, increasing the amount with the child's maturity and responsiveness. "Get the children hooked on books," became the byword at the project center.

Although the single-object-on-a-page, brightly colored picture book was generally voted the most successful in attracting the very young child, some became interested early in books showing many small objects to a page. They seemed to enjoy each object, isolating it from the others, naming it, describing it, then moving on to another.

Typically the child would sit in the tutor's lap, or beside her, and would be encouraged to handle the book and turn the pages. Relating familiar objects to the pictures was a necessary first step. Thus the tutor would point out that the ball in her hand and the flat round red disk in the picture were one and the same. The labelling games being carried on in the household were extended to books. "That's a chair. Let's find a picture of a chair. Look at those keys! Just like mine!" became a delightful game for a beginner when enlivened by an enthusiastic tutor. The children particularly enjoyed pretending to eat food represented in the pictures. Soon the bookwork progressed to making up stories about the pictures, using actions and people familiar to the child.

In time the children accepted books as a regular activity. Each book was used until it became familiar, or as long as it held the child's interest. After a while he was given freedom to choose a book from several offered. For most, the beginning of the session, when the child was neither over-stimulated nor fatigued from active play, proved the best time to read. At first interest was fleeting, but later some were able to spend entire sessions with books.

The language used and responses elicited became more complex as the child's vocabulary increased. The simple initial response of "choo-choo" to a pictured train was later expanded to include detailed accounts of a trip to the railroad station, or a discussion of what makes a train go. Special interests were indulged so that while one child would be enjoying a series of books about horses, another would be involved with foods. As the subjects grew older, books about cars, trucks, or almost anything on wheels were among the most prized. The child's favorite books frequently were left in the home.

Reading became more meaningful when pictures and stories related to at least some aspect of the familiar. The richer the child's experiences the greater became the possibility of interesting him in books and the more effective became their use. Using a book in combination with an experience helped to relate the abstract to the real; and rereading it the next day aided in recall of a pleasant experience. Building up associations between books and experiences continued throughout the tutoring.

Scrapbooks were considered important supplements to the reading and various kinds were made, sometimes with mothers joining in the fun. Pictures or drawings illustrating trips, or of animals, cars, or foods; mementoes of special holidays; photographs of the child and his family; the child's own finger paintings or drawings; pressed leaves or flowers — almost anything was used to increase the child's enjoyment in his "own book." Especially when related to a sequence of events or to various elements of a single activity, scrapbooks served as a link between the picture book and the story book.

Story books and recordings were used successfully in combination. For example, the story of Peter and the Wolf would be read by the tutor as the child looked at the pictures. Then the record would be played, with tutor and child listening to the sequence, pointing to the appropriate pictures, naming the characters, and identifying the actions in the recording.

EXPERIENCES

Although all events, including the entire tutoring program to which the child was exposed, could be included in the concept of experiences, this section is limited to events that occurred away from the subject's home which tended to broaden and enrich his understanding of his environment. Not only were excursions away from home considered a rewarding educational tool, they became indispensable where school-age children crowded the homes at vacation time.

Many neighborhood walks were taken, and activities during these walks included mailing a letter, watching the milkman make his deliveries, meeting another child, collecting brightly colored leaves, playing in the snow, feeding a squirrel or pigeon, noting the flight of a flock of starlings. Such walks often enabled a child who didn't have a pet to become acquainted with a cat or dog. If the animal appeared friendly, the child might be encouraged to approach it, pat it, note its eyes, nose, mouth, and hair. The walk might be to the playground, where the sandbox, swings, seesaw, the playhouse storing games and equipment, and the boys and girls of all sizes would provide substance for expanding knowledge and adding new vocabulary. A walk to a neighborhood store for an ice-cream cone or animal crackers was always a delight, and there were packages and materials on the shelves to be discussed. Visits were sometimes made to the home of the tutor or to a friendly neighbor, where the child might see objects or pets not in his own home. One child who loved horses was taken for pony rides and trips to see horses, finally getting a ride on a horse. Each child was taken to the public library so that he might have the experience of selecting a book, seeing it charged out by the librarian, and taking it home.

The children were brought into the center in small groups for birthday parties, and in large groups for holiday celebrations. There were picnics in the park with the families participating. Other trips included ones to the zoo, nature center, museums, aquarium, supermarket, 5¢-and-10¢ store, toy store, pet shop, gas station, construction site, bakery, dairy, police station, fire house, school, bus terminal, post office, airport, and the circus.

JIGSAW PUZZLES

Over fifty different jigsaw puzzles aided in developing perceptual and problem-solving abilities in the subjects while serving as stimulus materials for vocabulary development and concept formation. The difficulty of the puzzles varied in accordance with the number, size, and complexity of the parts. The simplest ones consisted of whole objects placed into matching spaces. One tutor developed eight recommendations for working with puzzles: 1. present puzzles as enjoyable games; 2. demonstrate how the pieces are placed; 3. give each puzzle piece a name; 4. begin by removing and replacing one piece at a time, gradually increasing the number; 5. finish one puzzle before starting another; 6. if the task proves too frustrating, change to a more relaxed activity; 7. praise the child's successes with a smile, applause, or a treat; 8. present puzzles already mastered for relaxation and reinforcement.

GAMES

As the spirit of the tutoring was one of fun, games, and cameraderie, much teaching was done through both improvised and traditional children's games. These began with simple peek-a-boo, pat-a-cake, and ball games and graduated to hide-and-seek, treasure hunts, guessing games, and sorting and matching games. Games helped to engage the many children in the environment as teaching aides. Concepts such as *up-down* were taught through Ring Around a Rosey, London Bridge, Skip to My Lou, and other circle games. Variations of musical chairs and finger games were popular.

MUSIC AND RHYTHM

Music was introduced through singing songs and listening to records. Subjects who were not particularly fond of musical activities were not forced to participate. The tutor and a subject, or a group, would become involved in such activities as clapping hands, swaying back and forth, walking fast and slow, marching, and hopping and running to music.

For more advanced musical activities, instruments such as bells, drums, tambourines, and musical sticks were used. These helped introduce the child to different kinds and qualities of sounds. Some instruments were bought; others were made by the tutors and children with the aid of oatmeal boxes, cans, jingle bells, paper plates, milk cartons, sticks, and the like. Instruments were usually introduced one at a time.

Music helped the children develop socially and was an integral part of group activities, such as at Christmas, Easter, and birthday celebrations. Nursery rhymes in song and the songs that accompanied circle games were the ones enjoyed most and were readily committed to memory.

TOYS

Children and tutors alike appeared to derive much happiness from commercial toys and equipment. Making toys out of materials already in the environment was seldom undertaken with great enthusiasm, the tutors being quick to point out the need for new and colorful objects in the drab environments.

The impact of toys on the program should not be overlooked or minimized. The toys and their uses were too numerous to describe here in detail, but each in its turn was utilized to support the relationship between tutor and subject and to promote language comprehension and learning. Included were pop beads and beads for stringing, dump-and-fill bottles, play dough and clay, building blocks, nesting toys, balls, puzzles, plastic bolts and screws, tinker toys, peg boards, pounding benches, gear-turning toys, lock-and-key boxes, toy telephones, musical instruments, record players, magnets, magnetic letters, prisms, flashlights, sandpaper, various household tools, balloons, spin tops, magnifying glasses, dolls, toy animals, digging and garden tools, a kiddy car, a tyke bike, a tricycle, a wagon, various mechanical toys, and a multitude of both books and art materials.

RESULTS

Pretesting of both the experimental and control groups on the Bayley Infant Mental Test at 14 months confirmed earlier research findings that low-socio-economic-status infants do not have low mental test scores prior to fifteen months of age. At 21 months the control group had a mean IQ of 90, which remained near that level through four years of age. This finding, that without intervention a relatively low but stable level of mental-test scores was established by 21 months of age, suggests that intellectual stimulation should begin prior to that time. The tutored group dropped slightly below norms by 21 months — Mean IQ = 97 — but with continued tutoring climbed to a mean Stanford-Binet IQ of 106 by 36 months of age. These findings suggest that, optimally, tutoring should begin before 14 months of age, a conclusion that was supported by the tutors' reports that some of the infants showed signs of early deprivation at the time tutoring began. The higher scores of the experimental as contrasted with the control subjects were shown for verbal, nonverbal, and memory components of the Stanford-Binet scores at three years, suggesting that the effects of tutoring were not limited to a single area of mental functioning. This conclusion was supported by findings of significant differences on The Johns Hopkins Perceptual Test and on the Peabody Picture Vocabulary Test. A cluster of task-oriented behavior ratings from the Bayley Infant Behavior Profile, including ratings of object orientation, goal-directedness, attention span, cooperativeness, and adequacy of the test, also showed significant differences between tutored and untutored infants at three years of age.

Although mental-test scores during and at the termination of the period of intensive tutoring supported the initial hypothesis that tutoring would increase mental-test scores, a year after termination of tutoring the approximately 17-point IQ difference between experimental and control subjects had dropped to 10 points, the experimental group dropping from a mean IQ of 106 to 100 on the Stanford-Binet. This drop in scores after termination of early education programs has also been reported by Caldwell and Smith (1968) and by Gray and Klaus (1969), although these authors also report residual differences between groups at followup. The need for evaluation of long-term as well as short-term effects of intervention is shown by these studies.

Ratings were made of maternal behavior with a revised version of the Maternal Behavior Research Instrument (Schaefer, Bell and Bayley, 1959) at 16 months and with a Maternal Behavior with Tutor and Child Inventory (Schaefer and Aaronson, 1966) at 30 and 36 months. Adjective rating scales on child behavior were completed at 16, 19, 22, 27, and 36 months, and a more detailed and comprehensive Infant Behavior Inventory (Schaefer and Aaronson, 1967) was completed at 36 months of age. From extensive statistical analysis, a cluster of ratings that define maternal hostile rejection was found at 16 months — Withdrawal of Relationship, Punishment, Use of Fear to Control, Irritability, and Punitiveness — and for the 30- and 36-month ratings — Hostile Involvement, Hostile Detachment, Low Interest in the Child's Education, Low Verbal Expressiveness, and Low Involvement with the Child. A cluster of ratings defining child hostility at 36 months was also isolated, and that included ratings of Hostility from the Adjective Rating Scales and Belligerence, Negativism, and Irritability from the Infant Behavior Inventory. Significant consistency in ratings of maternal hostility at 16, 30, and 36 months was found that supported earlier findings that a mother's behavior with her child tends to be stable through time (Schaefer and Bayley, 1967). The ratings of maternal hostility at the several age periods were also significantly correlated with ratings of the child's hostility at 36 months.

The findings that ratings of the maternal hostility and child hostility that were made by the tutors were significantly correlated with the independent ratings of the task-oriented behavior and with mental test scores at 36 months, confirmed the results of the Berkeley Growth Study (Schaefer and Bayley, 1963; Bayley and Schaefer, 1964). The finding that supplementary tutoring and maternal behavior have similar effects upon child behavior and mental-test scores provided further support for both findings. Examination of the cases suggested that the effects of maternal care and supplementary tutoring are additive, *i.e.,* the children who achieved the highest mental-test scores were those who received tutoring and had a positive relationship with the mother.

DISCUSSION AND CONCLUSIONS

Some of the major conclusions that were derived from this project that might influence the planning of future programs in early child care and education will be discussed. Although some of the conclusions are derived from the statistical data of this and other projects, other conclusions are based upon observations, interpretations of our experience, and reflections about the implications of research on early development. The first set of conclusions about intellectual development were derived from the statistical data of the project:

1. Negro children from lower-socio-economic-status families show above average mental-test scores when provided with appropriate intellectual stimulation. The differences between the tutored and untutored groups that were found in this study clearly indicate that children's potential for higher levels of intellectual functioning can be partially developed through even five hours a week of one-to-one tutoring. Of course the limits of intellectual development of the group have not been determined from this limited intervention. The finding that the lowest Stanford-Binet IQ – 89 – of the tutored group at three years of age was equal to the Mean IQ at three of the untutored group, indicates that additional stimulation can provide a substantial change in level of intellectual functioning.

2. The quality of maternal care, as well as supplementary tutoring, significantly influences early intellectual development. Data from this project have provided additional evidence that maternal positive involvement, interest in the child's education, and verbal expressiveness with the child are related to his early intellectual development. The description of a good mother-child relationship would probably also apply to the description of a good tutor-child relationship. The goals of the project and the methods used to achieve those goals were to some extent guided by previous research on parent behavior, child behavior, and intellectual development.

3. The child's social behavior and the child's early intellectual development show substantial intercorrelations. The relationship between a mother's acceptance of the child and her educational efforts is paralleled by the relationship between the child's competence and his adjustment. Perhaps the controversy between proponents of promoting the social and emotional development of children and of promoting the cognitive development of children is unnecessary, for an optimal education program can and should promote both competence and adjustment.

4. The child's education should begin prior to fifteen months of age. The most reasonable hypothesis would be that the development of early relationships and

interests during the first year of life can influence the child's later intellectual development. The importance of early exposure to language stimulation has not yet been definitely established, but some evidence that early vocalizations may be related to later intelligence would support the need for early language experience. The experience of this project would not support an emphasis upon promoting early sensory-motor development but would support the development of early relationships, interests, and language.

5. The need to plan for continuing education in order to maintain and increase intellectual functioning is strongly supported. The regression on mean IQ scores that was found after termination of intensive tutoring in this and other early-education projects suggests that brief early stimulation projects may have limited, if any, long-term effects upon intelligence. These findings suggest the need for planning for the total educational experience of the child rather than for limited periods. Clear evidence that early intellectual stimulation has more long-term effects than subsequent intellectual stimulation has not been presented. Clarke and Clarke (1960) have found that young, mentally retarded adults, after leaving severely deprived environments, have shown mean IQ gains of 16 points over a six year period. Klineberg (1935) and Lee (1957) have reported IQ gains during the elementary school years for Negro children who move into northern cities. These studies suggest a need to shift our emphasis from the need for early education to the need for early and continued education in the family as well as in the school.

The experience of the project also leads to conclusions about the needs of infant educators which might apply also to caretakers, parents, and teachers:

1. There is a need for training and experience in child care and education. The great variations in family care and education found in all social groups as well as in this study suggest that skills in child care must be developed through training and supervised experience. Although academic training might be helpful, apprenticeship training is probably necessary to learn the specifics of child care and education. The varied experiences in child care of the tutoring staff of this project contributed to the development of skills during the course of the project. If it were possible, it would be desirable to have a staff replicate a project to see if the experience they had gained led to increased effectiveness.

2. There is a need for supervision, guidance, and opportunities for consultation as well as sharing of experiences among tutors. The morale of the tutoring staff was exceptionally good throughout the course of the project, despite the difficulties encountered. Although the initial motivation of the staff was important, the opportunity to discuss their problems and successes, the shared experiences, the support from supervisors and colleagues, and the attitude that the staff was cooperatively engaged in an important contribution to education were also important for their continued enthusiasm. Would it be possible to organize similar

supportive groups for mothers or teachers in our educational institutions? The isolation of mothers in their homes and of teachers in their classrooms, with little opportunity for supportive consultation or sharing with peers, may be one of the major problems in child care and education.

3. There is a need for varied materials and methods and for a range of activities to maintain a high level of interest and enthusiasm of tutors. Throughout the course of the project, new toys and materials or an enthusiastic presentation of new methods would arouse renewed interest in the tutors. Field trips and birthday and holiday parties for the children and their parents were of much interest to the staff as well as the children. Changes in routines, and attractive materials, influence teachers and caretakers as well as children. Perhaps this conclusion would apply equally to mothers, classroom teachers, and other caretakers of young children. Would it be possible to develop inexpensive age-graded book and toy libraries and make them available to parents through neighborhood schools?

SUMMARY

A review of research on intellectual development prompted the development of this home-tutoring project for infants. Findings on the effects of tutoring and maternal care suggest a need for programs that will provide early and continued intellectual stimulation. The hope that enduring changes in the quality of parental care and education might provide continued stimulation suggests a need to supplement child-centered programs with parent- or family-centered programs in early education. The experience of the project also suggests some generalizations about the educational process that might guide future program development.

1. Education is a process that begins at birth and continues until death. The development of relationships, language, interests, task-oriented behaviors, and skills during infancy influences the child's success in academic education. Learning does not end with the completion of the school day, school year, or formal education but continues, with or without planning, throughout the life span.

2. The family is a major educational institution in our society. Statistical data indicate that schools do not change the rate of intellectual functioning that is developed by the family, despite the fact that disadvantaged children have higher intellectual potential than is being developed by their current environments. Support for the child's education in the family should supplement the current emphasis on the school.

3. Educational planning should recognize that each person is both a teacher and a student throughout the life span. Educators should assist in the development of the teaching skills of both parents and future parents and should coordinate the educational functions of the family and the school. Children should be given ap-

propriate training and supervised experience in teaching that will allow them to educate one another and will prepare them for adult roles as parent-educators.

4. The major contribution of this project is not the development of a limited curriculum, although specific methods and materials have been discussed, but rather the development of a different perspective on the educational process. Assumptions about the roles of relationships, of varied and increasingly complex experience, and of the language stimulation that accompanies those relationships and experiences have guided the development of the project and have been supported by the experience of the project. Both the short-term and long-term data of the project suggest the need for a comprehensive system of education that goes beyond the current emphasis upon academic education to include pre-academic, para-academic, and post-academic education in the family and community.

ACKNOWLEDGMENTS | 14

Regarding the Schaefer and Aaronson paper, the authors wish to acknowledge with gratitude the help of the many persons who have contributed to this project. The project was developed, with the support of Dr. David Shakow, while the authors were members of the Laboratory of Psychology, National Institute of Mental Health. The project was launched by Mary Leo Vincellete and was continued by Paul H. Furfey and Thomas J. Harte through a National Institute of Mental Health Special Grant to the Catholic University of America. Others to whom thanks are due are: the National Institute of Mental Health project officer, William C. Rhodes; project supervisor, Belford Fisher; educational supervisors: Maureen Nichols and Lillie Davidson; tutors: Lucille Banks, Jane Blais, Patricia Chernoff, Patricia Gentry, Bonita Jones, Veronica Lake, Betty Pair, Carolyn Parnell, Karen Salzmann, Joicey White, and Carol Zucker; research assistants: Julie Forrest and Betty Burgoon; and secretaries: Prudence Tucker, Terry Kidner, and Joe Quinn; all have made major contributions to the development of this program. The cooperation of the families and children in this educational innovation was essential.

REFERENCES | 14

Bayley, N. Comparisons of mental and motor test scores for ages 1-15 months by sex, birth order, race, geographical location, and education of parents. *Child Development*, 1965, *36*, 379-411.

Bayley, N. Consistency and variability in the growth of intelligence from birth to 18 years. *Journal of Genetic Psychology*, 1949, *75*, 165-196.

Bayley, N. Learning in adulthood: the role of intelligence. In H. Klausmeier and C. Harris, (Eds.) *Analyses of Concept Learning*. New York: Academic Press, 1966.

Bayley, N. and Schaefer, E. S. Correlations of maternal and child behaviors with the development of mental abilities: data from the Berkeley growth study. *Monographs of the Society for Research in Child Development*, 1964, *29*, No. 6 (Serial No. 97).

Bayley, N. and Schaefer, E. S. Relationships between socio-economic variables and the behavior of mothers toward young children. *Journal of Genetic Psychology*, 1960, *96*, 61-77.

Bradway, K. P. Predictive value of Stanford-Binet preschool items. *Journal of Educational Psychology*, 1945, *36*, 1-16.

Caldwell, B. N. and Smith, L. E. Day care for the very young: prime opportunity for primary prevention. Paper presented at the American Public Health Association Meeting, Detroit, Michigan, November, 1968.

Clarke, A. D. B. and Clarke, A. M. Some recent advances in the study of early deprivation. *Journal of Child Psychology and Psychiatry*, 1960, *1*, 26-36.

Cronbach, L. J. Year-to-year correlations of mental tests: a review of the Hofstaetter analysis. *Child Development*, 1967, *38*, 283-289.

Dawe, H. C. A study of the effect of an educational program upon language development and related mental functions in young children. *Journal of Experimental Education*, 1942, *11*, 200-209.

Fowler, W. Cognitive learning in infancy and early childhood. *Psychological Bulletin*, 1962, *59*, 116-152.

Francis-Williams, J. and Yule, W. The Bayley infant scales of mental and motor development: an exploratory study with an English sample. *Developmental Medicine and Child Neurology*, 1967, *9*, 391-401.

Gray, S. W. and Klaus, R. A. The early training project: a seventh year report. Nashville, Tennessee: John F. Kennedy Center for Research on Education and Human Development, George Peabody College for Teachers, 1969.

Hindley, C. B. Stability and change in abilities up to five years: group trends, *Journal of Child Psychology and Psychiatry*, 1965, *6*, 85-99.

Hofstaetter, P. R. The changing composition of intelligence: a study in T-technique. *Journal of Genetic Psychology*, 1954, *85*, 159-164.

Hunt, J. McV. *Intelligence and Experience*. New York: Ronald Press, 1961.

Hurley, J. R. Parental malevolence and children's intelligence. *Journal of Consulting Psychology*, 1967, *31*, 199-204.

Hurley, J. R. Parental acceptance-rejection and children's intelligence. *Merrill Palmer Quarterly*, 1965, *11*, 19-31.

Irwin, O. C. Infant speech: effect of systematic reading of stories. Journal of Speech and Hearing Research, 1960, *3*.

Kennedy, W. A., Van De Riet, W., and White, J. C., Jr. A normative sample of intelligence and achievement of Negro elementary school children in the southeastern United States. *Monographs of the Society for Research in Child Development*, 1963, *28*, No. 6, (Serial No. 90).

Kirk, S. A. *Early Education of the Mentally Retarded: an Experimental Study.* Urbana, Ill., University of Illinois Press, 1958.

Klineberg, O. *Negro intelligence and selective migration.* New York: Columbia University Press, 1935.

Lee, E. S. Negro intelligence and selective migration: a Philadelphia test of the Klineberg hypothesis. *American Sociological Review*, 1957, *16*, 227-233.

Milner, E. A study of the relationship between reading readiness in grade one school children and patterns of parent-child interaction. *Child Development*, 1951, *22*, 95-112.

Miner, J. B. *Intelligence in the United States.* New York: Springer, 1957.

Montessori, M. *The Absorbent mind.* Madras, India: Theosophical Publishing House, 1963.

Moore, T. Language and intelligence: A longitudinal study of the first 8 years. *Human Development*, 1968, *11*, 88-106.

Schaefer, E. S. Does the sampling method produce the negative correlation of mean IQ with age reported by Kennedy, Van De Riet, and White. *Child Development*, 1965, *36*, 257-259.

Schaefer, E. S. and Aaronson, M. Infant behavior inventory. Mimeograph, 1967.

Schaefer, E. S. and Aaronson, M. Mother's behavior with tutor and child during tutoring sessions. Mimeograph, 1966.

Schaefer, E. S. and Bayley, N. Maternal behavior, child behavior, and their intercorrelations from infancy through adolescence. *Monographs of the Society for Research in Child Development*, 1963, *28*, (No. 3, Serial No. 87).

Schaefer, E. S., Bell, R. Q. and Bayley, N. Development of a maternal behavior research instrument. *Journal of Genetic Psychology*, 1959, *95*, 83-104.

Skeels, H. M. and Dye, H. B. A study of the effects of differential stimulation on mentally retarded children. *Proceedings of the American Association on Mental Deficiency*, 1939, *44*, 114-136.

Skeels, H. M. and Harms, I. Children with inferior social histories; Their mental development in adoptive homes. *Journal of Genetic Psychology*, 1943, *72*, 283-294.

Skodak, M. Children in foster homes: A study of mental development. *Iowa Studies in Child Welfare*, 1939, *16*, No. 1.

Stoner, W. S. *Natural Education.* New York: Bobbs Merrill, 1914.

Terman, L. M. and Merrill, M. A. *Measuring intelligence: a guide to the administration of the new revised Stanford-Binet tests of intelligence.* Boston: Houghton Mifflin, 1937.

Van Alstyne, D. The environment of three-year-old children: factors related to intelligence and vocabulary tests. *Columbia University Teachers College Contributions to Education*, 1929, No. 366.

Palmer | *Introduction* | 15

The following program was implemented to determine "the effects of minimal intervention at age two and three upon subsequent intellective development." The program could be described as "minimal" when considering both the length of time the children participated, and when considering the scope of the curriculum. Each child participated in the program for two one-hour sessions a week over a period of eight months. The curriculum consisted of basic concepts — prepositions and adjectives which are used in all cultures and which were assumed to be prerequisite to most subsequent and more complex learning. The concepts were ordered by difficulty, as well as by meaningfulness.

The manner in which the concepts were taught was considered as important as the concepts themselves. A one-to-one Instructor-child ratio enables the establishment of an affective bond between child and Instructor and fostered the association of positive affect and the "learning" situation. It was also hypothesized that in such a situation, with interesting materials, the child would learn of the necessity to organize sensory or verbal input in order to make an appropriate response to another person, i.e., the Instructor. Care was taken to respond to the individual needs of each child, and children were entered into the training program at their current level of concept knowledge and proceeded through the curriculum at their own pace.

Perhaps one of the most interesting outcomes of this study is revealed in the comparison of the concept training group with another group, the Discovery Group. The latter group did not receive concept training, but spent an equal amount of time in a one-to-one relationship with an adult and with the same materials. Both groups showed improvement on criterion performance tasks and the Stanford-Binet, thus leading Palmer to assume that some factor other than the concept training, *per se*, was responsible for the improvement in intellectual functioning. The regular meeting with an adult, the positive affect developed in the one-to-one situation, or the reinforcement provided specifically when the child made an organized and appropriate response may all have played a role. Most apparent in Palmer's paper, as well as Schaefer's and Aaronson's papers, are the additive and interacting positive results attributed to the positive relationship between child and Instructor, and the close association between affect for the teacher and affect for learning.

Francis H. Palmer

Minimal Intervention at Age Two and Three and Subsequent Intellective Changes

15

A. DIAGNOSIS OF EDUCATIONAL NEEDS

It has been said that "compensatory education has been tried and has failed." While not many of us would accept this statement because the universe of strategies has hardly been exhausted, most would admit that when intervention programs have been adequately evaluated they have seldom met the investigator's expectation. For that reason, it appears to be worthwhile to describe an intervention program for children of ages two and three, which with subsequent evaluation appears to demonstrate that a little intervention can go a long way, given the right age and conditions.

Any given chronological age yields enormous intellective, social, and affective diversity across individuals. This is true of the preschool years as it is of later life. One only has to examine the vocabulary of two-year-olds to be struck by these differences. With further observation, one can become convinced that similar variability exists for almost any dimension of behavior.

Francis H. Palmer is at the State University of New York at Stony Brook. Printed by permission of the author. The research described in this paper was made possible by support from a grant from the National Institute for Child Health and Human Development (HD02253).

Few would question that variability in performance is a function of an interaction between genetic and experiential factors. However, while remaining cognizant of genetic determination, a child deserves the opportunity to search for his learning capability. It is the relationship between the stage of development of the child and the programming of subsequent experience to which preschool curricula should be directed.

At the Harlem Research Center, in 1965, we were interested in determining the effects of minimal intervention at age two and three upon subsequent intellective development. The curriculum developed to comprise the intervention made certain assumptions about the educational needs of the young child. Those assumptions are listed below:

1. EARLY INTERVENTION IS BETTER THAN LATER INTERVENTION

Intervention designed to change the intellective, affective, or social development of the child should occur as early in life as is administratively feasible, affectively tolerable, and intellectively consistent with the level of development when intervention begins. The basis for this assumption is found in the literature of early experience in animals and has been developed elsewhere by the author and others (Bronfenbrenner, 1968; Palmer, 1969). In summary, the inferences derived from that literature and relevant to children are: a. the infant organism has a drive for stimulation which increases with exposure to stimuli; b. the effects of stimulus deprivation increase as the organism becomes less passive and more actively engaged with his environment, c. the effects of deprivation increase with its duration until appropriate patterns of behavior are established, and d. as the phylogenetic scale is ascended, stimulus deprivation has increasingly severe effects, but the effect of remedial treatment also increases.

2. THERE ARE BASIC CONCEPTS PREREQUISITE TO MOST SUBSEQUENT LEARNING

There are symbols representing simple concepts which every child must learn as a prerequisite to understanding and describing his relationship with the world around him. These concepts are universal; they must be learned by the child in the altaplana of Peru, the kibbutzim of Israel, the krech of the Soviet Union, or the nursery school in Omaha. They are learned by almost all individuals sooner or later, and we assume that the earlier in life they are learned, the earlier the child is ready to acquire more complex concepts specific to the culture within which he is growing.

Examples of these concepts are symbolized by words such as *open, soft, big, black, rough, many,* etc. We have assessed large numbers of children at different preschool ages and have determined the proportion of children who can correctly respond to the various concepts. In this manner we have determined, for example, that 65% of 120 Black males at age two responded correctly to *open.* At two years and eight months of age another sample (n = 80) showed that 78% of Black males responded correctly to the same symbol. The concept *rough,* as in sandpaper, we have found to be more difficult for the two year old than *open,* since at 2/0 only 25% responded correctly, and at 2/8 40% responded correctly. A large number of such symbols have been presented to children age two to four years and eight months, and we now know the order of difficulty at various ages as well as the age at which almost all children comprehend them.

The curriculum described below is based on the assumption that if children are taught the simple but universally acquired concepts earlier than they would acquire them by interacting with their normal environment, they will be better able to acquire more difficult concepts with the same universal characteristics (e.g., *same, different, more than*), as well as other symbols specific to their culture (*subway, street, elevator*).

3. ORGANIZATION OF INPUT FOR A RESPONSE TO ANOTHER PERSON

It is essential for optimal intellective growth that environmental stimulation, *qua* input, be organized by the child in order to make a response to adults or peers. Stimulation is a necessary but not sufficient condition for the development of such responses. The distinction is similar to the difference between an adult reading a detective story for the almost exclusive purpose of self-gratification, without regard to use of the information derived, and an adult reading an article in a scientific journal which must be organized and integrated toward a response to others as well as himself. In the first instance, information is being received only; in the second, it is being received and organized in a manner appropriate for a deliberate response. We assume that this facility is learned, and the sooner it is part of the child's repertoire, the better for intellective development. Indeed, we suggest that this facility is a common denominator of intelligence, no matter how defined.

Furthermore, we assume that this facility is most easily learned in the presence of others under conditions which allow the child maximum opportunity for deriving rewards, namely, in a one-to-one teacher-child situation where interruptions are unlikely, and attention to the child (while requiring a response) is on a regular basis. "Supermothers" provide this opportunity. Many mothers, regardless of social class, do not.

We hypothesize that for the development of this facility the earlier years are more critical than others, and that it is characteristic of a high level of intellective development that this processing of information is learned early in life.

4. POSITIVE AFFECT AND INTELLECTIVE DEVELOPMENT

Sustained intellective growth requires that the child associate subsequent learning with positive affect. Positive affect at age two or three is best developed by interaction with a warm and relatively permissive person who relates with the child on a systematic schedule or strategy. Punishment is rejected as a means to modify learning not because it is not effective in specific situations, but because it is unlikely that it can contribute to the child's long term positive affect toward other learning situations. Furthermore, we assume that the desired positive affect can best be developed when the child has the opportunity to be with the adult under conditions which allow no interruption for extended periods of time, and which are systematically scheduled to provide for anticipatory responses. The child must be able to count on "his time" with the Instructor, and she in turn must take advantage of the situation and provide the conditions for learning.

It is questionable that these conditions can be achieved in group situations with the very young. Separation from the mother for even short periods of time is frequently trauma enough for a two-year-old, and to compound it by not providing an adequate or better substitute seems hardly conducive to a situation within which the desired learning could take place. It is reasonable to expect however, that given the conditions described above, the child will in time learn to forget the mother for the moment, accept the substitute, and over the course of an extended program and interaction with several teachers, learn to interact more readily with adults and with associations positively related to learning.

5. EACH CHILD TO BEGIN TRAINING AT HIS LEVEL AND PROCEED AT HIS OWN PACE

Each child in an intervention program should begin at his own level of development with respect to the contents of the curriculum, and proceed from there at a pace neither too rapid nor too slow for his capacity. That goal can be met only if 1. adequate information is available with respect to what knowledge the child brings to the program; 2. a curriculum is available, the difficulty of which can be adapted to his level of development; and 3. an adult is consistently present to pace his instruction. Presumably all three of these conditions can best be met with a one-to-one teacher-child ratio. As the number of children for which an individual Instructor is responsible at one time increases, we may anticipate that the conditions of appropriate beginning level and rate of instruction will be violated. Therefore, we assume that, in addition to providing the child with more opportunity to integrate information in order to form a response, and to facilitate positive affect associated with learning, the one-to-one ratio best enables the teacher to attend to the individual characteristics of the child. It is a vehicle through which the child's most important identifiable educational needs can be provided.

6. DURABILITY OF EFFECTS

Any increase in intellective functioning demonstrated as the result of a given treatment must be shown to be durable. It is to be expected that a large variety of intervention programs will demonstrate gains in intellective performance immediately following the termination of the program. The critical question for the investigators is: what are the conditions which provide for intellective change of an enduring quality?

7. MINIMAL INTERVENTION AT EARLIER AGES

Many children under four years of age should not be involved with intervention programs which separate them from their mothers for extended periods. Also, we assume that there is a maximum time span during which the child can learn efficiently, and this time span is a function of his age and level of intellective development. Finally, to provide the conditions of training which best meet the educational needs described, costs would mount rapidly as the amount of time the child is involved in individual instruction increases. Therefore, we conclude that there is a need for minimal intervention which can be demonstrated to have durable effects, for example, intervention which could be embedded in day care programs and nursery schools with relative ease, or which could be used independently of such programs.

8. ACCEPTABILITY TO MOTHER

No program or curriculum designed for the preschool child can be successful unless it has the trust and cooperation of the mother. She should be thoroughly oriented concerning the goals of the program and the experiences her child will have. She should have an opportunity to observe the learning situation and to ask questions about any aspect of the training she does not understand. Ideally, she should learn teaching procedures from observation and use them in the home.

9. SUMMARY OF EDUCATIONAL NEEDS

Our diagnosis of educational needs has identified eight broad goals required of an intervention program if it is to make a lasting change in intellective development. Intervention should occur early; it should involve training in certain basic concepts prerequisite to subsequent learning; it should facilitate the organization of input for responses to significant others; it should develop positive affect toward the learning experience; and it should be pitched to the child's level of development when he begins the program and should proceed at a pace neither too difficult nor too easy for him. Effects of the intervention should be durable to be of value. Intervention at the earlier years which requires minimal contact with the child is greatly needed. No program is likely to be successful without the active cooperation and trust of the mother.

B. FORMULATION OF BEHAVIORAL OBJECTIVES

We make no pretense to be testing the validity of the assumptions just described in the evaluation of this program. Certain behavioral objectives are tested, however, and information related to our assumptions may be implicit in the result of our evaluation. The curriculum and its associated training conditions are mediators between our assumptions and the behavioral objectives listed below:

1. To increase the child's knowledge of basic concepts.
2. To demonstrate that children who increase their command of these concepts exhibit generalization of effect to other behaviors.
3. To show that these effects are durable.
4. To examine the relative magnitude and durability of the effects and to determine what behaviors are most or least influenced by the intervention.
5. To show that effects are discernible throughout the range of socio-economic status.
6. To demonstrate that the curriculum and the training environment command the respect and trust of parents.

C. SELECTION OF CONTENT

1. CONCEPTS

Regarding children's learning, there is a rough sequencing of what is learned with increasing age. Individual words are learned before phrases or sentences: form discrimination is learned before color discrimination; and some prepositions and adjectives which relate the child to his environment are learned before others. Prepositions and adjectives form the core of the curriculum described in this paper. It should be noted that almost all children learn these concepts (i.e., prepositions and adjectives) sooner or later, and that the concepts are characterized by their universality across cultures.

In order to specify the concepts to be learned, a large number of words were arbitrarily selected from the verbalizations of two-and-a-half to four-year-old-boys — words such as *into, open, wet, soft, under, big, full, over, rough, short*, etc., ranging to more complex concepts such as *more than, many, same,* and *different.*

2. MATERIALS

Materials were then chosen which could be used for illustrating a specific concept. For example, *closed* was represented by a puppet whose mouth could be manipulated by the Instructor so that it was open or closed; for *wet*, two socks, one wet and one dry, were used; and for *soft*, a ball of cotton was employed. Most materials were selected from items which we assumed were present in the child's home and with which the child might already be familiar. A variety of such materials were accumulated for each concept. In this manner *soft* eventually was illustrated by not only the ball of cotton, but also by the Instructor's cheek, a piece of velvet, etc. When the words denoted action, such as *up* or *down*, appropriate toys and materials were identified and used. Certain toys, such as a small tow truck with a lifting rig on the rear, were used for more than one concept: e.g., up, down, forward, backward, fast, and slow could be demonstrated with the same tow truck.

3. TRAINING CUBICLES

Eight cubicles, roughly 7 × 9 feet, were built in the Harlem Research Center. Between each two was a 9 × 5 foot observation room with one way mirrors, providing vision into the adjacent cubicles. Microphones were suspended from the ceilings of the training rooms, and amplifiers and speakers were placed in the observation rooms. In this manner, parents, students, and staff could see and hear every aspect of training at any time without the child's being interrupted.

4. INSTRUCTORS

Instructors were selected for heterogeneity of educational background and ranged from those with only high school educations to doctoral candidates in psychology.

Roughly half were male and half female at any given time. All were White. They were selected by observing them in the training room with the child. Most of those rejected disqualified themselves after spending forty-five minutes in the cubicle with a two- or three-year-old.

D. ORGANIZATION OF CONTENT

The content of the curriculum has been defined as the concepts, materials, and procedures associated with instruction. The organization of that content required several deliberate steps: 1. initial assessment of each child to determine what knowledge he brought to the program with him, 2. ordering concepts within a written curriculum by difficulty and meaningfulness, 3. identification of the steps to be used in each training situation, 4. deciding how best to attend the needs of the individual child, 5. establishment of criteria for when a child had learned a concept, and 6. development of lesson plans and records.

1. INITIAL ASSESSMENT

Assessment measures will be covered in greater detail under the evaluation section of this paper. Only that measure used in assessment and related to the organization of the curriculum will be discussed here.

After each child had met the criteria for adaptation to the testing situation (Palmer, 1970) he was given the Concepts Familiarity Index (CFI), which was specifically designed to measure knowledge of those concepts to be used in the curriculum. The CFI provided a measure of what concepts each child knew when he entered the program. At age two most concepts were in pairs representing two poles of the same dimension, e.g., *up* and *down*. To measure the child's knowledge of *up* and *down*, two testing situations were devised so that both poles were illustrated in each situation (e.g., using the tow truck and a toy automobile: "make the car go *up*," and "make the car go *down*"). Each situation was repeated twice on different days of testing, once for measuring the child's knowledge of *up* and once for measuring *down*. Thus the combination of two concepts by two situations yielded four items in the CFI. A total of 46 concepts were used for a total of 92 items.[1]

At age two, presentation of the CFI in its original form required about six sessions of 45 minutes each after the child had met the criteria for being ready to

---

[1] The Concepts Familiarity Index has been shortened for age two by deleting items shown to be contributive to the measure on the basis of an item analysis, or by deleting items which the assessors felt were not measuring what the child actually knew.

test. During the adaptation period the child became familiar with the Center, its personnel, and most important, learned to interact with another adult with the mother absent. Also, during this period the mother was present in the observation room more often than not.

2. DEVELOPMENT OF THE WRITTEN CURRICULUM

The results of the assessment provided data regarding the proportion of children at age two (or three) who already knew a given concept when they first came to the Center. Concepts were sequenced in the curriculum roughly according to their difficulty, with those known by the largest proportion of children first. Exceptions to strict ordering of concepts by difficulty were made for considerations associated with three other strategies involved in the curriculum: Series, Levels, and Stages.

a. SERIES

The curriculum was organized on one dimension by subsets of concepts with a commonality of meaning. There were nine such subsets (Series) used in the curriculum: 1. Position (e.g., *on top of*); 2. Direction (e.g., *up*); 3. Sensory-Tactile (e.g., *soft*); 4. Quantity (e.g., *empty*); 5. Movement (e.g., *fast*); 6. Size (e.g., *little*). Each Series included several concepts, each of which was taught in situations different from that used in assessment for the same concept. In addition to the concept categories, the Series included Form Discrimination, and the matching of objects on the basis of Same and Different.

b. LEVELS

Instruction was divided into Levels of relative difficulty with respect to the concepts involved. Level I included concepts which the largest proportion of children knew when they arrived at the program. For example, in the Direction Series, Level I included *up, down, on top of, out of*; whereas Level III, representing more difficult concepts, included *around, through,* etc. Levels became increasingly more difficult until, for example, Level V included Sensory Tactile concepts *rough* and *smooth*; Quantity concepts all and none, and Size concepts *bigger than* and *littler than.*

c. STAGES

Within a Series concepts of increasing difficulty were categorized as Stages. Thus the Sensory-Tactile Series had several Stages: Stage I included *wet* and *dry* at Level II of difficulty; Stage II included *hard* and *soft* at Level III of difficulty; and

Stage III included *rough* and *smooth* at Level V of difficulty. Within a Series it was possible to have a Level of difficulty not represented by a Stage.

d. WRITING OF THE CURRICULUM

A single page was used for each concept in the curriculum. Pages were ordered according to Level, Series, and Stage. The page included a description of the concept and how it was to be taught, the relevant steps involved in the teaching, choice of toys or materials which might be used, and the situations within which the concept would be taught. (see Table I) Almost 100 pages were developed for ages 2/0 thru 4/0.

e. INSTRUCTOR'S MANUAL

An Instructor's Manual accompanied each copy of the curriculum and addressed in detail the purpose of the study and the assumptions on which the study and curriculum were based; it gave explicit instructions on how to handle situations related to both child and mother. Each Instructor had a copy of the curriculum and the Manual.

TABLE I
SPECIMEN PAGE OF CONCEPT CURRICULUM

HARD-SOFT

LEVEL III

SERIES   *Sensory-Tactile Concepts*

Stage 2   *Hard - Soft*

There are various ways of appreciating the differences between hard and soft objects; feeling the differences, hearing sharp or dull noises as the objects hit another object, etc. The following instructions provide as many approaches to perceiving such differences as were thought of. Try to use various methods while working with Steps 1 and 2. This can help the child not only learn the difference between hard and soft, but also learn that there is more than one way of telling the difference. It may be easier for some children if each word and its referent object are presented separately in Steps 1 and 2, i.e., take the soft object, feel it, label, (Step 1), then present it to the child for his inspection, and label, (Step 2). Then go through Steps 1 and 2 with the hard object.

Materials   Felt and Thin Logical Block (same shape and color)
(Situations)   Soft Sponge blocks and Wooden or Plastic ones (as close in
                    shape and color as possible.)
                  Cotton and Rock

TABLE I (Continued)
SPECIMEN PAGE OF CONCEPT CURRICULUM

Materials (Continued)	China figure and Rubber figure Clothes: materials vs. shoe, soles, or belt buckle Body parts: skull, nails, etc., vs. calf, cheek, etc. Objects in room: chairs, table, wall, floor, etc., vs. Kleenex, cloth, rubber animals, etc.
Situation 1	Felt and Thin Logical Block (same shape and color)
Step	
1	*T* feels each object. Can also rub them against face or arms. Can strike them with stick. Labels.
2	*T* labels materials appropriately as child feels them. Be sensitive to child's reaction to physical contact with the object, especially if the contact is initiated by *T*, since tension and fear reduce tactile perception and *pleasure*. Some children will imitate *T*'s actions spontaneously, others will need encouragement. A game of "peek-a-boo," hiding parts of your face behind objects and looking at yourself in mirror while doing so, might be an effective way to involve some children.
3	*T* asks child for hard, then for soft object or asks child to rub hard then soft object on self or *T*. Child responds correctly to *T*'s question.
Situation 2	Sponge blocks and Wooden or Plastic ones (as close in shape and color as possible).
Step	
1	Same as Situation 1. In addition, the differences in the properties of hard and soft objects such as noise and bounciness can be demonstrated by building towers and knocking them over, dropping the blocks, etc.
2	*T* labels as child plays with the objects.

3. *STEPS USED IN TRAINING FOR EACH CONCEPT*

Four steps were usually used for concepts involved in all Series except Form, Same, and Different:

   a. Instructor demonstrates with materials and labels his actions as they are related to the concept.

  b. Instructor has child perform an action related to the concept, and labels the child's actions for him.
  c. Child performs action related to concept at Instructor's command.
  d. Instructor asks child to label appropriately while he or child performs a task related to the concept.

When the child spontaneously performed the meaning of the concept in play, Instructors were told to omit a. above and move directly to b. Also, they were cautioned not to be overly rigid about following the steps at all times, but to be certain that steps c. and d. were used for each situation to which the child was exposed.

4. ATTENDING THE INDIVIDUAL CHILD

The Instructor was aware of what concepts the child had responded to correctly on assessment, and in training validated that knowledge quickly by exposing the child to a single training situation designed for the concept. If the single situation was responded to correctly, the Instructor checked off the concept as known; if incorrectly, the usual training situations were then used and followed by the learning criteria described below. In this manner the child moved to his level of attainment in the curriculum as rapidly as possible.

  Once the appropriate level was reached for standard training procedures the child was allowed to proceed through the curriculum at his own pace. If his attention wandered, the Instructor acted to regain his focus on the materials associated with the concepts. If he was obviously rejecting the situation for the day or the moment, or found a specific concept too difficult, she was encouraged to interrupt training and play with him for a while, and return to that concept later or on another day.

5. CRITERION FOR LEARNING A CONCEPT

After the child had been trained in two or more situations related to a single concept, and when the Instructor judged that he knew the concept, he was exposed to three situations different from those he had experienced in training, each of which he had to respond to correctly to reach criterion. Furthermore, all three could not be presented on the same day; criterion could be met only by correct response to situations presented during two successive training sessions.

6. LESSON PLANS AND RECORDS

Instructors were responsible for preparing lesson plans and recording the training activities covered for each session the child attended the Center. Prior to a session the Instructor checked the child's record to determine what four or five concepts were next in his sequence and what materials were to be used. She then planned her lesson on the Session Planning Sheet. Materials were placed in the cubicle before the child entered, and his choice of toys as he entered guided the Instructor with respect to which of the concepts should be used first in that session. After the training period, the Instructor recorded the concepts attempted and/or completed on the Record of Session Results.

Instructors were rotated from one child to another after six sessions. Routinely, the first session with a new Instructor was designated Free Play, to provide the child the opportunity to adapt to the new adult. During the 8 months, no Instructor saw a given child for more than one series of six sessions. The Sessions Planning Sheets and Record of Session Results were of particular value to an Instructor dealing with a child for the first time or to one substituting in the event of illness. At the end of six sessions and before the child saw his new Instructor, the old Instructor completed the Characteristics Index, a series of behavioral dimensions on which the child was judged on a seven point scale (e.g., how verbal was the child relative to others in the sample, how cooperative in the training situation, to what extent did he attend to the materials and the instructor, etc.).

E. SELECTION OF LEARNING EXPERIENCES

While there is implicit in the organization of the content of the program much which is consistent with the educational needs defined earlier, emphasis was placed, when training Instructors, on providing the child with specific learning conditions within which the curriculum should be used.

1. *EXPOSURE TO SYSTEMATIC INSTRUCTION AT AN EARLY AGE*

To satisfy the assumption that earlier intervention is better than later intervention we chose age two and age three so that the relative effects at those ages could be compared. Two was chosen as the earliest age at which our program was intellectively consistent with the child's stage of development, affectively tolerable, and administratively feasible.

At age two, most children are learning a vocabulary at a very rapid rate. Whether the child is talking or not, his reflective language, that ability to understand the speech of others and to respond, is already impressive. Pilot work had convinced us that with a sequence of training sessions his attention span could be increased to the point where forty-five minute instructional periods would be appropriate.

Also at age two, many children can be separated from the mother and interact with other adults. When the child resisted that separation, procedures were developed for having the mother withdraw gradually over as many sessions as were needed. All but 12 of the 120 children at age two were able to interact with the Instructor in the absence of the mother within three or four visits to the Center. Many did on the first or second visit.

Administrative feasibility is a matter of major concern when training very young children. When matters of scheduling, transportation, and routine child care are involved, the logistical complexity of a program dealing with a large number of children can endanger the goals of the program itself. The decision was made that age two was the earliest that the average child could be adequately supervised, transported, and provided with the desired intervention.

2. ORGANIZATION OF INPUT FOR A RESPONSE TO A SIGNIFICANT OTHER

We predicted that the one-to-one Instructor child ratio; forty minute periods of training in a cubicle providing for no interruption; an organized curriculum with interesting materials, and warm, responsive and firm Instructors would combine to provide conditions under which the child would be most likely to organize information in a manner conducive to responses to others. Given such conditions, he could extend his attention span and develop insight into the fact that he was not just a recipient of input provided by the Instructor and the materials, but that the Instructor expected something else from him, namely, that he respond to her relative to that input. Whether this facility be interpreted as an increase in attention span or as a cortical integrating process which can be learned only in the presence of another, this assumption and the conditions designed to provide for it remain a major part of the rationale for the program.

3. DEVELOPMENT OF AN AFFECTIVE BOND WITH SIGNIFICANT OTHERS

The conditions of training deliberately attempted to provide for the child an opportunity within which he could develop an affective bond for his Instructor. The latter were enjoined to be affectively responsive themselves, which most found was not a cross to bear when dealing with two- and three-year-olds. We hypothesized that as the child grew increasingly familiar with the environs of the Center and with its personnel, the change from one Instructor to another would become easier. Furthermore, we predicted that exposure to ten or more different adults during the eight months would make it easier for the child to respond to still another adult in a quite different environment such as a school system.

4. MINIMAL INTERVENTION

At age two, we did not (and do not) believe it was to the child's advantage to separate him from his mother for extended periods during the day, nor did we believe more than one hour for each session was optimal for providing conditions contrived to further his intellective and affective development. Consequently, over an eight month period, the child was provided with two one-hour training sessions each week, scheduled during the same hours each week (e.g., Tuesdays and Thursday at 10 a.m.). We had hoped that many children with that schedule would learn to anticipate the day and time they were to come to the Center, and in many cases that proved to be the case.

Thus the learning experience to which the child was exposed was relatively brief in total number of hours, involved a one-to-one child-Instructor ratio under conditions designed to provide for the development of positive affect between them, emphasized the learning of simple concepts, and provided for no interruption in a training session as well as for training over an extended period of time.

G. EVALUATION

1. DESIGN

The evaluation of the curriculum was designed longitudinally to provide for annual assessment until the children had completed the first grade. It covaried type of training (Training and Discovery), age of training (2 and 3), and socio-economic status (Categories I through V on the Hollingshead-Redlich Two Factor Scale of Social Class).

2. SUBJECTS

Subjects were 310 Negro males born in the hospitals of Manhattan in 1964. The 240 subjects who participated in the two training conditions were born in August-October of that year, and the 70 non-participating controls in November-December, so that the latter could be tested annually at the same age as the former, although they were actually assessed 2 months later each year.

Negroes were chosen as subjects to minimize the effects of child rearing practices across ethnic groups, and because a wide range of social class is available in Harlem where the study was conducted.

Birth records for the months indicated were examined, and the names of all males born who were over five pounds in weight, and whose mothers had no history of drug addiction, syphilis, or serious birth injuries, were recorded.

Mothers' names and addresses were subsequently sent to the U. S. Post Office. Where Post Office records indicated that mother and child still lived at the address where they were at the time of the child's birth, the mother was contacted and interviewed. Children from homes where a language other than English was spoken were dropped from the potential sample. Those mothers meeting the criteria of selection, which included the requirement of prescribed numbers at different levels of socio-economic status, were asked to sign a statement indicating willingness to participate in the program; then a time for further orientation was set. A more detailed report of the results of the selection process may be found in Palmer (1970).

One hundred and twenty of the 240 subjects who participated in the program began in September 1966 at age 2 (Alpha sample); the remainder began a year later at age three (Gamma sample). The 120 randomly selected to begin at age two were further selected for Concept Training or Discovery Training on the basis of social class and initial assessment score on the Concepts Familiarity Index. Identical practice was followed a year later when the three-year-olds began training.

The 70 non-participating Controls (Beta sample) were equated with the participating children on the basis of socio-economic status. They were first assessed at 2 years and eight months, simultaneously with the participating groups after training had been terminated.

Because the study was longitudinal and parental involvement was essential to minimize attrition, each mother was informed about the goals and procedures by the Principal Investigator or a member of the senior staff. Each mother was encouraged to accompany her child to the Center for the first six sessions of attendance, and to observe through the one-way mirror and audio equipment what the child was doing and what was being said to him.

B. TREATMENT CONDITIONS

a. CONCEPT TRAINING (N = 120)

As described in main section D of this paper.

b. DISCOVERY CONDITION (N = 120)

Subjects were not exposed to the curriculum. Instructors played with the children with identical toys and materials, but did not initiate verbal interchange related to the concepts. They were instructed not to initiate more conversation that a given child might receive from a teacher if he were in a nursery school class of fifteen. However, Instructors were told to respond to all questions asked verbally or by gesture, and to continue responding as long as the child persisted in his questions.

c. NON-PARTICIPATING CONTROLS
(N = 70)

These subjects were selected in a manner identical to the participating groups, were two months younger, and consequently were assessed two months after the participating groups each year. The question of how the mothers of the Control children were to remain motivated enough to return their children for annual assessment each summer for five years was a serious one. This problem was solved by informing each mother at orientation that by the time her son was ready for public schooling we would have a complete and long-time record of his intellective development. Those records would be available to school authorities or physicians only upon her request. Mothers have used these records extensively when problems associated with health or achievement have occurred. Attrition rates show that while the participating groups are somewhat less likely to drop out of the annual assessment program, differences between participating groups and Controls were not statistically different.

4. MEASURES OF PERFORMANCE

Effects of the treatment were measured annually from the age when training terminated (2/8 and 3/8) to age 4/8 (as of this writing). The battery was comprised of a variety of indices ranging from the CFI, directly related to what was taught in the Concept Training curriculum, to measures whose validity appeared to have little to do with what the child had experienced in training.

As the subjects increased in age, measures became more numerous and more complex, and the average amount of time required for assessment was inversely related to age and the number of measures used. At age two, only two measures comprised the battery, but an average of 9 one-hour sessions were required for completion; at age 4/8, 17 measures were used, requiring an average testing time of approximately six hours.

Instructors who had been involved in training were never allowed to assess. In most instances a single assessor gave the entire battery to each child.

An obvious problem of comparing participating groups with Controls was the length of adaptation to the Center given the former but not the latter. While it might be argued that adaptation itself is part of any preschool training, this was a matter of considerable concern at age 2/8, when the participating groups had had eight months adaptation time and the Controls only the number of sessions required for them to meet the criteria for readiness to test. For each annual assessment thereafter, however, this difference presumably became less of a problem for two reasons: a. each year the Controls increased their total adaptation time in the laboratory so that by age 3/8 assessment, they had already spent an average of 6 hours there, and by age 4/8 an average of 14, and b. each year the participating groups returned, the time had increased since their 8 months training and presumably their initial advantage had diminished. This problem is, of course, built into the intervention study, however designed, and was anticipated by including the Discovery group as another treatment condition to control for the Hawthorne effect.

5. RESULTS

The effects of the Training and Discovery treatments were determined by a wide variety of measures and by comparing those children involved in each treatment group with 70 Controls who had been exposed to neither. As indicated above, the measures used varied with age. A summary of performance on those measures is described below, and a more detailed analysis of the data will be reported separately (Palmer and Moren). Summary results will be reported in the order of behavioral objectives outlined in main section B of this paper:

1. Was the child's knowledge of basic concepts increased?
2. Did the treatment generalize to behaviors other than those taught in the concept training?
3. Were the effects durable over time?
4. Were specific behaviors more or less permanently effected by the intervention?
5. Were the effects discernible throughout the range of socio-economic status?
6. Did the program command the trust and respect of the parents?

A. WAS THE CHILDREN'S KNOWLEDGE OF BASIC CONCEPTS INCREASED?

To determine effects immediately following the eight months training, those children trained at age 2/0-2/8 were assessed at age 2/8, and those trained at age 3/0-3/8 were assessed at age 3/8. The Concepts Familiarity Index was designed as a measure of knowledge about the specific concepts taught in the Training condition and thus is the best available measure to answer the question raised in 1. above. All children were reassessed annually after the training period had terminated, through age 4/8 as of this writing. Thus for those children trained at age 2/0 both a one year and two year follow-up are available at this time, and for those trained at age 3/0 a one year follow-up is available.

1. IMMEDIATELY AFTER TRAINING

When those children trained at age two (Alpha sample) were assessed immediately after the training period was completed, both the Training and Discovery groups outperformed their Controls on the CFI. Furthermore, the Training group outperformed the Discovery group.

When those trained at age three were assessed at age 3/8, both participating groups again outperformed their Controls, and again the Training group outperformed the Discovery group.

Thus, not surprisingly, since a. the CFI measures specifically what was taught in the Training condition, and b. assessment occurred immediately after training, the order of performance was Concept Training, Discovery, and Nonparticipating Controls in descending order, with statistically significant differences between each pair of treatments.

2. DURABILITY OF EFFECTS ON THE CFI

a. *One year after treatment.* One year after treatment all children were assessed again. One year post assessment for the Alpha sample coincided with assessment after training for those in the program at age three (Gamma sample) and the second exposure to assessment for the Controls (Beta sample). Thus the comparison for one year durability of effects matches the Alphas at age 3/8 with the Betas at that age, and the Gammas at age 4/8 with the Betas at that age.

One year after training both Training and Discovery groups of the Alpha sample had higher means on the CFI than the Beta Controls, but only the latter was statistically significant. Thus the relative positions of the Training and Discovery groups were reversed from results immediately after training, with Discovery significantly better than the Training group.

When assessed at age 4/8, the Gamma sample maintained the order found immediately after training with the Training group, Discovery, and Control performing in that order. Both participating groups were significantly higher than the Controls, and Training was significantly higher than the Discovery.

b. *Two years after training.* At age 4/8, two years after the termination of the intervention, both Training and Discovery groups of Alpha attained higher mean scores than their Controls but neither was statistically significant. No differences existed between Training and Discovery groups.

Thus while the participating groups continued to score higher than Controls on each exposure to the CFI regardless of age, when individual samples were compared, the durability of effect did not reach statistical significance one or two years after training as had been true immediately after training.

We conclude that while the effects of Training diminished on the CFI with time and no further intervention, that the effects of participating in the program persisted over time. This conclusion is based on the probability of 0.15 that the mean scores of the participating groups would be higher in six assessments (Alpha Training and Discovery at 3/8 and 4/8, and Gamma Training and Discovery at 4/8), unless some factor other than chance was operating.

Clearly, however, the differences found between Training and Discovery groups on the CFI immediately after Training did not persist. Short term gains on knowledge of concepts can be attributed to the Training condition, but long term advantages must be ascribed to the conditions of participating in the program independent of the Concept Training itself.

B. WAS THERE GENERALIZATION OF EFFECT TO OTHER MEASURES OF BEHAVIOR?

At each age level the battery of measures used was deliberately designed to range in the behaviors from those specifically related to what was taught during Concept Training (the CFI) to some which had little face validity for what appeared to have taken place in the participating conditions, (e.g., delayed response, simple perceptual discrimination, etc.) In this manner it was hoped to identify behaviors which were affected by the intervention beyond what was specifically taught. The extent to which this was successful is described below.

1. *Immediately after training?*

a. *At age 2/8* the Alpha Training and Discovery outperformed their Controls on the Stanford-Binet IQ (96.43 vs. 93.31), on embedded figures, the ability to follow instructions, simple perceptual discrimination for both total score and time, motor coordination, labeling, body parts, and body positions at the .05 level of statistical significance. Their mean scores were higher for the Peabody Picture Vocabulary Test, persistence in a boring task, and delayed response, but those differences were not statistically significant. No differences existed between the participating groups and their Controls on location, simple form, varied form, and color discrimination.

The Training group outperformed the Discovery group only on the ability to follow instructions; Discovery was not significantly better than Training on any measure. Thus while those involved in the program consistently outperformed their Controls on measures not specifically related to the concept training itself, the Training conditions had no advantage over the Discovery at this age.

b. *At age 3/8* Gamma Training and Discovery groups were significantly better than their Controls on the Stanford-Binet IQ (99.29 vs. 93.31), simple perceptual discrimination score and time to completion, motor performance, labeling, and form problems. Their means were higher for a grouping task but the differences were not statistically significant. Control group means were higher for persistence in a boring task and sorting, but neither was significant. No differences between Training and Discovery groups existed. Here again, for measures of behavior not directly taught in the Concept condition, the participating groups were consistently higher than their Controls, but no differences between the participating groups existed.

2. *One year after treatment.*

   a. *Those trained at 2/0 (Alpha).* One year after the two-year-olds participated in the program, the Training group had higher means than the Control group on all measures except sorting, but they were significantly better only on time to completion of the simple perceptual discrimination task. The Discovery group, on the other hand, also had higher means than the Controls on all measures but sorting, and they were significantly better on simple perceptual discrimination score and time to completion, motor coordination, labeling, and form problems. However, no statistically significant differences existed between Training and Discovery groups. Simple perceptual discrimination persisted as the most reliable difference between participating groups and their Controls.

   b. *Those trained at 3/0 (Gamma).* A year after the program ended, those trained at age three consistently outperformed the Controls on each of eight measures in the battery, including all 12 of the subtests of the WPPSI. Of these, the Training group was significantly better than the Controls on the Stanford-Binet IQ (100.32 vs. 92.38), seriation modeling and seriation memory, and Information, Comprehension, Picture Completion, Mazes, Geometric Design and Block Design on the WPPSI.

   The Discovery group significantly outperformed the Controls on Seriation Modeling, Seriation Memory, and Classification, as well as Animal House, Picture Completion, Mazes, Geometric Design, and Block Design on the WPPSI. The Stanford-Binet IQ scores were higher but not statistically significant (97.22 vs. 92.38). No significant differences existed between Training and Discovery groups.

   Thus, for measures not specifically related to the concepts taught in the Training condition, the participating groups appear to have outperformed their Controls one year after training more significantly than was true for the Concepts Familiarity Index. But again, no consistent differences existed between Training and Discovery conditions.

3. *Two years after training.*

   In general, the Alpha sample showed greater superiority over their Controls two years after training than had been shown one year after. The Training group had significantly higher means than the Controls on Seriation Modeling, Seriation Memory, Classification, and within the WPPSI on Picture Completion and Block Design. The Controls were better on none.

   The Discovery group had significantly higher means than the Controls on Seriation Modeling and Seriation Memory, and within the WPPSI on Mazes, Geometric Design, and Block Design.

   Stanford-Binet scores two years after participating in the program were higher for the Alphas but not significantly so (94.51 vs. 92.38). Thus at age 4/8, one year after participating for the Gammas and two for the Alphas, the former outperformed the latter on the Stanford-Binet, 98.83 to 94.51.

Thus, to summarize the effects of test scores when the three groups were compared, it may be said that immediately after training, the participating groups outperformed their Controls, and those effects were generalized to include behaviors not specifically related to the Concept Training. Furthermore, some effects were durable for one year for those trained at both two and three years, and for those trained at age two, some were durable for two years. The Training group did not outperform the Discovery group, however, and we must conclude that the conditions of training other than the Concept Training itself must account for those differences.

C. WHAT SPECIFIC BEHAVIORS APPEAR TO HAVE BEEN MOST INFLUENCED OVER TIME?

The data described above indicate that for both participating groups the conditions of training independent of Concept Training itself increased performance in the behavioral domains of knowledge of basic concepts, simple perceptual discrimination, and to a lesser degree, language. In all comparisons at every age, the participating groups received higher means on the CFI than their Controls. A variety of measures related to simple perceptual discrimination consistently differentiated the participating groups from the Controls (e.g., at age 2/8 our measure of SPD both with respect to score and time to completion; at age 3/8 a more complicated version of the same measure both with score and time; and at age 4/8, those subtests of the WPPSI which appear to be most closely related to the SPD measure used at the earlier ages). The argument for change in language behavior is less convincing. At age 2/8 the participating groups were significantly better on a measure of labeling (presumably productive speech) and on the CFI (presumably comprehensive speech). However, the PPVT did not differentiate participating groups from the Controls. The Stanford-Binet did. At age 3/8 Labeling, the CFI, and the Stanford-Binet differentiated the Gamma group but not the Alpha group from the Controls. No differences existed on the PPVT. At 4/8 means favored the participating groups for the CFI, Labeling, and the Stanford-Binet, but the Controls did as well on the Vocabulary measure of the WPPSI.

D. WERE THE EFFECTS DISCERNIBLE THROUGHOUT THE SOCIO-ECONOMIC STATUS OF CHILDREN?

As has been reported elsewhere (Palmer, 1970) no differences by SES existed at age 2/0, 2/8, 3/0 and 3/8 on any measures used for children who a. were visiting the Training Center for the first time, or b. in the Control groups. Nor, it can be added, did differences exist by SES for the participating groups after training or in subsequent assessments up to and including age 3/8. At 4/8 differences did exist by SES on almost all measures of performance in all groups.

E. DID THE PARENTS TRUST
   AND RESPECT THE PROGRAM?

Two sources of data are relevant to the question of the respect and trust the parents had in the program — attendance records and attrition rates. During the two years that the program was active, 78% of all appointments were kept. At age 4/8, 100 of the Alpha sampled were assessed out of an original 123 who began training at 2/0, and 101 of 120 Gammas who began training at age three were located and assessed. Of the Control subjects, 48 of an original 68 were located and assessed. For a program which provided only eight months of training for children at age two or three, and required annual attendance each summer thereafter for assessment only, we have been gratified with the attrition rate. From this we assume that parental involvement was good and respect for the program considerable.

H. DISCUSSION

This study, funded by the National Institute of Child Health and Human Development, was designed as research to determine the effects of minimal intervention at ages two and three and the durability of those effects. The original rationale, curriculum, and procedures were adhered to throughout; no changes were made during the conduct of training which violated the original design. While the results indicate that our program did make a difference in intellective development and that the difference was durable, we have learned a considerable amount about ages two and three from 14,000 hours of individual training, and would suggest modifications in the curriculum and procedures to be used in day care centers, nursery schools and learning clinics.

With respect to meeting our behavioral objectives, it appears that they were met. The basic concepts were better known to the participating groups immediately after the program, those effects generalized to other behaviors, and many of the effects were durable. Simple perceptual discrimination appears to be enhanced most and with greatest permanence, but knowledge of basic concepts and expressive and reflective language were increased as well. The ability to follow instructions was higher among the participating groups, and it can be argued that an increase in attention span is, in fact, what accounted for higher performance across the measures used. That argument cannot be resolved from the present data, but for practical purposes it would seem irrelevant as to *why* the children in the program performed better when, in fact, they did. No interaction was found between increase in performance and social class, although by age 4/8 differences existed in both treatment groups as well as the Control group. This finding is consistent with the literature which demonstrates performance differences by SES at four and a half years; these differences cannot be attributed to the effects of the intervention itself.

From the investigator's point of view, the fact that no consistent differences were found between Training and Discovery conditions clearly refutes one of our original hypotheses, namely, that a structured training regime emphasizing basic concepts presumed prerequisite to subsequent learning would accelerate performance over the loosely structured Discovery condition. The data are clear that the results were independent of the structured training, and suggest that other characteristics of the program common to both treatments produced the effects. We believe this to be a powerful argument for use of the one-to-one situation with young children, and would advise day care centers and nursery schools to include systematic one-to-one interaction in whatever larger program they adopt. Furthermore, the findings do not denigrate the value of the curriculum although it was not the most effective aspect of the intervention. The Discovery treatment under research conditions was equally effective, but under operating day care procedures it may not be so if for no other reason than that the Instructor has no specific curriculum to keep her in continuous and uninterrupted interaction with the child during his session. Because the program was designed as a research project, our Instructors were highly trained and constantly supervised. Those precautions undoubtedly made for much more rigorous adherence to the needs of the child than would be found in many typical day care situations. The existence of the Concept Training curriculum and its carefully delineated procedures provide structure for the Instructor as well as the child, and while perhaps no better than another curriculum so deliberately conceived and which emphasizes another aspect of development (e.g., language), its use compels the Instructor to deal with the child in a prescribed and consistent manner.

Of the relationship between the findings of the study and the educational needs assumed in the beginning of this chapter, the following may be said:

1. EARLY INTERVENTION IS BETTER THAN LATER INTERVENTION

This study was designed to determine the relative effects of two forms of intervention introduced at two different ages, not to test directly the assumption that earlier intervention is better than later intervention. The data available as of this writing, however, suggest that the assumption has been refuted with respect to the specific interventions involved, since the Gammas have consistently outperformed the Alphas. For example, the Stanford-Binet scores have been consistently higher for the Gammas. Even allowing for the slightly higher pretraining assessment scores by the Gammas, which occurred in spite of the rigorous selection procedures and random assignment to groups, those trained at age three are superior as of this writing. While our ultimate criterion remains performance at the first grade level, and intermediate data must be treated for what it is, our present inclination is to delay the structured Concept Training for the average child until he is closer to age three, and to increase the number of sessions devoted to the Discovery condition at earlier ages. A new revision will incorporate for the earlier ages both conditions, with Concept Training to be introduced gradually from age two to three.

Either of the two interventions is better than none at age two and three. Particularly reassuring, because so large a proportion of the sample were ghetto children, is the average Stanford-Binet IQ of 100 for all children one year after training had ceased. In general, the literature (e.g., Deutsch, 1967; Kennedy, 1963) indicates that the IQ's of Negroes at age 4/8 are around 85-90. Our Controls at that age scored around 92, perhaps partly as a function of two previous exposures to the measure on previous assessments, and partly as a function of our systematically obtaining a representative sample of middle-class negroes. In any event, since the standardization means of the Stanford-Binet are around 100 for White children, our interventions at age three appear to have done something right.

These findings appear to be important for educational purposes, particularly since the design precluded subsequent intervention after the initial eight months was terminated. Presumably, any applied program designed for children of this age would not cease contact after the first eight months was completed. If funds were available, it would be important to validate the study as designed, with the additional intervention of one session every two weeks from the time the eight month treatment ended until the child entered the first grade.

When compared with intervention programs with older preschool children, our results are encouraging, particularly when the total number of hours of child contact is considered. The number of hours of actual contact with the child was indeed minimal when compared to many traditional programs. Absences, which ran about 20% throughout both years of training, and the time required for post and pre-assessment each year, limited the total time for training to about 42-45 sessions.

The question of training at two would then seem to focus on how much training and under what conditions. There is little question that many two-year-olds could be trained to remain in the instructional situation for periods longer than forty-five minutes, but what that optimal time is, and what deleterious effects extending that period might have, we do not know. Finally, at age two we must raise the question of how long a child should be separated from the mother.

Minimal Intervention at Age Two and Three

It is our prejudice that he should not be separated 30-40 hours per week; rather than that, we believe that 2-3 hours of intervention and a cooperating mother at home are best for the young child.

2. ORGANIZATION OF INPUT FOR RESPONSE TO AN ADULT

It is in the nature of longitudinally designed intervention studies with large samples that specific educational assumptions can seldom be directly tested. One has to accept behavioral objectives which appear to be related to those assumptions for evaluation purposes, and can only infer from the data to the assumptions themselves. We assumed a need for the young child to learn that information input alone is not sufficient to gain reward from an adult, and that he must learn to organize input in a manner conducive to responding with that information to an adult or peer. The question of what specifically brought about increased performance in the Training and Discovery groups is not resolved by stating that the Concept Training as such made no difference. The conditions of training common to both groups are complex and include: one-to-one interaction, systematically scheduled training periods, the affective relation between Instructor and child, the duration of the program over a period of eight months, and the specific physical attributes of the Harlem Training Center as a facility. Any one or all of these conditions could have brought about the increase in performance.

It is our belief that within the one-to-one interaction and the affective relationship, conditions were provided which allowed some children to learn that the acquisition of stimulation was insufficient to derive reward, that only by organizing that information in the form of a response was reward achieved. The ability to respond to training is partly a function of learning that the Instructor requires an organized response. We suggest that the training conditions used here provided an opportunity for more children to learn this than was true for the Control group. Some children did not learn this during training, as some adults presumably never learn it. One of the primary differentiators between intellective "haves" and "have nots" may have to do with whether this facility is learned at an early age.

One may ask how we are so convinced of the importance of this phenomenon since both Training and Discovery groups excelled, one in a structured learning condition and the other in a relatively permissive condition. Since ancillary studies during the Training showed that the Training Instructors did as they were asked, and, in fact, initiated around eight times the conversation as when they were teaching in the Discovery condition, we can only suggest that organization of input for responding to another occurred in both groups, but in different ways. The Training child was rewarded directly in a structured environment where the Instructor initiated conversation. As he saw the materials before him, attended to them on instruction, and responded, he was rewarded. At some point the achieving child learned to attend with the realization that only by doing so could he expect the reward. The Discovery child, on the other hand, also had to learn to attend to the material and to engage the attention of the Instructor before the latter would verbalize at all. If he persisted in asking questions about the materials, the Instructor continued to respond. If he stopped, she stopped. It is with respect to the conditions under which learning appears to progress best that the strategy associated with merely enriching the child's environment seems to be lacking. Visual, auditory, tactile, and other stimulation is a necessary but not sufficient characteristic to result in the ability to organize information and be able to respond. Social interaction, best provided by the dyadic relationship between Instructor and child under conditions precluding interruption and fostering positive affect, are necessary concomitants of stimulation for optimal effects to occur.

3. DEVELOPMENT OF AN AFFECTIVE BOND BETWEEN CHILD AND INSTRUCTOR

It was assumed that conditions providing for the development of positive affect by the child for a significant other was essential for sustained intellective development. That most children developed positive affect for Instructors specifically, and the Center in general, is suggested by mothers' reports, attendance records, and the behavior of children in the Center. Only rarely did a situation develop where the child appeared to be resistant to the Instructor as an individual, and when that did occur, the practice of substituting another Instructor of the opposite sex usually dispelled the resistance. As the program progressed and children were exposed to several Instructors, the routine changing from one Instructor to another after six sessions appeared to be increasingly easy for the child.

Admittedly, it is difficult to demonstrate that it was the child's development of positive affect for the Center and its Instructors which related to his progress in training. The conviction that it was an integral part of the conditions of training which led to superior learning as compared to the Controls remains a conviction, but it remains central to our explanation of why both treatments yielded desired results.

In conclusion, the results suggest that an exception has been demonstrated to the hypothesis that "compensatory education has been tried and failed." As a result of the four years we have followed these children and the data available, we are also convinced that the conditions of training rather than the specific materials and procedures in the curriculum brought about the durable effects. The great advantage of the curriculum and procedures is that they exist in considerable detail and have been shown to be effective when applied under the conditions for learning used in this study.

REFERENCES | 15

Bronfenbrenner, U. Early deprivation in mammals and man. In G. Newton (Ed.), *Early experience and behavior.* Springfield, Illinois: C. Thomas, 1968.

Deutsch, M. *The disadvantaged child.* New York: Basic books, 1967.

Kennedy, W. A., Van de Riet, V. and White, J. C. A normative sample of intelligence and achievement of negro elementary school children in the southeastern United States. *Monographs of the Society for Research in Child Development,* 1963, *28* (6, Serial No. 90).

Palmer, F. H. Inferences to the socialization of the child from animal studies. In Goslin, D. (Ed.), *Socialization theory and research.* New York: Rand McNally, 1969.

Palmer, F. H. Socioeconomic status and intellective performance among negro pre-school boys. *Develop. Psychology,* 1970, *2* (4).

Parker, Day | *Introduction* | 16

The purpose of this chapter is to compare the preschool programs described in this volume in order to highlight some of the similarities and differences among them. Reading this chapter, however, will not serve as a substitute for reading each of the program conceptualizations. Since much is necessarily lost when program characteristics are removed from context in order to be contrasted with one another, such comparisons may present an oversimplified view of the programs involved. Nevertheless, we hope this summary will provide a useful overview of the programs and clarify distinctions among them on several important dimensions, namely: 1. the foundations of the conceptualization; 2. goals and objectives; 3. implementation, 4. assumptions concerning the child's motivation, 5. teacher motivation, and 6. exportability.

Ronald K. Parker
Mary C. Day

Comparisons of Preschool Curricula

16

THE FOUNDATIONS OF THE CONCEPTUALIZATIONS

Most individuals concerned with the development and education of young children hold certain principles and beliefs about what children should learn and how this learning should take place. In many cases these principles and beliefs are implicit in the ways individuals interact with children; in other cases, curriculum developers, in presenting a particular curriculum conceptualization, have made their principles and beliefs explicit. The authors contributing to this volume have presented the explicit foundations of their curricula. For heuristic purposes these foundations can be examined along two dimensions: 1. the degree to which formal theory in child development influences the curriculum conceptualization and 2. the degree to which the empirical research literature influences curriculum conceptualization. Combining these two dimensions, we can conceive of a continuum of possibilities, ranging from a conceptualization grounded in a theoretical position which has strong empirical support, to one that ignores both theoretical systems and empirical literature in its formulation. The conceptual-

Dr. Ronald K. Parker is at the Center for the Advanced Study of Education, The City University of New York, and Mary Carol Day is a graduate student at the Harvard University Graduate School of Education. Printed by permission of the authors.

izations presented here include some based on a comprehensive formal theory of child development (e.g., those of Piaget and Montessori), some based on a set of principles inferred from the empirical literature (e.g., that of Schaefer and Aaronson), and some which minimize formal theory and the research literature while placing heavy reliance on personal experience (e.g., Weikart's unit-based program). In addition, some program developers draw from several theoretical positions, employing each theory to provide guidelines for one or two aspects of the program or drawing selectively from the vast research literature on child development.

The use of theory to guide the selection of content and instructional strategies and to foster and maintain teacher morale is discussed by several program developers. They emphasize that theory offers a framework for overall curriculum planning, while at the same time enabling teachers to make their own decisions, with reference to the theory, on a day-to-day basis. Both Piagetian and Montessori preschools are based on theories of the cognitive development of the child, as is Hooper's position concerning the timing and content of instructional sequences.

Kamii's Piagetian preschool is grounded in the work of the Swiss genetic epistemologist, Jean Piaget, and Montessori preschools are based on the work of the Italian doctor and educator, Maria Montessori. Kamii is explicit in her paper concerning the Piagetian principles which she feels are most relevant to designing and developing the ideal learning environment, curriculum, and instructional strategy. Her preschool program is based upon principles drawn from Piagetian theory (although Piaget himself offers few pedagogical principles), and the goals of the program are consistent with Piaget's developmental stages. Montessori preschools are based upon Montessori's developmental theory and the principles of instruction which Montessori herself carefully formulated.

Hooper endorses the organismic-developmental viewpoint exemplified by the theories of Piaget and Werner, and he also specifies those features of the theories that offer guidelines for content and instructional strategy. He points out the importance of 1. using the developmental acquisition sequence as a guide to both optimal content and optimal timing of particular content, 2. viewing the child as the self-correcting and self-pacing monitor of his cognitive development, and 3. planning peer group interaction.

There are several obvious similarities between preschool programs based upon Piagetian and Montessorian developmental theories. Both emphasize the importance of sensory-motor skills for later intellectual development, and both assume that the child will choose materials with which to work that are appropriate to his developmental level and that are interesting to him. Hence external motivating techniques are not necessary and feedback should be provided by the objects and activities themselves (except in the area of social knowledge, e.g., correctly naming objects). Neither theory stresses language development for the three to six-year-old child. However, the Montessori program's three-staged lesson does focus on teaching the labels for physical (e.g., perceptual, tactual) attributes, and Kamii notes the importance of "representation" in structuring and communicating knowledge to other people. Hooper's version of applied organismic-developmental theory differs from Kamii's in its focus on the relationship between language and logical operations and in its emphasis on the importance of contingent feedback from the teacher concerning the appropriateness of the child's responses on complex cognitive tasks.

The similarities in the Piagetian and Montessori preschools reflect the similarities in Piaget's and Montessori's thought about cognitive development. Elkind (1967) has summarized some of the ideas Piaget and Montessori held in common:

> *The first idea is that nature and nurture interact in a dual way. With respect to the growth of abilities, nature provides the pattern and the time scheduling of its unfolding while nurture provides the nourishment for the realization of this pattern. When we turn to the content of thought, however, just the reverse is true; nurture determines what will be learned while nature provides the prerequisite capacities. A second idea has to do with capacity and learning. For both Piaget and Montessori, capacity sets the limits for learning and capacity changes at its own rate and according to its own time schedule. Finally, the third idea is that repetitive behavior is the external manifestation of cognitive growth and expresses the need of emerging cognitive abilities to realize themselves through action. (pp. 543-544)*

The preschool programs described by Nedler, Robison, and Karnes, Zehrbach, and Teska each employ the theoretical positions advanced by more than one theorist in providing rationales for different aspects of the program and in pinpointing goals and objectives. Nedler and Robison relied on data from the empirical literature as well as on a variety of theoretical statements in formulating their objectives and in developing their programs. Nedler's approach was to conduct research surveys in the neighborhoods to be served by the project in order to identify the needs of the population. Nedler then reviewed the empirical literature, especially that related to language development and bilingualism. She cites Bruner, Hunt, and Blank as investigators who contributed to her conceptualization of a curriculum for low-income Mexican-American children. Also, the "levels of operations" in Guilford's "structure of the intellect" model provided dimensions to be used in formulating behavioral objectives.

Like Nedler, Robison also thoroughly reviewed the empirical literature in several areas (e.g., language, self-concept, cognition). In addition, Piaget contributed ideas concerning social interaction and active manipulation; O. K. Moore's emphasis on the importance of play was incorporated, and Bloom's model of "learning for mastery" offered suggestions for instructional strategy. One important point made by Robison was that the goals (in terms of program design and desired effect) of the CHILD Program did not require one particular curriculum design, the CHILD Curriculum being only one of several models that could have been developed. Robison stated that her long range goal of maximum cognitive functioning in school was a value decision, but that the theoretical statements and the research literature suggested objectives to help attain that long range goal.

Karnes, Zehrbach, and Teska, as well as Kamii, explicitly set forth the value of theory for the formulation of objectives, curriculum design, and teacher planning. After stating the primary goals and subgoals for the Ameliorative Curriculum, these program developers adopted process theoretical models to aid in the achievement of the goals. Psycholinguistic theory, as presented in the Illinois Test of Psycholinguistic Abilities (ITPA), is used in many ways to guide the language focus of the program. And Guilford's "structure of the intellect" model offers similar guidelines in the area of intellectual functioning. Karnes *et al.* considered the primary task in developing an effective preschool program to be "the formulation of principles for making decisions rather than the production of static curricular materials." Agreeing with Robison, they state that their curriculum represents only one of the curricula which could result from application of these principles.

Nimnicht's educational system can also be included among the programs employing several theoretical viewpoints. In his description of the New Nursery School (Nimnicht, McAfee, and Meier, 1968), which was a precursor to the program described in his present chapter, Nimnicht acknowledges the influence of Maria Montessori, Martin Deutsch, and O. K. Moore. Nimnicht's synthesis of these various viewpoints resulted in the formulation and development of a "responsive" model of education which requires that the educational system respond to the child, rather than rigidly requiring the child to respond to the educational system. Nimnicht's responsive program and the Montessori program are similar in regard to "freedom within limits" offered the child.

Theoretical systems played a lesser role in the remainder of the programs — those of Miller and Camp, Schaefer and Aaronson, Palmer, Anderson and Bereiter, Blank, Weikart, and Whitney and Parker.

Miller and Camp present the conceptualization of a preschool program that focuses on the development of the child's competence. They relied on research literature to identify the variables associated with the development of competence, dividing these variables into four categories: 1. cognitive variables, 2. motivational variables, 3. personal style variables, and 4. physical variables. A belief that the essence of competency is the ability to predict and control one's environment led to a focus on developing the child's ability to order and structure the environment and to the choice of an information processing model to guide the selection of objectives and the development of the curriculum.

Schaefer and Aaronson also relied on the research literature in choosing both the age of intervention (15 months) and the main thrust of their Infant Education Project. Review of the intervention research, and research on the correlates of early intellectual development, influenced the choice of subordinate objectives and suggested the major components of the program. The focus on language development in the Infant Education Project stands in marked contrast to the Piagetian and Montessorian emphasis on sensory-motor skills and manipulation.

The intervention program presented by Palmer is based on assumptions about the educational needs of the child. Some of these assumptions are firmly grounded in research data, while others are more speculative. The important thing to note here is that Palmer explicitly identified the assumptions made in the design and implementation of his program.

Anderson and Bereiter, who presented one component of a program, and Blank, who discussed techniques rather than presenting a description of her program, do not specify in their papers the influence of any theory. Anderson and Bereiter specifically state that "we have not begun with a theory of thinking. Rather the approach has been to first design a number of thinking tasks that seem reasonably teachable to young children and then to try them out." Blank's techniques of simplification were developed within a structured tutorial program for preschool children. In previous descriptions of her program, Blank (in press) has acknowledged the influence on her thinking of the developmental theories of Piaget, Vygotsky, and Yudovitch.

Weikart's unit-based program permits "the teacher to deal independently and intuitively with the educational program for children enrolled in her class. She does not follow a specified curriculum based on a specific cognitive theory or language theory. She does respond to the 'needs' of the children as seen from the vantage point of general knowledge of child development and personal wisdom and experience."

Whitney and Parker rank low on the importance of theory in their curriculum and high on the influence of research literature in helping shape the Discovery Program. Only one major theoretical position is presented in their paper — the principle of guided discovery learning. On the other hand, the research in child development was utilized at all times in their construction of the developmental and educational objectives.

GOALS AND OBJECTIVES

The second dimension on which preschool curricula may be compared concerns their goals and objectives. Both goals and objectives are the ends toward which a program is directed, with the former being more global, long-term aims constituting the major areas of curriculum focus (e.g., cognitive development). Objectives are more specific behavioral statements used to guide the educative process by setting the course and tone for instruction, as well as for evaluation, selection, and development of materials and procedures. Said another way, objectives are specific behavioral statements (like "the child is able to classify stimuli according to color") designed to help the staff work with the child to attain the long-term goals of a program. Objectives and goals of the various programs may be compared on three features: 1. explicitness (or operationalism), 2. breadth, and 3. emphasis on content or process.

EXPLICITNESS, BREADTH, AND CONTENT-PROCESS DISTINCTIONS

An objective or goal is explicit, or operational, if it specifies the *observable* change desired in a learner as a result of instruction. The *explicitness* with which goals and objectives are expressed varies in the program descriptions. Goals such as success in school, language competence, cognitive development, and socio-emotional development could all be defined and evaluated in quite different ways. For example, does a "successful program" result in the participants making "average" scores on various achievement tests, or do scores which are "significantly higher" than those of a control group yet lower than the national norms also constitute success? Although a complete failure to attain goals such as "success in school" would be quite obvious, decision rules concerning when a program is successful or unsuccessful in attaining broad goals are frequently not made prior to the operation and evaluation of a program.

As already mentioned, *objectives* express the specific behavioral achievements desired, and can be assessed and evaluated on a day-to-day basis. Behavioral objectives allow for continual evaluation by teachers in the daily classroom situation, enable diagnostic testing to determine the child's strengths and weaknesses in particular areas, and provide for sequenced instruction which builds new learning on the base provided by previous learning. One exemplary feature of most of the preschool programs described here is the organization and specificity of their behavioral objectives. Many of the programs with behavioral objectives used a task analysis or component analysis approach in defining the objectives; thus the objectives are sequenced in, at the minimum, on *a priori* levels of difficulty.

The programs of Kamii, Nimnicht, Schaefer and Aaronson, and the unit-based curriculum described by Weikart are those placing least emphasis on previously defined behavioral objectives for each child. Montessori is excluded from this group because the child's appropriate use of the Montessori materials, which are sequenced in order of difficulty, provides behavioral objectives. Kamii divided her goals of formal operations and socio-emotional maturity into subgoals, but her objectives remain internal processes rather than external behavior and she intentionally does not specify behavioral objectives or precise sequencing. Nimnicht's responsive environment allows the child to choose his own activities and to pace himself, while the teacher focuses on the possibilities that exist within the child's chosen activity for attaining one or two weekly objectives. The tutors of the Infant Education Project developed a list of toys, materials, and learning situations with graduated levels of difficulty, but they did not use a structured curriculum with a set of behavioral objectives. Finally, Weikart's unit-based curriculum did not specify behavioral objectives. In this program social and emotional development are considered primary, and planning is conducted on a day-to-day basis to meet the needs of each child. However, as the excerpt from the paper written by Weikart's teachers indicates, some of the teachers' weekly goals could be assessed behaviorally, e.g., naming body parts.

Breadth is the second feature on which the objectives of the various preschool programs may be compared. Breadth may be defined as the number of child development dimensions (e.g., cognitive, socio-emotional, sensory-motor, etc.) included in the objectives of the programs. It is important to notice that while the conceptualizations of some programs profess an interest in developing particular abilities, e.g., creativity or social skills, no precise behavioral objectives are defined for the ability. Thus, there is a difference in breadth of *stated* objectives and breadth of *clearly specified behavioral* objectives. The Discovery Program described by Whitney and Parker is the most complete in specifying behavioral objectives across a comprehensive set of developmental dimensions. Precise behavioral objectives are presented for every area or dimension of child growth considered important. In many cases, program designers have developed behavioral objectives for program areas ordinarily omitted. For example, Miller and Camp state that in their program contingent reinforcements for desired *attitudes* are systematically programmed. Also, Nimnicht lists *behavior* which is characteristic of the child who has a positive self-image with regard to learning and school activities. The breadth of *stated* program objectives can be ascertained by studying Table I.

Another main distinction between goals can be made on the basis of their focus on either *content* or *process*. Karnes, Zehrbach, and Teska define process as "the ability to obtain, organize, manipulate, synthesize, integrate, and communicate information" and content as "facts, information and concepts." Since both content and process are inextricably bound together in any learning setting, the distinction is one of relative emphasis rather than choice of alternatives. Most of the program developers represented in this collection have explicitly stated their positions; the majority of them agree that process is more important than content, but that content should be chosen carefully. The guideline offered by Karnes, Zehrbach, and Teska is that the characteristics of pupils should help to determine the position taken on the process-content continuum. "The Ameliorative Curriculum assigned top priority to process; however, since process can be developed through a variety of content and since disadvantaged children lack certain types of content, process was to be developed using that content which most effectively bridged the gap between the disadvantaged culture and school culture." Anderson and Bereiter also believe that "priorities are different for different groups of children, and more advantaged children may have already acquired those skills taught by the academic preschool." Other programs focus almost exclusively on process, viewing content as important primarily for its function in helping to develop process skills. Among these programs are Anderson and Bereiter's conceptual skills component, and Kamii's, Miller and Camp's, and Nimnicht's programs.

Several programs emphasize the importance of presenting the child with content which will be relevant to later school requirements. The primary goal of the Ameliorative Curriculum is to "prepare the child for effective participation in a standard school program." Thus the content of the Ameliorative Curriculum was selected for its relevance to local elementary school requirements. In addition, Bereiter and Englemann's academic preschool curriculum and Robison's CHILD Curriculum also focus on content areas typically considered "academic"; Robison provides a list of some of the advantages which she thinks a content-centered program has to offer.

Statements of conceptualization and outlines of curricula are not sufficient, however, to determine whether, in day-to-day operation, process or content is emphasized more. To adequately evaluate their relative emphasis, observations of the learning environments and of the manner of implementation of the curricula of the preschool programs are necessary.

MAIN PROGRAM OBJECTIVES

The main objectives of each preschool program may be categorized into five broad, rather loosely defined, and somewhat overlapping areas: 1. sensory-motor skills, 2. cognition, 3. language, 4. socio-emotional development, and 5. academic content. For example, "instruction giving" and "question asking" could be categorized as relevant for either language development, cognitive development or (and more accurately) both. Unfortunately, because different terms are used across papers to describe the same behaviors, and because differential importance is assigned to various objectives within each program, a precise comparison of objectives, considering importance, is very difficult. Nevertheless, Table I is an attempt to provide a useful reference for the major goals and objectives of each of the fourteen preschool programs. The objectives

TABLE I
MAJOR GOALS AND OBJECTIVES OF PRESCHOOL PROGRAMS

PROGRAM	MAJOR GOALS	SENSORY-MOTOR SKILLS	COGNITION	LANGUAGE	SOCIO-EMOTIONAL	ACADEMIC CONTENT
Anderson and Bereiter Conceptual Skills	Communication Thinking skills		Thinking, problem solving a. Relevance b. Truth and falseness c. Incongruities d. Defining solution sets e. Definitions	Communication Skills a. Instruction following b. Instruction giving c. Question asking		
Blank Based on description in Blank Tutorial Program	Abstract thinking	Cognitively directed perception, e.g., a. Selective attention	Coding Process, e.g., a. Development of verbal concepts b. Categories of exclusion c. Separation of word from its referent d. Relevant inner verbalizations		Independent work	

Hooper Logical Operations Instruction	Logical operations		b. Reduction of egocentric perspective c. Distinction between tangential and germane	Problem Solving, e.g., a. Cause and effect reasoning b. Imagery of future events c. Recognition of the incorrect d. Sequential ordering
			Classification Seriation Conservation	
Kamii Preschool Based on Piaget's Theory	Formal operations; Socioemotional maturity	Physical knowledge—enlarging repertoire of actions to be applied to objects	Physical knowledge; Social knowledge; Logico-mathematical knowledge a. Classification b. Seriation c. Numerical construction d. Space and time Representation (Indices, symbols, signs)	Socioemotional development a. Intrinsic motivation b. Controlling own behavior c. Relationship with peers d. Relationship with adults

Comparisons of Preschool Curricula

TABLE I (Continued)
MAJOR GOALS AND OBJECTIVES OF PRESCHOOL PROGRAMS

PROGRAM	MAJOR GOALS	SENSORY-MOTOR SKILLS	COGNITION	LANGUAGE	SOCIO-EMOTIONAL	ACADEMIC CONTENT
Karnes, Zehrbach, and Teska Ameliorative Curriculum	Content, Processes and Attitudes necessary for effective participation in a standard school program	Motor skills—control of bodily movements	Cognitive development Information processing skills	Language, e.g., a. Verbalizations b. Pre-Reading c. Sequencing events d. Visual-motor coordination	Motivation conducive to learning; Positive self-concept; Social and emotional development	Math concepts a. Basic number concepts b. Manipulative skills c. Vocabulary Science-social studies a. Vocabulary b. Classification c. Sensory discriminations Language
Miller and Camp DARCEE	"Coping" or information processing skills and sustaining attitudes	Sensory skills a. Orienting and attentional b. Discriminatory c. Relational d. Sequential Motor response skills	Abstracting and Mediating skills a. Conceptual b. Association c. Classification d. Sequencing e. Critical thinking	Verbal response skills a. Fluency b. Articulation c. Syntax	Attitudes to sustain and further skills, e.g., ability to delay reward, persistence, achievement motivation	

Montessori (as described by Banta)	Provide "freedom within limits" for the child to develop mental, physical, and psychological abilities	a. Small motor coordination b. Orientation Motor education—organization and control of spontaneous movements; Sensory education— a. Perception of touch, hearing, and vision b. Concepts of volume, length, weight, etc.	Intellectual abilities	Concentration Pride in successful completion of work; Cooperation	Math education a. Numerals b. Counting Language education a. Letters
Nedler Southwest Educational Development Laboratory	Acquisition of essential skills and concepts that underlie intelligent behavior	Visual skills, e.g., a. Perceiving position in space b. Figure-ground perception c. Spatial relationships Auditory skills, e.g.,	Reasoning and Problem Solving a. Describe objects b. Narrate events c. Generalize d. Explain and predict	Language skills a. Vocabulary b. Basic sentence patterns c. Syntactic structures d. Use of language in problem solving	

Comparisons of Preschool Curricula

TABLE I (Continued)
MAJOR GOALS AND OBJECTIVES OF PRESCHOOL PROGRAMS

PROGRAM	MAJOR GOALS	SENSORY-MOTOR SKILLS	COGNITION	LANGUAGE	SOCIO-EMOTIONAL	ACADEMIC CONTENT
Nedler (continued)		a. Auditory perceptual b. Discrimination c. Retention Motor skills, e.g., a. Body awareness b. Body control				
Nimnicht Far West Laboratory for Educational Research and Development	Develop intellectual ability and a positive self-image with regard to learning	Develop senses and perceptions	Problem Solving a. Non-interactional b. Interactional c. Affective Concept formation ability	Develop language ability	Positive self-image, e.g., a. Likes self and others b. Believes he can be successful in school c. Believes he can solve problems	

Nimmicht (Continued)			Positive self-image as regards learning, e.g., a. Express more confidence in answers b. Tardy less frequently	
Palmer Harlem Research Center	Increase knowledge of basic concepts		Basic concepts of: a. Position b. Direction c. Sensory-tactile d. Quantity e. Movement f. Size Organization of information for responses to others	Affective bond with tutor Positive affect toward learning
Robison CHILD Curriculum	Cognitive and language development	Sensory discrimination Physical manipulation	Cognitive development, e.g., a. Attentiveness, task mastery, problem solving b. Ordering, classification	Language development a. Development of spontaneous speech b. Standard English as second dialect	Social interaction; Rules of game; Autonomy; "Playfulness"; Experiences of success in cognitive tasks	Music, Language (includes pre-reading), Mathematics, Science, Sociology, Geography, Economics

Comparisons of Preschool Curricula

TABLE I (Continued)
MAJOR GOALS AND OBJECTIVES OF PRESCHOOL PROGRAMS

PROGRAM	MAJOR GOALS	SENSORY-MOTOR SKILLS	COGNITION	LANGUAGE	SOCIO-EMOTIONAL	ACADEMIC CONTENT
Robison (Continued)				c. Language uses for cognitive tasks d. Vocabulary expansion e. Experience with books, pictures, letters, numerals		
Schaefer and Aaronson Infant Education Research Project	Intellectual development and language skills		Intellectual development a. Language skills b. Concept formation	Language development a. Receptive and expressive language b. Basic vocabulary c. Acquaintance with books	Cooperation; Attentiveness; Persistence to task completion; Positive relationship between child and tutor; Feelings of competence	

Weikart Ypsilanti Pre-School Curriculum Demonstration Project Unit-Based Program	Social and emotional development		Teaching of cognitive activities was embedded in program, e.g., spatial relations, classification, temporal sequences	Ability to use sentences in conversation	Sustained attention; Persistence; Positive interactions with teachers and peers; Positive attitude toward school; Impulse control; Good manners; Sense of well being; Feelings of accomplishment
Whitney and Parker The Discovery Program	Cognitive, linguistic, affective, social, motivational, and physical development	Physical development, e.g., a. Eye-hand coordination b. Muscle tone c. Agility	Cognitive development, e.g., a. Solving problems b. Classifying c. Numbers d. Predicting and testing	Language development, e.g., a. Conversation b. Vocabulary	Affective support a. Positive adult-child relationships b. Identify emotions c. Role-play social skills Motivation, e.g., a. Self-confidence b. Creativity c. Responsibility	Preacademic skills, training

TABLE I (Continued)
MAJOR GOALS AND OBJECTIVES OF PRESCHOOL PROGRAMS

PROGRAM	MAJOR GOALS	SENSORY-MOTOR SKILLS	COGNITION	LANGUAGE	SOCIO-EMOTIONAL	ACADEMIC CONTENT
Whitney and Parker (continued)					Social development, e.g., a. Cooperation b. Resolution of personal and interpersonal problems	

listed are, in some cases, only a sampling of the total objectives listed in the program descriptions. In general, the terminology used in the descriptions of the programs is also used in the table. In some cases there are different categorizations for the same item (e.g., attention), following the categorization used by the program developer. The "cognition" category includes such objectives as information processing, ordering, thinking, and problem solving. The category entitled "academic content" lists subject areas within which objectives are defined in consideration of specific content that may contribute to success in elementary school. Whereas language may be one content area of an academically-oriented preschool, such as the Ameliorative or the CHILD Curriculum, the more precise objectives of the language curriculum are listed under "language" in the table.

Overall, most of the programs are quite comprehensive and take into consideration many aspects of the child's development. It is definitely apparent that programs presented here that focus upon academic or cognitive objectives do not, as an invariable consequence, neglect socio-emotional objectives. For example, Anderson and Bereiter state: "We cared about the children and we considered their emotional future as carefully as we considered their academic one. Concern for the child's emotional stability was the justification for such careful programming of skills — to make learning a less frustrating experience. In fact, it was considered so carefully that it went without saying." Schaefer and Aaronson comment on the intercorrelation between the child's intellectual development and his social and emotional development, similarly noting that "an optimal education program can and should promote both competence and adjustment."

IMPLEMENTATION

A second dimension on which preschool programs may be compared is implementation — the manner in which the curriculum is presented and how the classroom environment is organized. Type of instructional format, the teacher's role, grouping of the children, sequencing of content, and parental participation are five main aspects of implementation. Table II compares the fourteen programs on each of these and specifies the characteristics of the children who participate in each program. Since the table adequately presents the mode of grouping the children and the sequencing of content, only the remaining three aspects of implementation will be discussed below.

INSTRUCTIONAL FORMAT

Three broad categories of instructional format can be identified by focusing on the manner in which the curriculum is presented to the child. One technique is

TABLE II
IMPLEMENTATION OF PRESCHOOL CURRICULA

PROGRAM	CHILDREN	INSTRUCTIONAL FORMAT	TEACHER'S ROLE	GROUPING	SEQUENCING	PARENTAL PARTICIPATION
Anderson and Bereiter Conceptual Skills	Three to six-year-olds who have already learned the skills taught by the "academic preschool"	Direct instruction; Practice on thinking problems	Direct learning and provide practice on thinking problems	Small groups	Tasks arranged in order of difficulty; Sequenced behavioral objectives	
Blank Tutorial Program	Three and four-year-old low-income	Dialogue guided by the teacher and based on appropriate questioning; 15-minute sessions	Structure and guide the dialogue	Individual	Interaction structured to meet the ability level of each child; Simplification techniques vary from those requiring minimal to those requiring complex responses	

Hooper Logical Operations Instruction	Three and four-year-old middle-income	Teacher-directed small group activities with emphasis on peer group interaction; 20- to 30-minute sessions	Direct training sessions according to curriculum and provide feedback as to correctness of child's response	Group of four age-matched children	Tasks sequenced in order of difficulty; Sequenced behavioral objectives	Home visits for 90 minutes, every two weeks
Kamii Preschool Based on Piaget's Theory	Three to six-year-old low-income	Child chooses activity from group of teacher selected items, and teacher follows child's interests	Physical knowledge: encourage child to predict and experiment; Social: instruct and reinforce correct responses; Logico-mathematical: encourage reasoning, select materials, and diagnostically evaluate	Individual and group activity, with the former longer and considered more important	No predetermined, sequenced behavioral objectives or tasks; Teacher follows up on child's interests at his developmental level, using diagnostic evaluation	
Karnes, Zehrbach, and Teska	Three to five-year-old low-income	Structured game format;	Daily plan activities according to diagnostic evaluations	Primarily small groups, but also large groups and	Hierarchical order of behavioral objectives paired with	Parents work with children at home, teach in the classroom,

Comparisons of Preschool Curricula

TABLE II (Continued)
IMPLEMENTATION OF PRESCHOOL CURRICULA

PROGRAM	CHILDREN	INSTRUCTIONAL FORMAT	TEACHER'S ROLE	GROUPING	SEQUENCING	PARENTAL PARTICIPATION
Karnes, Zehrbach, and Teska (continued) Ameliorative Curriculum		20-minute structured learning period in each content area; Music period and directed play	and theoretical models; Guide learning in game format	individual; Grouped by ability within age levels	criterion performance tasks for content objectives; Process objectives sequenced using theoretical models; Individual diagnostic testing and prescription	and help other parents acquire teaching competencies
Miller and Camp DARCEE	Three to five-year-old low-income	Interrelated units with teacher-directed activities, structured learning experiences, and evaluation; Varied instructional activities, e.g.,	Direct activities and evaluations according to sequenced curriculum	Small groups of five children	Sequenced behavioral objectives; Programming of reinforcement schedules; Units progress from concrete, proximal to abstract, distal	Curricula for other members of family

		"plant walks," direct instruction, games			
Montessori	Three to six-year-olds Backgrounds vary with particular school	Planned environment with materials designed to hold child's interest, control for errors, and teach; Child chooses materials and paces himself	Prepare environment; Maintain order to facilitate development of concentration; Demonstrate use of materials; Diagnose degree of learning	Individual and small group but varies depending on particular classroom; Heterogeneous age grouping	Graded didactic materials from which child chooses; Sequence in introducing materials and questioning child
Nedler Southwest Educational Development Laboratory	Three to six-year-old Mexican-Americans	Units with daily lessons in each of five major areas; Alternating periods of direct instruction and self-selected activities	Direct instruction following lesson plan format; Assess attainment of objectives; Pace instruction	Small groups of six children and individual activity; Typical class: 18 children and 2 teachers	Sequenced lessons and behavioral objectives with assessment following instructional activities; Criterion performance tasks for appropriate pacing	Presently developing

TABLE II (Continued)
IMPLEMENTATION OF PRESCHOOL CURRICULA

PROGRAM	CHILDREN	INSTRUCTIONAL FORMAT	TEACHER'S ROLE	GROUPING	SEQUENCING	PARENTAL PARTICIPATION
Nimnicht Responsive Environment	Three to nine-year-olds from low-income or culturally and ethnically different homes	Learning environment allows free exploration, informs child of consequences of his action, is self-pacing, and is designed for making interconnected discoveries	Determine how room may be used to accomplish weekly objectives; Choose learning episodes; Observe and respond to children	Individual, small group and large group activities	Learning environment permits sequencing and pacing by the child	Parent/Child Toy Library; Parent involvement in decision making, e.g., culturally-relevant material and approach to language development
Palmer Harlem Research Center	Two and three-year-old Blacks; Hollingshead-Redlich Two Factor Scale of Social Class; Categories I-V	Direct instruction with child choosing from several sets of materials; Affective tie between child and tutor important	Demonstrate, label, and question child about concepts, following Instructor's Manual; Pace and sequence lessons appropriately for each child	Individual instruction	Concepts ordered by difficulty and meaning; Child proceeds at own rate	Familiarization with goals and techniques of program

488   The Preschool in Action

Robison CHILD Curriculum	Four and five-year-old low-income inner city	Spontaneous play, games, tutorial, and direct instruction; Emphasis on child autonomy	Plan each day's work, using teacher guides; Diagnostic testing and pacing	Groups of various sizes, independent activity, and tutorial; Grouped by grade level (i.e., age)	Behavioral objectives sequenced in hierarchical order; cross-references across content areas; Diagnostic tests determine pacing	Attempted to involve parents as volunteers in classroom, in discussions of curriculum, and in reinforcement of skills
Schaefer and Aaronson Infant Education Research Project	15-36 month-old Black children from low-income families	One-hour visits, five days per week; Variety of experiences and methods, including games, trips away from home, labeling objects, reading, music	Tutors vary methods to meet needs of each child; Develop curriculum items and teaching strategies; Interact with children in variety of ways	Primarily individual instruction; sometimes small groups	Lists of toys, materials, and learning situations sequenced according to level of difficulty, by no definite sequence of activities	Parents encouraged to participate in home visits; Conclusions focus on importance of "family centered programs"
Weikart Unit-Based Program	Three to six-year-old low-income	Unit themes; One-half hour structured Circle Time, free play,	Independently plan and direct all preschool activities; Initiate	Large group activity for one-half hour; Small groups and	No lists of sequenced behavioral objectives; Teachers tried	Home visits for 90 minutes every two weeks

Comparisons of Preschool Curricula   **489**

TABLE II (Continued)
IMPLEMENTATION OF PRESCHOOL CURRICULA

PROGRAM	CHILDREN	INSTRUCTIONAL FORMAT	TEACHER'S ROLE	GROUPING	SEQUENCING	PARENTAL PARTICIPATION
Weikart (continued)		directed activity; Permissive atmosphere but compliance required in routines, manners, and behavior control	teacher-pupil interaction when necessary; Plan activities but allow individual choices; Evaluate each child	individual activity	to meet needs of each child	
Whitney and Parker The Discovery Program	Two to six-year-old low- and middle-income	Planned activities alternated with self-chosen activities; Children not required to participate in planned activities	Initiate planned activities; Observe and evaluate skill acquisition	Heterogeneous age grouping; 2 staff members for 12 children; Group and individual activities	Sequenced behavioral objectives, classified into thematic skill areas and cross-referenced	Take-home materials, including booklets and other educational materials

direct instruction, whereby the teacher presents information to the child and directs the child's activities. A second technique is the use of *games* designed to teach specific information and skills, and a third is *exploratory learning* which allows the child to choose his activities from a variety of alternatives and to seek answers to questions for himself. Of course, there are variations on each technique, but, in general, the categories indicate the amount of freedom provided the child within the learning situation.

The child's freedom is limited to the extent that a planned, sequenced curriculum is implemented by the teacher. If a task analysis has been used to delineate specific behavioral objectives that are sequenced in order of difficulty and that correspond to specific instructional tasks, and if the teacher follows this instructional outline, the child's program is structured and he has relatively little freedom to choose his activities — although he may determine the pacing of the activities. If the child *does* have a choice, it is generally chosen from the three or four activities that are next in the instructional sequence, as is the case with Palmer's tutorial program. Both direct instruction and games may be used to implement a curriculum of this type. The programs of Anderson and Bereiter, Blank, Hooper, Karnes *et al.*, Miller and Camp, and Palmer provide a relatively high amount of structure for the child. Anderson and Bereiter, Hooper, and Palmer use a form of direct instruction, although it should be noted that in all three of these programs the child is an *active* participant. The Anderson-Bereiter and Hooper programs stress the importance of peer interaction. Karnes, Zehrbach, and Teska use a structured game format during three daily 20-minute learning periods. Miller and Camp utilize a variety of instructional activities, including direct instruction, games, and field trips (e.g., "plant walk"), all of which are directed by the teacher. Finally, Blank's tutorial interactions are structured by the teacher who introduces topics and materials, carefully poses questions, diagnoses the child's deficiencies, and guides the child toward answering the question or solving the problem posed (Blank and Solomon, 1969).

In addition to a teacher-imposed sequence of instructional activities, structure may be provided in the form of a carefully designed and controlled environment within which the child is free to choose his own activities and to pace himself. Montessori, Nimnicht, Kamii, and Whitney and Parker place great emphasis on designing the environment to foster the attainment of certain instructional objectives. But this emphasis does not necessarily exclude attention to teacher-child interactions. For example, Kamii's teachers are actively involved with the individual child. Although they do not use didactic methods, they introduce games and question the child to stimulate his thinking. Kamii holds that the choice of materials is crucial in the acquisition of physical and social knowledge, but the particular objects used for logico-mathematical development are not as important. "Planned environment" is the key Montessori idea, and the goal of Montessorians is "a carefully prepared environment which guarantees exposure to materials and experiences through which to develop intelligence as well as physical and psychological abilities." The two primary criteria for the materials are 1. ability to hold the child's interest and 2. power to teach (through built-in error control). In addition, the classroom atmosphere must be calm, orderly, and conducive to the child's concentration. Nimnicht's responsive environment also focuses on learning materials, which like Montessori's are autotelic and inform the learner immediately of the consequences of his actions. Nimnicht's teachers have one or two objectives each week, and they attempt to use the materials in the room and the child's interests in the materials to achieve the particular weekly objectives. The Discovery Program described by Whitney and Parker uses materials which have been evaluated for their role in learning, and the physical environments of the Discovery Centers are designed to foster the attainment of certain behavioral objectives.

Several of the programs alternate among various types of instructional format. Both the program described by Nedler and the Discovery Program employ periods of direct instruction and planned activities which alternate with periods of child-selected activities. The unit-based curriculum described by Weikart devotes the initial half-hour of the daily two-hour session to teacher-directed activities in a large group while children may choose, within the established routines, their activities for the rest of the day. Robison's CHILD Curriculum employs a variety of instructional formats. Much emphasis is placed upon the importance of play, games, and active experiences, and the child's autonomy in the selection of activities is allowed whenever possible. The Infant Education Research Project also employed a variety of instructional strategies, with the particular strategies used depending upon the responses of each child. Overall, Schaefer and Aaronson state, "the spirit of the tutoring was one of fun, games, and camaraderie"; thus, much instruction took place through improvised and traditional games.

In Table III the approximate location of each program on the structure continuum is presented diagrammatically. It should be remembered that a chart such as this necessarily oversimplifies the interaction that occurs between the teacher and the child and can only present the average degree and not the range of structure provided the child within the program. For example, the programs which alternate between direct instruction and child-selected activity are located in the "moderate" row. Each row represents the degree of structure provided for the child, and each column indicates the degree to which the teacher's role is structured (a topic to be discussed shortly). The order of programs within each cell is insignificant.

Structured and unstructured learning activities, where structure refers to the initiation and direction of learning activities by the teacher, have both potential advantages and potential disadvantages for the child. Some of the advantages of structure (and, by implication, the disadvantages of autonomy) are:

1. the child is directly taught those skills basic to his educational development, and there is no waiting and hoping that he will "discover" them for himself;
2. through the direct intervention of the teacher, the child is provided with adult models for behavior rather than being left solely to his own devices; and
3. the teacher can offer immediate answers to a child's questions as well as feedback to his responses.

On the other hand, the advantages of more child autonomy (and, by implication, the disadvantages of tight structuring) include the following: 1. autonomy allows and fosters the development of initiative and decreases pressure for con-

TABLE III
LEVEL OF STRUCTURE PROVIDED FOR THE CHILD AND THE TEACHER

LEVEL OF STRUCTURE
TEACHER

	Low to Moderate	Moderate	Moderate to High
Moderate to High		Blank Karnes, Zehrbach, and Teska	Anderson and Bereiter Hooper Miller and Camp Palmer
Moderate (CHILD)	Weikart's Unit Based	Kamii Robison	Nedler Whitney and Parker
Low to Moderate	Schaefer and Aaronson	Montessori Nimnicht	

LEVEL OF STRUCTURE CHILD

Comparisons of Preschool Curricula

formity; 2. it ensures a child's interest in his chosen activity where more structured tasks can decrease motivation by requiring attention to content in which he is not interested; 3. it increases the likelihood that the material he selects will be at his appropriate level of development rather than where the teacher thinks he *ought* to be; and 4. it affords him an opportunity for making decisions and discovering relationships and "laws" on his own, instead of always relying on the teacher for direction or advice.

THE ROLE OF THE TEACHER

The role of the teacher in each of the fourteen preschool programs reviewed here can be considered with respect to the amount of autonomy the teacher assumes in planning and implementing the preschool curriculum. The more the curriculum, behavioral objectives, and instructional format are specified for the teacher before he comes to the classroom, the more structured is the role of the teacher. Preschool programs can thus be classified according to the degree of structure for the teacher, just as they can be classified according to the degree of structure provided the child.

In the first and most structured category are preschool programs which have detailed curriculum guides, specific behavioral objectives, and highly delineated means of implementation and evaluation. In these programs the teacher's major responsibilities include presenting the materials and structuring the classroom in the specified manner, diagnosing the ability level of each child, reinforcing the children for correct or appropriate responses, and pacing the learning activities. Anderson and Bereiter, Hooper, Miller and Camp, Nedler, Palmer, and Whitney and Parker all describe programs which fall into this category. For example, in the Southwest Educational Development Laboratory's program described by Nedler, teachers receive lesson plan formats, each of which includes "a clearly stated behavioral objective, a description of the materials needed for presentation of the learning experience, and an outline of the teaching procedure designed to enable the child to achieve the specified objective." But "each teacher assumes the responsibility for decisions regarding pacing and spacing of activities within the program. She is the final judge of how best to achieve the match between the child's cognitive structures and the experiences he will encounter in the learning environment."

The second category is comprised of programs within which the *teachers* direct the learning situation and structure the environment *according to specific and carefully articulated principles or theoretical frameworks.* These programs differ in the amount of specification provided to the teacher, but all allow the teacher more autonomy than do the programs in the first category. The programs of Blank, Kamii, Karnes, Banta (i.e., the Montessori program), Nimnicht, and

Robison are of this variety. Because these programs are so diverse in the functions required of the teacher, a brief summary of the teacher's responsibilities is presented in the next two paragraphs. (Table II presents similar and at times additional information.)

Blank presents a number of principles and prescribes specific techniques (in this volume and in Blank and Solomon, 1968, 1969) for handling tutorial interaction, but the tutor is on his own in the difficult task of implementing these techniques. In the Ameliorative Program teachers select, from a variety of optional content areas, the content which they feel most competent to present. They conduct diagnostic evaluations, evolve appropriate curricula, select instructional strategies, and plan each day's activities with reference to the model provided by the Illinois Test of Psycholinguistic Abilities and Guilford's "structure of the intellect" model. Robison provides her teachers with a packaged curriculum consisting of statements of goals, of procedures, of material use, and of diagnostic testing; however, she stresses the teacher's central position in planning and pacing each child's activities while using the teacher guides to enlarge the teacher's repertoire of instructional techniques. In Nimnicht's program, guidelines, training units, and rather extensive training are provided to the teacher; but within the classroom setting the teacher must respond appropriately to the activities of the children in accordance with the program philosophy.

As Banta points out, the implementation of the Montessori preschool varies widely, but there are general principles and guidelines in which all teachers are trained. Montessori preschool teachers are farther removed from individuals who stand in a supervisory capacity to them than are many of the teachers of more recently developed programs. Thus, the Montessori teacher probably has more freedom to implement Montessori guidelines and to use Montessori materials in her own way. Finally, the role of the teacher in Kamii's Piagetian preschool is "to help the child control his own behavior and to build his own knowledge through his own actions on objects, his own reasoning processes, and his own curiosity and excitement." Fulfilling this role requires that the teacher "follow the learner's own way of learning and guide it." Thus, the teacher does not have a sequenced set of activities or behavioral objectives, but bases her interactions with the child and her manner of structuring the learning environment on principles drawn from Piaget's theory of cognitive development.

The third and final category consists of the programs within which the teacher has complete autonomy or only very general and abstract guidelines to aid him in developing curricula, selecting instructional format, and specifying objectives. In Weikart's unit-based program the teachers established objectives, developed the curriculum, and implemented it, depending heavily upon personal knowledge and beliefs about the needs of the child and the operation of a preschool program. The tutors in Schaefer and Aaronson's project were also responsible for developing the curriculum and devising various instructional formats which would meet the needs and interests of each child. Only general guidelines and the major goals of the project, were defined for the teachers.

Table III presents the relative location of the fourteen programs along a continuum which represents the level of structure provided to the teacher. In this chart, all programs which were described as belonging to the first category are positioned in the "moderate to high" column, those programs that comprised the second category are located in the "moderate" column, and the two programs that were classified in the third category are located in the "low to moderate" structure column.

From the foregoing discussion, it should be apparent that there are diverse resolutions to the structure-autonomy question, and that for teachers as for children there are advantages and disadvantages both to structure and autonomy. The advantages that *structure* affords teachers include the following:

1. Structure provides teachers with a concrete plan for the presentation of content. This helps them to attend more effectively to the child's *response* to content than to content *per se*. Without such structuring, there is the possibility that teachers will not know what to do and when to do it, or that they will be given general goals but no specified means of achieving them. Structure reduces planning time as well because the teachers are required to follow an essentially prescribed course of action.
2. Structure, requiring as it does prescriptive instruction based on an educational diagnosis, helps insure that a child is working with materials at an appropriate level of difficulty. Without such evaluative feedback, teachers may find that their presentation is ineffective, and that their goals and expectations as well as the tasks they set a child are inconsistent with, or irrelevant to, his needs and abilities.
3. Structure can enable inexperienced or semi-experienced teachers to become more proficient than if they are left primarily to their own devices and obliged to rely on intuition and common sense. Many such teachers may simply not know how to become more effective without some structured guidelines on curriculum implementation and the management of children.

The disadvantages of structure as opposed to autonomy for teachers are:

1. Structure often serves to limit or decrease the originality and spontaneity of a teacher's approach. In fact, the more structuring there is, the more this may prove to be the case — to a point where even a teacher's motivation can be affected. Greater autonomy, on the other hand, may make the teacher feel more like a professional and less like a technician going through predetermined behavior in rote fashion.
2. A structured program with specified objectives may well produce severe negative reactions in a teacher when she discovers that she is not operat-

ing as effectively as she has assumed. However, this statement is not meant to imply that teachers should be encouraged to become like ostriches, determined to avoid facing possible inadequacies in themselves and the need to change; nor is it being proposed that, at any cost, teachers must be sheltered. What we are suggesting is that, with fewer prescribed objectives to carry out, he may feel far less devastated by certain kinds of feedback that may cast some doubts on his overall effectiveness.

In regard to structure for the teacher, Banta has pointed out that a thorough knowledge of objectives and techniques with which to handle instructional situations leaves the teacher free to observe the child and his responses to educational materials. "The teaching day takes on meaning and direction; there are no large didactic holes to fill; and above all, the teacher is left free to attend to the child rather than the invention of teaching techniques and the mechanics of each lesson." Banta's statement could actually be used to describe any program whose teachers 1. plan each day beforehand to some extent and 2. *are experienced* with the educational approach they are using, or carefully study daily objectives and instructional techniques before entering the classroom.

The differences in effectiveness of structured and relatively unstructured classrooms, in terms of child development and motivation, have not been adequately assessed. In his paper Banta cites findings that led to the conclusion that "classrooms function on an either-or basis: either analytic thinking or curiosity and innovative behavior are improved. All classrooms do appear to improve conventional learning processes." Banta found that structured Montessori classes were more effective in increasing analytic thinking but decreased curiosity and exploratory behavior, whereas permissive Montessori classrooms had the greatest effect in increasing innovative behavior.

It is also likely that the effectiveness of different levels of structure varies with the particular characteristics of the children involved in the program. Bissell (1970) reanalyzed data collected by other researchers (DiLorenzo, 1969; Karnes, 1969; Teska, 1969; Weikart, 1969) in order to examine differential program effects as a function of socio-economic status. For the majority of families in each sample, neither parent had gone beyond high school in formal education and the father, if present, was unemployed or was employed in a blue-collar occupation. Ratings of socio-economic status (SES) were made on the basis of an equal rating of mother's and father's educational level, father's occupation, and number of children in the family. Children were separated into two groups on the basis of their SES rating; one group consisted of children with an SES rating in the bottom half of the sample and one of children with an SES rating in the top half of the sample.

Bissell found that directive, highly structured preschool programs tended to be *more* effective with those children in the lower half of the sample, or equally effective with all of the children in the sample; non-directive, less structured programs on the other hand, tended to be more effective with those children in the top half of the sample than with children in the lower half of the sample. Effectiveness was assessed by an increase in Stanford-Binet IQ scores. In general, the children in this sample benefitted more from structured, directive programs than from nondirective, less structured programs.

Parker and Day (1971) recently reported an interaction between age of the child and type of early education intervention program. Three ages were involved (3—3 1/2, 3 1/2—4, and 4—4 1/2 years), with one half of each age group receiving brief exposure to a highly structured cognitive training program embedded in an unstructured program, and the other half receiving only the unstructured enrichment program. For the two older groups of children, there was no differential impact as a result of the type of program. Program impact was measured by Palmer's Concept Inventory, described in his chapter in this volume. When the scores of the younger children were examined, however, differences in scores were found between participants in the two programs, with the program containing the embedded structured component producing the greater gains.

More studies similar to these are needed which examine the interaction between characteristics of the child and effectiveness of types of instruction. But such studies should go further. Socio-economic status and age are extremely global variables, and by themselves tell us little. What particular characteristics of the child, which are sometimes correlated with socio-economic status or age, interact with instruction? The need for more research to pinpoint relationships between teaching method and child growth in all aspects of development must be vigorously stressed.

PARENTAL PARTICIPATION

Parental involvement with and participation in the preschool program has become a major concern for many program developers. Two primary reasons for this concern are 1. the extreme importance of individuals both *having* and *feeling that they have* power and control over the events which influence their lives and the lives of their family, and 2. the need for an educational program to be supported and reinforced at home if it is to have a maximum and enduring impact.

Parental participation in preschool programs may take three forms: 1. familiarity with the content and techniques of the program, 2. involvement in parent education programs designed to provide parents with both general information about child development and specific information about their own children, and 3. participation in decision-making as regards the goals and operation of the preschool.

Familiarity with the preschool's activities and goals can be accomplished through visits to the center by the parents in order to help or observe, home visitation by the teachers, take-home materials for the children, or any combination of the three depending upon the extent of involvement desired. If formal parent education programs are undertaken, the staff should be certain that the program is meeting the *needs of the parents*. The form taken by parental participation in each of the preschool programs described here will be reviewed very briefly.

"To assure parental participation" is a subgoal of the Ameliorative Curriculum. The Ameliorative Program's family involvement component includes having parents work with their young children at home, teach in the classroom, help other parents acquire improved teaching competencies, and train older siblings to teach younger siblings. Robison tried to include parents as volunteers in the program, scheduled meetings for discussion of the CHILD Curriculum, and made suggestions concerning parental reinforcement of skills learned in school. Weikart's unit-based program and Kamii's Piagetian preschool included home visitation. Parents of children in these programs received a 90-minute home teaching visit by the preschool teacher every two weeks. The Parent-Child component of the Discovery Program represents a very sophisticated approach to parental involvement.

Schaefer and Aaronson's entire program consisted of home visits, during which the participation of the mother was encouraged. These researchers found a variety of different reactions to the invitation to participate, with some parents being enthusiastic and other parents showing little interest. Schaefer and Aaronson are emphatic in their statements concerning parent participation in educational efforts directed towards the child, heavily stressing the need to supplement child-centered programs with family-centered programs in early education. Two suggestions made by Schaefer and Aaronson concerned 1. the organization of supportive groups for mothers and teachers in educational institutions and 2. the creation of toy libraries.

Miller and Camp have developed curricula for other members of the child's "learning ecology." They see the child's instrumental environment ("world of people") as being extremely important for the child's development. "During the child's early formative years, the instrumental environment is primarily the family, and, more specifically, the effective instrumental agent is the mother." Miller and Camp thus feel that focusing on influencing the child's family as well as the child is vitally important.

Palmer stresses that the mother should know the goals of the program and the experience her child is having. He encouraged mothers to attend the center and to observe through a one-way mirror the interaction between their children and the tutors. Southwest Educational Development Laboratory is presently designing a parent education program.

Nimnicht involves parents in a variety of ways. The Parent/Child Toy Library lends parents both toys and games designed to improve specific skills and offers parents a ten-week course of instruction in the use of toys. In addition, the parents of the children participating in the Far West Laboratory's program have decision-making power. Nimnicht states that an educational system should be responsive in content and in procedure, and thus parents make decisions concerning content along with the staff. Two decisions which Nimnicht feels parents should make concern the amount of culturally relevant material to be included in the curriculum and the approach to language development to be employed (e.g., English as a second language).

Karnes, Zehrbach, and Teska offer three guidelines for parental involvement which bear repeating: "1. Greater concern must be expressed for the personal worth of parents. 2. Greater opportunities must be provided for parents to make choices regarding goals they want to work toward and how they want to include themselves. 3. Greater care must be used in applying procedures that might be viewed as entering the privacy of the individual." Hoffman *et al.* (1971) offer an additional guideline. Fathers as well as mothers have vital roles to play in the development of their children, and a special effort should be made to involve fathers in program activities. Tuck (1969) has designed a program specifically to help fathers interact with their sons and daughters in a variety of ways.

Given that parental participation is a desirable component of preschool programs and given that more and more program developers are viewing parental involvement as a *necessary* facet of preschool efforts, there is a need for evaluation of various parental involvement techniques. Which techniques appear to be most viable and effective in terms of meeting the needs of parents and in terms of beneficial results for the child's development? Preschool programs having identical classroom activities but varying type of parental involvement (e.g., take-home materials vs. home visits by the preschool staff) could be systematically compared in order to investigate the effects of various types of parental involvement.

MOTIVATION

THE CHILD'S MOTIVATION

The programs described in this volume vary somewhat in their assumptions concerning the child's motivation to learn. Most of the program developers assume that the child is intrinsically motivated, and that it is the teacher's job to find techniques and materials appropriate for utilizing and maintaining the child's natural curiosity and interest. While some programs rely primarily on the child's motivation *plus* the teacher's selection of appropriate materials for the classroom, others use a variety of additional motivational techniques, such as concrete reinforcers, social reinforcement, games, and multimedia.

The Montessori preschool and Nimnicht's responsive environment program concentrate on providing carefully designed materials and an atmosphere within which the child's natural interest and concentration will be fostered and maintained. The materials are designed to hold the child's interest and to teach; they have "built-in error control" and provide the only feedback to the child considered necessary. The child works for the sake of the activity itself, and the teacher does not intervene to reinforce the child.

Kamii's Piagetian preschool is similar in its assumptions concerning the child's "insatiable amount of curiosity about everything" and the crucial importance of the materials in the classroom. Kamii and Montessori are also similar in minimizing the distinction between work and play. Kamii holds that physical knowledge is attained through feedback from objects and the child's action on objects, while logico-mathematical knowledge is attained through the child's own reasoning processes. Although great emphasis is placed on materials, the role of the teacher in the Piagetian preschool seems to involve more interaction with the child than in the Montessori or responsive environment programs. The Piagetian teacher introduces activities, asks questions to learn how the child is thinking, and questions the child and poses problems to stimulate his thought.

None of the programs described in this volume rely heavily on extrinsic reinforcement. An example of a program which *does* emphasize immediate and *concrete* rewards for performance on learning tasks is Bushell's (1970) Behavior Analysis classroom. The Behavior Analysis classroom uses a token exchange system whereby children are given tokens for progress in various learning tasks. The tokens may later be exchanged for enjoyable events and activities of the child's choice. Of the programs presented here, Miller and Camp indicate that they initially use concrete reinforcers in the DARCEE program, providing a "careful programming of reinforcement schedules to move the child from a concrete and extrinsic reward system to an abstract and intrinsic one." Weikart also mentions the occasional use of concrete (e.g., paper hat) reinforcers by the teachers of the unit-based curriculum.

The motivational technique of contingent *social* reinforcement (i.e., praise) for appropriate responses is used by most of these preschool programs, and Karnes *et al.* advocate the additional importance of indicating the reasons for praise. Kamii, also, provides social reinforcement for *social* knowledge. According to Montessori, however, the teacher should avoid reinforcing the child, thereby disturbing his concentration.

A variety of additional techniques can be used to attract and maintain the child's interest in the learning situation. The most commonly used technique is that of matching the child's developmental level with appropriate materials. Indeed, almost every program developer mentioned the importance of careful observation and diagnosis to ascertain that the best "match" was being attained between the materials and the child's ability.

Games and play can be used as important motivational techniques. According to Kamii, "play is one of the most powerful allies on the teacher's side." Karnes, Zehrbach, and Teska point out that games provide for concurrent visual, auditory, motoric, and verbal behavior, enable repetition in a meaningful context, provide a positive approach to learning, and facilitate high motivation. Robison's program utilizes a variety of techniques but Robison emphasizes the value of play in terms of intensity of involvement, long attention span, and the intrinsic nature of the reward. Schaefer and Aaronson emphasize the "spirit of fun, games, and camaraderie" in the tutoring relationship and note the value of games in attracting other children in the environment as teaching aides.

The use of multimedia resources has great potential for motivating children. Planned educational experiences that involve all or many of a child's senses — seeing, touching, hearing, tasting, and smelling — are invaluable for creating maximum learning opportunities. Multisensory involvement should include activities which emphasize not only a different modality on different occasions but also a combination of modalities on a single occasion. Whitney and Parker present a description of the comprehensive and highly sophisticated multimedia system being used in the Discovery Program, and several of the other programs are using tape recordings, records, transparencies, and typewriters in instructional activities.

Grouping together children of different ages is a motivational technique utilized by Montessori, Whitney and Parker, and Weikart. Heterogenous age groupings offer the double benefit of 1. enabling younger children to learn from the older children (who may serve as models or teach directly) and 2. providing the older children with the opportunity to teach what they have learned, thus clarifying and strengthening their knowledge in the process.

THE TEACHER'S MOTIVATION

The teacher's commitment to the preschool program is undoubtedly a crucial variable in determining the success of a program. Weikart, for one, believes a key component of a staff model which will enable a curriculum to work is a "deep personal commitment of teachers to their program and children." Karnes parallels that belief in saying that "to ensure the success of a program, there must be a dynamic, professional growth program." The means of involving and maintaining the involvement of teachers in a program is vital.

In the initial stages of the programs discussed here, several program developers collaborated with teachers in developing both instructional strategies and instructional materials. The teachers of Weikart's unit-based program, for example, developed their own objectives, curriculum, and techniques. "Program decisions regarding actual curriculum plans were made on a practical intuitive basis rather than on a theoretical basis, making the particular curriculum a direct expression of their own views of preschool education." In this case operational procedures and staff model goals were the only external constraints placed upon the teachers. Schaefer and Aaronson also depended on their tutors to a great extent in formulating their program. The tutors were responsible for selecting both materials and techniques, and for varying the materials and techniques to meet the needs of each child.

However, once a program has been developed and curriculum and techniques precisely defined, what is the teacher's remaining challenge? Several program developers stress that the utilization of certain techniques is in itself a difficult and challenging task. Mastery of Blank's simplification techniques, to cite one example, is not easily accomplished. And the use of educational diagnosis, prescriptive instruction, and criterion performance objectives for each child necessitates decisions by the teacher concerning the pacing and presentation of materials. Robison points out that correct pacing of activities was performed with much more ease the second year than the first year by teachers who were employing individual diagnosis and behavioral objectives for the first time. Analysis of each child's progress as well as planning for the next day are both essential for effective individualized instruction, and this planning is done by teachers. Karnes reports that the use of models and highly specific objectives frequently stimulated teachers to develop new instructional materials. Thus, there is always a great deal of room for teacher decision-making even when techniques and curriculum content are specified in some detail. As Banta has said, the teacher is in the critical interface between the child and the method, and that gives him both tremendous responsibility and challenge.

EXPORTABILITY

The continuing rapid expansion of interest in preschool programs brings to the forefront a problem that will become more acute if some programs are eventually found to be more successful than others in fostering certain aspects of child growth (e.g., language, problem solving, pre-academic skills) or in developing a greater variety of the child's abilities. The problem is that of "exporting" programs for use in other geographic areas with other children and different staffs, while maintaining satisfactory effectiveness.

Necessary for successful exportation are conceptual statements and written curricula, characteristics of most of the programs included in this book. The development of a curriculum which is replicable and effective in various settings is no easy task. In her article presented in this volume, Nedler reviews step-by-step the effort which the Southwest Educational Development Laboratory exerts to develop a replicable, prototype curriculum.

Although a clear and explicit conceptual statement and a written curriculum with specified materials and instructional activities are necessary for implementation of a program by others, these two guidelines are insufficient. Teacher training programs are just as essential. The teacher who ultimately presents the program to the child cannot be expected to do so, in a manner characteristic of the program, without specific instruction. Teacher training programs seem to be the only means of insuring that a teacher comprehends and is able to use the techniques and materials of a novel or unique program.

The importance of the teacher's day-to-day implementation of the curriculum is stressed in many of the preceding papers. For example, Banta reports: "All other American Montessori Society functions, from an education perspective and from the child's perspective, are subordinate to teacher quality." Nimnicht similarly acknowledges the importance of good teacher training: "The first concern in evaluating the program is to determine how effective the training program is in producing the desired changes in teacher behavior." To these comments Robison would add: "One vital ingredient of such a design [to evaluate the CHILD Curriculum] must be a measure of the extent to which teacher behavior samples indicate that the curriculum is actually experienced by children."

At present, emphasis on the development of comprehensive and effective teacher training programs is just becoming widespread. Although many programs use a variety of teacher training techniques (e.g., workshops, videotape, observation, demonstration) for limited numbers of teachers in geographical proximity, few programs have advanced to the stage where the training of a large number of teachers to implement specific curricula can be successfully undertaken.

Among the programs which are involved in the training of a relatively large number of teachers are those of Montessori, Nimnicht, Weikart, and Whitney and Parker.

One of the primary objectives of Nimnicht's educational system is "to develop a model inservice training program for teachers," and the development of training procedures for teachers is currently in the performance testing stage for his Head Start program for three and four-year-olds. The Far West Laboratory plans to provide two years of intensive training (the time "required to obtain a high level of performance in 75% or more of the classrooms") and continuous inservice training to initially implement and maintain the program. A local individual trained by the Laboratory (Program Advisor) "works with teachers and assistants in ten classrooms to develop a quality program in the local community with limited support from the Laboratory."

The Discovery Program's training procedure follows a four-step plan with behavioral objectives specified at each step: 1. familiarization with the printed materials; 2. assignment to a fully operating Discovery Center for preservice training; 3. placement in an inservice training program using staff development modules composed of booklets, videotapes, and microteaching training materials; and, 4. field monitoring.

In his paper, Banta stresses the problems of quality control faced by the American Montessori Society, and these problems will exist for all programs which increase in number and spread geographically. Banta has also raised the question of the possibility of teacher training effectively overcoming initial differences in teacher style (although he feels videotape may be an effective tool). Data confronting this issue come from a study headed by Louise Miller (1970) in which four programs — Bereiter and Englemann, DARCEE, Montessori, and Traditional — were compared. In this study, training for teachers of three of the programs consisted of eight weeks of preservice training and inservice training, including two two-day workshops and bi-weekly meetings with the project directors. The teachers of the Bereiter-Englemann curriculum participated in only four weeks of preservice training but had the same amount of inservice training as the other teachers. To answer the question "Did the teachers really implement the program in which they were trained," the programs and teachers were evaluated by those who developed each program or were involved in the training. All programs received ratings above midpoint on a 0 (not at all) to 10 (best possible) scale, but the consultants for the Bereiter-Englemann program were least pleased while those for the Traditional program were most pleased. Results from in-class monitoring indicated that "despite considerable variation among teachers within each program, most of the salient characteristics of the programs which it was feasible to assess in this manner were clearly present, and to a sufficient extent to produce greater homogeneity within programs than between programs." (1970, p. 34) Later Miller states that: "Our results so far support the notion that regardless of differences in personality and formal education, the preschool teacher can be greatly influenced in her teaching methods by training which involves specific procedures, and provides the teacher with unambiguous instructions regarding techniques." (1970, p. 36) Thus, data resulting from Miller's comparisons are encouraging; training programs may indeed be effective in altering teacher techniques and behavior. However, the extent to which inservice training programs are necessary has not yet been established, and the maintenance of quality in a program will probably always require surveillance.

Research investigating training program effectiveness and the interactions between teacher performance and program characteristics is currently desirable. Are there certain personality characteristics or attitudes that militate against a teacher's effectively implementing a particular program? Do some programs require more extensive teacher training than others? Which programs are the easiest and which are the most difficult for inexperienced and for experienced teachers to implement? These are some of the questions for which there are no answers.

CONCLUSION

The evolution of curriculum development in early education has reached the point where a variety of curricula options exist. This volume has presented some of the best developed and most clearly conceptualized options. Elsewhere, Parker and Ambron (1972) reviewed approximately forty preschool curricula and both that review and the present review lead to the same conclusion: that the quality of preschool curricula has been increasing steadily over the last eight years. We may also note in concluding that the day has passed when a curriculum can gain wide acceptance without a specification of its conceptualization, behavioral objectives, and delivery system. The curricula presented in this volume attest to these facts.

The next decade of development in this field hopefully will focus on more careful component analyses of curricula (e.g., language development), using criterion performance tests in order to provide the data for curriculum evaluation and revision. It also appears desirable for considerable effort to be expended in the development of the component areas of social, affective, and physical development, as well as a continued emphasis on cognitive development.

The central purpose of this volume has been to focus attention on the status of curriculum development in preschool education, not to praise our efforts, but in order to stimulate the field to make greater strides in the near future.

REFERENCES | 16

Bereiter, C. and Englemann, S. *Teaching disadvantaged children in the preschool.* Englewood Cliffs, New Jersey: Prentice-Hall, 1966.

Bissell, J. S. The cognitive effects of pre-school programs for disadvantaged children. National Institute of Child Health and Human Development, 1970.

Blank, M. A methodology for fostering abstract thinking in deprived children. *Monograph, Ontario Institute Studies in Education.* In press.

Blank, M. and Solomon, F. A tutorial language program to develop abstract thinking in socially disadvantaged preschool children. *Child Development,* 1968, *39*, 379-389.

Blank, M. and Solomon, F. How shall the disadvantaged child be taught? *Child Development,* 1969, *40*, 47-61.

Bushell, D., Jr. *The Behavior Analysis Classroom.* University of Kansas Support and Development Center for Follow Through, 1970.

DiLorenzo, L., et al. Prekindergarten programs for educationally disadvantaged children. New York State Education Department, 1969.

Elkind, D. Piaget and Montessori, *Harvard Educational Review,* 1967, *37*, No. 4, (b).

Hoffman, D., Jordan, J., Moore, B., and McCormick, F. *Parent participation in preschool day care: Principles and programs.* Monograph No. 5. Atlanta: Southeastern Education Laboratory, 1971.

Karnes, M. B. *Research and development program on preschool disadvantaged children.* Washington, D. C.: Office of Education, 1969.

Miller, L. B. Experimental variation of Head Start curricula: A comparison of current approaches. Progress Report No. 5. Louisville, Kentucky: University of Louisville, 1970.

Nimnicht, G., McAfee, O., and Meier, J. *The new nursery school.* New York: General Learning Corporation, 1968.

Parker, R. K. and Ambron, S. (Eds.), *Child Development and Education Handbook: Preschool,* Vol. *II.* Office of Child Development, Department of Health, Education, and Welfare. Washington, D. C.: U. S. Government Printing Office, 1972.

Parker, R. K. and Day, M. C. Evaluation of the Home Visit Program of the Title III Brooklyn Block Preschool. Board of Education, New York, New York, 1971.

Teska, J. Success and failure in five different programs of preschool intervention with culturally disadvantaged children. Thesis presented to the University of Illinois, 1969.

Tuck, S. *A model for working with black fathers.* Chicago: Institute for Juvenile Research, 1969.

Weikart, D. A comparative study of three preschool curricula. A paper presented at the biennial meeting of the Society for Research in Child Development, Santa Monica, California, 1969.